AMSCO®

ADVANCED PLACEM

MW00849438

Psychology

PERFECTION LEARNING®

The cover image is an example of neurographic art, an expressive and therapeutic drawing technique that combines art and psychology to promote emotional well-being and self-discovery. Developed by Russian psychologist Pavel Piskarev in 2014, this method involves creating abstract patterns and lines that represent the subconscious mind's thoughts and feelings. By transforming chaotic and spontaneous lines into harmonious shapes, individuals can process emotions, reduce stress, and achieve a meditative state. Neurographic art encourages creativity and personal growth, offering a unique way to explore and understand one's inner world.

AMSCO *Advanced Placement* *Psychology* is one of a series of Advanced Placement* social studies texts first launched with the book now titled *AMSCO* *Advanced Placement* *United States History.*

Authors

Laura Brandt, *BA in Social Studies, MA in Psychology, MA in US History, EdD in Curriculum and Instruction*

Laura teaches AP Psychology and is chair of the Social Studies Department at Libertyville High School in the Chicago suburbs. She also teaches AP Psychology online for the Center for Talent Development through Northwestern University. She recently taught AP Psychology, IB Psychology, and AP Seminar at the College du Leman in Geneva, Switzerland.

Laura was the recipient of the 2012 APA Teachers of Psychology in Secondary Schools (TOPSS) Excellence in Teaching Award and later served on the executive board of that organization, which represents high school psychology instructors within the American Psychological Association. She has served in many roles for the AP Psychology exam reading and is also an examiner for IB Psychology. Laura is a co-creator of the iScore5 review app for the AP Psychology exam and a co-creator of the Books for Psychology Class blog, which reviews psychology-related books and provides classroom activities for teachers and students. Laura was an author of previous editions of this text and has served as a reviewer, contributor, and author on other educational materials related to AP Psychology.

Mike Hamilton, *BA in Education, MA in US History*

Mike has been teaching high school psychology for more than 20 years. He began in Iowa before moving to Massachusetts, where he currently resides and has taught at Hopkinton High School since 2005. Mike served on the AP Psychology Test Development Committee for six years and was co-chair from 2016–2020. He has also been involved in the AP Psychology Reading since 2011, first as a Reader, progressing to a Table Leader and Question Leader, and now serving as an Exam Leader.

Mike was the 2019 recipient of the APA's Society for the Teaching of Psychology Moffett Memorial Teaching Excellence Award. He was also the recipient of the APA TOPSS Excellence in Teaching Award in 2013. One of Mike's proudest accomplishments is founding the New England Teachers of Psychology (NETOP) workshop, which from 2012 to 2022 brought teachers from around the country together every year in August to share best practices and learn from regional university professors.

Contributing Authors

Jeffery Scott Mio, PhD, is an emeritus professor from the Psychology and Sociology Department at California State Polytechnic University, Pomona, where he served as Director of the M.S. in Psychology Program from 1995–2021. He was president of Division 45 of the American Psychological Association from 2002–2003 and president of the Western Psychological Association (WPA) from 2010–2011. During that same period, he was on the advisory panel for the development of the National Standards for High School Psychology Curricula. He served as the executive officer of the WPA from 2016-2018. He has published a number of books, including an undergraduate textbook on multicultural psychology from Oxford University Press, now in its sixth edition. Dr. Mio has won many teaching awards and has published more than 200 scholarly articles, many centered on issues of cultural diversity. Dr. Mio contributed to this book the features that develop cultural understanding as well as the topics on social psychology.

Regan Gurung, PhD, is an award-winning professor of psychology and the executive director of the Center for Teaching and Learning and the psychology program at Oregon State University. He is also the founding co-editor of the APA's *Scholarship of Teaching and Learning in Psychology* journal. In addition to his extensive scholarship, Dr. Gurung is a co-author of the popular book *Study Like a Champ* (APA) which represents the latest scholarship in learning science. He contributed the "Study Like a Champ with Dr. G." features to this program.

Corinne Schwarzrock, MA, MS, Graduate Certificate in Positive Psychology, is Division Leader of International Studies and AP Psychology/Dual Credit Psychology at Cary-Grove High School in Cary, Illinois. Corinne contributed the topic on positive psychology.

Charles Schallhorn, MEd, was a key contributor to previous editions of this book. Charles is the chair of the Social Studies Department and teaches AP Psychology at Mountain House High School in Mountain House, California.

sReviewers

Michael Berndt, MEd, Senior Reviewer, has taught psychology and AP Psychology for 26 years at Apollo High School in St. Cloud, Minnesota. He has attended the AP Psychology Reading every year since 2006 and has served as a Reader, Table Leader, and Question Leader. In 2023, he received the APA TOPSS Charles T. Blair-Broeker Excellence in Teaching Award.

Dana C. Melone
Cedar Rapids Kennedy High School
Cedar Rapids, IA
AP Psychology Teacher, Curriculum
Facilitator, and Table Leader

Amy Ramponi
Kimberly High School
Kimberly, WI
AP and Clinical Psychology Teacher
Former AP Reader

Heather Schroeder
William Fremd High School
Palatine, IL
Social Studies Dept. Chair
AP Psychology Teacher

Corinne Schwarzrock
Cary-Grove High School
Cary, IL
AP Psychology Teacher

Lisa Jensen Trelease
Herriman High School
Herriman, UT
AP Psychology Teacher, Coach, and Reader

Contents

Foundational Practices: The Science of Psychology

UNIT 1—The Biological Bases of Behavior — 117

Topic 1.1 Interaction of Heredity and Environment — 119

Topic 1.2 Overview of the Nervous System — 136

Topic 1.3 The Neuron and Neural Firing — 144

Topic 1.6 Sensation

Introduction

Studying Advanced Placement® Psychology

Our purpose in this book is to provide the detail of a standard textbook with engaging readability and relatable examples. Everything in the book either explains key concepts in psychology or provides examples to help you understand ideas in a meaningful context. The book presents the content of an introductory college psychology text but with a sharp focus on the AP® Psychology course learning objectives and essential knowledge. We recommend that you read this introduction twice: once when you begin the course and again when the test approaches. Some things will make more sense after you have finished the course.

The contents of this book are aligned with the College Board's 2024 Course and Exam Description. Individual teachers and professors may choose to approach the content differently, depending upon their unique philosophy and individual class characteristics. There is no one "correct" way to structure an introduction to psychology course. The content in the College Board framework gives students a broad introduction to the field of psychology as well as experience developing the foundational practices of the science of psychology.

As with almost all introductory texts, reading this book is analogous to wading in shallow water in a very big lake. Psychology as a field is deep and rich in detail; almost every unit in this book has at least one college-level, semester-long course with its own complete textbook full of more details than this book can cover. That is part of the beauty of psychology—no matter the level you study, there is always more to discover.

Course Description

In its 2024 Course and Exam Description, the College Board suggests dividing the AP® Psychology course into four main "practices" and five content units.

Foundational Practices: The Science of Psychology

The Science Practices outlined at the beginning of the Course and Exam description are foundational to the discipline of psychology. They are introduced at the beginning of this text in a section of their own, but they are developed throughout the program in the Think as a Psychologist features.

Practice 1: Concept Application Practice 1 introduces some of the key concepts of psychology and demonstrates how they can be applied to various scenarios.

Practice 2: Research Methods and Design Practice 2 introduces the scientific method and various research designs behind experimental and non-experimental research studies from which knowledge of psychology is drawn.

Practice 3: Data Interpretation Practice 3 explains how the numerical and descriptive data that are found through psychological studies can be understood in relation to key statistical concepts.

Practice 4: Argumentation Practice 4 introduces the key thinking strategy behind psychological science: proposing a claim and using evidence and reasoning to support it.

Five Content Units

The Course and Exam description identifies the core essential knowledge required for the course that is covered in the five units. It also suggests how the units might be paced over the school year. Each unit can range from 17 to 23 school days to cover.

Unit 1: The Biological Bases of Behavior Unit 1 explores the relationship between nature (our biological makeup) and nurture (our environment) and takes a close look at the structures and functions of the brain and the nerves that send signals to and from the brain. It also explores the natural, environmental, and cultural aspects of sleep and explains how our senses take in and interpret our surroundings.

Unit 2: Cognition Unit 2 takes a close look at how internal and external factors affect how we perceive our environment and identifies the processes we use to think, problem solve, form judgments, and make decisions. It explores the fascinating explanations of how memory works—and can fail—and looks at the concept of intelligence testing and its application in a diverse world

Unit 3: Development and Learning Unit 3 outlines the development of humans from birth through old age, exploring along the way the various aspects of human development—physical, gender and sexual orientation, cognitive, communication and language, and social-emotional. It then turns to an in-depth look at how humans and nonhuman animals learn via processes such as classical and operant conditioning as well as social and cognitive learning.

Unit 4: Social Psychology and Personality Unit 4 explores individuals in relation to groups—how and why we see others as we do. It also covers various theories of personality as well as what motivates us and how emotions differ from other mental processes such as reasoning and knowledge.

Unit 5: Mental and Physical Health Unit 5 introduces the field of health psychology and the power of positive psychology to enhance wellbeing. It also explores a variety of psychological problems and current interventions and therapies that can be used in the course of treating those varied problems.

The Advanced Placement Psychology Exam

The course description also indicates that each of the five units of the book counts for roughly the same percentage of questions on the multiple-choice questions on the exam and therefore the same "weight" in scoring. Questions on the content of each unit range from 15% to 25% of the exam score, and they form the foundation of a number of questions on the exam. The percentage of multiple-choice questions based on each practice is described below.

Practice 1: Concept Application 65%

Practice 2: Research Methods and Design 25%

Practice 3: Data Interpretation 10%

The AP® Psychology exam is composed of two portions. The first consists of 75 multiple-choice questions, representing 66.7% of your exam score. You will have 90 minutes to complete those. The second portion has two free-response questions (FRQs) which make up 33.3% of your exam score. You will have 70 minutes to complete those for a total of two hours and forty minutes for the entire exam.

Your score on the exam will fall into one of the following five categories, which reflect the assessment of your college readiness. Since the exam is normed, the cutoff for each level changes from year to year. Different colleges have different criteria for accepting College Board scores, so be sure to check with any college of interest to you to find out its policy. The College Board considers scores of 3 and above to be passing.

5 = extremely well qualified

4 = well qualified

3 = qualified

2 = possibly qualified

1 = no recommendation

The Multiple-Choice Portion

The multiple-choice section must be completed in 90 minutes, so you will have a little more than a minute per question. There is no penalty for guessing—scoring is done based solely on how many questions you get correct. The multiple-choice portion accounts for two-thirds of the exam's total score.

Types of Multiple-Choice Questions Every multiple-choice question has two parts: the stem, or question, and four alternative choices you have to answer the question. On the AP exam, all of the alternatives represent genuine psychological concepts, though there will be only one clearly correct answer. The questions are written for clarity in both the stem and the alternatives. The stem can appear in many forms. You are likely to have a mix of the following main types of multiple-choice questions. *Don't worry if you don't know the answers to these questions now—you will learn the background to all of them in this course.*

Concept Application questions typically provide a scenario and ask which term best applies or connects to that scenario. For example:

1. Lexie is training her golden retriever puppy, Sunflower, to roll over. When Sunflower makes a move in the right direction, Lexie rewards her with a treat and "Good girl!" praise. Lexie is applying which of the following perspectives to training her dog?*

   (A) Evolutionary approach

   (B) Biological approach

   (C) Behaviorist approach

   (D) Cognitive approach

   * **The answer is (C).**

2. A child watches her mother use a credit card at the grocery store, and later the child plays a game pretending to buy groceries with a fake credit card. This is an example of which type of learning?*

   (A) Direct instruction

   (B) Observational learning

   (C) Auditory learning

   (D) Inferential learning

   * **The answer is (B).**

Questions on Research Methods and Designs will often include a summary of a research study and ask you to identify some aspect of the study. Research Methods and Designs are covered extensively in Practice 2. Following is an example.

3. Psychiatrists Corbett H. Thigpen and Hervey M. Cleckley treated a woman named Chris Costner Sizemore. They diagnosed her with what is now known as dissociative identity disorder characterized by the presence of different personalities, or alters, that would come forward at different times. The psychiatrists believed the alters helped Sizemore cope with trauma she experienced in childhood. What type of research method did Thigpen and Cleckley use to reach their conclusion?*

(A) Correlational study

(B) Case study

(C) Experimental study

(D) Meta-analyses

* The answer is (B).

Questions on Data Interpretation will often present the results of a study in a graphic and ask you to interpret the findings. Data interpretation is covered extensively in Practice 3. Many psychological theories have principles that can be clearly expressed in graphics. For example, a graph might show how many repetitions over how much time a cat needed to discover that pressing a lever led to a reward. Throughout this book, you will see graphs showing research results, and these will help prepare you for such questions.
Following is an example.

4. The following graph shows the results of a study on depression and hours of sleep per night. What conclusion can be drawn from these findings?*

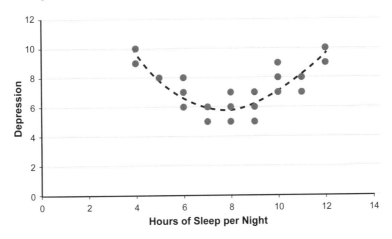

(A) The more hours people sleep, the less depressed they are.

(B) The fewer hours people sleep, the more depressed they are.

(C) There is no relationship between hours of sleep and depression.

(D) People who sleep between 7 and 9 hours a night have lower depression than those who sleep more or less.

* The answer is (D).

Some multiple-choice questions will be presented in sets, in which two to three questions will be based on the same scenario. These will appear as follows:

Questions 5 through 7 refer to the following.

Researchers wanted to know if suggestion could make people hear a sound that did not exist. Volunteers were randomized into two groups. Group 1 was told they would be taking a routine hearing test. Group 2 was told they would be taking a routine hearing test that made tones every five seconds. In actuality, both groups were given the exact same test with randomly timed tones. The chart below shows the results.

	GROUP 1	GROUP 2
Average percentage hearing loss at beginning of study	10	11
Number of tones that subjects missed	45	51
Tones that subjects claimed to hear but never occurred	6	74

5. Which psychological concept were the researchers testing?*
   (A) Perceptual set
   (B) Heuristics
   (C) Stereotypes
   (D) Person perception

   * The answer is (A).

6. What aspect of the study requires debriefing?*
   (A) The division of the groups
   (B) Hearing loss at the beginning of the study
   (C) The use of deception
   (D) The qualifications of the testers

   * The answer is (C).

7. What conclusion can be drawn from the study's findings?*
   (A) The difference in the participants' hearing loss at the beginning of the study explains why Group 2 heard more tones that did not exist.
   (B) The instructions to Group 2 led them to expect more sounds, which is likely why they thought they heard them.
   (C) Participants were not randomly assigned to groups.
   (D) Expectations did not influence participants' hearing of nonexistent tones.

   * The answer is (B).

Strategies for Answering Multiple-Choice Questions Following are strategies students have found useful for completing the multiple-choice portion of the exam.

- Although you have a limited amount of time, use it wisely by reading each question carefully.

- If you are confident of the speed of your reading, go through the multiple-choice section two times. The first time through, answer questions you are sure of and mark questions that you need to read again. When you do come back to them, something in the questions you completed may have triggered your memory.

- Read the stem of the question, and try to determine the answer without looking at the alternative responses. This strategy will allow you to recall an answer without getting confused by other alternatives. If you bring the answer to mind and it shows up as one of the alternatives, then you can move on to the next question. If you do not recall a response immediately, the alternative responses may help jog your memory.

The Free-Response Portion

The two free-response questions together are worth one-third of the overall score. Points are awarded for correct responses but not removed for incorrect material. Do not just write whatever comes to mind related to the question. Instead, thoughtfully provide a targeted response that shows clear understanding of the concepts in the question.

Topics of the FRQs Free-response questions are likely to include ideas from multiple units, asking about fundamental concepts in psychology that prepared students should be able to answer. Questions on perspectives of psychology and research methods are likely to be assessed. Be prepared with material from the entire course.

Two Types of FRQs You can, however, expect that there will be two different types of FRQs and you will have to answer one of each type. Each type is worth seven points.

The Article Analysis Question (AAQ) will provide a summary of a research study and directions for how to answer questions about it. The AAQ assesses Practices 2, 3, and 4. *You will have 25 minutes to answer it, including a suggested 10-minute period to read the summary and questions.*

Question 1: Article Analysis

Your response to the question should be provided in six parts: A, B, C, D, E, and F. Write the response to each part of the question in complete sentences. Use appropriate psychological terminology in your response.

Using the source provided, respond to all parts of the question.

(A) Identify the research method used in the study.

(B) State the operational definition of the participants' confidence in knowledge.

(C) Describe the meaning of the differences in confidence levels between the groups in the study.

(D) Identify at least one ethical guideline applied by the researchers.

(E) Explain the extent to which the research findings may or may not be generalizable using specific and relevant evidence from the study.

(F) Explain how at least one of the research findings supports or refutes the researchers' hypothesis that Internet users overestimate their personal knowledge.

Introduction
Researchers set out to explore the impact of Internet searches on individuals' perceptions of their own knowledge. The authors argue that searching the Internet for information leads people to overestimate their understanding of the topics they research, creating an illusion of knowledge. This phenomenon occurs because individuals mistake access to information for personal understanding.

Participants
The study involved 202 participants (119 men and 83 women, average age 32.59) from the United States who completed the study via Amazon's Mechanical Turk. Similar participant demographics and recruitment methods were used across subsequent experiments. Participants gave their informed consent.

Method
The study used several scenarios, each designed to investigate the effects of Internet searching on self-assessed knowledge. Participants were randomly assigned into two groups: one group used the Internet to search for explanations to common questions, while the other group did not. After the initial search task, both groups assessed their ability to answer unrelated questions in different domains on a scale of 1–7, with 1 indicating low confidence and 7 indicating high confidence. The researchers collected the participants' measures of confidence in their knowledge and analyzed the differences between the groups.

continued

Results and Discussion

The research demonstrated that participants who used the Internet to search for information rated their ability to answer unrelated questions significantly higher than those who did not use the Internet. Participants who had looked up explanations on the Internet rated themselves as being able to give significantly better explanations to the questions in the unrelated domains during the self-assessment phase (M = 3.61) than those who had not used the Internet (M= 3.07). The effect was observable across all six domains for which participants were asked to assess their knowledge. This effect was consistent even when controlling for variables such as time spent on the task and the content of the questions. The results indicate that the act of searching the Internet inflates individuals' self-assessed knowledge, leading them to believe they have a better understanding of various topics than they actually do.

The findings suggest that the Internet functions as a memory partner, where individuals rely on external sources for knowledge but fail to recognize the extent of this reliance. This overestimation of personal knowledge has implications for how people perceive their cognitive abilities and make decisions based on their perceived understanding. The study highlights the need for greater awareness of the limitations of personal knowledge and the potential pitfalls of over-reliance on external information sources.

Reference

Fisher, M., Goddu, M.K., Keil, Frank C. (2015). Searching for explanations: How the Internet inflates estimates of internal knowledge. *Journal of Experimental Psychology*, *144*(3), 674–687.

The points for the Article Analysis Question (AAQ) will be awarded according to the following general rubric.

Scoring Rubric

ARTICLE ANALYSIS QUESTION (AAQ)		
Elements of Research		
Reporting Category	**Scoring Criteria**	
Part A Research Method (0-1 points)	**0 points:** Does not accurately identify the research method used in the study	**1 point:** Accurately identifies the research method used in the study. EXAMPLE: The research method is an experiment.
Part B Research Variable (0-1 points)	**0 points:** Does not state a measurable or quantifiable definition of the identified variable used in the study.	**1 point:** States a measurable or quantifiable definition of the identified variable as used in the study EXAMPLE: Confidence was determined by self-rated ranking from 1 (low) to 7 (high).
Part C Statistical Interpretation (0-1 points)	**0 points:** Does not accurately describe the meaning of the differences in the participants' confidence.	**1 point:** Accurately describes the meaning of the differences in confidence between the groups. EXAMPLE: Participants rated their confidence higher if they had used the Internet (mean or average rating of 3.61 compared to 3.07 in the group not using the Internet) , suggesting an inflated sense of personal knowledge.

Part D	0 points: Does not	1 point: Accurately identifies at least
Ethical Guidelines	accurately identify at least one ethical guideline applied by researchers in the study.	one ethical guideline applied by researchers in the study.
(0-1 points)		EXAMPLES: Researchers obtained informed consent.
Part E	0 points: Does not propose a claim regarding the generalizability of the study to a population (general or specific)	1 point: Explains the extent to which the study is generalizable using specific and relevant evidence referencing participant variables from the study.
Generalizability		
(0-1 points)		EXAMPLE: The study is likely not generalizable because participants were not randomly selected.

Note: if the response states that the study is somewhat generalizable, it must support their assertion by explaining the ways in which it is and is not generalizable.

Reporting Category	Scoring Criteria		
Part F	0 points	1 point	2 points
Argumentation (0-2 points)	Does not accurately explain how the results of the study support or refute the psychological concept of hypothesis presented in the question.	Uses the results of the study but does not explain how the psychological concept or hypothesis is supported or refuted. **OR** Explains that the psychological concept or hypothesis is supported or refuted but does not use any results from the study.	Uses a specific result from the study to explain how the results support or refute the psychological concept or hypothesis presented in the question. The results are accurately interpreted. EXAMPLE: Since participants who used the Internet consistently rated their ability to answer unrelated questions higher, the study supports the hypothesis that external knowledge is often misperceived as personal knowledge.

The Evidence-Based Question (EBQ) will provide a summary of three research studies in the same format as the AAQ on related topics. They will be preceded by the directions for answering questions related to them. The EBQ assesses Practices 1 and 4. As the directions indicate, you must develop a defensible claim, identify evidence from the research studies related to it, and then use reasoning to explain the relationship between the claim and evidence. The reasoning must come from your knowledge of what you have learned in this course. *You will have 45 minutes to answer the EBQ, including a suggested 15-minute period for reading.*

The following example includes summaries of three different studies on the subject of the "spotlight effect," the belief that you are being noticed more than you really are. Since you are just beginning the course, you are not expected to be able to read these studies and then complete the evidence-based tasks. So here is an overview of these studies and how they relate to one another.

- **Source A** confirms the spotlight effect and examines different factors that could explain it as well as efforts people make to correct their first impression that people were paying more attention to them than they actually were.

- **Source B** considers the minority spotlight effect by examining how members of a minority group perceive they are being noticed when negative comments related to their group are made. In contrast to the previous study, in this study participants accurately gauged how much they were being noticed.

- **Source C** looks at both the spotlight effect and the illusion of transparency—the belief that one's internal states are more apparent than they are. Participants all had moderate to high levels of social anxiety. The results showed that when participants were placed in a context of high judgment (high social-evaluative context), they experienced higher levels of the spotlight effect and evaluated their performance on a task more negatively. Participants in a context of low judgment (low social evaluative context) reported higher levels of illusions of transparency than of the spotlight effect. The study adds to the understanding of the spotlight effect by showing how it can be influenced by social-evaluative concerns.

Together, these three studies offer slightly different takes on the spotlight effect. When you respond to the evidence-based question on the exam, you will draw on both similarities and differences in the sources to develop and support a claim—or position—related to the topic. For example, your claim might be that the spotlight effect, while widely experienced, can be influenced by factors unique to certain groups, situations, and anxiety levels. You might then find specific pieces of evidence from the studies to use to support your claim, and you would refer to them by saying something like, "Source B shows that for minority groups . . . ." You would then need to explain, using information you learned in this class, why the evidence supports the reasoning. By the time you take the exam, you will have learned about social psychology and might provide reasoning based on the concept of in-groups and out-groups.

Following is a complete question. A scoring rubric appears after it.

QUESTION 2: EVIDENCE-BASED QUESTION

This question has three parts: Part A, Part B, and Part C. Use the source provided to answer all parts of the question.

For Part B and Part C, you must cite the source that you used to answer the question. You can do this in two different ways:

- Parenthetical Citation
  For example: " . . ." (Source A)

- Embedded Citation
  For example: "According to Source A, . . ."

Write the response to each part of the question in complete sentences. Use appropriate psychological terminology.

Using the sources provided, develop and justify an argument related to [the topic of the studies]. (For this example, you might be asked to develop and justify an argument on the varied ways the spotlight effect is experienced by different groups.)

(A) Propose a specific and defensible claim based in psychological science that responds to the question.

(B) (i) Support your claim using at least one piece of specific and relevant evidence from one of the provided sources.

(ii) Use a psychological perspective, theory or concept, or research finding learned in AP Psychology to explain how your evidence supports your claim.

(C) (i) Support your claim using an additional piece of specific and relevant evidence from a different source than the one that was used in Part B (i).

(D) (ii) Explain how the evidence form Part C (i) supports your claim using a different psychological perspective, theory, concept, or research finding learned in AP Psychology than the one used in Part B (ii).

Source A

Introduction
The "spotlight effect" refers to people's tendency to overestimate how much others notice and remember their appearance and actions. This phenomenon stems from an egocentric bias, where individuals' rich subjective experiences make it difficult for them to accurately gauge others' perspectives. The study aims to provide empirical evidence for the spotlight effect through various experiments involving potentially embarrassing situations and group interactions.

Participants
The study included multiple groups of participants across different experiments. For instance, in Study 1, 109 Cornell University undergraduates participated, with 15 serving as target participants, 64 as observers, and 30 as controls. Participants were often recruited from university psychology classes and received extra credit or monetary compensation for their involvement.

Method
The research consisted of several experiments:

T-Shirt Experiment (Studies 1 and 2): Participants wore T-shirts with either an embarrassing image (e.g., Barry Manilow, a singer many considered uncool) or a positive image (e.g., Bob Marley, a singer widely loved) and estimated how many observers noticed the image.

Group Discussion Experiment (Study 3): Participants engaged in group discussions and later estimated how prominently their contributions and errors were perceived by others.

Anchoring-and-Adjustment Process (Studies 4 and 5): These studies investigated the cognitive processes behind the spotlight effect by asking participants to consider alternative estimates before finalizing their judgments and manipulating the time participants wore the T-shirts before encountering observers.

Results and Discussion

Studies 1 and 2: Participants overestimated the number of observers who noticed their T-shirts. The estimates were significantly higher than the actual number of observers who could identify the image on the T-shirt.

Study 3: Participants believed their positive and negative actions during group discussions were more prominent than others actually perceived them to be. This overestimation was consistent across various dimensions such as advancing the discussion and making speech errors.

Study 4: Participants typically considered higher values before adjusting their estimates downward, supporting the anchoring-and-adjustment explanation.

Study 5: Participants who had time to get used to wearing the embarrassing T-shirt estimated lower observer notice rates than those who encountered observers immediately.

The findings consistently supported the spotlight effect, demonstrating that people overestimate how much their actions and appearance are noticed by others. The results were attributed to an anchoring-and-adjustment process, where individuals' initial intense self-focus is only partially corrected for when estimating others' attention.

Reference

Gilovich, T., Medvec, V. H., & Savitsky, K. (2000). The spotlight effect in social judgment: An egocentric bias in estimates of the salience of one's own actions and appearance. *Journal of Personality and Social Psychology*, 5(7), 743–750. DOI: 10.1037//0022-3514.78.2.211

Source B

Introduction
The study investigates the Minority Spotlight Effect, where members of minority groups feel they are the focus of others' attention when topics related to their group are discussed. This sensation of being in the spotlight often comes with negative emotions. The research aims to understand this experience from the minority individual's perspective, examining their feelings of conspicuousness and emotional reactions in such situations.
Participants
The study involved three groups of participants: 1. **Study 1:** 41 Black students from Williams College. 2. **Study 2:** 82 Williams College students, including Black, Latino/Latina, and White participants. 3. **Study 3:** 154 Williams College students, with a mix of male and female participants from various racial backgrounds.
Method
Participants were placed in scenarios where their minority group status was made obvious. **Study 1:** Black students imagined being in a class where a provocative comment about race was made. **Study 2:** Participants listened to recordings on affirmative action (race-relevant) or carbon emissions (neutral) while two confederates directed their gaze according to a predetermined schedule. **Study 3:** Female participants listened to recordings about women's underrepresentation in STEM (gender-relevant) or carbon emissions (neutral). Participants then reported how much they felt they were the focus of attention and their emotional responses.
Results and Discussion
Study 1: Black participants felt more in the spotlight and experienced negative emotions when the professor made a race-related comment. **Study 2:** Minority participants felt they were looked at more and felt more in the spotlight when the recording was race-relevant, with accurate estimates of how much they were observed. **Study 3:** Female participants felt more in the spotlight and experienced negative emotions when the recording was gender-relevant, accurately estimating how much they were observed. The studies support the idea that minority individuals feel conspicuous and experience negative emotions when their group is made noticeable. This feeling is linked to the responsibility of representing their group and heightened self-awareness. Contrary to the general spotlight effect, minority participants accurately estimated others' attention, possibly due to increased vigilance. The research highlights the need for environments where minority group members do not feel isolated or overly scrutinized.
Reference
Crosby, J.R., King, M., & Savitsky, K. (2014). The minority spotlight effect. *Social Psychological and Personality Science.* 78(2), 211–222. DOI: 10.1177/1948550614527625.

Source C

Introduction
The study explores the concepts of the spotlight effect and the illusion of transparency in relation to social anxiety. The spotlight effect refers to the tendency of individuals to overestimate how much others notice their actions and appearance, while the illusion of transparency is the belief that one's internal states are more apparent to others than they actually are. The study investigates how these cognitive biases (distorted ways of thinking) contribute to the construction of the self as a social object in individuals with social anxiety.
Participants
The study included multiple groups of participants across different experiments. Participants were students from the University of Southampton who had completed the Brief Fear of Negative Evaluation Scale (BFNES), a psychological assessment tool designed to measure the fear of negative evaluation from others, which is a key component of social anxiety. It consists of 12 items, each rated on a five-point scale ranging from 1 (not at all characteristic of me) to 5 (extremely characteristic of me). A total of 60 students, with moderate to high levels of social anxiety, were selected for the study. The sample included 53 women and 7 men, divided into two conditions: a context with high social evaluation and a context with low social evaluation.
Method
The study used a between-subjects design, a type of experimental design in which different groups of participants are exposed to different conditions or treatments. This means that each participant experiences only one condition of the experiment, allowing for comparisons between groups rather than within a single group.
Participants were allocated to either a high or low social-evaluative condition. In the high social-evaluative condition, participants performed a memory task while being videotaped and told their performance would be evaluated by experts. In the low social-evaluative condition, participants performed the same task with the belief that their recall would be coded for significant events without evaluation. Participants completed the Self-Awareness and Task Performance Questionnaire (SATP-Q) and other measures assessing fear of negative evaluation and depression. An independent assessor rated participants' performance and self-awareness based on videotapes.
Results and Discussion
Participants in the high social-evaluative condition reported higher levels of the spotlight effect and evaluated their task performance more negatively compared to those in the low social-evaluative condition. However, there was no significant difference in levels of the illusion of transparency between the two conditions. Interestingly, participants in the low social-evaluative condition reported higher levels of the illusion of transparency than the spotlight effect, while those in the high social-evaluative condition reported the opposite. These findings suggest that the spotlight effect is more closely tied to social-evaluative concerns, whereas the illusion of transparency may be a more general feature of social anxiety.
Reference
Brown, M. A., & Stopa, L. (2007). The spotlight effect and the illusion of transparency in social anxiety. *Journal of Anxiety Disorders*, *21*(6), 804-819. DOI: 10.1016/j.janxdis.2006.11.006.

The points for the Evidence-Based Question (EBQ) will be awarded according to the following general rubric.

Scoring Rubric

FRQ: EVIDENCE-BASED QUESTION (EBQ)		
Reporting Category	**Scoring Criteria**	
Part A Claim (0-1 points)	**0 points** Does not propose a claim that is relevant to the question.	**1 point** Proposes a claim that is relevant to the question. EXAMPLE: Although the spotlight effect is widely observed, how it is experienced varies according to minority group status, the judgmental nature of certain contexts, and anxiety levels.

Note: A claim that meets the criteria can be awarded the points regardless of whether the responses in Parts B and C successfully support the claim.

Reporting Category	**Scoring Criteria**	
Part B (i) Evidence (0-1 points)	**0 points** Does not identify nor correctly cite one piece of specific evidence from one of the provided sources to support the claim. Any evidence provided is not relevant to the question.	**1 point** Uses one piece of correctly cited, specific, and relevant evidence from one of the provided sources to support the claim. EXAMPLE: According to Source B, when members of a minority group experience a negative comment, they accurately assess the degree to which they are noticed.

Note: Responses that use a correct citation style other than the methods prescribed by the question can earn the point for citing the source.

Reporting Category	**Scoring Criteria**		
Part B (ii) Explanation and Application (0-2 points)	**0 points** Does not explain the relationship between the evidence and the claim.	**1 point** Explains the relationship between the evidence and the claim.	**2 points** Applies a psychological perspective, theory, concept or research finding to explain how the evidence supports the claim. EXAMPLE: In-group/out-group theories in social psychology explain that when minority group members find themselves in settings dominated by majority group members, they are more likely to categorize themselves as part of the out-group. This categorization heightens awareness of their minority status and increases the perception of being watched.

Additional Notes:
- The explanation and application points can be earned even if the response did not earn the point in B(i) due to incorrectly cited and/or non-specific evidence.
- The psychological perspective, theory, concept, or research finding must be explicitly identified in the *AP Psychology Course Exam Description* (2024).
- The presence of a citation indicates the sentence or phrase is intended to be "evidence". All text prior to the citation will be considered "evidence". Text after a citation will be considered reasoning, unless accompanied by another citation.

Reporting Category	Scoring Criteria	
Part C (i)	**0 points**	**1 point**
Evidence (0-1 points)	Does not identify nor correctly cite one piece of specific evidence from one of the provided sources to support the claim. Any evidence provided is not relevant to the question.	Uses one piece of correctly cited, specific, and relevant evidence form one of the provided sources to support the claim. EXAMPLE: Source C shows that "participants in the high social-evaluative condition reported higher levels of the spotlight effect," adding the factor of a high-judgment situation to the occurrence of the spotlight effect.

Reporting Category	Scoring Criteria		
Part C (ii)	**0 points**	**1 point**	**2 points**
Explanation and Application (0-2 points)	Does not explain the relationship between the evidence and the claim.	Explains the relationship between the evidence and the claim.	Applies a psychological perspective, theory, concept or research finding to explain how the evidence supports the claim. EXAMPLE: Social anxiety disorder (social phobia) involves the intense fear of being judged or watched by others. It causes some people to become overwhelmed with anxiety and fear when in social situations. They have an intense fear of being criticized or embarrassed, so they avoid such social situations as large events or parties, public speaking, being on stage, or using public restrooms. This disorder helps explain why the spotlight effect is experienced at a high level in the study with social evaluative contexts.

Additional Notes:

- The explanation and application points can be earned even if the response did not earn the point in B(i) due to incorrectly cited and/or non-specific evidence.
- The explanation and application points can be earned if the response uses the same source in both Parts B and C, provided that the evidence used in Part B and C is different.
- The psychological perspective, theory, concept, or research finding must be explicitly identified in the *AP Psychology Course Exam Description* (2024) and is different from the perspective theory, concept or research finding used in part B.
- The presence of a citation indicates the sentence or phrase is intended to be "evidence". All text prior to the citation will be considered "evidence". Text after a citation will be considered reasoning, unless accompanied by another citation.

Task Verbs In its Course and Exam Description, the College Board® defines the task verbs used in the FRQs as follows. Be sure you understand what each question is asking you to do.

- **Describe:** Provide the relevant characteristics of a specified topic.
- **Explain:** Provide information about how or why a relationship, process, pattern, position, situation, or outcome occurs, using evidence and/or reasoning to support or qualify a claim.
  — Explain "how" typically requires analyzing the relationship, process, pattern, position, situation, or outcome;
  —Explain "why" typically requires analysis of motivations or reasons for the relationship, process, pattern, position, situation, or outcome.
- **Identify/State:** Indicate or provide information about a specified topic, without elaboration or explanation.
- **Propose:** Provide a claim for a specific topic using your own words.
- **Support or Refute:** Provide reasoning that explains whether a claim or evidence should be upheld or rejected.
- **Use evidence:** Provide information from a study (i.e., data, rationales, conclusions, hypotheses) that is specific and relevant to a given topic.

Strategies for Answering Free-Response Questions

Following are strategies to use when answering the free-response portion of the exam:

- Plan your time carefully. You may want to devote 25 minutes to the AAQ and 45 minutes to the EBQ, including reading time.
- Carefully read each question and identify exactly what is being asked before you start writing.
- Highlight the verbs that show what task(s) you are to complete: describe, explain, and draw a conclusion, for example.
- Write in complete sentences.

- Each answer should address the one particular point you are trying to earn. Devote a paragraph to each term or concept and clearly identify the concept the paragraph addresses.

- You do not need to write the type of essays you might write in your English classes, with an introduction stating a thesis statement or claim and a conclusion following from the evidence provided. There is no need to restate the question. The first sentence should be about the first concept in the question.

- Definitions alone do not score, but including a definition is always a good idea. Be sure to apply the terms to the scenario in the prompt.

- Avoid circular definitions, those that use the terms themselves in the definitions. For example, if you are defining the term cognitive dissonance, do not write, "Cognitive dissonance is when someone experiences dissonance in their cognition." Instead, look for synonyms. *Cognitive* relates to thinking, so use thinking in your response. *Dissonance* is about ideas clashing or conflicting. Use those words instead: Cognitive dissonance is the uncomfortable feeling that results when your thinking conflicts with your actions.

- Show your knowledge—use psychological terms and ideas for your reasoning and clear evidence from the text

Features of This Book
A number of features help you make the most of your learning experience.

- Each unit begins with a brief overview and then a listing of the **Learning Objectives** covered in the unit. The Learning Objectives directly align with those identified in the AP Psychology Course and Exam Description and provide a quick summary of the unit's contents, first to set your mind before you read and later to provide memory cues when you are reviewing for the exam.

- **Study Like a Champ with Dr. G.** (Dr. Regan Gurung) then provides you with science-tested strategies to learn and remember as much as you can in each unit.

- Each topic begins with an **Essential Question** to help you read with a purpose and focus your thoughts on answering that question.

- At the end of each topic, the **Reflect on the Essential Question** feature provides a suggested graphic organizer for you to complete as you take notes from each main part of the topic to answer the essential question. Completing the graphic organizers will help you consolidate the material, and the organizers will be a helpful review tool.

- Throughout the topics you will encounter many **Think as a Psychologist** features. These are activities to help you develop and strengthen the foundational practices you were introduced to in the front section of the book. You will be surprised at how good you get at applying psychological concepts, identifying elements of research designs, interpreting data, and proposing defensible claims.

- A chart at the end of each chapter with **Key Terms** lists the important terms, concepts, and people from the chapter to help you review before the exam. Within each topic, the key terms are presented in **bold type.** When you see that bold type, pay close attention, because you will be expected to know those terms.

- Each topic concludes with six or seven multiple-choice questions patterned after those you will encounter on the exam..

- At the end of the unit, more Study Like a Champ strategies help you pull together what you are learning.

- Each unit concludes with 15 multiple-choice questions and both types of FRQs—the Article Analysis Question and the Evidence-Based Question. In the first unit, the EBQ refers to just one study; in the second unit it refers to two, and in Units 3–5, three summarized studies are provided to use for the EBQ.

- **A full practice exam** at the end of the book gives you a "trial run" to help you identify any areas in need of extra review. **Two additional exams** are available for your teacher to download.

General Tips for Studying for the Exam

Preparing for the AP Psychology exam is like nothing else you have done (unless you have taken other AP exams). Although your teacher will likely give you quizzes and tests throughout the course on discrete topics, the AP exam itself requires comprehension and retention of five units' worth of information and learning. You cannot possibly memorize all the names, dates, and facts in this book—instead, you need to create a framework in your mind for them built on important and enduring concepts. Use every possible strategy to make the material your own—read it, take notes on it, talk about it, create visualizations of it, and relate the ideas in this book to your prior experience and learning. The following approaches will help you accomplish this goal:

- Form a weekly **study** group. Use the Essential Question from each chapter as the starting point for your discussion, focusing on how the material you learned during the week helps to answer that question, or work collaboratively on the graphic organizer at the end of the chapter. Ask questions about anything you do not understand. The weekly meetings ensure that you will prepare on a regular basis, and they also give you a chance to speak about and listen to the concepts you are learning in addition to reading and writing about them.

- Follow the clear, conversational advice below from an expert in learning strategies, Dr. Regan Gurung, to get the most out of this course.

STUDY LIKE A CHAMP WITH DR. G.

Forget everything you have been told about how to study! Unless a teacher or parent has kept up to date on the latest science on what best helps you learn, you have probably not been given all the facts. Let's change that.

Most students waste their time studying the wrong way. Beyond spending too much time scrolling reels on social media or texting, two major distractions which can derail studying plans (and which you should get under your control), the average person just does not know how best to study. Consider these two students:

Liam's approach is to read his material repeatedly. He highlights important points in a variety of colors, creates summaries and outlines, and then rereads his material again. Melina reads her material once, takes notes on the main points, and then tests herself on the material, often two to three times a week. Are you more like Liam or Melina?

The reality is both are using common study methods. Reading and rereading a text is perhaps the most common way to study. Spoiler alert! It is also one of the most *ineffective* ways to learn. Shockingly, so too is highlighting text and summarizing material. All these three techniques are extremely common, but years of psychological research have shown that they are not the best ways to study. Melina has it right. Be like Melina.

For over sixty years now, areas such as cognitive, developmental, social, experimental, and biological psychology (all areas you will learn more about in this book), have explored what helps people learn. As you get started in your quest to learn psychology for your AP exam and future coursework, here are the fruits of psychological science to help you do your very best. If you use the right study techniques, you will not only understand the material well, but you will also remember it for a long time. Our biggest challenge as humans is the first word of the first sentence in this Study Like a Champ guide. We *forget*. We hear information. We study information. We hope to know about it for years later (remember that great time you had on your eighth birthday?). Unfortunately, we forget.

The good news is that if you use the study techniques described here and throughout this book well, not only will you be able to learn a lot of material, but you will be able to remember it for a long time. Certainly, long enough for your AP exam, and if done well, long enough to apply the great content and improve your life. So what are the key techniques? First, let's look at your options.

Combined, Liam and Melina use many of the most often used study techniques: rereading, highlighting, summarizing, testing, and spacing out studying. There are more specifics of course. There is the use of memory shortcuts such as mnemonics (e.g., the acronym OCEAN for key human personality traits of openness, conscientiousness, extraversion, agreeableness, and neuroticism). There is making examples of what you are studying and elaborating on the material. There is mixing up what you study so each study session involves, say, some biology, some psychology, some math (a technique called interleaving). There is using flash cards to study key terms. Many of these work, but what's the best?

A group of psychological scientists asked exactly that question. They collected all the research they could find on all these study techniques and looked at which ones were most tied to students' learning. They read hundreds of studies. They even did some of their own research testing different techniques. I know, because I did a lot of that work myself with colleagues (see Gurung & Dunlosky, 2022). I am going to give it to you straight so you can use the best techniques to study for your AP Psychology (and any other) exam. Here it is.

Of all the study techniques, ONLY TWO are clear-cut winners. Your time studying is best spent in *retrieval practice* and using *spacing*. Let's unpack this.

Retrieval practice is what Melina did in the scenario above. You test yourself on the material you are trying to learn. Retrieval or "bringing back" is your seeing if you can pull the information from your head. When we learn something new, we can hold onto it for about 30 seconds before we lose it. This working memory is short term. Our challenge is to get it into long-term storage (a lot more on this in Unit 2 on Cognition). Research demonstrates that by testing yourself often, you help strengthen the memory in your long-term storage. The more you try to remember what you studied, the stronger the memory becomes. The single best thing you can do to learn well for an exam is to test yourself over and over and over.

This benefit of testing is so strong, that if you have a limited amount of time, you will learn and remember better if you test yourself repeatedly than if you spend that same time rereading the material. You can test yourself by having a friend ask you questions or working in a study group, by trying to write down material on a blank sheet without your textbook or notes present, or even have AI (e.g., ChatGPT) give you questions on the material.

Spacing is the second most important technique. In contrast to cramming or studying the whole day before an exam, you should spread out your studying. For every class, plan to study the material at least three times a week. This spacing out of your studying also strengthens memories. When you separate out when you study, evidence suggests that your brain is strengthening or consolidating the memories in between study sessions. Space out when you test yourself for best effects.

Of course, AP Psychology is not the only course you are studying for. Spacing out your retrieval practice works for any course, but to ensure that you do it, you need to plan well. Schedule out every hour of your week. Make sure you get enough sleep, have time for physical activity and time in nature, have time for friends and family, and most of all, have time to space out your studying. For specific tips on how to plan, measure your own current study technique, and even for TikTok clips on how to use and practice good study habits, check out all the links here: bit.ly/pipgurung. You will also be prompted at the beginning and end of each unit to use these tested strategies so you can study like a champ!

Finally, have fun with psychology. Those who study psychology can develop insights into themselves and others. This field of study has given us many "Aha!" moments in our lives, and we wish the same for you.

Laura Brandt

Mike Hamilton

Jeffery Mio

Regan Gurung

Practice 1

Concept Application:

Apply Psychological Perspectives, Theories, Concepts, and Research Findings

Practice 1.A Apply psychological perspectives, theories, concepts, and research findings to a scenario.

AT A GLANCE: KEY TERMS AND OVERVIEW

- **Psychological perspectives** refer to different frames of reference or approaches used to understand and explain human behavior and mental processes. Think of a perspective as a lens that filters the way a person examines people's and animals' thinking and behavior. Just as you would see the world as red if you looked at it through a red lens, a perspective changes how you see the world. For example, the *cognitive perspective* focuses on how people think, remember, and solve problems. A cognitive psychologist wants to understand how the mind works and shapes how people interpret the world around them. The *behavioral perspective* examines how people's actions are shaped by their environment and experiences and how they can change behaviors through rewards and reinforcements or punishments. These are just two of the psychological perspectives that have been developed over the years.

- **Theories** in psychology are organized sets of principles and propositions designed to explain and predict behavior and mental processes, such as Jean Piaget's theory of how thinking develops through different stages of life or different models of how our memory encodes, stores, and retrieves information.

- **Concepts** in psychology are fundamental ideas or constructs used to describe and understand psychological phenomena, such as perception, memory, emotion, motivation, and personality. You will likely find many concepts in this text that explain experiences you have had, but as you learn the language of psychology, you will also have the rationale and explanations behind these concepts. For example, when something in our life does not go as we hoped, we often blame external forces. When things go well, on the other hand, we often take personal credit. This concept is known as the *self-serving bias*, and we often use it to protect our fragile self-esteem so we can continue to believe we are capable and successful individuals.

- **Research findings** in psychology are the results obtained through empirical (verifiable by observation) investigation and experimentation, providing evidence to support or refute hypotheses, theories, and concepts. The findings in psychology are derived from the same processes as in any other scientific discipline. The difference is that psychologists study human and animal behavior and cognition. These findings contribute to the advancement of knowledge in various areas of psychology, from understanding psychological disorders to exploring thinking and language processes and social behavior.

- **Logical conclusions** are often the result of research. They are formed through reasoning based on information and evidence.

- **Objective conclusions** are those that are based on evidence, not personal beliefs, even when the evidence presents a conclusion you did not expect to support.

- A **scenario** is a description of a possible situation that a psychological principle or concept will help to explain.

The Development of Psychology

To learn the skills associated with Practice 1, you need at least an introductory understanding of the **psychological perspectives, theories, concepts,** and **research findings** to be able to apply them to a scenario.

The following brief overview of the development of psychology introduces the various perspectives, theories, concepts, and research findings that have helped shape the discipline. You will learn more about them in later units, and you will apply these perspectives, theories, and concepts to scenarios you encounter in this book. Try to apply them to your own life experiences, as well, because then what you learn is more likely to stick.

As you read about the development of psychology, note how one theory or perspective often arises to address weaknesses in another theory. This process is essential for the advancement of knowledge and understanding. Scientific theories are dynamic and subject to revision based on new evidence and insights. You will see that the theories you read about here are continually modified as researchers find out more about human and animal behavior and cognition and use more advanced technologies to study these phenomena.

Also note the inclusion of more female psychologists as the discipline developed and a gradual realization of potential biases in research, both reflecting changing social attitudes and the acceptance of multicultural differences—in simple terms, the realization that a "one-size-fits-all" approach to psychological perspectives, theories, and concepts was an unrealistic and unhelpful goal.

The Birth of Psychology as a Science

As you read the brief history of psychology that follows, don't worry about remembering names and dates. You will not be expected to know them. Instead, focus on the development of concepts and perspectives.

Psychology as a discipline was inspired by other scientific disciplines, such as biology and chemistry. Just as biology had developed a process for understanding plants and chemistry for understanding chemicals, psychology inspired the process for understanding more about human behavior and thought. The official "birth" of psychology is often attributed to the German philosopher, physician, and professor Wilhelm Wundt, who is known as "the father of psychology" because he was the first person to study humans in a laboratory setting. Wundt began studying people in his laboratory in Leipzig, Germany, in 1879. He wanted to move the field of psychology away from philosophy and make it a discipline that was more measurable and scientific (empirical). Chemicals and other elements were being studied in laboratories, and Wundt believed that humans could be studied in much the same way. To study them, Wundt used a process he called *introspection*, which required people to report their conscious experiences (sensations, perceptions, and first reactions) in relation to a number of different objects. Unfortunately, the process of introspection was unsuccessful in achieving his goal because people's responses were too subjective and, unlike chemicals, they changed from trial to trial.

Edward Titchener brought Wundt's ideas to the United States in 1892. Titchener worked at Cornell University and promoted the study of conscious experience by attempting to break it down into its most basic components or "structures" using Wundt's introspective techniques to understand the whole. He coined the term *structuralism* to identify this approach. Because it was so closely related to the work of Wundt, structuralism is sometimes thought of as the first "school" of psychology.

William James, an American philosopher, physician, and professor at Harvard University, was one of many who were critical of structuralism. James believed it made more sense to examine the *function* of consciousness—what purpose did it serve? Just as Wundt had been influenced by the objective measurement of other scientific fields, James had been influenced by the work of Charles Darwin and his *theory of evolution*—the view that organisms change over time as they adapt to their environment and that adaptations that serve the function of promoting survival are passed on to offspring. Rather than seeing consciousness as made up of "structures," James saw it as a continuous flow; he coined the term *stream of consciousness* to describe it. James saw the big picture and asked what its *function* was. James saw the function of consciousness as an evolutionary adaptation to the environment that made it possible for humans to thrive and continue to adapt. His approach became known as *functionalism*. James also wrote the first comprehensive textbook of psychology, *Principles of Psychology* (1890).

Mary Whiton Calkins received one-on-one lessons in psychology from James. She conducted early studies on memory and served as the first woman president of the American Psychological Association. She founded one of the first psychology laboratories in the country at Wellesley College. Today, more than half of all undergraduate and graduate degrees in psychology at all universities are granted to women.

Margaret Floy Washburn was the first woman to receive her Ph.D. in psychology (from Cornell University in 1894). Earlier, at Columbia University, she had studied under Raymond Cattell, a psychologist who had identified 16 discrete personality traits. Washburn was interested in animal behavior and wrote a book titled *The Animal Mind* (1908). She would later have an impact on behaviorists (see Topics 3.7 and 3.8), who conducted much of their research with animals. Washburn also served as the president of the American Psychological Association and taught psychology for many years at Vassar.

Max Wertheimer took the field in another direction in Germany in 1912. His approach became known as *Gestalt psychology* (*Gestalt* translates to "shape" or "form"). To understand this approach, look at the picture below. It is actually made of hundreds of photos, but our focus is drawn to the larger figures of the mother and daughter. While structuralists wanted to examine each small picture, metaphorically, Gestalt psychologists, like functionalists, encouraged looking at the shape or form of the whole.

Figure P1.1 Like humans, this collage can be examined by looking at its smallest parts (as structuralists might do) or by seeing the whole entity (as Gestalt psychologists would do).

Modern Approaches to Psychology

Structuralism and functionalism are foundational theories for understanding the origins of the discipline of psychology. They eventually gave way to modern approaches to psychology, which continue to evolve to help us understand human and animal behavior and the human mind. Each of the approaches briefly described below will be covered in much more detail in later units.

Psychoanalytic Approach Austrian neurologist Sigmund Freud studied medicine but soon discovered that not all ailments were physical. Psychological ailments, he believed, could be treated by what one of his patients identified as "the talking cure." The *psychoanalytic approach* Freud developed in the late 1890s emphasized the role of the *unconscious*, a repository of memories, feelings, and drives, many of them unwanted, that are beyond the reach of conscious awareness.

Freud posited that we have three conflicting parts of our personality. The *id* holds our wants and desires and is primarily motivated by sex and aggression. The *superego*, in contrast, acts as our conscience and leads us to "do the right thing." Freud believed that the id and superego were often at odds with each other. To negotiate the conflicting forces, the *ego* allows people to get what they want and desire within the confines set by society by acting on what Freud referred to as the *reality principle*. Freud also believed that our personality was shaped by the time we were 6 or 7 years old.

Because the unconscious cannot be studied objectively, psychoanalytic theory was criticized for its lack of scientific objectivity. Many also believe that Freud overemphasized the influence of the unconscious on behavior. A more modern take on Freud's ideas emphasizes the importance of childhood events but limits other aspects of his theories. This is known as the *psychodynamic approach*. (See Topic 4.4.)

Behavioral Approach The *behavioral approach* arose in 1913 from criticisms of the psychoanalytic approach. Rather than focus on one's unconscious, which cannot be studied empirically, behaviorists chose to focus on *observable* behavior. John Watson, like Wilhelm Wundt, believed behavior needed to be observable to be objectively and empirically measured. Watson built on the work of Edward Thorndike, who placed cats in puzzle boxes and found that once cats figured out how to escape from the puzzle box for a reward, they would repeat the behavior over and over again. He observed the *law of effect*—responses that produce a satisfying effect will likely be repeated; those that produce an undesirable effect will likely not be repeated. In a similar way, behaviorism rests on the tenet that behaviors that are rewarded will be repeated and those that are punished will eventually be extinguished. Behaviorism is often described as the study of *stimulus and response* learning.

Watson became infamous for asking the experimental question, "Can we condition fears in young children?" In a study (the ethics of which were highly questionable), Watson tested a young boy in his lab who became known as Little Albert. Little Albert had a particular affinity for a white rat. Watson presented Albert with the rat and at the same time made a loud noise, which scared Albert. After multiple pairings of the loud noise with the rat, Albert came to fear the white rat alone even when there was no frightening sound. This technique of paired associations is known as *classical conditioning*. In the early 20th century, Russian psychologist Ivan Pavlov devised experiments in classical conditioning, training dogs to salivate at the sound of a tone. (See Topics 3.7 and 3.8.)

Like Watson, B. F. Skinner believed that behavior should be studied objectively using the scientific method, and only what can be seen or observed is measurable. In the 1930s, he created an *operant conditioning chamber* (also known as a *Skinner box*) in which an animal—often a rat or a pigeon—would be trained to complete a voluntary behavior, such as turning around or pecking the corner of the cage. Once the behavior was completed, the animal would receive a reward, which often increased the likelihood of the behavior occurring again. This process became known as *operant conditioning*. Like Thorndike, Skinner believed that behavior that was rewarded would be repeated, while behavior that was punished would not be repeated. (Try to think of ways in which your own life has been shaped by seeking out behaviors for which you are rewarded and avoiding those for which you are likely to receive a punishment.) Because Skinner emphasized the importance of learning through rewards and punishments, he believed that people have no free will and essentially operate based solely on past learning, like robots.

The behaviorist approach is still popular today, but people have moved away from the radical approach taken by Skinner and Watson. While Skinner acknowledged that people had thoughts, he believed thoughts had little scientific value because, since they could not be observed, they could not be studied objectively.

Cognitive Approach By examining thinking and perception, the *cognitive approach* addresses the flaw Skinner identified in studying thoughts. The cognitive revolution in psychology took place in the mid- to late 1950s. Psychologists such as Harry Harlow and others began to wonder why behaviorists were studying rats and pigeons to learn about human behavior rather than animals that were closer to humans, such as primates. They also believed that, by failing to examine thought processes, the field of psychology was not addressing a major factor that drove behavior: thinking.

The cognitive approach studies how thinking and perception influence behavior. This field includes such topics as memory, problem-solving, decision-making, and perception. While cognitive psychologists do not necessarily discount observable behavior, they are more concerned with the internal functions driving behavior. Psychologists such as Jean Piaget studied how children's cognitive development unfolds. The cognitive perspective remains a strong approach today, and new methods allow more objective study of how people think, interpret information, and make decisions in given situations. (See Topic 3.4.)

Humanistic Approach In the 1950s, the *humanistic approach* also came to prominence. This approach addressed perceived flaws in both the psychoanalytic and behavioral approaches. The humanistic approach has a more positive outlook on people related to their motivation to fulfill their potential. In addition, humanists focused on a person's future rather than the past. This approach also took issue with the behaviorists' idea that humans have no free will and are driven only by past rewards and punishments. The humanists believed that people do have free will and ultimately are responsible for the decisions they make, regardless of what they may have learned in the past. Humanism focuses on the potential of people and their drive to be their best. (See Topic 4.4.)

Carl Rogers was one of the founders of the humanistic approach in the 1950s. Before Rogers went into the field of psychology, he was training to be a minister, a calling that perhaps helps explain his optimistic view of the world. Rogers did acknowledge that environments may not always be ideal and can prevent individuals from reaching their potential. Abraham Maslow built on these ideas and created a model of a *hierarchy of needs* (1954), in which people move from basic biological needs to their full potential, which he identified as self-actualization. Like Rogers, Maslow believed that people strive to reach their highest potential but can be limited by a poor environment.

The humanistic approach today remains strong in the field of therapy but is criticized for what many describe as an overly optimistic view of human behavior. Also, many say it works well as a general approach to life but is not inclusive enough to be considered an explanation of all human thought and behavior.

Sociocultural Approach The *sociocultural approach* emphasizes the impact of people's culture, religion, ethnicity, gender, income level, and overall environment on the individuals they become. To better understand the sociocultural approach, think about how your family, religion, high school environment, and peer group shape your beliefs and goals. Also, consider how you might be different if you practiced a different religion, grew up in a different neighborhood, or had a different ethnic background. (See Topics 3.4 and 5.3.)

Biological Approach This approach focuses primarily on examining how genetics, the nervous system, hormones, and brain structures influence a person's thinking and behavior. Damage to certain areas in the left hemisphere of the brain can result in a lack of language functioning; an excess of a neurotransmitter called dopamine may be a contributing cause of schizophrenia. These types of findings are the focus of the *biological approach* to psychology. While examining biological factors that may cause a lack of functioning, this approach also focuses on how biological treatments may improve certain conditions. Treatments primarily involve medication to regulate levels of hormones or neurotransmitters in the brain and body. As brain scanning techniques such as CTs and MRIs continue to improve, biological psychologists are learning more than ever about how the brain operates. (See Topics 1.4 and 5.3.)

Evolutionary Approach This approach dates back to Charles Darwin and his thoughts on *natural selection* and the *survival of the fittest,* the process by which the genes that are most beneficial for survival are protected and strengthened and the organisms that develop those genes survive and pass them to future generations. However, *evolutionary psychologists* think beyond

Darwin's famous study of the *physical* adaptations of finches to look for aspects of human thought and behavior that may give individuals or their genes a better chance for survival in the future. For example, evolutionary psychologists may examine why many people have an aversion to bitter tastes (they may have been an indication of poisonous foods that were dangerous to eat), or they may explain that we are attracted to those with certain physical traits because those traits tend to be associated with higher chances for successful reproduction. (See Topics 1.1 and 5.3.)

Biopsychosocial Model In the late 20th century, psychiatrist George L. Engel formulated a model of treating patients that looked for explanations of illness, as well as potential treatments, by examining the interactions of the patient's biology, personality, and social influences—the *biopsychosocial model.* While recognizing the biological and physiological elements of disease, Engel and others who followed believed that a patient's perception of an illness or condition and the social environment of the patient both have an influence on treatment outcome. The interaction of these elements can also help explain the onset of disease: Someone who grows up in a family of smokers (social) might be more likely to become a smoker because of a desire to belong (psychological), and smoking is a known disease-causing behavior (biological). Some psychiatrists and medical doctors believe that Engel's ideas have helped medical doctors see patients as whole beings rather than just biological systems. (See Topic 5.3.)

MODERN APPROACHES TO PSYCHOLOGY		
Perspective	**Image to Remember**	**Explanation**
Psychodynamic	Conscious Mind / The Unconscious Mind	The iceberg represents levels of consciousness and shows the scope of the unconscious mind compared to that of the conscious mind.
Behavioral		Behavior that is observable and measurable is scientifically useful. People learn through rewards and punishments.

MODERN APPROACHES TO PSYCHOLOGY		
Perspective	**Image to Remember**	**Explanation**
Cognitive		Thinking and perception influence behavior.
Humanistic		The flower is trying to reach its full potential and blossom. Even in a bad environment, it will try its best. People strive to be their best.
Sociocultural		Individuals are influenced by the people and culture that surround them.
Biological

Hypothalamus
Pituitary gland
Amygdala Hippocampus | Brain structures and the body affect behavior. |
| Evolutionary | | Evolutionary adaptations help explain human thought and behavior. |

MODERN APPROACHES TO PSYCHOLOGY		
Perspective	**Image to Remember**	**Explanation**
Biopsychosocial	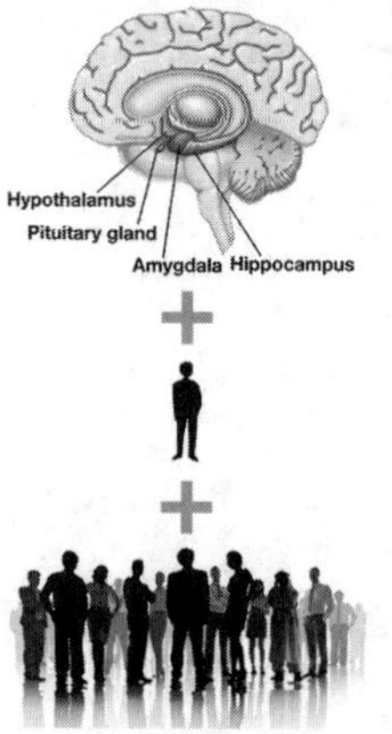 Hypothalamus Pituitary gland Amygdala Hippocampus + +	Interactions among a person's biology, personality, and culture help shape thoughts and behaviors.

Figure P1.2

The Strengths and Limitations of Perspectives

Perspectives in psychology, such as those you just read about, are like lenses or magnifying glasses. Lenses help us see things within the lens better, but things outside of the lens become less clear. Perspectives can make us blind to—or at least less aware of—other phenomena. For example, Freud's theory focused the lens on inner drives, taking little account of the kinds of influences the behaviorists examined. Humanism makes valuable contributions to understanding human potential but pays little attention to biological factors, beyond the requirement to meet basic needs.

In the following activities, you will use what you have learned about the various perspectives, theories, concepts, and research findings to illuminate some aspect of a scenario. You will also compare and contrast theories and perspectives and sharpen your logical thinking. Since each of these activities is a common practice among psychologists, the activities all begin with the same direction: **Think as a Psychologist.**

THINK AS A PSYCHOLOGIST

Explain How Psychological Perspectives, Theories, Concepts, and Research Findings Apply to a Scenario (Practice 1.A.1)

The theoretical perspectives you have read about in this section are general frameworks that are applied to specific instances for purposes of therapy or understanding. For example, behaviorism rests on the conviction that behaviors are shaped by punishments and rewards. A psychologist applying the concepts and perspectives of behaviorism to a classroom situation would look for ways in which undesirable behavior of a student is being reinforced through rewards and seek opportunities to extinguish it. The ability to apply a general concept to a specific individual or situation is critical to good psychological thinking.

Following is another example of applying the general concepts of behaviorism to a specific situation, this time related to a friend who always interrupts people. You become frustrated whenever Marcus interrupts you, so you try to apply the principles of reward/reinforcement and punishment.

- Whenever Marcus patiently waits for others to finish speaking without interrupting, you use positive reinforcement to acknowledge his patience by praising him or expressing appreciation.

- When Marcus does interrupt, you calmly but firmly redirect the conversation back to the person who was speaking. Removing the attention from Marcus can discourage the behavior over time.

The essence of Practice 1 is to understand a concept—in this case the concept of rewards and punishments—and apply it to a specific scenario—in this case Marcus's annoying interruptions.

Practice Applying Concepts to Scenarios

Choose the correct answer.

1. Katelyn is struggling in school and fighting frequently with her parents. She is not sure about her future and what she wants to study in college. Apply the concepts associated with humanistic psychology to offer an explanation of her behavior. Which of the following statements about Katelyn best represents the application of that concept to Katelyn's scenario?

   (A) Katelyn will work to the best of her ability to determine the best course of action for her future career and work hard to achieve that goal.

   (B) Katelyn has been shaped by her parents' dysfunctional relationship and will have a difficult time forming deep relationships in the future.

   (C) Katelyn is overthinking her problems, which are minor, and her misperception of the scope of the problems is inflating their importance.

   (D) Katelyn has learned from her peers to treat her parents badly and to not put forth her best effort in school. Because this behavior is rewarded by her friends and she has not yet faced any negative consequences, it will continue in the future.

Complete the following activity.

2. Eighteen-year-old Jennifer is afraid of heights. She has sought professional help to overcome this paralyzing fear but to little avail. When she is higher than two stories, she is reminded of a frightening trip to a high observation deck as a child. Each time Jennifer knows

she will be in a high place, she plans out her approach days ahead but is anxious and agitated until the moment arrives. She realizes her fears are irrational but cannot seem to stop her behavior. In a few sentences, apply the perspective of cognitive psychology to help Jennifer understand the cause of her fears.

THINK AS A PSYCHOLOGIST

Compare and Contrast How Perspectives or Theories Explain Behavior and Mental Processes (Practice 1.A.2)

You can also apply more than one perspective, theory, concept, or research finding to a scenario and, in so doing, show their similarities and differences in explaining behavior and mental processes.

For example, think about Jennifer and her fear of heights. You have already explored how cognitive psychology could help Jennifer understand the cause of her fears. How might other theories approach her problem, and how would those approaches be similar to or different from that of cognitive psychology?

After reviewing some of the perspectives or theories introduced in this section, you may make these observations:

- The psychoanalytic approach would suggest that Jennifer's intense fear of heights, while tied to an actual experience in childhood, may represent other memories that have been repressed in her unconscious mind. She may benefit from therapy that attempts to access those repressed memories through dream interpretation.

- The humanistic approach would stress that as someone with free will, Jennifer is not bound by fears she acquired in the past. She can look to the future and know she has the potential to overcome her paralyzing fear of heights and live a better life. She can seek professional help to overcome her fear and try to move toward reaching her potential.

- The behavioral approach would examine Jennifer's fear of heights by looking into the role of rewards and punishments to determine how these forces shaped her behavior. Behaviorists would identify the relief of Jennifer's anxiety when she came down from the high observation deck as a positive outcome (by removing the aversive stimulus of anxiety) and recognize that the law of effect would suggest that positive outcomes are likely to be repeated.

Don't worry if you find these applications too much to take in right now. In this section, you have read only a cursory overview of a very broad discipline. The perspectives of psychology will be woven throughout the text and will be reviewed and developed throughout each unit. Do your best to complete the following activities now. Answering questions about a subject before studying it formally can lead to deeper learning.

Practice Comparing and Contrasting Theories and Perspectives

Choose the correct answer.

1. How does the humanistic approach to psychology differ from the psychoanalytic approach?

    (A) The humanistic approach studies thinking, and the psychoanalytic approach focuses on learning through rewards and punishments.

    (B) The humanistic approach focuses on learning through rewards and punishments, while the psychoanalytic approach emphasizes the importance of the unconscious.

    (C) The humanistic approach focuses on striving to be one's best, while the psychoanalytic approach examines unconscious forces and the importance of sex and aggression.

    (D) The humanistic approach focuses on the good in all people, while the psychoanalytic approach emphasizes one's religion and peer group.

Complete the following activity.

2. Ana is having trouble adjusting after moving to a different country and changing schools. She is facing challenges with her mother at home. She also feels like she does not fit in with her peers at school and is struggling with the workload of her academic courses. Her classmates often ridicule her clothes and her accent. She feels embarrassed about this situation, but she is still attempting to make friends and is hopeful that she will eventually find a group that accepts her and allows her to be herself. In a few sentences, compare and contrast how the biological and sociocultural approaches to psychology would explain Ana's behavior.

Thinking and Reasoning

Practices 2, 3, and 4 lay the foundation for deriving logical and objective conclusions from research. However, even before you explore those practices, you can learn how to identify a logical and objective conclusion about behavior and mental processes, based on clear thinking and sound reasoning.

Logical Conclusions

Logical conclusions come from the process of reasoning, which can be broadly categorized into two types: deductive and inductive. Both methods are used to arrive at conclusions, but they operate in different ways.

Deductive reasoning starts with a general statement or hypothesis and examines the possibilities to reach a specific logical conclusion. It is often summarized as going from the *general to the specific*. If the premises are true and the reasoning is valid, the conclusion is necessarily true. The structure of deductive reasoning is such that, if the premises are true, then the conclusion must also be true. Here's a classic example:

- **Premise 1:** All men are mortal.
- **Premise 2:** Socrates is a man.
- **Conclusion:** Therefore, Socrates is mortal.

In this case, if both premises are true, the conclusion that Socrates is mortal must also be true. This is an example of a syllogism, a form of deductive reasoning.

Inductive reasoning works the opposite way, moving from *specific observations to broader generalizations and theories*. It involves making a series of observations and using them to make generalizations. Inductive reasoning is probabilistic, meaning that the conclusions reached are likely to be true but not guaranteed. Here's an example:

- **Observation 1:** The sun has risen in the east every morning so far.
- **Observation 2:** Today, the sun rose in the east.
- **Conclusion:** Therefore, the sun will rise in the east tomorrow.

With inductive reasoning, even if all the premises are true, the conclusion is not necessarily true, but it is likely. The conclusion is a **hypothesis** that, while supported by past observations, is still open to falsification by future evidence; that is, the hypothesis must be capable of being proven incorrect by observable evidence or experimental results.

A **logical conclusion**, therefore, is a statement that follows logically from the given premises. In deductive reasoning, if the premises are true and the logic correctly applied, the conclusion is certain. In inductive reasoning, the conclusion is probable, based on the evidence, but not absolutely guaranteed.

- **Deductive Conclusion:** Certain, based on the premises being true and the form of reasoning being valid.
- **Inductive Conclusion:** Probable, based on the observation of patterns or regularities, with the understanding that future evidence could potentially modify the conclusion.

Understanding the difference between these types of reasoning is crucial for critical thinking because it helps in evaluating the strength and validity of arguments and in making informed decisions based on evidence.

Objective Conclusions

To reach an **objective conclusion,** you need to focus on facts and evidence, not just what you hope or believe to be true. Here's how that concept applies to understanding mental processes and behavior in an objective, scientific way.

Being objective means being unbiased and not letting personal feelings, opinions, or prejudices affect your judgment. It's like being a referee in a soccer game: you're there to make calls based on the rules of the game, not on which team you want to win.

When psychologists aim to understand why people think, feel, or behave in certain ways, they try to be like that referee. They use specific methods to gather evidence and make conclusions based on what the evidence says, not what they hope it will say. Reaching an objective conclusion depends on following the steps below:

1. **Ask clear questions:** Start with a clear, specific question that can be tested. For example, "Does listening to music while studying improve test scores?"

2. **Collect data systematically:** Collect data in a way that is planned and consistent. This could be through experiments, surveys, or observation, but it has to be done in a way that is fair and not biased. For example, you might test a group of students with music and another group without music while keeping all other factors constant, such as time spent studying the material, external noise, and other environmental conditions.

3. **Analyze objectively**: Look at the data without letting personal beliefs influence their interpretation. Use statistics to see if the results are significant or if they could have happened by chance.

4. **Draw conclusions based on evidence:** Finally, make conclusions based on what the data show, not what you wanted them to show. If the evidence from the study shows that students who listen to music score better on tests, you might conclude that music has a positive effect on studying—but you should also consider limitations and suggest further research to determine if other studies reach the same conclusion.

THINK AS A PSYCHOLOGIST

Draw Logical and Objective Conclusions About Behavior and Mental Processes (Practice 1.A.3)

Arriving at an objective conclusion about mental processes and behavior is like solving a mystery with clues you've carefully collected and examined, making sure you're not jumping to conclusions based on what you personally believe or want to be true.

Objectivity is crucial because it ensures that the conclusions drawn about mental processes and behavior are based on evidence and are as accurate as possible. Objectivity helps build a reliable understanding of psychology that can be used to help people in practical ways, such as understanding what factors can contribute to improving education, health, and relationships.

Practice Drawing Logical and Objective Conclusions

Choose the correct answer.

1. During summer vacation, a group of high school students decided to start a small gardening project in their neighborhood. They noticed that the plants they watered in the morning seemed to be more vibrant and grow faster than those watered in the afternoon. Based on this observation, which of the following is the most logical conclusion?

   (A) Watering plants in the morning causes them to absorb water more efficiently because of lower temperatures and less sunlight, leading to better growth.

   (B) Plants prefer to be watered with cold water rather than warm water from the afternoon heat.

   (C) Watering plants in the afternoon is more time-consuming than watering them in the morning.

   (D) Plants grow faster in the summer regardless of when they are watered.

Complete the following activity.

2. A high school psychology teacher conducts a study to determine the effect of room color on students' test performance. Two identical rooms are used, with one room painted blue and the other painted red. Students are randomly assigned to take a math test in one of the two rooms. The difficulty level of the tests is the same for both groups. After the tests are graded, the teacher compares the average scores of students in the blue room against those in the red room. Based on the scenario, write an objective conclusion about the impact of room color on students' test performance.

Practice 1.B Explain how cultural norms, expectations, and circumstances, as well as cognitive biases, apply to behavior and mental processes.

AT A GLANCE: KEY TERMS AND OVERVIEW

- **Cultural norms** are unwritten rules and standards of behavior that are widely accepted within and between groups, influencing how individuals interact and conduct themselves in various situations.

- **Expectations,** in a cultural context, refer to the behaviors, roles, or outcomes that individuals or groups anticipate based on societal norms, personal beliefs, or situational factors.

- **Circumstances,** in psychology, encompass the specific conditions or context in which individuals find themselves, including environmental factors, social influences, and personal experiences, which can shape behavior and psychological processes.

- **Cognitive biases** are systematic ways people's thinking veers off track, usually to simplify impressions of people and events.

- **Confirmation bias** leads people to seek, interpret, and remember information that supports what they already believe and discount other information.

- **Hindsight bias** is the "knew-it-all-along" way of seeing past events as more predictable than they really were.

- **Overconfidence bias** is thinking that one's ability is greater than it really is, leading to overestimated outcomes and risk-taking.

- Biases might lead to the application of psychological concepts in a **discriminatory,** or inequitable, way.

Culture, Biases, and Discriminatory Treatment

The discipline of psychology is not complete if it does not consider how people, as individuals, are different from the groups to which they belong and how thinking and behavior are influenced by one's culture. It also must take into account ways in which people's thinking can show illogical bias. Those biases may sometimes lead to unfair treatment of groups of people.

Cultural Norms, Expectations, and Circumstances

Cultural norms are the shared standards and rules that guide behaviors within a society, affecting everything from communication styles to values, beliefs, and appropriate behaviors. Cultural norms significantly influence human behavior and mental processes, serving as the collective expectations that guide how individuals within a society should act and think. These norms encompass a broad range of behaviors and attitudes, from basic manners and communication styles to deeply ingrained values and beliefs about right and wrong. The impact of cultural norms on psychology is profound, since they set the stage for the socialization process, informing individuals about the roles they are expected to play and the behaviors that are seen as acceptable or taboo. For instance, norms related to individualism or collectivism (see Unit 4) shape how people view their identity in relation to the group, influencing everything from personal goals to how emotions are expressed and managed. Cultural norms can be influenced by immediate family, school environment, and the larger society.

Different cultures express and experience mourning in different ways. Many Mexicans create an altar for their deceased relatives (left) on *Día de los Muertos* (Day of the Dead), inviting their spirits back into their homes. After a mourning period immediately following a loved one's death, Jews light a candle that lasts for at least 24 hours on each anniversary of their loved one's death.

Cultural expectations add another layer to the interaction between culture and psychology. These expectations can determine the paths individuals take in their personal and professional lives, shaping ambitions, educational pursuits, and even personal relationships. For example, in some cultures, there is a strong expectation for children to put family responsibilities above individual desires, which can influence career choices, marriage decisions, and living arrangements. In other cultures, children are expected to focus on their education and their interests in sports, activities, and clubs. These expectations affect such mental processes as decision-making, ranking priorities, and resolving conflicts as individuals navigate the balance between fulfilling cultural expectations and pursuing personal desires.

Cultural circumstances, including historical, economic, and political contexts, further mold behaviors and mental processes. These circumstances can determine access to resources, exposure to stress, and the collective experiences that shape a community's worldview. For example, societies that have experienced significant hardship or conflict may develop a collective resilience and a strong sense of community, affecting how individuals cope with stress and adversity. These experiences can influence psychological traits such as optimism, trust, and the value placed on social support, illustrating how the broader cultural environment affects the psychological makeup of its members.

Understanding the relationships among cultural norms, expectations, circumstances, and behavior is crucial for a comprehensive understanding of human psychology, since behaviors and mental processes cannot be fully understood in isolation from the social and cultural circumstances that shape them. This awareness is vital for psychologists working in increasingly multicultural societies, where recognizing and adapting to diverse cultural norms and biases is essential for effective communication, conflict resolution, and therapeutic intervention.

THINK AS A PSYCHOLOGIST

Explain How Cultural Norms, Expectations, and Circumstances Apply to a Scenario (Practice 1.B.1)

Just as you can explain how a psychological theory or concept applies to a scenario, you can analyze a behavior or mental process based on external influences, such as cultural norms, expectations, and circumstances. For example, consider the following scenario.

Lulu is a high school student experiencing stress and anxiety. She is from a culture that values community and collective success over individual achievement, and she has moved to a country where individualism and personal success are highly prized. In her new school, she notices that students are encouraged to compete against one another for awards and recognition, a stark contrast to her previous experiences where group projects and team achievements were more common, and the entire group shared in success. Lulu feels conflicted; while she wants to adapt to her new environment, she also holds strong values from her upbringing that emphasize the importance of supporting her classmates and working together as a community.

While different psychological perspectives might look for internal explanations for Lulu's stress and anxiety, such as behavioral patterns she could modify, explaining the influence of cultural norms, expectations, and situations would do a better job of illuminating Lulu's discomfort.

Lulu might feel pressured to adopt the competitive behaviors of her peers, experiencing stress and anxiety as these behaviors conflict with her cultural values of community and collaboration. Her earlier cultural norms and expectations deeply influence her behavior and mental processes. Lulu is experiencing an internal conflict from the clash between her ingrained cultural values and the new cultural expectations she faces. This explanation best captures the psychological impact of navigating different cultural norms and illustrates the potential stress and anxiety that can arise when individuals' cultural background conflicts with their current environment. It demonstrates the challenges of cultural adaptation and the importance of acknowledging and respecting diverse cultural backgrounds in shaping behaviors and mental processes.

Practice Applying Cultural Norms, Expectations, and Circumstances to a Scenario

Choose the correct answer.

1. Juan, a Hispanic high school student, has recently moved to a new school in a predominantly non-Hispanic area. He is exceptionally respectful and formal in his interactions with teachers and school staff. He often addresses them with titles and uses formal language, an uncommon practice among his new classmates. Also, Juan tends to turn down invitations to social events on weekdays, explaining that he has family commitments, such as helping at home or attending family gatherings. His peers find this unusual, since they are more used to spending their free time with friends or engaging in after-school activities. How might cultural norms and expectations influence Juan's behavior and interactions at his new school?

   (A) Juan's formal way of addressing teachers and his prioritization of family commitments over socializing with peers on weekdays reflect his adherence to Hispanic cultural norms that value respect for authority and strong family ties.

   (B) Juan's behavior is an indication of his lack of interest in adapting to his new school's social environment and making new friends.

   (C) Juan's actions demonstrate a misunderstanding of the social norms at his new school, suggesting he is unaware of how to interact appropriately with teachers and peers.

   (D) Juan's formal interaction with teachers and commitment to family obligations are signs of his introverted personality.

2. Tasha, a woman in her thirties, has recently been finding it hard to keep up with her responsibilities at work. Despite being highly skilled and dedicated, she has been struggling with fatigue, which has affected her performance. Tasha lives in an under-resourced urban neighborhood where noise levels are high from constant traffic and occasional late-night disturbances. Her apartment next to a busy street lacks soundproofing, so the noise interrupts Tasha's sleep. Additionally, Tasha cares for her elderly mother, who lives with her and requires attention at various hours of the night. These circumstances have compounded, leaving Tasha feeling exhausted during the day. How do Tasha's living circumstances contribute to her struggle with fatigue at work?

   (A) Tasha's fatigue is primarily a result of her personal inability to manage her time effectively, indicating a need for better organization skills.

   (B) The high noise levels in Tasha's neighborhood and her responsibilities toward her elderly mother lead to poor sleep quality, directly contributing to her fatigue and affecting her job performance.

(C) Tasha's struggles at work are unrelated to her living conditions, suggesting that the real issue may be a lack of motivation or commitment to her job.

(D) Living next to a busy street has inspired Tasha to work harder and prove herself, meaning her fatigue must be due to reasons outside her control, such as workplace demands.

Cognitive Biases

Cognitive biases are ways of thinking that veer people away from strictly rational and objective conclusions. They are consistent ways that people make faulty assumptions about other people and situations. These biases influence how someone sees the world, often creating a personal version of reality based on their own perceptions, rather than on actual facts. This subjective view, rather than objective information, can drive how people act and what they believe about others' behavior. As a result, cognitive biases can sometimes cause skewed perceptions, faulty judgments, and flawed interpretations, all forms of irrational thinking. Despite these problems, cognitive biases occur frequently; as you begin your practice of thinking as a psychologist, be aware of these biases in an effort to avoid their influence. (See Topic 4.1 for more on cognitive biases.)

Confirmation bias is one type of cognitive bias. It refers to the tendency to search for, interpret, favor, and recall information in a way that confirms one's preexisting beliefs or hypotheses, while giving less consideration to alternative possibilities. For instance, consider a scenario in which someone holds a strong belief that left-handed people are more creative than right-handed people. These people are more likely to notice and remember information that supports this belief and ignore or forget information that contradicts it. This bias can significantly affect research outcomes: researchers might selectively collect data that support their hypothesis without paying due attention to data that contradict it. Great researchers look for reasons they may be wrong and only accept their hypothesis as correct when the data lead them to this conclusion.

Another example is **hindsight bias,** often referred to as the "knew-it-all-along" effect. It involves the tendency to see events that have already occurred as being more predictable than they were before they took place. For example, after attending a football game at which an underdog team wins, a person might insist they knew the outcome beforehand, despite not having predicted it. This bias can alter one's memory of past decisions and experiences, leading to overly simplistic explanations for complex events. It can also affect learning processes by assuming that events are more predictable than they truly are, potentially leading to a failure in accurately planning for future uncertainties. The hindsight bias occurs frequently in psychology.

Overconfidence bias is demonstrated when a person's subjective confidence in their judgments is reliably greater than their objective accuracy, especially when confidence is relatively high. Overconfidence bias is at work in scenarios in which individuals rate their knowledge or abilities higher than is warranted, which can lead to taking greater risks in their daily lives or making decisions based on overestimated outcomes. For example, a student might feel extremely confident about acing an exam without sufficient study, based on their belief in their intelligence or previous performances. That confidence may lead them to underperform because they didn't think they needed to study. If researchers fall victim to the overconfidence effect, they may find themselves unwilling to investigate other research studies that refute or challenge their own findings.

These cognitive biases can have an impact on behavior and mental processes by skewing perception, decision-making, and memory. Whether in personal life, professional settings, or social interactions, being aware of these biases is important for making more rational, objective decisions and for understanding the complexities of human thought and behavior. Recognizing and limiting the influence of biases can lead to improved judgment, better interpersonal relationships, and more effective problem-solving skills.

THINK AS A PSYCHOLOGIST

Explain How Cognitive Biases, Such as Confirmation Bias, Hindsight Bias, and Overconfidence Bias, Apply to a Scenario (Practice 1.B.2)

Understanding cognitive biases can help you explain the reasons for illogical or irrational behavior and conclusions. Consider this scenario.

Anjanie, an avid amateur photographer, enters a local photography contest. The theme of the contest is "Urban Life," and participants are required to submit photos that capture the essence of city living. Anjanie has won a few small online photography contests in the past, so she feels sure she has the skills and understanding of the theme to win the prize. She spends a day walking around the city, taking a handful of photos, believing that her natural talent and eye for photography will impress the judges.

She selects her favorite photo—a candid shot of people crossing a busy intersection—and submits it. Anjanie is sure that her submission will stand out for its authenticity and spontaneity. However, when the winners are announced, Anjanie's photo is not among them. The feedback from the judges notes that while her photo was good, it lacked the depth, composition, and innovative perspective that the winning entries showcased. The judges also mention that many entries, including Anjanie's, failed to fully explore and convey the theme of "Urban Life" beyond its most obvious aspects.

How does cognitive bias apply to this scenario?

Anjanie is surprised and disappointed by the outcome. She had been so confident in her abilities and her photo that she didn't invest time in researching past winners, seeking feedback before submitting, or critically assessing her own work to ensure that it met the contest's criteria at a high level. In this way, overconfidence bias affected her mental processes and rational behavior.

Practice Applying Cognitive Biases to a Scenario

Complete the following activities.

1. Mia and Noah are partners in a science fair project in which they have to predict the outcome of a chemical reaction between two substances. After conducting preliminary research, Mia suggests that the reaction will produce a color change to blue, based on the properties of the chemicals involved. Noah, however, is skeptical and suggests that the reaction might produce a different result, perhaps a temperature change instead of a color change, due to the volatility of one of the substances. They proceed with their experiment, and to their surprise, the reaction causes the solution to emit light, a phenomenon neither had predicted. After reviewing their results and the experiment, Mia remarks, "You know, when we think about it, the light emission makes total sense because of the energy levels involved in the reaction. I thought this could have been an option from the start given the chemicals we were working with." Noah is taken aback by Mia's comment, remembering their initial predictions and discussions, which had not even remotely considered light emission as a possible outcome of their experiment. Based on the scenario, what cognitive bias is Mia exhibiting? In a few sentences, explain how that bias affects the quality of her thinking.

2. Elena is passionate about nutrition and believes strongly in the benefits of a plant-based diet. She spends much of her free time reading articles, watching documentaries, and following social media influencers who advocate for the health advantages of avoiding animal products. When tasked with writing a research paper for her health class on the topic of dietary choices and health outcomes, Elena sees a perfect opportunity to explore and present evidence supporting the superiority of plant-based diets. Elena finds several studies that report positive health outcomes associated with plant-based diets, such as lower risks of heart disease and improved blood sugar control. She includes these findings in her paper, emphasizing the benefits of eliminating meat and dairy products. However, Elena encounters some high-quality research suggesting that well-balanced diets containing lean meats and dairy can also lead to good health outcomes and that the key might be more about overall diet quality rather than the exclusion of animal products. Elena chooses not to include these studies in her paper, reasoning that they are poorly researched and have small sample sizes. Based on the scenario, what cognitive bias is Elena demonstrating? In a few sentences, explain how the bias affects the quality of her thinking and research.

Applying Psychological Theories or Concepts in Inappropriate or Discriminatory Ways

Psychology is a helping science that seeks to eliminate bias and discrimination. Understanding how psychological concepts can lead to negative outcomes is imperative for the field of psychology and the many people who may benefit from the work of psychologists. Applying psychological concepts or theories inappropriately or in discriminatory ways can lead to a range of problems, from misdiagnosis and ineffective treatment in clinical settings to reinforcing stereotypes and biases in society at large. When psychological theories are used without regard to context, culture, or individual differences, they can perpetuate harm and hinder the progress toward a more inclusive and accurate understanding of human behavior and mental processes.

Misdiagnosis and Ineffective Treatment One of the most direct consequences of inappropriately applying psychological theories is in clinical settings, where it can lead to misdiagnosis and ineffective treatment plans. For instance, cultural differences in the expression of psychological distress are often overlooked, leading to incorrect diagnoses. The *Diagnostic and Statistical Manual of Mental Disorders*, which describes the criteria for diagnosing various disorders, has been criticized for its Western-centric perspective on mental health, potentially leading clinicians to treat behaviors that are culturally normal in non-Western societies as disorders when they are not. An example of this is the differing expressions of depression across cultures. While Western populations might emphasize sadness or guilt, non-Western individuals might report physical symptoms such as fatigue, back pain, or headache. These differences in symptoms may result in incorrect diagnoses. Applying a one-size-fits-all approach to diagnosis can overlook these crucial differences, leading to treatments that fail to address the patient's actual needs.

Reinforcement of Stereotypes and Biases The misuse of psychological concepts can also reinforce stereotypes and biases, further marginalizing certain groups. An example is the misuse of intelligence testing throughout history. Early intelligence tests were used to reinforce racial hierarchies, with biased items that favored certain cultural knowledge, leading to the false notion that some racial groups were inherently less intelligent than others. Such applications not only misrepresented the nature of intelligence, but also contributed to discriminatory educational and social policies.

Ethical Implications in Research Applying psychological theories without considering their ethical implications can lead to problematic research practices. An infamous example is the 1971 Stanford University prison experiment under the direction of Phillip Zimbardo, in which student participants were assigned roles of guards or prisoners. The study was meant to investigate the psychological effects of perceived power, but it led to abusive behavior and psychological harm. The experiment has been criticized for its ethical violations, including the lack of informed consent and adequate protection from harm.

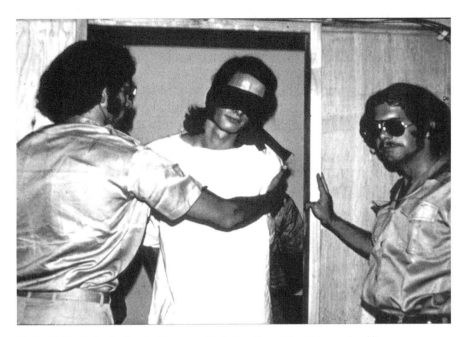

Credit: Phillip Zimbardo, Creative Commons Attribution-Share Alike 4.0 International license.
Guards in the infamous Stanford Prison Experiment were not given any specific directions—they were just told to do what they needed to, within reason, to maintain order. They were dressed in khaki uniforms and carried a whistle and a billy club. They became increasingly brutal in their psychological abuse of the prisoners and the experiment was stopped on the sixth day. Zimbardo later wrote a book about the experiment. In the preface he wrote, "It was emotionally painful to review all of the videotapes from the Stanford Prison Experiment." The abuses of the study inspired change in the ethical guidelines for research.

Cultural Insensitivity and Generalization Another issue arises when psychological concepts are generalized across different cultural contexts without considering specific differences among and within cultures. For instance, the concept of individualism versus collectivism (see Topic 4.3), while useful in exploring cultural differences in behavior and cognition, can be oversimplified or applied in ways that stereotype entire cultures as being one way or another. This oversimplification overlooks the diversity within cultures and the dynamic nature of cultural identities, potentially leading to misunderstandings and a lack of culturally competent care in psychological practice.

The possibility of misusing or discriminating with psychological theories shows why psychology needs to be more culturally aware, ethical, and sensitive to differences. Those working in the field must recognize that applying these theories without thought can cause harm, and they should aim for practices that honor personal and cultural diversity. Achieving this awareness involves ongoing learning about the cultural backgrounds of psychological theories, ethical guidelines for research and practice, and the need to critically evaluate biases and assumptions in psychological frameworks.

THINK AS A PSYCHOLOGIST

Explain Implications of Applying Psychological Concepts or Theories in Inappropriate or Discriminatory Ways (Practice 1.B.3)

Consider the following scenario.

Sixteen-year-old Ahniya has been experiencing symptoms of depression, including prolonged sadness, loss of interest in activities she used to enjoy, and difficulty concentrating on her studies. When she visits a psychologist for help, the psychologist concludes that Ahniya's symptoms are a result of teenage mood swings and a lack of discipline in managing her schoolwork and social life. The psychologist suggests that Ahniya should get more involved in her community and work harder at school. Ahniya tries these approaches, but her symptoms do not improve.

In this scenario, the psychologist's assessment of Ahniya's situation represents an inappropriate application of a psychological theory, particularly regarding depression. Depression is a complex mental health disorder characterized by persistent feelings of sadness, loss of interest or pleasure in activities, changes in appetite or weight, disturbances in sleep patterns, fatigue, feelings of worthlessness or guilt, difficulty concentrating, and thoughts of death or suicide.

The psychologist's attribution of Ahniya's symptoms solely to "teenage mood swings" and a lack of discipline overlooks the possibility of a legitimate mental health concern. Depression is not merely a result of normal teenage experiences or a lack of effort in managing one's life. Such an interpretation fails to recognize the seriousness of Ahniya's symptoms and the potential need for professional intervention and support.

Furthermore, the psychologist's suggestion for Ahniya to "get more involved" in her community and "work harder" at school implies a simplistic solution to what may be a complex psychological issue. While involvement in community activities and academic success can contribute to overall well-being, they are unlikely to help the symptoms of depression without addressing the underlying psychological factors.

Overall, the psychologist's assessment demonstrates a lack of understanding or consideration of the psychological theories and research on depression, leading to a dismissal of Ahniya's legitimate concerns and potential need for mental health treatment.

Practice Explaining Implications of Applying Psychological Concepts or Theories in Inappropriate or Discriminatory Ways

Complete the following activities.

1. During a school career day, a career counselor presents information about various professions. When discussing engineering and technology fields, the counselor focuses on the male students, suggesting these fields are more suited to men because they require "logical thinking and physical strength." Conversely, when discussing careers in nursing or teaching, the counselor directs attention to female students, citing these professions as a good fit due to their "natural nurturing abilities." In a few sentences, discuss how the career counselor's statements reflect the inappropriate use of psychological theories related to gender roles and abilities, reinforcing stereotypes and potentially influencing students' career aspirations in a discriminatory manner.

2. Dr. Lewis is conducting a study on the effects of sleep deprivation on cognitive performance. He recruits college students and informs them that they will be participating in a study related to sleep patterns, but he does not disclose that they will be intentionally deprived of sleep for 48 hours. During the study, several participants experience significant distress, including anxiety and hallucinations. Dr. Lewis believes that the ends justify the means, as his research could lead to important findings in the field of cognitive psychology. In a paragraph, analyze the ethical issues in Dr. Lewis's research study, focusing on the lack of informed consent and the potential harm to participants. Explain how this approach violates ethical principles in psychological research.

3. In a diverse school district, a new standardized testing system is introduced to assess students' abilities across various subjects. This test, however, was developed based on data and experiences predominantly from middle-class, suburban, and primarily White demographics. For this reason, many test questions inadvertently incorporate cultural references and scenarios familiar mainly to these groups, such as leisure activities, holiday traditions, or items commonly found in their upper-middle-class households. Ethan, a 14-year-old White student from a suburban background, along with many of his peers, finds the test relatable and in tune with his everyday experiences. The familiarity of the content gives Ethan a certain level of comfort and confidence, allowing him to perform exceptionally well. As a result, Ethan and similar students score higher on the standardized test, reinforcing perceptions of their superior academic abilities. This performance discrepancy not only highlights their achievements but also inadvertently sets a benchmark that places students from different cultural and socioeconomic backgrounds at a disadvantage, which may affect their academic placement and access to advanced educational resources.

In a few paragraphs, explain how the design and application of this standardized test provide an unintended advantage to students like Ethan, based on their cultural background and experiences. Discuss the implications of such an advantage in perpetuating educational disparities and the importance of incorporating a diverse range of experiences and perspectives in educational testing to ensure fairness and equality.

Practice 2

Research Methods and Design

Evaluate Qualitative and Quantitative Research Methods and Study Designs

Practice 2.A Determine the type of research design(s) used in a given study.

AT A GLANCE: KEY TERMS AND OVERVIEW

- **Qualitative research** is a method of studying people and their experiences by gathering nonnumerical data, such as words, images, or observations. It explores the depth of people's thoughts, feelings, and behaviors to understand their motivations, beliefs, and perspectives.

- **Quantitative research** is a method of studying people or other subjects by collecting and analyzing numerical data. It uses statistics and mathematical models to understand patterns, relationships, and trends.

- Research studies can use an *experimental methodology* or a *non-experimental methodology*. Throughout this course, you'll need to be able to distinguish the differences between them.

- **Experimental methodology** involves the use of independent variable(s) and random assignment to groups. Experimental methodology is a **quantitative research method** because it relies on measurement and numerical data.

- In an experiment, a **variable** is any factor or condition that can change or vary, and that is measured, manipulated, or controlled by the researcher. Variables can be classified into two main types:

  - The variable that the researcher deliberately manipulates or controls in order to observe its effect on another variable is the **independent variable**. It is the presumed cause or predictor of the outcome being studied. When trying to identify the independent variable in any experiment, ask yourself what the researchers are manipulating or what is changing between the groups in the study.

  - The variable that is observed, measured, or recorded to assess the effect of the independent variable is called the **dependent variable**. It is the outcome or response variable that may change due to variations in the independent variable.

- **Random assignment** is a method used in experimental research to ensure that each **participant**, or person or animal taking part in the study, has an equal chance of being assigned to any of the experimental conditions. It involves randomly placing participants in different groups or conditions in an experiment, such as a treatment group and a control group. The purpose of random assignment is to ensure that any differences observed between groups are due to the experimental manipulation rather than preexisting differences between participants. Random assignment is also unique to experiments; the other methods of research you will read about do not use random assignment to groups. This is the key component that allows researchers to determine cause and effect: did the independent variable cause the outcome of the study?

- **Non-experimental methodologies** include case study, correlation, meta-analysis, and naturalistic observation.

- **Case study** is a research method that involves an in-depth and detailed examination of a particular individual, group, event, or phenomenon. In a case study, researchers gather and analyze comprehensive information about the subject of interest, often using multiple sources of data such as interviews, observations, documents, and archival records.

- **Correlation** is a research method used to examine the relationship between two variables. In a correlation study, researchers measure two or more variables and assess how they are related to each other. A **positive correlation** indicates that as one variable increases, the other variable also tends to increase, while a **negative correlation** indicates that as one variable increases, the other variable tends to decrease.

- **Meta-analysis** is a research method used to synthesize and analyze the results of multiple studies on a particular topic. In a meta-analysis, researchers collect data from individual studies that have investigated the same or similar research questions. The data from these studies are pooled together and analyzed statistically to determine overall effect sizes (the degree of difference between two groups), patterns, or trends across the studies.

- **Naturalistic observation** is a research method used to study behavior in its natural environment without intervention or manipulation by the researcher. In a naturalistic observation study, researchers observe and record behavior as it occurs in real-life settings, such as schools, workplaces, or public spaces. The goal of naturalistic observation is to gain insights into naturally occurring behaviors, interactions, and phenomena in their natural context.

Types of Research Designs

How did people learn about everything that fills this psychology book and so many others? How did people learn how babies see the world, how children imitate aggressive behavior, how teenagers are not "morning people," how adults respond to authority, how people strive for fulfillment? The answer is through systematic, well-designed research studies using the scientific method. Knowing how to conduct strong research studies allows you to study any topic you are interested in, and all scientific disciplines use the same types of methodologies. Research is the underlying foundation of all that we know about psychology and other sciences.

The Scientific Method in Psychology

To gather information about how humans and animals think and behave, psychology, like any other scientific field, uses the **scientific method**—a process of systematic observation, measurement, and experiment to formulate and test hypotheses. The scientific method underlies both **experimental research** and **non-experimental research**.

The process of science always begins with a question. Researchers conduct preliminary studies to refine a question, make sure it is stated as clearly as possible, and connect it with related evidence or theories. Once they have refined the question, they restate it as a formal hypothesis and test it with an experiment or another type of research, such as observation. The result of this systematic procedure is **empirical data**, which is evidence that comes from observation or experimentation. After gathering empirical data, researchers analyze the results, draw conclusions, and communicate with other researchers about what they learned. The steps in the scientific method are shown in Figure P2.1.

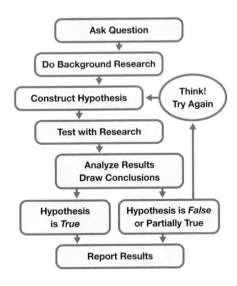

Figure P2.1 Scientific Method

The scientific method helps researchers think critically about the questions they are investigating and opens up the possibility for alternative answers to a question.

Hypotheses Researchers are curious by nature and may be tempted to begin a study as soon as they become interested in a psychological phenomenon. However, they must consider a number of factors and create a research plan before they begin. The first step is to restate the research question as a **hypothesis**, which is a specific and testable description of the expected outcome of a study. The hypothesis specifies the **variables**—anything that can change or be changed—and a relationship between them and describes the circumstances or conditions that affect the relationship.

Experimental Methodology The experimental methodology is the only type of research that allows psychologists to draw cause-and-effect conclusions. This is because researchers have control over the **independent variable**, the variable that the experimenter manipulates. The **dependent variable** is the variable that researchers measure. The hypothesis makes a prediction that the dependent variable will vary or be influenced by the independent variable.

Suppose, for example, that your school wants to test the effectiveness of a math tutoring program in increasing math test scores. Following are the basic elements of the experiment:

- **Hypothesis:** If students participate in the new math tutoring program, then their math test scores will improve.

- **Independent variable**: Enrollment in a math tutoring program. There are two groups—those enrolled in the tutoring program and those not enrolled.

- **Dependent variable:** Math test scores, measured using a standardized math test given at the end of the semester.

This experimental setup is designed to show cause and effect by controlling and manipulating the independent variable—the math tutoring program—and observing its direct impact on student test scores. Students are placed into either the tutoring program or a group without tutoring. It is essential that the participants are placed into groups using **random assignment**. This randomness helps eliminate any differences between groups. For example, if random assignment was used in this study, it should ensure that students from a wide array of math levels and classes were placed into both groups. In this way, if there are differences between the groups at the end of the study, it should be because of what researchers did to the independent variable, not because there were differences in the groups from the start.

The group without tutoring is called the *control group* because it allows comparisons to be made against those who are receiving the tutoring. Any difference in outcomes (math scores) between these groups can more confidently be attributed to the tutoring program itself rather than other external factors. The group that received the tutoring is the *experimental group*.

In an experiment, the experimental group(s) receives the independent variable (math tutoring program).

By measuring math scores before and after the tutoring program, researchers can assess the specific impact of the tutoring program over time. If the experiment concludes that the tutoring group significantly outperforms the control group in math tests, it would suggest that the tutoring program is the cause of improved math scores.

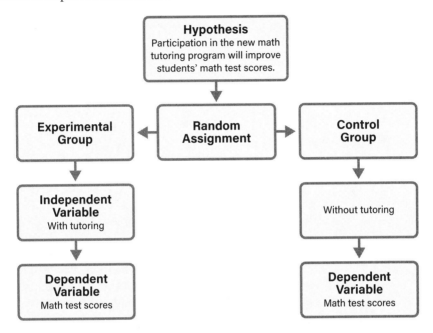

Figure P2.2

Non-Experimental Methodologies Suppose researchers want to study a question that has no quantitative or empirical evidence to draw on. For example, there is virtually no empirical evidence of the positive impact of dog training on a prison population, yet anecdotal reports from inmates, prison employees, and those who are given a service dog trained by inmates are consistently very positive. Any number of hypotheses can be developed from these observations: "If service dogs are trained by inmates, the results of the training are more effective than if they are trained by volunteers outside of prison" or "Prisons in which inmates have the responsibility to train service dogs experience lower levels of violence than prisons without such programs" or "If prisoners are given the responsibility to train service animals (first thing that can change), then social conditions in the prison (second thing that can change) improve." Note that the hypotheses include both of the variables. Hypotheses can support existing theories, lead to new theories, or reveal inaccuracies or errors in theories.

To support these hypotheses, researchers can use non-experimental methodology, using qualitative data to test them. For example, they might conduct a **case study** to explore the psychological, behavioral, and rehabilitating effects of dog training programs on prisoners. The participants would be a selection of inmates from a single prison who volunteer for the program. These participants would include individuals from various backgrounds and with different lengths of incarceration because, regardless of what type of research study is conducted, researchers want a random sample from the population.

Researchers would gather information through *interviews* with the participating inmates, program staff, and prison officials to gather personal perceptions and narratives about the program's impact. They would have regular *observations* of training sessions to document interactions between prisoners and dogs, noting changes in inmate behavior, mood, and engagement over time. They would also *analyze any relevant records*, such as accounts of behavioral issues, psychological assessments, and recidivism (rates of returning to prison) among participants, compared to a matched control group of inmates who are not participating in the program. (Most non-experimental studies, however, would not have a control group.)

Or researchers could design a **correlational study**. Such a study might draw from a large sample of inmates from multiple prisons that already offer dog training programs. This sample would ideally include a diverse group of inmates varying in age, gender, crime, and sentence length. Like an experimental study, the research would involve variables. The first variable would be participation in a dog training program. The second variable would be the measures of behavioral issues, psychological assessments, and rates of returning to prison among participants. Through extensive analysis, participants would be compared to a control group of inmates who are not participating in the program. Unlike an experimental study, however, it cannot determine cause and effect, because there is no way to determine which variable is the cause and which is the effect. It can only show correlation—how the two variables relate. If they have a positive correlation, then participation in dog training would show improvements in behavior, mental health, and staying out of prison. If they have a negative correlation, the trends move in opposite directions: participants in dog training would show worsened behavior, mental health, and repeat offenses.

A **meta-analysis** would carefully search existing studies and show ways in which they come to similar or different conclusions in order to better understand what the totality of the research reveals. Researchers would use a rigorous and structured approach to collecting, evaluating, and statistically analyzing data from multiple studies that have examined the relationship between dog training programs and prisoner rehabilitation outcomes. The meta-analysis would estimate the degree of difference between participants and nonparticipants of dog training programs and determine the consistency of the effect across studies. It would also identify which types of outcomes, such as behavior, mental health, and recidivism, are most significantly affected by these programs, and under what conditions.

A **naturalistic observation** study would allow researchers to study behaviors in their natural contexts without any manipulation or intervention. The study would take place in a prison that has an established dog training program. Observations would occur during the normal activities of the program, where prisoners interact with dogs under the supervision of program staff. Researchers would try to observe as unobtrusively as they can, using video recordings to capture the observations. They would set a duration limit to the period of observations that would allow them to compare prisoners at the beginning of the study and at the end.

These inmates at a U.S. federal prison are taking part in a dog training program.

THINK AS A PSYCHOLOGIST

Determine Whether a Study Is Using Experimental or Non-Experimental Methodologies (Practice 2.A.1)

Practice Determining the Type of Research Study

Review the Key Terms and Overview. Then answer the following questions.

1. A study titled "Impact of artificial intelligence on human loss in decision making, laziness and safety in education"[1] examines the effects of artificial intelligence (AI) on decision-making, laziness, and privacy concerns among university students in Pakistan and China. The study uses data gathered from 285 students. It finds significant impacts of AI on increasing human laziness, generating privacy and security issues, and diminishing human decision-making capabilities. The study suggests that while AI can significantly benefit the education field, it also raises substantial ethical concerns that must be addressed, emphasizing the need for careful design, implementation, and

---

1   Ahmad, S. F., Han, H., Alam, M. M. et al. (2023). Impact of artificial intelligence on human loss in decision making, laziness and safety in education. *Humanities and Social Sciences Communications*, *10*(1), 311. https://doi.org/10.1057/s41599-023-01787-8.

m anagement of AI technologies to lower these risks. The authors advocate for a balanced approach to AI use in educational settings, valuing human concerns and ethical considerations over other factors.

Is this study experimental or non-experimental? Explain your answer.

2. Researchers tried to answer two questions: (1) "Is exposure to violent media games associated with increased aggression?" (2) "How can such exposure increase aggression?" To find answers, they did an extensive review of research in the authoritative database *PsychInfo*, looking for articles on video games and aggression. Thirty-five articles were relevant. They included 54 samples and 4,262 participants. The studies found that there is a positive relationship between violent video game playing and aggression.

Is this study experimental or non-experimental? Explain your answer.

3. Researchers[2] set out to assess how group discussions influence participants' attitudes. They divided 310 college students into three different groups through random assignment. In the first group, participants debated in favor of "equal rights for men and women in the workplace." The second group discussed the topic "women should leave their jobs and return home if there is a high unemployment rate." The third group served as a control and did not participate in any discussion. Each group consisted of eight to ten members to ensure active participation from all individuals. The researchers observed that the discussions indeed had an impact on the participants' attitudes, as evidenced by immediate post-discussion assessments.

Is this study experimental or non-experimental? Explain your answer.

Practice 2.B Evaluate the appropriate use of research design elements in experimental methodology.

AT A GLANCE: KEY TERMS AND OVERVIEW

- A hypothesis must be **falsifiable**. That is, a hypothesis must be able to be proven false by an experiment or observation. A falsifiable hypothesis is one that allows for a situation or outcome that would contradict the predictions made by the hypothesis. It enables scientific inquiry and progress by testing and potentially disproving theories, paving the way for more accurate explanations and understanding. In fact, good researchers look for reasons their hypothesis might be wrong before accepting that it is right.

---

2 Echabe, A. E., & Castro, J. L. G. (1999). Group discussion and changes in attitudes and representations. *The Journal of Social Psychology, 139(1)*, 29–43.

- Clear and detailed statements about how the researcher will measure the data collected on the variables are called **operational definitions**. For example, to measure the success of service dog training by prisoners, researchers would need to develop an operational definition of success, such as, "Success is defined as a lower number of reported incidents of prison violence after the study was completed than before the study began."

- Both falsifiable hypotheses and clear operational definitions make it possible to **replicate**, or re-create, a study.

- Even when both the experimental and control groups are treated similarly, extraneous factors, called *confounding variables*, may interfere with the independent variable and, therefore, have an impact on the outcome of the study. A **confounding variable** is a hidden or unexpected factor that can influence both the independent and dependent variables in a study, creating a misleading association between them. It can distort or confuse the interpretation of results, leading to incorrect conclusions about cause and effect. A possible confounding variable in studies on dog training in prisons might be a participant's undisclosed prior experience with animals, although this should be controlled through the use of random assignment. Researchers have learned to take confounding variables into consideration.

Design Elements in Experimental Methodology

As you have read, the experimental method is the only methodology that can demonstrate **cause and effect** because it enables a researcher to manipulate one of the variables and observe the effect of that manipulation on one or more other measured variables. Research that uses the experimental method is sometimes known as *laboratory experimentation* and has been criticized for being too artificial to assess behaviors that most people usually exhibit. The argument is that people do not act the same way in a laboratory setting as they would in their day-to-day lives. To make sure experimental studies are as accurate as possible, researchers take great care in developing hypotheses, choosing participants, and controlling for bias.

Falsifiable Hypotheses

Research using the experimental method must be centered on a hypothesis that is **falsifiable**. For a hypothesis to be considered scientific, it must be testable through empirical methods and must clearly outline conditions under which it could be disproved. This concept emphasizes that for any hypothesis to be credible, it must be open to potential refutation under specific experimental conditions or empirical investigation.

Table P2.1 identifies the qualities a hypothesis needs to be falsifiable.

A falsifiable hypothesis . . .	
. . . makes specific predictions.	The hypothesis should make specific predictions about outcomes that are testable through observation or experimentation. It should clearly state an expected result that can be measured or observed in a way that is objective and consistent.
. . . identifies how it can be disproved.	The hypothesis must specify conditions under which it could be proven false. It should be clear what evidence would count against the hypothesis. If no possible evidence could contradict the hypothesis, it is not falsifiable.
. . . can be tested empirically.	The hypothesis must be testable using current scientific methods and technology. It must be built on concepts that are observable and measurable. If a hypothesis involves elements that cannot be observed or measured with current technology or scientific methods, it cannot be considered falsifiable.
. . . is logical.	The hypothesis does not include logical flaws or contradictions and cannot be modified to explain away any possible contradictory evidence.
. . . avoids vagueness.	The hypothesis should avoid vague terms and be as precise as possible. Vagueness can lead to interpretations that fit any possible outcome, which undermines the principle of falsifiability.

Table P2.1

THINK AS A PSYCHOLOGIST

Evaluate the Appropriate Uses of Design Elements in Experimental Methodology (Practice 2.B.1)

Practice Evaluating Design Elements

Read the research scenario below and answer the questions that follow it.

Researchers want to understand why teenagers seem to be so attached to social media. They have observed teenagers using social media, and they have interviewed a number of teen social media users. They want to explore their hunch that social media fulfills a deep-seated need to feel connected.

1. What is the researchers' likely hypothesis?

2. Is their likely hypothesis falsifiable? Explain your answer.

Experimental Hypotheses, Independent Variables, and Dependent Variables

As you have read, research begins with a hypothesis, a prediction about the result of the study. Researchers generally write a hypothesis for an experiment in the form of an "if-then" statement. For example, "If participants drink a 12-ounce cup of coffee before working on a puzzle (independent variable), then they finish the puzzle faster (dependent variable) than those who did not drink the coffee." An "if-then" statement makes it easy to identify the variables, the relationship between them, and the expected result of the experiment.

Psychological researchers study many variables that are more difficult to define and measure than the speed of completing a puzzle. Self-esteem, intelligence, or personality type are some examples. Clear, well-defined operational definitions are critical for helping other researchers understand how dependent variables are being measured in a study. These details are necessary for any attempt to replicate a study.

THINK AS A PSYCHOLOGIST

Evaluate the Appropriate Uses of Design Elements in Experimental Methodology (Practice 2.B.2–3)

Practice Evaluating the Appropriate Uses of Design Elements

Read the research scenario below and answer the questions that follow.

Suppose a team of sports psychologists who run noticed that they seem to run faster the day after eating a steak dinner. They decide to conduct an experiment to test their personal observations, and they write the following hypothesis for the experiment: "If people eat protein, then they run faster." This hypothesis specifies two variables, what people eat and running speed. It also specifies a cause-and-effect relationship between the two variables: running speed depends on what you eat. To test this hypothesis, the sports psychologists will vary what people eat and then measure how fast they run.

The researchers set up three groups to which the participants will be randomly assigned. One group will eat a high-protein diet the day before the run. A second group will eat a low-protein diet the day before the run. A third group will eat what they usually eat.

1. In the hypothesis ("If people eat protein, then they run faster"), which variable does the *if* part of the sentence identify, the independent or the dependent? Explain your answer.

2. What might be some consequences to the study if the researchers tell participants in the high-protein group to eat what they typically think of as a high-protein meal?

3. What are some possible operational definitions for the *if* part of that hypothesis to avoid the consequences from question 2?

4. The second part of the hypothesis is "… then they run faster." Which variable is identified in the *then* part of the sentence, the independent or the dependent? Explain your answer.

5. What are some potential consequences to the study if the researchers tell participants to measure their running speed in whatever way they usually do, such as by a fitness tracker, treadmill timer, or stopwatch?

Populations and Sampling

- The **population** of a study consists of all individuals who can potentially participate. Since they can't use every person who could potentially take part, researchers use a **representative sample** by randomly selecting from the population a sample that has characteristics that are similar to those in the population. When a study is conducted with a representative sample, researchers are able to **generalize** the results—that is, affirm that they apply—to the larger population. For example, if you wanted to examine a new school policy in your high school, it is unlikely you could speak to every student, so you could use a random number generator to randomly select 200 students' ID numbers. This process should result in all levels, classes, and ages of students being equally represented in your study.

Note: Random sampling is not the same as random assignment. Random selection should be used whenever possible in all types of research studies, randomly selecting the sample from the defined population. Random assignment is unique to experiments and involves randomly placing participants into a control or experimental group.

- **Sampling bias** is an error in the sampling process that allows some members of a population to be more or less likely than others to be included in a study. If, in the high school study mentioned above, you only talked to students in your AP Psychology class, you have sampling bias because this class does not represent all age levels or levels of classes in the building. If a study has sampling bias, one cannot generalize to the population defined for the study. To ensure that a sample is representative and to avoid sampling bias, researchers use a **random sample**, one in which each member of the population has the same chance of getting into the sample as any other member.

- In contrast to random sampling, researchers sometimes use **convenience sampling**. As its name suggests, convenience sampling is a sampling method by which the sample is drawn from a part of the population that is readily available and easily accessible. Convenience sampling is commonly used in exploratory research and pilot testing where the goal is to get an initial understanding of a hypothesis or phenomenon rather than to generalize the findings to the entire population. Because samples are not randomly selected, convenience sampling is prone to sampling bias, thus limiting the generalizability of the research findings. If you ask your friends to list their favorite television series, you have conducted a convenience sampling that cannot be generalized beyond the friends you asked.

- Research that can be **generalized** can be applied to other settings, populations, or time periods outside of the original conditions of the study.

Before conducting an experiment, researchers must also define the population to be tested, sometimes called the *population of interest*. The **population** consists of all individuals who can potentially participate in the study. Psychologists would like to apply, or **generalize**, what they learn to all people. However, most of the time, it would take too much time or cost too much money to include all potential participants in a study. Even if the population of interest is narrower than *everyone*—for example, only people who like to run—the time and cost of a study would still make it impossible to include *everyone who likes to run*. Therefore, researchers use a smaller group of the population, or a sample.

Researchers use a variety of techniques to make sure the results from the sample will apply to the population of interest. At the most basic level, researchers use a **representative sample**, a sample that has characteristics that are similar to those in the population. Without a representative sample, researchers are unable to generalize the results to the larger population.

Although people are unique, groups of people can share characteristics, such as sex, gender, age, socioeconomic status, and interests. If you asked for volunteers for your experiment on running or used a classified ad to recruit people, you might get a group of people sharing the characteristics of liking volunteer work, reading classified ads, running, and being mostly young middle-class adults. These samples would not be representative of the larger population, resulting in **sampling bias**, a flaw in the sampling method that causes certain individuals or groups within the population to have a higher or lower likelihood of being selected for the study. To obtain a representative sample and prevent sampling bias, researchers employ **random sampling**. Through random sampling, every individual in the population has an equal chance of being chosen for the sample. This is typically done by giving every participant an identifying code and then placing all potential participants into a computer's random number generator and selecting the number of participants you wish to be in your study. Any sampling method that introduces a systematic pattern, or results in a sample that exhibits a pattern, is not truly random. Techniques that do not use random selection can lead to sampling bias, reducing the extent to which the results of the study can be generalized to the broader population.

Beginning researchers may define the population to be studied too broadly, making random sampling problematic and limiting the generalizability of experimental results. If the population is too broadly defined—for example, all people in the United States—drawing a random sample from the population becomes virtually impossible. In the same way, if researchers want to determine whether eating a diet high in protein has an impact on running speed, defining the population as everyone who runs will make selecting a random sample virtually impossible. If, in contrast, the researchers defined the population as "all students at City High School," they could reasonably expect to draw a random sample.

When researchers use random sampling to select the participants in a study, they can generalize the results to the population they defined at the start of the study. This ability to generalize the results of a study to a larger population is called *external validity*. When researchers can establish external validity, they can apply the results of an experiment to other, similar populations. For example, if researchers used random sampling to select participants for a study of heartbeat recovery time of 12-year-old children after running on a treadmill for 15 minutes, they would be able to generalize the results to other 12-year-old children who were not in the study.

However, as you read earlier, there are certain instances in which researchers do not need their findings to be widely generalizable. In these cases, they may choose to use **convenience sampling**, drawing on participants who are nearby or easy to reach for some other reason. Convenience sampling is a practical choice in many research scenarios, and it is often used in qualitative research. For example, researchers studying psychological or social behaviors of college students often use convenience sampling to gather data from students on a college campus. This can involve surveys or experiments on topics such as stress management, study habits, or social interactions, where students who are readily available and willing to participate are selected. Companies conducting market research might use convenience sampling at retail locations to quickly gather customer opinions. For instance, customers present in a store might be asked to provide feedback on their shopping experience or on new products, which allows for immediate and relevant consumer insights.

Convenience sampling can be useful when speed, cost, practicality, and specific situational demands are critical factors. But it is prone to bias and is not very useful for generalizability.

THINK AS A PSYCHOLOGIST

Evaluate the Appropriate Uses of Design Elements in Experimental Methodology (Practice 2.B.4–7)

Practice Evaluating the Appropriate Use of Design Elements

Choose the correct answer.

1. Which of the following is the best example of random selection?

   (A) Selecting every 10th name from the census to determine who will be in the study

   (B) Splitting the alphabet in half to determine who will be in the experimental or control group

   (C) Arbitrarily selecting names from everyone in the population to determine who will be in the study

   (D) Determining all of the individuals who can potentially participate in the study

2. An experimenter wants to determine the impact of caffeine on attention span. Which of the following would achieve random assignment in this study?

   (A) Placing participants into either the caffeine or noncaffeine group without any set pattern

   (B) Offering different levels of caffeine to the participants

   (C) Observing the level of attention exhibited by participants given caffeine

   (D) Selecting who will participate in the study without any specific pattern

Read the following scenario and complete the activities.

Varad is a graduate student in psychology. He wants to study the impact of a high-protein diet on muscle tone in students on his college campus. He plans on providing some students with high-protein diets for six months while others will continue with their normal diets for the same time period. He will measure muscle tone at the start of the study and again at the end of the study. Varad wants to make sure that his results are generalizable.

3. Define random selection. Then explain one possible way Varad could achieve random selection in his study.

4. Define random assignment. Then explain how Varad could achieve that.

Experimental and Control Groups, Placebos, and Limiting Experimenter Bias

---

**AT A GLANCE: KEY TERMS AND OVERVIEW
(PRACTICE 2.B CONTINUED)**

- A **placebo** is a substance or treatment that has no therapeutic effect, often used as a control in testing new drugs. Sometimes, though, when people simply *believe* that an action or a substance will have an effect, it actually *does*. The explanation for this phenomenon is the **placebo effect**—a real response to an action or substance based solely on expectations, not on the actual properties of the action or substance.

- To eliminate the participant bias, researchers use the experimental methodology known as a single-blind study. A **single-blind study** is one in which the participants do not know whether they belong to the control group or the experimental group. For example, to test a new drug, researchers give the new drug to the experimental group and give a placebo pill—one that contains no active ingredient but looks like the new drug—to the control group. Neither group knows whether they have been given the actual drug or the placebo. The simple act of taking a pill, even one with no active ingredient, may cause improvements because of the placebo effect, so to prove the benefits of the new drug, the improvements in the experimental group must be substantially better than those of the control group.

- Drug studies also involve a double-blind procedure. When neither the experimenter nor the participants know to which group the participants belong, the experiment is called a **double-blind study**. Double-blind studies eliminate **experimenter bias**, an error resulting from the experimenter's unconscious expectations of results; while researchers try to be objective, we are all swayed by our own biases. If uncontrolled, experimenter bias can interfere with the objective outcome of a study because the researchers' expectations unintentionally interfere with how they treat participants in a specific type of experiment. As you have read, researchers' expectations can also lead to confirmation bias (see Practice 1.B.2).

Once researchers have randomly selected a sample of participants, they place them into the groups established by the independent variable and the methodology. To establish cause and effect in an experiment, researchers manipulate the independent variable in one or more **experimental groups**. They also measure the dependent variable in a **control group**, or comparison group that doesn't receive the experimental treatment.

Suppose a researcher is studying whether drinking a glass of milk before bed provides more restful sleep than not drinking the milk. The experimental group would drink a glass of milk before bed. The control group would drink something that looks and tastes like milk but is not actually milk.

Placebos and Experimenter Bias The people in the control group in the milk-at-bedtime experiment above might *think* they are drinking milk and might *think* it promotes restfulness. As a result of this *thinking*, they might actually *feel* more restful. This phenomenon is known as the **placebo effect**, by which changes in a person's physiology or health result from their expectations, not from the actual substance or treatment they receive.

A **placebo** is a substance or treatment with no healing effects, often used in medical trials to test new treatments. Although placebos contain no active medical ingredients, people sometimes get better just because they believe they are receiving an effective treatment. In drug studies, placebos are made to look identical to the real medication.

To rule out the placebo effect, researchers can conduct either a single-blind or double-blind study. As you have read, in the single-blind study, participants do not know if they are receiving the real treatment or a placebo. In the double-blind study, neither the participants nor the researchers know who is in the experimental group or the control group. Recall that this setup prevents experimenter bias.

THINK AS A PSYCHOLOGIST

Evaluate the Appropriate Uses of Design Elements in Experimental Methodology (Practice 2.B.8–9)

Practice Evaluating the Appropriate Use of Design Elements

Choose the correct answer.

1. Mary is an undergraduate student who has volunteered for a study her professor is running. During the study, Mary picks up on cues from her professor about the expectations he has regarding the outcome of the study. The professor does not realize he is giving these cues, and she does not realize that she is picking up on them, yet she behaves as he expects. Which of the following phenomena has occurred?

   (A) Mary's professor has demonstrated experimenter bias.

   (B) Mary's professor has experienced sampling bias.

   (C) Mary has displayed the placebo effect.

   (D) Mary has participated in a double-blind study.

Reread the scenario on page 43 about Varad's study and then answer the following question.

2. Define *double-blind study* and its purpose. Then explain how Varad could set up his study to achieve that.

Qualitative and Quantitative Measures

Determining whether experimental research uses qualitative or quantitative measures is important for several reasons. It affects how data are collected, analyzed, interpreted, and applied. Each type of measurement has strengths and limitations, and choosing the right one is necessary to achieve the study's objectives, address the nature of the research question, and state the kinds of conclusions that can be drawn. Table P2.2 shows the differences between them.

Factors	Qualitative Measures	Quantitative Measures
Research Goal	Ideal for exploratory research when the goal is to understand underlying motivations, opinions, or experiences in depth Qualitative methods such as structured interviews capture complex stories or the nuances of human behavior and social interactions that quantitative methods might miss. This is sometimes referred to as "rich data."	Ideal for quantifying variables and testing hypotheses with statistical methods Quantitative measures, like Likert scales, allow for precise measurement of variables and make statistical analysis possible, which in turn allows researchers to determine relationships between variables or compare groups effectively.
Data Analysis Techniques	Analyzed through methods such as identifying patterns and themes in the data	Subject to statistical analysis that can quantify differences or relationships and test the study's hypotheses with precision

Factors	Qualitative Measures	Quantitative Measures
Generalizability	Typically has limited generalizability because of the small, nonrandom samples often used The findings are more about depth of understanding than breadth. Qualitative methods set expectations about the type of conclusions that can be drawn and their applicability to broader populations.	Offers greater potential for generalization if the sample is large and representative enough Quantitative measurements can provide a broad overview of trends and patterns that apply to larger populations.
Accuracy	While offering in-depth insights, may face challenges in the consistency of the measurement over time and the extent to which it measures what it is supposed to measure, but can provide high validity in capturing the complexity of human experiences	Provide greater consistency because of the structured nature and repeatability
Resource and Time Demands	Generally require more time for data collection and analysis, given the need to conduct extensive interviews, transcribe them, and carry out detailed data interpretation	Can be streamlined in data collection (e.g., surveys) and analysis (using statistical software), making them more suitable for larger-scale studies or when resources are limited

Table P2.2

THINK AS A PSYCHOLOGIST

Evaluate the Appropriate Uses of Design Elements in Experimental Methodology (Practice 2.B.10)

Practice Evaluating the Appropriate Uses of Design Elements

Read the following research scenarios and determine whether they used qualitative or quantitative measures. Explain each answer.

1. In this investigation, the researcher aims to determine the effectiveness of a new online learning tool designed to improve reading comprehension skills among middle school students. A total of 200 students are randomly assigned to either use the new online tool or follow their regular classroom curriculum without the tool for a semester. The researcher measures the reading comprehension skills of all students using a standardized test before and after the semester. The results are then statistically analyzed to compare the average improvements in scores between the two groups, with the aim of determining the tool's impact on reading skills.

2. In this study, the researcher is interested in exploring how children from divorced families perceive their relationships with their parents as they transition into adolescence. The researcher conducts in-depth interviews with a group of adolescents, each session lasting about an hour, focusing on their emotional experiences and the quality of their interactions with both parents since the divorce. Participants are encouraged to share personal stories and feelings about changes in family dynamics. The data collected are transcribed and analyzed for common themes, such as feelings of attachment, how well supported the teens feel, and changes in family roles.

Representation, Peer Review, and Replication

A benefit of the experimental method is its ability to demonstrate cause and effect through the manipulation of an independent variable. With a solid research design, including random assignment to groups, the experimental method can be generalizable to wide populations and reported. See Figure P2.3 for the steps in the experimental process.

Appropriate Representation of Participants

Throughout experiments, participants are represented anonymously to preserve their privacy. In addition, taking care to represent participants appropriately has an impact on both research conduct and research outcomes.

Impact on Research Conduct Ensuring that participants are appropriately represented in psychological studies is key to upholding ethical standards. Inclusivity and fairness in participant selection, avoiding bias toward any group, and ensuring that no group bears undue risk or is systematically excluded, unless scientifically justified, are fundamental to appropriate representation.

Appropriate representation also affects the sampling process. The sample needs to reflect the diversity of the population to which the researchers intend to generalize their findings. Factors such as age, gender, ethnicity, socio-economic status, and other relevant demographic characteristics need to be thoughtfully considered.

Impact on Research Outcomes A study that appropriately represents its target population will have higher *external validity,* meaning its conclusions are more likely to apply to a broader audience.

Appropriate representation also helps reduce various forms of bias in the outcomes, including sampling bias and cultural bias. Sampling bias occurs when certain segments of a population are overrepresented or underrepresented, which can skew results. Cultural bias can result in misinterpretation or inappropriate generalizations if the sample does not adequately reflect cultural diversity.

With diverse participants, the data collected are more likely to accurately represent the range of human behaviors, experiences, and psychological processes. This diversity can help identify how different factors affect various groups differently, which is essential for developing effective psychological interventions. Further, research that accounts for a wide range of human experiences through appropriate representation gains credibility.

The research process is not over when the results are reported. If researchers want their work to be published, they need to submit it to a journal for **peer review**. Peer review is a process used to ensure the quality and credibility of published work. In this process, when an author submits a manuscript to a journal or conference, it is evaluated by one or more experts in the same field (the "peers"). These reviewers assess the study's methodology, conclusions, and relevance to ensure that the work is of high enough quality and rigor to merit publication. Peer evaluation helps editors decide whether the work should be accepted, revised, or rejected. Peer review is foundational to scholarly publishing and is key in maintaining scientific integrity.

Experimental Design

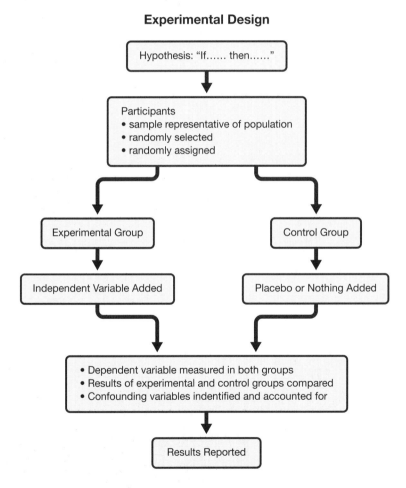

Figure P2.3

Even after publication, the process of scientific inquiry continues. **Replication**—conducting an experiment or study again to verify and confirm the original findings—is essential to ensure reliability and validity of scientific data. It helps identify any errors in the original research, contributes to the body of evidence supporting a hypothesis, and strengthens the overall conclusions drawn from the research. It is vital in the scientific process because it allows results to be verified, ensuring that findings are not due to chance, errors, or biases.

Replication helps strengthen the scientific community's confidence and allows further research to build on solid foundations. It also clarifies the body of evidence supporting a hypothesis and strengthens the overall conclusions drawn from the research. It is vital in solidifying the conditions and limitations under which findings hold and, in so doing, aids the refinement of theories. It spurs innovation by confirming reliable results, which directs resources and focus toward new questions.

Replication also plays a key role in preventing fraud, maintaining the integrity of scientific literature. Replication is increasingly recognized as a key for maintaining the robustness and self-correcting nature of science.

THINK AS A PSYCHOLOGIST

Describe the Impact of Appropriate Representation of Participants in Conducting Research and on the Outcomes of Research (Practice 2.B.11, 2.C.7) | Evaluate the Appropriate Uses of Design Elements in Experimental Methodology (Practice 2.B.12)

Practice Describing the Impact of Appropriate Representation and Evaluating the Appropriate Use of Design Elements

Complete the following activities.

1. Provide three examples of appropriate representation of participants and explain their importance in research studies.

2. Start a new graphic like Figure P2.3 that picks up from "Results Reported." In your graphic, show what follows after researchers submit their results, how the results get to appear in publication, and what happens after publication to keep the scientific process progressing.

Practice 2.C Evaluate the appropriate use of research design elements in non-experimental methodologies.

AT A GLANCE: KEY TERMS AND OVERVIEW

- Four common non-experimental methodologies are **case study, correlation, meta-analysis**, and **naturalistic observation**. (See page 30.)

- **Correlational studies** examine the relationship between two variables. In a correlation study, researchers measure two or more variables and assess how they are related to each other. Recall that a **positive correlation** indicates that, as one variable increases, the other variable also tends to increase, or that they are both decreasing, while a **negative correlation** indicates that, as one variable increases, the other variable tends to decrease. This is sometimes referred to as an *inverse relationship*.

- A **directionality problem** in correlational studies is the difficulty in determining the direction of cause and effect between two correlated variables. It is unclear which variable is the cause and which is the effect. In some cases, a third variable is the cause. Just as experiments can have confounding variables, correlational studies can have what is known as a **third variable problem**. This occurs when a variable outside of the study is affecting both variables. For, example, there may be a strong positive correlation between high levels of education and high incomes. The third variable problem in this scenario is socioeconomic status. If individuals were able to complete a college or post-graduate education, it may be because they had the money to pay for it, which in turn creates more money.

- Researchers using surveys take care that the wording of the survey does not lead to **self-report bias**, the errors and inaccuracies that can occur when individuals provide subjective accounts of their own behaviors.

- One type of self-report bias is **social desirability bias**. Participants may answer questions in a way that they believe others will view favorably. They may underreport undesirable behaviors or overreport desirable behaviors so they appear in a better light.

- Researchers also collect data with **structured interviews**, a method of assessment where all interviewees are asked the same set of predetermined questions in a specific order and manner. This approach ensures consistency and objectivity in how information is collected across different individuals.

Design Elements in Non-Experimental Methodologies

Non-experimental research designs are used to study relationships between variables without manipulating the variables themselves. This type of research is often observational and can provide valuable insights into phenomena where experimental manipulation is not possible because of ethical or practical reasons.

Despite their differences, non-experimental methodologies share key design elements with experimental methodologies. They have *hypotheses* that must be *falsifiable*. They have *operational definitions* to clarify what they are measuring. They have **variables of interest**—the variables that are the focus of the researcher's attention.

Case Studies

Some non-experimental researchers use **case studies** through which they conduct in-depth studies of either an individual or a group who share a common characteristic. Often, individuals who are featured in case studies have some unique characteristic that researchers want to investigate.

A case study generally involves numerous testing methods to gather as much data about the participants as possible. In his book *Awakenings*, neurologist Oliver Sacks describes an instance in which he undertook an in-depth *group case study* of individuals who had experienced years of paralysis. Many medical professionals had given up on these individuals, who were in a coma-like state, and believed that they could not interact with the outside world. Dr. Sacks evaluated their physical abilities and behavioral patterns and the individual differences within the group. He eventually treated them with L-dopa, a synthetic form of the neurotransmitter dopamine, and many found at least temporary relief from their paralysis.

In an *individual case study*, a school psychologist might evaluate a child for a special education program. The psychologist would give the child a full battery of cognitive assessments to rule out some types of deficits, determine if there are environmental or physical causes, and identify precisely where a learning deficit lies. The psychologist would then create an Individualized Educational Plan based on the student's unique needs and check in periodically to determine how the child is progressing.

Case studies can be extremely beneficial for the individual or group involved but often cannot be generalized to the larger population because of the unique characteristics of the individual(s) studied. They also cannot be replicated. However, case studies may help researchers generate hypotheses for experimental testing.

THINK AS A PSYCHOLOGIST

Evaluate the Appropriate Uses of Design Elements in Experimental Methodology (Practice 2.C.1–3)

Complete the following activity.

Read the following research scenario and answer the questions.

Researchers are studying the long-term effects of traumatic brain injury (TBI) on an individual professional athlete. They want to find out if athletes with TBI experience cognitive decline over a 10-year period after their injury. They decide to test the athlete once a year with a series of standardized assessments of cognitive abilities.

1. What is the likely hypothesis?
2. Explain whether the hypothesis is falsifiable.
3. What operational definition are the researchers using for measurement?
4. What are the variables of interest in this study?

Correlational Studies

Occasionally, researchers want to study questions for which manipulating an independent variable would be unethical or impossible. Some examples include studying the long-term impact of methadone as a treatment for heroin addiction or the impact of smoking on teenagers' lung capacity. A researcher cannot ethically provide participants with heroin, withhold methadone from other participants, or ask teenagers to smoke. They can, however, investigate individuals who currently use heroin, currently participate in methadone treatment for heroin addiction, or are already smoking. In these cases, the researchers cannot manipulate the independent variable (heroin, methadone, or smoking). However, they can use correlational studies to investigate the relationships among these users on methadone and see if there is a relationship with recovery.

Correlational studies allow researchers to determine if there is a relationship between two variables. These studies do not involve manipulation of variables as in an experiment. Rather, they seek to examine how variables are related, without interference on the part of the researcher. When reading about the methodology or results of a study, look for words such as *link* or *relationship* to identify a correlational study.

The correlational method of research cannot demonstrate cause and effect because no independent variable is manipulated. However, correlational studies are often used as part of a larger research program before conducting an experiment.

Two common types of relationships that can be determined from correlational research are positive correlations and negative correlations.

In a **positive correlation**, the variables move together in the same direction. If one variable increases, the other also increases; if one variable decreases, the other also decreases. If you were to examine the relationship between time spent exercising and fitness level, you would likely find that as time spent exercising increases, fitness level also increases. Likewise, you would find that the less time people spend exercising, the more likely their fitness level will be low. Do not get confused when the variables are decreasing. As long as both variables are decreasing together, the relationship is still positive. *Correlation coefficients* indicate the strength of the relationship between two variables. A positive correlation will fall between 0 and +1.0. (See Practice 3, page 94.)

In a **negative correlation**, the variables have an inverse relationship. For example, the more a person practices golf, the lower his or her game score will be. As the temperature decreases, the amount of clothing people wear generally increases. The key to identifying a negative correlation is that the variables move in opposite directions. The correlation coefficient for a negative correlation will be between 0 and −1.0. (See Practice 3, page 95.)

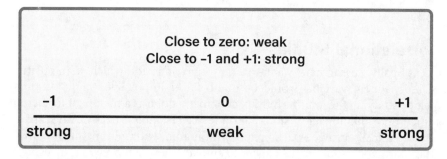

Figure P2.4 Correlation Coefficients

When analyzing relationships, draw arrows next to the variables. The directions of the arrows will indicate at a glance which type of relationship, positive or negative, you are considering. Avoid thinking of a positive correlation as indicating a "good" relationship and a negative correlation as indicating a "bad" relationship. The identifiers "positive" and "negative" simply indicate whether the variables move in the same or opposite directions.

Correlational studies are useful for making predictions—one of the goals of psychology—and decisions. For example, if parents learn that there is a positive correlation between playing football and having a concussion, they may think twice about allowing their children to participate on a football team. Colleges value SAT scores because they correlate positively to, and therefore predict, the grades students get in their freshman year.

Correlational studies are also useful to avoid unethical experiments that would expose participants to harm. For example, suppose a researcher wanted to know if the death of a family member had an impact on levels of depression the following year. It is impossible to manipulate the independent variable (the death of a family member) in this study. But finding out if there is a link may allow proactive interventions to take place, which may benefit family members at risk for depression. A correlational study provides an ethical way to study the level of depression people feel after the death of a family member.

Correlational studies may be misleading, however, because the relationship between the variables, especially which variable is affecting which, is sometimes hard to determine. This difficulty is known as a **directional problem**. For example, suppose there is a positive correlation between exercise and a good night's sleep. You cannot know if exercise causes better sleep or if getting better sleep provides more energy for exercise. It could be the case that both variables affect one another. Researchers also cannot rule out the possibility that a third variable causes both of the other variables to increase or decrease. For example, the temperature in the room may have more effect on the quality of sleep than exercise or drinking milk. This is known as a **third variable** activity. Links have been found between smoking and lung cancer, but it would be helpful to know if a third variable, such as genetic vulnerability to environmental factors or being raised in a home with smokers, is contributing to the link between these variables.

Despite these challenges, correlational research is used often and produces valuable information. Correlational studies assist in making predictions about relationships and establishing links between variables. Figure P2.5 will help you review the types of correlation that result from this research method.

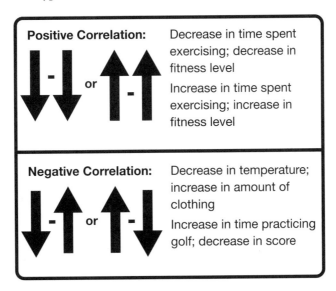

Figure P2.5 Types of Correlations

THINK AS A PSYCHOLOGIST

Evaluate the Appropriate Uses of Design Elements in Experimental Methodology (Practice 2.C.4)

Practice Evaluating the Appropriate Uses of Design Elements

Read the following research scenarios and answer the questions.

Educational psychologists are investigating the correlation between physical activity levels and academic performance in middle school students, believing that the more physical activity middle school students have, the better their academic performance will be. They plan to measure students' daily steps with a wearable tracker. They will measure students' academic performance by their grade point average at the end of the school year.

1. What is the likely hypothesis?
2. Explain whether the hypothesis is falsifiable.
3. What operational definitions are the researchers using for measurement?
4. What are the variables of interest in this study?

In another study focused on students' academic performance, researchers are trying to determine if there is a relationship between the amount of time students spend studying and their grades. At the end of the school year, they see a positive correlation between time spent studying and better grades. But they begin to wonder:

- Does spending more time studying cause better academic performance (more study leads to better grades)?
- Does better academic performance encourage students to spend more time studying (good grades motivate more study)?
- Does another factor (such as motivation, intelligence, or access to resources) influence both studying time and academic performance?

5. Explain how the nature of correlational studies can lead to such questions and what effect that has on proving cause and effect.

Collecting Data Through Surveys

Non-experimental studies sometimes gather data by asking participants to complete surveys. Surveys are inexpensive and can quickly gain information about people's opinions, attitudes, and perceptions. In a survey, participants receive a list of questions to answer. Survey research may be helpful in obtaining information about individuals' political views, what features of a new car they like or dislike, or what aspect of a marketing campaign is appealing. Surveys can be conducted face to face, by phone, through the mail, or online. Surveys are often completed using an interview format.

For example, if researchers want to know what students think about a proposed new attendance policy at their high school, they could send an electronic survey to all students. The results of this survey could quickly determine if the policy has the support of the student population, and that information could influence the administration's decision.

Other survey research occurs *after* an event, such as the review of a recently purchased product. Individuals who invested in a newly released smartphone may be asked what features they liked or did not like so that modifications can be made for future product releases.

As helpful as survey research is, it poses challenges. Participation in most survey research is not done by random selection. In many instances, people with extreme positions may respond to surveys. Often low response rates may cause survey results to not reflect the views of the population as a whole. Researchers conducting survey research can make efforts to use **random selection**, a technique for ensuring that all individuals in a population have an equal opportunity of being chosen to participate, to attempt to gather a variety of responses that reflect all views of a population. The Gallup Poll, for example, which conducts research about presidential elections, attempts to randomly call voters to predict who will win an upcoming election. This type of survey is, however, different from an experiment because, even if random selection or sampling is used, there is no manipulation of an independent variable and it cannot determine cause and effect.

Wording Problems Another challenge with surveys is that the wording or *framing* of the questions can have a strong effect on the way people respond, possibly skewing the results. For example, researchers have found that the words *forbid* and *allow* are especially potent in a question. In a now famous experiment from 1941, researcher Daniel Rugg posed a question two ways: (1) "Do you think that the United States should allow public speeches against democracy?" and (2) "Do you think that the United States should forbid public speeches against democracy?" When respondents were asked whether the United States should *allow* public speeches against democracy, 21 percent said yes and 62 percent said no, with the remaining percentage undecided or without opinion. When other respondents were asked if the United States should *forbid* such speeches, 39 percent opposed forbidding the speeches and 46 percent favored forbidding them. The difference between the responses is significant: 21 percent vs. 39 percent in favor of allowing and 62 percent vs. 46 percent in favor of forbidding. Many later experiments built on this one, and many possible explanations have been offered, some suggesting that it is not the wording itself but rather the simple "either-or" nature of the question that tipped the outcomes. Specific wording, the context of the questions, the order of questions, the presence or absence of alternatives, the order of the alternatives, if present, and whether problems were "framed" in terms of gains or losses all influenced survey results. (For more on framing and context and their effect on responses, see Topic 2.2.)

Other kinds of wording can also greatly influence how respondents answer, often leading to inaccurate responses and, therefore, faulty data. Answers can show bias in two common ways, among others. **Self-report bias** occurs when respondents answer questions inaccurately because of misunderstanding, forgetting, or personal biases. **Social desirability bias** occurs when respondents provide answers they think are more socially acceptable rather than truthful ones. They want to present themselves in the best possible light.

The following table shows the kind of wording that can bring out these biases.

Wording That May Lead to Self-Report Bias
Vague Time Frames: "How often do you exercise?" is open to wide interpretation. Respondents might think of different time frames (last week or last month, for example), leading to inconsistent and biased answers.
Leading Questions: "Given the known health benefits of exercising, how often do you exercise?" may lead respondents to exaggerate how often they exercise, since the first part of the question suggests a "correct" behavior.
Complexity: "How adequately do you feel the current Electoral College system represents the democratic intent of the U.S. constitutional framework in translating the popular vote into the presidential election outcome?" may confuse respondents, causing them to give answers that don't accurately reflect their understanding or opinions.
Wording That May Lead to Social Desirability Bias
Sensitive Topics: "Have you ever texted while driving?" may lead respondents to underreport undesirable behaviors to align with social norms.
Positively Framed Behaviors: "Do you recycle regularly to help the environment?" might lead to overreporting of recycling behavior because recycling is viewed positively.
Pressure for Conformity: "Most people feel that volunteering in the community is important. Do you volunteer regularly?" The pressure to conform to expressed social norms may cause respondents to overstate their volunteering activities.

Table P2.3

THINK AS A PSYCHOLOGIST

Evaluate the Appropriate Uses of Design Elements in Experimental Methodology (Practice 2.C.6)

Practice Evaluating the Appropriate Uses of Design Elements

Read the following 5-question survey for high school students about study habits. Explain the wording problem and identify the type(s) of bias each question is likely to bring out.

1. Do you always complete your homework on time, as responsible students should?

2. Would you say you are more disciplined than your peers when it comes to managing study schedules?

3. How frequently do you find yourself procrastinating on school assignments?

4. How often do you achieve the study goals you set for yourself each week?

5. Everyone knows that organizing your study space is key to learning efficiently. How organized is your study area?

Collecting Data Through Interviews

Interviews are another method for both formal and informal data collection. They can be conducted in a one-on-one setting or, less often, in groups. Like surveys, interviews can be useful for gathering much information quickly and relatively inexpensively. Interviews may be useful in developing an understanding of people's opinions and beliefs, and they make use of some of the same types of questions as surveys—with the same kinds of potential pitfalls in wording.

Interviews can be used for a variety of purposes. For example, they allow cognitive psychologists to understand someone's reasoning for choosing one answer over another on an exam. By interviewing the participants, researchers can know what participants experienced during a session, something a naturalistic observation study does not allow. Participants can report their experiences, thoughts, and feelings during or after a study. Finally, interviews may help psychologists gain an understanding of a wide variety of topics, such as decision-making, interpersonal attraction, and emotions.

a.bacall

"I'm an honest person but when I take an online survey, I'm a big liar."

A **structured interview** is a standardized set of questions in a specific order. Each interviewee is asked the same questions in the same way to ensure consistency and objectivity. Table P2.4 provides more information on structured interviews.

Key Features of Structured Interviews	
Consistency	The interviewer follows a script and does not stray from the predefined questions. This standardized approach helps minimize variations that could affect the reliability of the data collected.
Quantifiability and Comparability	Responses from structured interviews are easier to quantify and analyze statistically because the format of the questions and answers is consistent. This is useful in research settings where comparing data across many subjects is required in order to draw broad conclusions.
Reduction of Bias	By limiting the interviewer's ability to alter questions based on personal judgment or the interviewee's responses, structured interviews help reduce interviewer bias.

Table P2.4

THINK AS A PSYCHOLOGIST

Determine Whether the Measurement Instrument for Non-Experimental Research Was Qualitative or Quantitative (Practice 2.C.5)

Practice Determining Whether the Measurement Instrument Was Qualitative or Quantitative

Read the following research scenarios and then answer the questions.

Study One: Researchers want to explore how people in mental health therapy are recovering. They want consistent, in-depth data across a diverse group of participants. Participants will be asked preset questions in one-on-one settings about their emotional states and emotional state improvement since starting therapy. Researchers will analyze the data by identifying common themes and variations in factors that influence mental health recovery.

Study Two: Researchers seek to measure employee satisfaction levels within a large corporation and identify key factors influencing their workplace happiness. Workers will respond to an electronically distributed survey and report their level of satisfaction with various aspects of their job, including job security, work-life balance, and management support, using a 5-point Likert scale from 1–strongly disagree to 5–strongly agree. The survey will go to a large sample of employees, ensuring anonymity and encouraging honest responses. Data will be analyzed using statistical methods, pinpointing numerically the levels of satisfaction and identifying predictors of employee happiness within the workplace.

1. Which of the above studies used a qualitative measurement instrument? Explain your answer.

2. Which of the above studies likely used a Likert scale as a measurement instrument? Explain your answer.

3. What possible reasons might the researchers in both studies have had for choosing the measurement instrument they chose?

Meta-Analyses

For some topics of interest, many different researchers have published studies that use the same operational definitions of the independent variables. Each of these studies is useful in its own right, and together they provide even more insight into an area when someone examines the results of all of those studies to provide a better picture of the collective body of research on a given topic. The process of analyzing the results of many studies that have measured the same variables is known as **meta-analysis**.

Meta-analyses allow researchers to see the "big picture" by combining the results of similar studies. For example, if many different high schools adopt a bullying prevention program that intervenes proactively to prevent student bullying, each school could publish the results of its program. Then a meta-analysis could examine the published results from all schools that had introduced the program and analyze the results as a whole.

Because this process examines multiple studies together, it provides a more comprehensive view than a single study. But meta-analysis may become complicated when studies have measured the same variable but used different operational definitions or measured the dependent variable in different ways. For example, if one school in the bullying meta-analysis exposed students to one session of an intervention program and others exposed students to four sessions, comparing the studies would be difficult. It would be equally difficult to compare studies if one school measured reported bullying attempts while others measured students' responses to bullying on a survey.

THINK AS A PSYCHOLOGIST

Describe the Impact of Appropriate Representation of Participants in Conducting Research and on the Outcomes of Research (Practice 2.C.7) | Explain How Conclusions from Non-Experimental Research Evolve via Scientific Processes Such as Peer Review and Replication (Practice 2.C.8)

Practice Describing the Impact of Appropriate Representation of Participants

Complete the following activity.

In 2015, the Open Science Collaboration (OSC) published a report of their efforts to replicate 100 experimental and correlational studies published in three psychology journals. They had all been subject to peer review. The results of their meta-analysis sent shock waves through the psychology field: Only 39 of the studies were replicated successfully. The study became a landmark and created a "replication crisis" in the field of psychology.

Not so fast, said a team of professors and a graduate student from Harvard University (Daniel Gilbert, Gary King, and Stephen Pettigrew) and the University of Virginia (Timothy Wilson). Their study, published in 2016, revealed serious mistakes in the OSC study. For one, OSC failed to take into account that some replications would fail by chance alone, and in so doing they introduced statistical error into their findings. The team also found that some of the replications strayed too far from the original methods to be considered fair tests. Either of those alone would have been enough to call into question the OSC's findings. But the team also found that the OSC's study made a sampling error. In their choice of studies to replicate, they excluded many from subfields of psychology known for their rigorous methodology, thereby failing to select a random sample. Considering all these factors, the original studies failed only at the rate any group of studies would by chance.

They concluded "that the reproducibility of psychological science is quite high and, in fact, statistically indistinguishable from 100%. . . . The moral of the story is that meta-science must follow the rules of science."

The team critical of the OSC study stresses that they believe there was no intentional wrongdoing on the part of the OSC researchers—the scientists just made statistical and methodological mistakes, as scientists sometimes do. But they also note that the sensational headlines raising doubts about the reliability of psychological studies did harm to the field, creating a negative public perception.

1. Explain why the 2015 report was considered a "crisis" for the field of psychology.

2. Explain why random sampling is so important to research studies in general and why in this case it led to a sensational conclusion.

Naturalistic Observation

Another non-experimental methodology is **naturalistic observation**, the observation of human or animal behavior in its natural setting. Participants do not know that they are being observed, so they act naturally. For this reason, naturalistic observation avoids the criticism leveled against experimental research as being artificial because of the intentional manipulation of variables, the necessity for control, and the location of testing in a laboratory.

An example of naturalistic observation is observing student behavior in the cafeteria at lunch. You might observe how students interact with one another, where they sit, with whom they sit, how many buy lunch versus bring lunch from home, and other behaviors. Student behavior in this setting is likely to be different from behavior in a laboratory, and recreating the school lunchroom in a lab may be too artificial to obtain results that are reflective of what actually happens in the lunchroom.

Naturalistic observation has benefits when doing research with certain populations. This method may be helpful when conducting research with children who are too young to be interviewed or with animals that cannot be studied in a lab.

However, naturalistic observation may also lead to error. Although it allows researchers to obtain information that reflects the actual behavior of those being observed, it does not allow the researcher to interact with them. That lack of interaction may lead to erroneous conclusions about why the behavior occurred.

Along with case studies and the data collected in surveys and interviews, naturalistic observation is only descriptive; researchers cannot interfere, as they may be able to in an experiment, by adjusting variables. Careful and accurate observation is one goal of psychology.

Naturalistic observation has led to much information on the social life of coyotes. These three demonstrate one expression of a social order: the ears of the alpha male are upright, while the ears of the others, who acknowledge his leadership, are pinned back.

Use Table P2.5 to review the advantages and disadvantages of non-experimental research methods.

Types of Descriptive Research	Advantages	Disadvantages	Example
All	Avoids artificiality of highly controlled experiments	Cannot demonstrate cause and effect	Observations, case studies, surveys
Naturalistic Observation	Participants act naturally—no artificial conditions	Lack of interaction between experimenter and participants may lead to erroneous results May be subject to experimenter bias	Researchers observe the hunting behaviors of coyotes living in a specified area.
Case Studies (individual or group)	Collection of detailed in-depth information Opportunity to investigate unique illnesses	May be distorted by the expectations of the researcher Cannot be generalized to the population	Researchers study how a patient recovering from surgery to remove a brain tumor performs on cognitive, emotional, and physical tasks.
Meta-Analysis	Allows researchers to analyze data from a large sample	Time-consuming because data comes from diverse studies	A meta-analysis showed a strong relationship between physical attractiveness and good mental and physical health.
Interviews	Quick, easy, and inexpensive collection of data Information directly from the participant to eliminate experimenter guessing	Possibility of subjective self-reports Participants may lie Participants may be prone to demand characteristics Possibility of researcher asking leading questions	Researchers evaluate responses after a community tragedy.

Table P2.5

Practice 2.D Evaluate whether a psychological research scenario followed appropriate ethical procedures.

AT A GLANCE: KEY TERMS AND OVERVIEW

- **Institutional review** is a process by which prospective psychological studies are approved or rejected, based on how well they meet ethical guidelines. That institution may be a university, public health institute, or corporation.

- **Informed consent** is a signed statement indicating that a research study participant understands the components and the potential risks of the study and agrees to take part.

- **Informed assent** is an agreement necessary for a minor to participate in a study about which they have been fully informed. A minor would sign the assent form but also need a consent form signed by a parent or legal guardian. Minors cannot give consent; only parents and other legal guardians can provide consent for the participation of minors.

- **Deception** is misleading or withholding information from participants about the true purpose or nature of a study. Researchers use deception when knowing the true intent of the study might influence participants' behaviors and responses, potentially biasing the results.

- **Research confederates** are accomplices to those carrying out a study that requires deceiving participants. Sometimes they pretend to be research participants themselves.

- **Debriefing** occurs once a study is completed. At this point, researchers can give participants more details about the nature of the study than they would have been able to before the study began. If any deception was used during a study, researchers must immediately debrief participants to let them know they have been deceived.

Ethics Guidelines for Conducting Psychological Research

As psychologists explore human and animal thinking and behavior, they must abide by a code of ethics in the treatment of the participants. All institutions that conduct ongoing research have an **Institutional Review Board (IRB)** that reviews any study to determine if the proposal is ethical or if it poses risks to those involved. The IRB ensures the safety of those participating in research studies, and a study cannot begin until the IRB has given approval.

The American Psychological Association and other professional organizations that oversee and report on research have a number of specific criteria that must be followed in all research studies. Many institutional review boards have adopted the ethical guidelines set forth by the APA, but individual institutions may include additional guidelines or restrictions regarding what can and cannot be done with participants at their institutions.

The federal government also has regulations regarding ethical experimentation. In 1974, Congress passed the National Research Act, which authorized federal agencies to develop regulations protecting human subjects. Over the years, the regulations have been revised and updated.

Informed Consent

Humans participating in research studies must be participating by their own free choice. No *coercion*, or force, can be used to require individuals to comply with any aspect of a research design. Even after a study begins, a participant may decide that the topic of the study makes them feel uncomfortable or unsafe, and the participant may leave the study without at any time providing any reason or explanation.

Before the study begins, participants must be told all the details of the study and given a clear explanation of their role in the study, as well as the potential risks involved in participation. If the participants agree to take part in the study, they give their signed **informed consent** indicating that they understand the components and the potential risks of the study and agree to take part. Even if people have signed the informed consent form, they are not obligated to complete the study. For participants younger than 18, a parent or other legal guardian must sign an informed consent form before the study begins. Minors should be given the opportunity to provide **informed assent**, an agreement to take part after having been informed of the details of the study. In some cases in which a person is incapacitated or has cognitive decline and cannot consent for themselves, a family member or representative may give **consent by proxy**.

Minimizing Harm

The American Psychological Association (APA) has established ethical guidelines to ensure that research involving human participants respects and protects the individuals involved. A central ethical guideline is that researchers should take reasonable steps to avoid causing physical or psychological distress, harm, or suffering and to minimize harm if it is foreseeable and unavoidable. Researchers assess the risks before starting any study. They establish how likely the risks are and the degree of harm they could cause. Researchers must ensure that any risks are justified by the potential benefits of the research.

Confidentiality and Anonymity

The identities of participants in a study must be kept confidential. **Confidentiality** protects their private information. Typically, participants are also not identified by name. Instead, they are assigned a code or a number to protect their anonymity for the duration of the study. To prevent experimenter bias, even the researchers often do not know what data belongs with which participants. Once a study is complete, researchers must continue to protect the participants' anonymity and confidentiality; the information cannot be shared with anyone outside of the researchers without permission from the participants. For example, if researchers investigated the impact of teenagers' drug use on social relationships, they cannot release the names and drug use of individual participants during or after the study. There are exceptions to this, if the researchers find that the person is a danger to themselves or others, but these instances are rare.

Deception

Some studies require that the researchers mislead participants about the true nature of the study in order to test the phenomenon under study. In Stanley Milgram's famous research on obedience to authority, participants were told that they were involved in a test on learning and memory. They were told to administer what they thought were higher and higher levels of electric shock to another person, the "learner," who they believed was also a volunteer in the study but was actually a **confederate** (fellow researcher) of Milgram's.

Deception, which involves misleading participants about the nature of an experiment and its methodology, is acceptable when the researcher believes it is necessary for the efficacy of the study and the IRB agrees with the researcher's reasoning. IRB boards will generally not approve studies that use deception if the study can be done another way. Participants must be told as part of their informed consent that deception may be used. The APA guidelines set limits on the types of deception researchers can use. Researchers may not deceive participants about the risk factors of the study. They also may not deceive participants after completion of the study by falsifying the results. If researchers use deception in a study, they must conduct **debriefing** at the conclusion of the study to explain the deception. The participants should be told the true intention of the study as soon as reasonably possible. Regardless of whether deception was used in a study, debriefing should always occur at the conclusion of the study before the participant(s) leave the premises.

Milgram delayed debriefing participants in his studies because he was concerned they would share details of the study with their friends and neighbors in the small town of New Haven, Connecticut. Many of the participants in the study left without knowing that the individual posing as the learner was not harmed by the "electric shocks" they had administered (the person was never actually shocked). Some of the participants were deeply concerned because they believed that they had either harmed or possibly even killed the learner. Milgram sent a letter to all participants at the conclusion of the study. However, sending a letter is not sufficient to offset or diminish the risk faced by the participants. Some participants did not receive a debriefing letter until years after their involvement in the study. The use of such deception would be deemed unethical based on today's ethical guidelines.

The APA and IRB guidelines regarding debriefing participants were created to address ethical issues that became apparent in the wake of World War II and through Milgram's and others' research. Researchers and the IRB must consider both the physical and emotional risks of any study to be sure that neither will have a damaging impact on the well-being of participants.

Animal Research

Historically, animal experimentation has played a large role in research. Researchers from different areas within psychology often use animals for gathering information that may help us better understand human behavior. Behavioral psychologists, such as B. F. Skinner, worked with rats and pigeons to demonstrate the impact of rewards and punishments on behavior. Although cognitive psychology did not become a formal approach until the late 1950s, psychologists were studying cognitive phenomena with nonhuman primates beginning in the early 1900s.

Today, animals are still used in many studies, and they must be treated ethically in all research. Harming an animal or placing one in unnecessarily risky conditions is unethical. Universities that use animals in research must have a committee that evaluates the proposed studies. That committee, which is for nonhumans what the IRB is for humans, is called the Animal Care and Use Committee (ACUC). Review boards weigh the risks to the animal against the benefits of the research.

The American Psychological Association's Committee on Animal Research and Ethics (CARE) advocates for the ethical use of animals in research. The committee's main goals are to provide education on responsible research with nonhuman subjects and to establish clear guidelines about what ethical and responsible use of animals in psychological research means.

Technology has significantly transformed the use of animals in psychological experimentation, leading to both reductions in animal use and enhancements in the quality and ethical standards of research that still involves animals. For example, technology has made alternate research methods available using computer modeling. Technology has also improved the oversight of ethical compliance in laboratories through better monitoring systems and electronic record-keeping. This helps ensure that animal care guidelines are followed strictly and that any deviations are promptly addressed.

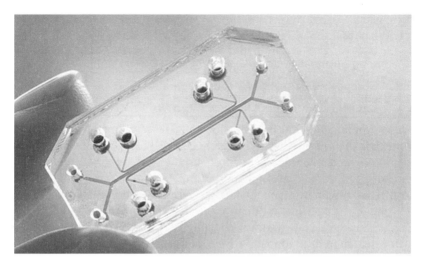

New technologies, such as this lung tissue on a chip, make it possible to study the interactions of cells and mimic blood flow, reducing the use of animals in experimentation.

THINK AS A PSYCHOLOGIST

Evaluate Whether a Psychological Research Scenario Followed Appropriate Ethical Procedures (Practice 2.D.1–6)

Practice Evaluating Ethics in Research

Read the following and answer the questions.

Hypothetical Experiment: "Peer Pressure and Conformity Test"

Objective: To investigate the extent to which high school students are willing to engage in unethical behavior under peer pressure.

Procedure:

- Researchers undertake the study independently, without review.
- Participants are groups of high school students who believe they are participating in a study about teamwork and decision-making.
- Each group is placed in a scenario where they must decide whether to cheat on a mock academic test to win a group prize.
- Unbeknownst to the participants, several members of each group are actually actors who subtly encourage the decision to cheat, claiming that "everyone does it" and that it's the only way to ensure that the group wins.
- The real participants' responses and discussions are recorded to analyze the influence of peer pressure on their decision-making.

Review the ethical guidelines in this section. Then identify at least three ways in which this experiment violates them.

THINK AS A PSYCHOLOGIST

Comparing Research Methodologies (Practice 2.C)

Practice Comparing Research Methodologies

Read the following and complete the activity.

The most fundamental question in choosing a research methodology is, "Will this method help achieve the research goal?" For the following scenario, determine which methods are most useful and appropriate, given the researcher's goals, resources, and ethical limitations.

Suppose researchers in Oklahoma are attempting to examine the effectiveness of a specific antidepressant as a treatment method for clinical depression in a local Native American tribe. They want to generalize the results of their research to the national Native American community. List the pros and cons of using experimentation, case studies, and correlational studies. To help organize your answer, create a chart like the one below, listing the pros and cons of each method. Determine which research method(s) would best suit the researcher's goals and whether the results would be generalizable. Write a paragraph explaining your answer.

Research Method	Pros	Cons	Generalizable?
Experimentation			
Correlational Studies			
Case Studies			

Practice 3

Data Interpretation:

Evaluate Representations of Psychological Concepts in Quantitative and Qualitative Research, including Tables, Graphs, Charts, Figures, and Diagrams

Practice 3.A Identify psychology-related concepts in descriptions or representations of data.

AT A GLANCE: KEY TERMS AND OVERVIEW

- Research studies produce a tremendous amount of data. **Data** are the facts collected in the course of research.
- Data can be described in words or represented in a graphic.
- Recall that a **variable** is any factor or condition that can change or vary and is measured, manipulated, or controlled by the researcher. Being able to **identify the variables** in descriptions or representations of data is the first step to understanding their relationship.
- Statistics is the science of collecting, analyzing, summarizing, and representing large amounts of data.
- Data can be represented in the following ways:
  - A **table** represents data in words or numbers in rows and columns.
  - A **graph** visually represents organized data so relationships are clear.
  - A **chart** visually represents data that may or may not be related.
  - A **diagram** is a simplified drawing representing data.
  - A **figure** can be any of the above representations.

The terms *graphs* and *charts* are sometimes used interchangeably.

Identifying Variables in Descriptions or Representations of Data

Consider the following hypothetical study. Note that it does not account for confounding variables.

Study Topic	The Impact of Sleep on Academic Performance
Research Question	Does the number of hours of sleep high school students get each night affect their performance on weekly math quizzes?
Study Design	• Participants: A group of high school students in the same class • Procedure: Students keep a sleep diary for four weeks, recording the number of hours they sleep each night. Each week, they take a math quiz. • Data Collection: Record the quiz scores along with the sleep data for each student. • Data Analysis: Calculate the average quiz score for students who slept different average amounts each night (e.g., 5–6 hours, 6–7 hours, etc.).
Results	During the study, students who averaged more hours of sleep per night got higher average scores on weekly math tests.

Table P3.1

Here is one way to describe that study in words: "A study was conducted among students to examine the relationship between the average number of hours they slept per night and their weekly math quiz score. Data were collected on students' nightly sleep hours and corresponding weekly math quiz score, which allowed researchers to analyze whether increased sleep time correlated with higher academic performance."

You might be able to see that the variables of interest are the average hours of sleep and the average quiz results, with a question about whether the first may influence the second.

The data can also be represented in a **table**. Note that the information in the following table is much more specific than it was when the variables were just described in words.

Average Hours of Sleep per Night	Average Quiz Score
5	65
6	70
7	75
8	89
9	85
10	88

Table P3.2

If you arrange the same data in a **line graph**, you can see at a glance the effect of sleep on academic performance.

Impact of Sleep on Academic Performance

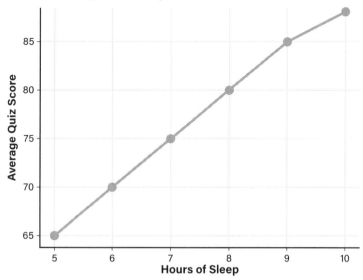

Figure P3.1

The horizontal line at the bottom of the graph is called the *x-axis*. In this case, the *x*-axis shows the hours of sleep, the variable believed to influence math scores. The vertical line ascending from the left corner of the *x*-axis is called the *y*-axis. (An easy way to remember this is "*y* goes to the sky." This will help you remember the orientation of the *x*- and *y*-axes in any graph.) In this case, the *y*-axis shows average quiz scores.

To interpret the graph, identify where the variables meet. For example, if you want to know the average score of a student who gets 7 hours of sleep, look up the *y*-axis to find where the *x*- and *y*-axes intersect. You will see that a student who averages 7 hours of sleep a night gets an average score of 75.

The value of a line graph is in being able to see trends and patterns. Because of the shape of the line, you can see the clear relationship between hours of sleep and quiz scores: the more sleep students get, the higher their quiz scores will be. The influence of sleep on quiz scores levels off somewhat after 9 hours of sleep. The quiz scores still rise, but since the slope of the line is not as steep between 9 and 10 hours of sleep as it is between 8 and 9 hours of sleep, you can see that they don't rise quite as fast.

A bar **chart** (or bar graph) is another way to visually represent the data from this simple study. It also uses the *x*-axis for hours of sleep and the *y*-axis for average quiz scores, but instead of starting at 65, the lowest average score among the students, the labeling of the *y*-axis starts at zero. The data represented this way makes the difference in quiz scores seem less dramatic than in the line graph. Presenters may manipulate the way the data are displayed to distort their findings, varying the increments in the *x*- or *y*-axis to make a trend look larger or smaller, as in Figures P3.1 and P3.2.

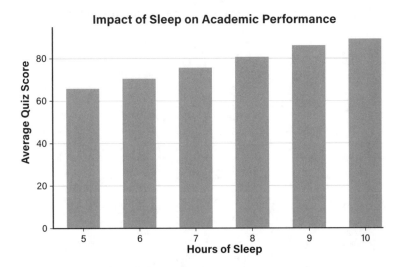

Figure P3.2

Another kind of chart that represents data is the pie chart. However, pie charts are typically used to represent proportions or percentages, which summarize information from a data set but do not demonstrate trends in the data. For this reason they are not ideal for showing relationships between variables like hours of sleep and quiz scores. However, if you want to represent the same data with a pie chart, you could focus on one variable, such as the distribution of sleep hours among the students in the study.

Distribution of Hours of Sleep Among High School Students

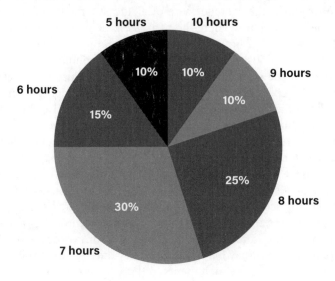

Figure P3.3

A Venn diagram can be used to illustrate the overlapping factors between sleep and academic performance.

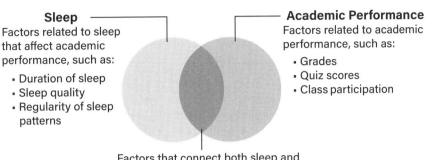

Sleep
Factors related to sleep that affect academic performance, such as:

- Duration of sleep
- Sleep quality
- Regularity of sleep patterns

Academic Performance
Factors related to academic performance, such as:

- Grades
- Quiz scores
- Class participation

Factors that connect both sleep and academic performance, such as:

- Alertness during class
- Memory retention
- Focus and concentration

Figure P3.4

When creating a bar graph for categorical data, leave space between the bars. This space between each of the bars signals that the data are *categorical* and measured on a nominal scale, one with no natural order or hierarchy and whose items are labeled. Figure P3.2 shows categorical data.

In a **histogram**, in contrast, bars touch one another to show *continuous* rather than discrete data. (See Figure P3.5.) Examples of data that can appear in histograms include time and age. For example, you could use a histogram to display the results of an experiment that measured the time it took rats to run through a maze. You would show equal segments of time on the *x*-axis and the number of rats running the maze within each time segment on the *y*-axis. The ages of students, lengths, weights, and heights can be grouped for display in a histogram. The histogram bars on the graph must touch one another to let viewers know that they are looking at continuous data.

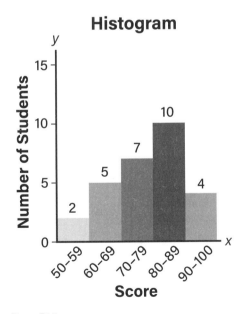

Figure P3.5

THINK AS A PSYCHOLOGIST

Identify Variables in Descriptions or Representations of Data (Practice 3.A.1)

Practice Identifying Variables in Descriptions or Representations of Data

Read the research scenario. Then answer the following questions.

How do you feel right before you have to get up and sing, speak, or perform in some other way in front of people? Anxiety is a common response, and it can sometimes get in the way of a good performance. A 2014 research study[1] explored whether reframing anxiety as excitement might enhance performance. The researcher designed a study in which participants were called in to sing a karaoke song that would be scored for accuracy by a Nintendo Wii device. Each participant was randomly assigned to say, when asked by a researcher, one of two responses: "I am excited" or "I am anxious." A third group was not asked that question. The researcher hypothesized that just saying the assigned words "I am excited" out loud might be enough to turn performance anxiety into excitement. The results of the study showed that people who were assigned to say "I am excited" got better singing scores.

1. What are the variables of interest in this study?

2. Look at the following graphic. How are the variables represented on the graphic?

3. Did participants score better when they said "I am anxious" or when they said nothing? Explain how the chart represents that information.

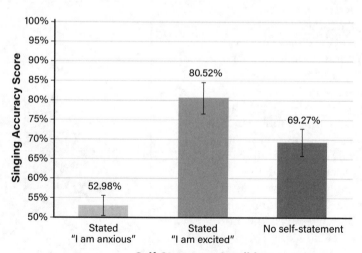

Error bars represent 5% confidence intervals around the means.

1 Brooks, A.W. (2014). Get excited: Reappraising pre-performance anxiety as excitement. *Journal of Experimental Psychology: General American Psychological Association, 143*(3), 1144–1158. 0096-3445/14/$12.00 DOI: 10.1037/a0035325

Identifying Statistical and Psychological Concepts Depicted in Graphics

Graphics can be especially clear ways to represent statistical concepts. For example, look again at the chart about excitement versus anxiety before a performance (page 76). The vertical lines in the middle of each bar, known as "error bars," extend 5 percent above and 5 percent below the average singing score. They express the idea that if the study is repeated, the result could vary by up to 5 percentage points above or below the reported value of the means.

A *scatterplot* is another type of graph. It is designed to display correlational data so that the relationship between the two variables is visible. The *y*-axis shows the values of one of the variables; the *x*-axis shows the values of the second variable. Each dot on the scatterplot is a pair of data points representing a participant in the study. Each point is plotted on the graph. A line of regression, or a line of best fit, is a straight line drawn through a scatterplot to represent the relationship between the two variables. The closer the dots are clustered to the line, the stronger the relationship between variables. The line or the orientation of the dots on the scatterplot represents the type of relationship and indicates the direction and strength of a correlation. The line of regression helps to p redict or explain how one variable changes in relation to another.

Once you have plotted all the data points on the scatterplot, you can evaluate whether a relationship exists between the two variables. A cluster of points that tips up to the right, as in the left scatterplot in Figure P3.6, indicates a positive correlation. If you drew a line through the center of the cluster, it would begin at the bottom left of the graph and move toward the top right corner. The steeper the line, the stronger the correlation.

Negative correlations have a cluster of points that tips up to the left. A line running through the center of the cluster begins at the top left of the graph and moves toward the bottom right (see the center scatterplot below). The steeper the line, the stronger the negative correlation. When the pairs of data points appear randomly scattered across the graph or do not form a cluster, as in the right scatterplot below, there is no relationship between the two variables

Scatterplots and Correlation

Positive Correlation   Negative Correlation   No Correlation

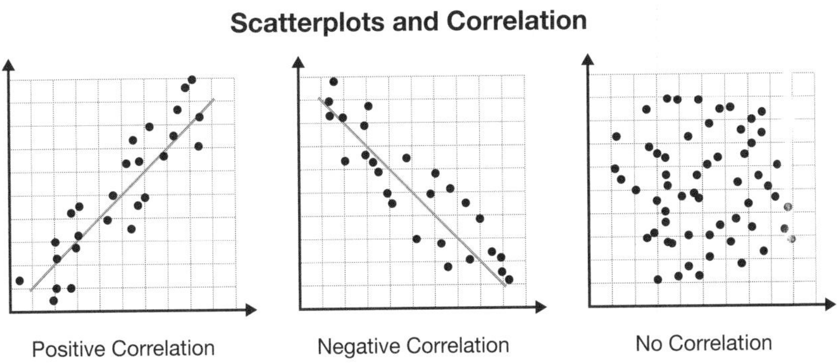

Figure P3.6

Visual representations can also clarify other statistical concepts, such as

- Probability—the percentage chance an event may occur
- Measures of central tendency—metrics that summarize or represent the center point or typical value of a data set; these measures are used to describe the average or most common value in a distribution (see next section, 3.B)
- Percentile ranking—the percentage of individuals in the distribution with scores at or below a particular value

Psychological as well as statistical concepts can also be clearly expressed in a visual representation. In Unit 1, for example, you will read about neurons, cells that transmit information throughout your body. These microscopic cells can be as small as one-tenth the diameter of a human hair. While they can be seen through powerful microscopes, labeled diagrams are helpful when learning about their structure (Figure P3.7). Often, seeing a visual depiction helps to provide another way to encode new information and, in many cases, can help you understand the connection between different concepts.

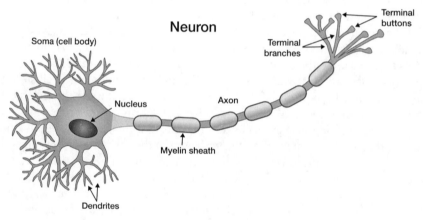

Figure P3.7

In Unit 2, you will read about memory and forgetting. Psychologist Hermann Ebbinghaus conducted studies to understand how and at what rate we forget what we have learned. The results of his studies are clearly and concisely expressed in the Ebbinghaus forgetting curve, a line graph that illustrates how information is lost over time when there is no effort to retain it. The x-axis shows the number of days elapsed. The y-axis represents how much of the memory is retained. The curve shows a steep decline in memory retention soon after learning, with the rate of forgetting gradually leveling off. According to the curve, the most significant drop in memory occurs within the first few hours to days, and after that, the decline becomes slower. Once you can understand how to read these types of graphs and charts, it often makes understanding the information much easier.

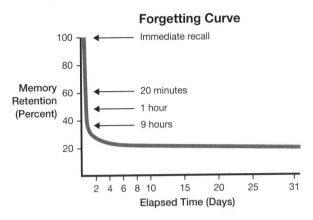

Forgetting Curve

Figure P3.8

In Unit 3 you will read about the psychological concept of *reinforcement* associated with behaviorists. That concept can be illustrated in a table or chart. For example, consider a table with two columns: "Behavior" and "Response" (Table P3.3). The table lists various behaviors exhibited by a group of children, the type of response or reinforcement they received (e.g., praise, reprimand, or no response), and the frequency of subsequent behavior. By examining this table, you can identify patterns of reinforcement and how they influence behavior. If the data show that certain behaviors are consistently followed by positive reinforcement and occur more frequently, this aligns with the concept of reinforcement in psychology.

Behavior	Response	Frequency of Subsequent Occurrences
Sharing toys	Praise	More
Interrupting	Reprimand	Less
Helping others	Praise	More
Not finishing homework	No response	More
Following instructions	Praise	More

Table P3.3

THINK AS A PSYCHOLOGIST

Identify Statistical and Psychological Concepts Depicted in a Table, Graph, Chart, or Figure (Practice 3.A.2)

Practice Identifying Statistical and Psychological Concepts Depicted in a Table, Graph, Chart, or Figure

Study the graphics and answer the questions.

1. A student wanted to know what chance she would have of a coin's landing on a head if she tossed the coin three times. She did some calculations and was able to represent her findings in a bar graph. What statistical concept does this graph show?

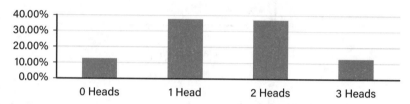

   (A) Correlation

   (B) Average

   (C) Margin of error

   (D) Probability

2. Tanya is helping the school's track and field coach recruit athletes for the upcoming season. She is timing her classmates as they run the 100-yard dash. She has tested 20 students so far and wants to show her coach the results. Which of the following would be the most appropriate way for Tanya to display her data for the coach?

   (A) A bar graph

   (B) A scatterplot

   (C) A histogram

   (D) A pie graph

3. Psychologists are interested in how people learn. Look at the following graph. What concept about learning does the graph convey?

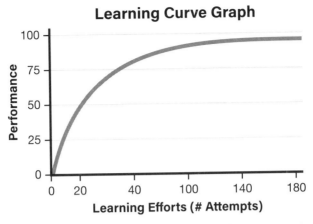

Learning Curve Graph

Graphical correlation between a learner's performance on a task and the number of attempts of time required to complete the task.

Practice 3.B Calculate and interpret measures of central tendency, variation, and percentile rank in a given data set.

AT A GLANCE: KEY TERMS AND OVERVIEW

- Researchers summarize the data they collect with a **measure of central tendency**, which indicates the point in a distribution of scores around which all the scores cluster.
- **Data sets** are collections of data gathered from an experiment, correlational study, naturalistic observation, or a case study.
- Among the measures of central tendency are
  - The **mean** is the average number in a data set.
  - The **median** is the middle number in a set of scores.
  - The **mode** is the most frequently occurring score in a data set
- **Measures of variation**, or variability, reveal how dispersed the data are.
  - The simplest descriptive measure of variability is the **range**, which represents the span of the scores in a data set.
- A **normal curve**, or symmetrical bell curve, is a graphic representation of a normal distribution.

- A **normal distribution** is a probability distribution that is symmetri about the mean, showing that data near the mean are more frequent in occurrence (because the *y*-axis displays frequency) than data far from the mean.

- **Standard deviation** is a statistical measure that quantifies the amount of variation or dispersion in a set of data values. It indicates how spread out the data points are around the mean (average) of a data set. The larger it is, the wider the curve. If the standard deviation is small, it means that scores are similar to one another. If the standard deviation is larger, scores are more widely dispersed.

- In a normal distribution, **the percentages of distributions across the curve** are as follows:

  — Approximately 68% of the data fall within one standard deviation of the mean.

  — Approximately 95% fall within two standard deviations of the mean.

  — Approximately 99.7% fall within three standard deviations of the mean.

  This rule is a quick way to summarize the distribution and gauge where most of the data points lie relative to the mean.

- **Skewness** in a graph refers to the degree of asymmetry of a distribution around the mean when the data displayed are not symmetrical.

- A **bimodal distribution** has two peaks (modes), which may indicate two different populations within the data set or a combination of two different distributions.

- **Percentile rank** refers to the percentage of scores in a given distribution that are the same as or lower than a particular score.

- **Regression to the mean** is the statistical concept that, when a variable is extremely high or low on its first measurement, it tends to be closer to the average (mean) on a subsequent measurement. It is a reminder that chance and variability are always factors with data measurements.

Calculating Mean, Median, Mode, and Range

After organizing and graphing data, researchers summarize the data with a **measure of central tendency**, which indicates the point in a distribution of scores around which all the scores cluster.

Mean The **mean** is the average number in a data set; it is the most commonly reported measure of central tendency. To calculate the mean, add all the scores in the data set and divide by the number of scores (N). The number of scores or data points often represents the number of participants in a study.

How is the mean helpful to people? If your parents want to know how much lunch money to provide to you each week, the mean can help them decide. They could use the mean amount you spent on lunch each week last year to determine what you generally spend on lunch.

A disadvantage of the mean is that extreme values can pull it in one direction or another. For example, suppose you purchased lunch for all your friends one week because they did not have money. The amount you spent that week will make the value of the mean higher than if you spent your usual weekly amount. In that case, the mean will not accurately reflect how much money you generally spend on lunch. The mean also will not accurately reflect what you generally spend if your parents include what you spent on lunch during school vacation week.

When a data set contains one or two extremely low or high data points, two other measures, the median and the mode, more accurately reflect its central tendency.

Median The **median** is the middle number in a set of scores. You calculate the median by determining the point in a distribution at which half of the scores fall above and half below.

Arranging the scores into a frequency distribution makes it easier to detect the middle number because the scores have already been arranged from lowest to highest or highest to lowest. For the data set 15, 17, 18, 21, 24, 26, and 28, the median or middle score is 21. Three numbers fall below 21 and three fall above. When the number of scores in the data set is even, you average the two middle scores to find the median.

When a data set has extreme scores, the median is a more useful measure to report than the mean because it is not as strongly affected by extreme scores. However, you always need to look at the data set to know whether there are extreme scores and what impact they may have on the median.

Mode The mode is the most frequently occurring score in a data set. The mode is not how many times the score occurs. Rather, it is the score itself. For example, if you track how many points an athlete scores per game in a basketball season, the mode might be 6. A mode of 6 means that the athlete most frequently scored 6 points per game.

Bimodal data sets are those that have two distinct peaks or modes. These peaks represent the values or ranges of values that occur most frequently in the data set. Essentially, in a bimodal distribution, there are two different groups within the data set that are separated by a gap where fewer values occur.

For example, imagine a grade 6–12 school with two very popular after-school programs: a robotics club and a drama club. The robotics club attracts younger students, mostly ages 10 to 12, while the drama club is popular with older students, ages 14 to 16. If we were to plot a histogram of the ages of students participating in these programs, we might see two peaks: one around the 11-year age group and another around the 15-year age group. This distribution shows two modes, one for each age group, making it a bimodal data set. In this case, the two modes reflect the different interests of different age groups within the school, showing how bimodal distributions can reveal underlying patterns or groupings in the data.

In the graph below, you can see two distinct peaks in the data: one for the Robotics Club, centered around ages 10 to 12, and another for the Drama Club, centered around ages 14 to 16. This visualization clearly shows the bimodal nature of the data, reflecting the different age groups that are most engaged in each club.

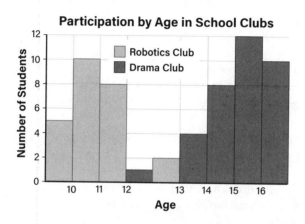

Figure P3.9

The mode is the most appropriate measure of central tendency to report for nominal data—data with no natural order or ranking, such as types of pets or eye color. The word *nominal* derives from the Latin word for "name," and nominal data are always labeled or named.

Which measure of central tendency is best depends on your research question, the data set, your purpose, or your audience. If a psychology instructor wants to boost students' spirits about an exam on which a few students scored poorly but most scored well, she might report that the median score was an A. The median is useful in this case because it is not affected by extreme scores. However, if the instructor reported that there were two modes, 77 and 82, on the exam, students might end up confused because it does not give them a clear picture of the performance of the class as a whole.

THINK AS A PSYCHOLOGIST

Calculate Mean, Median, and Mode from a Set of Data (Practice 3.B.1)

Practice Calculating Mean, Median, and Mode from a Set of Data

Read the following scenario and complete the calculations.

A psychologist is conducting a study to understand the mood variations in teenagers. Each participant in the study is asked to rate their mood on a scale from 1 to 10 at the end of each day, where 1 represents a very poor mood and

10 represents an excellent mood. The study was conducted over a week with seven teenagers. The results are below:

- Teenager 1: 7, 7, 8, 8, 9, 7, 8
- Teenager 2: 5, 5, 6, 5, 6, 5, 5
- Teenager 3: 8, 8, 9, 8, 8, 9, 8
- Teenager 4: 4, 5, 5, 4, 5, 4, 4
- Teenager 5: 6, 7, 7, 6, 6, 7, 6
- Teenager 6: 3, 3, 4, 3, 3, 4, 3
- Teenager 7: 9, 9, 10, 9, 10, 9, 9

Complete the following calculations. Create a table like the one below to record your calculations,

1. Calculate the mean mood rating for each teenager.
2. Determine the median mood for each teenager.
3. Identify the mode mood for each teenager.

Teenager	Mean	Median	Mode
1			
2			
3			
4			
5			
6			
7			

Measures of Variability

Measures of central tendency provide basic information about a data set—a snapshot—but do not reveal how spread out or dispersed the data in the distribution are. **Measures of variability** serve this purpose.

The simplest descriptive measure of variability is the **range**, which represents the span of the scores in a data set. You find the range by subtracting the lowest score in a data set from the highest score. In the data set 31, 44, 45, 48, 53, 57, the range is 26 (the highest score, 57, minus the lowest score, 31).

The range shows only the distance between the lowest and highest scores. It cannot reveal the average distance from the mean or other significant relationships between data points.

The **variation** of a data set indicates how widely spread scores are from one another and the mean. Typically, researchers report the measure of variability called the **standard deviation (SD)**, the average distance from the mean for a set of scores. The standard deviation becomes its own unit of measure, represented as a *z-score*—the number of standard deviations from the mean. A z-score of −1SD means a score is one standard deviation *below* the mean; a z-score of +1SD means a score is one standard deviation *above* the mean.

If you take future statistics classes, it will be necessary to know the steps to compute a standard deviation, but since you cannot use a calculator in the AP Psychology exam, you can use deductive reasoning to come up with the standard deviation of a data set.

Let's say you have rats run down a short length of a track and record their times in seconds, which are listed below. You may want to report a measure of central tendency (likely the mean) and a measure of variance (likely the standard deviation) for this data set.

DATA SET: LENGTH OF TIME IN SECONDS FOR RATS TO RUN THROUGH A MAZE				
Rat #1	Rat #2	Rat #3	Rat #4	Rat #5
10	5	6	10	4

The first step in determining the standard deviation is to compute the mean by adding up all of the scores (35) and then dividing by the total number of scores (5). This is the mean, which in this data set is 7. If you know that the standard deviation is the average distance from the mean for a set of scores and you do not know the formula, simply determine how far each data point is away from the mean, which you can see in the chart below.

DISTANCE FROM MEAN FOR EACH DATA POINT				
Data Point #1	Data Point #2	Data Point #3	Data Point #4	Data Point #5
3	2	1	3	3

Even without knowing the formula to compute standard deviation, you can see that the average distance from the mean for this data set is somewhere between 2 and 3 and in fact the standard deviation is 2.82.

Normal Distribution

Some variables, such as intelligence test scores and the heights or shoe sizes of a large group of people, produce a symmetrical distribution. In a symmetrical distribution, the pattern of scores on one side of the mean is a mirror image of the pattern on the other side of the mean. Distributions of this sort are known as **normal distributions** and are sometimes referred to as a "bell curve" because of the shape of the distribution when graphed.

Normal distributions are useful because they are predictable. The data in a normal distribution fall around the mean in the same way each time. For example, Figure P3.10 shows that 68 percent of the scores in a normal distribution fall between –1 standard deviation (below the mean) and +1 standard deviation (above the mean). Fewer than one percent of the scores fall in the tails of the distribution. Because of this consistent pattern, you can use a normal distribution to understand some of the basic information a data set can communicate.

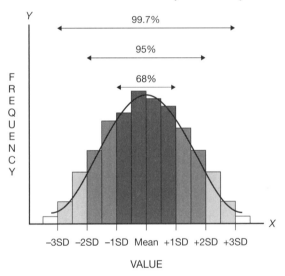

Normal Distribution (Bell Curve)

Figure P3.10

You can also use the normal distribution and the standard deviation to understand a score's **percentile rank**, the percentage of scores in a distribution that a particular score falls above. To determine the percentage of scores that fall between the mean and the standard deviation or to determine the percentile rank of a score, you need to know

1. that the scores are normally distributed

2. the mean

3. the standard deviation

If you don't have access to a graph like the one in Figure P3.10, you also need to know the percentage of scores that fall between each pair (between -1 and +1) of standard deviations around the mean, as shown in Table P3.4.

PERCENTAGE OF SCORES FALLING BETWEEN PAIRS OF STANDARD DEVIATIONS AROUND THE MEAN	
Standard Deviations Around the Mean	Percentage of Scores
Between –1 and +1	68%
Between –2, and +2	95%
Between –3 and +3	99.7%

Table P3.4

The following mnemonic can help you remember the percentage of scores for a normal distribution:

One 68-year-old threw a huge birthday party for two 95-year-olds. The three went all out for the event, hiring radio station 99.7 to DJ the party.

Working through a hypothetical example will help you learn how to use the normal distribution to find the percentile rank of a score in a data set. For example, scores on the ACT exam are normally distributed. Suppose that for a particular set of ACT scores, the mean is 21 and the standard deviation is 3. This is all the information you need to determine the percentile rank of any score on the test. To find the percentile rank of a score, start at the center of the distribution. An ACT score of 21 is in the center of the distribution. It has a percentile rank of 50, which means that half the scores are above 21 and half are below. Because the standard deviation is 3, a score of 24, which equates to a z-score of +1 (21 + 3), would have a percentile rank of 84. To see why, look at figure P3.11, which shows that 34 percent of the scores fall between the mean and 1 standard deviation above the mean. If a score of 21 has a percentile rank of 50, a score of 24 has a percentile rank of 50 + 34, which equals 84. Likewise, a score of 27 (21 + 2 standard deviations) has a percentile rank of 97 (50 + 47.5). This 47.5 is half of the 95% which is equally distributed on both sides of the mean.

You can see that a data point of +3 SD (3 standard deviations above the mean) has a percentile rank of 99.7. A data point of –3 SD (3 standard deviations below the mean) has a percentile rank of 0.2. A data point of +3 or –3 is rare and is referred to as an outlier. *Outliers* are data points that fall beyond 3 standard deviations from the mean. In some cases, these data points are just very different from the data points in the rest of the distribution. For example, on the ACT scores depicted above, if someone fell asleep shortly after the test began and only answered one question correctly, they would be an outlier and might not be included in the data set, as it could distort the results, depending on how large the data set was. In other cases, outliers may cause researchers to question the validity of their data collection. Before disregarding the outliers in a data set, researchers need to consider how the data were collected and if the measurement can be considered valid.

Percentages in a Normal Distribution

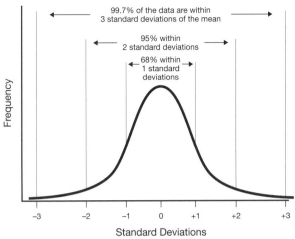

Figure P3.11 The percentages shown in the figure above apply to any data set that is normally distributed.

Normal distributions have one additional important feature. The measures of central tendency in a normal distribution are all the same and all fall directly in the center of the distribution. That is, in a normal distribution, the mean, median, and mode have the same value. Not all distributions are normally distributed, so you can use this fact to quickly assess whether a data set is normally distributed. When a data set is not normally distributed, the majority of the data points fall to one side or the other of the distribution.

Skewed Distributions

If your psychology instructor gave your class the Advanced Placement Psychology exam on the first day, you might expect that most students would perform poorly. Perhaps two students in your class took Introductory Psychology at the local community college over the summer, and their scores were high. If your psychology instructor gives your class a practice AP exam two days before the actual exam, most students would do well. There may be a few students who perform poorly because they were absent often during the year. In each case, the AP exam scores would pile up at one end of the distribution or the other. These types of distributions are referred to as **skewed**. Measures of central tendency are more variable in skewed distributions than in a normal distribution. The mean is most affected by extreme scores, so it is pulled toward the side of the distribution where most of the scores fall. In a **positively** (right) **skewed** distribution, the mean falls to the right of the median and the mode. In a **negatively** (left) **skewed** distribution, the mean falls to the left of the median and the mode. (See Figure 3.12.)

A distribution in which there are many low scores and a few high scores is known as a positively (right) skewed distribution. The skew is defined by the slope of the graph, not the side to which most data points fall. Positive in this case does not mean "good"; rather, it indicates the side of the graph on which the slope falls. If you compare the values of the measures of central tendency, the mode will be less than the median, and the median will be less than the mean.

Skewed Distributions

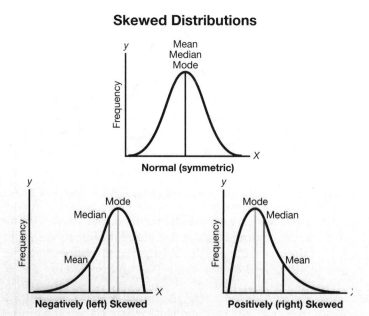

Figure P3.12

To determine the skew, look for the tail, the part of the graph where there are relatively few scores. The side on which the tail is located determines the skew.

A negatively skewed distribution occurs when the majority of data points are high and a few data points are low. In a negatively skewed distribution, the scores pile up on the right side of the graph and the slope falls on the left. The mean will be less than the median, and the median will be less than the mode.

A visual image can help you remember the difference between a positively skewed and a negatively skewed distribution. A positively skewed distribution looks like your right foot, with your big toe on the left side and a slope on the right. A negatively skewed distribution looks like your left foot, with your big toe on the right and the slope on the left.

THINK AS A PSYCHOLOGIST

Calculate Mean, Median, Mode, and Range from a Set of Data (3.B.1) | Explain the Elements of the Normal Curve Including Percentages of Distributions of Scores Across the Curve, How to Interpret Skewness in a Graph, and How to Interpret a Bimodal Distribution (3.B.2) | Interpret Mean, Median, Mode, Range, Standard Deviation, and Percentile Rank from a Set of Data (3.B.3)

Practice Calculating and Interpreting Measures of Central Tendency and Distribution Curves

Choose the correct answer.

1. Which of the following statements can be made about a normal distribution without knowing specific information about the data set?

   (A) The mean will be pulled to the right by extreme scores.

   (B) Eighty-four percent of the population will score at or below a +1 standard deviation.

   (C) Ninety-five percent of the population will score within one standard deviation of the mean.

   (D) The mean and median will be higher than the mode.

2. Jessica's chemistry instructor told the class that the results of the final exam were normally distributed. Because Jessica had been paying attention in her psychology class, she knows what this means. The instructor hands back the exams, telling the students that the mean was 80 and the standard deviation was 4. Jessica's score on the exam was 88. She wants to compute her percentile rank to see how she did in comparison to her classmates. Which of the following is correct about Jessica's exam score?

   (A) Jessica's percentile rank is 99.85.

   (B) Jessica's percentile rank is 84.

   (C) Jessica's percentile rank is 0.015.

   (D) Jessica's percentile rank is 97.5.

3. Which of the following is true about a negatively skewed distribution?

   (A) There will be a very small standard deviation.

   (B) The mode will be lower than the mean.

   (C) The mean will be lower than the median.

   (D) The mean, median, and mode will all be the same.

4. Varun is graduating from college. He is excited to have received a job offer from a small accounting firm near his home. During his research on the company, he found that most of the firm's 50 employees are recent college graduates like himself who make $43,000 per year. There are five managers who make $80,000 per year, a vice president who makes $120,000 per year, and a CEO who makes $300,000 per year. Which of the following best represents Varun's findings on the salaries of the employees at the accounting firm?

(A) A positively skewed distribution

(B) A normal distribution

(C) A correlation coefficient of –0.67

(D) A negatively skewed distribution

Read the following scenario and answer the questions.

Mr. Jones has just given a review test in preparation for the AP Psychology exam in May. He wants to be certain that he can provide those who need extra assistance the opportunity to attend a study session if they don't do well on the practice test. During the study session, he will review the topics covered by the exam. Mr. Jones is going to ask any student whose score is more than one standard deviation below the mean on the review test to attend the study session. As an expert statistician, you will be asked to examine the data provided below, which represent the students' scores, and make a recommendation to Mr. Jones regarding who should attend the study session.

Student #1	Student #2	Student #3	Student #4	Student #5
97	78	92	88	67

5. For the population above, determine the following and indicate which each of the scores represents.

- The mean
- The median
- The range
- The standard deviation

6. Recommend to Mr. Jones which students should attend the study session.

7. Explain which type of graph would be best to summarize the information from this data set.

8. Graph the data, labeling the axes and title.

Regression Toward the Mean

Regression toward the mean is a statistical phenomenon that occurs when subsequent measurements of a variable show a tendency to be closer to the average or mean of the population, especially if the initial measurements are extreme. As the data set gets larger, the mean gets closer to the anticipated mean.

- Initially, if a measurement of a particular variable (like test scores, for example) is unusually high or low—referred to as an "extreme score"—it may not be a true representation of the individual's typical performance or the average situation. If you gave an IQ test to a group of NASA astronauts, they would likely score far higher than the average IQ score.

- When additional data points are collected, these new measurements are likely to be less extreme (closer to the average) than the first measurement. If you then give the IQ tests to a random group of individuals from around the country to add to the data set, it will likely come closer to the mean of 100, as we would expect for IQ scores. The reason for this change is the built-in variability in the data and the fact that extreme deviations from the mean are less probable.

- As more measurements are taken, they typically average out. Extreme values (both high and low) become diluted by more average values. The average of the collected data points will naturally tend to move toward the mean of the population from which the samples are drawn.

- The first extreme measurements might be influenced by random fluctuations, measurement errors, or specific unusual conditions. As more data are gathered under varying conditions, these random effects and outliers have less influence on the overall data set's average, pulling the average closer to the population mean.

Here's an example: Suppose a student scores exceptionally high on a difficult exam, possibly because of a favorable mix of questions that matches well with what the student focused on during study. If the student takes several more exams of similar difficulty but with different mixes of topics, their scores on these subsequent exams are likely to be closer to their true academic level (the mean), rather than the initial high score.

This effect is crucial in research and data analysis because it shows that an extreme observation may not be a true reflection of the underlying reality and that more data can provide a more accurate and less biased view. It also cautions against making predictions or decisions based solely on extreme values.

THINK AS A PSYCHOLOGIST

Explain How Regression Toward the Mean Occurs as More Data Are Collected (3.B.4)

Practice Explaining How Regression Toward the Mean Occurs as More Data Are Collected

Rachel, a high school student, decides to try out for the school's track team. During the initial time trials, Rachel, who usually finishes a 400-meter dash in about a minute, unexpectedly clocks an impressive time of 52 seconds, one of the fastest times among the hopefuls. This extraordinary performance is far better than Rachel's usual practice times.

Excited by the prospect of being one of the top sprinters on the team, Rachel prepares for the final selection trials held a week later. However, during these trials, she runs the 400-meter dash in 58 seconds, which aligns more closely with her usual performance average. Rachel cannot understand how her performance had declined.

Complete the following activity.

1. Explain to Rachel the statistical reason her time in the tryouts was closer to her usual times.

Practice 3.C Interpret quantitative or qualitative inferential data from a given table, graph, chart, figure, or diagram.

AT A GLANCE: KEY TERMS AND OVERVIEW

- **Inferential data** refers to the information obtained from analyzing larger population. This type of data is used to make educated guesses or inferences about characteristics of the population based on the data collected from the sample.

- A **correlation coefficient** is the statistic used to describe the strength and direction of the relationship between two variables.

- **Effect size** is a numerical measure of the strength or magnitude of the relationship between variables or the size of the difference between groups in a study, regardless of sample size. Effect sizes are used to interpret the real-world, practical impact of research findings and are valuable for comparing results across different studies or contexts.

- **Statistical significance** is the demonstration that the results of a study are not just the results of chance. It helps researchers understand if the patterns or differences they see in their data are strong enough to conclude that they reflect a real effect in the population being studied rather than just random fluctuations.

Trends and Relationships in Variables

In the first section of Practice 3 (3.A), you read about positive and negative correlations. Review page 77 to be sure you can tell the difference. Recall also that *correlation does not prove causation* between variables, only whether they are related or linked.

The statistic used to describe the strength and direction of the relationship between two variables is called a **correlation coefficient (*r*)**. The value of a correlation coefficient falls between −1.0 and +1.0. A correlation coefficient with a value falling between 0 and +1 indicates a positive relationship between two variables. A negative relationship has a correlation coefficient between −1 and 0. The closer the value of a correlation coefficient is to +1.0 or −1.0, the stronger the relationship between the variables. For example, a correlation coefficient of +0.34 indicates a moderately positive relationship between two variables, and a correlation coefficient of +0.78 indicates a stronger positive relationship. The strongest positive relationship between two variables is +1.0, although it is rare to find correlation coefficients above +0.80 in the field of psychology.

Look again at the scatterplots in Figure P3.6, reproduced below.

Scatterplots and Correlation

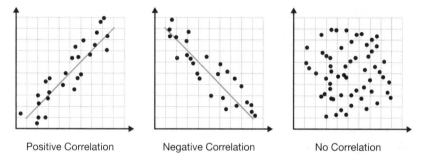

Positive Correlation   Negative Correlation   No Correlation

Even when a correlation coefficient and scatterplot indicate a strong relationship between two variables, you cannot assume the relationship is causal. It simply means that the variables are moving together or inversely to one another. A third variable that is related to the original two variables may be responsible for the strong correlation.

THINK AS A PSYCHOLOGIST

Describe Trends in and Relationships Between the Variables as Depicted In the Data Presented, Such as Interpreting Correlational Data from a Scatterplot, Including the Correlation Coefficient (3.C.1)

Choose the correct answer.

1. Paul has run a correlational study and found that as people age, their ability to hear high-pitched sounds decreases. While you do not have a written copy of Paul's study in front of you, which of the following correlation coefficients likely describes the finding of Paul's study?

(A) –1.02

(B) +1.24

(C) –0.48

(D) –0.05

1. A fitness club studied the relationship between hours exercised per week and stress levels. The results are shown below. Describe the trend in the scatterplot.

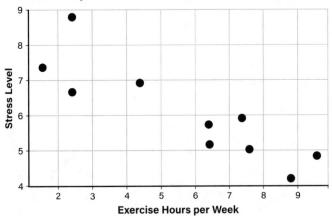

Relationship Between Exercise Hours and Stress Levels

Inferential Statistics: Statistical Significance and Effect Sizes

While descriptive statistics provide basic information about a data set, such as measures of central tendency and variance, inferential statistics provide tools for determining causality and drawing conclusions from a data set. **Inferential statistics** are methods for determining the likelihood that the result of an experiment is due to the manipulation of the independent variable or variables or is due to chance.

Statistical significance is one type of inferential statistic. Significance is reported as a *p-value*, which is the probability of getting the experimental results. The closer the *p*-value is to zero, the less likely the result is due to chance. It is always possible that a variable outside the experimental manipulation is influencing the results. A *p*-value of zero, which would indicate 100 percent certainty that the result is due to the experimental manipulation, is therefore impossible.

In the field of psychology, a *p*-value of 0.05 or less is acceptable for results to be considered statistically significant. When $p \leq 0.05$, a researcher can conclude that the result is unlikely to have occurred by chance and, in an experiment, it is likely that the result is due to the manipulation of the independent variable.

Effect size is a statistical concept that quantifies the strength of the difference between two groups, such as the control group and the experimental group. Unlike statistical significance, which shows if an effect exists, effect *size* identifies the size of the effect: Is the difference big enough to really matter in practical terms? It helps researchers understand whether a finding is meaningful and has real-world applicability. For example, if you took the ACT and fell directly at the mean, you would have a percentile rank of 50, with 50 percent of all test takers scoring above you and 50 percent scoring below. If you went to a tutor who worked with you for six weeks and then took the test again, if the effect size was +1.0, that means that the tutor helped you move one standard deviation up in your time together. While this may not seem like a big deal, it is, because this means your score will have moved from the 50th percentile to the 84th percentile.

Consider a study investigating the impact of a new reading program on student performance. The study involves two groups: one using the traditional method (control group) and the other using the new reading program (experimental group). At the end of the semester, both groups take a standardized reading test. The mean score for the traditional group is 70 with a standard deviation of 10, while the mean for the program group is 75 with a standard deviation of 10. If using Cohen's *d*, a standardized effect size measure, an effect size of 0.5 is calculated, which is considered a moderate effect. This suggests that the new reading program results in a moderate improvement on student reading scores compared to the traditional method. Such a finding can influence educational policies and resource allocation, emphasizing the value of measuring effect size to gauge the real-life significance of research outcomes.

THINK AS A PSYCHOLOGIST

Interpret Results from Research that Could Be Expressed as Effect Sizes or Statistical Significance (3.C.2)

Practice Interpreting Results from Research that Could Be Expressed as Effect Sizes or Statistical Significance

Choose the correct answer.

1. Alice has just found that the study she has been conducting over the last two years has yielded statistically significant results. She wants to tell her parents about her exciting news, but they do not know much about statistics. Which of the following statements can Alice share with her parents to summarize the meaning of statistical significance?

(A) The results are unlikely due to chance.

(B) The results will be an important contribution to the field of psychology.

(C) The independent variable is fully responsible for the result.

(D) The dependent variable is fully responsible for the result.

Read the following scenario.

A school district has implemented a new mathematics curriculum in some of its schools to see if it can improve student performance on standardized math tests. The district conducts a study with two groups of students:

- Group A: Students who continue with the traditional math curriculum.
- Group B: Students who use the new math curriculum.

At the end of the school year, both groups take the same standardized math test. The results are as follows:

- Group A (Traditional Curriculum):
  — Mean score: 78
  — Standard deviation: 8
- Group B (New Curriculum):
  — Mean score: 83
  — Standard deviation: 8

Complete the following activity.

Calculate the effect size using the differences between groups to determine the effectiveness of the new curriculum.

Step 1: Subtract the smaller mean from the larger mean.

Step 2: Divide the difference in means by the shared standard deviation.

Step 3: Use the following ranges to determine if the effect size is small, medium, or large.

- **Small effect size:** $d = 0.2$ or less
- **Medium effect size:** $d = 0.5$
- **Large effect size:** $d = 0.8$ or more

Practice 4

Argumentation:

Develop and Justify Psychological Arguments Using Evidence

Practice 4.A Propose a defensible claim.

AT A GLANCE: KEY TERMS AND OVERVIEW

- A **claim** is a statement in which a person takes a position they believe to be true. It is unlike a fact, which is known or can be proven to be true.

- A claim needs to be **defensible**. That is, it must be able to be supported with convincing evidence and reasoning. It is unlike an opinion, which can't be proved true or false. A claim should be able to be supported by evidence that is not simply opinion.

Proposing a Defensible Claim

Imagine you are in your room listening through headphones to one of your favorite songs. When the chorus comes around, it always stirs feelings in you:

> For you, I'd scale the highest ridge, I'd brave the wildest tide,
> Sacrifice whispers softly in shadows where it hides
> I'd trade all my tomorrows to give you this one day,
> In the quiet shade I've cast may you brightly find your way.

You could say many things about this song:

- "I like it better than 'Take My Hand,' the track before it on the album." This is an *opinion* about the song—there would be no way to prove it and no way to argue against it.

- "The first line of the chorus includes the words *highest* and *wildest*." This is a *fact:* you need only look at or listen to the lyrics to see that it is true. Again, there is no way to argue against it. Facts can be quickly proven true or false through observation or research.

There's more you can say about it, though. One day when you're listening to the song and the chorus is just ending, your brother barges into your room saying, "What did you do with my phone? I can't find it!" Usually, you resent when your brother tries to blame you for something that is really his problem, but today you turn off the music, remove your headphones, and say sympathetically, "I didn't do anything with it, but I'll help you find it if you want."

Here's another thing you could now say about the song:

- "After listening to that song, I was nicer to my brother than I usually am when he blames me for something." This is an *observation*, something that you noticed or witnessed.

Now you begin to wonder: "Did listening to those lyrics of loving sacrifice affect the way I treated my brother?" If you feel that may be true—not just for you but for other people as well—you might express it as a **claim**—a statement asserted to be true but still needing reasons and evidence to show why. You might express it this way:

Claim: Listening to music with prosocial lyrics—those about helping other people—leads to an increase in prosocial behavior.

A claim expresses a position with which people might disagree. It becomes part of an ongoing conversation on a subject to which different thinkers and researchers have contributed a variety of perspectives, some of which may challenge your claim. To qualify as a claim, then, a statement needs to be **defensible.** A defensible claim is one that people may disagree with but that can be supported as reasonable with facts and other evidence. A strong defensible claim is also clear and specific.

Defensible claims also make a connection between two parts or elements within them. In the example about prosocial lyrics, the two parts are listening and behavior. In experimental terms, you might think of these as the independent and dependent variables. ("*If* people listen to prosocial lyrics, *then* they engage in prosocial behavior." See Practice 2.)

THINK AS A PSYCHOLOGIST

Propose a Defensible Claim (Practice 4.A)

Propose a defensible claim on each of the following subjects. You can base the claim on your knowledge, experience, or observations. Make your claims clear and specific. View them as hypotheses.

1. Taylor Swift's influence on girls

2. Exercising to music

3. Friends and common interests

4. Schools confiscating cell phones every morning and returning them after school

5. Mandatory coed school sports teams

Taylor Swift accepts the Album of The Year award for *Midnights* onstage during the 66th GRAMMY Awards in 2024.

Olivia Rodrigo calls herself Taylor Swift's biggest fan and has been greatly influenced by Swift's music.

The song "We Shall Overcome" became an unofficial anthem of the civil rights movement and stirred compassion and a sense of unity. Dr. King called music "the soul of the movement." About 250,000 people attended the 1963 March on Washington at which Dr. Martin Luther King Jr. gave his famous "I Have a Dream" speech.

Practice 4.B Provide reasoning that is grounded in scientifically derived evidence to support, refute, or modify an established or provided claim, policy, or norm.

AT A GLANCE: KEY TERMS AND OVERVIEW

- **Reasoning** in the context of argumentation is the explanation of the relationship between evidence and a claim.

  — **Reasoning used to support** a claim, policy, or norm would help to show why it is sound or logical.

  — **Reasoning used to refute** a claim, policy, or norm would help to show that it is flawed, unreasonable, or wrong.

  — **Reasoning used to modify,** or change, a claim, policy, or norm would provide alternate data or reasoning to show that some part of the claim, policy, or norm is flawed, even though other parts of it are supported.

- **Scientifically derived evidence** refers to data—and conclusions drawn from that data—in studies that have carefully followed the rigors of the scientific method. This evidence is available in books, journal articles, and other sources that have been vetted by experts in the field.

- A **policy** is a plan developed and upheld at an institution to meet certain goals and guide decision-making in areas of concern. You may be most familiar with school policies, such as those outlining the rules for attendance and behavior.

- A **norm** is an accepted standard, practice, behavior, or expectation within a specific group, society, or context. A norm can describe an accepted practice or indicate what the practice *should* be.

- An **established claim** is one that has been tested and found to be sound and is widely accepted.

- A **nuance** is a subtle distinction or shade of meaning.

Gathering Scientifically Derived Evidence

Suppose you want to evaluate your claim about prosocial music ("Listening to music with prosocial lyrics leads to increased prosocial behavior") to see how well it might hold up in the ongoing conversations on that subject. You start doing some research and find that it is a subject that has been extensively studied from many different angles. Your evidence may include the following three pieces of evidence.

Evidence for Claim on the Effect of Prosocial Music on Behavior	
Source 1	An early experiment[1] studying this phenomenon showed that randomly grouped people in a restaurant in France who were exposed to songs with prosocial lyrics left larger tips than those who were exposed to songs with neutral lyrics or to no music at all.
Source 2	In experiments where participants in the workplace listened to songs with "happy" lyrics, they were more likely to choose cooperative solutions in subsequent tasks compared to those who listened to songs with neutral or unhappy lyrics.[2]
Source 3	Another study[3] demonstrated that people who listened to prosocial music and were paid for their participation in the study actually gave less of their earnings when given the chance to donate to charity than people who listened to music with antisocial lyrics.

Provide Reasoning that Supports, Refutes, or Modifies

You have your claim: "Listening to music with prosocial lyrics leads to increased prosocial behavior." You now have scientifically derived evidence from credible sources to use to develop your claim. However, the evidence alone is not sufficient. For example, you cannot prove anything by stating that listening to music with prosocial lyrics leads to prosocial behavior simply because a study in a French restaurant showed that people gave more generous tips after hearing music with prosocial lyrics. That leaves too great a gap in logic between the claim and evidence. Reasoning bridges that gap. An argument needs all the following elements.

ELEMENTS OF AN ARGUMENT		
Claim	**Evidence**	**Reasoning**
Prosocial music promotes increased prosocial behavior.	At least one (or more) references to information drawn from a credible source.	Explanation of how the evidence supports, refutes, or modifies the claim.

NOTE: The Evidence-Based Free-Response Question on the AP Psychology exam will provide you with a summary of three psychological studies and ask you to develop a defensible claim citing **evidence from the studies** *and using* **knowledge you have gained in this course** *to provide the reasoning. You will use your knowledge from psychology class (terms, theories, phenomena) that relate to the claim you have made and evidence you have cited. While the evidence comes from the source, the reasoning comes from your own mind.*

1 Jacob, C., Guéguen, N., & Boulbry, G. (2010). Effects of songs with prosocial lyrics on tipping behavior in a restaurant. *International Journal of Hospitality Management, 29*(4), 761–763. https://doi.org/10.1016/j.ijhm.2010.02.004.

2 Kniffin, K. M., Yan, J., Wansink, B., & Schulze, W. D. (2017, March) The sound of cooperation: Musical influences on cooperative behavior. *Journal of Organizational Behavavior, 38*(3), 372–390. doi: 10.1002/job.2128. Epub 2016 Aug 9. PMID: 28344386; PMCID: PMC5347889.

3 Ganser, J., & Huda, F. (2010). Music's effect on mood and helping behavior. *UW-L Journal of Undergraduate Research XIII.*

Reasoning that Supports Claims Reasoning is a powerful tool for supporting claims, since it helps build the logical and coherent argument that can convince others of a claim's validity. The following chart shows different ways you could use reasoning to support the claim about prosocial music and prosocial behavior.

Using Reasoning to Support Claims	
Making Logical Connections	Reasoning helps establish logical links between different pieces of information or observations. By showing your thinking about how one idea logically follows from another, reasoning strengthens the argument and makes the claim more persuasive.
Example *Listening to music with prosocial lyrics naturally leads listeners to reflect on the positive messages, which can influence their actions toward others. With constant exposure to themes of kindness and cooperation, listeners may be more inclined to emulate these behaviors.*	
Applying Concepts	Reasoning can support a claim by linking it to a broader concept or established theory. In this way it lends the authority of the wider theoretical framework or concept to the claim. You have practiced applying concepts in Practice 1. You will learn many more concepts throughout this course, including the concept of priming in Topic 2.2. Priming refers to the process by which exposure to one stimulus influences the response to a subsequent stimulus, without conscious awareness. You will also learn about social learning theory (Topic 3.9), which suggests that people learn behavior by observing and imitating models. As you have read, the Evidence-Based Question requires that you use information you learned in the course as your reasoning.
*Example (**Applying the Concept of Priming**) The psychological concept of priming can explain how the stimulus of prosocial lyrics leads to prosocial behavior as a response to that stimulus. Priming is a memory technique that allows memories and information or feelings to be recalled more easily. Prosocial lyrics prime listeners to think and act in a cooperative and positive manner, which increases their prosocial interactions with others.*	
*Example (**Applying the Concept of Social Learning Theory**) The causal relationship between prosocial music and behavior can be seen through the lens of social learning theory (Topic 3.9), which suggests that people learn behavior by observing and imitating models. Prosocial lyrics serve as a model of positive behavior that listeners may imitate.*	
Anticipating Disagreements or Counterclaims	Effective reasoning anticipates possible objections or counterarguments and addresses them within the argument. This supports the claim by showing that it can withstand criticism.
Example Some may argue that the effects of music are too fleeting to significantly influence behavior. However, repeated exposure to prosocial messages in music can reinforce and strengthen these behavioral tendencies over time.	
Synthesizing Information	Reasoning involves synthesizing, or piecing together, diverse bits of evidence to support a claim. By integrating different sources of data or perspectives, reasoning provides a comprehensive argument that convincingly supports the claim. In the Evidence-Based Question, you will need to synthesize the ideas in the three studies to develop a solid and defensible claim.

> **Example** *Synthesizing the results from various studies, examples of behavioral change, and psychological theories reveals that prosocial music has a tangible and beneficial impact on listener behavior. The consistent pattern across different contexts supports the claim that prosocial lyrics lead to prosocial behavior.*

Table P4.1

Reasoning That Refutes Claims When you **refute,** or disprove, a claim with reasoning, you can use some of the strategies in the previous table as well as those that follow. Even when your intention is to support a claim, understanding ways in which it might be refuted will be necessary to defend the claim well.

Using Reasoning to Refute Claims	
Offering Alternative Explanations	Cause and effect in human behavior is rarely straightforward, because so many factors can influence any given behavior. Recall that just because two things happen together (correlation) does not necessarily mean one causes the other (causation).
Example *It's possible that people who are already inclined to behave prosocially are more likely to seek out, appreciate, and respond to prosocial music, so the music itself may not be causing the behavior. This reverse causality suggests that personal traits may dictate music preferences more than music may cause a change in behavior.*	
Providing and Explaining Conflicting Evidence	Reasoning often involves providing additional empirical evidence that may conflict with the original evidence and explaining why that conflicting evidence needs to be considered.
Example *Another study[4] demonstrated that people who listened to prosocial music actually donated less money from their earnings for participation in the study than people who listened to music with antisocial lyrics and reason that even one exception makes the original claim too weak to stand.*	
Questioning the Universality or Generalizability	Reasoning can be used to show that what may be true in one or a few cases may not necessarily apply to others.
Example *The effect of prosocial music might not be universal. Cultural differences, personal preferences in music, and differences in context and age can all influence how or whether music affects behavior. For these reasons, prosocial effects may not be consistent across different groups or situations.*	
Applying Concepts	Reasoning can refute a claim by linking it to a different and possibly more relevant broader concept or established theory.
Example (Applying the Concept of Confirmation Bias) *Consider the concept of confirmation bias, which you read about in Practice 1.B. This bias demonstrates that people might give more weight to evidence that supports their existing beliefs and disregard evidence that contradicts them. Fans of prosocial music may be more likely to report positive effects of the music on their behavior, skewing the perceived effectiveness of these songs.*	

Table P4.2

---

4   Ganser, J., & Huda, F. (2010). Music's effect on mood and helping behavior. *UW-L Journal of Undergraduate Research XIII.*

Reasoning that Modifies a Claim When you **modify** a claim, or show that it is partly true and partly flawed and propose a refinement that corrects that, you attempt to refine the statement to better align with available evidence, acknowledge limitations, and address complexities that may have been overlooked in the original claim. You may use a different set of reasoning strategies, as shown in the following table.

Using Reasoning to Modify Claims	
Limiting the Scope or Extent	You might modify a claim by pointing out that it may be valid only under certain circumstances or for defined lengths of time, or may be one of several possible explanations.
Example To modify the claim about the effect of prosocial lyrics on prosocial behavior, you might limit the scope and change it to: "Under certain conditions, listening to music with prosocial lyrics leads to prosocial behavior." The first phrase limits the scope of the claim. You might add another phrase at the end: "at least in the short term" to limit the duration of the effect.	
Suggesting the Need for Additional Empirical Evidence	You might modify a claim by emphasizing that, while some studies support the claim, more research is needed to understand all the factors involved.
Example Further empirical research is necessary to determine any possible long-term impacts of prosocial music on behavior. Experiments should also control for variables such as how often and for how long people are exposed to the music and what the listeners' initial attitudes are toward helping behaviors.	

Table P4.3

The following table summarizes the different strategies of supporting, refuting, and modifying claims.

GOAL	SUPPORTING A CLAIM	REFUTING A CLAIM	MODIFYING A CLAIM
Strategies	• Making logical connections • Anticipating disagreements • Synthesizing information • Applying concepts	• Offering alternative explanations • Providing and explaining conflicting evidence • Questioning the universality or generalizability • Applying concepts	• Limiting the scope or extent • Suggesting the need for additional empirical evidence

THINK AS A PSYCHOLOGIST

Identify Reasoning that Supports, Refutes, or Modifies an Established or Provided Claim, Policy, or Norm (Practice 4.B.1)

Practice Providing Reasoning That Supports, Refutes, or Modifies an Established or Provided Claim, Policy, or Norm

Read the following claim. Then complete the activities.

Claim: Rap music is a positive force for identity and education among adolescents.

1. Provide reasoning that supports this claim.

2. Provide reasoning that refutes this claim.

Read the following policy recommendation. Then complete the activity.

Policy Recommendation: State literacy, math, science, and civics assessments should be reformed to integrate Hip-Hop culture.[5]

3. Provide reasoning that modifies this policy.

Read the following educational norm. Then complete the activity.

Educational norm: Students should not be allowed to perform original rap songs in school.

4. Provide reasoning that refutes this policy.

One aspect of Hip-Hop culture some educators would like to see in schools is the use of mentors to encourage and support young learners.

---

5   Collins, J. E. (2024). Education policy reform for the Hip-Hop era. *Kappan, 105*(7), 60–61.

Explaining Nuances of Claims, Policies, or Norms with Scientifically Derived Evidence

In psychology, delving into the **nuances** of claims, policies, and norms through scientifically derived evidence allows for a sophisticated understanding of arguments put forward in psychological research. Research questions rarely have one answer. The claim you developed after observing your behavior with your brother, for example—that listening to prosocial lyrics leads to prosocial behavior—has dozens, if not hundreds, of ways it could be qualified, or modified, depending on how it is understood and studied. Recall that all scientific inquiry becomes part of ongoing conversations on subjects that have been studied by many people, often over many years. Understanding nuances in these conversations ensures that knowledge is thoughtfully refined, that interpretations are based on solid empirical data, and that conclusions are not based merely on subjective perceptions or anecdotal evidence. In the following representation, each aspect of the claim is open to many different nuances.

ELEMENTS OF A CLAIM		
Basic Claim	**How or Why**	**Why It Matters**
Prosocial music promotes prosocial behavior.	What explains why or how prosocial music has this effect	How can the knowledge be put to good use in the real world, and how does it relate to what we already know?

Table P4.4

Categories of Nuances

Nuances in research may show up in several different ways. One category of nuance is *process*—the ways in which the research study was conducted. A second category of nuance is *findings*—the conclusions researchers draw from their studies. (You may wish to review the "At a Glance" sections in the shaded boxes in Practices 2 and 3 to refresh your memory about research methodologies and data interpretation.)

Nuances in Process You may find nuances related to the process of a research study. Suppose, for example, you learn that the study that showed that listeners of prosocial music giving less money was done under very controlled circumstances in a classroom, in contrast to the real-life setting of the restaurant in France for the prosocial experiment on tipping behavior. You might explain the difference in outcomes, at least in part, by the nuanced difference in context.

The researchers of the classroom study also noted in the Limitations section of the study that they were present when the participants chose how much money to give, while in other studies researchers were not present. That also represents a nuance of process that may have had an effect on outcome. The participants may have wanted to look good in front of others, which affected how much money they gave and may have had more influence than the type of music they listened to.

Nuances in Findings Researchers may draw conclusions that are only slightly different from, or slightly similar to, the findings of others. For example, suppose you find a study from Australia about how music choices in adolescents can predict behavior.[6] This study categorizes music into four main types and finds that two of them were more aligned with the quality of *empathy*, the ability to understand and share the feelings of another. The researchers suggest that adolescents who preferred these forms of music might be more likely to exhibit prosocial behaviors than those who preferred the other music types.

This study provides several nuanced distinctions from other studies and nuanced interpretations.

1. This study, as opposed to others mentioned, addresses only adolescents, so its generalizability to an adult population is not possible.

2. Whether music with prosocial lyrics leads to prosocial behavior in adolescents may depend on what their preferred music style is.

Since all the above examples and types of nuances rely on aspects of research studies, they all qualify as being based on **scientifically derived evidence.**

THINK AS A PSYCHOLOGIST

Explain Nuances of Claims, Policies, or Norms with Scientifically Derived Evidence (Practice 4.B.2)

Practice Explaining Nuances of Claims, Policies, or Norms with Scientifically Derived Evidence

Read the following briefs of studies already mentioned (Source A and Source B) and one new one (Source C). Then answer the questions.

NOTE: You will encounter research summaries in the following format in the free-response portion of the AP Psychology exam. Get used to reading them in this format by taking your time to absorb each part. You will also see research summaries in this format at the end of each unit in this book so you will have more opportunities to become familiar with the summary style.

---

6 Clark, S. S., & Giacomantonio, S. G. (2015). Toward predicting prosocial behavior: Music preference and empathy differences between late adolescents and adults. *Empirical Musicology Review, 10*(1), 50.

Source A (Prosocial Music and Tipping Behavior)

Introduction

Researchers wanted to explore the influence of background music with prosocial lyrics on tipping behavior in a restaurant setting. Previous studies have shown that music can affect purchasing behavior and prosocial behaviors in controlled environments. This study aims to investigate whether these effects translate to naturalistic settings, like restaurants, where multiple external factors are present.

Participants

The study involved 786 customers (432 males and 354 females) of a restaurant in Vannes, France. These participants were randomly assigned to either dine alone or in groups and were unknowingly part of the study, which examined their tipping behavior under different musical backgrounds.

Method

The experiment used three types of background music conditions: prosocial lyrics, neutral lyrics, and the restaurant's usual music. All the songs were in French. Over 6 weeks, excluding Sundays, music was played during lunch and dinner times in a randomized order. The impact of the music on tipping behavior was measured by tracking whether customers left tips and, if so, how much. In France at the time, a 12 percent tip was required by law to be added to the check. The measured tips in this study were those above the required amount.

Results and Discussion

The findings appear below.

Table 1 Mean of the proportion of patrons who left a tip

	Prosocial Lyrics	Neutral Lyrics	No Music
Lunch	37.46	28.09	21.71
Dinner	32.64	20.89	26.41
TOTAL	35.05	24.48	24.06

Table 2 Mean of tip given in Euros (At the time, 1 Euro equaled 1.33 US Dollars)

	Prosocial Lyrics	Neutral Lyrics	No Music
Lunch	1.22	1.23	1.15
Dinner	1.53	1.21	1.26
TOTAL	1.38	1.22	1.21

The findings revealed that prosocial lyrics significantly increased both the likelihood of customers leaving an extra tip and the amount of the tip compared to neutral or no music conditions. This suggests that prosocial lyrics may enhance empathetic feelings and prosocial behavior, leading to higher tips. The study supports the hypothesis that music influences customer behavior, even in a busy restaurant environment, and highlights potential managerial implications for enhancing employee income through strategic music selection.

Reference

Jacob, C., Guéguen, N., & Boulbry, G. (2010). Effects of songs with prosocial lyrics on tipping behavior in a restaurant. *International Journal of Hospitality Management*, 29(3), 761–763. https://doi.org/10.1016/j.ijhm.2010.02.004

Source B (Prosocial Music and Buying Fair-Trade Coffee)

Introduction
Researchers wanted to find out if there was a positive impact of music with prosocial lyrics on everyday behavior, specifically focusing on the effects such music has on increasing prosocial behaviors in a natural setting. The research hypothesizes that exposure to prosocial lyrics can enhance prosocial purchasing behavior, contrasting with existing literature that often emphasizes the negative effects of music.
Participants
The field experiment involved 256 participants (66% female) who were guests at a café. These participants were unaware that they were part of a study designed to observe their purchasing behavior under different musical conditions.
Method
Participants were randomly assigned to one of two conditions: prosocial lyrics or neutral lyrics. The experiment was conducted in a real-world café setting, where two observers discreetly monitored and recorded the participants' behaviors. The key behaviors measured were the purchasing of fair-trade products versus regular products and tipping behavior. Two separate playlists of 18 songs in English were developed for the background music in the café. One included only well-known songs with prosocial global themes, such as John Lennon's *Imagine* and Michael Jackson's *Heal the World*. The other included songs by the same artists that had neutral lyrics. Researchers set up the experiment so that all customers saw a chalkboard displaying information on fair-trade coffee—coffee bought through trading groups that support coffee farmers and sustainable growing methods and that prohibit child labor. Fair-trade coffee costs more because of these protections. Waiters allowed six minutes to pass before taking customers' orders so customers would have a chance to hear at least two songs. Customers who were present when the prosocial songs were played bought more fair-trade coffee, even though it cost more, than customers who heard the neutral playlist. However, they did not tip more.
Results and Discussion
The results demonstrated a significant positive relationship between prosocial lyrics and prosocial behaviors ($r = .12$; anything above $r = .08$ was considered significant), with guests exposed to prosocial lyrics more likely to purchase fair-trade products compared to those who listened to songs with neutral lyrics. This finding suggests that music with prosocial lyrics can effectively influence purchasing decisions in everyday scenarios. Although the mechanisms behind this influence remain under-researched, the results indicated that prosocial media can foster prosocial outcomes in naturalistic settings.
Reference
Ruth, N. (2016). "Heal the World": A field experiment on the effects of music with prosocial lyrics on prosocial behavior. *Psychology of Music, 45*(2), 298–304. DOI:10.1177/0305735616652226

1. Explain one difference or nuance in the *process* of Source A and Source B.

2. Explain one difference or nuance in the *findings* of Source A and Source B.

Source C (Prosocial Music and Rice Donations)

Introduction
The study examines how songs with prosocial lyrics influence prosocial behavior, specifically online charitable donations. Building on the general learning model (GLM), the research aims to understand how such songs impact empathy and subsequent prosocial actions. The GLM is a framework that explains how media exposure, such as songs or videos, can influence behavior. It suggests that repeated exposure to certain types of media content can shape a person's thoughts, feelings, and behaviors by creating mental scripts and reinforcing specific attitudes. The model emphasizes the role of cognitive, emotional, and social processes in mediating these effects, leading to changes in real-world behaviors, such as increased empathy and prosocial actions.

Participants
Study 1: 203 Chinese college students (107 females) randomly assigned to three groups: prosocial songs, neutral songs, or prosocial lyrics
Study 2: 137 Chinese participants (72 females) assigned to prosocial or neutral songs groups

Method
Study 1: Participants listened to either prosocial songs, neutral songs, or prosocial lyrics without music in a laboratory setting in this double-blind study. Participants listened to the music (or lyrics) attentively through over-ear headphones while being seated in individual compartments. The setup ensured that participants focused solely on the songs or lyrics, without any background distractions. After they listened, participants completed an online charity task. The operational definition of prosocial behavior was how much time participants spent playing a game on the website play.freerice.com. Every correct answer donates rice to people in need through the UN World Food Programme. The more time spent playing the game, the more food gets donated, so the larger the prosocial effort.
Study 2: Replicated Study 1 but with songs played as background music. Empathy was measured using the Interpersonal Reactivity Index-C (IRI-C). The IRI-C is a questionnaire consisting of 22 items that participants rate on a scale from 1 (does not describe me well) to 5 (describes me very well). The IRI-C includes scales for Perspective Taking (understanding others' viewpoints), Empathic Concern (feeling sympathy for others), and Personal Distress (feeling discomfort in response to others' distress). Higher scores indicate stronger empathy in these areas.

Results and Discussion
Study 1: Participants exposed to prosocial songs or lyrics donated significantly more rice compared to those who listened to neutral songs. There was no significant difference between the prosocial songs and prosocial lyrics groups.
Study 2: Listening to prosocial songs increased empathy and led to more donations compared to neutral songs. Analysis showed that empathy mediated the relationship between song type and charitable behavior.
The findings suggest that prosocial songs enhance empathy and prosocial behavior, with potential applications in promoting charitable actions in real-world settings.

Reference
Hong, M., Liang, D., & Lu, T. (2023). "Fill the world with love": Songs with prosocial lyrics enhance online charitable donations among Chinese adults. *Behavioral Sciences, 13*(9), 739. https://doi.org/10.3390/bs13090739

3. Explain two differences or nuances between Source C and either or both of Source A and Source B.

4. Develop a claim about prosocial music and prosocial behavior based on the evidence in these three sources. Select one piece of evidence from at least two of the sources to support your claim.

Explaining the Effectiveness of Claims, Policies, or Norms with Scientifically Derived Evidence

Recall the brief overview of psychological perspectives you read about in Practice 1. That was a summary of just the most prominent voices in the ongoing conversations about how and why people think, behave, and feel as they do. One way to look at the progression of those perspectives is by examining the core *claim* of each perspective, the *challenges* to each claim, and the *scientifically derived evidence* used to support the challenges. You might even want to picture some of the key participants in this conversation— Sigmund Freud, B. F. Skinner, Jean Piaget, Carl Rogers, and Charles Darwin—sitting around a table talking. Although some were from different times and places, each stepped into an ongoing conversation that had started long before they joined. And each at some point said, "But I don't agree, and here's why."

Charles Darwin   Sigmund Freud   Jean Piaget   B. F. Skinner   Carl Rogers

What would the conversation be like among these key modern psychologists? How might they challenge one another's claims? How might the psychologists on the next page challenge their claims?

Consider the following **claim**. How might you challenge its effectiveness based on the studies you have read about in this section?

Listeners pay far more attention to the musical content of a song than to the lyrics. In fact, most people don't even really listen to lyrics.

One of the first questions you may have about this claim would be what evidence the person making the claim has about the proportion of listeners who focus on music instead of lyrics. Even if you do not know that, however, you can still evaluate the effectiveness of that claim with the scientifically derived evidence you do have. You now know, for example, that studies have shown that prosocial behavior tends to correlate with the listening of prosocial songs, which are defined as prosocial most clearly by their lyrics. So clearly people are not only *listening* to the lyrics but also paying attention to their meaning,

Kenneth and Mamie Clark

Carol Gilligan

George I. Sánchez

Mary Whiton Calkins

These scholars brought diverse voices to ongoing conversations in psychology. Mary Whiton Calkins (page 4) contributed ideas on memory. Kenneth and Mamie Clark (page 476) studied the effect of segregation on Black children. Carol Gilligan studied morality and promoted women's voices in research. George I. Sánchez focused on mental measurements and bias in standardized testing. Derald Wing Sue is a leader in the field of muticultural counseling and has shed light on microaggressions, subtle discriminatory messages.

Derald Wing Sue

developing feelings of empathy as a result, and acting generously. So even if the person making this claim could provide scientifically derived evidence that most people pay more attention to the music than to the lyrics, the claim would still need to account for why lyrics can move people to prosocial behavior.

Explaining the effectiveness of claims does not require challenging them, however. You can also join the conversation by using scientifically derived evidence to *support* them. For example, suppose you came across this **policy** as you are researching places to work during summer break. The job at this organization requires making calls to solicit contributions to charitable causes and then entering the results in a database.

> **Policy:** Employees may not use personal listening devices on the job, but "easy listening" music is piped in throughout the office and can be heard when employees are not making calls.

How might you evaluate the effectiveness of this policy using scientifically derived evidence? Without knowing exactly what "easy listening" music consists of, you might infer thatg, because it is "easy," it does not rock the boat or raise conflicts and more likely presents a positive message. Even if the lyrics may not be explicitly prosocial, you might conclude this is an *effective* policy, based on your knowledge from scientifically derived evidence that listening to happy music affects mood, and a better mood may make the job of soliciting money for charity easier.

THINK AS A PSYCHOLOGIST

Using Scientifically Derived Evidence, Explain How or Why a Claim, Policy, or Norm Is or Is Not Effective (Practice 4.B.3)

Practice Explaining the Effectiveness of Claims, Policies, or Norms with Scientifically Derived Evidence

Complete the following activities.

1. Read the following claim from a research article on how people evaluate songs on their personally created playlists.[7] An evaluation of the entire study would be needed to definitively support or challenge this claim. For this activity, use scientifically derived evidence you already know to explain whether the claim is effective. Explain your answer.

   Claim: "People . . . associated a track with a setting and used their imaginations to create a scenario that the music represents."

2. Read the following claim. Use the provided evidence from scientific research in the bullet points that follow it to write an explanation of whether the claim is effective.

   Claim: Hip-Hop is unique in its portrayal of women as unequal to men and may contribute to antisocial behavior.

   - A majority (57%) of rock videos portrayed women as "passive, dependent on men, accenting physical appearance."[8]
   - Two-thirds of country music songs cast women in subordinate roles.[9]

---

7 Sanfilippo, K. R. M., Spiro, N., Molina-Solana, M., & Lamont, A. (2020, February 6.) Do the shuffle: Exploring reasons for music listening through shuffled play. *PLoS One, 15*(2): e0228457. doi: 10.1371/journal.pone.0228457. PMID: 32027672; PMCID: PMC7004375.
8 Alexander, S. (1999, Fall). The gender role paradox in youth culture: An analysis of women in music videos. *Michigan Sociological Review, 13*, 46–64.
9 Andsager, J., & Roe, K. (1999). Country music video in country's year of the woman. *Journal of Communication, 49*(1), 69–82.

- "The following music genres were statistically significant and have a positive correlation with altruism [prosocial behavior]: Alternative, Country, Classical, and Emo. In addition, the following genres had marginal positive correlation with altruism: Hip-Hop, Gospel, and 80s Rap. Furthermore, there was a relationship found in this study between listening to Aggressive, Positive, and Deep/Thought-Provoking lyrics and Altruism scores."[10]

Singer John Legend and rapper Common joined forces at a benefit for an organization that provides support for under-resourced fathers, mothers, and caregivers to help lift them out of poverty. They also cowrote with rapper Rhymefest the award-winning song "Glory" from the 2014 movie *Selma*.

10 Hippler, C. (2011). The relationship between genre choice of music and altruistic behavior. Thesis. University of Central Florida.

UNIT 1: Biological Bases of Behavior

Unit Overview

Have you ever wondered what makes you who you are? What guides your personality, sense of humor, intelligence, fears? Is it the genes you inherited from your parents, or is it the influence of your friends, the environment in which you were raised, the larger culture? Psychologists try to answer these types of questions, and Unit 1 will help you begin to understand the biological components of the puzzle of who you are.

The debate between nature and nurture and the exploration of the nervous system and brain are central to understanding human behavior and mental processes. The debate about nature and nurture examines how genetic inheritance (nature) and environmental influences (nurture) shape our personalities, intelligence, behavior, and mental health. This debate shows the complexity of psychological development and the many different influences that determine who we are. The nervous system serves as the body's communication network, and the brain serves as the command center. Both play pivotal roles in how we perceive through our senses and interact with and interpret our surroundings. These biological systems not only govern physical operations but also influence our emotions, thoughts, and behaviors, showcasing the links between our biological makeup and our psychological experiences.

To capture the essence of this intricate relationship, psychologist Donald Hebb memorably asked: "Which contributes more to the form of a rectangle, its length or its width?" This question, often paraphrased in discussions of nature and nurture, highlights how inseparable and equally important genetic and environmental factors are in shaping human development.

LEARNING OBJECTIVES

- Explain the relationship between heredity and environment in shaping behavior and mental processes. (1.1.A)
- Differentiate among the subsystems of the human nervous system and their functions. (1.2.A)
- Explain how the structures and functions of typical neurons in the central nervous system affect behavior and mental processes. (1.3.A)
- Explain how the basic process of neural transmission is related to behavior and mental processes. (1.3.B)
- Explain how psychoactive drugs affect behavior and mental processes. (1.3.C)
- Explain how the structures and functions of the brain apply to behavior and mental processes. (1.4.A)
- Explain how the sleep/wake cycle affects behavior and mental processes throughout the day and night. (1.5.A)

- Explain how the process of sensation is related to behavior and mental processes. (1.6.A)
- Explain how the structures and functions of the visual sensory system relate to behavior and mental processes. (1.6.B)
- Explain how the structures and functions of the auditory sensory system relate to behavior and mental processes. (1.6.C)
- Explain how the structures and functions of the chemical sensory systems relate to behavior and mental processes. (1.6.D)
- Explain how the structures and functions of the touch sensory system relate to behavior and mental processes. (1.6.E)
- Explain how the structures and functions of the pain sensory system relate to behavior and mental processes. (1.6.F)
- Explain how the structures and functions that maintain balance (vestibular) and body movement (kinesthetic) relate to behavior and mental processes. (1.6.G)

Source: AP® Psychology Course and Exam Description

STUDY LIKE A CHAMP WITH DR. G. | BEGIN WITH A PLAN

Here you go. You have five units ahead of you. Prepare your mind to take it all in and amplify your **metacognitive skills**. That jargony word, *metacognition*, basically means "thinking about thinking." When you are aware of what you know and what you do not know, you are in a better position to close the gaps.

There are three main parts to metacognitive excellence. You plan. You monitor. You assess. Throughout the unit and at the end, you will have a chance to monitor and assess. **For now, focus on the plan**. Explicitly set up a schedule for when and how you are going to study. Use your class's syllabus to plan. See how long you have for Unit 1. Select which days you will first read a topic, then which ones you will test yourself on the material (retrieval practice). Make sure you build in some gaps between the days you study Unit 1 material (spaced practice). (See pages xliv–xlvi.)

Good planning does not need fancy apps or a big board with multicolored sticky notes. The key is using a planning strategy that works for you and that you will use.

What activities do you need to plan? Essentially, everything. First, plan when you are going to study your psychology. Which days? What times? How long? Also, make sure to plan for all the other things you have to do. When will you eat? When will you hang out with your friends? When will you study for your other classes?

The best plan includes all 7 days of the week and all 24 hours of each day. Yes, block in when you are going to sleep, too. When you anticipate all you need to do, sticking to your plan is a lot easier. If you do not plan in advance to have fun, for example, then when you accept an invitation from friends to do something fun, your study plans for that time will be disrupted. If, on the other hand, you have figured in fun and you stick to the fun plans, you will be more likely to stick to your plans to study as well.

You may really love biology and chemistry; if so, the material in Unit 1 will zip by. If those are not your favorite subjects, having a plan that establishes how long you will stick with it will make it more likely you will not only get through it all but even learn it.

Topic 1.1

Interaction of Heredity and Environment

"For the longest time, the nature-nurture debate has been cast as a kind of contest between genes and experiences. . . . [But n]ature and nurture are always working together to produce all of our traits."

—David S. Moore

Essential Question: How do biological and environmental factors interact to influence our behaviors and mental processes?

In an article called "My Genome, My Self," psychologist Steven Pinker explores the field of behavioral genetics—the study of ways in which human behavior is determined by biology. "Of course, genes can't pull the levers of our behavior directly," he writes. "But they affect the wiring and workings of the brain, and the brain is the seat of our drives, temperaments and patterns of thought." In this unit, you will explore the "wiring and workings of the brain" as well as a persistent question of psychological studies: How much of our behavior is "nature"—determined by biology—and how much is "nurture"—the result of our environment?

Heredity and Environmental Factors

Throughout the history of the field, psychologists have studied the genetic basis of behavior. Some researchers claim that behavior is determined by biology; not surprisingly, they are known as biological determinists. Others claim that behavior occurs as a response to an organism's environment and surroundings; they are known as environmental determinists. Over time, researchers have come to believe that both are correct—nature, or **heredity** (a person's biological makeup), and nurture, or the **environment** (including life experiences, family, and education), both play roles in influencing behavior. Researchers have identified predictable patterns of behavior that develop because of interactions between what people inherit and the surroundings in which they grow up. The field called *behavioral genetics* focuses on discovering how genes and experiences interact and lead to specific behaviors and mental abilities.

Every individual has a unique *genome,* the entirety of that individual's hereditary information, as well as a unique *genotype,* the specific genes for particular traits. While our genes may predispose us to grow to a certain height, the environment might moderate that, leading us to be slightly taller or slightly shorter. People growing up in impoverished environments might be shorter than they would have been had they lived in an environment with more resources, despite a genetic predisposition to a certain height.

Sometimes, an individual inherits genes from parents that lead to the development of disorders or diseases, and sometimes genes are damaged during prenatal development. Some examples of genetic disorders include cystic fibrosis, neurofibromatosis, and Down syndrome (in which an individual has an extra chromosome). Some congenital disorders (i.e., disorders that are due to a genetic problem or that occur during prenatal development and are present at birth) may have a genetic and/or an environmental link, including hydrocephalus (often known as "water on the brain" but actually an accumulation of cerebrospinal fluid) and microcephaly (underdevelopment of the brain).

Gene-Environment Interactions

Genes set a blueprint for development, but the environment also plays a key role. Think about how someone building a house starts with blueprints but may make modifications and alterations over time. In the same way, your environment can make slight alterations to your genes. For some behaviors or physical characteristics, a particular environment is important at a particular time in life for the genetic information to be expressed. This time in life is known as a sensitive or critical period because the organism has increased sensitivity to environmental influences during this time. For example, children have sensitive periods for the development of binocular vision (i.e., focusing both eyes to see depth), hearing, and learning the sounds of their first language. Another well-known example of this type of sensitive period is Konrad Lorenz's study of imprinting in ducks and geese. Hatchling chicks are genetically driven to bond to and follow a "parent"—that is, the first large moving object they see. In Lorenz's study, goslings without an adult goose imprinted on Lorenz himself. During a sensitive period, some connections between neurons in the brain become stronger, and some unnecessary or unconnected cells die or are pruned away.

Konrad Lorenz and the geese that imprinted on him during their sensitive period.

Another example of gene-environment interaction is the development of personality. Every individual has a genetically influenced temperament. In other words, we each have our own patterns and characteristic ways of responding to the environment. The New York Longitudinal Study (1956–1988)[1] revealed that temperamental characteristics appear right at birth and include how sensitive, irritable, distracted, approachable, or moody we are. Some children (about 40 percent) show an overall pattern known as an easy temperament. They are relaxed and agreeable. Others (about 10 percent) are described as difficult; they tend to be moody, intense, and easily angered. Another group of children are considered "slow to warm up." These children tend to be restrained, unexpressive, and shy.

Our temperaments influence how we react to, and, therefore, how we in turn affect, our environments. For example, consider how a parent might respond to his two children, one of whom is easily distracted and irritable and one of whom is slow to warm up. That parent might act differently during play sessions with each child—the irritable one might need more direction or intervention, whereas the slow-to-warm-up child might need quiet time to get used to an activity. The temperamental characteristics of the children influence the parent's behavior, and the parent's behavior simultaneously influences the development of the child's personality. If you have grown up with siblings, consider how adults in your household may treat each of you differently based on their response to your unique personalities. *Reciprocal determinism*, a concept developed by researcher Albert Bandura, theorizes that influence from personal, behavioral, and environmental factors interact. In other words, by interacting with the world around us, we have a role in changing the environment in which we live. (See Topic 4.5.)

Evolutionary Psychology

Evolution is the study of inherited traits over successive generations of a species, and **natural selection** is the process that governs evolution. As Charles Darwin demonstrated, the basic principle of natural selection is that, given a range of possible inherited trait variations, those traits that lead to increased reproduction and survival of the species are most likely to be passed down to generations that follow. Think about how this might apply in your own life or to the people you know. Someone with an outgoing personality may meet more people and be more likely to meet someone they want to marry and have children with, thus passing their genes to the next generation. The process by which an organism or species becomes better suited for life in its environment is known as *adaptation*, and the specific traits that make the organism or species better suited are known as *adaptive traits.*

Evolutionary psychology is the study of the evolution of mind and behavior based on principles of natural selection. Evolutionary psychologists ask, "How have the principles of adaptation served to create the current range

---

1   Thomas, A., Chess, S., Lerner, R., & Lerner, J. (1998). New York longitudinal study, 1956–1988. https://doi.org/10.7910/DVN/CIGGJY, Harvard Dataverse, V2.

of behaviors and responses that humans have? How are those behaviors helpful for the organism to live within the environment?" In general, these scientists agree that "only the strong survive" is a myth—it's the organisms with the most adaptive traits for their environments that survive and reproduce.

The Process of Natural Selection With every generation, random errors in gene replication lead to changes in a species. These errors are known as *genetic mutations*. Sometimes these mutations lead to the development of a trait that is adaptive for the organism; the organism lives effectively in the environment and passes that trait down to the next generation. For example, for some people with obesity, a particular mutation decreases their likelihood of developing diabetes. If mutations lead to traits or behaviors that are adaptive, as in this case, the organisms with those genes may live to pass them on. In contrast, a gene mutation may lead to sickle cell anemia, causing poor blood flow and chronic pain. If the adaptations make life difficult, the organisms may die without reproducing.

The evolutionary success of the traits that most humans possess helps explain the similarities of people around the world. Because emotions, drives, and reasoning are similar across many cultures, evolutionary psychologists conclude that they have been adaptive in the past and perhaps are still adaptive now. The nausea of pregnant women, especially after eating bitter or strongly flavored food, provides one example of a universally adaptive response. Bitter tastes often accompany poisonous foods, so developing nausea will increase the likelihood that the woman will spit the poison out. Historically, then, when people lived as hunter-foragers, women with strong responses to bitter tastes were more likely to survive, but women without strong responses often died, reducing the likelihood that future generations would have a weak response to these flavors.[2]

Human mate preferences provide another example of the impact of natural selection through the lens of evolutionary psychology. Both men and women look for physical signs of a strong and healthy mate, including symmetry in face and body, healthy skin, certain ratios of shoulders to hips, and muscle strength. Some evolutionary psychologists argue that a male's evolutionary goal is to procreate as much as possible; therefore, men would seek out many partners. Females have different evolutionary goals, including finding one suitable mate with good genes who can be a good protector and provider for future children. Women, then, are more likely to have fewer partners than men and likely only one at a time.[3]

Some previously adaptive behaviors no longer serve us. For example, eating sweets was once an adaptive behavior. In hunter-forager societies, fruits were relatively rare. People ate fruits when they were available and over time

---

2 Curtis, K. S., Davis, L. M., Johnson, A. L., Therrien, K. L., & Contreras, R. J. (2004). Sex differences in behavioral taste responses to and ingestion of sucrose and NaCl solutions by rats. *Physiology & Behavior. 80*(5), 657–64. doi: 10.1016/j.physbeh.2003.11.007. PMID: 14984799`

3 Buss, D. M., & Schmitt, D. P. (1993, April). Sexual strategies theory: An evolutionary perspective on human mating. *Psychological Review, 100*(2), 204–232. https://doi.org/10.1037/0033-295X.100.2.204

developed a taste for sweets. This adaptive behavior was especially useful in periods with little or no food because fruits and other sweets are typically high in calories. These natural sweets were never in such abundance that they could lead to such health problems as diabetes or obesity. However, they are very abundant now, and this taste for sweets has led to the production of processed foods, which are associated with health problems today, especially in the United States.

Another simple example of an outdated behavior is the fight-flight-or-freeze response. Neanderthals and early humans were wary of the dark and developed a fear of potentially dangerous noises. Those who responded strongly to these potential dangers were more likely to survive and reproduce, so the trait was passed along to future generations. Those without the trait were more likely to die or not reproduce. In our modern world, people generally do not need that intense level of response. People who do show that intense response to potential dangers are often diagnosed with anxiety disorders.

In early genetics studies, some researchers believed that an individual's genes could change as a result of behavior. For decades, this idea was rejected by the scientific community. Research over the past few decades, however, has shown that how we live our lives can indeed influence whether genes become active or stay inactive—that is, whether they are expressed or not. An individual could change gene expression to adapt to the environment without having to wait generations for a trait to become active through the DNA. This emerging field of study is known as *epigenetics.*

Evolutionary psychologists examine traits, such as memory, perception, and language, always asking what their evolutionary advantage might have been. Consider our ability to infer or interpret emotions of others, discern kin (family) from nonkin, identify and prefer healthy mates, and cooperate with others. Which human psychological traits, tendencies, and behaviors are evolved adaptations—that is, the products of natural selection? Our cognitive processes may have been adaptive at one time in our history, but how are they affecting us now? Does our attempt to simplify a complex world contribute to prejudice and war? Evolutionary psychologists hope to help answer these questions.

Criticisms of Evolutionary Psychology Evolutionary psychology identifies modern traits and looks backward to propose an explanation for how these traits developed. This type of explanation is sometimes called a *hindsight explanation.* Hindsight explanations are not testable scientifically, no matter how much intuitive sense they may make.

Critics of the field ask about the social and moral implications of the evolutionary psychology perspective. Could evolutionary psychology be used to justify such practices as high-status men mating with a series of young, fertile women? What about cultural differences that seem to work against evolutionary explanations, such as limiting the number of children that can be born in a family?

Some theorists have, in fact, controversially attempted to apply these principles to justify discrimination and social hierarchies. A practice known as **eugenics** aimed at improving the genetic quality of the human population.

Eugenics, derived from the Greek words meaning "good birth," emerged as a "scientific movement" in the late 19th and early 20th centuries. The core idea behind eugenics was to encourage the reproduction of individuals with desirable traits (positive eugenics) and discourage or prevent the reproduction of those with undesirable traits (negative eugenics). Desirable traits were often defined in terms of physical health, intelligence, and moral character, but these criteria were heavily influenced by the prevailing social, cultural, and racial biases of the time and were subjective at best.

The application of eugenics led to a range of discriminatory practices. In the United States, for example, eugenic policies resulted in the forced sterilization of thousands of people deemed unfit to reproduce, including those with mental illnesses, disabilities, and those belonging to racial and ethnic minority groups who faced unfair stereotypes. Similarly, in other parts of the world, eugenic ideologies contributed to racial hygiene theories that culminated in atrocities like the Holocaust.

While the overt eugenics movement has largely been discredited and condemned for its unethical practices and discriminatory ideologies, the intersection of genetics and psychology continues to raise important ethical considerations. Advances in genetic engineering and reproductive technologies revive debates about the potential for new forms of eugenics under different circumstances. The challenge remains to ensure that the application of evolutionary and genetic insights into human behavior and reproduction respects human rights and values diversity.

Evolutionary psychologists recognize these criticisms and continue to develop techniques and research programs to respond to them.

Research on Heritability

Ask yourself: Would you be the same person if you had been raised in a different family? A different culture? On a different continent?

Research on heritability can help answer questions like those. The word *heritability* is often confused with the word *inherited*, but the two words have very different meanings. *Heritability* is a statistic used to determine how much of the variation among members of a group is attributable to genes. The heritability of a trait may vary, depending on the range of populations and the environments studied. Heritability involves comparisons of specific traits among populations, *genotypes* (genetic makeups), and *phenotypes* (outward physical manifestations of characteristics).

Heritability is a way to discuss how these differences play out in a population. As an example, consider that some humans in a population are taller than others. Heritability attempts to identify the extent to which genetics causes a part of the population to be extra tall and the extent to which extra height is influenced by the environment. Studies on twins, families, and adoptions have led to greater understanding of heritability and the gene-environment interaction.

Twin Studies

Researchers who are interested in the interaction of genes and environment often study twins. To understand why, consider the difference between identical and fraternal twins. Identical twins are also known as monozygotic (MZ) twins because one fertilized egg (known as a zygote) splits in half and develops into two people. Monozygotic twins have identical genotypes—the same genes, although not necessarily the same number of copies of those genes. Fraternal twins, in contrast, develop from two separate fertilized eggs and so are known as dizygotic (DZ) twins—two zygotes. On average, dizygotic twins have 50 percent of their genes in common, the same as other non-twin pairs of siblings.

Because monozygotic twins share the same genetics, any differences between them are most likely—though not certainly—caused by interaction with the environment. Because shared genes can also mean a shared experience, most, not all, monozygotic twins share placentas and genders and are treated similarly by people in their worlds.

Twin studies offer insights into the nature and nurture debate.

This close interaction between genetics and environment creates a prime research opportunity for psychologists. In recent years, researchers have learned a number of things from twin studies, including the following:

- A person whose identical twin has schizophrenia has a 30 to 50 percent chance of developing the disorder as well.
- If one twin is on the autism spectrum, an identical twin is on the spectrum 70 percent of the time.
- A person whose identical twin has Alzheimer's disease has a 60 percent chance of developing it, but a person whose fraternal twin has Alzheimer's disease has only a 30 percent chance.
- Identical twins are more alike on measures of extroversion and emotional stability than fraternal twins.

As always, any conclusions need to be evaluated based on the methodology of obtaining them. Systematic research, for example, carries a different weight from that of anecdotes (i.e., stories or reports that aren't scientifically evaluated). Consider the case of the famous set of twins, the Jim Twins, who were separated at birth and reconnected after 38 years. They weren't systematically studied, but reports show they were very much alike. Both were named Jim (Lewis and Springer). Both liked woodworking, driving their Chevys, watching stock car races, and drinking the same brand of beer. Their voices were nearly identical, and they had similar personalities, intelligence, heart rates, and brain waves. Does this story suggest that shared genes are much more influential than different environments?

Geneticists and other systematic researchers are working to answer this question. Any answer, however, is bound to be incomplete. We know that families, peer groups, and other aspects of our lives influence our attitudes, values, manners, religious beliefs, and political viewpoints.

Family Studies

Family studies have also been instrumental in exploring the genetic basis of behavior and mental processes by examining patterns of traits and disorders among relatives. Unlike adoption studies and twin studies, which can more directly disentangle genetic from environmental influences, family studies look at the prevalence of traits and disorders within a biological family to infer genetic contributions. Following are a few notable examples of family studies in the field of psychology and behavioral genetics:

- **Schizophrenia and Psychiatric Disorders** One of the most well-documented areas of family studies involves schizophrenia and other psychiatric disorders. Research has consistently shown that schizophrenia is more common in the biological relatives of a person with schizophrenia than in the general population. The risk increases with genetic closeness, suggesting a strong genetic component. Similar patterns have been observed for bipolar disorder, major depressive disorder, and anxiety disorders, indicating that these conditions have a heritable component.

- **Intelligence and Cognitive Abilities** Family studies have also been used to investigate the heritability of intelligence and cognitive abilities. Studies show that IQ scores are more similar among closely related family members than among more distantly related or unrelated individuals. This similarity suggests that genetic factors play a significant role in cognitive abilities, although these studies also highlight the influence of shared family environment on IQ scores.

- **Personality Traits** Research on personality traits, such as the Big Five (openness, conscientiousness, extraversion, agreeableness, and neuroticism; see Topic 4.5), has benefited from family studies. These studies have found that certain personality traits have a genetic component, with family members more likely to share traits than would be expected by chance. However, the environment shared by family members also contributes significantly to personality development.

- **Substance Abuse and Addiction** Family studies have contributed to understanding the genetic basis of substance abuse and addiction. These studies have found higher rates of substance abuse disorders among relatives of individuals with these disorders compared to the general population. This pattern indicates a genetic predisposition to addiction, although environmental factors and family dynamics also play critical roles.

- **Alzheimer's Disease and Dementia** Family studies have helped identify the genetic risk factors for Alzheimer's disease and other forms of dementia. These studies have shown that having a first-degree relative with Alzheimer's significantly increases one's risk of developing the disease, leading to the identification of genetic mutations associated with increased risk.

Family studies have provided valuable insights into the genetic influence of various behaviors and mental processes. By examining the occurrence of traits and disorders across generations and among relatives, researchers have been able to infer the contribution of genetic factors. However, these studies also confirm that both genetics and environment shape human behavior and mental processes.

Adoption Studies

While some adoption studies focus on twins, most studies compare adopted persons with their biological and adoptive families to assess how much of their behavior can be attributed to genetic inheritance and how much to the environment provided by their adoptive families. Key findings from adoption studies include the following:

- **Intelligence** Studies have found that adopted children have intelligence scores more similar to those of their biological parents than their adoptive parents, a finding that again demonstrates a strong link to biology in intelligence. Recent research has also found that as people age, the similarities to biological relatives in intelligence increase. However, the environment also matters, especially in early childhood, as evidenced by the fact that adoption from a deprived environment to a nurturing one can lead to increases in IQ.

- **Mental Health Disorders** Adoption studies have provided evidence for the genetic basis of various mental health disorders, including schizophrenia, bipolar disorder, and depression. For instance, individuals who are adopted away from a biological parent with schizophrenia have a higher risk of developing the disorder than the general population, indicating a genetic vulnerability.

- **Personality Traits** Studies on adoptees have also shed light on personality traits. Traits such as extraversion and neuroticism show a significant genetic component, with adopted individuals displaying personality traits that are more similar to their biological relatives than to their adoptive family members.

- **Environmental Influences** While showing the importance of genetics, adoption studies also highlight the role of environmental factors. The difference in outcomes between adopted individuals and their biological families can often be attributed to the environment. Nurturing, education, and socioeconomic status play crucial roles in development.

- **Gene-Environment Interaction** Adoption studies have helped highlight gene-environment interactions, showing that effects of genetic influences on behavior and mental processes can be moderated or strengthened by environmental conditions. For example, a supportive environment can reduce the risk of developing mental health issues for people with genetic vulnerabilities.

Overall, adoption studies, like twin studies and family studies, continue to provide compelling evidence that both genetic and environmental factors are crucial and often interact in ways that challenge any overly simplified debate between nature and nurture. These findings have important implications for understanding individual differences in psychological traits, an understanding that can be put to use in developing effective approaches to education, mental health treatment, and the nurturing of children's potential.

All the studies reinforce one key understanding: Behaviors themselves are not inherited, but genetic predispositions that might lead to the behaviors may be. For example, a person with a predisposition to anger may be more likely to divorce than a person who is not predisposed to become angry during conflicts and can instead work through problems.

Genes, then, are part of the story of why we are the way we are but not the whole story. Genes and environments work together like two hands clapping; the genes in any organism must interact with the environment. Interaction is the interplay when the effect of one factor (such as the environment) depends on another factor (such as heredity). Genes point a person in one direction, drawing particular responses from others that reinforce the genetic direction. For example, a happy baby draws in adults who respond to the happiness with warmth of their own. This interaction can become a cycle, with the happy baby becoming more outgoing and socially confident and then interacting more with the environment. Environment-gene interaction plays a role in the development of almost any trait or behavior. Even if you cannot yet answer the question of whether your own traits are a result of nature, nurture, or both, you may now have a better understanding of how psychologists go about trying to find those answers.

THINK AS A PSYCHOLOGIST

Determine the Type of Research Design Used in a Given Study (2.A) | Apply Psychological Perspectives, Theories, Concepts, and Research Findings to a Scenario (1.A)

Identical female twins were born in South Korea in 1974. At age two, one of them was separated from her sister and grandmother at a market. Her family searched desperately for the child, but they could not find her. She was placed first in foster care and then adopted by a family in the United States. For this reason, in the study she is known as US. Her twin, who remained in South Korea, is known as SK.

In 2018, US sent a DNA sample to a South Korean program that tries to reunite children who are adopted into different families. That is when US learned about her biological parents and her twin sister. When Nancy Segal, director of the Twin Studies Center at California State University, Fullerton, learned about the twins raised in different cultures, she contacted her colleague Dr. Yoon-Mi Hur, director of the Kookmin Twin Research Institute in Seoul. They agreed to study the twins—Segal studied US and Hur studied SK. Each twin was assessed with a standard IQ test. Each also completed interviews, self-surveys, and questionnaires covering a range of factors—including personality, family life, job satisfaction, individualism-collectivism values, and self-esteem. The results were then compared.[4]

The results of the study indicate both strong genetic influences and notable cultural differences in various aspects of the twins' lives.

Genetic Influence

- **Personality Traits:** Despite being raised in different environments, the twins exhibited similar personality profiles. They were both notably high in the quality of conscientiousness, indicating a shared genetic predisposition toward being purposeful, organized, and achievement-oriented. This consistency suggests a strong genetic influence on personality traits.

- **Mental Health:** Both twins scored within the normal range or slightly below average on clinical scales assessing mental health, indicating a shared genetic resilience to mental health issues. Despite US experiencing a difficult home environment and divorce, her scores did not suggest higher levels of clinical symptoms, so there appears to be minimal influence of rearing-family environment on adult mental health in this case.

- **Self-Esteem:** The twins had identical scores on the Rosenberg Self-Esteem Scale, indicating similar levels of self-worth. This finding suggests that self-esteem is more influenced by genetic factors than environmental differences.

---

4 Segal, N. L., & Hur, Y.-M. (2022, August). Personality traits, mental abilities, and other individual differences: Monozygotic female twins raised apart in South Korea and the United States. *Personality and Individual Differences, 194*(5), 111643.

- **Job Satisfaction:** While the twins had different occupations with varying working conditions, they both expressed a high degree of job satisfaction. The similarity in job satisfaction suggests a genetic component in how individuals perceive and respond to their work environment.

Cultural Influence

- **Individualism-Collectivism:** The twins showed differences in their scores on the Individualism-Collectivism Scale, reflecting their respective cultural backgrounds. US had a stronger belief in individual autonomy and equality, which aligns with American cultural values. In contrast, SK had a stronger sense of belonging to a collective and accepting hierarchy and inequality, consistent with South Korean cultural norms. These differences highlight the influence of cultural climates on individuals' values and beliefs. (See Topic 4.3.)

- **Family Environment:** The twins were raised in significantly different family environments. SK regarded her home environment as harmonious, while US characterized her home environment as more challenging. These differences reflect the cultural and familial contexts in which the twins were raised and demonstrate the impact of cultural upbringing on family dynamics and values.

- **Intelligence:** SK scored notably higher on an IQ test than US, suggesting a combination of genetic predispositions, environmental influences, cultural factors, and individual differences in shaping cognitive development and academic achievement.

Practice Identifying Research Methods

Choose the correct answer.

1. Which of the following research methods was used in the twin study?

   (A) Experimental

   (B) Longitudinal

   (C) Naturalistic observation

   (D) Case study

2. Explain your answer.

Practice Applying Psychological Perspectives, Theories, Concepts, and Research Findings to a Scenario

Complete the following activity.

3. Identical twins Alex and Jamie were separated at birth and adopted into different families. Alex was raised in a bustling city with access to top-tier educational resources, while Jamie grew up in a rural area with

limited educational opportunities. Now, at the age of 18, Alex and Jamie are preparing to take an intelligence test as part of a research study investigating the influence of genetics and environment on cognitive development.

Based on the twin study cited, which twin would likely score higher on an IQ test, Alex or Jamie? Apply the research findings from the twin study to explain your answer. Be sure to address genetic, environmental, psychological, and socioeconomic factors in your response.

THE BIOLOGICAL BASES OF BEHAVIOR: *A MULTICULTURAL PERSPECTIVE*

What if you went to school in a different country? Or what if your learning came mainly from outside of formal schooling? Would you still be you? Education systems around the world differ greatly in their structure, content, and cultural emphasis. These interact with genetic predispositions (nature) to shape cognitive abilities and academic achievement, which in turn help shape a person's development.

For example, in many East Asian cultures, Confucian values place a strong emphasis on education and academic success. These cultures typically have highly structured education systems with rigorous academic standards and significant parental involvement. For instance, China, Japan, and South Korea place a high value on rote learning, discipline, and respect for teachers. This nurturing environment fosters high academic achievement and cognitive development, possibly strengthening genetic predispositions for intellectual capabilities.

In contrast, some Western cultures, such as those in Finland and other Nordic countries, adopt more holistic and student-centered approaches to education. These systems emphasize creativity, critical thinking, and individual learning styles over rote memorization. The Finnish education system, for example, is known for its flexible curriculum, low-stakes testing, and a strong emphasis on well-being and equity. This nurturing environment supports a wide range of cognitive abilities, encouraging students to explore their interests and develop their unique strengths. The interaction between a supportive educational environment and genetic predispositions in these cultures may result in a balanced development of both cognitive and noncognitive skills.

In many indigenous cultures, education often takes place outside formal school settings and is deeply intertwined with cultural traditions and community practices. Knowledge is passed down through generations via oral traditions, hands-on learning, and communal activities. For example, among the Maori in New Zealand or various Native American tribes, learning is a communal activity that includes storytelling, rituals, and practical skills. This form of education emphasizes cultural identity, social cohesion, and practical knowledge. These nurturing practices help preserve cultural heritage while fostering cognitive abilities relevant to the specific environment and society.

The varying emphasis on academic achievement, creativity, and cultural practices across different educational systems demonstrates that nurture plays a crucial role in the expression of innate abilities.

Develop a Claim

Based on your reading about cultural differences in education, develop a claim about the impact of an educational system (environment/nurture) on the expression of genetic features (nature).

REFLECT ON THE ESSENTIAL QUESTION

Essential Question: *How do biological and environmental factors interact to influence our behaviors and mental processes?* Using the Key Terms, complete a chart like the one below to gather details to help answer that question.

Behavioral Genetics	Evolutionary Psychology

KEY TERMS

environment	evolutionary psychology	natural selection
eugenics	heredity	

MULTIPLE-CHOICE QUESTIONS

1. Jennifer and Emily are identical twins. Jennifer was adopted as an infant into a loving home with a high socioeconomic level. She interacts with her family and friends often and loves to socialize. Emily was raised by her biological single mother in impoverished circumstances. She moves often and struggles to make enduring friendships at school. If there are reasonably large differences between Jennifer's and Emily's IQs at age 18, which of the following can be concluded?

   (A) Environmental factors can directly alter genetic expression.

   (B) Genetic factors are more influential than environmental factors.

   (C) Only nurture plays a significant role in psychological development.

   (D) Nature is solely responsible for psychological traits.

2. Dr. Bouchard has been working with twins for many years to determine the origins of different traits. He has arrived at the concept of gene-environment interaction for nearly every trait he has studied. Which of the following expresses his conclusion?

   (A) Environmental factors exclusively dictate the genetic expression of traits.

   (B) While genetics provide the potential for certain traits, the environment influences the extent to which these traits are manifested.

   (C) Genetic predispositions negate the influence of different environments on behavior and traits.

   (D) Similarities in behavior and traits are coincidental and not indicative of underlying genetic influences.

3. Frederick is an evolutionary psychologist. Which of the following might be an explanation for the development of fear that would be consistent with his perspective?

   (A) We develop fear from our brain's connections between two experiences or stimuli.

   (B) We acquire fears exclusively through punishments we receive in life.

   (C) We develop fears because they can keep us alive for longer since they lead us to avoid potentially dangerous situations.

   (D) We learn fears from watching others in our environment act fearfully toward objects or events.

Questions 4 through 6 refer to the following.

Jian and Lei are siblings adopted by the Chen family. Despite growing up in the same household, they have developed vastly different academic interests and personalities. Lei excels in mathematics and enjoys solitary activities, while Jian excels in the arts and is very social. Their adoptive parents, both engineers, provide a home environment rich in educational resources and social opportunities.

4. Considering Jian and Lei's development, which of the following most accounts for their differing academic interests and personalities?

   (A) The influence of genetic predispositions on their individual development

   (B) The dominant role of the home environment provided by the Chen family

   (C) The impact of epigenetic changes due to their unique experiences

   (D) The critical period of development in early childhood shaping their interests

5. What would provide the strongest evidence that the environment played a key role in Mei's and Jian's differing personalities?

   (A) Discovering that their biological parents had similar personalities to Mei and Jian

   (B) Learning that Mei and Jian had different sets of friends and extracurricular activities

   (C) Finding out that their biological parents also excelled in different academic fields

   (D) Knowing that the Chen family encouraged both children equally in all subjects

6. Why is research on twins such as Mei and Jian conducted as correlational studies rather than experiments?

   (A) Because correlational studies demonstrate cause-and-effect relationships

   (B) Because correlational studies provide in-depth information about a small group

   (C) Because correlational studies combine data from multiple studies to demonstrate an overall effect size

   (D) Because purposely removing children from their homes to create two different groups necessary for an experiment would be unethical

7. Below is a graph from a twin study with monozygotic and dizygotic twins comparing similarities in personality characteristics known as the Big Five. Based on the results displayed, which characteristic is most likely to have the highest level of genetic influence?

(A) Agreeableness

(B) Conscientiousness

(C) Openness

(D) Neuroticism

Twins and Personality Traits

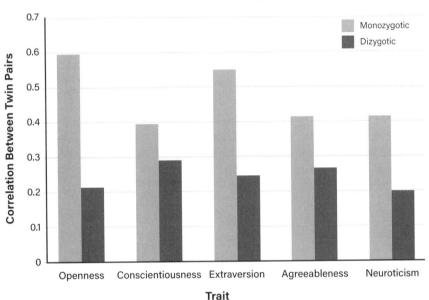

Source: Jang, K. L., Livesley, W. J., & Vernon, P. A. (1996, September). Heritability of the big five personality dimensions and their facets: a twin study. *Journal of Personality, 64*(3), 577–91.

Topic 1.2

Overview of the Nervous System

"If the nervous communication be cut off between the brain and other parts, the experiences of those other parts are nonexistent for the mind. The eye is blind, the ear deaf, the hand insensible and motionless."

—William James

Essential Question: What are the different parts of the nervous system and what are their respective functions?

"Everything psychological is simultaneously biological." This commonly cited quotation suggests that everything people think, feel, and do has biological roots—everything. From daydreaming to sleeping, from practicing jump shots to rehearsing lines in the school play, the brains of humans and other animals are constantly at work, operating behind the scenes and making decisions. In fact, a person's brain has made some decisions even before that person becomes aware that he or she is thinking or feeling something. How does the brain do this? A tour through the nervous system illustrates how the brain and the rest of the nervous system work to direct behavior and play important roles in a person's daily life.

Subsystems of the Human Nervous System

Neuroanatomy is the study of the structures of the nervous systems, which include the brain and the nerves that run throughout the body. Figure 1.2.1 shows the basic organization of the nervous system and its subsystems.

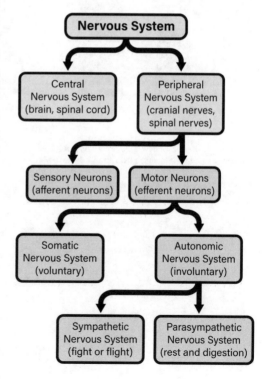

Figure 1.2.1

The Central Nervous System

The **central nervous system (CNS)** is literally "the brains of the operation"—it coordinates the actions and interactions of the other systems in the body. The **brain** is the dominant part of the CNS. The **spinal cord** is the avenue through which the brain communicates with the rest of the body.

The Brain Inside a person's skull is arguably the most fascinating and complex structure in the universe, the human brain. The brain has a role in every thought, emotion, and action that a person expresses. It processes information and experiences, often before we are even aware that we experienced something.

Researchers are still discovering the complexities of this wondrous organ. They have learned more about the brain in the last 50 years than had been learned in the entirety of human history before that point.

The brain makes up about 2 to 3 percent of a person's total body weight, uses about 20 percent of a person's total oxygen consumption, and consumes about 17 percent of the glucose (energy) the body uses. It is composed of many billions of cells and connections among cells (see Topic 1.3) and surrounded by three protective layers. The hard skull and a cushion of cerebrospinal fluid that surrounds the brain provide further protection.

The spinal cord extends down from the medulla oblongata (brain stem) and descends through the center of the vertebral column (backbone). Pathways within it carry sensory messages to and motor messages from the brain. The spinal cord is also enclosed in protective meninges and surrounded by cerebrospinal fluid.

The Peripheral Nervous System

The **peripheral nervous system (PNS)** includes the nerves outside the brain and spinal cord that connect the central nervous system to the rest of the body. The peripheral nervous system relays messages from the central nervous system to the rest of the body. To help you remember this, note that the word *periphery* means "outside the center," and the peripheral nervous system is outside of the central nervous system. The PNS has two major divisions: the sensory pathway and the motor pathway. Signals from sensory receptors travel via sensory nerves from the body to the brain via the sensory pathway. Signals from the brain travel via the motor pathway and then to muscles or glands to influence behavior.

The motor pathway of PNS contains two subsystems, or divisions:

- The **somatic nervous system** includes the nerves that transmit signals from your brain to the skeletal muscles to allow voluntary movement. For example, when you raise your hand, walk, jump, wave to a friend, or end a text, the brain sends signals through the somatic nervous system to initiate these movements. If you get up and get a snack before finishing this topic, your somatic nervous system is hard at work.

- The **autonomic nervous system (ANS)** controls functions that we do not have to think about. These functions are automatic and involuntary:

breathing, blood pumping through the veins and arteries, digestion, gland functioning, the work of other internal organs. People can choose to influence and sometimes override these basic signals, such as by slowing down breathing or by increasing heart rate through exercise, but for the most part, this system operates without intervention.

THINK AS A PSYCHOLOGIST

Apply Psychological Perspectives, Theories, Concepts, and Research Findings to a Scenario (1.A)

Tonya, a thrill-seeker, decides to spend her Saturday afternoon at the amusement park. She eagerly heads straight for the tallest roller coaster in the park, known for its breathtaking drops and loop-the-loops.

As Tonya waits in line, her heart begins to race with excitement. Her pupils dilate, allowing more light to enter her eyes, enhancing her vision to take in the surroundings. Meanwhile, her heart rate increases, pumping more blood to her muscles to prepare for physical exertion.

Finally, it's Tonya's turn. She takes a seat in the roller coaster and feels her body tense with anticipation. As the coaster ascends the first steep incline, Tonya's skin feels the rush of wind and the exhilarating feeling of acceleration.

As the roller coaster hurtles down the first drop, Tonya throws her arms up in the air, laughing with delight.

Throughout the roller coaster ride, Tonya's body remains in a state of heightened arousal, with an increased heart rate and dilated pupils.

As the roller coaster comes to a stop, Tonya's heart rate gradually returns to normal, and she steps off the ride with a wide grin on her face, exhilarated by the adrenaline-pumping experience.

Practice Applying Psychological Concepts to a Scenario

Complete the following activity.

Go step by step through Tonya's experience riding the roller coaster, explaining how the somatic and autonomic nervous systems are shaping Tonya's experience. Refer to Figure 1.2.1 as you answer the question.

Two Divisions of the Autonomic Nervous System

The autonomic nervous system has two further subdivisions.

- The **sympathetic nervous system** is the emergency response system. When a person is frightened by a loud sound or startled when someone sneaks up from behind, the sympathetic system goes to work (i.e., is activated). The person's heart rate increases, attention becomes more focused, digestion slows, muscle tension increases, and adrenaline flows into the bloodstream. The system enters "fight, flight, or freeze" status.

- The **parasympathetic nervous system** is the default condition of the ANS. It functions to calm the person, reduces energy expenditure, decreases blood sugar, increases blood flow to the digestive organs, and decreases heart rate, among other things. It allows us to rest and digest, relax and recuperate. It returns the body to a state of balance or *homeostasis*.

The two systems work together to balance energy use and energy conservation. Figure 1.2.2 shows the detailed connections between the brain and spinal cord (i.e., the CNS) and the organs in the body, by way of the two divisions of the autonomic nervous system.

Parasympathetic and Sympathetic Nervous Systems Regulating Organs

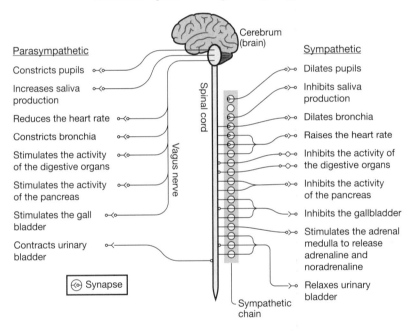

Figure 1.2.2

THINK AS A PSYCHOLOGIST

Identify Psychology-Related Concepts in Descriptions or Representations of Data (3.A) | Apply Psychological Perspectives, Theories, Concepts, and Research Findings to a Scenario (1.A)

How do you feel when you're sitting in a dentist's chair about to have your teeth cleaned or a cavity filled? Researchers wanted to quantify the answer to that question from the point of view of both children and adults. One of the measurements they made during their experiment was of patients' pulse rates at different times of the procedure. Study the results in the graph. The *y*-axis shows the change in the number of beats per minute. The *x*-axis shows where in the procedure the changes took place.

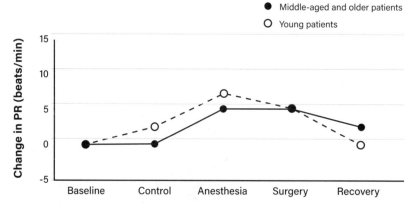

Matsumura, Kiyoshi et al. "Changes in blood pressure and heart rate variability during dental surgery." American journal of hypertension 11 11 Pt 1 (1998): 1376-80.

Practice Identifying Psychology-Related Concepts in Representations of Data

Complete the following activities.

1. Summarize the overall findings by answering these questions:

   How did heart rate change for adults from the beginning of the procedure to the end?

   How did heart rate change for children from the beginning of the procedure to the end?

2. Explain the roles the parasympathetic and sympathetic nervous systems played in the changes in heart rate.

3. Draw a logical and objective conclusion from these findings.

REFLECT ON THE ESSENTIAL QUESTION

Essential Question: *What are the different parts of the nervous system and what are their functions?* Using the Key Terms, complete a chart like the one below to gather details to help answer that question.

Central Nervous System	Peripheral Nervous System

MULTIPLE-CHOICE QUESTIONS

1. Brett's friends convinced him to try skydiving. He is very nervous but decides to try it anyway. How will his autonomic nervous system respond, first, when he jumps out of the plane, and second, when he safely lands on the ground?

   (A) His sympathetic nervous system would first activate the fight-flight-or-freeze response, while his parasympathetic nervous system would return his body to a state of calm.

   (B) Both systems would activate simultaneously to produce a moderate physiological response to stress.

   (C) His parasympathetic nervous system would increase physiological arousal to match that of the sympathetic nervous system during stress.

   (D) His sympathetic nervous system would decrease heart rate and breathing to conserve energy in response to stress, and then his parasympathetic system would compensate by increasing his heart rate and breathing.

2. Jenessa is trying to hold perfectly still because she is playing a game of "statue" with her nieces. She has a terrible itch on her nose and finally lifts her arm to scratch it. Which part of the nervous system aids in her ability to lift her arm to scratch her nose?

   (A) Central

   (B) Parasympathetic

   (C) Somatic

   (D) Sympathetic

3. Dulcina is studying to be a doctor and must therefore memorize much information about the body. As she studies for her anatomy exam, she cannot recall where in the nervous system the nerves of the brain and spine belong. Help Dulcina match these nerves to the correct nervous system.

(A) Somatic

(B) Central

(C) Sympathetic

(D) Parasympathetic

Questions 4 and 5 refer to the following.

After an intense basketball game, Kim and Jordan sit down to rest. Kim, feeling exhilarated from the win, notices her heart rate slowing down, her breathing becoming more regular, and a feeling of calm returning. Jordan, who missed the final shot, experiences a slower return to a relaxed state, ruminating over the game's last moments, but she gradually begins to feel her body relaxing.

4. Which part of Kim's nervous system is primarily responsible for reducing her heart rate and promoting relaxation after the game?

(A) The central nervous system, through direct control of heart and lung function

(B) The sympathetic division of the autonomic nervous system, by decreasing activity

(C) The parasympathetic division of the autonomic nervous system, by restoring the body to homeostasis

(D) The somatic nervous system, by voluntarily controlling breathing to induce calm

5. Jordan's prolonged stress response after the game illustrates the interaction of which systems?

(A) The sympathetic nervous system's extended activation and the slow intervention of the parasympathetic nervous system because of the rumination about the missed shot

(B) The central nervous system's inability to process the emotional aspect of the game

(C) The somatic nervous system's dominance over autonomic responses in stressful situations

(D) The parasympathetic nervous system's immediate activation to counteract stress, which fails to engage

6. Justin just finished a delicious pizza and tater tot lunch from the school cafeteria. As he sits in his next class, his body is digesting the food, but Justin does not even have to think about what is happening. Which of the following nervous systems is assisting with the food digestion?

(A) Somatic

(B) Parasympathetic

(C) Sympathetic

(D) Central

7. Examine the bodily changes indicated in the diagram. Which nervous system is represented?

(A) Sympathetic

(B) Central

(C) Somatic

(D) Parasympathetic

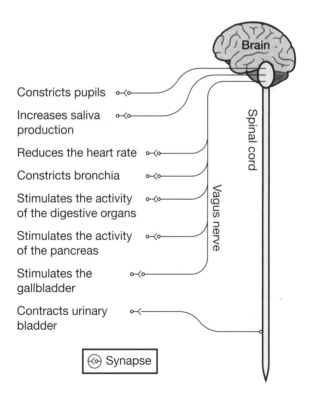

Topic 1.3

The Neuron and Neural Firing

"A typical neuron makes about ten thousand connections to neighboring neurons. Given the billions of neurons, this means there are as many connections in a single cubic centimeter of brain tissue as there are stars in the Milky Way galaxy."

—David Eagleman

Essential Question: How do the structures, functions, and processes of neurons as well as psychoactive drugs affect behavior and mental processes?

In Topic 1.2, you read about the structures and organization of the nervous system, which includes the brain and the nerves that run throughout the body. Topic 1.3 will explore neuroanatomy on a cellular level—what types of cells make up the nervous system, how they are organized, and how they communicate.

Neuroanatomy: The Structures and Functions of Nerve Cells

The brain is composed of hundreds of billions of cells that connect to and communicate with one another in intricate networks. Arguably, the most important of those cells are the **neurons**—the basic units on which the entire brain and nervous system are built: no neurons, no messages getting to and from the brain. The structures and functions of typical neurons in the **central nervous system** affect how messages travel around the body and, in turn, affect behavior and mental processes.

Neurons and Glial Cells

Nerves are bundles of neuron axons—slender protrusions from the cell body, often called *fibers*—outside of the brain and spinal column. Cranial nerves are nerves that come out of the brain and generally send messages to the head and neck, (*Cranium* is another name for the skull.) Some bundles of neuron axons (called *tracts* in the brain and spinal cord) join together in the brain stem; as those tracts exit the brain, they become a major part of the spinal cord. Figure 1.3.1 shows how other nerves then extend through the body.

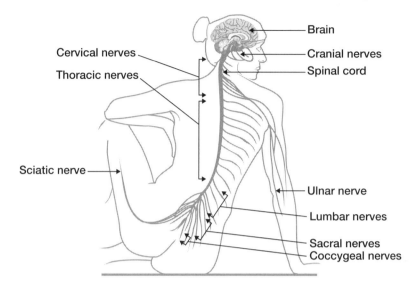

The Nervous System of the Human Body

Brain

Cervical nerves

Thoracic nerves

Cranial nerves

Spinal cord

Sciatic nerve

Ulnar nerve

Lumbar nerves

Sacral nerves
Coccygeal nerves

Figure 1.3.1 Pairs of spinal nerves extend from both sides of the spinal column.

But neurons aren't the most abundant cells in the brain. They are outnumbered by as many as 50 to 1 by **glial cells**. Glial cells provide nutrition and protection for the neurons. The glial cells function like glue to hold the neurons together (in fact, *glia* comes from the Greek word meaning "glue"). Glial cells provide structure, insulation, communication, and waste transport. These types of cells form the basis of the nervous system and are the building blocks of all behavior and mental processes.

The Reflex Arc

Neurons come in many shapes and sizes; they can be as small as four microns (4/100 of a millimeter) or as large as 100 microns (1/10 of a millimeter). They also have varying functions:

- **Sensory neurons** take input received through sensory receptors throughout the body, such as in the skin, eyes, nose, ears, and tongue, and pass it *toward the brain and spinal cord* to initiate a response. These neurons are made up of bundles of axons called afferent nerve fibers.

- **Motor neurons** transmit signals *away from the brain and spinal cord* to our muscles and other organs. Motor neurons are bundles of axons called efferent nerve fibers that carry motor commands from the central nervous system to other parts of the body.

- **Interneurons** are relay neurons, or connectors, allowing for information to pass between neurons *within the brain and spinal cord*.

Not all incoming messages will make it to the brain. For those that do not, the spinal cord controls what is known as the **reflex arc**. A reflex arc occurs when a signal is sent from a sensory organ to the spinal cord, which processes the information instead of passing it on to the brain. A reflex is then carried out by motor neurons. For example, when a person touches a hot surface with a finger, sensory cells in the skin pass the information ("Hey, that's really hot!") to the spinal cord, which responds immediately with a message to initiate action ("Get your hand off that thing right now!"). This system is faster than if the signal had to travel to the brain to make a decision about how to respond to the sensation.

Neural Structure

In general, every neuron has the same basic structure. If you have taken biology or anatomy/physiology, you may recognize that neurons are similar in many ways to other cells in the human body. However, they also have distinct parts that play key roles in the communication process.

The body of a nerve cell is known as the soma (the name *soma* comes from the Greek word for "body"). The soma contains the nucleus and other parts that are important for the creation of proteins and membranes needed for a neuron to function. Cell bodies can vary in size and shape, as you can see in Figure 1.3.2.

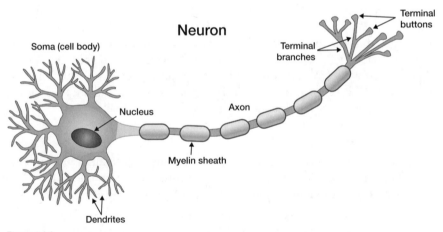

Figure 1.3.2

Treelike protrusions extending from the cell body are known as *dendrites*, a name derived from the Greek word *dendron*, meaning "branches." The dendrites receive signals from other cells. Each neuron can have hundreds or thousands of dendritic spines, each of which may make multiple connections with other neurons.

Messages from the soma travel down the length of the axon, where it branches out. The terminal branches end in little bulbs called terminal buttons. The terminal buttons have small sacs, known as vesicles, that contain chemicals (called **neurotransmitters**) that are necessary to pass on the signals between neurons.

Because the axons carry electrical charges, they need to be insulated. Glial cells help to perform this function in the central nervous system (CNS), developing into a covering known as **myelin**. In the **peripheral nervous system (PNS)**, glial cells form a myelin sheath around the axons. This outer covering of the myelin protects the cell and creates a tunnel for regenerating the nerve fiber after damage. The protective sheath also helps increase the speed of conduction of the signal along the axon.

Neurons do not typically touch one another. They communicate electrically within a neuron and chemically between neurons across very small gaps called **synapses** (Figure 1.3.3). Neurotransmitters from the terminal buttons of one cell are released into the synapses between that cell and other cells.

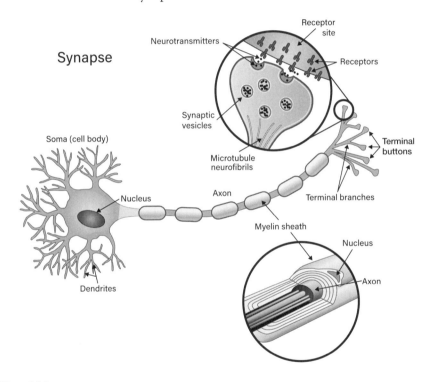

Figure 1.3.3

Neural Transmission

Neural transmission is a fundamental process that underlies all aspects of behavior and mental processes, serving as the primary means of communication within the nervous system. Understanding how neurons communicate with one another helps to explain the biological basis of thoughts, emotions, behaviors, and various psychological phenomena. Neural communication usually occurs in an orderly, systematic way. Each part in the neural structure plays a role in this communication. Disruptions to this orderly, systematic process could lead to disorders, including multiple sclerosis and myasthenia gravis. (See pages 151–152.)

The Process of Neural Transmission

Neural conduction is the process by which information travels through a neuron. This process is commonly known as **neural firing**. Neural firing is both electrical (within the neurons) and chemical (between neurons).

The Electrical Component: Resting and ActionPotentials Input from the environment is received by sensory receptors, passed on to the dendrites, and then sent to the cell body in the form of electrical impulses. As you may recall from other science classes, cell bodies contain various charged particles called ions. Some ions have positive charges, and others have negative charges. Neurons are no different. When a neuron is in a resting state, it has an overall negative charge, at –70 millivolts (mv). The inside of the neuron contains more potassium and chloride ions than the outside, which contains more sodium ions than the inside. Because this imbalance creates a *possibility* of voltage change, the resting state is called **resting potential**. In this state, the neuron is inactive and not in the process of transmitting a message.

An easy way to remember resting potential is "salty bananas." Bananas contain lots of potassium. If you dip the banana into a tub of salt water (sodium), the banana is in its resting state—the inside has lots of potassium, and the outside has lots of salt. If you then peel the banana and take a bite, it might taste a little salty because a banana peel is semipermeable, which means that some ions can pass through it. The "peel" or membrane of a neuron is also semipermeable, so that sodium and potassium can move in and out. This movement is altered when gated sodium and/or potassium channels are opened. Continuous, tiny pumps in the cell membrane move sodium ions out of the cell and potassium ions into the cell.

When an electrical impulse reaches the cell body, gated channels open up and allow sodium ions to rush into the cell. This increase in sodium alters the balance of charge, making the cell more positive than it was when it was resting (–70mV). This change in charge is known as **depolarization**. The brief positive charge creates an electrical impulse known as an **action potential**. The action potential, the message the neuron is sending, travels down the axon as a voltage spike, like a chain reaction of dominoes falling, as the energy moves down the neuron.

Action potentials follow the **all-or-nothing principle:** Cells either fire (if the electrical charge inside the cell reaches a **threshold** of about –55mV) or they don't fire, and when an action potential does occur in a cell, it always occurs with the same charge. Some people describe the process as similar to turning on a television. Either the TV is on or it is off. A TV can't be partially on.

For a brief moment after firing, the neuron is in its **refractory period**, during which it is not able to fire again. The neuron needs a short period of time to reset itself. If you have ever tripped a breaker in your house, you may have had to reset the electrical outlet, which takes a short time to be ready to go again, just as the neuron does.

A neural impulse might speed through your nervous system in an autonomic response to a sudden pain stimulus—when you feel a shooting pain from a leg cramp, for example. Less urgent messages that require processing and thought, such as those from your eyes to your brain about the words on this page, take longer. The speed of a neural impulse can range from 2 to 200 miles per hour,

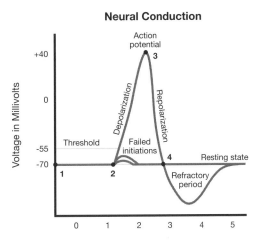

Figure 1.3.4 Neural Conduction

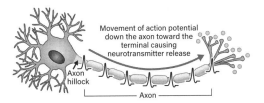

Figure 1.3.5 The Path of an Action Potential

depending on a number of factors, including the size of the nerve fiber and the type of signal. Researchers usually record the speed in milliseconds, or thousandths of a second.

By age 4, children's nerve speed is the same as that of adults. Conduction speed in some nerves, such as the nerve that runs through the elbow, slows as people age.

The Chemical Component: Neurotransmitters When a neuron fires, the electrical charge from its action potential travels all the way down the axon. When this charge gets to the vesicles in the terminal buttons, the neuron releases its neurotransmitters—the chemical component—into the synapse. Neurotransmitters that enter the synapse are picked up by receptors in the dendrites of adjoining neurons. These neurons are sometimes referred to as postsynaptic neurons because they come into play after the neurotransmitters enter the synapse. If enough neurotransmitters are received by the dendrites to change the ionic balance of these new neurons, the cycle begins again.

After they complete their work at the receptor cells on the dendrites, the neurotransmitters are reabsorbed by the presynaptic neuron in a process called **reuptake**. In other cases, an enzyme breaks down the neurotransmitters in the synapse.

Consider what happens when cells in the eye respond to light. The light is taken in by sensory receptors, passed on to the dendrites, and then sent to the cell body in the form of electrical impulses, which ripple down the axon through the terminal branches, buttons, and vesicles. They are then sent on their way by neurotransmitters, which are released into the synapses. An overview of the process is described below.

{sensory receptor}→ {dendrites of cell #1}→ {soma}→ {axon}→ {terminal branches}→ {terminal buttons}→ {vesicles}→ {neurotransmitters released into the synapse}→ {dendrites of cell #2}→ {soma}

Functions of Neurotransmitters

Once a message or action potential arrives at the end of a neuron, it needs a "ride" across to the next (postsynaptic) neuron. At this point, chemical messengers known as neurotransmitters play an important role. Some neurotransmitters are classified as **excitatory neurotransmitters**. When these chemicals are released from the terminal buttons, they excite connecting neurons and cause them to fire. Others are classified as **inhibitory neurotransmitters**. These inhibit (prevent) the next neurons from firing. Inhibitory and excitatory neurotransmitters balance each other out, attempting to create a homeostasis, or equilibrium, within the brain and body.

Often, neurotransmitters work in concert with other neurotransmitters, but the focus here is on the primary responsibilities and functions of some of the most important neurotransmitters.

Acetylcholine The first neurotransmitter discovered was **acetylcholine** (**ACh**). It is active in both the peripheral and central nervous systems. ACh is connected to movement; its primary function in the somatic nervous system is to activate muscles and carry out voluntary movements. It is involved in decreasing heart rate, increasing sweat and saliva, and increasing muscle contractions. Acetylcholine also plays a role in learning and memory. Levels of ACh can drop up to 90 percent in people with Alzheimer's disease.

Figure 1.3.6 shows ACh being released into the synapse and activating the skeletal muscle cell in the neural communication process. If key receptors for ACh are blocked, paralysis may result, which is what happens when a snake's venom temporarily paralyzes its prey. Because the ACh cannot bind to the receptors, the motor neurons don't get the message to fire, and the somatic nervous system is paralyzed. Various tribal groups in Central and South America have paralyzed their prey for hundreds or even thousands of years with curare, a poison that blocks the acetylcholine receptors in motor neurons.

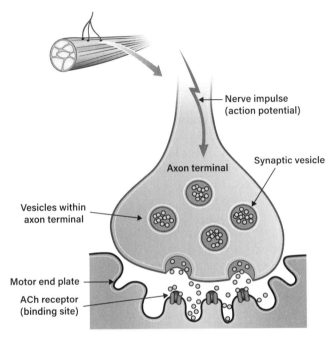

Figure 1.3.6 ACh being released into the synapse

Disruption in the orderly process of neural transmission is the cause of several serious conditions. One is **myasthenia gravis (MG),** an autoimmune neuromuscular disorder characterized by weakness and rapid fatigue of any of the muscles under voluntary control. In a healthy neuromuscular junction, nerve endings release acetylcholine (ACh) into the synapse, which then binds to acetylcholine receptors on the muscle cell surface. This binding causes ion channels to open, leading to muscle contraction. After the action, acetylcholine is broken down by the enzyme acetylcholinesterase, ensuring the muscle does not remain in a constant state of contraction.

In myasthenia gravis, the body's immune system produces antibodies that attack the acetylcholine receptors or the functional structure of the junction where the neuron meets the muscle. This attack reduces the number of acetylcholine receptors available for binding or alters their function, making it more difficult for the nerve signal to effectively trigger muscle contraction.

The hallmark of MG is muscle weakness that worsens with activity and improves with rest. This condition can affect various muscles, including those that control eye and eyelid movement, facial expression, chewing, swallowing, speaking, and breathing. The degree of weakness varies throughout the day and may fluctuate over time.

By interfering with the normal process of neuromuscular transmission, myasthenia gravis leads to significant muscle weakness and fatigue, profoundly affecting the quality of life. However, with appropriate treatment, many individuals with MG can lead relatively normal lives, although managing the condition requires ongoing care and monitoring to adjust therapies as needed.

Another condition brought on by the disruption of the orderly process of neural transmission is **multiple sclerosis (MS)**. In a healthy nervous system, myelin sheaths wrap around nerve fibers (axons), making possible the rapid and efficient transmission of electrical signals along the nerves. This myelination ensures quick communication between the brain, spinal cord, and the rest of the body, enabling smooth and coordinated movements, sensation, and other critical functions.

In MS, the immune system mistakenly attacks and damages the myelin sheath in a process known as *demyelination*. This damage can also extend to the underlying nerve fibers. The areas where myelin is lost (plaques or lesions) disrupt the normal flow of electrical impulses along the nerves, leading to a range of neurological symptoms. These include fatigue, walking difficulties, numbness or weakness in one or more limbs, electric shock sensations with certain neck movements, tremor, lack of coordination, unsteady gait, vision problems, slurred speech, and cognitive disabilities.

The disruption of neural transmission in MS due to demyelination and nerve damage is the underlying cause of its diverse and unpredictable symptoms, which can come and go. Advances in treatment and management strategies have significantly improved the quality of life for many people with MS, allowing them to manage symptoms and maintain functional abilities.

Serotonin One of the most important neurotransmitters is **serotonin**, which is connected to mood, emotion, appetite, sleep, and sexual desire. High levels of serotonin in the brain increase happiness, and low levels are associated with depression, anger control, obsessive-compulsive disorder, and potentially preoccupation with suicidal thoughts.

Depression is often treated using drugs called SSRIs (selective serotonin **reuptake inhibitors**). These drugs work by blocking the reabsorption or reuptake of the serotonin into the sending neuron, leaving it in the synapse longer and thus allowing the neural signal to continue repeatedly, increasing its effect on lifting mood, increasing appetite, and regulating sleep and wake cycles.

Dopamine Sometimes called the pleasure chemical of the brain, dopamine is released into the pleasure centers of the brain, specifically the nucleus accumbens and hypothalamus, which are part of the mesolimbic or "reward" pathway.

Dopamine plays a role in a number of behaviors related to reward and motivation. For example, dopamine is released when we anticipate something pleasurable, such as making a long-desired purchase, winning a game, or—for addicts—getting the next hit of heroin or winning when gambling. This anticipation releases dopamine, which makes us feel better temporarily.

Low dopamine levels have been connected to addictive behaviors, including drugs, gambling, and sex. Dopamine also affects alertness and happiness, reduces hunger, and helps with fine motor coordination.

Dopamine is also connected to muscle control, specifically the lack of it. People with Parkinson's disease (for example, actor Michael J. Fox or the late, famous boxer Muhammad Ali) exhibit tremors and loss of key motor skills because their brains have stopped producing adequate supplies of dopamine. A potential treatment for Parkinson's disease is a drug that stimulates creation of dopamine. On the other hand, excessive levels of dopamine production in the limbic system have been linked to positive symptoms of schizophrenia. (See Topic 5.4.)

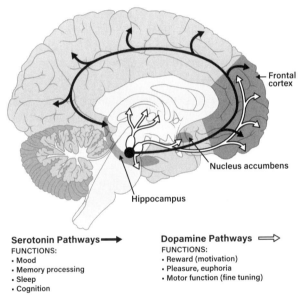

Figure 1.3.7 Dopamine and Serotonin Pathways in the Brain

Norepinephrine Norepinephrine is active in the sympathetic nervous system's response to danger. Higher levels of norepinephrine increase alertness, blood pressure, and heart rate. Norepinephrine also releases glucose stores (energy) so that a person can respond quickly, as in the **fight-flight-or-freeze response**, which occurs when people encounter something dangerous or even life-threatening. **Norepinephrine** is involved in developing fears, and low levels of norepinephrine are connected to depression. One treatment for depression is a selective norepinephrine reuptake inhibitor (SNRI). Like SSRIs, SNRIs are drugs that reduce the reuptake of the neurotransmitter, leaving it in the synapse longer and allowing the neural signal to continue repeatedly.

GABA The primary inhibitory neurotransmitter that slows things down, calming the central nervous system, is **gamma-aminobutyric acid,** commonly known by its acronym **GABA**. It is sometimes considered a natural tranquilizer. GABA increases sleepiness and decreases anxiety, alertness, memory, and muscle tension. Too little GABA is associated with anxiety disorders, and anti-anxiety medication will raise levels of GABA in the brain, thus "cooling down" the overactive brain and relieving symptoms of anxiety. Without GABA, neurons fire too easily and too often, destabilizing the brain systems.

Glutamate Glutamate, the major excitatory neurotransmitter, is the opposite of GABA. It is involved with most normal operations of the brain, including thinking, memory, and learning. It plays a key role in **long-term potentiation (LTP),** a pattern of neural firing that strengthens synaptic connections over time. As we repeat a behavior or a cognitive task, we make the connections in our brains stronger. Glutamate facilitates this process.

Other chemicals are also involved in the electrochemical process. **Endorphins** relieve pain and stress. Endorphins, which are released by the pituitary gland, are often called the brain's natural aspirin. You may have heard about people getting an "endorphin rush" while participating in physical activities such as running. If you have ever hurt yourself while playing a sport and not initially felt the pain, it may be because your endorphin levels were high.

Substance P Substance P is a neuropeptide, a type of neurotransmitter, which plays a crucial role in the body's pain perception and the transmission of pain signals to the brain. It is composed of a chain of amino acids and is found throughout the brain and spinal cord (central nervous system) as well as in some peripheral tissues.

One of the primary roles of substance P is to convey pain information from the peripheral nervous system to the central nervous system. When tissue damage occurs, substance P is released from the terminals of specific sensory nerves, contributing to the transmission of pain signals to the spinal cord and brain, where the sensation of pain is perceived.

Research suggests that substance P is also involved in regulating mood and anxiety. Elevated levels of substance P have been found in individuals with depression and anxiety disorders, indicating it may play a role in the diseease processes of these conditions.

Agonists and Antagonists Sometimes neurotransmitters help to activate a message on a postsynaptic neuron, and other times neurotransmitters inhibit a postsynaptic neuron from firing. **Agonists** activate the receptors for certain neurotransmitters and ultimately make the effects of the neurotransmitters stronger. Well-known agonists include **heroin**, oxycodone, methadone, hydrocodone, opium, and morphine, which mimic the actions of endorphins throughout the entire nervous system. **Antagonists** are chemicals that inhibit or oppose the actions of neurotransmitters. Often, they sit in receptor sites and block the neurotransmitter from binding with the receptors on the dendrites.

An example of an antagonist is haloperidol, a drug that blocks dopamine and is used to treat schizophrenic symptoms.

The Endocrine System and Behavior

Whereas the central and peripheral nervous systems communicate using nerve impulses transmitted in the brain, spinal cord, and nerves, the slower-acting *endocrine system* sends its signals by passing **hormones** through the bloodstream. Because many hormones can also be neurotransmitters, to tell the difference always ask yourself if the chemical originated in the nervous system (neurotransmitter) or glands (hormone). These hormones are secreted (produced and passed on) from a number of different parts of the body and select parts of the brain. The endocrine system plays a critical role in raising and lowering a person's blood sugar (glucose) levels, making a person feel hungry or full, regulating metabolism and sleep, and determining sex drive. While the endocrine system is slower to operate than the CNS, its effects last longer.

Figure 1.3.8 shows some of the glands that make up the endocrine system, along with the hormones that each gland secretes. The parts of the system work with the nervous system as an interconnected team.

The **hypothalamus** signals the **pituitary gland**. The pituitary gland regulates stress, growth, and reproduction. The pituitary gland sends signals to other glands, including the testes, ovaries, and thyroid gland, which then release their own hormones. The pituitary gland is often referred to as the "master gland" because it controls the working of other glands in the endocrine system.

Major Glands and Hormones

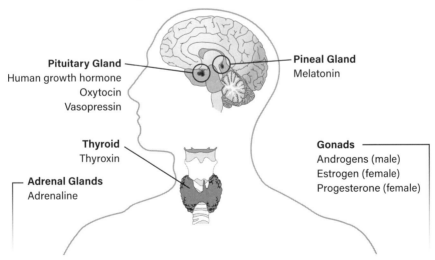

Pituitary Gland
Human growth hormone
Oxytocin
Vasopressin

Pineal Gland
Melatonin

Thyroid
Thyroxin

Adrenal Glands
Adrenaline

Gonads
Androgens (male)
Estrogen (female)
Progesterone (female)

Figure 1.3.8 The Endocrine System

The table below identifies some hormones and their relation to behavior and mental processes. These hormones illustrate the interactions between the endocrine system and the nervous system. As you review the table, look for ways chemical messengers can influence our behaviors, emotions, and overall mental health.

Hormones and Their Effect on Behavior and Mental Processes	
Adrenaline	**Adrenaline** in the endocrine system is associated with energy; in the sympathetic nervous system, it is associated with response to high-emotion situations, such as emergencies. Adrenaline affects behavior by enhancing alertness and physical readiness for immediate action, which can be crucial for survival. Adrenaline is the same chemical as epinephrine. People with serious allergies are often prescribed a device to inject epinephrine. Epinephrine reduces life-threatening responses, such as swelling, difficulty breathing, and a drop in blood pressure. It opens the airways and increases blood pressure by reducing the size of the blood vessels.
Leptin	Secreted by fat cells, **leptin** is involved in regulating energy balance by inhibiting hunger, which in turn diminishes fat storage. Leptin communicates with the brain about the body's energy status, influencing appetite and food intake. Changes in leptin levels can affect mood and motivation related to eating behaviors and are involved in the long-term regulation of body weight.
Ghrelin	Often called the "hunger hormone," **ghrelin** is produced in the stomach and signals the brain to stimulate appetite. It plays a key role in meal initiation, as its levels increase before meals and decrease after eating. Beyond its effects on hunger, ghrelin has been linked to reward mechanisms in the brain, influencing pleasure-related eating behaviors.
Melatonin	This hormone is produced by the pineal gland in response to darkness, helping regulate the sleep-wake cycle. **Melatonin** influences circadian rhythms and is crucial for healthy sleep patterns. Disruptions in melatonin secretion can affect sleep quality and mood, contributing to disorders such as insomnia and seasonal affective disorder (SAD).
Oxytocin	Often dubbed the "love hormone" or "social bonding hormone," **oxytocin** is released in response to various forms of social interaction and bonding activities, such as childbirth, breastfeeding, and physical touch. It facilitates attachment and trust, plays a role in romantic attraction and parental behaviors, and can influence social recognition and anxiety. Oxytocin's effects on social behaviors have implications for understanding such conditions as autism and social anxiety disorders.

Table 1.3.1

Effect of Psychoactive Drugs on Behavior and Mental Processes

Psychopharmacology is the field of study that examines changes induced by drugs in mood, thinking, and behavior. Synthetic drugs and those derived from natural sources have various effects on the body; they can slow it down or speed it up. Humans have been using consciousness-altering substances for all of human history. Humans are not the only ones to seek alternatives, it seems. Elephants are known to raid fermented alcohol reserves, most cats are attracted to catnip, and reindeer ingest a mind-altering mushroom.

Most cats find catnip irresistible.

Psychological and Physiological Effects of Psychoactive Drugs on Neurotransmitters

Psychoactive drugs are chemical substances that alter perceptions, mood, or behavior. These chemicals can change consciousness by changing brain chemistry through their specific effects on neurotransmitters. Psychoactive drugs affect nerve synapses and neurotransmitters in three ways: They bind with receptors (agonists) on cell surfaces to support an action, block receptor sites (antagonists) to suppress an action, or block the reuptake of neurotransmitters by certain neurons. All mind-altering chemicals are able to pass through the blood-brain barrier, a semipermeable membrane that protects the brain from substances that may cause brain injury.

Tolerance, Addiction, and Withdrawal If a chemical is being supplied synthetically by a psychoactive drug, after long-term use the brain then produces less of that specific neurotransmitter, causing the user to develop a **tolerance** to the drug. The tolerance creates a need for increasing amounts of the drug to experience the same effects the brain would normally produce on its own. The impact of the drug also weakens over time, and increasing doses are required to achieve the same effect a lower dose once provided.

Tolerance is a phenomenon commonly associated with addiction. **Addiction** is a complex condition characterized by compulsive drug seeking, use, and dependence, despite harmful consequences. It is often marked by an inability to control drug use, intense cravings for the desired substance, and continued use despite negative effects on physical health, mental well-being, relationships, and other areas of life.

Withdrawal—a set of symptoms associated with discontinuing a drug—reverses neuroadaptation. Symptoms may include cravings, tremors, anxiety, depression, seizures, and even death. Withdrawal symptoms vary by drug but can be psychological, physical, or both.

Drug Categories

Psychoactive substances exert a profound influence on the functioning of the human mind and body. Among the diverse array of psychoactive drugs, stimulants, depressants, hallucinogens, and opiates stand out for their distinct effects on neurotransmitter systems and cognitive processes. Understanding the pharmacological properties and psychological effects of these drug categories is essential for comprehending their widespread use, potential for abuse, and impact on mental health and behavior.

Stimulants Caffeine, nicotine, cocaine, and amphetamines are all **stimulants**—drugs that speed up the body's functions. Stimulants provide users with a sense of increased energy, mental alertness, and forced wakefulness. All stimulants can cause dependence, tolerance, withdrawal, and psychological addiction as well as irreversible changes in mood.

- **Caffeine** is the most used drug in the world. It affects *adenosine*, a central nervous system neuromodulator that has receptors to slow a person down and induce sleepiness. Caffeine acts as an adenosine-receptor antagonist. That is, caffeine slows down the impact of adenosine, thus increasing levels of alertness.

- Nicotine imitates acetylcholine by attaching to a type of acetylcholine receptor (AChR) called a nicotinic receptor. These receptors connect to the nucleus accumbens, the reward center in the brain, and increase activation in dopamine pathways, making a smoker feel good. Though nicotine is the addictive substance, tar in tobacco is cancer-causing (carcinogenic), compounding the health risks of smoking.

- **Cocaine** is an illegal substance that blocks the reuptake of neurotransmitters such as dopamine, serotonin, and norepinephrine. Rather than being reabsorbed by the sending neuron, the chemicals stay in the synapse, acting as an agonist and increasing their effects on the next neuron. This interaction creates dopamine dependency, boosting feelings of confidence and pleasure with serotonin and generating more energy with epinephrine. The result is an immediate rush—and an eventual crash.

- Amphetamines are drugs used to increase wakefulness and enhance cognitive performance. Prescribed as racemic amphetamine (trade name: Adderal®), amphetamine is used to treat ADHD and narcolepsy. Amphetamine works by increasing the concentration of dopamine in brain synapses, which increases metabolism and mental clarity and creates wakefulness. Amphetamine has a high potential for abuse and dependence. With its euphoria-inducing properties, Adderal has become a relatively cheap addictive substance. When used properly, it reduces symptoms of the disorders for which it is prescribed. However, it is often abused by college students and other individuals who need to stay awake for hours beyond normal sleep time. High doses can cause an irregular heartbeat, anxiety, and even psychosis with delusions and paranoia.

- Methamphetamine is an illegal substance, a "super" stimulant used mainly as a recreational drug and not prescribed medically. While it is chemically similar to amphetamine, its differences are significant. Unlike amphetamine, methamphetamine is faster acting, more potent, and more dangerous. One specific methamphetamine (MDMA), nicknamed Ecstasy, was used originally in therapy sessions in the 1960s but became a street drug in the 1980s at raves, music festivals, and concerts. Feelings of euphoria, an increased sensitivity to light and touch, and reduced inhibitions are produced as MDMA increases serotonin levels released into synapses of the brain and blocks reabsorption. Increased norepinephrine increases energy while increased dopamine creates euphoria. The dehydrating effect of this drug is exacerbated by an increase in body heat, made worse during dancing. This, in turn, increases blood pressure and may result in death. MDMA also suppresses the immune system, impairs memory, and disrupts sleep. Long-term use reduces serotonin production and may lead to depression.

Depressants and Sedatives These drugs lower neural activity and slow body functioning. All **depressants** can cause dependence, tolerance, withdrawal, and psychological addiction. Examples include alcohol and barbiturates.

- **Alcohol** slows neural processing and thinking and impairs motor coordination. It does so by reducing activity in the prefrontal cortex and the cerebellum, parts of the brain responsible for controlling inhibitions and making judgments. Alcohol reduces self-awareness and impairs memory by suppressing the processing of events into long-term memory. Alcohol also impairs REM sleep, further interfering with memory storage. Alcohol also disrupts neurotransmitters. It intensifies the effects of gamma-aminobutyric acid (GABA), an inhibitory neurotransmitter in the brain—hence the characteristic sluggish movements and slurred speech of someone who has had too much to drink. Alcohol also reduces glutamate, an excitatory neurotransmitter, slowing down reactions and impairing judgment. Alcohol affects balance and fine motor coordination, which is why drinking and driving are so dangerous. Alcohol also causes the release of dopamine in the reward system of the nucleus accumbens.

- Sedatives, sometimes called tranquilizers or hypnotics, are drugs that reduce anxiety or induce sleep. These include barbiturates, drugs that depress the activity of the central nervous system, reducing anxiety while also impairing memory and judgment (e.g., phenobarbital and Seconal®). Sedatives work by making receptor sites more efficient, thereby increasing the efficiency of GABA, inhibiting brain functions, and exerting a calming effect.

- Benzodiazepines are antianxiety drugs (e.g., Valium® and Xanax®). They work by slowing the central nervous system, leading to muscle relaxation and sedation. They also depress heartbeat and breathing. These depressants can be lethal in overdose, and they interact with other drugs, especially alcohol, impairing memory and judgment.

Hallucinogens Drugs that cause hallucinations and distort perceptions of reality are known as **hallucinogens** (psychedelics). Primary examples are LSD (lysergic acid diethylamide) and marijuana. MDMA/Ecstasy is sometimes considered a hallucinogenic drug as well as a stimulant.

- LSD effects vary from person to person, influenced by context and environmental factors, but common experiences include hallucinations (visual, auditory, and tactile). Many users have had a "near death" type of experience related to oxygen deprivation. LSD can cause physiological dependence/tolerance and psychological dependence.

- **Marijuana**, or cannabis, refers to the leaves, stems, resin, and flowers from the hemp plant that, when smoked, lower inhibitions and produce feelings of relaxation and mild euphoria. THC (delta-9-tetrahydrocannabinol) is the active ingredient of cannibus. The sensations of mild euphoria, relaxation, and increased auditory and visual perceptions are products of cannabinoid receptors in the brain. The neurotransmitter anandamide, called the "bliss molecule," binds to the THC receptors. Anandamide also appears to be involved in regulating mood, memory, appetite, pain, cognition, and emotions. When cannabis is ingested, THC can interfere with all of these functions. Chronic cannabinoid use also disrupts memory function, lowers attention, and impairs learning ability. In addition, lung damage can result from inhalation of the smoke. Marijuana can cause physiological dependence/tolerance and psychological dependence.

Opioids Drugs that reduce neurotransmission and temporarily lessen pain and anxiety include **opioids**. They work by reducing GABA, the inhibitory neurotransmitter that normally slows the release of dopamine in the nucleus accumbens. Without that controlled release, the brain releases more dopamine, creating a euphoric feeling.

The body produces natural opiates called *endogenous opioid peptides*, better known as endorphins. Endorphins regulate reaction to pain and also influence hunger, thirst, and mood control. Opiates from outside the body, such as opium, morphine, and the prescription drug OxyContin™, bind to the same receptors as endorphins, essentially as endorphin agonists. With continued use of opiates over time, the brain eventually stops producing dopamine and natural endorphins. When dopamine production stops, people may experience a condition called anhedonia, the inability to feel pleasure physically.

Psychoactive Drugs and Dependence or Addiction

The Diagnostic and Statistical Manual of Mental Disorders, 5th edition (DSM-5), the official guide to diagnosis published by the American Psychiatric Association, lists addiction in the substance-related and addictive disorders category, describing substance abuse and addiction as follows:

> All drugs that are taken in excess [activate] the brain's reward system, which is involved in the reinforcement of behaviors and the production of memories. They produce such an intense activation of the reward system that normal activities may be neglected. . . . The pharmacological mechanisms by which each class of drugs produces reward are different, but the drugs typically activate the system and produce feelings of pleasure, often referred to as a "high." Furthermore, individuals with lower levels of self-control, which may reflect impairments of brain inhibitory mechanisms, may be particularly predisposed to develop substance use disorders, suggesting that the roots of substance use disorders for some persons can be seen in behaviors long before the onset of actual substance use itself.

Addictive behaviors replace healthy behaviors and self-care actions. People who are addicted will have altered motivations, making the substance the primary reward, rather than other motivators such as relationships, career, and family. Addicts ignore negative memories resulting from addiction as well as positive memories before addiction began. Addicts also lack impulse control, the frontal lobe inhibitor to make proper judgments about what to do and not do. The DSM has also applied the idea of addiction to behaviors such as exercise, gambling, or shopping, though this application is still controversial.

Psychological dependence occurs when drugs that reduce stress become an increasingly important part of a user's life, often as "self-medication" to relieve negative emotions. Drug addiction or abuse of any substance is a brain disorder, and medical and/or psychiatric treatment is needed for those who abuse drugs.

While there may be as many reasons for taking drugs as there are drug users, several sociocultural, psychological, and biological factors may play a role in drug use and abuse.

Sociocultural factors, especially for teens, include the effect of drugs on friendships and other relationships. Drugs and alcohol lower inhibitions, so they might help people overcome shyness and make friends more easily. If their friends are taking drugs and drugs are readily available in their neighborhood, young people might become drug users to feel a sense of belonging and fitting in. Rebelling against parental and societal norms may be another sociocultural factor in taking drugs. Also, teens encounter so many of life's challenging situations for the first time—relationships, deaths of friends and family members, dysfunctional families, bullying—that they may experience significant stress and adopt avoidance behaviors, including drug use, to cope.

Many psychological factors are at play as well during adolescence. Feeling a lack of purpose in life, a relatively common experience in teens as they figure out who they are, can lead to experimentation. The prefrontal cortex, which controls impulsivity and evaluates consequences, is not fully developed in teenagers, perhaps explaining why teens tend to take more risks than older people, especially with drugs. Those with a sensation-seeking personality may take risks even beyond those of the average teen. Adrenaline junkies often like to do exciting things—driving at high speeds, skydiving, spending time in dangerous situations, or taking drugs—to feel more alive. Some people with untreated mental illnesses may self-medicate, using illicit drugs to treat the pain from their psychological disorder, especially anxiety and depression.

Finally, brain biology may be involved in addiction, since genes influence neurotransmitter production in our brains and endocrine systems. Some people are born with genetics that, in certain environmental conditions, make initial experiences with drugs especially pleasant. People with those same gene combinations, however, may never become users, let alone addicts, because they never have the "right circumstances" in which to begin drug use. Some people can be mild to moderate users of a drug, while others become addicted after the first use. Our brain biology can make us more susceptible to addiction, but genetics alone cannot explain it.

THINK AS A PSYCHOLOGIST

Determine the Type of Research Design Used in a Given Study (2.A)

Imagine for a moment that you are a laboratory rat. What kind of life do you imagine? Are you bored? Scared? Lonely? What would it take to have a happy life as a rat?

Researcher Bruce Alexander conducted a study in the late 1970s using laboratory rats to explore the nature of addiction and how it might worsen in isolation or, in contrast, how it might wane with social connectedness in what he imagined would be an ideal environment for rats. In the study, one group of rats was caged in isolation. Another group was allowed free access to a large area—Rat Park—with other rats, stimulating toys, and the freedom to interact sexually with other rats. Both groups were given two sources of water: one filled with plain water, and one laced with morphine. The results showed that most of the rats in isolation became addicted to the drugged water and chose it over plain water, relentlessly drinking the drugged water until they died. The rats in Rat Park, with a positive, low-stress environment with social connections, drank less than a quarter of the drugged water the isolated rats drank. None of the socially connected rats died.

As promising as the results seemed to be for an understanding of addiction, the study lost funding after a few years because of difficulty in replicating the results. In addition to the problems with replication, this experiment, like all animal experiments, raised questions about the extent to which animal studies apply to the science of human behavior.

Practice Determining the Type of Research Design Used in a Study

Answer the following questions.

1. Which of the following best describes the research method of this study?

   (A) Naturalistic observation

   (B) Cross-sectional

   (C) Experimental

   (D) Case study

2. What might the hypothesis have been?

THINK AS A PSYCHOLOGIST

Identify Psychology-Related Concepts in Descriptions or Representations of Data (3.A) | Apply Psychological Perspectives, Theories, Concepts, and Research Findings to a Scenario (1.A)

The bar graph that follows provides information on student dropouts and substance abuse. Carefully study the graph.

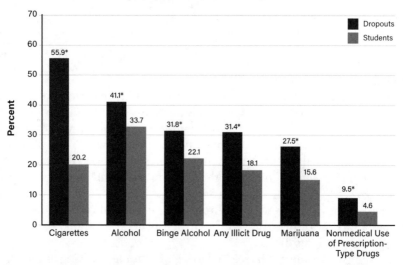

Past Month Substance Use among 12th Grade Aged Youths, by Dropout Status: 2002 To 2014

*Difference between 12th grade aged students and 12th grade aged dropouts is statistically significant at the .05 level.

Source: SAMHSA, Center for Behavioral Health Statistics and Quality, National Surveys on Drug Use and Health (NSDUHs), 2002, 2005, 2006 to 2010 (revised March 2012), and 2011 to 2014.

Practice Identifying Psychology-Related Concepts in Descriptions or Representations of Data

Answer the following questions.

1. Summarize the overall results of the survey data.

2. Identify one sociocultural factor that may help explain the results.

Practice Applying Psychological Research Findings to a Scenario

Answer the following questions.

3. How might the work of Bruce Alexander on Rat Park theoretically help explain the findings of the dropout and substance abuse surveys?

4. What might be a limit of the application of Rat Park findings to understanding dropouts and drug use?

REFLECT ON THE ESSENTIAL QUESTION

Essential Question: *How do the structures, functions, and processes of neurons as well as psychoactive drugs affect behavior and mental processes?* Using the Key Terms, complete a chart like the one below to gather details to help answer that question.

Neural Structure	Neural Communication	Psychoactive Drugs

KEY TERMS

NEURAL STRUCTURE

central nervous system
glial cell
interneuron
motor neuron

myelin
neuron
neurotransmitter
peripheral nervous system

reflex arc
sensory neuron
synapse

NEURAL COMMUNICATION

acetylcholine (ACh)
action potential
adrenaline
all-or-nothing principle
depolarization
dopamine
endorphin
excitatory neurotransmitter
fight-flight-or-freeze
   response

GABA (gamma
   aminobutyric acid)
ghrelin
glutamate
hormone
hypothalamus
inhibitory neurotransmitter
leptin
long-term potentiation
   (LTP)
melatonin

multiple sclerosis (MS)
myasthenia gravis (MG)
norepinephrine
oxytocin
pituitary gland
refractory period
resting potential
reuptake
threshold
serotonin
substance P

PSYCHOACTIVE DRUGS

addiction
agonist
alcohol
antagonist
caffeine
cocaine

depressant
hallucinogen
heroin
marijuana
opioids
psychoactive drug

reuptake inhibitor
stimulant
tolerance
withdrawal

1. Chelsea is making a plaster cast of her hand in art class. A classmate pours clay over Chelsea's hand, which causes Chelsea's sensory neurons to create an action potential. What is happening in Chelsea's neurons at this moment?

   (A) The interior of the neuron is filling with potassium and chloride.

   (B) Sodium ions are rushing into the neuron in the process of depolarization.

   (C) The neurotransmitters are returning to the presynaptic axon terminals.

   (D) The process of repolarization is taking place.

2. Martha is 60 years old and has recently experienced difficulty walking. She is also experiencing slurred speech, difficulty making facial expressions, and shortness of breath. Her doctor diagnosed her with myasthenia gravis. What is the likely cause of her disorder?

   (A) Lack of long-term potentiation

   (B) Disruption of neural communication due to damage of the myelin sheaths

   (C) Antibodies attacking acetylcholine receptors, disrupting neural transmission

   (D) Disruption of neural transmission as a result of drug use

3. Arturo, a professional chef, has just cut himself with a knife. Which of the following neurotransmitters is primarily responsible for transmitting pain messages from sensory neurons to the central nervous system?

   (A) Acetylcholine

   (B) Dopamine

   (C) Glutamate

   (D) Substance P

4. Jason, a 14-year-old, is having trouble sleeping, and his doctor thinks it might be related to a hormonal problem. Which hormone is likely involved in this issue?

   (A) Ocytocin

   (B) Melatonin

   (C) Leptin

   (D) Ghrelin

John, a college student, decides to experiment with psychoactive drugs during a party. He consumes a pill, and as the drug takes effect, John begins to experience feelings of euphoria, pleasure, and heightened energy levels.

5. Which category of psychoactive drug is John most likely using?

   (A) Stimulant

   (B) Depressant

   (C) Hallucinogen

   (D) Opiate

6. Which neurotransmitter is likely influencing the increased pleasure John is experiencing?

   (A) Serotonin

   (B) Dopamine

   (C) GABA

   (D) Acetylcholine

7. John continues to use drugs and finds that over time he needs greater amounts of the drug to get the same effect. What phenomenon causes that increased need?

   (A) Symptoms of withdrawal

   (B) Psychological dependence

   (C) Addiction

   (D) Tolerance

STUDY LIKE A CHAMP WITH DR. G.

How is your study plan progressing? Have you been able to stick to it? Give yourself a little time to get used to it. But if you see it is consistently not working, try another plan.

Topic 1.4

The Structures and Functions of the Brain

"The brain is more than an assemblage of autonomous modules, each crucial for a specific mental function. Every one of these functionally specialized areas must interact with dozens or hundreds of others, their total integration creating something like a vastly complicated orchestra with thousands of instruments, an orchestra that conducts itself, with an ever-changing score and repertoire."

—Neurologist Oliver Sacks

Essential Question: How do the structures and functions of the brain affect behavior and mental processes?

The human brain, a three-pound marvel of biological engineering, serves as the command center for the entire nervous system, orchestrating a wide array of functions that enable thought, emotion, behavior, and perception. Understanding the structure of the brain is fundamental to grasping how it processes information, regulates bodily functions, and responds to the environment. The brain's architecture is intricate, with complex networks of neurons and specialized regions responsible for memory, language, and decision-making. Understanding the structures and functions of the brain provides insights into the biological underpinnings of psychological phenomena, laying the groundwork for a deeper comprehension of human behavior and mental processes.

The Structures of the Brain

Although the brain has discernible parts, it is best thought of as a single organ because its parts are so tightly interconnected. In addition, although it's common to say that a brain part is responsible for a specific function, brain-behavior connections are far more complex than that would suggest. The brain's circuits are constantly communicating with one another, and no part works in isolation. This complexity means that an introduction to the structure of the brain will necessarily be simplified, and not every part or function can be included. The following discussion reflects how the organization of the brain is usually discussed and what researchers currently believe about the function of some key areas of the brain.

The Brain Stem

The oldest part of the brain is the **brain stem**, which is shown below. The brain stem connects the spinal cord to the brain and is responsible for sending messages received on the right side of your body to the left hemisphere and those received on the left side of the body to the right hemisphere. That pattern of messages is called cross-lateral. The hemispheres of the brain will then connect with one another to transfer the message between hemispheres.

One critical part of the brain stem, the **medulla oblongata** (sometimes just called the *medulla*), is responsible for maintaining and regulating heart rate, breathing (respiration), digestion, swallowing, and even sneezing. Damage to the medulla often results in death.

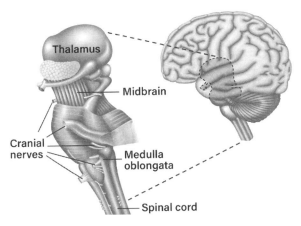

Figure 1.4.1 The Brain Stem

Above the medulla is the pons, a mass of nerve fibers that serve as relay stations, sending information from the brain stem to the cerebellum and cortex. The pons also plays an important role in sleep and dreaming.

The midbrain, located just above the pons, is involved in vision, movement, hearing, and muscle coordination, although it is not the central processing unit. Rather, the midbrain is an assistant, just one part of the circuitry that makes up brain function. Think of the midbrain as a point guard that gives lots of assistance to teammates but does little of the scoring itself. It connects both sensory inputs to motor outputs and connects the hindbrain to the forebrain.

Reticular Activating System and Reward Center

The **reticular formation** is a network of nerves that carry messages between parts of the brain stem. It helps regulate the intensity of pain and controls some parts of the body. The reticular formation also helps people focus on useful sensory input while filtering out unnecessary stimuli. For example, activity in the reticular formation allows people in a train station to hear a baby crying but at the same time ignore the sound of the train on the tracks.

The reticular activating system (RAS) and the brain's reward center are two critical components of the neural architecture that underpin a wide range of psychological functions, from basic physiological processes to complex behaviors and emotional responses. Each of these systems plays a unique role in how we interact with our environment, learn, and maintain motivation.

Reticular Activating System (RAS) The RAS, part of the reticular formation, is a network of neurons located in the brain stem that extends into the thalamus (see page 171) and plays a crucial role in regulating wakefulness and sleep-wake transitions. It turns the processing of sensory stimuli on (when we need the sensory information) and off (when we need to sleep). Should you start dozing off during class, the RAS is likely to blame. If a person's RAS is damaged, that person typically falls into an irreversible coma.

This system is fundamental in maintaining consciousness and is involved in the process of arousal from sleep. Remember the reticular activating system as regulating levels of alertness and arousal. The more messages coming to the brain through the RAS, the more alert a person will be.

Brain's Reward Center The brain's **reward center** is a collection of structures that are key to the experience of pleasure, motivation, and reinforcement learning. The reward system is deeply intertwined with the neurotransmitter dopamine, which signals the occurrence of a rewarding stimulus.

Cerebellum

The **cerebellum**, often referred to as the "little brain" because of its distinct structure and location at the back of the brain, plays a pivotal role in coordinating muscle movement, maintaining balance and posture, and contributing to various forms of **procedural learning**. Despite its smaller size compared to the cerebrum, the cerebellum contains about half of the brain's neurons, indicative of its complexity and the intricacy of its functions. If the cerebellum is damaged, a person might experience problems with balance and coordination, judging distances, and knowing when and where to stop moving forward. Some people with cerebellar damage have trouble walking in a straight line, and many also develop tremors.

The cerebellum's contributions to coordination, balance, and procedural learning underscore its importance not just in voluntary motor activities but also in cognitive functions related to planning, verbal fluency, and possibly even emotional regulation. It plays an integral role in the complex network of brain functions that support everyday life and learning.

The Limbic System

The **limbic system** sits at the top of the brain stem. The limbic system is sometimes called the mammalian brain because other mammals (but not reptiles, for example) have a similar structure in their brains.

The limbic system includes the thalamus, hippocampus, amygdala, and hypothalamus. Together, they help us to process pleasant emotions like joy, happiness, excitement, or pleasure and unpleasant emotions like fear, anger, desperation, or nervousness.

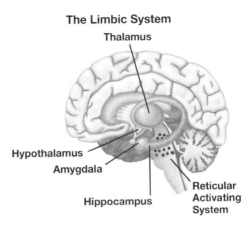

The Limbic System

Figure 1.4.2

The **thalamus** serves as a relay station between the brain stem and the cerebral cortex. For example, sensory signals are sent from the sense organs through sensory neurons, up the spinal cord, through the brain stem, and on to the thalamus. The thalamus then sends signals to different lobes of the cerebral cortex (see pages 173–175). Signals from the eyes, ears, skin, and mouth are ultimately processed in these lobes. Think of the thalamus as the post office of your brain, guiding both incoming and outgoing messages to their proper location.

The **hippocampus** (Latin for "seahorse" because of its shape) is a rounded part of the limbic system near the center of the brain. The hippocampus plays an important role in transfering some short-term memories into long-term storage and in recalling facts and events. Damage to the hippocampus can result in serious cognitive problems. For example, British musicologist, conductor, and pianist Clive Wearing contracted a virus that damaged his hippocampus, and he is now unable to convert any new information into lasting memories. Although he has memories of people and friends he knew before his illness, he has difficulty conversing because he can't remember what another person said only a few seconds earlier. To help make sense of his life, he keeps a journal, but almost all the events are repetitions of "2:15 I am awake now," which would later be crossed out and followed with "3:30 I am fully awake now." He will have no recollections of making these notations, even a few seconds after he finishes. He can, however, still read music (because he was able to do this before his illness), and sometimes when he sits down at the piano, he can play a familiar piece, sometimes even with comic flourishes at the end. Although he cannot make new memories and has no store of episodic memories, he retains procedural memory. Wearing's story has been the subject of a number of documentaries and articles, and his wife Deborah, whom Wearing greets with excitement and love after even brief partings, wrote a book about it called *Forever Today: A True Story of Lost Memory and Never-Ending Love*.

Whereas the hippocampus is primarily involved in cognitive processes, the **amygdala** is primarily involved in processing emotion and survival responses (*amygdala* comes from the Latin word for "almond," which this cluster of cells resembles). The amygdala becomes active during potentially threatening situations, such as when a person is focused intently on something and is unexpectedly startled or even when a person is watching a scary movie. A moment of silence on screen builds anticipation, and if a quick movement is paired with a loud sound or music, the movie watcher jumps high and spills popcorn everywhere, thanks to the activation of the amygdala.

When scientists create lesions in parts of an animal's amygdala (see page 185), the animal becomes excessively tame. It seems as if all aggressiveness is gone. Humans with lesions or tumors in the amygdala show similar behavior: flat affect, very little emotion, either positive or negative. (See Topic 1.4 for the role of the amygdala in survival.)

Another part of the limbic system that plays a major role in survival drives is the hypothalamus. The **hypothalamus** is one of the most important parts of the brain, working in conjunction with many other brain parts to regulate the autonomic nervous system. The hypothalamus sends signals of arousal to the **pituitary gland**, which then releases chemicals into the bloodstream. It releases hormones that are important for feeling sexually attracted to others (oxytocin) and bonding emotionally with others (oxytocin and vasopressin). The hypothalamus also helps to regulate body temperature and plays a role in sleep and fatigue.

Two nuclei (a **nucleus** is a bundle of cells that work together) in the hypothalamus, the lateral hypothalamus (LH) and the ventromedial hypothalamus (VMH), play a key role in eating. Remember, however, that hormones, habits, culture, and many other factors also play a role in hunger. The lateral hypothalamus plays a role in the initiation of hunger. The ventromedial hypothalamus, in contrast, regulates feelings of fullness (satiety). Individuals with damage to the VMH never feel full. They continue eating well beyond when most people would stop, consuming much more food than they need to survive and typically gaining massive amounts of weight. The LH and/or the VMH may potentially play a role in eating disorders such as bulimia nervosa and anorexia nervosa.

The nucleus accumbens is located near the hypothalamus but is a part of the frontal lobe (and is a part of the basal ganglia, which are connected to learning habits and motor skills). It has a primary role of cognitive processing of pleasure, aversion, motivation, learning, and reward. It is where dopamine is released when we experience pleasure. Therefore, it plays a role in addiction.

Forebrain Structures and Functions

No two brains are exactly the same, but every intact brain has some distinguishing features. First, the brain (cerebral cortex or cerebrum) has two **hemispheres**, which are sometimes referred to as the "left brain" and the "right brain." The two hemispheres are similar, but not mirror images; for example, some areas in one hemisphere are bigger than in the other hemisphere. While there is some localization of function whereby one hemisphere is primarily responsible for certain actions, this idea has been overstated in popular culture. It is not correct to say that people are "right-brained" or "left-brained."

In general, the left hemisphere controls the right side of the body, and the right hemisphere controls the left side of the body. For example, when a right-handed person is writing, the left hemisphere is more involved than the right hemisphere in coordinating the hand movements. However, the right hemisphere isn't uninvolved in the writing process, and it communicates with its partner on the left by passing information through the **corpus callosum** (Latin for "tough body"), a bundle of nerve fibers that connects the two hemispheres. Messages also move from one side of the brain to the other in the brain stem, where the motor and sensory "crossover" occurs. Visual signals cross in the optic chiasm, a structure at the base of the brain. (See Topic 1.6.)

The outer layer of the brain is the **cerebral cortex**, which covers the cerebrum. The tissue of the cerebral cortex is folded in on itself, forming peaks and valleys. Squeezing the skin on the back of your hand can provide an analogy: You'll see ridges and grooves similar to those in the brain. This folding and wrinkling allows for more surface area of cortex to fit into the skull. The more wrinkles, the more tissue surface the brain has to work with and the more computational power the organism has. A rat brain is almost smooth on its cortex. Compared to dogs, cats, and even dolphins and primates, the human brain has a more wrinkly cortex. If a scientist unfolded a monkey's brain so that the peaks and valleys became flat, the unfolded brain would have roughly the surface area of an 8.5 × 11 piece of paper. The human brain has even deeper sulci and gyri, and when spread out flat, a typical human brain has a surface area similar to four sheets of paper. That translates into a lot of computational power.

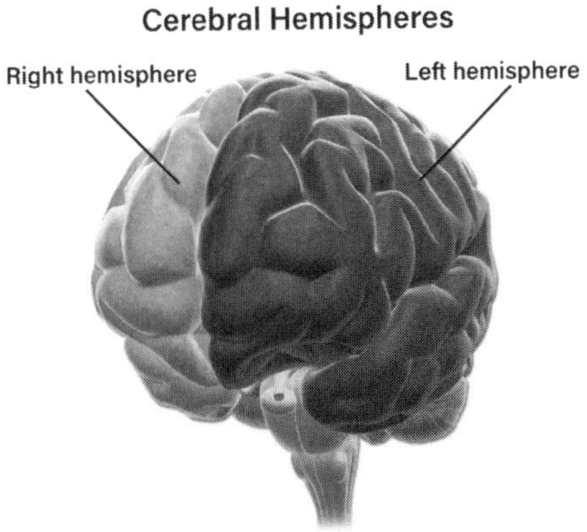

The cerebral cortex is divided into distinct **lobes**, or areas of the cerebral cortex, distinguished by their locations and primary functions. In graphics, the lobes are often color coded, but in reality, the edges aren't always clear because the cortex looks mainly uniform throughout. Even brain surgeons cannot always tell just by sight—patients undergoing brain surgery are often conscious so that the neurosurgeon can temporarily stop activity in a section of the brain and see how behavior is affected so they can identify the lobe of the brain before making any permanent incisions.

Cerebral Hemispheres

Right hemisphere

Left hemisphere

Figure 1.4.4

Figure 1.4.5 shows the four lobes—the occipital lobe, temporal lobe, parietal lobe, and frontal lobe—and the primary functions they serve. All four lobes also contain **association areas**; in fact, association areas take up more space by far in the cerebral cortex than the areas devoted to processing sensory and motor signals. Association areas process higher-order functions—thinking, remembering, planning, forming judgments, and speaking. These association areas are not initially responsible for any specific functions; instead, they are malleable, based on a person's experiences in life. As you will see, other areas of the brain are more specified to the function they serve.

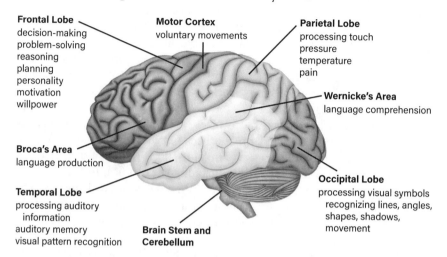

Figure 1.4.5 Lobes and Functions

The Occipital Lobes At the back of each hemisphere lies the **occipital lobe**. This lobe processes visual signals and coordinates various aspects of vision. The part of the occipital lobe at the very back, directly behind the eyes, is the primary visual cortex, which has an important role in taking information from the eyes and interpreting it so that a person knows what he or she is seeing. Another part of the occipital lobe, the visual association cortex, helps us recognize lines, angles, shapes, shadows, and movement. (See Topic 1.6 for more on the visual system.)

The Temporal Lobes The **temporal lobes** are near the ears; they are important for processing auditory information and auditory memory. One major role of the right temporal lobe is processing the melody and tonal changes in music. Part of the left posterior temporal lobe is known as Wernicke's area, which is important for language comprehension. (See Figure 1.4.7 on page 177 for more brain functions.)

The lower part of each temporal lobe is responsible for some visual processing, in particular the processing of patterns. Some people can see faces—they can point out ears, eyes, mouth, and other facial parts—but they cannot identify the person whose face it is. In fact, when shown photos, they can't even recognize people they know very well. This condition is sometimes referred to as facial blindness and can be caused by damage to the right temporal lobe in an area known as the fusiform gyrus. Brain scientist and author Oliver Sacks, mentioned earlier, suffered from facial blindness.

The Parietal Lobes Behind each frontal lobe—roughly on the top of the head—is the **parietal lobe**. This area of the brain is important for processing certain sensory signals from the body: touch, pressure, temperature, and pain. Remember from Topic 1.3 that sensory neurons bring messages toward the brain, and these messages are often headed for the **somatosensory cortex**, a specific area of the parietal lobe. The somatosensory cortex has been carefully mapped by surgeon Wilder Penfield to show where signals from each body part are received.

Think about how different areas of your body are more sensitive than other areas: your face, for example, and more specifically, your lips. One reason people kiss on the lips is that lips are much more sensitive. Look at the figure below and notice how much space is devoted to your face on the somatosensory cortex versus how much space this takes up on your body.

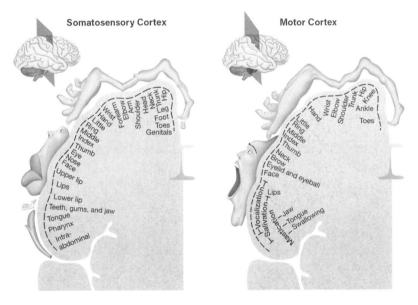

Figure 1.4.6 The image of a homunculus, or "little person," is distorted so that its body parts map to the region of the sensory or motor cortex that receives that part's signals. The figure is an aid for remembering what regions of the brain process which sensory and motor signals.

The Frontal Lobes The **frontal lobe**, which is the part of the brain directly behind the forehead and above the eyes (in each hemisphere), is "command central" for decision-making, problem-solving, reasoning, planning, personality, and language. These cognitive processes are often called **executive functions**. The frontal lobe is also important for motivation and the exercise of willpower, guiding the ability to say no to unhealthy foods or yes to challenging activities such as studying or exercising when it would be easier to sit on the couch and relax. The memory and problem-solving skills required to answer the questions at the end of each topic engage the executive functioning skills of the frontal lobe; so does the experience of figuring out whether you can afford to buy groceries or whether you should go skydiving with your friends.

Many scientists believe that the sophistication of the frontal lobe is what makes humans different from animals with simpler brains. Our hopes and dreams for the future, our awareness of eventual death, and our ability to reflect on our past are complex thought patterns that other animals do not seem to have.

The frontal lobe is also where the **motor cortex** is located. It is found in the very back of the frontal lobe, abutting the somatosensory cortex in the parietal lobe. The motor cortex plays a large role in voluntary movements, receiving information from and working with other parts of the brain. As with the somatosensory cortex, the parts of your body that you can move in more ways than others (face and hands, for example) will take up more space on the motor cortex.

THINK AS A PSYCHOLOGIST

Apply Research Findings to a Scenario (1.A)

Since the 1960s, knowledge of the brain has vastly expanded, in part because of neuroscience research made possible by advances in technology. Scientists have used detailed imaging and mapping to understand the brain. (See pages 180–185 for more on ways to study the brain.) Much of what we now know about the structures and functions of the brain came from that research.

Practice Applying Research Findings to a Scenario

Choose the correct answer.

As a result of a surgical procedure, Hakim's career as a violinist is over. He finds that he can no longer comprehend or compose music. When he tries to play, he gets confused because he can't retain what he hears. What part of the brain has likely been impacted?

(A) Occipital lobes

(B) Temporal lobes

(C) Reticular formation

(D) Parietal lobes

The Dynamic Brain

The human brain's ability to adapt and function is central to neuroscience. It is demonstrated in split-brain research, brain plasticity, and various methods for studying the brain, including brain scanning technologies. Split-brain research reveals how the brain's hemispheres can operate independently yet in coordination. Brain plasticity, or neuroplasticity, demonstrates the brain's flexibility in adapting to new learning or recovery from injury. Such technologies as MRI, EEG, and newer imaging technologies allow precise observation and manipulation of brain activity. Together, these topics provide insight into the brain's dynamic nature and the tools used to study its complexities in depth.

Split-Brain Research

Research on split-brain conditions, in which the corpus callosum (the bridge between the brain's hemispheres) is severed—commonly as a treatment for intense epilepsy—has revealed that the right and left sides of the brain may be specialized for distinct activities and functions.

The Divided Brain   As you have read, each of your cerebral hemispheres is performing its own primary set of functions. For many tasks, one hemisphere is more active than the other. This division of labor is called *brain lateralization* or **cortex specialization**. Remember, however, that the two hemispheres are connected via the corpus callosum, and information passes from one side to the other. All people with intact (i.e., not damaged) brains use both hemispheres and have access to the abilities that are dominantly controlled by each.

For most people, the left hemisphere of the brain controls most actions for the right side of the body; as you read earlier, the information crosses over in the brain stem. In addition, for most people, the left hemisphere is more active than the right when people engage in language skills.

Because of this dominance, many people refer to the left hemisphere as the "language side" of the brain. Similarly, the right hemisphere of the brain controls most actions for the left side of the body. It is more active than the left for some kinds of cognitive tasks and spatial abilities, as shown below.

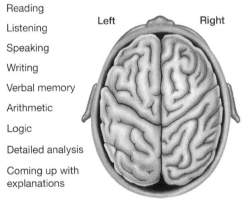

Reading
Listening
Speaking
Writing
Verbal memory
Arithmetic
Logic
Detailed analysis
Coming up with explanations

Recognizing faces
Interpreting emotions (emotional cognition)
Seeing and comprehending patterns
Making inferences
Processing spatial relationships (such as determining the location and relationships of objects in space)
Mentally rotating objects
Processing nonlinguistic sounds, including music
Recognizing and interpreting rhythms
Creating a sense of self

Figure 1.4.7 Hemisphere Functions

In general, the right side is more influential for global, intuitive, spatial, and creative tasks, while the left side is more active for tasks that are logical, verbal, and linear. Ultimately, an intact brain processes information in both hemispheres—but what about a brain that's not intact?

Cutting the Corpus Callosum During most cognitive tasks, the two hemispheres of the brain communicate seamlessly, with information passing back and forth via the corpus callosum. When the two hemispheres can't communicate, each side of the brain seems to act independently, seemingly without awareness or knowledge of the other. This intriguing phenomenon, known as the **split brain**, has been demonstrated in a series of well-known studies.

Epilepsy is a medical condition that involves a disruption of communication pathways in the brain, resulting in abnormal, "out of control" electrical activity that leads to seizures. This condition provided an opportunity for researchers to study a split brain. Research with nonhuman animals suggested that seizures might be eliminated if the defective pathway were destroyed entirely; in other words, if the scientists cut the corpus callosum so that the two hemispheres were isolated, or "split." Because epileptic seizures can be severe and debilitating, neurosurgeons made the decision to try this unconventional approach with humans who had not responded to more conventional treatments for epilepsy. Roger Sperry was the first person to conduct this research and, as he had predicted, the surgery reduced or eliminated the epileptic seizures, and for the most part, the split-brain patients appeared able to function effectively in their daily lives. They could talk and walk, they remembered events from the past, and they could make new memories. In most ways, life seemed normal—except, in certain ways, it wasn't.

For example, Jody Miller was diagnosed with Rasmussen's syndrome (an autoimmune disorder with severe seizures) at age 3. Her doctors and family chose to remove her right hemisphere in an effort to control the disease. Jody grew up with some motor coordination challenges, but she later became a successful college student.

A series of clever experiments with split-brain patients took advantage of the brain's **contralateral hemispheric organization**. *Contralateral* means "occurring in conjunction with the opposite side." Neuroscientists Roger Sperry and Michael Gazzaniga showed that some information, in particular visual information, seemed to get "stuck" in one hemisphere. This phenomenon is partly due to the anatomy of the visual system. Although each hemisphere generally controls the opposite side of the body, the visual system works a bit differently. Each eye takes in information from an entire scene, known as the **visual field.** All information about the right side of the visual field is sent from each eye to the left hemisphere, and all information about the left visual field is sent to the right hemisphere. The information is then combined in an intact brain because the signals from each hemisphere can cross via the corpus callosum.

The researchers asked patients with a severed corpus callosum to focus on a single spot in the center visual field, and then they presented a stimulus—a pencil or an apple, for example—in the far right (apple) or the far left (pencil) of the visual field, or sometimes both at once. Then, when the researchers asked the people to report what they saw, the patients said they saw the apple but they didn't mention the pencil. However, when asked to draw what they saw and instructed to draw with their *left* hands, they drew a pencil. When asked to pick up what they saw, both hands reached out—the right hand picked up the apple, and the left hand picked up the pencil. Many of the participants were surprised by the actions of their hands.

The apple in the *right visual field* is seen by both eyes, but a representation of the apple is sent only to the *left hemisphere*, which controls speech processing. Thus the person can say, "It's an apple." At the same time, a representation of the pencil in the *left visual field* is sent only to the *right hemisphere*, which controls the motion of the *left hand*. Thus the left hand will draw the pencil.

Split-Brain Experiment

The study participant with a severed corpus callosum takes in the visual information in the right visual field, which is processed in the left hemisphere.

Now the study participant cannot say what item is in the left visual field, because the visual information is processed in the right hemisphere. Because of the severed corpus collosum, information cannot be shared across the hemispheres as it would be in an intact brain.

The participant is able to speak the word "Apple" because the left hemisphere controls speech processing.

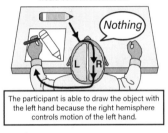

The participant is able to draw the object with the left hand because the right hemisphere controls motion of the left hand.

Figure 1.4.7 Split-Brain Experiment

Case studies have also revealed knowledge of the brain. Physician Paul Broca studied patients who had lost the ability to speak after meeting a patient who could only repeat the word *tan*. Carl Wernicke studied patients who had lost the ability to understand language. Because of these case studies, parts of the frontal lobe, typically on the left side, are now known as **Broca's area** (which moves the muscles to create speech) and **Wernicke's area** (which processes both spoken and written language).

Damage to Broca's or Wernicke's areas can lead to distinct types of **aphasia**, which are conditions that affect an individual's ability to communicate. These areas are located in the brain's left hemisphere for most people, which is generally responsible for language and speech.

Broca's Aphasia Broca's area, located in the left frontal lobe, is associated with speech production and articulation. When Broca's area is damaged, individuals may experience difficulty speaking. Their understanding of language remains relatively intact, but they struggle to form complete sentences or find the right words. Their speech may be nonfluent, labored, and broken into very simple sentences. Their grammar is often simplified, with a reliance on key nouns and verbs, omitting smaller words and inflections that convey grammar and tense. They are aware of these difficulties, which can lead to frustration.

Wernicke's Aphasia Wernicke's area is crucial for language comprehension rather than production. Damage to Wernicke's area, located in the left temporal lobe, results in difficulties with understanding spoken or written language. Individuals can produce fluent, grammatically correct speech, but it often lacks meaning or contains nonsensical words and phrases. They might have difficulty understanding others' speech and may not realize their speech is incomprehensible to others.

Both types of aphasia highlight the complexity of the brain's language network, where distinct regions control different aspects of language function. Damage to these areas from stroke, head injury, or other neurological conditions can severely affect an individual's communication abilities, often necessitating speech and language therapy for rehabilitation.

Brain Plasticity

In some rare cases, more dramatic surgery is necessary to help the patient. This drastic measure, a *hemispherectomy*, is only used when no other alternative is available. The dramatic surgery may in fact "save" a hemisphere of a child's brain by protecting it from the seizures. This can only be done if the seizures are originating from one single hemisphere.

A hemispherectomy is the removal of one of the halves (i.e., hemispheres) of the brain. Hemispherectomies have been successfully used to control seizures in people who have epilepsy, with fewer side effects than those resulting from severing the corpus callosum. In fact, when a hemisphere is removed from a young child, that child develops what would otherwise be lateralized skills in the remaining hemisphere. This incredible ability to recover from having only "half a brain" is an example of **plasticity**—the reorganization of neural pathways as a result of experience. Plasticity is stronger when we are young and reduces as we age, so many older adults experiencing a stroke never recover full functioning. Nevertheless, even adult brains are plastic to some degree. (See page 222 for more on neuroplasticity.)

Methods for Understanding the Brain

People have tried many ways to understand their own and others' behavior. As researchers began to recognize an important link between behavior and the brain, they wanted to find ways to see what happens inside the skull. Today, scientists use a variety of techniques to examine and learn about the structures and functions of the brain. Following is a brief look at the techniques most commonly used.

Case Studies Before modern brain scanning techniques, studies of individual cases were the primary means to understand brain functions. Detailed descriptions of case studies allow professionals and students alike to wonder at the complexity of the brain. Often these case studies involved someone who had experienced some type of trauma to the brain. One early case study was that of Phineas Gage. In 1848, Gage was working as the foreman of a crew cutting a railroad line in Cavendish, Vermont. He was packing blasting powder into a hole in the rock with a tamping iron when, unexpectedly, the powder exploded. The tamping iron shot upward, traveling through his left cheek, passing behind his eye, and protruding out of his skull. The force of the explosion and the speed of the rod seem to have generated enough heat to cauterize (seal off) many of the blood vessels, preventing him from dying instantly. In fact, he remained conscious—he walked over to a cart so he could be taken to a doctor.

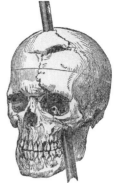

Figure 1.4.8

For many years, popular press articles and most introductory psychology textbooks reported that Gage had a severe change in his personality following the accident, in particular that he became loud and socially uninhibited, acting in ways that were seen as inappropriate at the time. Although recent reports suggest that this belief may not be accurate, it is certain that Gage was not able to go back to his job as a foreman and had difficulty holding new jobs. Recent research using new technology suggests that Gage probably lost about 4 percent of his cerebral cortex, including about 11 percent of the frontal lobe. Additionally, the connections between Gage's thinking frontal lobe were severed from his emotional limbic system, causing him to be controlled by his emotions. The changes in his behavior and the location of the damaged parts of Gage's brain have helped scientists understand where certain functions are located in the brain.

Other case studies also revealed knowledge of the brain. You have already read about the findings of Paul Broca and Carl Wernicke, whose names are now associated with the areas in the frontal lobe that control the production of speech (Broca's area) and the comprehension of language (Wernicke's area). More recently, Oliver Sacks published a number of books telling the case stories of individuals with unique neurological disorders. Possibly his most famous is about the man who mistook his wife for a hat. In this case study, Dr. P. is a music teacher with a peculiar neurological condition. Despite being successful in his field and highly functioning in many areas of his life, Dr. P. suffers from a condition that impairs his ability to recognize faces and objects correctly. This condition leads him to interpret his wife's head as a hat, and he attempts to lift it and place it on his head.

Brain Scanning

Scans of the brain provide information about how the different structures of the brain work and how the brain functions together as a whole. This section presents the most common imaging methods for studying the brain.

X-rays primarily show bones and other solid structures. They are especially useful when a person has broken bones. When a head injury occurs, an x-ray can show skull fractures. However, an x-ray will not show details of the soft tissue in the body, so it can't be used for a complete evaluation of ligaments, tendons, or brain tissue. As a result, other methods of investigating the brain have been developed.

Scientists use the process of **electroencephalography** to measure electrical activity in the brain (brain function). The brain communicates with the body via electrical and chemical signals (see Topic 1.3). The electricity in the brain at any one time is enough to light a bulb from 10–25 watts! To create an **electroencephalogram** (EEG), technicians attach electrodes to a person's scalp to record the waves of electrical activity that travel across the brain's surface during various states of consciousness (discussed in more detail in Topic 1.5). Brain waves should be occurring at predictable patterns, so if neurologists see abnormal patterns, they can make inferences about the patterns of behavior that may be caused by the unusual electrical activity.

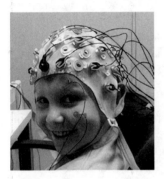

An Electroencephalogram (EEG)

Figure 1.4.9   Figure 1.4.10

A common use of EEG is to measure a person's brain waves while the person is asleep. Different sleep stages have different brain waves (see Topic 1.5), which can be seen in the EEG recording. An EEG can help to identify the occurrence of disorders, such as sleep apnea or seizures.

Computerized axial tomography (CT or CAT scan) involves taking two-dimensional x-ray photographs from different angles and using them to create a three-dimensional representation of an organ or other body part. CT scans can detect brain damage and measure blood flow in the brain, but the most common and probably most effective use is to identify a muscle or bone disorder, a tumor, or a blood clot. CT scanning is often used in emergency rooms because the technique helps doctors to identify critical problems in the lungs and abdomen very quickly. A major advantage is that the CT scan can examine bones, soft tissue, and blood vessels all at the same time.

Magnetic resonance imaging (MRI) is an imaging technique that uses a magnetic field and pulses of radio waves to generate detailed images of parts of the body made up of soft tissue, so they are especially useful when it's necessary to see the *structure* of the brain or other internal organs (Figure 1.4.11). CT scans also show brain structure, but MRIs provide increased detail. You may be familiar with MRIs because they are often used to show damage to ligaments and cartilage after a sports injury, such as a severely twisted knee or ankle. MRIs can be used to help diagnose strokes, tumors, inner ear and eye disorders, aneurysms, and spinal cord injuries. MRIs are also used in the diagnosis of multiple sclerosis to identify areas of myelin loss.

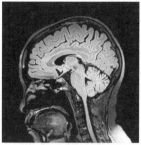 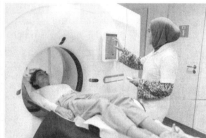

Figure 1.4.11 MRI   Figure 1.4.12 An MRI machine

Functional magnetic resonance imaging (**fMRI**) is a variation on the MRI process that involves using magnetic resonance imaging to visualize blood flow and oxygen metabolism to infer brain activity (Figure 1.4.13). No matter what activities a person is engaged in, blood is carrying oxygen to the brain. An fMRI will show where the oxygen is taken up from the blood during any particular activity, and scientists can then identify the parts of the brain that are involved in that activity. The development of fMRI technology has allowed scientists to create 3-D activation maps of the brain in real time. This is the only type of brain scanning that can detect both *structure* and *function*.

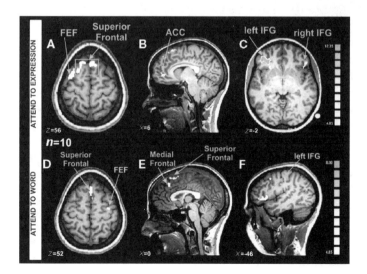

Figure 1.4.13 Functional Magnetic Resonance Imaging

Positron emission tomography (PET scan) images allow researchers to visualize slices of the brain to examine deep brain structures that had previously been reachable only via invasive procedures such as surgery. During a PET scan, scientists inject a radioactive "tracer" molecule into a person's bloodstream. This molecule is taken up by the body's cells in the same way that glucose is. The brain uses glucose as a form of energy, so blood carrying the tracer flows to parts of the brain that need energy to support its activity. The radioactive "glucose" will be carried to the active parts of the brain via the bloodstream and its path can be "traced" via the positrons (charged particles) that show up on the scan (Figure 1.4.14).

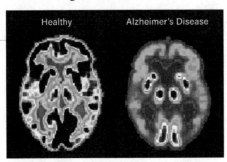

Figure 1.4.14 PET Scan: Researchers use PET scans to measure the amount of energy the brain uses during particular activities and to identify the parts of the brain that are active during different tasks. Doctors may also use PET scans to diagnose illnesses.

Another imaging type, electromyography (EMG), is used to assess the health of muscles and the nerve cells that control them, aiding in the diagnosis of myasthenia gravis and in imaging studies that rule out other conditions. EMG measures the electrical activity of muscles in response to stimulation. The test is performed using a device called an electromyograph, which records this activity. The test can help distinguish between muscle conditions in which the problem begins in the muscle itself and nerve disorders that cause muscle weakness or paralysis, such as myasthenia gravis.

Damaging or Stimulating Parts of the Brain Brain surgery (psychosurgery) typically involves destroying parts of the brain, usually to control or eliminate some unwanted behavior. *Ablation* is the process of removing or destroying some brain tissue, leaving behind **lesions**, or tissue damaged from the surgery.

A historic and ill-advised operation called a *prefrontal lobotomy* used ablation to control behavior. Developed in the 1930s, this process involves disconnecting the **prefrontal cortex**, a part of the brain directly behind the forehead, from the rest of the brain. Early lobotomies involved drilling holes on each side of the forehead just behind the hairline and injecting alcohol, which destroyed the brain tissue in that area. Other methods involved inserting sharp tools into

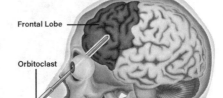

Figure 1.4.15

the brain and removing some brain tissue. A later method was to insert an ice pick-like instrument through the orbital bones (i.e., the eye socket) into the frontal lobe. Dr. Walter Freeman was the first to perform the transorbital lobotomy in 1946. After he was kicked out of most hospitals, he traversed the country in his "lobotomobile" conducting lobotomies and then often leaving town. He performed the surgery on hundreds of patients.

As you might expect, after this type of surgery, patients did show behavior changes: Many stopped acting out, but many also had personality changes, loss of long-term memories, and loss of emotional expressiveness.

Deep brain stimulation is a newer, less invasive method of altering the brain to eliminate behavioral symptoms. A surgeon first creates an opening in the skull and then carefully inserts an electrode through the opening and deep into the brain, all the way down into the brain stem. The electrode doesn't damage the brain, but rather, it stimulates a specific area. This stimulation interrupts communication in that area of the brain, reducing or eliminating behavioral symptoms that are associated with that area. Deep brain stimulation has been used to treat epilepsy, Parkinson's disease, tremors, acute depression, and Tourette syndrome.

Transcranial magnetic stimulation (TMS) is a noninvasive technique that alters brain activity. TMS involves the use of an electromagnetic wand that alters the magnetic fields that affect how the brain processes emotions and moods. TMS is sometimes used to treat depression.

Autopsy—a postmortem examination to determine cause of death—offers another tool for brain study. For example, when the brain is removed from the casing of a deceased person's skull, a brain specialist can examine slices of the brain under a microscope to look for evidence of Alzheimer's or for the level of beta-amyloid plaques that often show repeated brain injuries in chronic traumatic encephalitis (CTE). Currently, autopsy is the only way to determine these brain disorders. In nonhuman subjects, **lesioning**, or purposefully damaging certain parts of the brain and noting changes in behavior, has also been used as a research tool.

THINK AS A PSYCHOLOGIST

Evaluate Whether a Psychological Scenario Followed Ethical Procedures (2.D) | Identify Psychology-Related Concepts in Descriptions or Representations of Data (3.A)

In the 1980s, many professors assigned students the task of performing brain surgery on rats. The purpose was to replicate previous experiments.

One such professor did not have students go through an Institutional Review Board (see Practice 2.D). In his class, each student in Group 1 performed a lesioning of the lateral hypothalamus in a rat and placed an electrode into the skull and turned it on. Group 2 students performed a "sham lesioning," which included everything Group 1 did except the lesioning and turning on the electrode. The rats were weighed for two weeks after the surgeries.

		GROUP 1 AVERAGE WEIGHT OF RATS IN GRAMS	GROUP 2 AVERAGE WEIGHT OF RATS IN GRAMS
Presurgical Weights		400	450
Weights Postsurgery	Day 3	380	430
	Day 6	360	435
	Day 9	320	440
	Day 12	280	450
	Day 14	260	450

Practice Evaluating Ethical Procedures of an Experiment

Choose the correct answer.

1. If an Institutional Review Board had reviewed the proposal for this experiment, what would its likely response have been?

   (A) As long as the rats were otherwise treated humanely, the experiment could proceed.

   (B) Its replication value is limited and does not justify the harm to the rats in Group 1.

   (C) It would not be allowed because students are not skilled practitioners.

   (D) It would not be allowed because no experiments may harm animals.

Practice Identifying Psychology-Related Concepts in Representations of Data

Choose the correct answer.

2. Which of the following concepts is reflected in the data in this experiment?

   (A) The lesioning in Group 1 stimulated the release of serotonin.

   (B) The lesioning in Group 2 shows that the hormone leptin increases hunger.

   (C) The results confirm the role of the lateral hypothalamus in increasing appetite.

   (D) The results confirm the role of the lateral hypothalamus in decreasing appetite.

Going for a Drive: An Example of Brain Processing

Now that you know the basic functions of the brain structures, you can take a look at how each part of the nervous system plays a role in your behavior. Consider the example of going for a drive with your best friend. What is your brain doing during this driving experience? Initially, as you're making the decision to go on this drive, your *frontal lobe* is active, helping you plan out your trip. As you get into the car, your legs and back feel the pressure from the seat. The seat belt comes across your chest. These sensations are passed, *via sensory nerves in the peripheral nervous system,* to the *spinal cord* and then the *brain (the central nervous system).* The *thalamus* processes the information and then sends it to the *somatosensory cortex,* the part of the brain that ultimately processes the meaning in the message. The *cerebellum* helps keep you vertical, assisting your balance and helping you to coordinate all your movements. You are not feeling dizzy, so you can maintain your balance.

Because you have driven many times, you hardly have to think about putting the key into the ignition and turning the key (or maybe you have to push a button). Turning on the radio requires the *motor cortex* and the *cerebellum,* and you realize that you don't even remember starting the car. Your *basal ganglia* took care of that basic repetitive motor function for you.

As the music plays, you recognize the song because your *thalamus* sent the signals to the *temporal lobes,* which worked hard to help you identify the melody. The *left hemisphere* is especially active in processing the lyrics; with help from the *hippocampus,* it pulls information from the *cerebral cortex* so you can sing along. When your friend asks, "Who sings this song?" *Wernicke's area* helps you to recognize the words, and your *frontal cortex* is active as you formulate a response. *Broca's area* helps you say the name of the artist, and as soon as it's out of your mouth, you realize that your *frontal lobe* let you down, allowing you to miss the forthcoming comeback: Your friend says, "Then shut up and let them sing it!" As you realize that you just walked into that joke, your *frontal lobe* begins to feel a bit of shame for having fallen for such a transparent and predictable put-down of your singing skills.

Now you are ready to pull out of the driveway. Your *parietal lobe* helps you to judge the distance and speed as you move backward into the street, but first your eyes must process the signals of light bouncing off all the surfaces. As you look at the car, the rearview mirror, and out the back window, your eyes are bringing all that data into the *thalamus* and then the *occipital lobe*, where all that visual data is processed.

Your arms are controlling the steering wheel and gearshift, thanks to your *motor cortex* working as you switch from reverse to drive. The pressure you feel on the bottom of your foot as you move from the brake to the accelerator pad is processed by the *somatosensory cortex,* and the *hippocampus* is busy searching your memory for information about which roads to take to get to your destination.

As you are driving and talking, the *lateral hypothalamus* processes a signal from your body and messages your *frontal lobe*, which lets you know that you feel hungry. You ask your friend, "Hey, wanna get something to eat?" When your friend says, "I could go for some tacos," your *frontal cortex* helps you evaluate the possibilities for restaurants. The *hippocampus* is at work again, searching for the two best choices. You recall that the taqueria where you most recently ate had the best salsa you've ever had. Your *frontal lobe* goes into action and you respond, "Let's go to the taqueria on Main Street."

On your way, another favorite song comes on the radio. You both are singing and laughing. As your attention is diverted from the road, you do not notice the cars stopped in front of you. Out of the corner of your eye, you see lights and movement *(eyes, thalamus, occipital lobe)*. The *thalamus* and the *RAS* help focus your attention. Your *amygdala* activates the *sympathetic nervous system* via the *hypothalamus. Adrenaline* pours into your bloodstream. Your body knows what to do; you hit the brakes. You begin to sweat as your muscles tense and your body temperature rises. You somehow swerve to the right and avoid hitting the cars in front of you. The *frontal lobe* is working overtime to get you to stop on the side of the road. You pull over and turn on the hazard lights, but you are still breathing heavily and stunned about what just happened. Your *frontal lobe* sends the signal, and you realize everyone is safe. Your friend, and your *parasympathetic nervous system*, help to calm you down—your breathing slows, the chemicals move out of your bloodstream, and your body resets itself. The *sympathetic nervous system* sends a signal telling you that digestion isn't a priority right now, and you realize you're no longer hungry.

You reflect about the near accident, with your *frontal lobe* humming as you process all the activities that were going on during the drive. Your *hippocampus* helps you to remember and second-guess every decision you made—from the music to the singing, even to having your friend in the car. As you review everything, your *cerebral cortex* is working to make those memories into long-term ones: the melody of the song, the smell of the burning rubber, the squealing of the tires, the feeling of your body in the danger zone, and the sense of relief as you realize it was not an actual crash, only a near one.

THINK AS A PSYCHOLOGIST

Apply Concepts to a Scenario (1.A)

Practice Applying Concepts to a Scenario

Complete the following activity.

Develop your own explanation of what your brain is doing when you perform a routine task, such as jogging outdoors while listening to music or responding to a funny video someone posted on social media. Write out a brief description like the preceding example of your brain going for a drive.

REFLECT ON THE ESSENTIAL QUESTION

Essential Question: *How do the structures and functions of the brain affect behavior and mental processes?* Using the Key Terms, complete a chart like the one below to gather details to help answer that question.

Brain Structure	Studying the Brain
Brain Stem/Lower Brain	
Hemispheres	
Cerebral Cortex	

KEY TERMS

FRAMEWORK OF BRAIN ANATOMY

amygdala	hippocampus	pituitary gland
aphasia	frontal lobe	plasticity
association area	hemisphere	prefrontal cortex
brain stem	hippocampus	procedural learning
Broca's area	hypothalamus	reticular activating system
cerebellum	limbic system	(RAS)
cerebral cortex	lobe	reticular formation
contralateral hemispheric	medulla oblongata	reward center
organization	(medulla)	somatosensory cortex
corpus callosum	motor cortex	split brain
cortex specialization	nucleus	temporal lobe
epilepsy	occipital lobe	thalamus
executive function	parietal lobe	Wernicke's area

TECHNIQUES FOR STUDYING AND TREATING THE BRAIN

electroencephalography/	functional magnetic	lesion/lesioning
electroencephalogram	resonance imaging	
(EEG)	(fMRI)	

STUDY LIKE A CHAMP WITH DR. G.

Completing the activity associated with Reflect on the Essential Question is a powerful way to test what you know about what you have read. It offers good retrieval practice, and even if you have to look something up in the course of completing it, you are still cementing your learning.

1. Liz is a high school tennis player who started to lose weight rapidly during the season. Which part of the brain are new studies focusing on in understanding the role of the brain in changes in the desire to eat?

   (A) Hippocampus

   (B) Hypothalamus

   (C) Thalamus

   (D) Brain stem

2. Harold, who is 82, recently experienced a stroke. His body has mostly recovered, but he seems unable to understand why he is in the hospital or to learn the names of the nurses who care for him every day. He does, however, remember the names and details about his wife and children. Which of the following brain areas was most likely affected by Harold's stroke?

   (A) Hippocampus

   (B) Cerebellum

   (C) Thalamus

   (D) Brain stem

3. Lately, Maria has not been sleeping well. It seems like she hears everything at night. Even the faintest noises, such as the refrigerator humming and the toilet down the hall flushing, wake her up. If she does fall asleep, she has a very hard time getting up. Maria is desperate for some rest. Which of the following brain parts would be most involved in this scenario?

   (A) Cerebellum

   (B) Somatosensory cortex

   (C) Reticular activating system

   (D) Corpus callosum

Questions 4 through 6 refer to the following.

Valeria is a professional dancer who has been dancing for years. During a recent competition, the dance floor was slippery, and Valeria fell hard on her head and was temporarily unconscious. Now, Valeria has problems dancing. She knows the correct steps she must make, but she feels as if her legs and arms are moving as if directed by someone else. She often finds her movements choppy and feels off-balance.

4. What area of her brain was likely damaged by her fall?

(A) Wernicke's area

(B) Hippocampus

(C) Broca's area

(D) Cerebellum

5. Doctors want to determine if there is indeed structural damage to Valeria's brain and also determine if it is functioning properly when presented with different stimuli. Which of the following brain scanning techniques would you recommend they use?

(A) X-ray

(B) MRI

(C) EEG

(D) fMRI

6. If Valeria's experience is studied in detail and the findings lead to recommendations for increased safety precautions in the dancing industry, what type of research would have been conducted?

(A) Experiment

(B) Case study

(C) Naturalistic observation

(D) Meta-analysis

7. Maureen is 6 years old and has started having terrible seizures. She can no longer attend school because of the frequency of the seizures, and her parents are concerned that her brain will be permanently damaged. Her neurosurgeon determined that Maureen is eligible for a split-brain surgery procedure because all the seizures are starting in one side of her brain. After surgery, which of the following might you expect Maureen to experience?

(A) If an object is displayed for a short time in Maureen's right visual field, she will be able to select it from a number of items presented.

(B) There is no way either internally or externally for Maureen to get messages to both sides of her brain.

(C) Maureen's ability for higher-order thinking will be compromised.

(D) If an object is displayed for a short time in her right visual field, she will be able to say what she has seen.

STUDY LIKE A CHAMP WITH DR. G.

Using these practice questions is a good way to test yourself on what you have learned.

Topic 1.5

Sleep

"Now I do not know whether I was then a man dreaming I was a butterfly, or whether I am now a butterfly, dreaming I am a man."

—Chuang Chou

Essential Question: How does the sleep/wake cycle affect behavior and mental processes throughout the day and night?

As you read in Practice 1, American philosopher and physician William James saw consciousness as a continuous flow, a "stream of consciousness." Influenced by the work of Charles Darwin and his theory of evolution, James saw the function of consciousness as an evolutionary adaptation to the environment that made it possible for humans to thrive and to continue to adapt. James began to explore the nature of consciousness, but his efforts were cut short because he lacked the appropriate tools to adequately examine these ideas. Only since brain scanning was introduced in the 1990s have scientists been able to answer questions about human consciousness as it occurs. However, even with this capability, the study of consciousness is still in relative infancy.

Consciousness

Consciousness is our state of awareness of our existence, sensations, thoughts, and environment. We are conscious to the degree that we are aware of what is going on both inside and outside our bodies. Psychologists examine our waking consciousness and compare it to other levels of consciousness, including sleep, hypnosis, and altered states of consciousness achieved through meditation and drug use. Philosophers have continued to examine the nature of consciousness, asking such questions as: "What is the mind? Does the brain create the mind? Does the mind exist independently of the brain? Does the mind—or consciousness—exist beyond death? Does the mind influence the body, the body influence the mind, or are they interdependent?" In philosophy, *dualism* holds the point of view that mind and brain are distinct entities; the mind (nonphysical) is one thing, and the brain/body (physical) is another. Neither mind nor brain can be inferred from the existence of the other.

As you read this passage, you are conscious of the words on the page and what they mean. You may be less aware of movements like adjusting your glasses, tapping your foot, or wiggling in your seat. If you check the time or begin to focus on how warm the room has become, your awareness may shift, and you may suddenly lose track of what you are reading. Although several biological activities—cognitive and physical—may be happening simultaneously in a given moment, your awareness is directed toward only one at a time.

Consciousness has a single focus. We give our attention to one thing at a time, focusing our entire awareness on something within ourselves or in the environment outside ourselves. New things and novel ideas tend to capture our attention because our sensory systems are built to identify change. Have you ever noticed a new building or business on your way to school? Is it really new, or has it been there for months and you just never focused on it before? Suppose your family has just purchased a new blue Chevy Bolt, and now, suddenly, you see blue Chevy Bolts on every street. Although these vehicles have been popular for a while, having one in your family has clearly shifted your conscious awareness. You can be sure, however, that your focus will shift again. Once we are exposed to a stimulus repeatedly, we often begin to ignore it or to become habituated.

The different levels of consciousness that have been identified and named are described below.

- Conscious awareness includes all the sensations, perceptions, memories, and feelings you are aware of at any given moment. **Wakeful consciousness** is your normal, alert awareness that includes your working memory.

- The preconscious level includes stored information about yourself or your environment that you are not currently aware of or thinking about but can easily call to mind when asked. At the preconscious level, you can easily recall your favorite childhood spot to play or your embarrassment at being locked out of your school when you arrived after the late bell.

- The **unconscious** level was once the territory of Sigmund Freud's id (life and death instincts, immediate gratification, pleasure-seeking), superego (societal or parental standards that we try to live up to), and ego (self-image and reality-based part of the mind that tries to balance the id and superego). Today psychologists see the unconscious as the mental processing of learning, memory, perception, thought, and language that takes place without our awareness.

LEVELS OF HUMAN CONSCIOUSNESS	
Conscious Awareness	All the ideas in your immediate awareness, such as your thoughts, feelings, senses
Preconscious	Thoughts and memories not currently in conscious awareness but that can be retrieved into consciousness with focused attention
Unconscious	Mental process of learning, memory, and perception of which we are unaware

Table 1.5.1

The Sleep/Wake Cycle

Sleep is another type of consciousness. Since people spend nearly a third of their lives sleeping, psychologists find sleep a worthy topic of investigation. During sleep, our awareness of the external environment is reduced or absent, and our perception of time, self-awareness, and cognitive functions are altered. While some level of consciousness persists during sleep, it is different from the waking state. However, sleep itself is a complex physiological process involving various stages and cycles, regulated by the brain and influenced by factors like circadian rhythms, neurotransmitters, and environmental cues.

The human body experiences various biological rhythms (see Figure 1.5.1 below) that are not detected by our conscious awareness. For example, we are not usually aware of normal changes in body temperature, hormone levels, or energy levels during the day. Night owls and early risers do exist, but how do most humans operate in their daily wake/sleep cycle?

Waking and sleeping fall into a biological rhythm known as the **circadian rhythm**. Defining the sleep/wake cycle, the circadian rhythm ebbs and flows for roughly twenty-four hours without external cues.

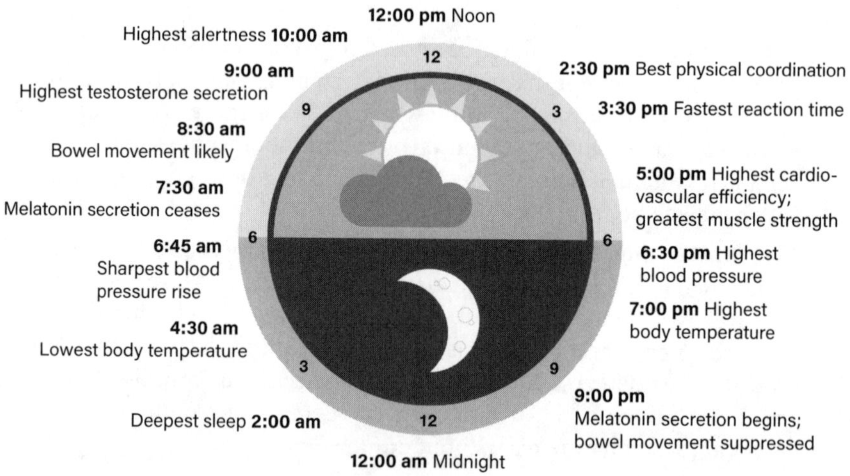

Circadian Rhythms

Figure 1.5.1

Human circadian rhythms are day-long biological patterns. Our cycles are roughly 24, with 16 hours awake and 8 hours asleep. Humans are considered *diurnal* creatures because we are typically awake during the day. Many other animals are *nocturnal,* meaning that they do most of their foraging and hunting at night and sleep during the day. Bats, lions, tigers, and many rodent species are nocturnal animals (along with fictional vampires). If you've ever had hamsters, gerbils, or rats as pets, you've probably been awakened by the various noises they make at night.

Brain Waves—The Key to Sleep Studies

Learning about the different wave patterns present in each known level of consciousness helps us understand the mind, the brain, and their interactions. **Electroencephalography (EEG)** was introduced in the 1950s to measure electrical currents in the brain, recording them as a visual tracing called an *encephalogram*. Researchers first began to use this measurement technique to examine the brains of people with epilepsy and, in time, began to focus on evaluating sleep. During a sleep study, electrodes are attached to the scalp to measure the brain's electrical currents during sleep and compare the results to those recorded during waking hours. Since the brain is electrochemical, EEG measures electrical currents produced as brain cells communicate with one another. EEG measures wave patterns in hertz (Hz). Brain waves are categorized by their speed.

MEASUREMENT OF ELECTRICAL ACTIVITY IN THE BRAIN		
Types of Waves	What They Show	EEG Tracings
Beta waves	Awake, alert, anxious	
Alpha waves	Relaxed, ready for sleep	
Theta waves	Stages 1 and 2 of NREM sleep	
Delta waves	Deep sleep; stage 3 of NREM	

Figure 1.5.2

If we are awake, alert, or anxious, we display *beta waves*—quick, rapid brain waves. If we are relaxed and possibly ready to fall asleep, we display *alpha waves*. Our minds wander and are more open to reflection, while our bodies' internal states begin to slow down. We may even experience hallucinations just before falling asleep. At some point, we shift from being awake to being asleep, but we do not perceive that moment of changeover. An EEG, however, can detect the wave changes in this period of sleep onset.

Stages of Sleep

In studies in which participants were prevented from exposure to outside light so they had no way to tell the time of day or what day it was, subjects still exhibited 21- to 28-hour internal clocks, averaging close to the actual 24-hour day. However, for the rest of us, environmental cues signal our brains that it's time to sleep. The first cue is our ability to perceive nighttime. As daylight lessens, the eyes (rods/cones in the cornea) detect lower light levels, and cells in the retina (ganglion cells) communicate directly with the suprachiasmatic nucleus (SCN), or "master clock." The SCN resides in the hypothalamus, a gland that also regulates hunger, thirst, body temperature, sex drive, and more. It interprets information taken from the eye and signals the pineal gland to secrete melatonin—the sleep hormone—into the bloodstream. Melatonin production increases naturally at night as darkness falls and then decreases during the day when the light returns. Interestingly, you may notice that it is easier for you to stay up late into the night than it is for your parents. Young people generally produce melatonin later and can, therefore, stay up later. The result on the other end of the sleep cycle is that young people generally also sleep later.

Falling Asleep As we transition from wakefulness to sleep, we experience **hypnagogic sensations**, particularly during Stage 1 of the sleep cycle. These sensations can include vivid imagery, auditory hallucinations, or sensations of falling or floating. They are often described as dream-like and can vary widely from person to person. Hypnagogic sensations are thought to arise due to the brain's transition from a state of wakefulness to sleep, during which sensory input becomes less reliable, and the brain begins to generate its own internal experiences. They are a normal part of the sleep onset process and typically last for only a few minutes before deeper sleep stages are entered. As brain waves start to prepare the body for sleep, alpha waves begin to appear. A good way to remember this is that you have **a**lpha waves when you are "**a**lmost **a**sleep."

Non-REM Sleep Once asleep, we enter Stage 1, or **non-REM (NREM) sleep**. (REM stands for Rapid Eye Movement and represents what is known as "dream sleep.") In Stages 1 and 2 of NREM sleep, our brains produce high-frequency/low-amplitude *theta waves*. As these waves begin to slow down, progressing into slow-wave sleep, the sleep spindles and k-complexes of Stage 2 begin to appear. Sleep spindles are slower-paced waves with spikes comparable to the low-amplitude theta waves of Stage 1. Sleep talking is associated with sleep spindles. K-complexes are large, high-voltage waves that often appear in response to such outside stimuli as sounds. These unique sleep waves are characteristic only of Stage 2 of sleep, which is a traditional stage of sleep between light Stage 1 sleep and deep Stage 3 sleep.

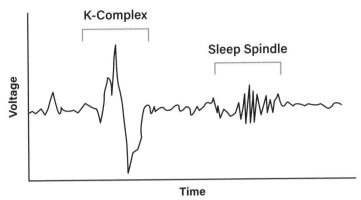

Figure 1.5.3

As we move into Stage 3, slow-wave sleep, delta waves begin to appear more often, hormones are released into the bloodstream for growth in children, our immune system refreshes itself, and sleep is so deep that we cannot be easily awakened and are completely unaware of our environment. This deep stage of sleep is essential for good health. Without such deep sleep, we are at greater risk for illness and may have difficulties with concentration and coordination throughout the day.

REM Sleep About 45 minutes into a sleep cycle, you will have the deepest sleep of the night. You will then start to move back to Stage 2 sleep and eventually have your first official dream state of the evening during **rapid eye movement (REM) sleep**, about 90 minutes after falling asleep. Despite popular belief, you are in a light stage of sleep in REM sleep.

REM sleep is often called the **paradoxical stage** because brain waves move as if we are awake, but our body is paralyzed. Though the brain is active, the brain stem acts to block communication between the cerebral cortex and the motor neurons to produce **REM paralysis** so our bodies remain still during dreams. We do, however, experience muscle twitches. Sleeping dogs moving their legs in running motions are in REM sleep. We also have vivid dreams while in REM sleep, and our heart rate, blood pressure, and breathing rate may become irregular. If we do not experience REM sleep one night, we may make up for it the next with **REM rebound**—more REM sleep—to help the body recover.

The process of sleeping follows this pattern: sleep onset, Stage 1, Stage 2, Stage 3, Stage 2, REM, and repeat. The pattern occurs three to five times per night of sleep in roughly 90-minute segments (see Figure 1.5.4). Notice that the amount of Stage 3 sleep declines during the night and REM and Stage 2 increase. In other words, you have far more deep sleep (Stage 3) early in the night than you do closer to the morning, when you are in far lighter stages of sleep (Stage 2 and REM).

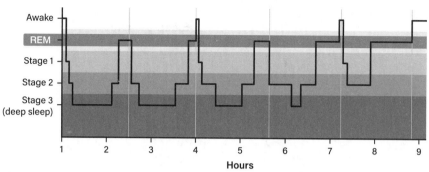

REM Sleep over Eight Hours

Figure 1.5.4

Why We Dream

Although researchers do not fully understand all the functions of REM sleep and consider REM to be somewhat mysterious, evidence shows that REM sleep plays a role in memory formation and consolidation, specifically for procedural and emotional memories. The **consolidation theory** of dreams posits that one of the primary functions of dreaming is to aid in the consolidation and processing of memories. According to this theory, during sleep, particularly during the rapid eye movement (REM) stage, the brain actively processes and integrates newly acquired information with existing knowledge, which helps in strengthening memory traces and facilitating learning. Dreams are believed to be a reflection of this memory consolidation process, as the brain replays and organizes memories in a manner that promotes memory retention and learning. This evidence may explain why infants, who are so busy processing new information, sleep sixteen hours a day, half of it in REM sleep. The percentage of REM sleep reduces considerably as we age. Research on the precise function of REM sleep continues.

The Activation-Synthesis Theory The **activation-synthesis theory** of dreams comes from a purely physiological/biological point of view. During sleep, the pons sends signals to the cerebral cortex, creating what we perceive as dreams. Neural activity during REM sleep periodically stimulates the brain. The activation-synthesis theory views dreams as the mind's attempt to make sense of random neural firings in the brain as we sleep. However, the activation-synthesis theory says there is nothing to interpret. Dreams are meaningless.

Why We Sleep

Many different theories attempt to explain why we sleep, but no single theory holds all the answers. These are just a few of the theories briefly described:

- From an evolutionary perspective, sleep kept us safely "tucked away" during the hours when our vision was limited and predators were active.

- Sleep helps restore health and efficiency. NREM sleep helps restore physiological functions; REM sleep helps restore mental processes. Recent evidence suggests that during sleep, the brain removes neurotoxic waste.
- Sleep helps us consolidate the information of the day and supports long-term memory. (See above.)
- Sleep helps us replay and process stressors from the day through dreaming.

Sleep Disruptions

Some of what researchers theorize about why we sleep comes from research into what happens when we are deprived of sleep. Research has shown that **sleep deprivation** contributes to many negative outcomes, including memory impairment and moodiness. Lack of sleep is also associated with overeating and eating unhealthy foods. If lack of sleep becomes habitual over time, we experience what is called a *sleep debt*. Chronic sleep deprivation can lead to chronic irritability, lack of motivation, anxiety, an inability to concentrate, reduced vigilance, longer reaction times, distractibility, reduced energy, restlessness, lack of coordination, poor decision-making, increased errors, forgetfulness, and physical symptoms such as high blood pressure, high blood sugar, and obesity.

Circadian Rhythm Disruption An out-of-sync sleep/wake cycle is called *circadian rhythm disruption*. Jet lag, for example, occurs when you travel across several time zones. Imagine you are traveling from Chicago to London. You leave from Chicago during the day and arrive in London the next morning. You were not able to fall asleep on the plane, remaining awake during your normal "night's sleep," and yet you arrive in London on the same day you left, with a six-hour shift in time zones. Your new 7 a.m. is actually 1 a.m. Chicago time! Adjusting to the time change mentally and physically may take you more than a week. This type of circadian disruption also happens every spring in geographic areas that shift from standard time to daylight saving time. As time shifts "forward," people need to wake up an hour earlier—a challenge as people adjust their circadian clocks. The somewhat minor disruption in circadian rhythm is even associated with an increase in automobile accidents in the few days after the time change.

Studies show that shift work and sleep deprivation are almost synonymous and are challenging for mind and body. Shift workers are prone to sleeping on the job, making mistakes, and taking frequent sick days. People driving home after evening and night shift work are more likely to fall asleep at the wheel and have auto accidents.

Most people find that changing from working days to working early evenings is easier than changing from working days to working the night shift. Shifting employees back and forth between shifts is disorienting to the employees—and a sure way to encourage them to leave their jobs.

In our 24/7 world, people work in the evenings and even overnight. Firefighters, police, nurses, doctors, and assembly workers often do shift work, sometimes working three twelve-hour shifts instead of a standard workday of eight hours. Nurses and other hospital personnel who work shifts suffer high rates of sleep deprivation and poor concentration; their lack of attention is even known to reduce the quality of patient care.

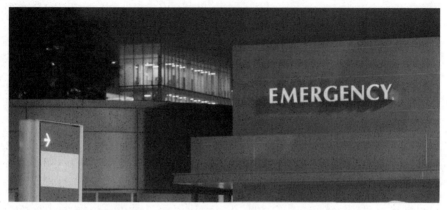

Many medical workers have to work the night shift. Researchers have found that workers who are exposed to intermittent bright lights during their shift, wear sunglasses while driving home, and sleep in a dark room at home can counteract the disruption to their circadian rhythms.

THINK AS A PSYCHOLOGIST

Evaluate Whether a Psychological Research Scenario Followed Appropriate Ethical Procedures (2.D) | Make a Defensible Claim (4.A)

In the 1970s, sleep studies were conducted at the Willowbrook State School, a residential institution for children with intellectual disabilities in New York. Dr. Saul Krugman, along with other researchers, conducted these studies to investigate the sleep patterns and disturbances among children at the facility.

Researchers monitored the sleep patterns of children using various methods, including observation, EEG recordings, and sleep questionnaires. They sought to understand the prevalence and nature of sleep disorders in this population. They deliberately deprived students of sleep by keeping the children awake for extended periods, often through various means such as bright lights, loud noises, and other disruptive stimuli. Some reports suggest that children were also subjected to physical manipulation to keep them awake, such as being forcibly kept upright or engaged in strenuous activities. These methods were employed to observe the effects of sleep deprivation on the children's behavior and cognitive functioning. The results revealed the significant short- and long-term negative effects of sleep deprivation on behavior, cognitive functioning, and emotional regulation.

Students at Willowbrook were also the subjects of experiments to study hepatitis transmission and develop a vaccine. Parents signed a consent form that said their students could attend the school in exchange for receiving vaccines. In fact, without their knowledge or the knowledge of their parents, students were deliberately infected with viral hepatitis as part of an experiment to develop a vaccine. They were given chocolate milk to which feces from infected people had been added. The research sped up the development of a vaccine for hepatitis B.

Practice Evaluating Ethical Procedures

Complete the following activty.

1. Review the ethical guidelines in Practice 2.D. Write two or three sentences evaluating the ethics of the Willowbrook studies using those guidelines.

Practice Making a Defensible Claim

Complete the following activity.

2. Develop a claim about experiments involving vulnerable populations. Identify what evidence and reasoning you can use to defend your claim.

Willowbrook State School

Sleep Habits

Adequate sleep may be the single best indicator of your overall health. The sleep habits you develop throughout life play a vital role in both your physical and psychological well-being, allowing you to function at your best.

Sleep Habits and Culture

How many people have been taught the importance of getting a solid eight hours of sleep? With this as a mandate, waking up in the middle of the night and not falling back to sleep right away could cause stress. However, eight hours is a culturally developed norm, and people in all parts of the world have their own sleep patterns without necessarily experiencing sleep deprivation.

In our culture today, sleep deprivation may be the result of keeping lights on all night, including lights associated with television, computers, tablets, and cell phones. Although we may want to sleep, we maintain a certain level of alertness for that text signal or that social media message from our friends. We do not unplug and, therefore, may not sleep—or may not sleep as deeply as the body requires. Be honest. Do you sleep with your phone close? Is the volume up? Is the vibrate on? Do you wake up to respond to messages? If so, you may be making challenging sleep issues even worse.

Good sleep habits emphasize behaviors that promote good health. Regardless of what other great information you learn in this psychology class, using the following recommendations can literally change your life!

- Stick to a regular sleep schedule, even on weekends. Go to bed and wake up at the same time every day.
- Avoid ingesting stimulants (caffeine, for example) for at least six hours before bedtime.
- Avoid taking extended naps during the day. No naps after 3 p.m.
- Reserve your bedroom for only sleeping. Keep your cell phone and other electronics away from your bed—they can interfere with sleep.
- Make sure your sheets are clean, and shower before bed to relax the body.
- Avoid eating large meals before bedtime and make evening snacks easy to digest (no cheese, meat, or nuts, for example).
- Make sure your room is dark and at a cool temperature (low to upper 60s).
- Develop and follow a relaxation ritual to prepare your mind for sleep.

THINK AS A PSYCHOLOGIST

Explain How Cultural Norms, Expectations, and Circumstances Apply to Behavior and Mental Processes (1.B) | Evaluate the Appropriate Use of Research Design Elements in Non-Experimental Methodologies (2.C)

In a recent article,[1] researchers focused on cultural factors influencing sleep in young people, specifically those aged 18 and younger. The study highlighted sleeping arrangements as a frequently studied aspect. The survey found notable differences in co-sleeping practices between regions, with infants in Europe, North America, and Australasia less likely to share a room or bed with parents compared to those in Asia. These distinctions likely stem from culturally ingrained values and beliefs regarding interdependency and parent-child bonds. In cultures where co-sleeping is encouraged, such as those in

1   Jeon, M., Dimitriou, D., & Halstead, E. J. (2021, February 19). A systematic review on cross-cultural comparative studies of sleep in young populations: The roles of cultural factors. *International Journal of Environmental Research and Public Health, 18*(4), 2005. doi: 10.3390/ijerph18042005. PMID: 33669583; PMCID: PMC7922907.

Asia, it is seen as fostering stronger familial connections, while in regions valuing individualism, like Europe and North America, independent sleeping is favored due to concerns about safety and promoting autonomy. Additionally, the cultural context appears to influence the association between co-sleeping and sleep duration/disturbances, with infants in Europe, North America, and Australasia experiencing longer nocturnal sleep duration and fewer night awakenings when falling asleep alone, a trend not observed in Asian infants. These findings suggest that cultural norms play a significant role in shaping sleep practices and outcomes in young children.

Practice Explaining How Cultural Norms Apply to Behavior and Mental Processes

Answer the following question.

1. Was (or is, if you have younger siblings) co-sleeping practiced in your household? If you don't remember, ask the adults in your home to remind you what the sleeping arrangements were when you were a baby. Also, ask what reasons your caregivers had for the sleeping arrangements they chose. Explain the factors that may have led to those sleeping arrangements. How might these sleeping arrangements early in life impact sleep later in life?

Practice Evaluating the Appropriate Use of Research Design Elements in Non-Experimental Methodologies

Researchers for this study gathered their information by searching seven journal databases with carefully chosen search terms and identified 1,213 articles in peer-reviewed publications. Then, they included only those that met certain requirements, such as being "either an observational or experimental study using a quantitative or qualitative approach," including "a comparison of populations between two or more countries," and using "one or more measures of sleep duration . . . and/or sleep disturbances." That filtering process left them with articles that were specifically related to the content and purpose of their study.

They next had to evaluate the *quality* of the studies. They used 12 criteria to make that evaluation, and 25 studies ended up fulfilling all requirements.

Complete the following activity.

2. Think of as many criteria as you can that might qualify a study for inclusion in this review on the basis of its quality. Use your knowledge of research methods and review Practices 2 and 3 to help you develop your list. Consider such issues as sound design, sampling, external validity, reliability, and bias. Share your list with the class and compare notes.

Sleep Disorders

Have you ever been so excited about an upcoming event that you slept very little the night before? Have you ever been so stressed that you took more than an hour to fall asleep? If so, you are normal. These sleep issues happen to nearly everyone at some time. However, while most of us are inconvenienced by occasional sleep irregularities, we do not experience the degrees of distress that sleep disorders such as the following create:

- **Insomnia**, the inability to fall asleep or stay asleep, can be temporary or chronic. Roughly 10 to 20 percent of the population experience insomnia from time to time or chronically. Insomnia can be caused by many factors, including underlying medical or psychiatric conditions, stress, emotional or physical discomfort or pain, use of medications or stimulants, or disruptions to the normal sleep cycle, such as shift work.

- **Narcolepsy** is a disorder in which a person suddenly falls into REM sleep during waking hours. These sudden sleep episodes can occur either during periods of excitement or periods of low activity—from laughing or cheering at a ball game to sitting quietly during a lecture or concert. Some people with narcolepsy also experience cataplexy, the sudden loss of muscle tone. Lack of activity and staying still for long periods can make narcolepsy symptoms worse. The condition occurs because the brain does not produce enough orexin, a neuromodulator that influences wakefulness, arousal, and appetite.

- **Sleep apnea** is a condition in which breathing stops and starts repeatedly during sleep. A person may fall asleep normally but awaken suddenly when breathing stops in order to gasp for breath and resume breathing.

In the most common type of sleep apnea, obstructive sleep apnea, the throat muscles relax and decrease the opening of the esophagus, disrupting normal breathing. People who are overweight and obese are especially susceptible to obstructive sleep apnea because excess fat presses on the airway and cuts off oxygen (a condition called anoxia). Sleep apnea can also be caused by a lack of signals from the brain to the muscles that control breathing, a condition called *complex sleep apnea syndrome*. Diagnosis of sleep apnea is done in a sleep lab using EEG and EMG to measure brain waves and muscle movement. Apnea can be treated with a breathing device that helps force air into the lungs through a mask. While the mask may be uncomfortable at first, most people with sleep apnea readily adjust to the mask because they are eager to get a good night's sleep and avoid exhaustion.

- **Somnambulism** (sleepwalking) occurs in NREM sleep during Stage 3, deep sleep. Sleepwalking is more common in children, and most will grow out of it. Because this occurs during deep sleep, most sleepwalkers will be unaware of their nocturnal travels when they wake up in the morning. Contrary to myth, no harm will come to sleepwalkers if you wake them while they are walking. Simply wake the person if needed and direct them gently back to bed. Sleep talking is speaking while asleep and also occurs in NREM sleep.

- **REM sleep behavior disorder** is a disorder in which the body is not motionless or "paralyzed" during REM sleep, and the person can physically act out dream behavior. Movements can include punching, kicking, jumping from bed, acting out the actions of a violent dream, making noises, talking, laughing, and shouting. People have harmed their partners during episodes, though they are actually asleep. This disorder is rare; the vast majority of people exhibit paralysis in REM sleep.

REFLECT ON THE ESSENTIAL QUESTION

Essential Question: *How does the sleep/wake cycle affect behavior and mental processes throughout the day and night?* Using the Key Terms, complete a chart like the one below to gather details to help answer that question.

Wakefulness/Day	Sleep/Night

MULTIPLE-CHOICE QUESTIONS

1. Carlos, a university student, is participating in a research study on dreaming. The researchers ask him to learn a complex sequence of motor tasks right before he goes to sleep. The tasks involve playing a series of notes on a piano, which he has never played before. The next morning, he is tested again on the piano sequence. What would the consolidation theory of dreaming predict about Carlos's performance on the piano sequence?

   (A) It will deteriorate.

   (B) It will be about the same.

   (C) It will improve.

   (D) It will be forgotten.

2. An office worker is concerned about constant sleepiness. Her doctor refers her to a sleep clinic, where they discover her sleep is interrupted by gasping for breath, waking up, and falling back to sleep dozens of times each night. With which of the following disorders would her doctor diagnose her?

   (A) Sleep paralysis

   (B) REM sleep behavior disorder

   (C) Sleep apnea

   (D) Night terrors

3. Nathaniel fell asleep about 90 minutes ago. What would Nathaniel likely experience at this point in his sleep?

   (A) Hypnagogic jerks

   (B) Stage 2 sleep

   (C) Stage 3 sleep

   (D) REM

Questions 4 and 5 refer to the following.

Rokheem, a college student, has been struggling to stay awake during his morning classes. The term has just started, and Rokheem is used to staying up late. He notices he feels most alert and awake during the evening and late at night, but he often feels groggy and tired during the early morning.

4. What phenomenon does Rokheem's grogginess reflect?

   (A) Insomnia

   (B) Sleep apnea

   (C) Circadian rhythm disruption

   (D) Sleep paralysis

5. What physiological process is primarily responsible for regulating Rokheem's sleep-wake cycle?

   (A) Serotonin production

   (B) Pineal gland activity

   (C) Glucose metabolism

   (D) Adrenaline release

6. As Kyra begins to awaken in the morning, she tries to move her legs to get out of bed but finds that she cannot move. This paralysis lasts only a few seconds before her motor abilities are fully restored. Kyra's experience is most closely linked to which of the following sleep stages?

   (A) NREM 1

   (B) NREM 2

   (C) NREM 3

   (D) REM

7. Studies on sleep deprivation have found an increase in accidents among workers who have six or fewer hours of sleep. Among individuals who sleep fewer than six hours, accidents skyrocket. What research method do these studies use?

   (A) Correlational

   (B) Naturalistic observation

   (C) Case study

   (D) Experiment

STUDY LIKE A CHAMP WITH DR. G.

Try to test yourself at least three times a week, including on topics you have already finished.

Topic 1.6

Sensation

"All our knowledge begins with the senses, proceeds then to the understanding, and ends with reason."

—Immanuel Kant

Essential Question: How do we process the information we receive from our environments?

Daniel Kish was barely a year old when he lost both of his eyes to retinal cancer. Yet, by developing a system of echolocation—the process bats use to "see" in the dark—now, as a grown man, he is able to detect the presence of a building 1,000 feet away, go mountain biking, and do many other things sighted people can do. He sends out sounds by clicking his tongue and then listens for echoes. Scientists who have studied his brain scans have found that even though he uses the sense of hearing to receive and draw information from the echoes, the part of the brain that is responsible for vision shows activity when he is using echolocation. Other studies confirm that the brain remodels itself after the loss of a sense. This topic will examine **sensation**, the process by which our brain and nervous system receive input from the environment through our five senses.

The Process of Sensation

Sensation is the initial step in the complex process of perception by which our sensory organs detect information from the environment and convert it into neural signals that the brain can interpret. This process, known as **transduction**, involves converting various forms of stimuli, such as light, sound, or pressure, into electrochemical messages that can be understood by the brain. As you have read, neurons communicate through these electrochemical messages. The **absolute threshold** represents the minimum intensity of a stimulus needed for our sensory systems to detect it reliably. It's like the faintest sound or the dimmest light that we can perceive. When a stimulus reaches this threshold, it triggers a response in our sensory receptors, initiating the process of sensation and ultimately leading to perception in the brain. The lower the absolute threshold, the sooner a person can detect a stimulus. Because young people generally have strong senses, they will be able to detect high-pitched sounds, faint smells, or distant objects better than older people.

Detecting Information from the Environment

Ernst Weber was a German physician whose study of sensation using strict experimental techniques brought scientific credibility to psychology in the mid-1800s. It also cemented his place as a founder in the field of *psychophysics*, the study of the relationship between external stimuli and our responses to those stimuli. In examining weights, he found that while we can detect differences between the weights of two items, we cannot determine the degree of difference. However, the greater the difference in the weights of the items, the easier it is to discriminate between them. For example, you would likely be able to notice a difference between an 8- and a 10-pound weight, but you would likely not be able to tell how much difference it was. You could, however, tell more easily the difference between a 4- and 10-pound weight. Weber looked for the smallest amount two stimuli had to differ for us to be able to tell them apart—the **difference threshold**, or the **just noticeable difference (JND)**. He found that to be perceived as different, two stimuli must differ by a constant percentage (rather than a constant amount). The amount of change needed to produce a constant JND is a constant proportion of the original stimulus intensity. Gustav Fechner, who was also studying the relationship between stimuli and sensation, called this finding **Weber's Law**.

Absolute thresholds are our lowest levels of awareness of faint stimuli with no competing stimuli present. In order to meet the threshold, the stimulus has to be detected at least 50 percent of the time. In vision, the absolute threshold is the equivalent of seeing a candle 30 miles away in a perfectly dark night—any farther than that and we see nothing. In hearing, it is the equivalent of registering a watch ticking 20 feet away (but not 20.5 feet). The absolute threshold for smell is the equivalent of a drop of perfume diffused in a three-room apartment; for taste, it is a teaspoon of sugar in a gallon of water. The level for touch is the equivalent of a wing of a fly dropped on your cheek from one centimeter.

To help differentiate between an absolute threshold and a difference threshold, determine if you are moving from detecting *no* stimulus to detecting *something*. If so, what you detect is the absolute threshold. If, on the other hand, you have already detected a stimulus and note that it is changing slightly (getting heavier or louder), this is the difference threshold.

Signal (or Stimulus) Detection Theory The **signal detection theory** is a way to measure how we discern a faint stimulus (signal) that conveys information and separate it from random background stimulation (noise). Because this concept relates to initially detecting a weak signal, it is associated with the absolute threshold. A key component of this process is separating the important information from the irrelevant information we are sensing all around us. This theory assumes that detection depends partly on a person's experience, expectations, motivation, and alertness. For example, a new parent will be much more sensitive than the average person to the stimulus of a baby's cry.

Sensory Adaptation People can also become less sensitive to a stimulus that is consistently present. For example, when you first walk into a room that has a candle burning, you may notice the smell, but after you have been in that room for a while, the smell will be less noticeable. If you leave and return, you will again notice the smell. Our sensory systems are set up to respond to change; this keeps us alert and often alive. **Sensory adaptation** occurs when sensory receptors respond less to unchanging stimuli. Another example of sensory adaptation would be feeling cold when you first jump into water but, after a time, no longer feeling cold because your body has adapted to the temperature.

Sensory habituation is a slightly different phenomenon and occurs in the brain rather than in the body's sensory receptors. Our perceptions of our senses depend on how focused we are on them. For example, you may no longer hear nearby traffic after living in an area for a time. Or, you may stop noticing the train going by since it no longer grabs your attention. You are shifting your attention away from the stimulus and onto something else. The stimuli haven't gone away, but your brain has determined that they are no longer a threat and do not need your attention. Consider this example: If you clap loudly when your pet is taking a nap, they will jump to attention. If you continue to clap loudly, though, they will realize that this loud noise is not a danger and may go back to sleep. However, the sensation you get from a stimulus can come back once you attend to it again.

Sensory Interaction As part of a holistic system, your senses almost always experience stimuli together. The sense of taste is heavily influenced by the sense of smell. Think of a time you had a bad cold and could hardly taste your food. Try holding your nose and closing your eyes while someone you trust feeds you various foods. You will have a hard time telling apples from raw potato. Steak is similar to a piece of cardboard. Cold coffee will seem the same as a sports drink. **Sensory interactions** reflect the way your brain assembles stimuli from different sensory systems to make sense of experience. For some people who have symptoms of long COVID, their inability to smell dramatically inhibits their ability to taste.

Synesthesia, which affects 2 to 4 percent of the population, is a condition in which the stimulation of one sensory pathway will automatically trigger the stimulation of another sensory pathway. That is, while experiencing a stimulus in one modality, such as sight, a person with synesthesia (a synesthete) will experience the stimulus in another modality as well, such as hearing. Smells and tastes can occur when a synesthete sees letters or numbers or hears words. Examples include: (1) seeing every number in a different color when viewing numbers that are actually printed only in black typeface; (2) seeing colors (hearing in color) or experiencing smells while hearing certain notes; and (3) experiencing a certain taste or scent when hearing voices.

Advertisers have used promotions calling for synesthesia. Skittles® uses the tagline, "Taste the rainbow." Pepsi® used "You've never seen a taste like this." Coca-Cola® had "Life tastes good." Authors often use cross-sense descriptions such as "bitter cold" and "loud colors" to intensify their points.

The Visual Sensory System

Many animals primarily use smell, sound, or touch to understand and evaluate their environments. Humans use these senses, too, but for sighted individuals, none as much as vision. For this reason, a very large part of our brain is devoted to processing visual inputs through the process of transduction, which transforms one form of energy into another. In the case of vision, transduction transforms electromagnetic light waves received by our sense of vision into electrochemical energy our brains can understand.

Visual Processing

Energy moves in waves in an *electromagnetic spectrum*, each type of energy having a different **wavelength**, the distance from one wave peak to the next. The **intensity** of a wave is the amount of its energy measured by amplitude or height. The visible region of the electromagnetic spectrum of energy is known as visible light. White light has a range of different wavelengths. When white light travels through a medium—air, water, or glass, for example—it is refracted (bent). The refraction separates the colors of light into their specific wavelengths. This is why, as a beam of white light passes through a glass prism (which refracts the light), the result is a rainbow of colors. The human eye has millions of **photoreceptor** (light receptor) cells that transduce light energy into electrochemical energy (nerve impulses). **Hue**, the color we experience, comes in the basic colors of red, green, or blue.

Compared to other animals, humans may be seen as having fairly limited vision. Figure 1.6.1 shows that the band of wavelengths we can see, called the *visible spectrum,* is small, whereas some other animals can see further up or down the spectrum. For example, some fish can see *infrared* (IR) light, which can help them navigate murky waters (infrared light waves travel well through mud and dirt). And cats, dogs, cattle, and many other animals can see *ultraviolet* (UV) light, an ability known as having *night vision*.

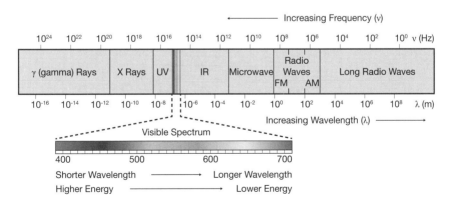

Figure 1.6.1 Visible Spectrum

Structure of the Eye Figure 1.6.2 shows the parts of the eye. Each has a different function in relation to processing light waves. The outer layer is the *cornea,* a transparent, convex structure that covers the front part of the eye. The shape of the cornea bends light toward the center of the eyeball. If you wear contacts, you place them on top of your cornea. The *iris,* or colored part of the eye, is a muscle that adjusts by opening and closing (dilating and constricting) in response to the brightness in the environment to let in more or less light. Think of a time when you walked outside on a bright, sunny day. Your iris constricts to limit the amount of light entering the eye. When you get up in the middle of the night, the iris contracts to allow all available light to activate the photoreceptors in your retina. The opening the iris creates is the *pupil,* the black part at the center of the eye. Light then passes through the *lens,* a transparent structure behind the pupil that is curved and flexible and changes its curvature to help focus images. The bending of the lens to focus information on the correct area of the retina is known as **accommodation**. Light waves then pass through a jellylike fluid called the *vitreous humor* before hitting the **retina**, the **photosensitive**—or light sensitive—surface at the back of the eye. Before passing through to the retina, the lens flips an image and focuses the inverted image.

Nearsightedness and farsightedness are refractive errors caused by the shape of the eye. In **nearsightedness,** the eyeball may be longer than normal or the cornea or lens too curved, making distant objects appear blurry. If you wear glasses or contact lenses, you are likely nearsighted.

In **farsightedness,** the eyeball may be shorter than normal or the cornea too flat. This variation causes light rays to focus behind the retina instead of directly on it, making close-up objects appear blurry. As people age, their lens often becomes less flexible, which means that visual images are not yet focused when they reach the retina. This condition often creates the need for reading glasses to see close images.

These conditions occur because of abnormalities in the shape of the eyeball or the curvature of the cornea, which lead to improper focusing of light onto the retina.

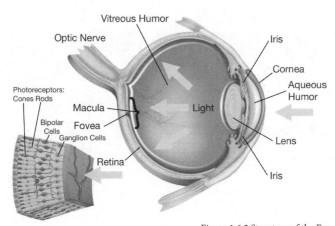

Figure 1.6.2 Structure of the Eye

The retina contains *photoreceptor cells* called rods and cones. The **rods** are photoreceptors that lie in the periphery of the eye and detect shapes and movements, but not color. Rods are activated in very dim light for night vision. It might seem strange, but you can actually see better at night in your peripheral vision because of the location of the rods on the sides or periphery of your fields of vision. Nocturnal animals such as possums and raccoons have rods that are far more sensitive, making their nighttime vision far superior to that of humans.

Dark Adaptation One feature our eyes possess is the ability to adapt to quickly darkening conditions such as when we go from daylight into a dark movie theater. This ability is called **dark adaptation**. In addition to the pupil opening quickly to allow for more light waves to enter the eye, this shift in available light creates increased retinal sensitivity in the rods. *Rhodopsin* is a light-sensitive pigment in the rods that helps the rods deal with low-light conditions. The eyes adapt similarly when going from a dark condition to one with more light. The chemical changes in the retina allow us to adapt quickly to changes in light as the pupil constricts.

The **cones** are photoreceptors that function only in bright light. Rods and cones are responsible for transforming (or *transducing*) electromagnetic energy into electrochemical energy that the brain can translate. There are more than 120 million rods and 5 million cones in each eye. They can be damaged easily from excessive exposure to light (e.g., staring at a solar eclipse or into the sun directly). Some people assume that we would have far more cones than rods but, because of the sensitivity of the cones, we need fewer of them than the less sensitive rods.

Cones are located primarily in and around the **fovea**, the central point of the retina which is found directly opposite the lens in the retina. Three types of cones—red, green, and blue—allow us to perceive all different colors of light. The brain is able to determine the wavelength by how active each of the color cones is. The more active, the more of that color is perceived. If a large enough number of rods and cones fire, then *bipolar cells* are activated. If enough bipolar cells are activated, ganglion cells, which meet at the back of the eye at an *optic disc*, fire and leave the eyeball at that point. Axons of the ganglion

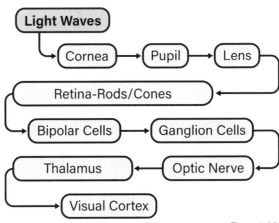

Visual Processing

Figure 1.6.3

cells comprise the **optic nerves** (the nerves that send signals from the eyes to the brain). Some of the fibers from each optic nerve cross into the opposite side of the brain (the thalamus) at the **optic chiasm**. From there, the signals travel to the occipital lobe, the primary visual cortex, and the visual association cortex.

Blind Spot The disc where the ganglion cells meet at the back of the eye is a hole in the retina where the visual nerve exits the eye. There are no photoreceptors there, and a **blind spot** is created in your field of vision. This "spot" is literally a place where you cannot see. As mentioned above, this is the point at which the optic nerve leaves the retina to carry messages to the brain. But the brain fills in the gaps in the incomplete retinal images to perceive a relatively complete picture of the world.

Figure 1.6.4

To see how the blind spot works, close your left eye and hold the page about 10 inches from your face as you focus your right eye directly on the plus sign in Figure 1.6.4 above. Slowly adjust the distance from your face until the emoji disappears. You can do the same experiment all around the circle of your blind spot.

Theories of Color Vision

We can perceive color only within the visible wavelengths of light, ranging from violet to red. There are two different, though complementary, theories explaining why this is so.

Trichromatic Theory The earliest theory about why we can see color only within the visible spectrum is called the trichromatic, or Young-Helmholtz, theory. The **trichromatic theory** explains a process that takes place within the eye. It hypothesizes that the three cone types in the retina, each producing only red, green, or blue, work together to let us perceive a range of colors. The colors that we see represent different wavelengths, with blue representing short wavelengths, green representing medium wavelengths, and red representing long wavelengths. Because these three colors represent the range of colors visible by the human eye, the combination of these three cones allows us to see the entire range of the color spectrum. Blue and red make purple, for example, and red and green make yellow. Black and white are produced by rods. When all three cones are equally active, we see white or gray.

Opponent-Process Theory Have you ever wondered why we can't see reddish green or bluish yellow? The second theory, **opponent-process theory**, answers this question by focusing on what happens in the brain rather than in the eye. It postulates three "systems" or opponent channels (red-or-green, blue-or-yellow, black-or-white). The theory states that light waves will excite one color in a pair (red, for example), which will then inhibit (prevent) the excitation in its opposing color (green). The black-white set are achromatic (or without color) and detect luminance (light-dark changes).

Both the trichromatic and opponent-process theory are correct—they just explain color vision on different levels.

Afterimages A phenomenon known as **afterimage** (a visual sensation that remains after the stimulus is removed) can be explained by the opponent-process theory. Staring at one color will fatigue the sensors for that color. If you were to stare long enough at an American-style flag with black and green stripes, a yellow upper left square, and black stars, and then look at a white page background, you would see a fuzzy American flag. This fuzzy perceived image is known as an afterimage, specifically, a negative afterimage. If you have ever worked with photography, you know that a negative is the opposite of the picture you have taken.

The phenomenon of afterimages can be explained in part by the activity of ganglion cells in the retina. When you stare at a colored stimulus, such as a red object, for an extended period, the ganglion cells sensitive to that color become fatigued or adapt to the constant stimulation. As a result, when you shift your gaze to a neutral background or a surface with a complementary color, such as green, the opponent ganglion cells that were inhibited by the red stimulus become more active. This increased activity relative to the surrounding cells creates the perception of a green afterimage until the cones for red can be replenished.

Similarly, if you stare at a green stimulus, the red-sensitive ganglion cells become fatigued, leading to increased activity in the green-sensitive ganglion cells when you look at a neutral background or a surface with a complementary color, such as red.

Color Vision Deficiency The inability to perceive color difference, or **color blindness**, is really a misrepresentation of the condition, because few people are born without any cones. This condition is caused by a lack of short-, medium-, or long-wavelength cones in the fovea. In **dichromatism**, only two types of cone cells function in the retina instead of the normal three. As a result, people with dichromatism are typically unable to distinguish between certain colors. The most common form of dichromatism is red-green color deficiency, which makes it hard to differentiate between red and green hues. This condition is more prevalent in males than females and can vary in severity.

Monochromatism, also known as *total color blindness*, is a rare condition in which an individual possesses only one type of functioning cone cell or lacks cone cells altogether. People with monochromatism typically see the world in shades of gray, as they lack the ability to perceive colors. Monochromatism can be further classified into two types: cone monochromatism, where only one type of cone cell functions, and rod monochromatism, where neither cone nor rod cells function properly, leading to extreme light sensitivity.

Both dichromatism and monochromatism result from genetic mutations affecting the cone cells in the retina, leading to deficiencies in color perception. These conditions can affect various aspects of daily life, including tasks that rely on color differentiation, such as driving, selecting clothing, and interpreting visual information accurately.

Brain Damage and Vision Disorders

Some people experience agnosia, a condition in which familiar objects become unrecognizable. One particularly dramatic form of agnosia is **prosopagnosia**, also known as **face blindness**. People with prosopagnosia can see faces—they can point out ears, eyes, mouth, and other facial parts—but they cannot identify the person whose face it is. In fact, when shown photos, they can't even recognize people they know very well. Brain scientist and author Oliver Sacks had prosopagnosia. Like many disorders, this is a spectrum disorder, with some people having some difficulty recognizing others and some not even able to recognize themselves.

Blindsight is a condition in which individuals who are blind because of damage to the visual cortex of the brain demonstrate some ability to respond to visual stimuli without consciously perceiving them. Despite being unable to consciously see objects or events in their visual field, people with blindsight may still exhibit certain visually guided behaviors, such as accurately reaching for objects or detecting movement. This ability suggests that some visual processing occurs in subcortical areas of the brain, bypassing the damaged visual cortex. Blindsight provides insight into the complex and multifaceted nature of human perception and consciousness, challenging traditional notions of how vision operates in the brain.

THINK AS A PSYCHOLOGIST

Calculate and Interpret Measures of Central Tendency, Variation, and Percentile Rank in a Given Data Set (3.B)

Five students participated in a psychology experiment investigating reaction times to visual stimuli. Each student was seated in front of a computer screen and instructed to press a button as quickly as possible whenever a specific visual cue appeared on the screen. The experiment was designed to measure the speed of processing visual information among the participants. The students were unaware of the exact purpose of the experiment to prevent any bias in their responses. After completing the task, the reaction times of each participant were recorded in milliseconds.

Data set: Reaction times (in milliseconds) of 5 students to visual stimuli.

{230, 250, 210, 260, 240}

Practice Calculating and Interpreting Measures of Central Tendency, Variation, and Percentile Rank

Answer the following questions.

1. What is the mean reaction time?
2. What is the median reaction time? Explain how you determined that.
3. What is the mode reaction time?
4. What is the range?
5. If a student has a reaction time of 255, which is one standard deviation below the mean, what is the percentile rank for this student?

The Auditory Sensory System

If a tree falls in the forest and there is no one around to hear it, does it make a sound? Take a moment and ponder that. Certainly, sound waves are created. But the answer depends on how we define the concept of sound. In psychology, in order for something to be a sound, it has to be perceived. So, if no one (or no animal) is around to hear it, a falling tree makes only waves, not sound. **Audition** is the biological process by which our ears process sound waves.

Using specialized brain and body parts, not only are we able to understand sound waves that move through the air, but we also can determine their original source and the source's direction, and we can understand and appreciate sophisticated combinations of sound such as language and music.

Sound waves are vibrations of molecules that travel through the air. They move much more slowly than light, which explains why you can see lightning but not hear the accompanying thunder until several seconds later. Sound waves are created by vibrating objects such as a plucked guitar string, vocal cords when air passes over them, or one object (e.g., a drum) that has been struck by another (e.g., a drum stick). Sound waves can also be created by forcing air through a chamber, such as a flute, or by releasing a burst of air, such as when air whooshes out of a popped balloon. These waves are characterized by their amplitude, and wavelength.

Amplitude affects the psychological quality of *loudness* (sound pressure or intensity)—how much pressure is being forced through the air. The intensity or power of sound is measured using a scale of *decibels* (dB). Decibels at 120 or higher can cause immediate damage to one's hearing, and one's eardrum will rupture at 150 dB. For each 10-decibel increase, the loudness increases by ten times; that is, 110 dB is ten times louder than 100 dB, and 100 dB is ten times louder than 90 dB.

The wavelength of sound waves affects the **pitch** (or note, A through G in various octaves). A sound's **frequency** is the number of wavelength cycles in a unit of time (i.e., the number of wavelengths per second). These are measured using hertz (Hz). Sound is perceivable by humans only in a range from 20

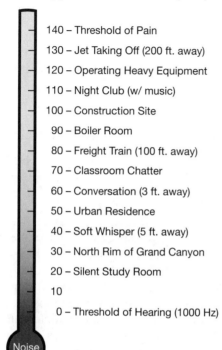

Typical Sound Levels (dBA)

140 – Threshold of Pain

130 – Jet Taking Off (200 ft. away)

120 – Operating Heavy Equipment

110 – Night Club (w/ music)

100 – Construction Site

90 – Boiler Room

80 – Freight Train (100 ft. away)

70 – Classroom Chatter

60 – Conversation (3 ft. away)

50 – Urban Residence

40 – Soft Whisper (5 ft. away)

30 – North Rim of Grand Canyon

20 – Silent Study Room

10

0 – Threshold of Hearing (1000 Hz)

Noise

Figure 1.6.5 Sound Levels

Hz to 20,000 Hz. One hertz is one vibration per second; 20 Hz is 20 vibrations per second. Toward each end of the spectrum, sound is more difficult for humans to detect, but some animals are able to hear in these ranges. For example, elephants are able to create *infrasound*, a low, rumbling sound humans cannot perceive. Some researchers assert that infrasound is associated with earthquakes, because the strange way some animals act before an earthquake would suggest they are detecting something that humans are not.

On the other end of the sound spectrum, some animals can hear high-frequency sounds that humans cannot. For example, dogs can hear a dog whistle, but humans cannot, and bats can use high-frequency sounds to navigate in the dark (this is called *echolocation*).

Beyond 20,000 Hz is the *ultrasound* range. Ultrasound machines use sound waves to determine tissue density and blood flow, and navies around the world determine the location of objects under the water using sonar (short for SOund Navigation And Ranging).

As with visual waves, sound waves go through a series of "steps" before they become neural impulses. The cone-shaped outer ear is called the pinna. It has a design that allows it to catch sound waves and direct them into the ear canal, also called the auditory canal. Next, the waves make the tympanic membrane (often called the eardrum) vibrate. This series of vibrations is called *conduction*. You may have noticed your older relatives and friends cupping their ear and turning it toward you in order to hear you better (to "catch" sound better). Many other animals have the ability to move their pinna in the direction of a sound.

Sound waves then travel to the middle ear where they vibrate the bones (*auditory ossicles*) of the ear. These typically unbreakable bones are called the *malleus* (hammer), the *incus* (anvil), and *stapes* (stirrup). These bones concentrate the vibrations of the eardrum on the cochlea's oval window, allowing information to enter the inner ear.

The inner ear begins where the stapes meets the oval window as part of the snail-shaped organ called the *cochlea* (pronounced "coke-lee-uh"). The inner surface of the cochlea (*basilar membrane*) resonates to different sounds in different locations. On the top of this membrane, along with dendrites of auditory nerve fibers, is the organ of Corti which contains *hair cells* (receptor cells). Transduction occurs when these hair cells convert vibrations into nerve impulses and send them to the auditory nerve.

From the auditory nerve, the new neural signals travel to the *thalamus* (sensory relay station) via the brain stem and then on to the temporal lobe's *auditory cortex*, where your brain perceives and makes sense of what you just heard.

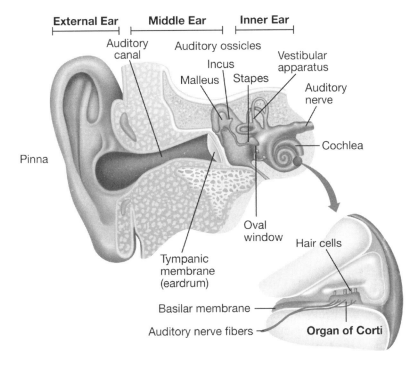

Figure 1.6.6 Ear Anatomy

Theories of Sound and Hearing

How do we hear certain pitches or tones? The first theory to describe this process was **place theory**, proposed by Hermann von Helmholtz. It says that higher and lower tones excite specific areas of the cochlea along the basilar membrane, each location (place) responding differently to different pitches. As sound waves enter the cochlea, higher-pitched sounds displace the fluid in the inner ear, making the stiffer *cilia*—the microscopic hairs on sensory cells—vibrate in the narrow beginning, whereas the lower frequency sound waves travel down the length of the cochlea and stimulate the softer cilia in the wider rear, or apex, of the cochlea. Older people often have a more difficult time hearing high-pitched noises because the cilia (hair cells) for high-pitched sounds have been damaged over time.

A second theory, **frequency theory**, suggests that as a pitch rises, the entire basilar membrane vibrates at that frequency, with nerve impulses that correspond with the frequency of the pitch traveling up the auditory nerve, enabling us to perceive pitch in a kind of frequency coding.

Researchers have determined that these two theories are similar to the trichromatic and opponent-processes of vision in that together they can be used to describe how pitch is perceived. Current conclusions show that pitch perception depends on both place *and* frequency coding. Frequency coding is used for sounds under 1000 Hz. For sounds between 1000 and 5000 Hz, a combination of frequency and place along the basilar membrane seems to work. And sounds over 5000 Hz appear to respond to the place along the basilar membrane.

A third theory is the volley theory. The **volley theory** of pitch perception is a hypothesis that explains how we perceive the pitch of sound waves with frequencies higher than 1000 Hz, which is the upper limit for the frequency following response observed in individual auditory neurons. According to the volley theory, groups of neurons in the auditory system fire in rapid succession to encode the frequency of these higher-pitched sound waves.

Rather than relying on individual neurons to fire at the exact frequency of the sound wave, groups of neurons work together in a coordinated manner, like a volleyball team working together. Each neuron fires at a slightly different phase of the sound wave, but together they produce a combined pattern of neural firing that corresponds to the frequency of the sound wave. This synchronized firing allows the auditory system to accurately perceive the pitch of higher-frequency sounds.

The volley theory highlights the importance of neural cooperation and time coding in pitch perception, particularly for frequencies beyond the range of individual neuron firing rates. While the volley theory provides a plausible explanation for how the auditory system processes higher-pitched sounds, it is just one of several theories proposed to explain pitch perception, and ongoing research continues to refine our understanding of this complex process.

Locating Sound

You are walking across campus and you hear someone call your name. It gets louder, but where is it coming from? Is the voice in front of you? Behind you? Off to one side? **Sound localization,** or determining where a sound originates, requires your ears to attend to two things. The first is loudness—the louder the sound, the more likely it is to be closer. The second concerns the timing of when each ear receives the sound. There will be a greater intensity of the sound in the ear closer to the source of the sound because it hears it first and therefore hears a slightly stronger signal. The brain puts all this together to determine the approximate or even exact source of the sound. We are pretty accurate in locating sounds except when they come from directly in front of us, directly behind us, or directly above us. In these cases, the timing and intensity are experienced as the same in each ear, leaving the brain without the detailed information needed to make the judgment about where the sound is originating.

Problems in Hearing

Conduction deafness is a condition in which there is a poor transfer of sounds from the tympanic membrane to the inner ear. Just as the lens in the eye ages, so do the bones in the middle ear. As a person ages, the vibrations need to be louder to activate the hammer, anvil, and stirrup to initiate those incoming vibrations to be transferred to the inner ear. Conduction deafness is common as people get older, but hearing aids can compensate for the loss.

Nerve deafness is caused by damage to hair cells or the auditory nerve. Hearing aids are ineffective in these cases since no auditory messages can reach the brain. However, people with nerve deafness can receive a *cochlear implant*. An "electrode array" is surgically placed within the cochlea of the affected ear, and an external device is placed behind the pinna to collect and process sounds and transmit the signals to the cochlear implant, which stimulates the auditory nerve. Small children whose hearing problems cannot be solved otherwise often receive cochlear implants.

Figure 1.6.7 Cochlear Implant

Sensorineural deafness is caused by damage to the inner ear (the cochlea or the hair cells), the auditory nerve, or auditory processing areas of the brain. The hair cells can be abnormal at birth, or infection or trauma can damage them, but once damaged, they are dead and can no longer function or be replaced.

Roughly 90 percent of sensorineural hearing loss is preventable. This kind of damage was once caused primarily by frequent exposure to excessively loud sounds—from rock concerts, airplane engines, and explosions, for example. However, hearing damage has increased significantly in the past few decades with the invention of earbuds-style headphones that channel intense sound directly down the auditory canal. Normal aging reduces the number of hair cells too. By age 65, 40 percent of hair cells are gone. Their loss leads to a reduction in the ability to perceive higher-pitched sounds.

THINK AS A PSYCHOLOGIST

Develop a Defensible Claim (4.A)

You read earlier about Daniel Kish, who lost his vision as an infant and developed echolocation to "see" with his ears. Like Kish, Ben Underwood lost his eyes to cancer early in life, but by age 5 he began "seeing" with echolocation as well. By the time his friends were riding their bikes and shooting baskets, so was he.

The brains of people without vision who have mastered echolocation, such as Underwood and Kish, hold a key to solving some of the mysteries of sensation and perception, because they demonstrate the ability of the brain to rewire itself and the ability of neurons to perform different functions. Neuroscientists call this ability *neuroplasticity.*

Many experiments have confirmed the hypothesis of *cross-modal recruitment*—the brain's recruitment of neurons associated with another sense after the loss of one sense. For example, temporary disruption of the visual cortex of blind, Braille-proficient subjects with transcranial magnetic stimulation (TMS) led to impaired Braille reading. In other words, when there was disruption to their *visual* cortex, these subjects felt the effects in their *tactile* sensation. Other studies showed that people who lost vision at an early age and had it restored much later demonstrated many difficulties in visual processing, suggesting that their visual processing neurons may have deteriorated after having been recruited to support another sense. PET (positron emission tomography) studies with profoundly deaf people who received a cochlear implant show that those whose auditory cortical areas showed a near-normal metabolism, suggesting they were actively recruited for another sense, had poorer speech performance outcomes because their brains were so well rewired in support of another sense.

Practice Developing a Defensible Claim

Complete the following activity.

Consider this scenario: At age 2, Ahmal lost his hearing after being too near a blast. Think about what is likely going on in Ahmal's brain to compensate for that loss. Develop a claim to address this question: As a teenager, how well might Ahmal respond to a cochlear implant or other rehabilitative efforts? Cite one piece of information from the paragraphs above that provides evidence for your claim.

Chemical Sensory Systems

Each of our other senses has its own specialized name. Smell is **olfaction**, or the olfactory sense. Taste is **gustation**, or the gustatory sense. Smell and taste work together and are known as the **chemical senses** (or *chemoreception*).

Smell

Smell is the most evocative of the senses. Smells can bring back long-forgotten memories of childhood or people—the smell of your grandmother's house when she was cooking holiday dinner or the smell of the cologne your father or grandfather wore. You can smell those again and be immediately transported back in time. So how does smell work?

Evocative aromas from a cookout can bring back memories of family times together.

Olfaction begins with receptors in the mucous membrane in the upper nasal cavity. Hundreds of different kinds of receptors may exist. Olfactory nerve fibers respond to gaseous molecules in a "lock and key" system. Each receptor can be triggered when a chemical "key" fits the "lock" of the receptor. Odors are related to the shape of the molecules that create the smells. Each nasal cavity has roughly five million receptors which then send nerve signals through the nerve fibers to the amygdala and then to the hippocampus (where emotions and memory are processed). Recall from earlier in the unit that the thalamus serves as the "post office" of the brain, but it does not process smell. Smell is processed in the olfactory bulb and may have served an evolutionary benefit of quick processing and great recall, helping us avoid and remember situations that might be dangerous.

Pheromones are airborne chemical signals that animals can perceive. You may have heard the word used in relation to animal mating. When dogs meet, they sniff each other, their hind quarters in particular. Male dogs typically know when a female dog is in heat (ready to mate) because of the pheromones her body gives off. The *vomeronasal organ* in the nose senses pheromones. Since humans have this as well, we are susceptible to the smell of pheromones.

Diane Ackerman, in *A Natural History of the Senses*, describes the tendency of ancient males to heavily scent themselves: "In a way, strong scents widened their presence, extended their territory . . . . mint for the arms, thyme for the knees, cinnamon, rose, or palm oil for the jaws and chest, almond oil for the hands and feet, and marjoram for the hair and eyebrows." That book contains hundreds of fascinating examples of people modifying their scents. Manufacturing the right scent is big business. Research departments at perfume and food companies work hard to determine what particular smells, and in what quantity and combination, will produce the best-selling products. And restaurants will often pump out smells in order to draw you in.

Our ability to smell peaks between ages thirty and fifty, and women tend to be able to smell more accurately than men at all ages. After fifty, our sense of smell declines, and we adjust how much perfume or cologne we wear as well as how much spice we put on our food, since our sense of taste decreases with age as well. Without smell, everything becomes bland, because much of what we experience as taste is actually the result of smell. Even Disney World pumps the smell of fresh baked goods onto Main Street to increase hunger, but when visitors go into the shops, they find all of the food is wrapped and prepackaged.

Taste

If you look closely at your tongue, you will see small bumps on the surface. These are called *papillae*, the taste receptors on the tongue. These receptors absorb the chemical molecules of what we eat and drink. The signals are then routed to the thalamus and then to the cortex. The more papillae we have, the more packed together they are, and the more chemicals that are absorbed, the more intense the taste. Our perception of taste quality appears to be connected to complex patterns of neurons firing.

Gustation, the sense of taste, has six sensations—**sweet, salty, sour, bitter, umami** (this is a brothy, meaty, savory flavor), and **oleogustus** (fatty). The last one has only recently been added to the range of taste sensations after experiments in which researchers found tasters could identify a unique fatty taste. However, it's not the creamy, rich taste often associated with high-fat foods. Instead, it is unpleasant and usually causes a gag reaction in tasters. Humans are most sensitive to bitter and least sensitive to sweet. Tastes serve specific survival functions. Sweet foods such as fruit provide a source of energy (glucose). Salty foods help us maintain the sodium that we need for our basic physiology (recall that proper brain function requires sodium). Sour helps us perceive a potentially toxic acid, while bitter alerts us to a potential poison. And umami (often found in foods with monosodium glutamate, or MSG) helps us identify food with proteins for growth and tissue repair.

Dr. Linda Bartoshuk has performed extensive research on **supertasters**, people with particularly dense papillae-filled tongues (which appear to be genetic). While non-supertasters may try a food and not have any idea of the levels of sweetness or bitterness in it, supertasters will be able to detect those levels. Supertasters are very picky about the amount of specific spices in their foods because they are much more sensitive to chemicals, like capsaicin in hot peppers. They can taste the smallest changes in flavor and may insist on modifying recipes because of them. Recall the earlier discussion of absolute and difference thresholds. Supertasters can identify an ingredient in a product (absolute threshold) and tell the difference between two cookies in the amount of added sugar. In his book *Outliers*, Malcolm Gladwell describes two women who had such a great sense of taste that they could identify the difference in taste of the same brand of cookies made in different factories. **Medium tasters** are neither overly sensitive nor insensitive to taste sensations. A medium taster may be able to discern subtle differences in taste but may not have the same level of acute sensitivity as a supertaster, nor the same level of tolerance as a nontaster. **Nontasters**, who make up about the same percentage as supertasters, like spicy foods and tend to crave sweets.

THINK AS A PSYCHOLOGIST

Interpret Quantitative or Qualitative Inferential Data from a Given Table, Graph, Chart, Figure, or Diagram (3.C) | Evaluate the Appropriate Use of Research Design Elements in Experimental Methodology (2.B)

In 2022, researchers published a study examining the association between taste and smell sensitivity, preference, and quality of life in healthy aging.[1] The scatterplots below show some of their findings.

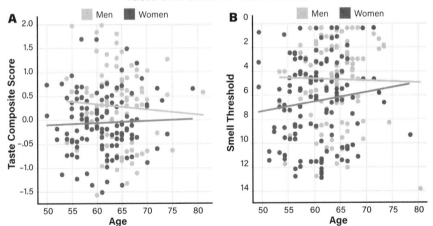

Scatterplot A shows the average of the separate taste tests given to each subject between the ages of 50 and 80. The lighter colored dots are women; the darker colored dots are men. Each dot is an individual's data point. Scatterplot B shows the smell thresholds of men and women in the same age group. Again, each dot is an individual's data point.

---

1   Lim, S. X. L., Höchenberger, R., Busch, N., Bergmann, M., & Ohla, K. (2022, March). Associations between taste and smell sensitivity, preference and quality of life in healthy aging—The NutriAct Family Study Examinations (NFSE) cohort. *Nutrients. 14*.(6), 1141. 10.3390/nu14061141. https://creativecommons.org/licenses/by/4.0/

Answer the following question.

1. Which of the following best explains the correlations shown in the scatterplots?

    (A) There is a positive correlation between aging and taste sensitivity.

    (B) There is a positive correlation between taste sensitivity and smell threshold in aging adults.

    (C) There is a negative correlation between both taste sensitivity and smell threshold and aging.

    (D) There is no significant correlation between either taste sensitivity or smell threshold and aging.

Practice Evaluating the Appropriate Use of Design Elements in Experimental Studies

Answer the following question.

2. The study authors got results that differed from those of most other researchers. What are two possible reasons, based on the research design, that might explain why their results differed?

The Body Senses

The body senses include touch, the vestibular (balance) system, and the kinesthetic (movement) system. The body senses collectively contribute to our ability to understand and interact with our environment. Each system provides crucial information that the brain integrates to form a cohesive understanding of bodily interactions and spatial orientation. This integration enables coordinated responses to external stimuli, helps maintain balance and posture, and ensures appropriate reactions to potential threats or injuries.

The Touch Sensory System

The senses of the skin allow us to feel light touch, pressure, pain, cold, and warmth. Inside the layers of the skin (the epidermis and dermis), there are several different kinds of cells that sense pressure. They are spread out and perceive constant pressure as force. Structures within the skin and brain process and/or transduce touch stimuli. The sensation of "hot" is produced by the activation of warm and cold receptors in the skin. Multiple receptors respond to fluctuations in temperatures. Signals received by the receptors are sent to the thalamus and then to the corresponding part of the somatosensory cortex at the front of the parietal lobe. The more receptors there are in a given body area, the more brain area there is devoted to it.

The Pain Sensory System

Despite being unpleasant to feel, pain can serve important functions. It can be a good warning system—it demands your attention, makes you focus, and communicates that damage may be occurring to your body. It can also be a good reminder that you have an injury, prompting you to treat an affected area of the body carefully or give it rest. The firing of smaller nerve fibers creates a slower, nagging, aching, widespread pain that serves this purpose.

The **gate-control theory of pain** posits that the more neurons fire in response to a pain stimulus, the more intense the pain. The theory also says that pain messages from different nerve fibers pass through the same neural "gate" in the spinal cord. If the gate is closed by one pain message, other messages may not be able to pass through. For instance, when scratching an itch, messages are stronger for the scratch than the itch, so the scratch messages get through, reducing the message of the itch.

Other factors also influence the degree to which we feel pain. Fear, high levels of anxiety, and memories of pain nearly always increase pain perception. If we expect high levels of pain with our upcoming root canal or wisdom teeth removal, we will likely experience more pain, both immediate and residual. Also, if people around us tend to be in pain, we might experience pain ourselves as we sympathize with others, a phenomenon that demonstrates a psychosocial influence on pain.

If you can learn to regulate a painful stimulus, you have control over it. One way to regulate pain is through distraction. Athletes often play on in a game even though they experience pain. Women in childbirth sometimes meditate or use deep breathing to distract themselves from labor pains. As you read earlier, pain is also influenced by neurotransmitters, with substance P helping to carry messages for pain to the brain and endorphins acting as natural opiates that temporarily reduce feelings of pain.

How you interpret pain stimuli can also affect pain levels. For example, after a strenuous workout, your muscles may feel tired and sore. At the same time, however, beta-endorphins may give you the upbeat feeling known as the runner's high. To which stimulus do you give the most importance? If you interpret your muscular pain as the result of life-affirming activity and focus on the feeling of well-being you experience, your pain levels are likely to go down.

Phantom limb pain is a phenomenon experienced by people who have undergone limb amputation or have lost a limb because of injury. Despite the absence of the limb, the person continues to perceive pain or other sensations originating from the missing body part. This pain can vary widely in intensity and character, ranging from mild discomfort to severe, debilitating sensations.

The exact cause of phantom limb pain is not fully understood, but it is believed to involve complex changes in the brain and nervous system. One theory suggests that after amputation, the brain continues to receive signals from nerves that used to supply the missing limb. These signals may be misinterpreted by the brain as pain, leading to the sensation of discomfort in the absent limb.

Additionally, alterations in the brain's sensory and motor cortex, which previously processed information from the amputated limb, may contribute to phantom limb pain. This reorganization of neural pathways can lead to abnormal sensations and pain perception.

Phantom limb pain can have a significant impact on quality of life, affecting the ability to perform daily activities and causing emotional distress. Treatment options for phantom limb pain include medications, physical therapy, nerve stimulation techniques, and psychological interventions aimed at addressing the emotional aspects of the condition.

Balance, Movement, and Our Bodies in Space

Balance is the **vestibular sense**, and movement is the **kinesthetic sense**. The vestibular system helps us sense our balance, gravity, and the acceleration of our heads. The sense of balance is located in the inner ear, which is sensitive to movement and acceleration. The *semicircular canals* are three fluid-filled tubes located adjacent to the cochlea and arranged at right angles to one another. Movement of the fluid within each gives the brain a sense of where we are in space and helps us keep our balance. To help you keep these concepts separate from one another, think of a yoga pose. In a pose known as "tree pose," you place your foot on your opposite knee and slowly raise your hands above your head in the shape of a V (vestibular). This pose takes much balance and is a great example of how keeping the head, and thus the inner ear, still aids in balance.

Kinesthesis is the body's ability to sense the position and movement of its own parts without relying on visual feedback. This sensory system provides information about the relative position of body parts and the effort required to move them, enabling coordinated movement and spatial awareness.

Imagine walking down a flight of stairs without looking at your feet. Kinesthesis allows you to sense the position of each step and adjust your movements accordingly, without the need to visually monitor the placement of each foot. Similarly, when reaching for an object, kinesthetic feedback informs you of the position and orientation of your arm and hand, guiding your movements to grasp the object accurately.

Kinesthetic receptors are located in muscles, tendons, and joints throughout the body. These receptors detect changes in muscle length, tension, and joint angles, sending signals to the brain to create a mental map of the body's position in space. This feedback loop helps coordination and smooth, fluid movements.

Without kinesthesis, activities like walking, running, and even simple tasks like typing on a keyboard would require constant visual attention, making movement less efficient and more cumbersome. By integrating kinesthetic feedback with visual and vestibular (balance) cues, the body can move with precision and grace, even in the absence of direct visual input.

THINK AS A PSYCHOLOGIST

Apply Psychological Perspectives, Theories, Concepts, and Research Findings to a Scenario (1.A)

Sometimes there is a mismatch between information from vision, the vestibular system, and kinesthesis. The *sensory conflict theory* proposes that motion sickness arises from a discrepancy between sensory information related to movement. When the information received by different sensory systems, such as the visual system and the vestibular system (inner ear), is contradictory, the brain becomes confused, leading to symptoms like nausea, dizziness, and disorientation. For example, when you spin and then stop your body, the fluid in the semicircular canals is still spinning, but your head is not. This mismatch leads to motion sickness. If you've ever watched dancers or skaters as they do pirouettes, you will notice they quickly move their heads to the same direction while their bodies play catch up. Their heads do not move at the same pace as their bodies in order to reduce the potential for motion sickness or dizziness.

Practice Applying Theories to Scenarios

Answer the following questions.

Imagine Deiondre sitting on a crowded subway train during rush hour, surrounded by the noise of the train's rumbling, the chatter of passengers, and the occasional screeching of brakes. As the train accelerates and decelerates rapidly, Deiondre begins to feel increasingly queasy and disoriented.

1. Why might Deiondre be experiencing motion sickness on the subway train, despite being surrounded by familiar urban surroundings?

    (A) Deiondre is feeling anxious about using public transportation, leading to psychosomatic symptoms of nausea.

    (B) The loud noises on the subway train are overwhelming Deiondre's auditory senses, causing nausea.

    (C) The rapid acceleration and deceleration of the subway train are disrupting Deiondre's inner ear balance system.

    (D) Deiondre is feeling claustrophobic due to the crowded conditions on the subway train, triggering symptoms of motion sickness.

2. Identify the theory that led you to your answer and explain how it applies to Deiondre's experience.

REFLECT ON THE ESSENTIAL QUESTION

Essential Question: *How do we process the information we receive from our environments?* Using the Key Terms, complete a chart like the one below to gather details to help answer that question.

General Process of Sensation	Thresholds	Theory	Adaptation and Interaction
Senses	How Stimuli Are Detected	How Stimuli Reach Brain	How Brain Interprets Stimuli
Vision			
Audition			
Olfaction			
Gustation			
Touch			
Vestibular Senses			
Kinesthesis			

KEY TERMS

DETECTION

absolute threshold
difference threshold
just noticeable difference (JND)

sensation
sensory adaptation
sensory interactions
signal detection theory

synesthesia
transduction
Weber's Law

VISION

accommodation
afterimage
blind spot
blindsight
color blindness
cones
dark adaptation
dichromatism

farsightedness
fovea
hue
intensity
monochromatism
nearsightedness
opponent-process theory
optic chiasm

optic nerve
photoreceptor
prosopagnosia (face blindness)
retina
rods
trichromatic theory
wavelength

HEARING

amplitude
audition
conduction deafness
frequency

frequency theory
nerve deafness
pitch
place theory

sensorineural deafness
sound localization
volley theory

CHEMICAL SENSES

bitter
chemical sense
gustation
medium taster
niontaster

oleogustus
olfaction
pheromone
salty
sour

supertaster
sweet
umami

BODY SENSES

gate-control theory of pain
kinesthesis

kinesthetic sense
phantom limb pain

vestibular sense

1. Tyler is looking at a piece of modern art that is entirely green and yellow. She stares at the piece for quite some time because she is intrigued by the design. When she looks away to the white walls of the art museum, she is surprised to find that she sees red and blue in the same design as the piece of art. Which of the following best accounts for this phenomenon?

   (A) Dichromatic color perception

   (B) Color detection by rods

   (C) The opponent-process theory

   (D) The trichromatic theory

2. Jason is 45 years old and has started to notice his vision is declining. He has more difficulty seeing close objects clearly and now needs reading glasses for small print. Which of the following likely accounts for this decline?

   (A) As you get older, the lens stiffens and accommodation becomes more difficult.

   (B) As you get older, the optic nerve frays, leading to partial blindness.

   (C) As you get older, the number of rods on the retina sharply decline.

   (D) As you get older, the muscles around the pupil atrophy, which leads to visual disruptions.

3. Jandy was born without the ability to detect sounds. For the first two years of her life she could not hear anything. What is the source of Jandy's condition?

   (A) Neurons firing in rapid succession

   (B) Conduction deafness

   (C) Replication of the sound in nerve impulses sent to the brain

   (D) Sensorineural deafness

Ibrahim, an avid cook, wanted to understand how different flavors and aromas influence the perception of a dish. He prepared four variations of a soup, each with a distinct combination of spices, to serve at a family gathering. Before serving, he explained that each soup highlighted a particular taste or smell to see if these changes would alter their experience of the meal. The family members noted their observations about the effect of each soup's flavor and aroma on their enjoyment.

4. Which part of the nervous system is primarily responsible for processing the flavors and aromas Ibrahim's family experienced during the tasting?

(A) The parasympathetic nervous system, since it integrates sensory information and contributes to flavor perception

(B) The autonomic nervous system, because it regulates involuntary actions that occur when tasting food

(C) The somatic nervous system, since it controls the movements involved in tasting and smelling

(D) The peripheral nervous system, specifically the sensory neurons involved in taste and smell

5. The ability of family members to detect the varied herbs and spices in each group most clearly relies on which of the following?

(A) Sensory adaptation

(B) Difference thresholds

(C) Absolute thresholds

(D) Synesthesia

6. Ibrahim takes the ages of his family members and compares their ability to identify the different tastes. He wants to plot the results to see how age might correlate with taste distinctions. Which should Ibrahim use to plot his data?

(A) Bar graph

(B) Histogram

(C) Scatterplot

(D) Frequency distribution

Your first unit is almost done. Congratulations! How did your plan work? Did you stick to studying on the days you planned to study? Planning is the first part of metacognition (thinking about thinking). Now is a good time to practice the two other parts.

The next step in metacognition is to **monitor** your learning. Do you remember the nature and nurture debate? What is the relationship between biological systems and mental processes? If your plan went well, you should have read the material and then tested yourself on it according to your plan. When you did, how confident did you feel about your answers? Ask yourself questions like these when you practice metacognition and try to take the pulse of your learning. Monitoring your confidence with the material—and how well your plan is working—is a good habit to get into, especially now when there are still four units to go.

Once you monitor your learning and your plan, **assess** your learning. If you have not already accounted for it in your plan, carve out time to complete the reflections on essential questions and multiple-choice questions at the end of each topic and the free-response questions in the unit review. Make sure time for assessing is part of your plan.

If your monitoring and assessment suggest your plan is not working well, change it immediately. Maybe you need to change *how* you plan. If you don't check an app on your phone very often, then consider switching to a paper calendar or a wall poster. If your plan to study at a certain time of the day or day of the week is consistently not working, change the time or days. Do not stick with a plan long after it is not working.

Plan. Monitor. Assess. This explicit focus on the PROCESS of studying can be critical to learning well.

UNIT 1: Review

MULTIPLE-CHOICE QUESTIONS

1. Seth and Anthony are identical twins who were raised in different households, but their personalities, intelligence scores, and temperaments are similar. However, Anthony is interested in math and science and is very outgoing, while Seth is interested in social studies and is more introverted. Which of the following conclusions can be drawn from this information?

   (A) Heredity sets limits on the influence of the environment.

   (B) Environmental factors have a greater impact than hereditary factors.

   (C) Heredity and environmental factors interact to influence behavior.

   (D) Behavioral traits are determined primarily by hereditary factors.

2. Huma has been assigned a project in which she has to describe each part of the nervous system and find a visual representation of each of its divisions. She is having trouble creating a visual depiction of the parasympathetic nervous system. Which of the following would be most accurate?

   (A) A person playing basketball to represent all the different voluntary movements involved

   (B) A person running away from a tiger to represent the fight-flight-or-freeze response

   (C) A parachute to represent gradually returning to a state of homeostasis

   (D) A brain to represent thinking and problem-solving

3. Huma did a great job on her nervous system presentation, and for her next project, her teacher has asked her to teach her classmates about neurotransmitters. Which of the following statements should she use to introduce the topic?

   (A) Neurotransmitters enter the axon during depolarization.

   (B) Neurotransmitters serve as the brain's main source of energy during neural firing.

   (C) Neurotransmitters are released into the synaptic gap to transmit signals between neurons.

   (D) Neurotransmitters physically connect neurons to allow for direct electrical conduction.

4. Hanan is a college student. After experiencing a head trauma, Hanan's vision is greatly disrupted. The damage Hanan experienced most likely occurred in which of the following lobes of the brain?

(A) Parietal lobes

(B) Hippocampus

(C) Occipital lobes

(D) Frontal lobes

5. Using the figure below on sleep stages, which of the following conclusions can you make?

(A) Sleep gets lighter as a person gets closer to the end of a night's sleep.

(B) REM occurs in a deep stage of sleep.

(C) Deep sleep does not occur until about 4 hours into the sleep cycle.

(D) Stage 2 of sleep is replaced by REM until the person wakes in the morning.

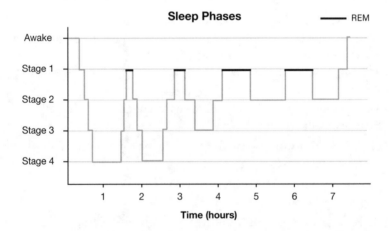

6. An hour after Dwight told his 13-year-old son to go to bed, Dwight thinks he might hear the faint sound of his son watching videos on his phone instead of getting to sleep. When he goes to check, he discovers he is right. Which psychological phenomenon explains Dwight's ability to hear this faint sound?

(A) The absolute threshold

(B) The just noticeable difference (JND)

(C) Sensory adaptation

(D) Habituation

7. Janice is creating an interactive exhibit of her art. She wants the patrons to see her paintings and sculptures under all different combinations of colored lights. She is currently working to place filters into the projector. Which distinct colors should she select?

(A) Red, blue, and yellow

(B) Yellow, blue, and green

(C) Red, blue, and green

(D) Yellow, green, and red

Questions 8 through 10 refer to the following.

Sua, a high school student, has been experiencing significant changes in sleep patterns due to the stress of upcoming exams. Lately, Sua notices a heightened sensitivity to light and sound around bedtime, making it difficult to fall asleep. This change in sleep has affected Sua's daily functions, including concentration and memory retention in class. Sua decides to seek help from a doctor. Her doctor wants to help more teens like Sua, so he asks her to participate in a small study with eight other teens experiencing similar symptoms. They go through a battery of tests, including brain scans, sleep and stress questionnaires, and one-on-one interviews to try to help determine the cause of their sleep disturbances.

8. What part of Sua's nervous system is directly involved in anticipating the stress of upcoming exams?

(A) The somatic nervous system, by controlling voluntary muscle movements

(B) The central nervous system, by processing the information and coordinating a response

(C) The sympathetic division of the autonomic nervous system, by preparing the body for a stress response

(D) The parasympathetic division of the autonomic nervous system, by calming the body down after stress

9. Because Sua's lack of sleep is caused by stress and the emotional issues surrounding her responsibilities, which of the following brain areas is likely to be active as she tries to go to sleep?

(A) Amygdala

(B) Thalamus

(C) Corpus callosum

(D) Cerebellum

10. Given the impact of Sua's changed sleep patterns on daily functioning, which part of the brain is most crucial in regulating sleep and wakefulness, potentially affected by stress?

(A) The amygdala, as it processes emotions that could affect sleep patterns

(B) The hypothalamus, which includes areas that regulate sleep and wake cycles

(C) The frontal lobes, responsible for critical thinking and planning that could keep Sua awake

(D) The cerebellum, involved in motor control and possibly affecting relaxation techniques before bed

Questions 11 and 12 refer to the following.

Researchers examined the relationship between participation in school music programs and academic performance among 1,000 middle school students. They analyzed how involvement in music classes such as band, orchestra, and choir aligned with grades in core subjects and standardized test scores. The hypothesis suggested that increased exposure to music education would be associated with higher academic performance.

11. What type of study did these researchers conduct?

(A) Experiment

(B) Cross-sectional study

(C) Correlational study

(D) Case study

12. Suppose the researchers in the study on music education were trying to convince schools to expand music education. They notice only things that support their position about music education while ignoring other factors that might affect academic achievement. Their behavior most clearly reflects which of the following biases?

(A) Hindsight bias

(B) Confirmation bias

(C) Social desirability bias

(D) Self-serving bias

13. Kirby had a massive seizure that affected his left frontal lobe. Which of the following is Kirby most likely to experience as a result of the seizure?

    (A) Kirby would lose his ability to produce speech.

    (B) Kirby would lose his ability to recognize the faces of his friends and family.

    (C) Kirby would lose the ability to process incoming sensory information.

    (D) Kirby would lose the ability to conduct smooth and coordinated movements.

14. Which brain scanning technique that traces electrical currents in the brain might Kirby's doctors have used to locate the area of his seizure?

    (A) fMRI

    (B) CT scan

    (C) MRI scan

    (D) EEG

15. Jazmine is trying out for the dance team. Her coach keeps telling her that she needs to hold her arms and hands in a particular position. Finally, the day before tryouts, Jazmine is able to do this without looking at her arms. Why is she able to do this?

    (A) The vestibular sense keeps her balanced.

    (B) Place theory grounds her in her environment.

    (C) Kinesthesis allows her to detect movement in her body.

    (D) A rush of pheromones gives her confidence.

QUESTION 1: ARTICLE ANALYSIS QUESTION (AAQ)

1. Your response to the question should be provided in six parts: A, B, C, D, E, and F. Write the response to each part of the question in complete sentences. Use appropriate psychological terminology in your response.

Using the source provided, respond to all parts of the question.

(A) Identify the research method used in the study.

(B) State the operational definition of the impact on rats' brains.

(C) Describe the meaning of the differences between the groups in the study.

(D) Identify at least one ethical guideline applied by the researchers.

(E) Explain the extent to which the research findings may or may not be generalizable, using specific and relevant evidence from the study.

(F) Explain how at least one of the research findings supports or refutes the researchers' hypothesis that an enriched environment would positively affect rats' brain functioning.

Introduction
The Rosenzweig et al. (1962) study investigated the effects of environmental enrichment or deprivation on the development of rats' brains. Previous research had suggested that environmental factors could influence brain structure and function, but this study sought to provide empirical evidence and further insights into these effects, with the belief that an enriched environment would increase brain functioning. The researchers hypothesized that rats raised in enriched environments would exhibit structural differences in their brains compared to those raised in deprived environments.

Participants
Thirty-six rats were selected from a larger population of laboratory rats. To reduce variability between subjects, the rats used in the study were young, healthy, and genetically similar. They were then randomly allocated to the different experimental groups (enriched, standard laboratory, and deprived environments). Twelve rats were allocated to each condition.

Method
The rats were housed in three different environments: enriched, standard laboratory, and deprived. Rats in the enriched environment were provided with toys, tunnels, and daily handling, while rats in the deprived environment were isolated with minimal stimulation. Rats in the standard laboratory environment served as a control group. The rats were raised in these environments from 10 weeks. The welfare of the animals was ensured throughout the experiment, with appropriate housing conditions and access to food and water. The researchers minimized stress and discomfort for the rats, adhering to ethical guidelines for animal research. Additionally, efforts were made to minimize the number of animals used and to maximize the scientific value obtained from each individual.

Results and Discussion
The researchers discovered significant differences in brain anatomy between the groups. Rats raised in enriched environments had thicker cerebral cortices, larger synapses, and more extensive dendritic branching compared to rats in standard or deprived environments. The sensory cortex was 5% heavier in the rats in the enriched environment (15.5 milligrams) than those in the isolated environment (14.8 milligrams). This suggested that environmental enrichment led to structural changes in the brain, particularly in regions associated with learning and memory. The study provided compelling evidence for the role of environmental stimulation in brain development. It suggested that an enriched environment could enhance cognitive abilities and promote neuroplasticity. These findings have had profound implications for various fields, including education, psychology, and neuroscience, highlighting the importance of providing stimulating environments for optimal brain development.
Reference
Rosenzweig, M. R., Bennett, E. L., & Diamond, M. C. (1962). Effects of environmental complexity and training on brain chemistry and anatomy: A replication and extension. *Journal of Comparative and Physiological Psychology*, *55*(4), 429–437.

QUESTION 2: EVIDENCE-BASED QUESTION (EBQ)

2. This question has three parts: Part A, Part B, and Part C. Use the source provided to answer all parts of the question.

   For Part B and Part C, you must cite the source that you used to answer the question. You can do this in two different ways:

   - Parenthetical Citation
     For example: " . . ." (Source A)

   - Embedded Citation
     For example: "According to Source A, . . ."

   Write the response to each part of the question in complete sentences. Use appropriate psychological terminology.

   Using the provided source, develop and justify an argument related to the degree to which genetic and environmental influences control the development of an individual.

   (A) Propose a specific and defensible claim based in psychological science that responds to the question.

   (B) (i) Support your claim using at least one piece of specific and relevant evidence from the provided source.

       (ii) Use a psychological perspective, theory or concept, or research finding learned in AP Psychology to explain how your evidence supports your claim.

Source A

Introduction
The Bouchard twin study spanned the years 1979–1990 to examine the nature-nurture debate in identical twins raised apart and then compared this group to those raised together. The study was conducted at the Minnesota Center for Twin and Adoptive Research. It highlights the limitations of earlier studies and the need for large-scale twin studies to address these limitations. The specific aims and hypotheses of the study deal with the investigation of the heritability of intelligence, personality traits, and other behavioral characteristics.

Participants
The study contained 100 sets of twins and triplets who were raised apart since childhood (average age of separation 5 months) who share 100% of their DNA. These were compared to dizygotic twins who share 50% of their DNA, the same shared with non-twin siblings. Participants came mainly from the United States and the United Kingdom. Snowball sampling was used to recruit twins for the study, with someone finding out about the research and passing on the information to other twins separated at birth. Some twins contacted the Minnesota Center for Twin and Adoptive Studies in order to find their twin. The average age was 41.

Method
The twins and triplets were rated on a number of measures, such as personality, temperament, occupation, leisure interests, and social attitudes. The tests took roughly 50 hours to complete. The results were triangulated. For example, three separate IQ tests were used to check for validity and reliability. Additionally, two different researchers conducted the tests to increase confidence in the results.

Results and Discussion
Bouchard and his colleagues found that similarities in twins raised apart were extremely high. Bouchard estimated that roughly 70% of the difference in identical twins raised apart was due to genetic similarities and the roughly 30% difference was due to environmental factors. This suggests that genetic factors may also influence the environment and that the factors examined had high levels of heritability. Some other researchers believe that the 70 percent similarities may not be entirely due to genetics. For example, since this study was also an adoption study, most twins and triplets were adopted into upper-middle-class homes in which the children would have been exposed to an enriched environment and would have likely experienced similar educational opportunities and access to extracurricular activities.

Source
Bouchard Jr, T. J., Lykken, D. T., McGue, M., Segal, N. L., & Tellegen, A. (1990). Sources of human psychological differences: The Minnesota study of twins reared apart. *Science, 250*(4978), 223–228.

UNIT 2: Cognition

Unit Overview

Have you ever thought about your thoughts? Did you ever wonder about how and why you remember some things and people, but other things just do not stick, no matter what strategies you try? This unit not only examines how memory works, but also provides some proven strategies to improve your memory for better performance in all your classes and success in later endeavors. It also examines cognition, the activity that occurs in our heads, directed by our brain, that allows us to identify, process, and interpret experiences. The philosopher René Descartes famously said, "I think, therefore I am," meaning, "I think, therefore I have self-awareness, so I must exist." The ability to solve problems, be aware of our own existence, anticipate possibilities, and even ponder our own mortality is the result of a complex series of intellectual activities that most other animals do not possess (as far as we know).

Cognition is the mental activity associated with thinking, knowing, remembering, and communicating. While that definition may seem simple, cognition is a deeply complex set of activities that allows us to interpret what we perceive through our senses, process new information, solve problems, create new ways of seeing things, and even think about thinking, which is known as *metacognition*. Cognition defines much of who we are and how we function as social animals.

LEARNING OBJECTIVES

- Explain how internal and external factors influence perception. (2.1.A)
- Explain how visual perceptual processes produce correct or incorrect interpretations of stimuli. (2.1.B)
- Explain how psychological concepts and theories account for thinking, problem-solving, judgment, and decision-making. (2.2.A)
- Explain how the types, structures, and processes of memory work. (2.3.A)
- Explain how different encoding processes work to get information into memory. (2.4.A)
- Explain how memory storage processes retain information in memory. (2.5.A)
- Explain how memory retrieval processes get information out of memory. (2.6.A)
- Explain possible reasons why memory failure or errors may occur. (2.7.A)

- Describe how modern and historical theories describe intelligence. (2.8.A)
- Explain how intelligence is measured. (2.8.B)
- Explain how systemic issues relate to the quantitative and qualitative uses of intelligence assessments. (2.8.C)
- Explain how academic achievement is measured and experienced as compared to intelligence. (2.8.D)

Source: AP® Psychology Course and Exam Description

STUDY LIKE A CHAMP WITH DR. G. | PRETESTING

You are in for a treat. This unit will introduce you to the wonders of the mind and reveal secrets of how we think. Correspondingly, you will get the backstory behind a lot of my study tips. In the front section of this program, I introduced our main challenge when we want to learn: We need to move information from sensory and short-term memory to long-term memory. Storing it in long-term memory (and storing it well) ensures that we remember it for days and years to come. You are more likely to do well on your exams, whether the AP exam for Psychology or any other exam, if you store material well. The material in Unit 1 gave you a sense of the biological bases of learning (your hippocampus and amygdala are key brain structures for that). Unit 2 will give you a sense of the cognitive bases of how we learn as you study memory and thinking. This means you are ready for the next key study trick.

So far, I hope you have been testing yourself often (retrieval practice) and spacing your studying (distributed practice). Now try this: pretesting. Pretesting involves quizzing yourself on material *before you have even studied it*. I will admit this sounds wild, but research shows it to be effective. If you test yourself on what you will soon be studying, your memory for it when you do study it improves. Cognitive science, the material in this unit, suggests the reason for this is that by pretesting, you help your brain develop an expectation of what is to come so when you read new material, you automatically organize it better. In many ways, by pretesting you are creating a framework or support structure that you then use for the new material.

Practically, this means that even before reading Unit 2, you should try to answer the questions at the ends of the topics or in the Unit 2 Review. This seems unheard of, I know, but trust the science and give it a try. The score you get does not matter. You can even test yourselves a few times, which may better prepare you to absorb the material when you read it or hear about the material in class. Try to work pretesting into your study schedule.

Topic 2.1

Perception

"There are things known and there are things unknown, and in between are the doors of perception."

—Aldous Huxley

Essential Question: How do internal and external factors influence perception?

In Unit 1, you read about how the body brings stimuli from the outside world into the brain through the senses. This chapter explores how the brain interprets and makes sense of those stimuli. A key aspect of our human experience, **perception** is the mental process of organizing sensory input into meaningful patterns. Estimates suggest that we process between one and ten million bits of information through our senses every second. We also compare this information to other information we have acquired in the past to allow for quicker processing and evaluation of the world around us.

Perceptual Systems

One set of systems takes external stimuli and converts the energy into neural messages the brain can understand. But our brains still need a way to reduce that huge amount of input into manageable bits. To help with that process, another set of systems selects, analyzes, and condenses information to form patterns or perceptions. These processes are not as straightforward as they may seem though, for what we *sense* is not always what we *perceive*.

Processing Incoming Information

If you looked at an unfamiliar object, what would you do first? Would you mentally search for a match with broad patterns from your experience before you discern the specifics of the object? Or would you start by looking at specific details and then piece them together to form an overall understanding of what you are seeing? Both are methods of filtering the sea of information in which our senses are always swimming.

Bottom-Up Processing One approach to information processing is called **bottom-up processing** because it starts by noticing individual elements and then zooms out to appreciate the whole picture. Inductive reasoning—an approach to logical thinking that begins with specific details or observations and forms broad perceptions or generalizations based on those observations—is an example of bottom-up processing. (See Practice 1.)

In contrast to top-down processing, which begins in the mind with previous knowledge, bottom-up processing begins with **external sensory information** and works up to mentally organizing them into a whole.

A good example of bottom-up processing is the way people with only rudimentary knowledge of a different language try to understand the meaning of a message. They will try to pick out words they understand and piece the overall message together to get a sense of what is being communicated.

Top-Down Processing Another approach to processing, as mentioned above, is **top-down processing.** This approach is guided by our thoughts and higher-level mental processes—we move from the general concept to the specific example. We use top-down processing when we create perceptions from our senses, drawing on our experience and **internal prior expectations**. When we use top-down processing, we look at the whole big picture, try to find patterns in it to make meaning, and then examine the details. We use background knowledge to fill gaps. Deductive reasoning—an approach to logical thinking that begins with a general idea, such as a hypothesis, and then develops specific evidence to support or refute it—is an example of top-down processing. (See Practice 1.)

You may have seen examples that demonstrate top-down processing on the Internet. Here is one that shows how our brains rely on experience and context for perceiving meaning in words:

Aoccdrnig to rscheearch, it deosn't mttaer in waht oredr the ltteers in a wrod are, the olny iprmoatnt tihng is taht the frist and lsat ltteers be at the rghit pclae. The rset can be a toatl mses and you can sitll raed it wouthit porbelm. Tihs is bcuseae the huamn mnid deos not raed ervey lteter by istlef, but the wrod as a wlohe.

Our top-down processing lets us bring past experience to bear on making meaning out of these words with mixed-up letters. Though reading this way is clearly a little more difficult than reading a regular passage, even a seven-year-old would be able to do it because they are still developing their reading skills and rely more on bottom-up processing.

Bottom-up and top-down processing work together. An example of what can happen when they don't work together is the case of a man named John who suffered a stroke and is unable to recognize faces (a condition called *prosopagnosia*). When he looks at himself in the mirror, he can see eyes, glasses, ears, nose, mouth, and jaw, but he has absolutely no idea who he is looking at. John's bottom-up processing allows him to see features, but because of the stroke, his brain can no longer provide the higher-level mental processing needed to achieve the perception of faces. He can see the pieces, but not the whole.

How We Perceive the World

Our experience of the world is shaped by internal models that are based on our prior experiences. These models, in turn, influence how our brains process information and how we interpret it.

Schemas The mental frameworks or structures that help us organize and interpret information about the world are called **schemas**. Schemas have a significant influence on our perceptual sets, and they vary from person to person as well as from one culture to another. For example, in some cultures, direct eye contact is seen as a sign of respect and attentiveness, while in others, it may be considered rude or confrontational. Misunderstandings can arise if individuals interpret behavior based on their own cultural schemas rather than understanding the cultural context of the other person.

Schemas help us organize and understand new information or experiences. Jean Piaget coined this term to explain how schemas build upon one another. If a child has a schema or understanding of his mother and father, he may begin to call all females he meets "mommy" and all males "daddy." Eventually, the child will come to understand that these schemas are not sufficient, and he needs new schemas for uncles, aunts, cousins, neighbors, and siblings. Connecting new information to pre-existing schemas also makes the new information easier to remember. When information is inconsistent with our schemas, we may dismiss or misremember this information because it does not adhere to our schemas or expectations.

Perceptual Set A top-down mental processing skill, **perceptual set**, refers to our disposition to perceive one aspect of a thing and not another, and it influences nearly everything we perceive. A perceptual set creates an expectation, and that expectation greatly influences how we experience a stimulus. For example, someone who is passionate about art may notice intricate patterns, colors, and compositions in everyday objects or scenes that others miss. Or a teenager listening to a song called "Heartbeat" may mishear the quickly sung lyric "Hear the beat, it's gone too far," as "Hear the beat of my guitar," expecting the song to fit the typical narrative of romance and use the metaphors of personal expression common to pop songs.

Context, Expectations, and Cultural Effects

Our tendency or bias to perceive some aspects of stimuli and ignore others can be influenced by our expectations, emotions, motivation, and culture. Our moods and circumstances can also create some top-down processing errors. For instance, have you ever been in a bad mood and thought someone disrespected you when, objectively, the person actually just said something neutral or even positive? How much is real, and how much is your emotional **context** affecting your perceptions?

Expectations also affect perception. If you have been told that a concert you are going to is in a bad neighborhood, if you feel unsafe or out of place when you get there, you may see other people looking at you strangely or threateningly. How much of what you are noticing is really people's response to your own appearance of feeling uncomfortable?

Cultural expectations affect perceptions as well. Not all cultures perceive the same stimuli in the same way. For example, a team of researchers from the Netherlands found that speakers of Persian, Turkish, and Zapotec (indigenous people of Mexico) do not perceive musical pitch as high or low as do English and Dutch speakers; they hear the different sounds as thin or thick.

Culture directs our attention, tells us what is important to notice and what is funny or offensive, and can even shape stereotypes. We change our perceptions to make the stimulus fit what we think it should be. Reality is not reality. Reality is what we think it is, regardless of the objective facts in front of us. Becoming more aware of this tendency can help double-check your perceptions to make sure you are not jumping to conclusions.

Gestalt Psychology

Understanding perceptual set helps us see how our minds are prepared to interpret sensory data in certain ways based on our prior beliefs and experiences. *Gestalt psychology* extends this understanding by exploring the fundamental rules that our minds use to organize sensory information.

Gestalt is a German word meaning "pattern" or "whole." Gestalt psychologists study the brain's tendency to integrate pieces of information into meaningful wholes. This perception, or interpretation, of the external world is done in predictable ways, and Gestalt psychologists describe several patterns through which we see the world.

Figure and Ground In **figure-and-ground perception,** the figure is what is focused on and the ground is the blurry background, which is likely ignored. As a demonstration, hold your finger out in front of you at eye level. Focus on it. Your finger is the figure. But now change your focus and look past your finger and focus on the other side of the room. That wall/bookcase/window becomes the figure as your finger becomes the ground.

Figure 2.1.1 The figure and ground are obvious in this photograph.

Figure 2.1.2 Reversible figure and ground

When you look at the image in Figure 2.1.2, however, the figure and ground are ambiguous. You might see the white vase as the figure and the black as the ground. Or maybe you see two facing profiles as the figure and the white as the ground. Viewers can see both images, but not at the same time. They need an attentional shift to go back and forth. This classic example of *ambiguous figures* is yet another way our brains can be fooled when examining our external reality.

Grouping Gestalt psychologists posited that our brains have a tendency to organize stimuli into groups, called **grouping**, in order to process the complexity of the world. Three types of grouping patterns demonstrated in Figure 2.1.3 are common to everyone.

Grouping

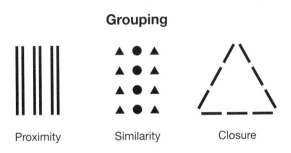

Figure 2.1.3

- **Proximity**—We see three sets of parallel lines rather than six unrelated lines because of the nearness, or proximity, of the pairs of lines.
- **Similarity**—We note two columns of triangles and a column of circles rather than three columns of shapes because we group similar items or items that share characteristics.

- **Closure**—We see a triangle rather than a series of broken lines in the form of what could be an unfinished triangle because we fill in the missing pieces to form a whole.

Using closure, our brains will envision things that are not even there. For example, what do you see in Figure 2.1.4? Do you see two triangles surrounded by three gray dots? Take away the dots, and the overlaying white triangle disappears. Your brain made that triangle. It does not exist outside of your brain. This is called an *illusory figure*.

Illusory Figure

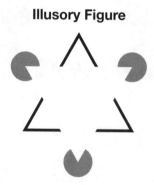

Figure 2.1.4

Attention

We cannot perceive all sensory stimuli at once, nor would we want to. We would drown in a sea of sensory stimuli, and nothing would make sense. The basic function of perception is to help make sense of our world. Toward this goal, our brains automatically pay attention to just one thing at a time. **Attention** is an interaction of sensation and perception affected by both internal and external processes. For example, when we pay attention, our brains (internal) must ignore all the other stimuli that are occurring at the same time (external). While we can perform some simple motor skills simultaneously (like the famous walking and chewing gum), for more cognitively complex tasks, we can focus on only one thing at a time. When people think they are multitasking, they are actually using divided attention—focusing on two or more tasks or stimuli. Some tasks, such as singing along with music while driving, are possible to perform with divided attention because one of them—in this case singing—does not require much thought. Both driving and singing rely on automatic processing. We don't need to focus our full conscious stream of attention on either.

However, our brains can focus well on only one thing at a time. We have an especially difficult time when the incoming stimuli are similar to one another. For example, try to read while someone is talking to you or the television is on. Even if you can get through a few pages, your reading speed and accuracy will be greatly reduced.

So, how does attention work? How much can we pay attention to at once? While our brains are processing upward of one million to ten million bits of information, we can consciously process only a few dozen at most.

Selective Attention With **selective attention**, we focus on one particular stimulus in our environment, such as a cat meowing, birds chirping, muscles tensing in our left leg, the pressure of our watch, or the sound of our own breathing. We can flit from stimulus to stimulus consciously while our brain processes everything else (filtering in relevant information and filtering out irrelevant information).

A classic example of selective attention is called the **cocktail party effect**. When talking at a party or someplace with a lot of background noise, like the school cafeteria, our attention can be drawn away from selectively attending to our own conversation if we hear our own name said by someone across the room. The stimulus of our name immediately demands our attention and produces the effect. This effect works because we have been "primed" to hear our name, having responded to it for many years. The cocktail party effect may even occur when you hear names that are similar to yours.

Another demonstration of factors that affect our ability to directly attend to (pay attention to) information is called the Stroop effect. When asked to read the words for colors printed in black ink, you can read them more quickly and with fewer errors than if they are presented in incongruent colors—that is, if the words *red*, *blue*, or *green* were presented in non-matching colors. Our brains recognize the color of the word first, which interferes with our ability to decode the word itself, and this interference pattern slows down our ability to read the word aloud. To correctly respond to each incongruent word, the brain has to compete between two automatic processes. It must suppress the easier perceptual process, which is identifying the word, in order to correctly identify the color of the word, which takes longer. This inhibition of the easier perceptual process requires selective attention.

Inattentional Blindness When our focus is directed at one visual stimulus (selective attention), leaving us blind to other stimuli, we are experiencing **inattentional blindness**. Classic research that demonstrates inattentional blindness involved showing subjects a film clip of a group of people tossing around a basketball. Subjects viewing the film were asked to count how many passes were made by the team wearing white shirts. The subjects' responses to this task were pretty accurate. But the film clip included other images as well—a woman with an umbrella and even someone in a gorilla suit. Few subjects noticed these. Their attention was fixed on counting the passes of players in white shirts, and they were blind to other stimuli. They selectively attended to only those people and demonstrated inattentional blindness to people in black, including the person in the gorilla suit. Magicians take advantage of inattentional blindness to successfully perform their magic tricks. For instance, because an arc movement of one's hand will distract a person's attention, magicians often use this maneuver to distract you from what the other hand is doing (e.g., picking your pocket or making something "disappear").

This is a screenshot from a video of the invisible gorilla experiment. You can see the whole video at www.dansimons.com. The citation for the published study is Simons, D. J., & Chabris, C. F. (1999). Gorillas in our midst: Sustained inattentional blindness for dynamic events. *Perception*, 28, 1059-1074. Figure provided by Daniel Simons.

Change Blindness One type of inattentional blindness, **change blindness**, is the inability to see changes in our environment when our attention is directed elsewhere. The TV series "Brain Games," which ran on National Geographic Television from 2011–2022, demonstrated this phenomenon multiple times. In one scenario, people were signing up at a desk to be on television. When one person went below the desk level to get a pen, a different person appeared back up with the pen. Few people noticed that it was a different person. Change blindness is slightly different from inattentional blindness because change blindness requires you to remember something. In the "Brain Games" example, it was necessary to remember what the original person looked like to identify the person popping up from the desk as different.

Visual Perceptual Processes

Visual perceptual processes involve how our eyes, the neural pathways that relay visual information to our brain, and the brain's own processing work together to help us understand the world around us. This process can lead to both accurate and inaccurate interpretations of what we see, depending on several factors. The combination of incoming sensory information, the basic processing of this data (bottom-up processing), the influence of our expectations and knowledge (top-down processing), how we organize what we see, our focus, and other mental factors all play a role in shaping our visual perceptions. Typically, accurate perceptions occur when we effectively process the sensory data, integrate the context and what we already know, and follow basic principles of perception. However, mistakes in what we perceive can happen due to illusions, biases, or distractions.

Depth Perception The ability to see the world in three dimensions and accurately judge the distance of objects is called **depth perception.** How, and at what point in life, do we gain depth perception? Researchers Eleanor Gibson and R. D. Walk conducted an experiment in 1960 to find out if depth perception is inborn. In their experiment, they created a *visual cliff*, a table with one half of the top appearing solid and the other half made of clear Plexiglas®. The meeting of the solid side with the clear side created the appearance of the drop-off of a cliff. Babies from six to fourteen months of age were placed on the "solid" side of the table, and their mothers stood at the other end of the table beyond the "drop-off," encouraging their babies to crawl toward them. The babies experienced increased heart rate moving over the perceived drop-off, indicating they perceived a difference in depth and potential danger.

Figure 2.1.5 The baby in this photo has to make a decision: Is there a drop-off, or is it safe to crawl forward?

Binocular Depth Cues With **binocular depth cues**, we use both of our eyes (*bi-* means two) together to judge depth and distance. One cue is **retinal disparity**—the difference between the images the eyes perceive because of their slightly different perspectives, or angles. The greater the disparity between what the eyes are taking in, the closer the stimulus is to us. A second cue, called **convergence**, is the merging of the retinal images by the brain. It is based on how far inward the eyes need to move when focusing on an object. To demonstrate, take an index finger and hold it as far away from your face as you can. Then slowly bring it closer to your nose. As it gets closer, your eyes begin to cross, or converge onto the same location. The more convergence the eyes must use, the closer the object is. If, on the other hand, you are looking at mountains far in the distance, you will notice very little convergence, and if you close one eye and then the other, the image will be nearly the same. This is a good example of a negative correlation—the less convergence, the more distant the object. (See Practice 3.)

Monocular Depth Cues If you were to lose the use of an eye, you would not lose all your depth perception because you would still have **monocular depth cues**, or depth perception cues that require only one eye. There are several types of monocular cues (five of these are demonstrated in Figure 2.1.6):

- **Linear perspective** is a depth cue that makes parallel lines appear to come together in the distance. The closer the lines are, the greater the apparent distance. As we are standing on railroad tracks while looking down the tracks into the distance, we can see this easily. The farther the distance, the closer the sides of the tracks appear to be. Because of Gestalt principles and linear perspective, we perceive that the point at which the black line leading to the mountains in Figure 2.1.6 is most narrow is the farthest away.

- **Interposition** is the partial blocking of one object by another object, leaving the viewer with the perspective that the blocking object is closer. If you see a chair blocking a complete view of a table, you know the chair is closer to you than the table. Interposition in Figure 2.1.6 leads us to believe that the female on the far left is in front of the man with the dog—closer to us—because her hand blocks his.

- **Relative size** is a depth cue that causes us to perceive something as farther away because it looks smaller than an object in the foreground that we assume is similar in size. In Figure 2.1.6, we perceive the people in the background as more distant, not smaller, than the man and the woman with the dog because of the relative size cue.

- **Relative clarity** is a cue that makes clear objects appear closer than blurry or fuzzy objects. The farther something is from us, the less detail it conveys. In Figure 2.1.6, the blurry female in the center left appears farther away and taller than the female next to her because of relative clarity cues.

- **Texture gradient** relies on the principle that the texture of surfaces appears to change as distance from the observer increases. Specifically, objects or surfaces that are closer to the viewer appear to have more detailed texture, while those that are farther away appear to have less detailed texture. Take a look at the floor nearest you. It will likely have some kind of texture—carpet fibers, wood patterns, or tile designs. The closer the object is, the clearer the gradient, or degree of detail. The farther away it is, the smoother and less detailed the texture becomes.

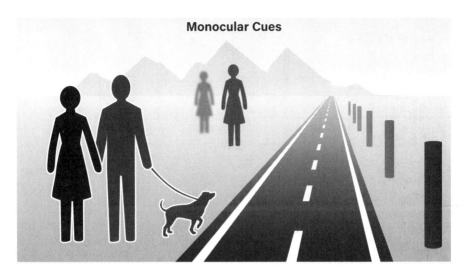

Monocular Cues

Figure 2.1.6 Monocular Cues and Gestalt Principles

Visual Perceptual Constancies

Perceptual constancy is our ability to perceive objects as unchanging even as changes may occur in point of view and illumination. Our brain makes adjustments and interpretations, without our awareness, to perceive the objects as remaining the same, because otherwise our world would not make sense.

Color constancy is the perception that the color of an object remains the same even if lighting conditions change. For example, a person can walk in and out of the shade on a sunny day. The light reflected from their clothing will change depending on whether they are in the sun or the shade, but our brain does not conclude that the color of the person or the person's clothes has changed.

Size constancy is the tendency for the brain to perceive objects as the same apparent size regardless of their distance from us. When someone walks away from us, the retinal image is shrinking, but we do not think the person is getting smaller. Our brains make this determination automatically. Our visual system infers the size of an object using cues from the image.

Shape constancy occurs when our viewing angle changes or an object rotates, and we still perceive the object as staying the same shape. For instance, if you look at a computer monitor straight on, it appears to be a rectangle that is wider than it is high. If looked at from the side, however, it appears to be a very thin rectangle much taller than it is wide. You know that the monitor has not changed the shape; you are just seeing it from a different angle.

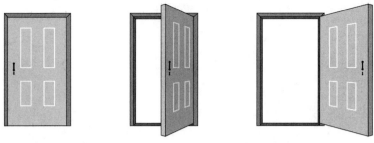

Figure 2.1.7 Because of shape constancy, you know that no matter what position the door is in, it is still the same shape.

Lightness constancy occurs when our perception of the whiteness, blackness, or grayness of objects remains constant, no matter how much the illumination has changed. We perceive lightness based on the intensity of light reflecting off an object. In other words, we see a constant *proportion* of lightness reflected rather than a total amount. Objects that look black reflect little light, and we will see them reflecting that same proportion of light whether they are outside in bright sunlight or inside in a dim room. White objects reflect the most light, and again we see the same proportion of light reflecting off of white despite varying lighting. A white rose appears white under both sunny skies and cloudy skies.

Apparent Movement

Apparent movement is the visual perception of movement when objects are not actually moving. The human visual system can process up to 10 to 12 images per second and still perceive the images as individual pictures.

The movement of a series of pictures at a rate that suggests motion is called *stroboscopic movement*. Motion pictures are a familiar example—old-fashioned film projectors displayed a series of still images at a rate of 24 frames per second. Digital "film" works at 29.95 frames per second, and Blu-ray machines project images at 60 frames per second. Our brains do not perceive these as still images but rather as movement on the screen.

The *phi phenomenon* allows us to perceive movement in stationary lights because of the pattern of their illumination. Picture a circle made up of eight lights. Only one light is lit at a time. Every time a light in the circle turns off, the light to the right of it turns on, all around the circle. That pattern of briefly lit lights will make it appear as if the lights are moving in a circle. You may have seen lights on signs spelling out words that appear to move across the sign. There is no actual movement—the lights are just blinking on and off according to a prearranged pattern.

THINK AS A PSYCHOLOGIST

Explain How Cultural Norms and Circumstances Apply to a Scenario (1.B)

Most people have seen the Müller-Lyer illusion (ML). In this illusion, two lines of equal length have arrowheads that go inward toward the middle of the line or arrowheads that go outward away from the line:

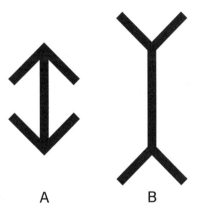

A   B

Most people perceive the center line in Figure B to be longer than the middle line in Figure A despite the fact that they are the same length. However, researchers found that some cultures in Africa and Australia do not see this illusion. Instead, they see the center lines to be equal in length. Researchers have wondered what about their cultures can explain this curious difference between their perception and ours.

One explanation is that the people who do not see the difference between the two lines come from cultures where their dwellings are huts made from fronds from trees, so people are not used to seeing angular connections.

Researchers[1] call these "carpentered" vs. "non-carpentered" cultures. We are in a carpentered culture, one in which the built environment is characterized by straight lines, right angles, and rectangular shapes, such as those commonly found in modern urban settings. As someone in a carpentered culture, if you were to look up at where two walls meet the ceiling, you would see lines that look like the lines in Figure B, whereas if you were to look at a square pillar, the lines formed where the sides meet the ceiling look like the lines in Figure A. In other words, Figure B looks like it is receding, whereas Figure A looks like it is jutting forward. For that reason, Figure B looks like it is farther away from you, which makes you perceive the line as longer.

Non-carpentered cultures are those in which the built environment and commonly seen objects lack the straight lines, right angles, and rectangular forms that are typical in more urban, industrialized settings. These cultures might feature more irregular, rounded, or organically shaped structures in their architecture and everyday objects. People in non-carpentered cultures may see the angled lines at both ends of lines A and B as nothing more than decorations and, therefore, have no distance cues that would make line B appear longer. Thus, even though basic experiences such as visual perception may seem like they are universal, culture can have a profound effect on these basic properties.

Practice Explaining How Cultural Norms Apply to a Scenario

Answer the following question.

Think about what life may be like in thickly forested jungle cultures. What is another possible reason people in those cultures may not learn visual cues that tell them if an object is close to them or farther away?

REFLECT ON THE ESSENTIAL QUESTION

Essential Question: *How do internal and external factors influence perception?*
Using the Key Terms, complete a chart like the one below to gather details to help answer that question.

Internal Factors	External Factors

---

1   Ahluwalia, A. (1978). An intra-cultural investigation of susceptibility to "perspective" and "non-perspective" spatial illusions. *British Journal of Psychology, 69*(2), 233–241.
    Segall, M. H., Campbell, D. T., & Herskovits, M. J. (1966). *The influence of culture on visual perception.* New York: Bobbs-Merrill.

MULTIPLE-CHOICE QUESTIONS

1. In this photograph, the flowers at the bottom of the frame in front of the lake appear in greater detail than the trees in the distance. This illustrates which monocular cue?

(A) Relative brightness

(B) Linear perspective

(C) Texture gradient

(D) Motion parallax

2. Kiley is an outfielder playing softball, and when a batter hits a ball to her, Kiley focuses her eyes on the approaching ball. As it gets closer, her eyes gradually turn inward, helping her judge how far the ball is away from her. This example demonstrates which of the following depth cues?

   (A) Texture gradient

   (B) Retinal disparity

   (C) Interposition

   (D) Convergence

3. As Ashley looks at the poster (depicted below) in the front of her psychology classroom, she initially sees only two faces looking at one another, while the white fades away. This poster illustrates which of the following Gestalt principles?

   (A) Figure and ground

   (B) Closure

   (C) Similarity

   (D) Proximity

4. When looking at the book in front of you, you probably perceive it as rectangular rather than trapezoidal, as it appears on your retina. This is due to which of the following?

   (A) Visual perceptual constancy

   (B) Selective attention

   (C) Retinal disparity

   (D) Proximity

5. Trisha was watching a scary movie while home alone. She heard a storm rattling the windows and interpreted that as the sound of an intruder trying to break in. What perceptual influence led her to make that interpretation?

(A) Apparent movement

(B) Gestalt principles

(C) Bottom-up processing

(D) Perceptual set

Questions 6 and 7 refer to the following.

Fifty university students participated in a study[2] and were exposed to ambiguous stimuli in different scenes. They were asked to identify the ambiguous object in the scene that they were given. For example, when viewed in a kitchen scene like the one below, the target object, a mailbox, was often interpreted as a loaf of bread, demonstrating consistency with the scene.

6. What perceptual issue is addressed by this study?

(A) The impact of selective attention on perception

(B) The impact of context effect on perception

(C) The impact of shape constancy on perception

(D) The impact of bottom-up processing on perception

7. If this study was run as an experiment, identify the independent variable.

(A) The different ambiguous stimuli presented

(B) The way in which the participant identified the ambiguous object

(C) The number of participants who identified the object as bread

(D) The scene that was presented

2   Palmer, S. E. (1975). The effects of contextual scenes on the identification of objects. *Memory & Cognition, 3*(5), 519–526.

Topic 2.2

Thinking, Problem-Solving, Judgments, and Decision-Making

"We cannot solve our problems with the same thinking we used when we created them."

—Albert Einstein

Essential Question: How do psychological concepts and theories account for thinking, problem-solving, judgment, and decision-making?

When we think about our thinking—whether we are acquiring information or thinking critically or creatively—we are using *metacognition,* the active control and awareness of our own thinking. Metacognition is a complex process during which we examine how we are thinking, the cognitive steps we take, the biases we may have, and our approach to learning a task. We may also use metacognition to test ourselves to see how much we learned, examine our choices, and figure out how to change our thinking in the future.

Concepts and Prototypes

One way in which we make sense of our environment and experiences is to form concepts. **Concepts** are mental groupings of similar objects, events, ideas, or people. The concept of "chair," for example, recognizes high chairs, recliners, dentists' chairs, classroom chairs, desk chairs, dining room chairs, and many other types of chairs as fitting the "chair" concept.

We are also able to form category hierarchies from concepts. For example, the field of psychology is one discipline within the overarching field of social sciences. You may recall from Unit 1 that psychology itself is an overarching discipline in which behavior can be viewed from a variety of perspectives and scientific approaches. That hierarchy, reflecting only a few of the perspectives, is represented in Figure 2.2.1. The expansion of concepts into hierarchies or subdivisions is an important element of learning. This structuring helps us to categorize and organize information, which also makes the information easier to retrieve.

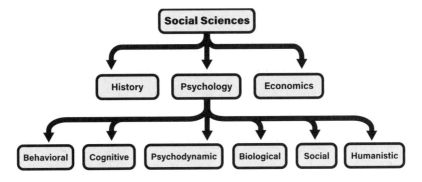

Figure 2.2.1 Category Hierarchy. There are many more social sciences and many more psychological perspectives than those represented in this category hierarchy.

Another tool we use for organizing and interpreting new information is the **prototype**, a mental image of the best example of a specific concept or category. The prototype contains the essential aspect of the concept. Matching new items to a prototype gives us a quick and easy method by which to sort items into categories. For example, if we encounter an unusual feathered creature, we may draw on our image of a prototypical bird, such as a robin, to categorize it. Our prototypical image of a dog might be the German shepherd, and we might compare all other similar creatures to the shepherd to see if there is a match.

The prototypes we hold in our minds are influenced by our social background, culture, and language. Together, these facets of our lives create a context and set of expectations that we apply to understand our world.

Critical Thinking

When we go beyond acquiring new information using concepts, prototypes, and other cognitive activities and develop opinions and beliefs about that information, we are engaging in **critical thinking**. Critical thinking means different things to different people. Psychologist Jane Halonen explains it as "[t]he propensity and skills to engage in activity with reflective skepticism focused on deciding what to believe or do." While people have differing definitions of critical thinking, they recognize common themes. One is skepticism, the unwillingness to blindly believe a claim just because someone says it is so. Critical thinkers question everything and everyone, including themselves. Psychology, like other disciplines that use the scientific method, has a "show me" or a "prove it to me" attitude, which leads practitioners to look beyond the conclusions to how the conclusions were reached, assessing claims and making objective judgments. Claims should be assessed based on evidence and strongly supported reasoning, not emotion, anecdotes, and stories. (See Practice 1, Skill 1.A.3 for deductive and inductive reasoning, key strategies in critical thinking.)

Forming and Modifying Schemas

As you learned earlier in this unit, a **schema** is a mental representation of a set of connected ideas. The mind uses schemas to make sense of the world and simplify it. The brain looks for patterns in the environment, whether they exist or not. When you look up at the clouds and see some shapes, your brain is working with your schemas to make sense of randomness. Your brain is trying to make sense of the world by finding patterns. Schemas provide a framework for thinking.

We form and modify schemas through assimilation and accommodation. We are always facing novel situations or experiencing new foods, new ideas, and new challenges. We try to adapt to place these novel experiences into our preexisting schemas. **Assimilation** allows us to make sense of new situations by relating them to prior experiences and their existing schemas without changing those schemas. For example, a person who has never seen a zebra may categorize it as a horse with stripes until he learns that it is actually a completely different type of animal. Another example of assimilation applies to academic learning. Students learn about a particular scientific concept in class and understand it within the context of their existing knowledge framework. When they encounter new information related to that concept, they are able to assimilate it into their existing understanding, refining and expanding their knowledge base.

Sometimes we must create new categories because our current classification is inadequate. This process is known as **accommodation**. To accommodate, we take in new information and change the schema to incorporate that new information. If a child sees the ocean for the first time and calls it a lake, she is assimilating prior experience. When she no longer makes this mistake and calls the body of water an ocean, she has accommodated by differentiating between situations and creating new categories. Children accommodate often as they learn language that helps them differentiate among objects. Similarly, as we grow older, we must accommodate changes in social roles and expectations. For example, transitioning from the role of a student to that of a professional requires accommodating new responsibilities, norms, and behaviors associated with the workplace environment.

We all have our own schemas about such characteristics as gender, appearance, and ethnicity; what we see when we are in love; our views as students or children; and our views as teachers or parents. These schemas are influenced by our assumptions, stereotypes, and expectations of how things should be and how we expect ourselves and others to act. Schemas can also act as mental filters by allowing some information to pass through, so we pay attention to it, or blocking other information from our awareness, so we ignore it. Schemas, then, influence what we remember and what we forget.

Executive Functions

While schemas help us quickly interpret vast amounts of data by fitting new experiences into preexisting categories, our brains need to adapt as our environments evolve and we encounter situations that don't neatly fit into these established schemas. This is where executive functions come into play. **Executive functions** are a set of cognitive processes that help us manage and coordinate our thoughts and actions and achieve goal-directed behavior. These functions include the ability to adapt to new situations, plan and organize activities, prioritize tasks, solve problems, control impulsive behaviors, and regulate emotions to achieve our goals. The prefrontal cortex of the brain plays a key role in these processes, which are vital for carrying out complex behaviors and engaging in thoughtful decision-making.

For example, executive functions are at work when a student plans their study schedule before exams, balancing studying with breaks and other commitments. They are also used when someone adapts their plans because of unexpected events, such as changing an essay's thesis statement in response to new information. Additionally, these functions help us think critically about the information we encounter, allowing us to solve problems effectively and make well-informed decisions.

Regular practice, targeted cognitive exercises, and strategies that enhance our awareness and control over our own thinking processes can improve these functions. Enhancing executive functions can lead to better performance in academic, professional, and personal settings, since they are integral to navigating the challenges and complexities of everyday life effectively.

Solving Problems

The way humans have used their thinking abilities to solve problems is the cornerstone of human progress and a key distinction between humans and other animals. Psychology focuses on three main kinds of **problem-solving**: trial and error, algorithms, and heuristics.

Trial and Error

The first method we use is typically trial and error, a process by which we try different solutions until we find one that works. This strategy works best when a problem has relatively few solutions. For example, if you are looking for one puzzle piece to fit a certain blank out of only four that remain, trial and error should be fairly quick. However, if you are trying to compute the best speed for a spacecraft reentering orbit, trial and error is impractical, since there are endless ways to compute the formula.

Algorithms

A second strategy is to use algorithms. An **algorithm** is a specific set of step-by-step instructions designed to perform a task or solve a problem. For example, if you wanted to know the sum of all the numbers from 1 to 100, you could add them one by one: 1+2=3; 3+3=6; 4+6=10, and so on. Eventually, you would get an accurate answer, assuming your math was correct, because you used the algorithm of adding one number to another and then adding that sum to the next number. A recipe is an example of an algorithm in everyday life. A recipe consists of a set of steps that can be followed by anyone. If you want to make lasagna, you will probably have more success if you follow a recipe than if you just use trial and error.

Heuristics

A third way to solve problems is to use **heuristics**, which are "rules of thumb." This simple thinking strategy often allows us to make judgments and solve problems efficiently. For example, if you usually agree with the positions of a political party and vote for candidates in that party without considering their individual positions, you are using a heuristic. When choosing a restaurant, you would be using a heuristic if you based your choice on which one had the most cars in its parking lot or the longest wait for a table, since those might suggest the restaurant is very popular. The strategy of using heuristics is usually speedier than using algorithms—imagine reviewing every single restaurant in your area before making a choice, as you would do with an algorithm. Heuristics allow the user to discard more options easily and use fewer data than algorithms, and they are often right.

However, in contrast to algorithms, heuristics may lead to incorrect outcomes. For example, one heuristic you might use when applying for jobs would be to avoid considering a job if the advertisement for it has spelling and grammar errors—those might suggest a sloppiness that could carry over to other parts of the company. While this supposition about the company might be true, it could also be true that it is a good company that just made a small error but would otherwise be a good match for you. You might miss a good opportunity with this heuristic.

A few kinds of heuristics can occasionally lead us astray in problem-solving in specific ways. One is the **representativeness heuristic**, with which we judge how closely something represents, or matches, our prototype for a given category. In research by Amos Tversky and Daniel Kahneman, the representativeness heuristic was illustrated with the following example. A former neighbor described Steve this way: "Steve is very shy and withdrawn, invariably helpful, but with little interest in people or in the world of reality. A meek and tidy soul, he has a need for order and structure, and a passion for detail." Is Steve more likely to be a farmer or a librarian? If you use the representativeness heuristic with Steve, his personality would more likely fit the stereotype of a librarian than a farmer. However, nothing in that description of Steve provides any career information. In fact, there are many more farmers than librarians, so there's a better chance that Steve is a farmer than a librarian.

Or how about a woman who wears glasses and loves to read? Is she more likely to be a teacher or a biker? That description fits our stereotype of a teacher, but there are only 3.1 million teachers in the United States and about 6 million bikers. The numbers suggest that despite our stereotypes, the woman is more likely to be a biker. The representativeness heuristic leads us to judgments that are based on how well people fit into our preconceived notions of groups to which they might belong. Our rule of thumb of how well people fit into our prototype misleads us into reaching the wrong conclusion.

Yet another example uses appearances to possibly mislead. When we look at a school with a trimmed lawn, painted and neat classrooms, and a polite and helpful office staff, do these appearances mean the school is well managed? Are appearances reflective of reality? If we conclude the school is well managed based on these outer signs, we are falling to the idea that these traits are connected to good schools. The reality is that some beautiful schools are terrible learning environments, and some schools are amazing despite less-than-ideal buildings.

Figure 2.2.2 A well-trimmed lawn and fresh paint do not make a reliable heuristic about school quality.

The **availability heuristic**, which estimates the likelihood of events based on their availability in memory, is another heuristic that can lead to incorrect assumptions or conclusions. If instances come readily to mind (perhaps because they are vivid or highly emotional), we presume such events are common. Two classic examples follow:

- Are there more words that begin with the letter *K* or more words with *K* as the third letter?
- Which is more dangerous, flying or driving?

We can easily and quickly think of many words that begin with the letter K (*koala, kind, kid, kangaroo, kitchen*), but words with *K* as the third letter are less easily available to our brains (*bake, cake, make*, for example). The same goes for the second question. The news and social media report plane crashes, but we rarely learn of all the traffic accidents that occur. Related examples of the availability heuristic include fear of planes because of a few highly publicized incidents that are easy to recall. Heuristics are usually right, but in some cases, we might reach wrong conclusions.

Problems in Problem-Solving

If we know how to solve problems, why we are often so bad at it? One reason is we might be out of practice in the necessary skills. When you were younger, for example, you no doubt had your multiplication facts memorized. Now, you might have to stop, think, and then respond, possibly even needing to reach for your phone or a calculator. Without using our problem-solving muscle—the brain—our skills diminish. Even if we are not out of practice, however, there are predictable ways we fail to solve problems. They involve succumbing to cognitive biases—ways of thinking that veer us away from strictly rational conclusions.

Confirmation bias is the tendency to search for information that supports our preconceptions and to ignore or dismiss contradictory evidence. Our confirmation bias is at work when we are in love and ignore all the negatives about our potential life-mate. It is at work when we see others through the filter of stereotypes and prejudice. It is at work when we allow information in that justifies or confirms our bias and ignore or reject information that counters our belief. For those conducting psychological research, confirmation bias is dangerous because the data, not preexisting ideas, should drive what we know about human behavior. The best researchers look for reasons they might be wrong before they accept that they are right.

THINK AS A PSYCHOLOGIST

Evaluate the Appropriate Use of Research Design Elements in Non-Experimental Methodologies (2.C.5) | Explain How Cultural Norms, Expectations, and Circumstances, as Well as Cognitive Biases Apply to Behavior and Mental Processes (1.B.2)

Researchers Daniel Kahneman and Amos Tversky conducted several studies to explore common tendencies that humans use in making decisions. As you have read, in one study, they asked participants the following question: "If a random word is taken from an English text, is it more likely that the word starts with a K, or that K is the third letter in that word?" The researchers found that, overwhelmingly, people believed that K was more likely to be the first letter of words in English. In reality, the letter K is two to three times more likely to appear as the third letter of English words. This study provided evidence that people often rely on the availability heuristic in their decision-making process.

Practice Evaluating Research Design Methods and Explaining Biases

Answer the following questions.

1. Based on the description above, did the researchers utilize a quantitative or qualitative instrument for measurement?

2. Upon learning about this research, a college student claims that this is an obvious finding that anyone could have easily predicted. This student's thinking most clearly demonstrates which of the following?

(A) Mental set

(B) Confirmation bias

(C) Hindsight bias

(D) Representativeness heuristic

Making Decisions

Problem-solving and **decision-making** are related. While you cannot solve a problem without making a decision, not every decision involves a problem. Every day we are faced with a myriad of decisions. Some of them, such as deciding what to wear or what to order for lunch, are trivial. Other decisions, such as choosing whom to date or deciding where to go to college, may have life-altering significance. Many factors go into the decision-making process. For example, intuition allows our experience with the world to work its way through our unconscious mind to assist us in decision-making. It can guide us in situations where we have limited information or when we need to make a quick decision. A number of cognitive biases influence the decision-making process. Being aware of these biases and actively challenging them can help us make more flexible, adaptive, and effective decisions.

Mental Set

A **mental set** is a tendency to approach decision-making in a particular way based on past experiences, habits, or previously successful strategies. It is a cognitive framework that guides how we perceive, interpret, and respond to various stimuli. Mental sets can influence the decision-making process in several ways: by directing our attention toward information that is consistent with existing beliefs or strategies while downplaying conflicting information, and by using decision-making heuristics to simplify complex problems. They can, however, create resistance to change by reinforcing familiar patterns of thinking and behavior so that we may be hesitant to consider new information or alternative perspectives. And they can both facilitate and inhibit creativity and flexibility in decision-making. For example, if your computer freezes and you rebooted the last time that happened, you would likely use the same tactic again, especially if it was successful.

Try this exercise: Create a formula to combine the amount in Jugs A and B to equal Jug C. Number 1 has an example to help you get started.

	Jug A	Jug B	Jug C	Formula
1	9	6	12	2(A)–B=C
2	7	3	11	
3	5	2	8	
4	2	2	4	

Table 2.2.1

The formula given to you in example 1 works to solve each of these problems, but you used a mental set if you continued the same formula for all four questions. In question 4, it would have been much more efficient to simply add 2+2 to arrive at the correct solution. Because the formula 2(A)–B=C worked for the earlier questions, many people will apply that for question 4 as well, without seeing the easier solution.

The Influence of Circumstances

Circumstances significantly shape decision-making since they provide the context within which choices are made. Priming and framing are two psychological mechanisms that further influence decision-making within these circumstances.

Priming The mechanism called **priming** involves exposing people to certain stimuli that unconsciously influence subsequent behavior or decisions. It works by activating associations in memory through words, images, or sensory stimuli just before a task or decision, shaping perceptions and behaviors in subtle yet significant ways. Because it operates at an implicit level, we may not be consciously aware of how the priming stimulus is influencing our decisions.

For example, if you are trying to choose between answers A and C on an exam, you might look at the board where, several weeks ago, your teacher had written the information you need to retrieve, and that act may help prime your memory and bring back the information. Smelling a perfume that your grandmother wore may prime emotional memories associated with your grandmother. If you smell that perfume on someone walking by, you might be primed to remember it's your sister's birthday and stop to pick up a card.

Framing The mechanism called **framing** exerts a similar kind of influence on decision-making and behavior. It is a cognitive bias in which the way information is worded (the "frame") influences how people perceive it and the decisions they make related to it. Essentially, framing involves presenting information in a way that emphasizes certain aspects or perspectives while downplaying or omitting others.

For example, imagine if a friend asked you to go skydiving. If they told you there was a 97 percent chance that everything would go smoothly, skydiving would sound pretty safe. However, if they told you 3 percent of skydivers' parachutes do not open, suddenly skydiving sounds far more dangerous.

Framing can also have significant implications for policy and political decisions. Politicians and policymakers often use framing techniques to shape public opinion and gain support for their policies or agendas. By framing issues in a certain way, they can influence how people perceive and respond to those issues. For example, some politicians might frame health care issues as a basic human right, whereas others might claim that government-provided health care is expanding the arm of government into the private sector.

Other Cognitive Biases

As you have read, biases can lead people to deviate from rational decision-making principles and make decisions that are not in their best interest. Recognizing these fallacies and understanding the underlying cognitive processes can help people limit their effects and make more informed decisions.

Gambler's Fallacy The **gambler's fallacy** is a cognitive bias that occurs when people believe that the outcomes of random events are influenced by previous outcomes, even when they are actually independent. In other words, people mistakenly believe that if a certain event hasn't occurred recently, it is more likely to occur in the future, or vice versa.

Consider a series of coin tosses. If a coin lands on heads five times in a row, someone succumbing to the gambler's fallacy might believe that the next toss is more likely to land on tails because "it's due." However, in reality, each toss of the coin is an independent event, and the probability of its landing on heads or tails remains the same for each toss (50-50), regardless of previous outcomes.

Gamblers often fall victim to the gambler's fallacy. For instance, if someone playing roulette sees the ball land on black several times in a row, they might incorrectly believe that red is "due" to come up next and, therefore, bet on red. However, as with the coin toss, each spin of the roulette wheel is independent, and the outcome is not influenced by previous spins. Recognizing and understanding the gambler's fallacy can help people make more rational decisions, particularly in situations involving chance or probability.

Sunk-Cost Fallacy The **sunk-cost fallacy** is a cognitive bias that occurs when people continue investing time, money, or effort into a project or endeavor because they have already invested significant resources, even when continuing to invest would not be rational based on the current circumstances. In other words, people are influenced by the sunk costs they have already incurred rather than an objective evaluation of the potential future costs and benefits.

For example, suppose someone has a great idea for a business to sell refilled ink cartridges for printers at a lower cost than new ones. This person invests a lot of money, gets a loan to cover production and distribution costs, and even invests their own money. Six months later, though, it becomes clear that the business will not succeed. Printers are being designed to reject refilled cartridges, so the market has dried up. Yet this startup owner has invested so much time, money, and energy that they are determined to succeed and continues to borrow money to find more cost-effective ways to deliver the product, hoping they will be able to get back all that they invested. This decision is driven by the sunk-cost fallacy: the person is prioritizing the sunk costs over the potential future costs and benefits.

The sunk-cost fallacy can lead to irrational decision-making and can result in a person continuing to invest resources into projects that are no longer viable or profitable. To avoid falling prey to the sunk-cost fallacy, people need to focus on the potential future costs and benefits objectively and to recognize that sunk costs should not influence decision-making.

THINK AS A PSYCHOLOGIST

Explain How Cognitive Biases Apply to Behavior and Mental Processes (Practice 1.B)

A schema, as you have read, is a mental set of related items, and heuristics are "rules of thumb" used to make judgments or assessments. Our experience tells us that heuristics are generally correct, but sometimes they can be wildly wrong.

Combining the concepts of schemas and heuristics can provide insight into stereotypes. For example, stereotypes can have an element of truth to them, but this "truth" is an average (or the "statistical mean"). Therefore, when we apply a heuristic to a schema, we are applying it to the statistical mean. While many people in a group are bunched up near the statistical mean, some are farther away from the mean. The application of a heuristic will be perceived as racially (or culturally or group) insensitive if it is applied to all people in the group.

Practice Explaining How Cognitive Biases Apply to Behavior and Mental Processes

Answer the following questions.

1. Think about the representativeness heuristic, a cognitive shortcut for making decisions or judgments based on how much a person or group resembles or is representative of the schema we have about a person or group. The extent of the similarity then affects how we make an assessment of the likelihood of a description being true. Take the case of a woman we will call "Susan." We learn that she is single and outspoken, took many women's studies courses in college, and engaged in many protests against injustice. If we were asked if it is more likely that Susan is a banker or a banker who is a feminist, what would we be likely to say? Explain your answer.

2. Now consider the availability heuristic, another mental shortcut by which we overestimate the occurrence, prominence, or importance of a person or event based on how easily something comes to mind. If it is more available, it must be more important, or so goes the fallacy. Suppose you are asked whether drug use is more common among minority teens who live in inner cities or among White teens in the suburbs. How might you answer, and how might the availability heuristic have influenced your answer?

Creativity

Cognitive biases lead us to conclusions based on flawed assumptions. While these biases can limit our perspective by funneling our thinking along predetermined paths, there's an interesting flip side to consider: the realm of creativity. By understanding and acknowledging our cognitive biases, we can consciously break away from them, using them as springboards rather than barriers to creative solutions.

Creativity is the ability to produce novel and valuable ideas within any discipline, including art, music, architecture, mathematics, science, and engineering. Any profession that involves solving problems or creating new ideas or new products relies on individual creativity.

This artwork of a fish stranded at low tide, made from pieces of plastic washed up out of the sea, uses sea garbage in a creative way to comment on the problem of ocean pollution.

What characteristics or components make up creativity? One is expertise—a strong base of knowledge about a topic or a high level of aptitude for certain skills. Another is high intelligence. Imaginative thinking skills and an ability to look at subjects from different perspectives can also contribute to creativity. While some visual artists are exceptionally good at reproducing pictures or images they see, others are able to create new representations of features, traits, or images to create an original work of art that has never before been imagined. An adventurous personality—one comfortable with change, ambiguity, and risk—may also contribute to creativity.

The most creative people are also known to have high levels of intrinsic motivation and to thrive in environments designed to spark, support, and refine creative ideas. Several companies in Silicon Valley (Google®, Apple®, and Pixar®, for example) have unusual workplaces in which the design and style of work is intended to foster creativity. Pixar, for example, provides a friendly and relaxed atmosphere, including a cereal bar with 14 kinds of cereals, other food and alcohol bars, the Smile Squad to help visitors find their way around, in-house aerobics classes, and improvisation classes. Workers are also encouraged to personalize their own workspaces, as well as to use the pool, play basketball and volleyball, and jog the trails. The company complex is open twenty-four hours a day, and employees can choose to work in whatever time period they prefer. Corporate culture supports the idea that mistakes are not only allowed but actually encouraged as part of the creative process.

Two kinds of thinking also influence creativity. **Convergent thinking**, in which a question invites only one correct answer, limits creativity. One example of convergent thinking is that which is required to answer a multiple-choice question, such as those on the AP test for this course. Each question is designed to have only one answer, which is known through reading comprehension and interpretation of data and concepts, with no creativity involved. Similarly, math questions have a single correct solution. A second kind of thinking is much more compatible with creativity. **Divergent thinking** is required when a question or problem can have several or many possible responses. A standard creativity question is, "How many uses can you think of for a brick (or paperclip)?" Even on weekends when you are bored, you may think divergently when you ask, "What should I do next?" because there may be many possibilities.

Psychologist Mihaly Csikszentmihalyi (pronounced "CHIK-sent-me-hi-ee") wrote the following about creativity:

> When we're creative, we feel we are living more fully than during the rest of life. The excitement of the artist at the easel or the scientist in the lab comes close to the ideal fulfillment we all hope to get from life, and so rarely do. Perhaps only sex, sports, music, and religious ecstasy—even when these experiences remain fleeting and leave no trace—provide a profound sense of being part of an entity greater than ourselves. But creativity also leaves an outcome that adds to the richness and complexity of the future.

Figure 2.2.4 Artists at their easels may feel the excitement and fulfillment of creativity.

Functional fixedness is a cognitive bias that limits a person's ability to see alternative uses for familiar objects or to think about problems in novel ways because they are fixated on the common use or function of those objects, as if they could have no other functions. The lack of creativity associated with functional fixedness can be an impediment to creativity. To avoid it, try thinking of other uses than the original use for objects. For example, the main use of a credit card is to pay for goods and services. But if you are locked in a room without a key, you could see a new function for a credit card and use it to slide the latch open. Or you could use a high-powered fan as a leaf blower or coffee mugs to hold office supplies. Breaking out of functional fixedness allows you to see objects in new and different ways and opens up a whole world of opportunities not bound by their most common uses.

REFLECT ON THE ESSENTIAL QUESTION

Essential Question: *How do psychological concepts and theories account for thinking, problem-solving, judgment, and decision-making?* Using the Key Terms, complete a chart like the one below to gather details to help answer that question.

Thinking	Problem-Solving	Judgment	Decision-Making

KEY TERMS

accommodation	decision-making	priming
algorithm	divergent thinking	problem-solving
assimilation	executive functions	prototype
availability heuristic	framing	representativeness
concept	functional fixedness	heuristic
convergent thinking	gambler's fallacy	schema
creativity	heuristics	sunk-cost fallacy
critical thinking	mental set	

1. Lonnie enjoys solving anagrams. Today's anagram is DFRIAA. She tries every letter combination and is able to successfully identify the word as *afraid*. Which problem-solving technique has Lonnie employed?

   (A) An availability heuristic

   (B) An algorithm

   (C) A prototype

   (D) Trial and error

2. Caroline works for an advertising firm, and her manager wants her team to use a divergent thinking approach to create a new ad campaign for a client. Which of the following should Caroline use with her team?

   (A) Focusing on ideas within a category of associated solutions

   (B) Devising as many solutions as possible

   (C) Arriving at a single, possible solution

   (D) Solving a problem with functional fixedness

3. Darian, a teenager, was given a new phone as a gift and thought the old phone should be recycled, not realizing that the old phone could be used as a music player to avoid taking up space with music on the new phone. Darian's inability to realize this possibility is likely due to which of the following?

   (A) Insight

   (B) Divergent thinking

   (C) Functional fixedness

   (D) Incubation

4. Caitlin is purchasing a gym membership that has a three-year minimum. The membership coordinator tells her there is an 85 percent likelihood that fees will not increase year-to-year. Which psychological concept best explains why he did not tell her there was a 15 percent likelihood that fees would increase?

   (A) Priming

   (B) Mental set

   (C) Framing

   (D) Sunk-cost fallacy

5. A teenager believes very strongly that a certain pro basketball player should not play on his favorite team. Over the course of the season, the teenager focuses on every mistake, turnover, and missed shot the player makes. However, the teen does not notice how well the player passes, helps the other teammates, and rebounds. This teenager's behavior illustrates which of the following?

(A) Confirmation bias

(B) The availability heuristic

(C) An algorithmic error

(D) Metacognition

Questions 6 through 8 refer to the following.

Researchers are interested in finding out if students who take more art classes demonstrate higher levels of creativity. The researchers are given permission to speak to 12th-grade students at two local high schools. They ask students to report the number of semesters of art class they have taken and then ask them to complete the Purdue Creativity Test, which provides ambiguous objects and asks students to come up with as many possible uses for each object in 2 minutes. Once the results are tabulated, they find that the more art classes a student took, the more uses for the objects they could identify.

6. What type of research has been conducted in this study?

(A) Case study

(B) Meta-analysis

(C) Experiment

(D) Correlational study

7. What conclusion can be drawn from this research?

(A) Students should take more art classes.

(B) Art classes cause increases in creativity.

(C) Students who take more art classes tend to be more creative.

(D) More research is needed to draw a conclusion.

8. What type of graph would be best to display this type of data?

(A) Bar graph

(B) Histogram

(C) Scatterplot

(D) Frequency polygon

Topic 2.3

Introduction to Memory

"A memory is what is left when something happens and does not completely unhappen."

—Edward de Bono

Essential Question: How do the types, structures, and processes of memory work?

What did you have for dinner yesterday? How about two weeks ago Wednesday? What did you wear three weeks ago Tuesday? Chances are you do not recall details much further in the past than a few days ago. Do you recall your first day of second grade? How about your first kiss? The first time you drove a car? The smell of bread baking or cookies at your grandmother's house? What about the time you were embarrassed by something a friend posted on social media? How accurate are those memories from childhood?

Those last ones you might remember better because we can often remember things that have emotional meaning for us. As we go through life, we begin to evaluate and assign importance to the ideas we encounter, the people we meet, and the things we do. Those things determined to be less important are more easily forgotten. But can you trust your memories? The events you recall—did they really happen? Or happen the way you remember them?

How Memory Works

For psychologists, **memory** has a specific meaning: It is learning that has continued over time. The general model of memory psychologists use, the information-processing model, is a three-step process:

- The first step is for the brain to receive information in a usable form in order to maintain it in consciousness or prepare it for storage in a process called **encoding**.
- The second step is the manipulation and rehearsal of information for **storage**.
- The final step is the **retrieval** of the information, recalling stored memories.

As you experience your daily world, your brain operates in parallel processing, interpreting numerous events and stimuli at the same time. As you are reading this passage, for example, you are seeing and interpreting the words on the page, but you may also be hearing household sounds around you or smelling your freshly bathed dog. To be able to understand everything, your brain runs all the information through its schemas in an effort to connect new information to older, established information. Making these connections consciously enables a person to improve memory and learning. You filter in the relevant information and filter out what you do not need.

The brain's ability to handle several different stimuli at once depends on **automatic processing**, information processing of much-repeated or well-learned activities that occurs without our awareness. For example, a basketball player at the free-throw line may have conscious attention focused on the basketball and the hoop. At the same time, however, the player's brain is automatically processing several other inputs without the player's awareness: the flexing of muscles to bend the knees and elbows, the force exerted on the ball, the motion of the arms and hands, the noise of the crowd, the distraction of fans waving behind the basket, and the sounds of the coaches yelling instructions to the other team. A brain deals with all that at once, even though attention is focused on one thing at a time.

Memories for learned knowledge, events, and experiences are differentiated by how they are processed by, stored in, and retrieved by the brain. Short-term memory (STM), as its name implies, holds small amounts of information for a short period of time. Long-term memory (LTM) can store information indefinitely.

Long-Term Memory

Long-term memory is divided into two types: explicit ("knowing that") and implicit ("knowing how").

Explicit Memory In contrast to automatic processing, **effortful processing** is encoding that requires attention and conscious effort. If you were asked to recall basic multiplication facts or what the main perspectives in psychology are, you would be using **explicit memory**, past knowledge that is consciously brought to mind. How did that information get into your brain? You did not learn it automatically but rather had to make an effort to learn it. You may have practiced your multiplication facts over and over again until you mastered them. Explicit memories are out in the open, recalled clearly in detail. They are the facts and experiences that we consciously know and can declare. We encode explicit memories through conscious, deliberate, effortful processing. Two types of explicit memory are episodic memory and semantic memory.

- **Episodic memories** are the stories of our lives and experiences that we can recall (like episodes of a television show) and tell to someone else. When people recount something that happened to them or someone else, they are using their episodic memories. There are many high school events, such as school dances or graduation, that will likely be lifelong episodic memories.

- **Semantic memories** are impersonal memories that are not drawn from personal experiences but rather from common, everyday kinds of knowledge, such as the names of colors, the names of the states, and other basic facts you learn over the course of your life. Take a minute to try to identify all of the countries in South America. If you learned the information at some point in a geography class, those items that you remember are semantic memories.

Figure 2.3.1 Episodic memory of a life event, such as a bat mitzvah

Figure 2.3.2 Semantic memory of math formulas

Implicit Memory Memories we retain without conscious effort and often without our awareness are **implicit memories**. Implicit memories are unconsciously retrieved. Your memories of how to do something, such as ride a bike, bake cookies, create code for a computer, tie your shoes, and all the other tasks you have learned, are known as **procedural memories**. It is likely that procedural memories were not always implicit but rather became so over time. For example, the first time you tried to ride a bike, it took much effort and concentration. If you have recently learned to drive, you may have experienced the same deep concentration when first learning. Procedural memories, when well practiced, become implicit, and even if you have not been on a bike or behind the wheel of a car for years, it will be easy to get back into the routine. Procedural memories are also unlikely to be affected by amnesia, since these types of memories are held primarily in the cerebellum. You may recall from Topic 1.4 that the cerebellum is responsible for balance and fine motor coordination, which underlies many procedural memories.

Figure 2.3.3 Procedural memory for riding a bike is unconsciously retrieved.

How do we retrieve implicit memories from our long-term memories? One way is *priming*, using cues to exploit the associative nature of memory to activate hidden memories. When we experience an event or learn something new, our brain forms connections between various elements of that experience. These connections create associations that link different pieces of information together. Priming works by presenting cues that are associated with specific memories or concepts, which in turn activate related information stored in long-term memory. Students will often use priming by quizzing each other verbally right before an exam to make sure all the ideas are reviewed.

Prospective Memory Most discussions of memory are related to experiences or information we learned in the past, but **prospective memory**

is a type of "memory of the future" with which one recalls or remembers to do something in the future. Examples include remembering to turn in a paper online for a class, remembering to take out the garbage before leaving, and, for high school seniors, remembering to fill out and submit college applications to their favorite schools before the deadline. At the end of each school day, you may be thinking of all the things you have to take care of that evening to be ready for the next day. This, too, is an example of prospective memory.

Long-Term Potentiation

As you may have expected, biology and the brain play a key role in memory formation, as well as in forgetting and amnesia. This biological role occurs at the level of both the neurons and the larger structures of the brain. At the neural level, a lasting strengthening of synapses between neurons that increases neurotransmissions is currently believed to be a biological basis for learning and memory. That lasting strength of synapses between neurons is called **long-term potentiation (LTP).**

The process of strengthening synapses can be improved by practice. Suppose you want to improve your tennis serve. If you practiced that serve repeatedly, you would be strengthening neural networks that would help this motion become a more intuitive action. In a similar way, you can improve cognitive skills with practice. Going over terms and relating them to your prior learning will strengthen neural networks and create long-term potentiation by physically changing pathways in your brain. Much of LTP occurs in the hippocampus, the brain structure most associated with emotion and the transfer of information from short-term memory into long-term explicit memory.

Most long-term memories are located in the cerebral cortex, but they are not all in the same location. Different parts of the cerebral cortex have smaller bits of information. For example, when we put "apple" into our brains, different aspects will go to different parts of the cortex. The shape, color, smell, texture, and memories associated with "apple" will all go to different parts of the brain. The part of the frontal lobe on the inside near the central fissure is thought to be involved in declarative and episodic memory. The amygdala is the primary processor of highly emotional memories.

Inside the cortex of the frontal lobe is a set of neurons called the basal ganglia, which play an important role in memory retrieval and procedural memory. The basal ganglia are key to creating and maintaining habits. Early research showed that when rats were working through a maze for the first time—sniffing, touching, and viewing each part of the maze—their brains were very active. After they were exposed to the maze hundreds and even thousands of times, their overall brain activity decreased, especially in the decision-making parts. The parts of the brain related to smell and touch were also far less active. The rats had internalized the maze with the basal ganglia, which were discovered to store habits by recalling patterns and acting on them. This internalization is known as a *cognitive map,* which you will learn more about in Unit 3.

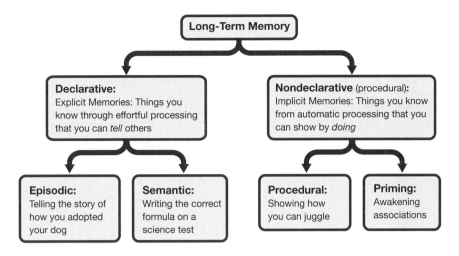

Figure 2.3.4 Types of Long-Term Memory

Short-Term and Working Memory

Short-term memory (STM) is a part of the memory system that holds small amounts of information for a short duration, typically a few seconds to a minute. It holds information long enough for immediate tasks, such as remembering someone's name after being introduced or following instructions. You might think of short-term memory as a "sticky note." Like a sticky note that you quickly jot information on for temporary use—a phone number or a grocery list item—short-term memory holds details briefly before they are either discarded or transferred to long-term memory. Sticky notes are handy for short reminders, but they aren't meant for long-term storage, just as short-term memory isn't designed for retaining information over extended periods.

Working memory refers to the part of short-term memory that is responsible for the temporary holding and processing of information. It is used to manage, manipulate, and act on information in the short term, enabling activities such as reasoning, learning, and comprehension. Working memory is crucial for tasks like problem-solving, maintaining attention, and following instructions. Instead of a sticky note, you might think of working memory as a "desk." Just as a desk allows you to keep essential documents and tools handy for immediate tasks, working memory holds information temporarily for quick access and use. You can think of it as a workspace where your brain organizes and processes information, making decisions, solving problems, and planning actions based on the materials spread out in front of you. Like a desk that can hold only so many papers before becoming cluttered and less efficient, working memory also has a limited capacity, beyond which it becomes harder to manage and use information effectively.

Several different theories or models have been developed to explain how information in short-term memory is transferred to long-term memory—or is forgotten.

Working Memory Model

The **working memory model** is a theoretical framework proposed by psychologists Alan Baddeley and Graham Hitch in 1974 to explain how short-term memory functions. The model proposes that short-term memory is a complex system with multiple components. This system temporarily stores and processes information while performing mental tasks. According to this model, short-term memory and working memory are closely related but distinct components of the memory system. While they both involve the temporary storage and manipulation of information, they serve different functions and have different characteristics.

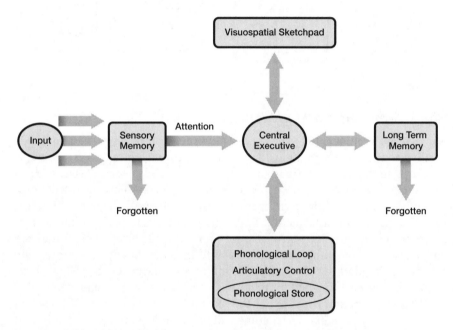

Figure 2.3.5 Working Memory Model

As you have read, short-term memory primarily serves as a temporary storage buffer for information that is currently being attended to or processed. Working memory goes a step further: It allows us to hold information in our mind while simultaneously performing mental operations on that information, such as categorization, comparison, or transformation. In 1956, George Miller found that the average person can only hold about 7 (plus or minus 2) items in working memory at a time.

The working memory model emphasizes the active nature of short-term memory, with information being constantly processed and manipulated to support ongoing cognitive tasks. It has been influential in understanding various cognitive processes, such as problem-solving, decision-making, and language comprehension.

The working memory model consists of several components:

- The **central executive** is the main component of working memory, responsible for coordinating cognitive processes. It allocates attention to different tasks, decides which information to focus on, and integrates information from the other components. It doesn't store information itself but controls attention and coordinates the activities of the other subsystems. It determines, for example, whether incoming information is auditory or visual and then sends it on to the proper system.

- The **phonological loop** deals with auditory and verbal information. It consists of two subcomponents, the phonological store (or inner ear), which holds auditory information in a speech-based form for a brief period (2 seconds or so), and the articulatory control process (or inner voice), which is involved in the rehearsal of verbal information, helping to refresh and maintain it in the phonological store.

- The **visuospatial sketchpad** is responsible for processing visual and spatial information. It is involved in tasks such as mental imagery, spatial reasoning, and navigation.

- The **episodic buffer** is a temporary storage system that integrates information from the phonological loop, visuospatial sketchpad, and long-term memory into a single representation. It acts as a backup store and provides a temporary workspace for holding and manipulating information from multiple sources.

Transferring to Long-Term Memory To transfer information from working memory to long-term memory, active rehearsal and elaboration techniques are often employed. *Rehearsal* involves repeatedly exposing oneself to the information, which strengthens connections between neurons associated with that information. *Elaboration* involves making connections between new information and existing knowledge, thereby facilitating its integration into long-term memory. Making personal connections helps connect new information with the information already held in long-term memory. When needed, the stored information can be retrieved from long-term memory and brought back into working memory for use. *Retrieval* involves reconstructing the stored memory based on cues or prompts from the environment.

Memory processes are highly complex and still not fully understood. The transition from working memory to long-term memory involves interactions among various cognitive and neural processes, and can be influenced by factors such as attention, motivation, emotional significance, and individual differences in cognitive abilities.

The Multi-Store Model

The currently accepted model of memory, originally theorized by psychologists Richard Atkinson and Richard Shiffrin, is known as the **multi-store model**. Its three stages are clearly delineated: sensory memory, short-term memory, and long-term memory.

Sensory Memory The first stage of their multi-store model is **sensory memory** (sensory register), during which we process everything we sense—an activity that takes less than a second to several seconds. Fleeting visual images in sensory memory are called **iconic memory**, and auditory signals are called **echoic memory**. This information will leave our brains unless we attend, or pay attention, to it (more on the issue of attention later). You will not remember the thousands of pieces of clothing people were wearing in the hall at school today or the hundreds of conversations you heard. Unless you immediately attend to these pieces of information, they will be gone in a few seconds and never transferred to long-term memory. If we do not attend to the information, it is lost. If you have ever wondered what your instructions are in class, even though the teacher just explained them, you know that when you don't pay attention, you don't remember.

Short-Term Memory (STM) Once information is attended to, it can be moved into the next stage—short-term memory. In the Atkinson and Shiffrin model, small amounts of information are stored for up to thirty seconds or so in short-term memory. A newer understanding of STM, however, focuses on the conscious, active processing of auditory as well as visual-spatial information along with information retrieved from long-term memory. This stage of the memory process is a kind of mental "scratch pad." Short-term memory is very sensitive and vulnerable to interruption or interference. If you are ordering pizza with some friends and are interrupted while dialing the number, it is unlikely that you will still recall the number after the interruption.

Long-term memory (LTM) is the final stage and the type of memory that can store information indefinitely, often based on its relative importance to the individual. To make it to LTM, stimuli must be encoded. Encoding is taking stimuli from the environment and converting them into a form or construct that the brain can understand and use. This conversion takes place by comparing new information to information previously learned. If the stimuli are not encoded, they will be forgotten. Once memories make it to long-term memory, they can potentially remain for a lifetime.

Human memory works very differently from the memory on your computer hard drive, which can reach capacity. We do not know of any upper-level capacity for long-term memory. People can continue to add new neural networks and new memories throughout their lives.

Figure 2.3.6 represents the stages in the process of moving stimuli into memory or forgetting them. If they are not attended to, they do not make it to short-term memory. If they are not encoded, they do not make it to long-term memory. The key to getting information into LTM is the coding for storage, or rehearsing the information enough so that it sticks.

Spend a few minutes looking at this diagram. Let's say you are trying to remember five people's names in your science class. Go through the model step by step to identify what would help or hinder you from getting this information into long-term memory and potentially retrieving it should you work in a group with one of them later in the semester.

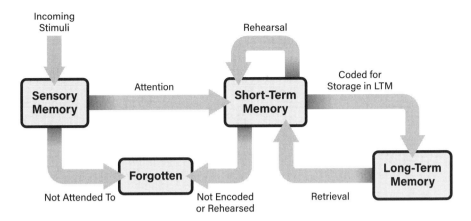

Figure 2.3.6 Memory Processes

The Levels of Processing Model

While short-term memory holds only limited amounts of information for up to 30 seconds, long-term memory can hold an unlimited amount of information for an unlimited amount of time. Critics of the multi-store model, however, say there are more factors involved in creating long-term memories than the model describes. One critique focuses on different levels of processing and their effect on moving information into LTM. When we simply try to memorize something without attaching meaning to it, we use **shallow processing** (trying to learn ideas on a superficial level, only memorizing) and tend to forget the ideas quickly. In contrast, elaborative rehearsal, linking new information with existing memories and knowledge in LTM, is a good way to transfer information from STM to LTM. When we make new information meaningful to ourselves, we remember it more effectively.

The **levels of processing model** suggests that the depth of processing affects the encoding and subsequent retrieval of information. According to this model, there are three main levels of processing.

- **Structural Encoding**: At the structural level, processing involves encoding the physical characteristics of stimuli, such as their appearance, shape, or sound. This level of processing focuses on superficial features of the stimulus without considering its meaning. For example, when presented with a word, structural encoding involves processing the visual appearance of its letters and their arrangement without considering its meaning. Structural encoding typically leads to shallow processing because it involves only surface-level analysis of the stimulus.

- **Phonemic Encoding**: Phonemic encoding involves processing the sound or pronunciation of a stimulus, such as a word or a phrase. At this level, we may focus on the phonological characteristics of the stimulus, such as its rhyming pattern, syllable structure, or phonetic components. For example, when presented with a word, phonemic encoding involves considering its sound and how it relates to other words with similar phonetic properties. Phonemic encoding is deeper than structural encoding but still involves relatively shallow processing compared to semantic encoding.

- **Semantic Encoding**: Semantic encoding involves processing the meaning of a stimulus and its relationship to other concepts and information stored in memory. At this level, we engage in deep processing by actively relating the stimulus to our existing knowledge, experiences, and understanding of the world. Semantic encoding leads to a richer and more elaborate representation of the stimulus in memory compared to structural and phonemic encoding. For example, when we are presented with a word, semantic encoding involves understanding its meaning, associations, and implications within a broader context. Within semantic encoding, self-referent encoding refers to applying information that you want to remember to your own life. Every time you learn a new psychological concept, try to create your own personal example, and you may be surprised at how much you remember. **Deep processing** involves elaborative rehearsal, along with a meaningful analysis of the ideas and words being learned.

As you move through each section of this book, try to make connections to what you have learned in earlier topics. This is a process called *interleaving* that is well established as helping students remember information at a deeper level. This process is especially important in psychology since nearly all the ideas can be connected to other ones. The more you study psychology, the more interconnectedness you will find among the perspectives, the processes, and the basic understandings. One simple example is the term *schema*. When you examine different psychological perspectives, such as psychodynamic, behavioral, and humanistic, you will realize that each one uses its own schemas to filter in and filter out information about behavior. Connections among concepts made through deep processing are everywhere in academic study.

THINK AS A PSYCHOLOGIST

Apply Psychological Perspectives, Theories, Concepts, and Research Findings to a Scenario (1.A.1) | Determine the Type of Research Design(s) Used in a Given Study (2.A.1)

Dr. Nandini conducted a study with her college Introduction to Psychology course. Her goal was to demonstrate to her students that some memory strategies are much more effective than others. In her class of 100 students, she randomly assigned 50 to be in Group A and 50 to be in Group B. Both groups were assigned the same set of 25 concepts to learn over the course of a week. During that time, Group A was instructed to learn the material by using strategies that included explaining the concept to a friend, relating the concept to a specific event in their lives, and picturing how that concept could influence their life in the future. Group B learned the same concepts, but they were instructed to create notecards that included the concept on the front of the card and the definition on the back of the card. Each group was given two hours to study over the course of a week. A month later, the two groups were assessed using the same test, which included multiple-choice questions and an application essay. The results of the study are in the table below.

	Mean Score on the Assessment	Standard Deviation
Group A	78.32	5.8
Group B	57.91	11.7

Practice Applying Theories and Determining the Type of Research Design

Answer the following questions.

1. Which research method did Dr. Nandini use in her study? Explain your answer.

2. The results of this study most clearly demonstrate the difference between which of the following?

   (A) Semantic and episodic memory

   (B) Shallow and deep processing

   (C) Explicit memory and automatic processing

   (D) Structural encoding and procedural memory

3. What can you conclude based on the differences in standard deviation between the groups?

REFLECT ON THE ESSENTIAL QUESTION

Essential Question: *How do the types, structures, and processes of memory work?* Using the Key Terms, complete a chart like the one below to gather details to help answer that question.

Type	Structure	Processes

MULTIPLE-CHOICE QUESTIONS

1. Jaxon is trying hard to learn all the formulas for his physics class. He creates flashcards, quizzes himself on each formula, and completes a number of practice problems. Which memory process is he using?

   (A) Automatic processing

   (B) Episodic memory

   (C) Echoic memory

   (D) Effortful processing

2. While reading a novel at a rate of nearly 500 words per minute, Megan effortlessly understands almost every word. This ability highlights the importance of which of the following?

   (A) Short-term memory

   (B) Iconic memory

   (C) Automatic processing

   (D) Semantic encoding

3. Gerard is trying to learn the notes to a new song on his guitar. He plays the song over and over as he practices to see if he can match the sound. According to the working memory model, where will this be processed?

   (A) Long-term memory

   (B) Phonological loop

   (C) Visuospatial sketchpad

   (D) Central executive

4. Marissa is a camp counselor and must make sure that everything is prepared for the day for activities, supplies, and lunches before her campers arrive. As Marissa drives to work, she is thinking of all the items on her "to-do" list. What type of memory is Marissa using?

(A) Implicit

(B) Echoic

(C) Semantic

(D) Prospective

5. Jonathan has a vivid memory of his fifth birthday party. He can remember the cake, the presents he received, and the people who attended. Jonathan's memories most clearly represent which of the following?

(A) Episodic

(B) Procedural

(C) Semantic

(D) Sensory

Questions 6 and 7 refer to the following.

To test the multi-store model of memory, cognitive psychologists randomly assign participants to one of two groups without disclosing which experience they will have. The researchers have all participants try to learn a 20-digit number in 10 seconds. In one group, the researchers ask the participants a question during this time, and in the other group, participants have an uninterrupted 10 seconds to try to learn the number. The results demonstrated that those in the uninterrupted group remembered more digits (mean 12.6) than the group that was interrupted (mean 8.7).

6. How did researchers try to eliminate participant bias in this study?

(A) By randomly assigning the participants to groups

(B) By using a double-blind study

(C) By not telling the participant their hypothesis

(D) By using a single-blind study

7. If researchers wanted to generalize these results to a high school population, what would they have to do?

(A) Take a random sample from a clearly defined high school population

(B) Randomly assign the participants to groups

(C) Take a sample size of over 1000 students

(D) Have results that are statistically significant

Topic 2.4

Encoding Memories

"Rhyme is a mnemonic device, an aid to the memory. And some poems are themselves mnemonics, that is to say, the whole purpose of the poem is to enable us to remember some information."

—James Fenton, poet

Essential Question: How do different encoding processes work to get information into memory?

For thousands of years, the Aboriginal people of Australia have committed vast amounts of knowledge to memory and passed it down to successive generations. Their highly detailed and complex oral traditions have survived accurately for centuries. Aboriginal elders say that they encode this knowledge in song, dance, story, and place. That last—associating a memory with a place—is just one of many ways we use to encode information.

As you read in Topic 2.3, **encoding** is the way information is transformed and placed in the memory. Encoding takes place in differing ways depending on the type of information being processed. Semantic encoding, for example, assigns meaning or relevance to information, often by relating it to prior knowledge or personal experiences. Other types of encoding processes involve encoding information based on sensory stimuli. Acoustic encoding is based on sound, visual encoding on sight, and tactile encoding on touch or physical sensation.

These encoding processes can occur simultaneously or independently, depending on the nature of the information and a person's cognitive processes. As you read in the last topic, the effectiveness of encoding depends on factors such as attention, rehearsal, and the depth of processing, with deeper levels of processing typically leading to more durable memory traces. Memory traces are the changes in the neural architecture of the brain that take place during learning and memory formation. Scientists believe that memory traces strengthen synapses, change neurotransmitter levels, and alter neural connectivity. They can vary in strength and durability, depending on many factors, such as the intensity of encoding, the frequency of retrieval, and the passage of time.

Encoding Processes

Encoding involves the conversion of sensory input into a form that can be stored in memory. Different processes and strategies contribute to effective encoding, but with varying degrees of effectiveness. Emotionally charged experiences tend to be encoded more effectively due to heightened arousal and attention. Emotional events are often vividly remembered and retained over time. There are, however, limits to this type of encoding. If you are in a terrifying situation, for example, emotions take over and this may cause errors in encoding.

Paying attention to information is essential for encoding to take place. Selective attention filters relevant information from the environment and directs cognitive resources toward it. The more attention we allocate to incoming stimuli, the more likely they are to be encoded effectively. Remember from the last topic that attention was necessary to move information from sensory to short-term memory. Semantic encoding focuses on the meaning of information to aid encoding. It involves processing the meaning and significance of information, which leads to deeper and more durable memory traces compared to shallow, surface-level processing.

Repeating or rehearsing information helps reinforce its encoding. Maintenance rehearsal involves simple repetition and will result in a shallow level of processing that is easily forgotten, while elaborative rehearsal involves deeper processing by relating new information to existing knowledge or personal experiences. Elaborative rehearsal is generally more effective in creating long-lasting memories. (You will learn more about maintenance and elaborative rehearsal in the next topic.)

Organizing information into meaningful patterns or categories enhances encoding. Associating information with specific contexts or environments can aid encoding and retrieval. Context-dependent memory suggests that recalling information is more effective when we are in the same context or environment where it was initially learned. Creating mental images or visual associations can enhance encoding. Visual encoding takes advantage of the brain's ability to store and recall visual information effectively.

The effectiveness of encoding processes and strategies can vary depending on individual differences, the nature of the information being encoded, and the context in which encoding occurs. Generally, strategies that promote deeper processing, such as elaborative rehearsal and semantic processing, tend to result in more durable and accessible memories. As you read through these strategies, think of how you can use them in your own learning. These strategies can help you study efficiently and effectively when put to good use.

Mnemonic Devices

Mnemonic devices, such as acronyms or visual imagery, provide organizational structures that make information more memorable. They aid in encoding information into both working memory and long-term memory in several ways. Mnemonic devices link new information to existing knowledge or experiences through association. By connecting the new information to something familiar or meaningful, mnemonic devices provide a mental anchor that facilitates encoding and retrieval. This association can be based on similarities, contrasts, or other relationships between the new information and familiar concepts. By making information more memorable and accessible, mnemonic devices help us encode and retain a wide range of information more effectively.

Many mnemonic devices involve repetition, which reinforces the encoding process. By repeatedly engaging with the mnemonic device, we strengthen the connections between the new information and the memory cues provided by the device. This repeated exposure helps consolidate the memory and makes it more resistant to forgetting. One way of repeating information is the acronym technique, in which the first letter of each word in a list or sequence is used to create a memorable acronym. To remember the names of the Great Lakes, for example, many schoolchildren have learned to think of *HOMES*, for Huron, Ontario, Michigan, Erie, and Superior. A psychology-related mnemonic that may help you remember the different types of neurons is *SAME*: Sensory neurons have Afferent nerve fibers and Motor neurons have Efferent nerve fibers. In Unit 4, you will learn about the Big 5 personality characteristics of Openness, Conscientiousness, Extraversion, Agreeableness, and Neuroticism; *OCEAN* is a useful mnemonic to help remember these characteristics.

Mnemonic devices often involve creating vivid mental images that represent the information being encoded. Visual imagery is a powerful tool for memory, as the brain tends to remember visual information more easily than abstract concepts. By converting abstract information into memorable images, mnemonic devices make it easier for the brain to encode and recall the information later. One mnemonic technique, the **method of loci**, converts the items to be remembered into mental images and associates them with specific positions or locations. (This is one of the methods Aborigines use to remember their long oral history.) For example, to remember a shopping list, you could imagine each item in a different location at your house. Try this now with the list of words below. Place each item you want to remember in the location identified in your house. Try to create a vivid image of the grocery items in that location in your home. When you are done, test yourself and see how many items you are able to remember. Then try again in a day or two. First identify the location in your house and next identify what you need from the grocery store. You might be surprised how easy the list of items is to recall.

Location in Home	Item From the Grocery Store
Kitchen counter	Broccoli
Kitchen table	3 heads of lettuce
Kitchen Sink	Strawberries
Front door	Granola bars
Bathroom	Soap
Sofa	Carrots
Television	Kleenex
Bed	Peanut butter
Pillows	Bread
Closet	Almonds

Mnemonic devices can be personalized to suit individual preferences and learning styles. By tailoring the mnemonic device to align with personal interests, experiences, or sensory preferences, we can enhance our engagement with the material and improve our encoding and retrieval of the information. For example, we might create a personalized story or narrative that incorporates the information we want to remember. By infusing the story with personal details, experiences, or interests, we make the information more relevant and memorable to ourselves. The way in which you remembered the items from the grocery store will differ from that of your classmates, but this unique and personalized way of remembering should help you recall these items more easily.

Chunking, Categories, and Hierarchies

One way to increase the amount of information stored in STM at one time is a process called **chunking**—combining or grouping bits of related information into meaningful chunks. An example of chunking is to try to recall this 20-digit number: 1 7 7 6 1 8 1 2 1 8 6 1 1 9 1 4 1 9 4 1. Not so easy. However, if you were to chunk that into five groups, you could recall it more easily: 1776 1812 1861 1914 1941. When chunked, those numbers represent the dates of wars in which the United States was involved.

Or think about American football games, with 22 moving people, each with a role. Novice viewers typically focus all their energy on following the ball. Experts, in contrast, already know where the ball is likely to go and will be able to use chunking to see not only the running back carrying the ball to a particular spot but also the guard pulling to block as well as the slot receiver crossing over to block the middle linebacker.

Categories organize information into groups or classes based on shared characteristics or features. For example, you may create a category for cognitive biases. That structured framework for information makes it easier to retrieve related items from memory; when you think of one cognitive bias, another comes more easily to mind.

Hierarchies organize information into a multi-level structure, where items are usually arranged from more general to more specific. For example, you may create a hierarchy on levels and types of long-term memory starting from the general concept and moving to specific types (see Figure 2.3.4).

The Spacing Effect

Another method of encoding is known as the **spacing effect** or spaced repetition. It refers to the fact that information is better retained and recalled when it is studied or rehearsed over multiple spaced intervals of time, referred to as **distributed practice**, compared to being studied or rehearsed all at once, which is known as **massed practice**. The spacing effect is particularly applicable to academic study. You have likely heard that cramming for exams is not the most effective method of studying and that is correct. There are several reasons for this.

- When information is initially encoded, memory traces are relatively weak. However, spaced repetition reinforces these traces repeatedly over time. Each time the information is revisited, the memory becomes stronger, leading to more durable retention.
- The spacing effect suggests that there is an optimal interval between study sessions for maximizing memory retention. Typically, shorter intervals (such as studying an hour a day) are more effective than longer intervals (such as studying several hours once a week), but the exact spacing depends on factors such as the nature of the material and individual differences.
- Spaced repetition strengthens the memory cues associated with the information. By revisiting the material multiple times across spaced intervals, you strengthen the connections between the cues and the encoded information, reinforcing long-term potentiation and making it easier to retrieve the information from memory.
- Spaced repetition helps prevent cognitive overload by distributing study sessions over time. Instead of trying to cram a large amount of information into a single study session, break up your study sessions into smaller, more manageable chunks, allowing for better encoding and retention.
- One of the key benefits of the spacing effect is its ability to promote long-term retention. By spacing out study sessions, you are more likely to retain the information over extended periods, rather than forgetting it shortly after learning it.

The spacing effect improves learning and memory by spreading out study sessions over time. This approach takes advantage of how our memories solidify and how well we can retrieve information later. As Dr. G. explains in the *Study Like a Champ* features, revisiting material repeatedly at intervals can strengthen our ability to remember and understand it better in the long run. To apply this in your own life, try to read one section of this book instead of a whole unit or multiple topics at a time. Take a few minutes each day to read over the notes you took in class that day and quiz yourself on what you know and do not know. This practice has years of research and hundreds of studies to back it up. It does not take any more study time, but it does take a plan and proactive action to prepare for assessments.

The Serial Position Effect

What we remember is also shaped in part by the order in which information is presented. We tend to remember information presented at the beginning and end of a list better than information presented in the middle of a list that exceeds what we can hold in short-term memory. This phenomenon, known as the **serial position effect**, has been widely studied since it was first identified by the German psychologist Hermann Ebbinghaus in the late 19th century.

It is typically observed in tasks involving the presentation of a list of items for memorization, such as word lists or number sequences. Our tendency to remember the first piece of information is called the **primacy effect**. The cognitive bias in which we remember information that came last more clearly than earlier information is known as the **recency effect**.

Psychologists believe the primacy effect occurs because items presented early in the list have more time for rehearsal and encoding into long-term memory. These items receive more attention and are more deeply processed, leading to stronger memory traces. On the other hand, they believe the recency effect results from the fact that the items at the end of the list are more readily accessible in short-term memory because they were more recently encountered. The middle items of the list tend to be overshadowed by the stronger primacy and recency effects. They receive less attention and rehearsal and may not be as effectively encoded into memory. As a result, they are often not remembered as well.

THINK AS A PSYCHOLOGIST

Apply Psychological Perspectives, Theories, Concepts, and Research Findings to a Scenario (1.A.1) | Evaluate the Appropriate Use of Research Design Elements in Experimental Methodology (2.B.1, 2.B.3) | Calculate and Interpret Measures of Central Tendency, Variation, and Percentile Rank in a Given Data Set (3.B.1)

Mrs. Berndt is conducting an experiment to investigate how various encoding strategies affect her students' performance on a unit exam. Her U.S. History class has 20 students whom she randomly assigns to one of two conditions. Group 1 is instructed to study for the upcoming test in a single two-hour chunk the night before the exam. Group 2 is instructed to spend 20 minutes studying each night over the course of six nights. Both groups took the same unit exam, which was scored on a scale from 1–10. The results are in the table below.

Group 1	Score	Group 2	Score
Student 1	7	Student 1	9
Student 2	5	Student 2	6
Student 3	3	Student 3	8
Student 4	7	Student 4	7
Student 5	6	Student 5	10
Student 6	2	Student 6	10
Student 7	4	Student 7	5
Student 8	7	Student 8	7
Student 9	1	Student 9	6
Student 10	8	Student 10	7

Practice Applying Research Findings, Evaluating Design Elements, and Calculating Measures of Central Tendency

Complete the following activities and answer the question.

1. Calculate each of the measures of central tendency (mean, median, mode) for group 1.

2. State a possible hypothesis for Mrs. Berndt's experiment.

3. Identify the independent (IV) and dependent (DV) variables in this experiment.

4. Which of the following is a logical conclusion that Mrs. Berndt could draw from the results of this experiment?

   (A) Maintenance rehearsal leads to stronger learning than elaborative rehearsal.

   (B) Group 1 performed less well because they used chunking as an encoding strategy.

   (C) Utilizing the spacing effect created stronger memories than massed rehearsal.

   (D) Group 2 benefited from the serial position effect more than group 1.

REFLECT ON THE ESSENTIAL QUESTION

Essential Question: *How do different encoding processes work to get information into memory?* Using the Key Terms, complete a chart like the one below to gather details to help answer that question.

Process	How It Works

KEY TERMS

category	hierarchy	primacy effect
chunking	massed practice	recency effect
distributed practice	method of loci	serial position effect
encoding	mnemonic devices	spacing effect

1. Students often remember more information from a course that spans an entire semester than from a course that is completed in an intensive three-week learning period. This illustrates the importance of which of the following?

   (A) Distributed practice

   (B) Chunking

   (C) The serial position effect

   (D) Implicit memory

2. Sarah is an art history major and needs to know the names of many artists, the pieces they created, and the genre of art each piece is associated with. Sarah went to the art museum to see in person many of the pieces she needed to know, and while at the museum she studied all of the aspects she needed to know. Unfortunately, when she took her exam in her art history classroom, she only had clear memory of the first 25 paintings she saw at the museum. Her experience demonstrates which of the following memory principles?

   (A) Primacy effect

   (B) Massed practice

   (C) Semantic encoding

   (D) Maintenance rehearsal

3. Spring break is rapidly approaching and Tanisha will be traveling to her favorite beach. Her family is leaving a few hours after she arrives home from school, so she needs to pack quickly. Tanisha goes through each of her classes throughout the school day and mentally places a few items that she needs to remember to pack. When she arrives home, she goes through each class in her mind and is easily able to remember everything she wants to take on her trip. Which memory aid did Tanisha employ to help her pack efficiently?

   (A) Chunking

   (B) The spacing effect

   (C) Method of loci

   (D) Semantic encoding

4. Jacques is a race car driver preparing for a Grand Prix race through a large city he does not know well. The course is over 160 miles and does 4 loops of the city. Jacques wants to make sure he knows every turn of the course, but as he makes his test runs he quickly finds himself overwhelmed and cannot remember anything. After he regroups, he decides that he will try to remember the course in 10-mile segments. This strategy is much more successful, and Jacques is able to place in the race. Which memory aid helped Jacques memorize the course?

(A) Chunking

(B) Spacing

(C) Mnemonic device

(D) Semantic memories

Questions 5 through 7 refer to the following.

A restaurant owner is trying to cut costs. The electronic tablets she issued each server to take orders often break down, and they are expensive to replace. The restaurant often serves large groups coming from local businesses. She encourages her servers to try to just remember the orders until they can punch them into a register that sends the orders to the kitchen. The graph below indicates the percentage of orders remembered for each person in the large groups.

5. Which of the following concepts best explains the results of this cost-saving measure?

(A) Long-term potentiation

(B) Misinformation effect

(C) The spacing effect

(D) Serial position effect

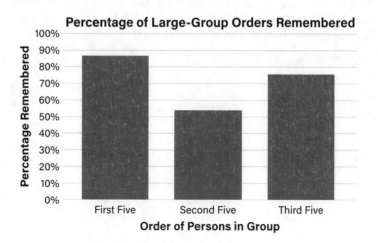

6. Which of the following most accurately describes why the research presented above is not experimental?

(A) The servers are not a representative sample of the target population.

(B) This scenario requires a double-blind procedure, which the restaurant owner did not use.

(C) The servers were not randomly assigned to an experimental or control group.

(D) The type of research used relied on survey data, and many of the servers may have exhibited the social desirability bias.

7. Based on the results of this trial period, what conclusion could the restaurant owner reasonably make?

(A) The money saved by not using tablets should not make a big difference in the servers getting the orders correct.

(B) If there are small groups (under five), the servers may be able to successfully remember their orders without a tablet.

(C) If the groups are very large, the servers will not be able to remember anyone's order.

(D) The servers will remember the orders for patrons at the beginning or in the middle of a group but are likely to forget the last orders they take.

STUDY LIKE A CHAMP WITH DR. G.

This topic offers more detailed information—"the backstory"—on the study suggestions provided in each unit. These accepted practices for remembering over a long period of time have been backed up by hundreds of research studies. Make use of the practices!

Topic 2.5

Storing Memories

"The memories which lie within us are not carved in stone; not only do they tend to become erased as the years go by, but often they change, or even increase by incorporating extraneous features."

—Primo Levi, chemist, author, and Holocaust survivor

Essential Question: How do memory storage processes retain information in memory?

You read about how memories are encoded in Topic 2.4 and will read about how they are retrieved in Topic 2.6. *Memory consolidation* is the process by which newly acquired information is stabilized and integrated into existing memory networks. It involves the transfer of information from short-term memory to long-term memory through synaptic changes and neural reorganization. Psychologists believe that consolidation takes place over time and may be facilitated by processes such as rehearsal and sleep.

In this topic, you will read about the processes that aid in memory storage. **Memory storage processes** are complex and dynamic, involving interactions among various brain regions and cognitive processes. These processes allow us to acquire, retain, and retrieve information, forming the basis of human cognition and behavior.

How Do We Remember?

As you read in Topic 2.3, psychologists recognize several main categories of memory. *Sensory memory* briefly holds incoming sensory information from the environment. *Short-term memory (STM)* holds information that is currently being processed. Working memory plays a crucial role in tasks such as reasoning, comprehension, and problem-solving. And *long-term memory (LTM)* stores information for long-term retrieval.

Differences in Memory Storage

These four types of memory differ in many ways. Each type of memory differs in **duration** (how long it lasts), **capacity** (size of storage), and the nature of the **content** (type of information) it holds.

Sensory Memory Sensory information from the environment in its raw form, is stored in **sensory memory.** For example, sensory memory stores visual information in iconic memory and auditory information in echoic memory. It has a large capacity but only holds a small amount of information at any given moment. Information is stored very briefly, typically only a fraction of a second to a few seconds.

Short-Term Memory Information that is currently being attended to or actively processed, such as digits in a phone number or words in a sentence, is stored in **short-term memory.** It has limited capacity, holding around 5 to 9 items (7 plus or minus 2) of information, and typically lasts around 15 to 30 seconds without rehearsal.

Working Memory In addition to holding information currently in use, as does short-term memory, **working memory** also involves mental processes such as reasoning, problem-solving, and decision-making. Like STM, it has limited capacity, but it involves active manipulation of information, typically holding around 4 chunks of information. Storage duration is similar to STM, lasting around 15 to 30 seconds without rehearsal.

Long-Term Memory Information from STM that has been encoded and consolidated for long-term storage is stored in **long-term memory**. The types of information it stores include explicit memories such as facts and events and implicit memories such as skills and habits. LTM has virtually unlimited capacity, and thus is capable of holding a vast amount of information. Its storage duration is potentially indefinite, lasting from minutes to a lifetime.

Prolonging Storage of Memories

Several strategies and techniques can help prolong memory storage and enhance retention of information over longer periods of time. You read about some of these in Topics 2.3 and 2.4. Two cognitive strategies for memory retention are maintenance rehearsal and elaborative rehearsal. They differ in their depth of processing and effectiveness in encoding information.

Maintenance rehearsal involves simple repetition or rote memorization of information without necessarily engaging deeply with its meaning or significance. This strategy helps keep information active in short-term memory but is less effective for transferring information into long-term memory. Maintenance rehearsal is like holding information in your mind temporarily, but it may not lead to lasting memory storage unless it is combined with other encoding strategies. If you are trying to remember your three friends' coffee orders, you may repeat them to yourself so that you can keep them in your short-term memory until you order.

Elaborative rehearsal involves actively engaging with the material and making meaningful connections between new information and existing knowledge or experiences. This strategy encourages deeper processing of information by relating it to personal experiences, semantic knowledge, or visual imagery. Elaborative rehearsal enhances encoding by creating more elaborate memory traces and associations, leading to better memory retention. By elaborating on the meaning, context, or significance of the information, people create stronger and more durable memory representations. If you are trying to remember that the hippocampus plays a role in transferring short-term to long-term memories, you may try to remember where it is located in the brain and what function the areas near the hippocampus serve (association), and then picture hippos on a college campus. This visual imagery is a type of elaborative rehearsal.

Autobiographical Memory

The memory system that contains information about ourselves, including personal experiences, events, and facts from our lives, is called **autobiographical memory**. It encompasses both memories of specific events or experiences (episodic memories), and general knowledge about ourselves and our lives (semantic memories). Autobiographical memory works through a complex process of encoding, storage, and retrieval. Biological processes, including genetics, may account for the fact that some people have highly superior autobiographical memory storage. Overall, the biological basis of superior memory storage in autobiographical memory involves a complex interplay of brain structures, neurotransmitter systems, neuroplasticity, as well as genetic factors. Understanding these biological processes is essential for making clear the mechanisms underlying autobiographical memory and memory enhancement strategies. Individuals with this unique ability are able to remember every day of their lives in great detail. They can tell you what they ate for lunch on a specific day over a decade ago and what they wore on any given day, and they can recall nearly every conversation.

However, this seemingly beneficial ability has drawbacks. Marilu Henner, an actress who has **highly superior autobiographical memory**, describes her two divorces that occurred in part because she could never forget an argument she had with her former spouses. Sometimes a bit of forgetting can be beneficial.

Autobiographical memory is dynamic and subject to change over time. Memories may be modified or distorted. Additionally, the interpretation and reconstruction of memories may be influenced by factors such as mood, motivation, and personal beliefs. Overall, autobiographical memory plays a central role in shaping our sense of identity, self-concept, and understanding of the past. It allows us to reflect on our life experiences, learn from past events, and navigate our present and future.

Factors That Negatively Affect Memory Storage

Physical impairment and developmental limitations can negatively affect memory storage processes. Physical impairments such as blindness or deafness can restrict the amount or quality of sensory information available for encoding memories. Other physical impairments affecting motor skills may limit the ability to engage in activities that aid memory formation, such as exploration and manipulation of objects. Developmental limitations may affect attention span and the ability to focus, making it challenging to encode information effectively into memory. And difficulty in language acquisition or communication can hinder the encoding and retrieval of verbal memories.

Amnesia is a condition characterized by partial or complete loss of memory. It can be caused by various factors, such as brain injury, neurological disorders, psychological trauma, or certain medical conditions. The severity and duration of amnesia can vary widely depending on the underlying cause and individual factors.

As you read in Topic 1.0, injury or trauma can create problems with various brain functions. One such problem is **retrograde amnesia**, or forgetting events that occurred before an injury or trauma. You may have seen old television shows in which characters would have coconuts drop on their heads and then forget who they were. Though a silly premise for a television show, that result can actually occur when the impact causes real brain damage. Usually, a brain part other than the hippocampus is affected and the individual loses episodic memories, not basic facts or language abilities. You likely know that the prefix *retro* means "old." In this case you are forgetting older memories or memories from before the brain trauma or infection. An individual with retrograde amnesia can still make new memories.

Anterograde amnesia occurs when the hippocampus is damaged, resulting in the inability to "create" long-term memories and forcing a person to always live in the present. Henry Gustav Molaison, a much-studied man known in scientific journals simply as H.M., was the first to be associated with this disorder. In an effort to stop his debilitating epileptic fits, H.M. had an operation to remove medial structures, the hippocampus, and the surrounding cortex, in both the left and right hemispheres. The operation succeeded in greatly reducing his seizures, but it permanently prevented his formation of long-term memories. Long-term memories acquired before the damage remained intact, but no new memories could be created. He was completely dependent on others because he could not remember if he had eaten meals or where he was going or who people were. H.M. did, however, know people from his past and he could even mow the lawn. Ironically, he did learn procedural memories, like drawing a star using a mirror (backwards and upside down). He got better and better at doing this even though he had no recollection of engaging in the task. This is likely because the area in which procedural memories are stored (cerebellum) was not damaged in his surgery.

Figure 2.5.1

Think back to the earliest memory that you recalled at the start of the memory section. How old were you? Adults are typically unable to recall early memories from infancy and early childhood, before the age of 3 or 4. This is referred to as **infantile amnesia**. While infants and toddlers are capable of forming memories, these memories tend to fade as they grow older. The exact reasons for infantile amnesia are not fully understood, but some theories suggest that it could be due to the immaturity of the brain regions responsible for memory formation during early childhood, as well as the lack of language skills to encode and retrieve memories effectively.

Some older adults develop a brain condition known as dementia, in which thinking, memory, and behavior begin to deteriorate. The frontal lobes of the brain begin to deteriorate to some extent in all adults over age 50. About 14 percent of Americans over the age of 71 are diagnosed with a specific form of dementia known as **Alzheimer's disease**, a degenerative disease in which memory loss is progressive and plaques accumulate in nervous system tissues. The age of onset is generally after 65, although some will experience early-onset Alzheimer's disease. Chances of developing Alzheimer's disease doubles every 5 years until age 85. Lower levels of the biochemical acetylcholine have been found to be associated with Alzheimer's disease, as well as the presence of a specific genetic trait (i.e., ApoE4 allele on chromosome 19). Signs of Alzheimer's may include problems speaking or writing, misplacing items, confusion with time or place, and the inability to complete familiar tasks. People with Alzheimer's disease also may experience extreme changes in personality and, in advanced stages, have trouble recognizing family and friends and often have difficulty remembering recent events.

THINK AS A PSYCHOLOGIST

Apply Psychological Perspectives, Theories, Concepts, and Research Findings to a Scenario (1.A.1) | Evaluate the Appropriate Use of Research Design Elements in Non-Experimental Methodologies (2.C.7)

Dr. Irving was called to examine a 35-year-old, Shana, who woke up in the hospital after a car accident that resulted in a concussion. She was very confused and distressed that she could not recall events before the accident as well as many facts about her past. Her family was notified, and when her husband arrived to visit, she did not recognize him and seemed to have no recollection of being married. As Dr. Irving continued neurological testing, he realized that she was able to create new memories of episodic and semantic material. That, coupled with various brain scans, allowed Dr. Irving to conclude that the hippocampus had not been damaged in the accident. When recovered enough to return home, she faced profound challenges. Returning to work was especially difficult. She couldn't remember the colleagues she had once been close with, and her ability to perform her job was greatly impeded. Dr. Irving worked with Shana for the next 18 months, gradually exposing her to elements of her life that had been forgotten. That exposure helped, and some memories slowly returned. Her recovery was not total after 18 months, but the progress made left both Shana and Dr. Irving hopeful that over time she would make a complete recovery.

Practice Applying Concepts and Evaluating Elements of Research Design

Answer the following questions.

1. Shana's condition can best be characterized as which of the following?

   (A) Retrograde amnesia

   (B) Anterograde amnesia

   (C) Infantile amnesia

   (D) Alzheimer's disease

2. Which of the following describes why Dr. Irving cannot generalize the results of his research with Shana?

   (A) Dr. Irving did not obtain informed consent and therefore cannot generalize the results of the study.

   (B) Generalization can only come from experimental research, and there is not an independent variable being manipulated in this study.

   (C) This study is based on correlation research, and a study cannot be generalized unless the findings indicate a causal relationship between variables.

   (D) Dr. Irving's research is based on a single investigation and the findings cannot be generalized to a population without using a random sample of subjects.

REFLECT ON THE ESSENTIAL QUESTION

Essential Question: *How do memory storage processes retain information in memory?* Using the Key Terms, complete a chart like the one below to gather details to help answer that question.

Memory Process	How It Works

KEY TERMS

Alzheimer's disease	duration	maintenance rehearsal
amnesia	elaborative rehearsal	memory storage process
anterograde amnesia	highly superior	retrograde amnesia
autobiographical memory	autobiographical memory	sensory memory
capacity		short-term memory
content	infantile amnesia	working memory
	long-term memory	

1. Mr. Humphries recently had a terrible seizure that damaged the interior of his temporal lobe, including his hippocampus. What memory issues might be expected as a result of this damage?

   (A) The inability to see properly

   (B) The inability to engage in higher-order thinking

   (C) The inability to make new memories

   (D) The inability to recall information from his past

2. Suzette has a highly superior autobiographical memory but does sometimes make a mistake in recalling the details of past events. Which of the following cognitive biases is most likely to occur because she usually is correct in her memories?

   (A) Confirmation bias

   (B) Belief perseverance

   (C) Hindsight bias

   (D) Overconfidence

3. Josephine is trying to remember the word *fête*. She knows French and knows the word she is looking for means "celebration" or "festival" in French. She also pictures the word written in fancy script and pictures people in very formal clothing at a large party. What technique is Josephine employing?

   (A) Sensory memory

   (B) Chunking

   (C) Elaborative rehearsal

   (D) Maintenance rehearsal

4. Leo is nearly 90 years old. He has had difficulty remembering where he put his wallet and has found himself lost on streets in his neighborhood. He does not remember that he was married, although he recognizes his adult children. He often is confused about what time of day it is and talks about getting a job, even though he has been retired for nearly 30 years. What may be a diagnosis that is consistent with Leo's symptoms?

   (A) Retrograde amnesia

   (B) Alzheimer's disease

   (C) Infantile amnesia

   (D) Anterograde amnesia

Questions 5 through 7 refer to the following.

5. The following graph indicates the age of onset of memory issues and the diagnosis of a memory disorder. What conclusion can be drawn from this data?

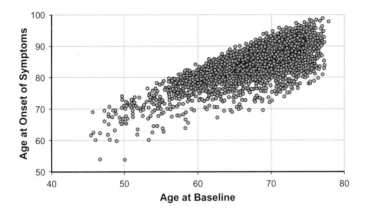

(A) A large proportion of people experience early-onset memory loss.

(B) There is a positive correlation between age at the baseline of the disorder and age at diagnosis.

(C) There is a negative correlation between age at the baseline of the disorder and age at diagnosis.

(D) There is no correlation between age at the baseline and age at diagnosis.

6. What type of research has been conducted to get the results depicted in the scatterplot above?

(A) Case study

(B) Cross-sectional

(C) Naturalistic observation

(D) Correlational study

7. Why is this study unsuitable to conduct as an experiment?

(A) Because it would be unethical to purposely inflict memory loss on individuals, which would be the manipulation of the independent variable

(B) Because it would not be possible to get enough individuals to generalize to the population

(C) Because all studies on Alzheimer's patients must be conducted as case studies

(D) Because there is no way to objectively measure the dependent variable

Topic 2.6

Retrieving Memories

We've forgotten how to remember, and just as importantly, we've forgotten how to pay attention. So, instead of using your smartphone to jot down crucial notes, or Googling an elusive fact, use every opportunity to practice your memory skills. Memory is a muscle, to be exercised and improved.

—Joshua Foer, 2006 USA Memory Champion

Essential Question: How do memory retrieval processes get information out of memory?

How do you study for tests? If you are like most students, you reread the textbook and your notes. In a survey, 84 percent of college students said they used rereading as a study strategy; 55 percent said rereading was the strategy they used most often and consistently. After students reread—with the expectation that rereading will result in the greatest learning—they may test themselves with chapter-ending questions or practice tests to see how well they do. What many do not realize, however, is that the real learning takes place during those self-quizzes, when their brains retrieve information. Indeed, research has repeatedly shown that rereading has little to no effect on learning, while retrieval, especially when it is spaced out, results in solid learning. If the retrieval is done repeatedly but over a short period of time, as a student might do when cramming for an exam, its impact is also negligible. This does not mean you should stop reading your book. You shouldn't. You should read it one time very closely and take good notes or make good annotations so that you have gathered all the key points and do not have to go back and reread the text again.

How does memory retrieval actually work? In the following pages, you will not only learn this, but also how you can enhance your memory retrieval skills.

Memory Retrieval Processes

Memory retrieval is the process of accessing stored information from memory when needed, allowing us to access past experiences, knowledge, and skills, forming the basis of human cognition and behavior. Memory cues activate neural networks in the brain that are associated with the encoded memory. The process involves retrieving and integrating the different components of the memory. During this process, the brain may fill in gaps or inaccuracies in the memory based on prior knowledge, expectations, or contextual information.

The success of memory retrieval depends on various factors, including the strength of the memory trace, the effectiveness of the memory cues, and the degree of interference or inhibition from competing memories. Factors such as recreating the environmental or situational context in which the memory was encoded, emotional arousal, and rehearsal can also influence retrieval success.

Memory Cues

Any stimulus associated with a memory is called a **memory cue**; because such cues usually enhance the retrieval of a memory, they are also referred to as **retrieval cues**. Often, when we forget something, the problem is that the cues that would help us recall the information are simply missing. If the cue is present, recall increases, although there are most certainly times that we failed to encode something in the first place or that it was not stored properly and therefore we cannot retrieve the memory. It is not always possible to know where the breakdown in the process takes place. The role of memory cues is one reason why it is often helpful to go back over the actions you were taking before entering the room if you forget why you walked into the room. Sometimes the cues are all you need to recall your reason. Memory cues also help explain why priming is a great activity before an exam, since in the process of priming, you are creating cues for yourself to help recall needed information.

Recall and Recognition

Two key concepts of memory are recognition and recall. **Recall** is the direct retrieval of facts or information without memory cues. In school, you use recall on fill-in-the-blank tests without word banks or possible choices and on essay questions. Students must take all the information from their brains to respond to the prompt for an essay. Recall is more difficult than recognition.

Recognition, which does rely on memory cues, is the correct identification of previously learned material. Think of how often recognition occurs while you read. You do not have to look up each word: you have already learned the meanings, so you can quickly identify the meanings and move on. In school, recognition is the process that helps you identify the correct answer on multiple-choice exams. You will see a question stem and four or five possible answers, one correct one and three or four included as distractors (false items included with a correct item). These serve as the memory cues. Your ability to recognize the correct response corresponds to how well you learned the material.

Figure 2.6.1

If these actresses look familiar to you, you are remembering them using recognition. If you correctly identify them by name (Salma Hayek, left; Penelope Cruz, right) you are remembering them using recall.

Enhancing Memory Retrieval

Memory retrieval is most efficient when we are in the same state of consciousness as when the memory was formed. This phenomenon is called **state-dependent memory**. For example, if you learn information while slightly caffeinated, you theoretically should be able to recall that information while in a similarly caffeinated state. State-dependent memory refers to your internal physical state. If you stay up until 3 a.m. studying for an exam you are going to take at 10 a.m., it will likely not be very useful, since you will be in an entirely different physical state.

A subcategory of state-dependent memory is **mood-congruent memory**, the recall of information while in a mood similar to when it was acquired. Mood-congruent memory applies only when the moods are genuine and authentic, not temporary states. You are more likely to recall happy memories after a great day than you are on a day you found out you failed three tests.

Context-dependent memory is the recall of information while in the same context or environment in which it was acquired. You are likely to show a slight improvement on test scores when you take an assessment in the same location in which you learned the material you are being tested on. It is likely that there are more triggers to prime your memory and the familiarity of the space may help as well.

THINK AS A PSYCHOLOGIST

Identify Psychology-Related Concepts in Descriptions or Representations of Data (3.A.1)

Seniors in a high school social studies class were asked to write out as many concepts as they could remember from their 7th-grade geography class. Next, the students returned to the room where they learned geography in middle school and were once again asked to identify as many concepts as they could. The average scores for the two conditions are in the table below.

Number of Concepts Initially Recalled	Number of Concepts Recalled in the Room They Learned Geography
Mean = 11.3	Mean = 21.9

Practice Identifying Concepts in Descriptions of Data

Answer the following question.

1. These results most clearly provide evidence of which of the following psychological concepts?

   (A) Context-dependent memory

   (B) Mood-congruent memory

   (C) State-dependent memory

   (D) Prospective memory

Retrieval Practice Processes

The testing effect and metacognition are two processes that can work together to help enhance memory performance through active engagement, monitoring, and regulation of learning processes. By incorporating both processes into learning activities and study strategies, educators and students can enhance memory retention, improve learning outcomes, and foster a deeper understanding of the material.

The Testing Effect The **testing effect** involves actively retrieving information from memory through testing or self-assessment, which has been shown to improve long-term memory retention better than passive study alone. By engaging in retrieval practice, you not only strengthen memory traces but also activate metacognitive processes involved in monitoring and evaluating your memory performance.

Metacognition The process of thinking about thinking is called **metacognition.** During retrieval practice, you can use metacognition to evaluate the effectiveness of your retrieval strategies and identify areas for improvement. By reflecting on the effectiveness of different retrieval strategies used during testing, you can identify which strategies were most effective in helping retrieve memories and adjust the intensity, frequency, or type of retrieval strategies based on your performance and learning needs.

THINK AS A PSYCHOLOGIST

Apply Psychological Perspectives, Theories, Concepts, and Research Findings to a Scenario (1.A.1)

Practice Applying Concepts

Complete the following activity.

As Dr. G. has explained, one scientifically demonstrated way that you can improve your learning is to regularly engage in metacognition. Write two or three sentences reflecting on how you prepared for your last psychology exam. What did you do well? What could you do to improve? Are there other strategies that might yield benefits to your overall performance?

THINK AS A PSYCHOLOGIST

Describe Trends in and Relationships Between the Variables as Depicted in the Data Presented, Such as Interpreting Correlational Data from a Scatterplot, Including the Correlation Coefficient (3.C.1) | Identify Statistical and Psychological Concept(s) Depicted in a Table, Graph, Chart, or Figure. (3.A.2)

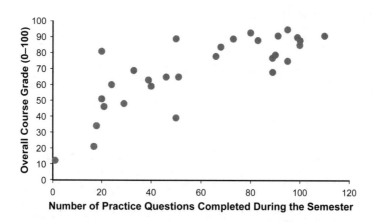

Practice Describing Relationships and Identifying Statistical Concepts

Answer the following question.

1. Briefly describe the relationship between the variables in the above scatterplot.

2. The results in the above scatterplot provide evidence that supports use of which of the following?

    (A) Testing effect

    (B) Metacognition

    (C) Mnemonics

    (D) Serial position effect

REFLECT ON THE ESSENTIAL QUESTION

Essential Question: *How do memory retrieval processes get information out of memory?* Using the Key Terms, complete a chart like the one below to gather details to help answer that question.

Memory Retrieval Process	How It Works

KEY TERMS

context-dependent memory	metacognition	retrieval cue
memory cue	mood-congruent memory	state-dependent memory
memory retrieval	recall	testing effect
	recognition	

1. Group 1 is asked to write down the names of the seven deadly sins. Group 2 is asked to look at a list of possible names of the sins and circle the correct seven. Why might Group 2 be more likely to recall more sins?

   (A) Implicit memories are easier to recall than are explicit memories.

   (B) Knowledge of the seven deadly sins is a type of episodic memory.

   (C) It demonstrates a failure of proper encoding.

   (D) Group 2's list provides more retrieval cues, making this recognition task easier for them.

2. Joyce has just had a fight with her parents. She is angry, and as she sits in her room, she thinks about all the other times her parents have been unjust and unreasonable in the rules they set for her. Which memory phenomenon is Joyce experiencing?

   (A) The recency effect

   (B) Context-dependent memory

   (C) The primacy effect

   (D) Mood-congruent memory

3. Josiah takes as many practice exams as possible before his AP biology exam and he earns a 5 on the exam. What technique did Josiah use?

   (A) Metacognition

   (B) Testing effect

   (C) Chunking

   (D) Elaborative rehearsal

4. Luca is on a tour of an old English castle. The tour guide wants to place the castle in the proper context in history and asks Luca, who mentioned his love of English history earlier in the tour, to provide a run-down of all the kings of England. What retrieval practice is the tour guide asking Luca to utilize?

   (A) Recall

   (B) State-dependent memory

   (C) Recognition

   (D) Context-dependent memory

Questions 5 through 7 refer to the following.

A government teacher is interested in finding out her students' knowledge of politicians. She randomly breaks her class into two groups. The first group is shown pictures of 20 U.S. senators and asked a yes or no question to indicate if they recognize each of them. The second group sees the same 20 senators but are asked if they know their names. The average scores out of 20 for both groups are depicted in the table below.

Participant #	Group 1	Participant #	Group 2
1	11	11	7
2	12	12	1
3	9	13	3
4	11	14	4
5	4	15	7
6	17	16	6
7	9	17	4
8	12	18	1
9	12	19	0
10	14	20	4

5. What type of research was the teacher conducting?
   (A) Experiment
   (B) Correlational study
   (C) Case study
   (D) Meta-analysis

6. What memory technique was Group 1 asked to utilize?
   (A) The testing effect
   (B) Recognition
   (C) The primacy effect
   (D) Recall

7. What is the mode of scores in Group 2?
   (A) 3.8
   (B) 6
   (C) 4
   (D) 2.3

Topic 2.7

Forgetting and Other Memory Challenges

"Your memory is a monster; you forget—it doesn't. It simply files things away."

—John Irving, novelist

Essential Question: Why do memory failure or errors occur?

Memory failure can be caused by many different factors, both internal and external. It can be the result of an encoding failure, or it may be the result of interference from new information, decay through lack of rehearsal, emotional arousal, or neurological factors such as brain damage.

Forgetting

Why do we forget? In 1885, psychologist Hermann Ebbinghaus was the first to conduct experimental studies on memory to help answer this question, using himself as the subject. He devised lists of nonsense syllables: meaningless, three-letter combinations such as FEJ and QUF that test learning and forgetting without interference or association with previous knowledge (so syllables such as DOT or BAT were not used). He set about trying to memorize these lists of nonsense syllables and found that the more times he tried to remember the entire list, the better he got at remembering, until finally he had the list mastered. The relationship between the number of repetitions and his success with remembering the syllables was an early demonstration of the learning curve, the relationship between the increase of learning and experience.

The Forgetting Curve

Ebbinghaus's most famous and enduring idea is known as the **forgetting curve**, or the exponential loss of information shortly after learning it. For example, think of a world language class you may have taken in middle school. You probably forgot most of what you learned from that class shortly after you learned it (though things like greetings and how to say your name were likely rehearsed frequently and are now in long-term memory). Though Ebbinghaus focused on very specific aspects of memory and used only himself as a subject, later research confirmed his findings.

In Figure 2.7.1, the amount of information retained immediately after learning or studying is about 100 percent. The graph also shows the amount retained after 20 minutes, 1 hour, and 9 hours. After 20 minutes, for example, only about 60 percent is retained, and after 9 hours less than 40 percent is retained. After that, retention rates decline more gradually over 31 days.

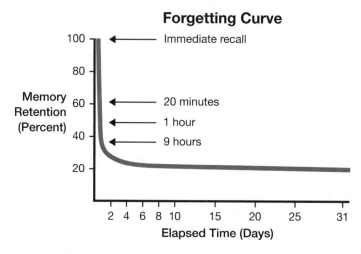

Figure 2.7.1 Ebbinghaus Forgetting Curve

Theories of Forgetting

There are many theories that offer different perspectives on the mechanisms underlying forgetting and provide insights into the complex nature of memory. No single theory can fully account for all instances of forgetting.

Encoding Failure Ebbinghaus showed that people forget at a predictable rate. But why? One reason is **encoding failure**, which occurs when a memory was never formed in the first place. The phrase "in one ear and out the other" is a great metaphor for encoding failure. We cannot learn or recall what we do not perceive and attend to. As you may recall from the multi-store model of memory, in order to transfer information from sensory to short-term memory, we must attend to the information (Topic 2.3). If we are focused on checking our phones, we cannot simultaneously be listening to our parents or teachers. This failure to encode leads to frustration and arguments when one person in the communication pair is not focused.

Interference Theory Another theory of forgetting is interference theory, which posits that there are two ways to interfere with the creation of new memories. One way is for new memories to impair retrieval of older memories. This process is called **retroactive interference**. This process helps explain why a teacher you had just a few weeks ago may forget your name. Once teachers are introduced to 175 or so new names of students at the beginning of a semester, the names of students they may have had as recently as just two weeks ago get pushed out or interfered with, and teachers have difficulty recalling them. A second kind of interference is **proactive interference**, a process by which prior learning inhibits or interferes with the recall of later learning. Have you ever called a new dog or cat by an old pet's name? If so, you have experienced proactive interference.

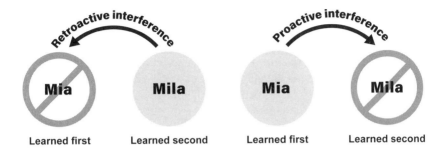

Figure 2.7.2 Retroactive and Proactive Interference

Proactive interference happens when previous information blocks the new information. Retroactive interference happens when recent information blocks old information. As in retrograde amnesia, in retroactive interference it is the older information that is forgotten. The difference is that in amnesia there was likely trauma causing the loss of memory and in interference it is because you have learned newer, similar information that is pushing out the older information. In other words, in proactive interference, the old information interferes with the new.

Tip-of-the-Tongue Phenomenon You've no doubt experienced this: "I can almost think of the name of that movie—it's on the tip of my tongue!" **Tip-of-the-tongue (TOT) phenomenon** is the feeling that a memory is available but not quite retrievable. People often experience this phenomenon when trying to recall a particular word or name. They know they know it, but they cannot bring the word to conscious awareness. It's often frustrating, but it is a normal part of memory and recall. You may experience this when a teacher asks you a direct question in class and you cannot come up with the concept they are asking for, despite knowing the answer.

Defensive Forgetting

Psychologist Sigmund Freud had a controversial theory of forgetting called **repression**, the pushing of painful, embarrassing, or threatening memories out of awareness or consciousness. In his theory, the ego—the conscious, reality-based part of the mind—represses painful memories to reduce anxiety and emotional pain, and it does so without a person's being aware of it. This process is also sometimes called *motivated forgetting*. Freud's repression theory has been extensively examined and researched over the past 80 years, but it lacks empirical support. For example, in a study of Holocaust survivors, most recalled their time in the camp in vivid detail but did not often speak of the events of this time because of the pain they experienced when bringing back the memory. (For more on repression, see the discussion on Elizabeth Loftus under Misinformation Effect.)

Ebbinghaus's forgetting curve was accepted in psychology for decades. However, Frederic C. Bartlett took a different approach to memory. Bartlett (1932) studied unusual stories that were unfamiliar to Western ears to see how Westerners would remember them. His most famous story was "The War of the Ghosts," which was a Yup'ik story from Alaska about a man who traveled with warriors on a river from his village to another area and was shot by an arrow but did not feel any pain. He returned to his village and told his story to his friends around a fire. The villagers said that he must have been fighting in the war of the ghosts. In the morning the man fell down, something black emerged from his mouth, and he died. The names of the village, river, and warriors were unfamiliar, and the sentence structure of the translated story was non-Western.

While Bartlett found a forgetting curve similar to that of Ebbinghaus, he also discovered that certain things from the story were forgotten and certain things were remembered consistently across his research participants. For example, most of the formal names (e.g., the name of the river, the name of the village) were forgotten, but the essence of the story was remembered. Participants all tended to retell the story in a more familiar Western structure rather than preserving the original Yup'ik sentence structure.

After Bartlett's study was published, researchers reexamined Ebbinghaus's studies on memory. They discovered that Ebbinghaus himself tended to remember nonsense syllables that resembled real words or were just pronounceable, whereas he tended to forget nonsense syllables that were truly nonsensical (e.g., he tended to remember PYK, ZAN, and BRN, but he tended to forget the nonsense syllables of PDG, AKQ, and XGI; the first three nonsense syllables are at least pronounceable). This discovery suggests that memory is dependent upon fitting new information into preexisting information. The nonsense syllables most easily remembered were those that resembled words Ebbinghaus knew. This insight helps explain why experts in a field can remember more from a lecture in their field than nonexperts can.

Bartlett's study illuminated differences in Western and non-Western populations. Western researchers typically find a phenomenon within our own culture and then try to see if this phenomenon is observed in other cultures. However, it should not be surprising that these other cultures might perform more poorly on the tasks or at least very differently from what has been discovered in our Western cultures, just as Westerners were unable to remember all the details of a story in an unfamiliar narrative structure with unfamiliar names.

Develop a Claim

After reading about studies on memory, consider how cultural differences might influence memory processes. Develop a claim that articulates this relationship, using evidence from the text or related studies.

Unreliable and False Memories

Some types of memories are not prone to being forgotten, but they are remembered in a way that makes them unreliable. These types of memories may be consistent with what we think happened but often are riddled with errors. The following memory types fall into this category.

Misinformation Effect Psychologist Elizabeth Loftus has done extensive research on memory construction and false memories and on how memory is malleable, or changeable, how it is not always accurate, and how it can have inaccurate attributions. Early in her career, Loftus did a study on how memory can change after information is shared with eyewitnesses after an event (in the original study, the event was an automobile crash). For example, if two people witnessed a mugging and disagreed on the color of jacket the culprit was wearing, they might eventually adopt the other person's version of events and convince themselves that they thought the person was wearing a red jacket all along. Loftus built on previous work that found memories were not always accurate, like recordings, but rather were constructed after the fact. In a 1974 study, Loftus and her colleague J. C. Palmer showed that the way in which eyewitnesses were asked questions could change their responses and memories. They showed participants the same video of a car crash and then asked questions about what they witnessed. Participants were then asked the same question: "Did you see how fast the cars were travelling when they . . . the other car." The verb in each sentence was the only thing that changed; some participants heard *crashed, hit, smashed, contacted,* or *collided.* Each word prompted different speed estimates from the eyewitnesses. They also discovered that giving witnesses misleading information or asking leading questions altered the memories of witnesses. In a follow-up study, participants were asked if they saw any broken glass when the cars either hit or smashed into one another. Those that heard the word *smashed* were far more likely to report having seen broken glass than those in the *hit* group, even though there was no broken glass in the video they watched. The word *smashed* seemed to activate a schema for a more severe accident that involved broken glass. This process, in which new information alters the way previous information is held in memory, is called the **misinformation effect**. This phenomenon is connected to retroactive interference, since new information alters the way in which the previous information is held in memory.

The impetus for the research of Elizabeth Loftus came from her own life. She was fourteen when her mother drowned in a swimming pool. Thirty years later, Loftus's uncle told her that she was the one who found her mother's body. She had vivid recollections of the traumatic event and began to bring back memories of finding her mother floating in the backyard pool. Soon after, her uncle called to let her know he was mistaken, that it was actually her aunt who had found her mother. She realized that misinformation had implanted a false but seemingly very real memory.

In an attempt to show how easily memories can be implanted, a student of Loftus's created what has come to be known as the "lost in a mall" experiment, in which a person can become convinced that he or she had a childhood experience of being lost in a shopping mall and may even be able to describe various details about the experience. The only problem: It never occurred. It was an implanted memory. The false memory was implanted through leading or suggestive questions.

Constructive Memory The process by which memories are actively reconstructed, elaborated on, or modified during retrieval is called **constructive memory.** It involves the integration of new information, beliefs, or experiences into existing memories and can result in memory distortions, errors, or inaccuracies as memories are shaped by factors such as imagination, suggestion, and inference. Constructive memory illustrates how memories can be shaped by external factors and previously held schemas.

Memory consolidation is the process by which newly formed memories are stabilized and integrated into long-term memory. It begins in the first few hours after learning. Memory consolidation takes place when we learn a new skill, such as playing a musical instrument or learning a foreign language; when remembering an important event, such as a wedding; or when studying for an exam. Even as you read this unit you are consolidating what you are learning and reading about with older memories. This process is strengthening neural connections through long-term potentiation, which you read about earlier in Topic 2.3. New skills become easier and more automatic with practice as they are consolidated in memory. Memories of important events may become more vivid and detailed over time as they are consolidated in memory. And information that is repeatedly reviewed and practiced is more likely to be consolidated in memory and therefore more easily retrieved during an exam. Memory consolidation that occurs during waking periods is known as *active consolidation,* while *sleep-dependent consolidation* occurs during sleep.

Imagination inflation refers to the phenomenon whereby repeatedly imagining or elaborating on an event can lead to an increased confidence in the event's occurrence, even if it never actually happened. Constructive memory processes play a role in imagination inflation by blurring the distinction between imagined events and real memories. Repeatedly imagining a fictitious event or elaborating on a real event can lead to the creation of false memories that seem just as real and vivid as genuine memories, leading to confusion between those memories and reality. Imagination inflation illustrates the malleability of memory and the reconstructive nature of memory processes. Understanding this phenomenon is important for evaluating the reliability of memories and eyewitness testimony.

A related concept, **source amnesia,** is the inability to remember the origin of a memory while retaining its substance. Think of all the places that you get your information—television, class, social media, textbooks, peers, family members. We often remember the information that we acquired but cannot recall where that information came from. Many teachers give lectures on a topic they learned about from many sources, but when asked where the information came from, they may not be able to identify the initial source.

Think of memory like Play-Doh: Each time you retrieve the memory, it can be molded and remolded. For example, if your team narrowly misses out on a state championship, there may be many conversations about this event over time, and the details may begin to shift. You may start to create a story about a referee who made a bad call, even if this was not part of your original memory.

THINK AS A PSYCHOLOGIST

Evaluate the Appropriate Use of Research Design Elements in Experimental Methodology (2.B.2, 2.B.5) | Apply Psychological Perspectives, Theories, Concepts, and Research Findings To A Scenario (1.A.1)

Professor Cassidy put an ad in the campus newspaper indicating that he is looking for students to volunteer for an experiment exploring memory processes. Fifty students volunteered, and Professor Cassidy randomly assigned them to two groups. Both groups did a memory experiment in which they learned to pair a musician with the name of one of that musician's albums (for example, Taylor Swift and *Folklore*). Group 1 learned 100 such pairings and then took a test two weeks later to see how many pairings they remembered. Group 2 did the same task, but two days after learning the initial pairing they were exposed to a second set of 100 pairings that contained different musicians, each paired with an album. Two weeks after the initial list was introduced, both groups took a simple recall test where they were asked to write down as many musician/album pairings from the initial list as they could remember. The mean number of accurate musician/album pairings for each group can be found in the table below.

Mean Number of Musician/Album Pairings Accurately Identified by Each Group	
Group 1	Group 2
Mean = 58.31	Mean = 36.26

Practice Evaluating Research Design Elements and Applying Concepts

Answer the following questions.

1. What is the operational definition of the dependent variable?

2. Identify why Dr. Cassidy will not be able to generalize his findings.

3. The results of the experiment are most likely due to which of the following?

   (A) Group 2 recalled less because Dr. Cassidy introduced misinformation that interfered with subjects' memory of the initial task.

   (B) Group 2 found the task overwhelming and stressful, which led them to repress the experience.

   (C) Group 2 likely experienced retroactive interference, which impeded their memory of the first list.

   (D) Group 2 used elaborative rehearsal more effectively than Group 1.

THINK AS A PSYCHOLOGIST

Develop and Justify Psychological Arguments Using Evidence (4.A)

Practice Developing and Justifying an Argument with Evidence

Complete the following activity and answer the question.

Using Topic 2.7 as a source, make a defensible claim addressing the following question: What is the most significant reason that we forget things in life?

1. Propose a claim identifying the factor you believe is most significant.

2. Why do you believe that is the most significant factor in forgetting?

REFLECT ON THE ESSENTIAL QUESTION

Essential Question: *Why do memory failure or errors occur?* Using the Key Terms, complete a chart like the one below to gather details to help answer that question.

Internal Factors	External Factors

KEY TERMS

constructive memory	memory consolidation	retroactive interference
encoding failure	misinformation effect	source amnesia
forgetting curve	proactive interference	tip-of-the-tongue (TOT)
imagination inflation	repression	phenomenon

MULTIPLE-CHOICE QUESTIONS

Questions 1 and 2 refer to the following.

Several students witnessed and have since been discussing an accident that happened in the cafeteria. Louis is certain that he saw Emma rush to help Isaac after he slipped and fell, but Bridget insists that it was Sophia who came to Isaac's aid first. When Bridget and Louis talk to the school nurse later in the day, Bridget tells him that it was Emma who helped Isaac up.

1. Which memory error has Bridget encountered?

   (A) Encoding failure

   (B) The misinformation effect

   (C) Inadequate retrieval

   (D) Retrograde amnesia

2. Students all over the school discussed the details of Isaac's fall, who was involved, what happened, and what recognition the helping students might receive. McKenzie told some of her friends that one of the students involved will be featured as "Student of the Week" on the school website. When asked whom she heard that from, she cannot recall but is confident that this information is correct. What memory challenge has McKenzie experienced?

(A) Anterograde amnesia

(B) Mood-congruent memory

(C) Constructive memory

(D) Source amnesia

3. Ewa is a talented actor who is often in the school's plays and musicals. Production has just started for the winter play and, despite having spent hundreds of hours preparing for the fall play just a few months ago, she finds that she can remember only her lines for the current play, and the lines from the previous play are gone from her memory. What psychological phenomenon could help explain Ewa's experience?

(A) Retrograde amnesia

(B) Retroactive interference

(C) Proactive interference

(D) Anterograde amnesia

Questions 4 through 7 refer to the following.

Professor Rosso wants to examine how long students retain material after leaving his class. To conduct the study, he recruits 10 volunteers from his class. He gives a 10-minute lecture that contains 20 pieces of information he wants students to remember, and after 15 minutes he tests them on how many they recall out of the 20 items. He then shows them a 15-minute sitcom and tests them a second time on their recall of the 20 pieces of information. After another 15-minute sitcom, he tests the students a third time on their recall of the 20 pieces of information. The results of the study are depicted below.

Participant	Trial #1 Info Recalled	Trial #2 Info Recalled	Trial #3 Info Recalled
1	17	14	11
2	14	12	11
3	15	15	14
4	19	17	12
5	20	19	15
6	20	18	13
7	17	14	11
8	12	9	9
9	19	19	16
10	18	16	14

4. For Trial #3, identify the range of scores.
   (A) 12.6
   (B) 12.5
   (C) 7
   (D) 14

5. The results of the study are depicted in the graph below. What is the most likely correlation coefficient for the findings in this study?

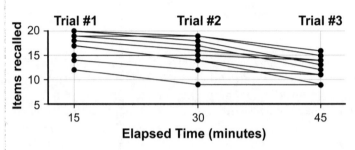

   (A) r = +1.25
   (B) p = .05
   (C) n = 30
   (D) r = −.64

6. Which of the following statements accurately explains the ability of Professor Rosso to generalize from this study?
   (A) Professor Rosso cannot generalize because he did not take a random sample of participants from his classes.
   (B) Professor Rosso cannot generalize to his classes because he did not include enough students in his sample.
   (C) Professor Rosso can generalize to his classes because he has only used students from his classes in his sample.
   (D) Professor Rosso can generalize to his classes because he did not mandate that students participate but instead took volunteers.

7. The graph of the results from Professor Rosso's study looks most like which psychological concept?
   (A) The learning curve
   (B) The normal curve
   (C) The forgetting curve
   (D) The serial position effect

Topic 2.8

Intelligence and Achievement

"I know that I am intelligent, because I know that I know nothing."
—Socrates

Essential Question: How do modern and historical theories describe intelligence?

While most agree that intelligence exists, just what is it and how can we clearly categorize the skills associated with it? Some consider **intelligence** to be related to success, others believe it reflects one's ability to successfully navigate day-to-day life, and yet others believe that intelligence refers to one's ability to solve novel problems or to be nimble in the face of new challenges. This topic will explore how individuals have attempted to define the components they believed make up one's intelligence. As you read, consider what factors you believe make up intelligence and which assessment techniques you believe best capture this abstract construct.

The qualities believed to make up intelligence differ from culture to culture. What it means to be "smart" can vary considerably depending upon the skills and talents a society values, which can vary over time and place. A culture's definition of intelligence will in many ways also define how intelligence is measured in that culture. For this reason, when tests of intelligence are used on cultural groups other than the one for which the test was written, the results may be low scores that are likely to be misleading or inaccurate. For example, tests with inflexible time restrictions are not well received by cultures that take an unrushed approach to problem-solving. Likewise, tests with only a single possible correct response for questions are not well received by cultures that tend to practice divergent thinking (a creative problem-solving approach aimed at coming up with several possible good answers; see Topic 2.2). Cultural differences in defining and measuring intelligence provide a challenge in developing culturally fair tests.

Theories of Intelligence

Both modern and historical theories have attempted to define intelligence, although they vary in emphasis and approach. Historical theories often focused on identifying the components or types of intelligence, while modern theories tend to adopt a more multifaceted and multidimensional view, acknowledging the complexity and diversity of human cognitive abilities.

Historical Efforts to Define and Measure Intelligence

Many historical theories proposed a unitary concept of intelligence, suggesting that it is a single, general ability. Early theorists had a relatively limited understanding of the cognitive processes underlying intelligence. Some of them viewed intelligence as a fixed and innate trait determined primarily by genetics and relatively stable throughout life.

Heritability Sir Francis Galton was one of the first to attempt to measure levels of intelligence. Galton was a statistician who created the concept of correlation and coined the name for the now well-known debate of nature and nurture. Galton, a cousin of Charles Darwin, fell decisively on the side of nature, believing that intelligence is inherited rather than influenced by environment. In his 1869 book *Hereditary Genius*, he laid out his thoughts regarding the heritability—genetic basis—of intelligence. He even went so far as to suggest ideas that would lead to the field of eugenics (see Topic 1.1), promoting reproduction for the highly intelligent and potential sterilization for those with "less desirable traits."

Galton believed that tests of physical and sensory strength would reveal mental capacity. He measured individuals' sensory abilities, bodily proportions, sensitivity to high-pitched sounds, and reaction times. Not surprisingly, given his thoughts about genetics, Galton's test indicated that upper-class males scored higher on these intelligence assessments than other groups. His methods of testing and clear bias for white males have been challenged by more recent and empirically sound research. Many modern researchers attribute Galton's findings to confirmation bias because he may have unknowingly created tests that would favor subjects who ultimately scored well. (See Practice 1.B to review confirmation bias.)

Factor Analysis In the early 1900s, Charles Spearman discovered that individuals who score high on one measure of intelligence (vocabulary, for example) often also score well on other measures of intelligence (such as arithmetic). This positive correlation was the impetus for Spearman's idea that all the specific skills (*s*) that comprised intelligence come together to make up one's overall intelligence, which Spearman described as general intelligence (***g***). This has since come to be known as the *g*-factor. To make a modern-day analogy, if you have ever taken an ACT, PSAT, or SAT exam, you know that you receive a subscore in each area of the test (*s*, specific skill), as well as an overall test score (*g*, general intelligence). While these are not intelligence tests, this is the specific-to-general breakdown that Spearman was interested in exploring. The statistical procedure Spearman created to analyze correlations between different measures is known as *factor analysis*. If various measures of intelligence correlated positively, they likely were all related to some other variable that was not measured, which is the *factor*. For example, you may find that some people in your class who do well in math are the same people who do well in English or social studies. The factor to which these abilities are all related is general intelligence (*g*).

Contemporary Intelligence Research and Theories

Contemporary theories recognize that intelligence is a many-sided concept that encompasses a wide range of cognitive abilities, skills, and capacities. These theories emphasize the existence of multiple forms of intelligence beyond the traditional notion of general intelligence.

Multiple Intelligences Howard Gardner of Harvard University expanded on the idea that intelligence is made up of more than a single factor. He criticized traditional intelligence tests for placing too much emphasis on those skills that are generally associated with school success, such as verbal and mathematical abilities. He believed that there are multiple intelligences that are relatively independent of one another and combine to identify intelligence in numerous different settings. Gardner's theory, published in 1985, identified eight different types of intelligence, as shown in Figure 2.8.1.

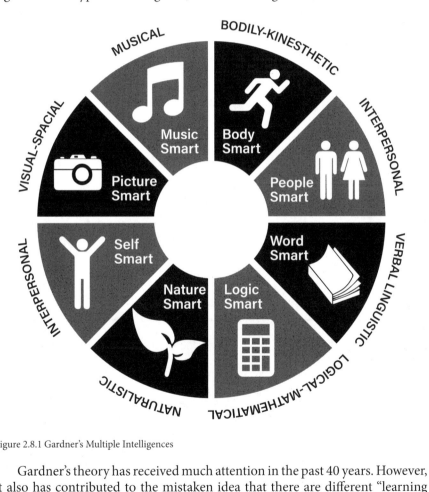

Figure 2.8.1 Gardner's Multiple Intelligences

Gardner's theory has received much attention in the past 40 years. However, it also has contributed to the mistaken idea that there are different "learning styles" and that educators should teach according to each individual's learning style. While people may have ways in which they are more comfortable learning, their education may be better served by attempting to identify areas of weakness in individuals' learning and having those individuals practice these areas so that they can become more capable of learning in all ways.

Gardner's theory has also received criticism for its lack of empirical support. It is very difficult to test these different proposed intelligences in a standardized format, and since Gardner does not believe in standardized testing, it does not appear that empirical support is forthcoming from his research. Many also have questioned whether his categories are actual intelligences or simply talents, which raises the question of whether there is truly a difference between the two. Still others question whether spreading the concept of intelligence too far will dilute the concept and reduce the significance of what we take intelligence to mean.

Triarchic Theory of Intelligence Robert Sternberg agrees with the basic premise of Gardner's theory—that traditional intelligence tests are not particularly good at assessing overall intelligence, and that intelligence is made up of multiple factors. However, he disagrees with the division of intelligence Gardner proposed because he believes the categories are too specific. In 1988, Sternberg proposed three larger categories under which different types of intelligence could be categorized. This is known as the triarchic theory (Figure 2.8.2).

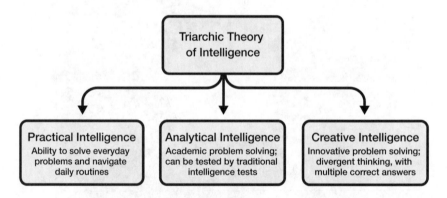

Figure 2.8.2 Sternberg's Triarchic Theory of Intelligence

Modern intelligence researchers and psychometric psychologists continue to debate the definition of intelligence and how to assess it properly and fairly. Some argue that the identification of intelligence as a single number cannot provide a complete summary of one's intelligence, and that what it means to be smart is too diversified to carry a single label.

Measuring Intelligence

Psychometric psychologists focus on measuring and assessing a number of traits, including intelligence. Psychometric psychologists are skilled mathematicians who statistically analyze the results from intelligence and other types of tests, such as personality inventories. They devise **intelligence tests** to measure individual differences by comparing one's results to those of others who have taken the same exam.

Early Intelligence Tests

The Binet-Simon intelligence scale was developed by Alfred Binet in partnership with his colleague Théodore Simon in 1905 to identify for the French government those children who would benefit from extra help before the start of their formal education. This assessment is often considered the first modern-day intelligence test. The test provided children with a **mental age**, allowing the assessor to identify if children were ahead of or behind their peers. For example, a 5-year-old child of average intelligence would receive a mental age of 5, whereas a child who is 5 years old but does not score as well as peers might receive a mental age of 3. The test was fairly successful at identifying those who needed extra help academically and correlated well with teachers' feedback regarding students' progress.

The belief that students would benefit from extra training before enrolling in school to help them catch up with their peers was a move away from Galton's theory that intelligence was entirely genetically inherited. Binet used the term "mental orthopedics" to express the idea that children can improve their attention and self-discipline with practice. This view prompted researchers in the field to recognize the importance of the environment's role in influencing subjects' levels of intelligence and introduced a shift away from the sole focus on genetic influence.

Reading to very young children helps their language growth, literacy, and reading achievement, but it also benefits children 6 to 12 years of age whose IQ may increase as a result.

Stanford-Binet Intelligence Test Lewis Terman, a professor at Stanford University, wanted to bring intelligence testing to the United States. Since the Binet-Simon scale had predicted academic success relatively well, Terman was interested in modifying it to apply to a wider population, so he adjusted the test to be more appropriate for an American audience of varied ages and a broader range of subjects. In 1905, Terman identified the new version of the exam as the Stanford-Binet intelligence test.

German psychologist William Stern created a formula in 1912 to compute one's **Intelligence Quotient (IQ)** by taking the mental age (provided by the exam) divided by the **chronological age** (the actual age of the child) multiplied by 100. The results would immediately show if children were ahead of or behind their peers. This formula set the standard for intelligence scores to have a mean (average) of 100. While this formula has since been replaced by more modern methods, a score of 100 still represents an average intelligence score.

$$IQ = \frac{\text{mental age}}{\text{chronological age}} \times 100$$

Figure 2.8.3 IQ Formula

Terman believed that intelligence is genetically determined, and he was particularly interested in studying those who had extremely high intelligence scores. Terman began one of the most well-known and longest lasting longitudinal studies in the history of psychology. His hypothesis sought to determine if those with high IQs led lives that were significantly different from others. Terman had a large sample of roughly 1,500 individuals with IQs of 150 or above. (Those whom Terman studied became known as "Termites.")

Despite some of his subjects perhaps earning slightly better salaries and having above average reports of happiness, they did not report having lives that were significantly different from others, as Terman had expected. They were, however, found to be above average in height, weight, physical strength, and emotional adjustment.

Wechsler Intelligence Scales David Wechsler believed that the widely used Stanford-Binet assessment did not measure all of a person's intelligence. He created different forms of his own intelligence assessments for children and adults—the Wechsler Intelligence Scale for Children (WISC) in 1945 and Wechsler Adult Intelligence Scale (WAIS) in 1955. (If you have ever taken an IQ test, this is likely the assessment you took, either in part or in whole.) He believed the Binet-Simon and Stanford-Binet tests were too dependent on verbal ability, so he added a performance scale that measured perceptual organization and processing speed—the time it takes to complete certain cognitive tasks—as well. The specific tasks involved in this new performance measurement included such abstract tasks as block design (matching visual patterns), picture completion (recognizing what is missing in a picture of an object), matrix reasoning (visual-spatial problems to solve), digit-symbol coding (remembering symbols and their matching numbers), and symbol searching (finding a designated symbol in a group of symbols). The digit-symbol coding and symbol searching measure processing speed. Wechsler retained the verbal scale, which included the more traditional intelligence components such as verbal comprehension and working memory, which he assessed by testing one's understanding of such subjects and skills as vocabulary, arithmetic, and digit span. Today a Wechsler test might be administered when a student is being evaluated for a special education program (e.g., extra services for students performing well below or above their classmates).

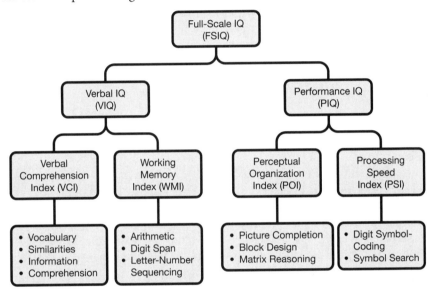

Figure 2.8.4 Wechsler Intelligence Scale

These types of performance tasks on the Weschler test were very different from what traditional intelligence exams had tested, but Wechsler believed that this assessment represented a more complete view of intelligence. (See Figure 2.8.4.) Wechsler also modified the way in which intelligence scores were reported. Instead of using the traditional formula created by William Stern, he proposed that, through the use of *norming*, an individual's scores be compared to others' using a percentile rank. The normal distribution that Wechsler used to compare intelligence scores is still used today. (See Practice 3 for more on standard distributions.)

Principles for Psychological Assessments

Just as defining intelligence can be tricky, constructing tests that can accurately measure intelligence poses its own challenges. How can we be sure that we are measuring what we intend to measure? This is made more difficult, as you have already read, because not all psychologists agree on the factors that contribute to intelligence. How can we be sure the same test will work for all subjects, in all situations, time and again? To address such challenges, all psychological assessments, including intelligence tests, should adhere to sound **psychometric principles,** fundamental features that an assessment must meet to be considered as high quality. This section explores these principles.

Standardization and Norms You have likely taken many standardized tests in your life. The AP Psychology exam you are preparing for in this course will be yet another example of this type of exam. The standardization process makes comparisons between test results from different test takers easier and more accurate.

Standardization refers to the procedures by which an exam is created, administered, and scored. For **standardized tests,** all factors regarding timing, directions, setting, seating, and monitoring should be the same for all test takers. It would be unfair if the proctor for your AP exam never gave you a time limit for completing the exam when test takers at all other schools had to complete the 75 multiple-choice questions in 90 minutes. If you could review answers and take all the time you wanted, your results would likely be higher than those with time restrictions and, for this reason, it would not be appropriate to compare your score to those of others who experienced different test conditions.

A college entrance exam such as the ACT or SAT mandates that the proctor read very specific directions and even tell you when you can open your test booklets. Once you complete a section of the exam, you are not permitted to go back and work on that section. All these measures have been put in place to standardize the exam and make sure your score can be compared with those of thousands of others who take the exam on the same day, with the same guidelines and under the same conditions.

Standardized tests also use test norms—the distribution of scores of a clearly defined group. The group from which norms are determined must be carefully identified by age, gender, and any other relevant factor to accurately serve as a sample for the entire population taking the test. A norm-referenced test is one that allows you to be compared to this sample group of test takers and determine your relative position in the testing group. If you received an ACT score of 28, you could not gauge how well you did on the exam until you knew that the highest possible score was 36, the state average was 21, and the school average was 24, for example.

To further describe one's score in comparison to others, percentile rank is used to indicate the percentage of people in a population who scored at or below an individual's score. Using the example above, in 2023 an ACT score of 28 translated to a percentile rank of 88. That percentile would indicate that you scored better than 88 percent of the students taking the same form of the test on previous test dates. Today, percentile rank is also used in reference to a person's score on an intelligence test.

Validity Validity is the degree to which assessments succeed in measuring what they are designed to measure. There are several different kinds of validity.

When a test measures the content or subject that it was designed to measure, it has *content validity*. If a test in your English class on *Beowulf*, which your class just finished reading, included questions related to *Beowulf*, it would have a high degree of validity. If it had instead included questions on geometry, you could rightly challenge the validity of the exam.

The above examples are exaggerated, and content validity is usually more challenging to determine. To properly assess whether a measure contains content validity, an expert should carefully examine all aspects of the concept the test developers are attempting to measure. For example, intelligence tests are strictly timed and, as a result, may be a good measure of speed of processing. However, if researchers do not believe that processing speed is an important component of intelligence, they may question the content validity of that intelligence test.

The degree to which a test appears valid to the test taker is called *face validity*. A test has face validity if it appears at first glance to measure what it sets out to measure. For example, because you now know that psychology involves the analysis of data and thus involves statistics, you could see a graph of a normal distribution on a unit exam in psychology and determine that at least that part of the test has face validity. However, a friend who has not taken psychology might take a quick look at the exam and claim that it is not a psychology test but is instead a math test. Your friend, a nonexpert who did not look at the exam closely, is questioning the face validity of the exam, when the exam actually has both face and content validity.

Almost everyone would agree that people have personalities and intelligence. Personality, intelligence, and other hypothetical concepts, such as self-esteem, are *constructs*, ideas or theories typically considered to be subjective and not based on empirical evidence For example, although we cannot pinpoint where in the brain or person such traits as personality and intelligence reside, we acknowledge their existence and try to assess and measure them. Constructs are more difficult to define operationally than concepts such as height and weight, which exist in the physical world and can be seen and touched. Researchers need to be very clear about how they plan to measure a given construct because others may have very different perspectives regarding what comprises that characteristic. For example, Wechsler believed that a good intelligence test must include both performance and verbal measures. For this reason, he questioned the construct validity of the Stanford-Binet test, which did not include any performance measures. **Construct validity** requires an assessment to be based on the entire range of theoretical concepts that underlie the subject.

On occasion, an individual may get a different result on two (or more) assessments that claim to measure the same construct. For example, if you took five different assessments, all of which claimed to measure intelligence, and four reported that you had an IQ between 115 and 120 but the fifth test claimed your IQ was 85, we would question the concurrent validity of the fifth test. Only a highly positive correlation between assessments that claim to measure the same component can establish *criterion validity* for those tests.

If an assessment accurately forecasts performance on a future measure, it has **predictive validity**. For example, thousands of high school students take the EXPLORE and PLAN aptitude tests to predict how they will perform on the ACT. The ACT, in turn, claims to predict one's success in the first year of college. Other tests that claim predictive validity are assessments for careers and those that focus on the ability to problem-solve in the future, using questions the test takers have not seen before rather than ones on the extent of the knowledge they already have.

Reliability Consistency and stability of results are an assessment's reliability. Like validity, reliability has several different types. Following are those that are often found in standardized assessments (see Figure 2.8.5).

The degree to which an assessment yields similar individual results each time it is taken is called **test-retest reliability**. For example, you may know people who took the ACT or SAT multiple times, trying to improve their scores, only to receive the same scores each time or improve by a single point. This example demonstrates high test-retest reliability.

Two Parts of a Test A less well-known type of reliability, **split-half reliability**, is the degree to which two halves of an exam have equal difficulty. In one sitting, test takers are told to answer only the odd-numbered questions. In another sitting, they would be instructed to answer the even-numbered questions. If the scores from both halves of the test are comparable, the exam has internal consistency and a high degree of split-half reliability.

Reliability and Validity of Intelligence Testing Do IQ tests actually measure what they are designed to measure? The validity of intelligence tests is up for debate. When evaluating intelligence tests based on their ability to predict school performance, they stand up fairly well. IQ scores and school grades generally correlate well. However, they do not correlate as well to careers that involve physical strength or endurance. In fact, it is estimated that as much as 75 percent of one's performance—physical or otherwise—is unrelated to IQ. For example, a worker may have great intellectual ability but not much conscientiousness (work ethic and ability to follow through on tasks). That worker may arrive late to work and meetings and not complete assigned projects. This performance is not related to the worker's level of intelligence but will most certainly have an impact on job success.

Some correlations regarding the consistency (test-retest reliability) of IQ test results over time are as high as 0.90 (remember that the highest positive correlational coefficient that can exist is 1.0). For test takers distracted by a personal matter or unusually tired on testing day, there will likely be lower levels of reliability from one test to the next. Those who are in a testing environment they find comfortable may score slightly higher than if they are in a setting in which they are nervous or distracted. Both environmental and personal factors need to be taken into account when examining the results of assessments of intelligence. All these variables help to explain why the validity of intelligence tests is open to debate.

Assessing the Range of Intelligence

What does it mean to be of "normal" intelligence? Understanding the basics of intelligence standards and extremes requires an understanding of statistics.

Normal Distribution The application of intelligence tests to the normal distribution has all three components needed to work with any normal distribution. First, and most important, we always know that the scores of an IQ test will result in a normal distribution. Second, we know that the mean (the average score in a population) is 100. Third, we know that the standard deviation (the average distance from the mean) is 15.

One benefit of working with a normally distributed population is that the distribution of the population is predictable. With a normal distribution, approximately 68 percent of the population will fall within one standard deviation of the mean (covering IQ scores between 85 and 115), about 95 percent of the population will score within two standard deviations of the mean (covering IQ scores between 70 and 130), and 99.7 percent of the population will score within three standard deviations of the mean (covering IQ scores between 55 and 145). Only 0.15 percent of the population will have an IQ score of below 55, and 0.15 percent of the population will have an IQ score above 145. (See Figure 2.8.5.)

Percentages in a Normal Distribution

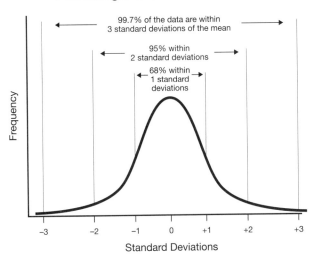

Figure 2.8.5

Percentile Rank Once you know how the percentage of the population is distributed in the normal distribution, you can start to compute the percentile rank for a given IQ score. Remember that *percentile rank* indicates the percentage of people who scored at or below a given score. If a person has an IQ score of 100, their score falls directly in the middle of the population, giving them a percentile rank of 50 because he scored better than 50 percent of the population.

When working with a normal distribution, remember that z-scores represent how many standard deviations a score is away from the mean. For example, if an individual had an IQ score of 130, her z-score would be +2 because her score is 2 standard deviations above the mean. If her IQ score was 100, the z-score would be 0 because she is directly at the mean. Z-scores are useful because they provide a succinct method of describing where a person's score falls in comparison to others in the normal distribution.

The normal distribution is predictable, and often large-scale tests like IQ scores and SAT or ACT scores turn into a predictable bell-shaped curve. While this allows for the computation of percentile and comparison across large groups, not all distributions are normal. Refer back to pages 89–90 for a review of positively and negatively skewed distributions.

Sociocultural Concerns

While intelligence testing is still commonly used today to identify those who may need extra assistance or more challenging work in school—or even just for those who are curious about intelligence—the widespread use of intelligence testing has received much criticism. One reason is because individuals from minority groups (in particular, Hispanics and African Americans) are far more likely to be identified as having lower intelligence scores than Caucasians. This finding could potentially be caused by something called **stereotype threat**: If a member of a group believes their group traditionally scores poorly on an assessment, this knowledge may cause anxiety, which in turn may cause the person to fulfill the poor expectation and score poorly. This performance does not reflect ability; this is about "performing down." Stereotype threat is not an issue when one does not know that one's group tends to score poorly on a given assessment.

Stereotype threat has also been demonstrated to have an impact when there are expectations about performance for a given gender. A number of studies have shown that when females are told that as a group they perform less well than males on math tests, test results reflect that their performance declines. However, when no stereotype threat is activated, females perform equally to males on average. This equivalent performance once again indicates that the issues is not of females' knowledge of math; it is an issue of the expectations others hold or that they are reminded of shortly before the exam.

Stereotype lift, in contrast, is a phenomenon in which individuals from stereotyped groups perform better on tasks when positive stereotypes about their group are activated. Unlike stereotype threat, stereotype lift occurs when individuals experience a boost in performance due to positive expectations associated with their social group. For example, if female students are reminded of the stereotype that women often perform better on assessments related to verbal tasks, they may perform better on a verbal test. Similarly, if African American students are exposed to positive stereotypes about academics, they may perform better on standardized tests because the negative stereotype has been removed.

To reduce stereotype threat, stereotype lift, and other possible inequities, researchers attempt to develop **socioculturally responsive assessments**. Often, however, bias in the design of an assessment is not identified until a certain group has scored significantly differently on it (usually lower) than other groups. Questions using regional language or references to events or objects with which one may not be familiar put some groups at a distinct disadvantage. An intelligence test should assess one's ability to solve problems rather than what one already knows. Good tests of intelligence must provide all test takers, regardless of their racial, ethnic, or socioeconomic background, an equal chance to demonstrate their problem-solving abilities. While intelligence tests have improved in this area, it is unlikely that bias has been eliminated entirely, so test makers continue to work on making these assessments fairer.

The single number provided by an intelligence test may also be problematic. Because there is a margin of error for all exams, scores reported in a range may be more useful. Genes provide a person with a range of intelligence, and the environment helps to determine whether a person falls at the low or high end of that range. This concept is known as *reaction range* and has moved the discussion of intelligence away from the single-number approach. Tests of intelligence may eventually come to reflect a range rather than focus on a single number.

Systemic Issues and the Uses of Intelligence Assessment

Systemic issues—those that are deeply embedded within the structures and processes of society—have shaped both the quantitative and qualitative interpretations of intelligence scores. Quantitative measures, as you have read, rely on standardized assessments and statistical analysis to arrive at an objective measure. Qualitative measures, in contrast, focus on the descriptive and interpretative aspects of intelligence rather than numerical scores. In addition to using descriptive analysis and case studies, qualitative measures consider the environmental, cultural, and educational contexts of the test taker. This approach recognizes that cognitive abilities cannot be fully understood in isolation from these contexts. Systemic issues related to differences in generations and differences in cultural background are central to today's academic conversations about intelligence.

The Flynn Effect—Generational Changes

As you have read, results of modern-day intelligence tests are displayed as a normal distribution. Each year, the test is renormed to keep the mean (average) numerical value of intelligence at 100. If these tests were not renormed each year, those who took intelligence tests years ago might appear less intelligent than those who take intelligence tests today. The **Flynn effect**, named after the New Zealand psychologist James Flynn, who identified the phenomenon, claims that people are getting "smarter," or at least increasing their quantitative scores.

There are many possible qualitative explanations for the Flynn effect, such as better nutrition early in life, which may allow for early brain development and development of neural networks, and access to better health care. Students today also take far more standardized tests to quantify what they know than did students in the past, so perhaps students are just getting better at taking these types of tests. In addition, the wealth of information available on the Internet and through personal devices today allows younger people access to far more information than their counterparts had even a generation earlier. All these factors may contribute to the improved scores. While the origins of the effect are not yet definitively understood, the scores of intelligence tests are moving upward, and, for this reason, one's results can be compared only to those in the group who took the exam at the same time. Comparing one's score to those who took the exam many years ago would provide misleading results and would be a misrepresented comparison if the tests were not continually renormed.

Scores Within and Between Groups

In their controversial 1994 book *The Bell Curve,* authors Richard Herrnstein and Charles Murray assert the now discredited claim that average IQ differences between racial and ethnic groups are partly genetic in origin. In fact, numerous studies across diverse populations consistently find that the range of IQ scores *within* any given racial, ethnic, or socioeconomic group is much broader than the differences in average IQ scores *between* these groups. In the same way, research in genetics and intelligence also indicates that while there are genetic components to intelligence, the vast majority of genetic diversity exists *within* populations rather than *between* them. This genetic diversity contributes to significant variations in IQ scores within any defined group.

Personal and Sociocultural Bias Additionally, the interpretation of individual IQ scores is susceptible to personal and sociocultural biases. These biases can come from multiple sources, including the test designers, administrators, interpreters of the results, and the cultural norms of the society in which the tests are used.

- **Personal bias** may develop through examiner expectations, which may lead the examiner to unconsciously give more favorable interpretations or additional encouragement to certain individuals based on their own biases or expectations. Confirmation bias occurs when those interpreting IQ scores seek information that confirms their pre-existing beliefs or hypotheses about a test taker, such as expecting lower or higher performance based on socioeconomic background, ethnicity, or gender.
- **Sociocultural biases** show in IQ test items that reflects the dominant culture's values and knowledge, which can disadvantage individuals from different cultural backgrounds. How IQ scores are used can also reflect sociocultural biases. For instance, decisions about educational

tracking, special education placements, or eligibility for gifted programs often rely on these scores. If the tests or their interpretations are biased, systematic inequalities in educational and occupational opportunities result.

IQ Scores and Other Outcomes *The Bell Curve* also sought to associate IQ scores with other life outcomes. These too have been discredited but offer an example of how the interpretation of IQ scores and other outcomes can reinforce certain stereotypes or misconceptions, potentially leading to decisions and policies that disproportionately affect certain groups. Thus, it's important to approach the analysis and application of IQ testing with a critical understanding of these underlying biases to ensure fair and equitable treatment across diverse populations.

Factors That Negatively Influence Intelligence Scores

Poverty, discrimination, and educational inequities in the United States and all around the world can have strong negative effects on intelligence scores. These factors of environment play an especially important role.

- **Poverty**: Poverty is associated with food insecurity and inadequate nutrition, which can lead to malnutrition and lack of nutrients crucial for brain development and cognitive functioning, particularly during critical periods of growth and development in early childhood. Just as James Flynn found that good nutrition early in life can contribute to raising IQ scores, the opposite can be true for a lack of nutritious food during the same critical period. Malnutrition can impair cognitive abilities such as memory, attention, and problem-solving, potentially lowering intelligence scores. People living in impoverished environments may be exposed to environmental toxins, pollutants, and stressors, such as air and water pollution, lead exposure, noise, and overcrowded living conditions. These environmental stressors can have a negative effect on brain development and cognitive functioning and contribute to lower IQ scores.

- **Discrimination**: As you have read, discrimination based on race, ethnicity, gender, socioeconomic status, or disability can have a negative impact on cognitive performance and intelligence scores. Stereotype threat and culturally biased test items contribute to lower scores, as do the cultural relevance of test items, language barriers, and unfamiliarity with testing. These results of discrimination undermine the validity and fairness of intelligence scores.

- **Educational Inequities**: People living in poverty often lack access to quality education because of inadequate school facilities, lack of qualified teachers, and insufficient resources. People from disadvantaged backgrounds may also have limited access to enriching and stimulating environments that promote cognitive development, such as books, educational toys, extracurricular activities, and cultural experiences. Lower-quality education and an impoverished environment can hinder cognitive development and academic achievement and affect intelligence scores.

Controversial Uses of Intelligence Test Scores

Imagine walking into a room knowing that a single number assigned to you could determine the course of your life. This is not the plot of a dystopian novel; it's a reality for many when it comes to intelligence scores. Throughout history and across various sectors—military enrollment, job qualifications, immigration processes, and educational admissions—intelligence tests have been a gatekeeper, often deciding who gets in and who is left out.

This practice of using IQ scores as a critical filter began in earnest during the early 20th century. For instance, during World War I, the U.S. military used intelligence tests developed by eugenicist Henry Goddard to sort soldiers into different roles and ranks. Even today, recruits with higher scores may be favored for certain roles or ranks within the military, while those with lower scores may be limited in their opportunities for advancement. The use of intelligence tests in military contexts has raised concerns about fairness, equity, and diversity within the armed forces.

Scores from intelligence tests have historically been used in various contexts to limit access to jobs, military ranks, educational institutions, and immigration to the United States.

In the job market, certain high-stakes professions use these scores to evaluate potential employees' suitability and assess applicants' cognitive abilities and suitability for specific job roles. However, the use of intelligence tests in employment settings has been criticized for perpetuating biases and discrimination, particularly against minority groups, and providing little relevant information on how a person will perform on the job. Test scores have been used to justify discriminatory hiring practices and to exclude individuals from employment opportunities.

In the realm of education, schools and universities often rely on standardized test scores, akin to IQ tests, to make decisions about admissions, sometimes determining a student's educational path from a young age. Test scores may be used to determine eligibility for gifted and talented programs, advanced placement courses, special education services, or admission into college. However, the use of intelligence tests in education has been criticized for reinforcing inequalities and perpetuating disparities in academic achievement, particularly for marginalized and disadvantaged students.

Aspects of immigration law have also considered the intellectual "fitness" of potential migrants, influencing who is allowed to enter and settle in a country. One of the most dramatic examples of testing immigrants occurred during the early 1900s when Goddard administered his intelligence tests to immigrants at Ellis Island. He determined that nearly 80 percent of Eastern and Southern European immigrants, most of whom had not yet learned English, were "feebleminded" in what was more of a case of confirmation bias than a test of IQ. Intelligence tests are no longer used in immigration policies.

The use of intelligence test scores in these ways has been controversial and fraught with ethical, legal, and social implications. Critics argue that intelligence tests may be culturally biased, lack validity and fairness, and perpetuate systemic inequalities and discrimination. As a result, there has been ongoing debate and scrutiny surrounding the use of intelligence tests in decision-making processes.

THINK AS A PSYCHOLOGIST

Propose a Defensible Claim (4.A) | Provide Reasoning That Is Grounded in Scientifically Derived Evidence to Support, Refute, or Modify an Established or Provided Claim, Policy, or Norm (4.B.1) | Evaluate Whether a Psychological Research Scenario Followed Appropriate Ethical Procedures (2.D) | Explain How Cultural Norms, Expectations, and Circumstances, as Well as Cognitive Biases, Apply to Behavior and Mental Processes (1.B.3)

Read the following abstract of a study exploring ethical issues in IQ testing.

Abstract.[3] Intelligence tests are widely used both in research and in practice (education, clinical, human resources). We begin to feel the huge stakes of intelligence tests in childhood. In some education systems, good IQ scores determine placement of children in special classes. Admission to prestigious universities also depends on the level of IQ. Later in adulthood, IQ can increase or decrease an individual's chance of getting a better job, or obtaining a satisfactory standard of living. In research, IQ determination for large groups of people or whole nations may result in a better public image for those with high scores, and stigma and discrimination for those with lower scores. We believe, therefore, that measuring IQ is a major issue of ethics, primarily through its impact on individual lives, and secondly because of the dangers that might result (discrimination against immigrants, women, and disadvantaged persons, and prejudice against certain races). Therefore, we propose the analysis of the most important dilemmas of using intelligence tests in research and practice and outline courses of action to avoid potential ethical slippage.

Practice Developing Claims, Using Evidence, Evaluating Research, and Explaining Cultural Norms

Complete the following activities.

1. Propose a defensible claim about the use of intelligence testing based on the above abstract.

2. Find a piece of evidence in Topic 2.8 that would support your claim. Cite the page number where you found that evidence.

---

3 Popa, C., Ciobanu, A. M, & Ionescu, B. (2017). Ethical dilemmas of using intelligence tests in practice and research. *Cercetări filosofico-psihologice, IX*(2), 67–69.

3. Provide a specific ethical guideline that researchers would need to follow if they wanted to conduct a study about the effects of IQ testing in American schools and explain why it is necessary.

4. Cite two ways reported in Topic 2.8 in which the study of intelligence and intelligence testing has been used in discriminatory ways.

Academic Achievement versus Intelligence

Academic achievement and intelligence are related but distinct concepts. *Academic achievement* involves mastering specific academic (subject-matter) content and skills within a school setting, while intelligence covers a wider range of cognitive abilities. Intelligence is generally seen as stable, reflecting deep cognitive skills that aid in problem-solving and adapting to new situations.

Academic achievement develops mainly in educational environments where students engage in various learning activities and assessments to show their knowledge and skills. Academic achievement can vary depending on factors such as teaching quality, student motivation, socioeconomic status, and cultural background. It is influenced by both internal factors, such as effort or cognitive abilities, and external factors, such as family support systems and educational resources.

Students' performance on tasks, tests, or assessments specific to a subject area or curriculum is the most common way of measuring academic achievement. These assessments aim to gauge mastery of academic content and the ability to apply knowledge, understanding, and problem-solving abilities in academic areas. Scores on standardized tests, such as the ACT or SAT, course grades, and completion of educational milestones, such as graduating from high school or college, are also measures of academic achievement.

Assessment Measures

Two common types of assessments are achievement and aptitude tests. **Achievement tests** identify what individuals know and test their skill levels in different areas. Unit or final exams in your classes are likely to be achievement tests. Your upcoming AP Psychology exam is an achievement test as well, because your test writers want to measure your level of knowledge in the topics you studied and your skill in applying that knowledge to unique situations.

While achievement tests focus on what a person has already learned, **aptitude tests** measure ability in a certain area, such as numerical, verbal, or mechanical reasoning; problem-solving in work-related situations; and spatial awareness. Strength in certain areas can help indicate one's potential vocational or professional direction. For example, those who show high aptitude for spatial awareness may do well as designers, engineers, and architects.

Fixed versus Growth Mindsets

A person's beliefs about whether intelligence is fixed from birth (**fixed mindset**) or malleable due to experience (**growth mindset**) can affect academic achievement. A fixed mindset may lead to avoidance of challenges and limited progress, while a growth mindset fosters resilience, effort, and a love of learning, ultimately leading to greater academic success and fulfillment. Individuals with a fixed mindset feel no sense of confidence in their abilities and do not believe that anything they do will change a situation. In the world of learning, sentiments expressing a fixed mindset may include, "I'm terrible at math," "I just can't understand physics," or "No matter what I do, I cannot learn a second language." The fixed mindset is essentially a form of learned helplessness (see Topic 3.8).

Those with a fixed mindset believe that they are born with their abilities and should not have to work that hard to surpass them. This mindset leads to stagnation and limits their potential to grow.

People with a growth mindset, in contrast, understand that perfection of a skill will not occur immediately or even soon, but the right practice will lead to it. Carol Dweck from Stanford University, who has conducted much research on mindsets, believes that a growth mindset has far more weight in a person's success than their intelligence. She believes that those with perseverance and grit who do not back down in the face of setbacks will continue to grow and develop their skills even when things get hard.

REFLECT ON THE ESSENTIAL QUESTION

Essential Question: *How do modern and historical theories describe intelligence?* Using the Key Terms, complete a chart like the one below to gather details to help answer that question.

Theory	Description

KEY TERMS

achievement tests	growth mindset	reliability
aptitude tests	intelligence	socioculturally responsive
chronological age	Intelligence Quotient (IQ)	split-half reliability
construct validity	intelligence test	standardized tests
discrimination	mental age	stereotype lift
educational inequities	personal bias	stereotype threat
fixed mindset	poverty	systemic issue
Flynn effect	predictive validity	test-retest reliability
g	psychometric principle	validity

1. Rachel is taking the ACT for the third time in the hopes of improving her score by five points so that she can attend the school of her choice. When she receives her test result, she finds she has received exactly the same score as the first two times she took the ACT. This indicated that the ACT has which of the following?

   (A) Construct validity

   (B) Content validity

   (C) Test-retest reliability

   (D) Split-half reliability

2. When Paula takes her AP Psychology exam, the proctor reads from a set of instructions, which all students are told to follow precisely. Her friend taking the same exam at the same time in a different location was given the same instructions. Which of the following is best described in this scenario?

   (A) Predictive validity

   (B) Construct validity

   (C) Interrater reliability

   (D) Standardization

3. At Jackie's high school, students are placed in physical education classes based on a rigorous battery of tests. Jackie has placed into the highest-level physical education class. When she arrives to class, she finds that she is one of two girls in the class. The teacher explains that any time girls have been in this level P.E. class, they usually cannot handle it and drop to a lower level. Jackie knows she has been placed correctly, but as the activities begin, she finds herself lacking speed and coordination. Which best explains Jackie's performance?

   (A) Jackie has a fixed mindset.

   (B) Jackie is experiencing decrease in general intelligence.

   (C) Jackie is struggling with context-dependent memory.

   (D) Jackie is experiencing stereotype threat.

4. The past four generations of Lonnie's family had taken IQ tests. Why is it not recommended to compare Lonnie's IQ scores with those of previous generations?

(A) IQ scores change what they measure about every 20 years.

(B) The Flynn effect suggests that IQ scores are steadily rising, making for an inaccurate comparison.

(C) The serial position effect suggests that IQ scores of the middle generations would be lower than those in the early and later generations.

(D) Earlier generations would have higher IQ scores because our dependence on technology has diminished memory capacity in recent years.

Question 5 through 7 refer to the following.

Justine is a psychometric psychologist who is evaluating IQ scores for a group of children who have just tested. The results from the group of students are normally distributed with a mean of 100 and a standard deviation of 15.

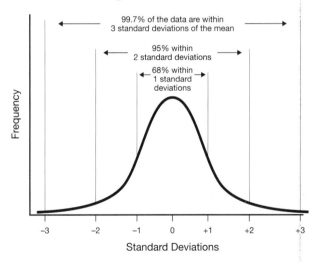

Percentages in a Normal Distribution

5. The first step in Justine's analysis is to add the scores for each standard deviation away from the mean (z-score). What is the z-score for a student who scored 130 on this IQ test?

(A) –2

(B) –1

(C) +1

(D) +2

6. If David scored 70 on this IQ test, what is his percentile rank?

(A) 2.5

(B) 16

(C) 50

(D) 84

7. In this data set, which of the following represents the median score?

(A) 85

(B) 68

(C) 100

(D) 130

STUDY LIKE A CHAMP WITH DR. G. | DO YOU REMEMBER?

Like many at the same point in high school as you, you probably have habits for studying. The material in this unit gives you a good sense of how those habits interact with the mental processes you have. The problem with habits is we stick to them even if they are not useful. In the unit opener I asked you to try something new. Remember what that was? (Yes, retrieval practice.)

I shared that one of the hot-off-the-press findings from cognitive science is that pretesting, testing yourself on material before you have studied it, increases memory for the material. I hope you tried pretesting for each of the sections of this unit. If you did not, it is not too late to change your study habits before you start on the next unit. It is also a good time to adapt your study plans to not only solidify when you practice retrieval and how you space out your studying, but to also add pretesting to your mix of study habits. With these three techniques, you will truly be on the way to studying like a champion, and you will start to see the positive results on tests you take. Keep practicing these techniques so you go beyond just rereading the material to systematically enhancing your cognitive skills.

UNIT 2: Review

MULTIPLE-CHOICE QUESTIONS

1. You see a friend approaching from the far end of the school courtyard. He looks small, but you assume he is his usual height because of which of the following?
   - (A) Weber's law
   - (B) The phi phenomenon
   - (C) Shape constancy
   - (D) Size constancy

2. A painter who wants to show that one figure is closer to the viewer than another, partially blocked, figure standing slightly behind it is using which of the following principles?
   - (A) Relative height
   - (B) Interposition
   - (C) Relative clarity
   - (D) Relative size

Questions 3 through 5 refer to the following.

Brewer and Treyens (1981) asked participants to wait for a short time in an office-like room. Unbeknownst to the participants, this was part of the actual study. Participants were in the room for 35 seconds and then taken to another room and asked to identify everything they recalled from the first room. The results found that participants were more likely to correctly remember items like a pencil or desk that were consistent with their existing schemas for an office. Participants were less likely to recall items that were inconsistent with their schemas for an office (skull, wine bottle, picnic basket) that had been placed around the room. Participants also identified items that were not in the room but that were consistent with their pre-existing schemas, such as books or a lamp. The results found that the stronger the level of expectancy, the stronger the level of recall of items in the office.

3. The research above used which of the following methods?
   - (A) Correlational study
   - (B) Naturalistic observation
   - (C) Case study
   - (D) Experiment

4. What type of measurement did this study use?

   (A) Qualitative

   (B) Cross-sectional

   (C) Quantitative

   (D) Longitudinal

5. Which concept best explains why participants remembered items that were not actually present in the office?

   (A) Source amnesia

   (B) Imagination inflation

   (C) Retrograde amnesia

   (D) Constructive memory

6. Todd was daydreaming in his calculus class when the teacher called on him and asked him to repeat what had just been said in class. Todd clearly had not been paying attention, but to his surprise he was able to repeat the last idea that had been said. Todd's experience is most likely due to which of the following?

   (A) Echoic memory

   (B) Iconic memory

   (C) Procedural memory

   (D) Semantic memory

7. The following graph represents what people believe about recent crime rates compared to what is actually happening with recent crime rates. Which psychological concept best explains the difference in perception and reality?

(A) Representativeness heuristic

(B) Gambler's fallacy

(C) Algorithm

(D) Availability heuristic

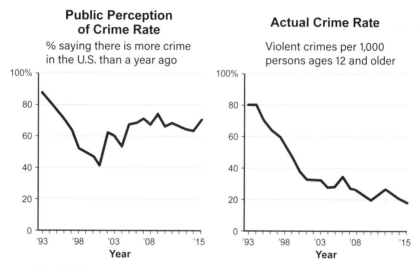

Public Perception of Crime Rate

% saying there is more crime in the U.S. than a year ago

Actual Crime Rate

Violent crimes per 1,000 persons ages 12 and older

Note: 2006 BJS estimates are not comparable with those in other years.
Source: Gallup, Bureau of Justice Statistics.

8. A local police force wanted to see if an increased police presence would deter crime. They partnered with a university to run a rigorous experiment in which they increased police presence in randomly selected areas of town and compared crime rates in those areas that did not receive an increased police presence. If the study found statistically significant results, what does this mean?

(A) Crime rates went down in all areas of the city.

(B) The results are likely due to the increased police presence and not likely due to chance.

(C) The results from both areas are comparable in terms of the level of crime.

(D) There is a negative correlation between crime rates and police presence.

9. Neve believes in the working memory model. What process does she believe analyzes visual information?

(A) Visuospatial sketchpad

(B) Central executive

(C) Prospective memory

(D) Phonological loop

Questions 10 and 11 refer to the following.

Libby's teacher runs a class demonstration on the levels of processing to test a hypothesis. She randomly assigns 10 students to look at each of 15 words in a list (Group 1) and another 10 students to make a personal connection to the word presented (Group 2). The results are depicted below, identifying how many words out of 15 each participant remembered.

Participants	1	2	3	4	5	6	7	8	9	10
Group 1	10	8	7	4	8	11	4	7	9	12
Group 2	8	14	12	11	12	15	9	11	14	12

10. According to the levels of processing model and the results of this study, which is the best method to use to increase recall?

(A) Creation of hierarchies

(B) Primacy effect

(C) Semantic encoding

(D) Structural encoding

11. What is the mean of the participants in Group 1 and Group 2 respectively?

(A) 8; 12

(B) 9; 12

(C) 8; 11.8

(D) 7; 1236

12. If a rat learned a maze shortly after receiving an injection of adrenaline, research indicates that the rat would have better memory for that maze when the rat was again experiencing a high level of adrenaline. This supports research on which of the following?

(A) Context-dependent memory

(B) State-dependent memory

(C) Implicit memory

(D) Episodic memory

13. Each time Lizzy learns a new concept in her psychology course, she tries to come up with examples of how that concept either has influenced or might in the future influence her life. Lizzy is utilizing which of the following?

(A) Elaborative rehearsal

(B) Mnemonic devices

(C) Shallow processing

(D) Structural encoding

14. Zeda was doing some construction in her garage when she realized she did not have a hammer to nail two boards together. She quickly realized that she could instead use her steel wrench to nail the boards together. Which of the following statements accurately represents this scenario?

(A) Zeda was stuck in a mental set.

(B) Zeda was able to overcome functional fixedness.

(C) Zeda overcame her confirmation bias.

(D) Zeda utilized the representativeness heuristic to solve the problem.

15. Marcie took her first SAT a few weeks ago. Her counselor told her that the results were normally distributed and she scored one standard deviation above the mean. Marcie wants to share the information with her parents but they do not know much about SAT scores, so instead she reports her percentile rank so they will know where she fell compared to all other students who took the exam that day. What is Marcie's percentile rank on the SAT?

(A) 50

(B) 16

(C) 84

(D) 97.5

Question 1: Article Analysis Question (AAQ)

1. Your response to the question should be provided in six parts: A, B, C, D, E, and F. Write the response to each part of the question in complete sentences. Use appropriate psychological terminology in your response.

   Using the source provided, respond to all parts of the question.

   (A) Identify the research method used in the study.

   (B) State the operational definition of facial recognition.

   (C) Describe the meaning of the differences between the conditions in the study.

   (D) Identify at least one ethical guideline applied by the researchers.

   (E) Explain the extent to which the research findings may or may not be generalizable using specific and relevant evidence from the study.

   (F) Explain how at least one of the research findings supports or refutes the researchers' hypothesis.

Introduction

Humans have typically lived in groups of fewer than 100 people. The rapid increase in densely populated cities changes the demand for the human ability to recognize faces. For protection purposes, it may be more useful to rapidly recognize faces in our personal environment to identify individuals as friend or foe. However, human facial recognition ability equips us to recognize far more than this number of faces. There has not yet been a study of how many faces a person can recognize. This study aimed to investigate the average number of faces known to individuals. This study will also investigate the difference in perception among familiar faces.

Participants

Participants were 25 undergraduate or postgraduate students at the University of Glasgow who engaged in 5–6 hours of testing and were paid $30 for their time. Participants were also provided with a cash bonus based on their performance in the facial recognition tasks.

Method

As participants arrived for the study, they were provided with informed consent forms, which contained information on the facial recognition tasks they would engage in during the study, the amount of time involved with the study, and the right to withdraw at any time during the study. This was a repeated-measures design, a type of study in which the same participants are tested multiple times under different conditions or over time. In this study, students participated in both conditions.

Task 1: Personal Recognition

Participants were then provided response sheets that were organized into 14 headed columns: family, friends of family, own friends, family of own friends, school (including staff), colleagues, locals (neighbors, etc.), retail staff, sports friends, social circles (e.g., church, athletics), commuters, students, professionals (e.g. doctors, dentists), and people met on a holiday or trip. They were encouraged to divide their lives into autobiographical chapters and to use a separate worksheet for each such chapter. The intention was to maximize recall by prompting participants to consider all the different social settings in which they might have acquired personally known faces and to repeat this systematically for each autobiographical chapter. Participants were then asked to identify individuals in each category by name as they created a mental picture of each person. To be clear about task demands and to foster consistency across participants, researchers provided written criteria specifying what counts as knowing a face. We stipulated that the participant should (1) be able to form a clear mental image of the face, or (2) believe that they would recognize the face if they saw it. We accepted identifying semantic descriptions (e.g. school janitor) in cases where the name could not be retrieved or was never known. Participants completed this task individually and in silence, entering items into the spreadsheet continuously for 60 minutes. We automatically saved the spreadsheet data every 5 minutes, allowing us to reconstruct the rate at which new items were generated.

Task 2: Famous Recognition

The research team compiled the names of 3441 public figures. We collected two different photographs of each public figure by entering their names as search terms in Google Images. To structure participants' recall, and to assist them in conducting an exhaustive memory sweep, we provided response sheets separated into twelve categories—arts and media, business, fashion, film, historical figures, music, politics, royalty, science, sports, TV, and other. We constructed two versions of a face-recognition test. Version A contained the first image of each person (3441 images); version B contained the second image of each person (also 3441 images). In each test, the 3441 images were presented sequentially on screen, with a different random order for each participant. For each image, the participants' task was to indicate via keypress whether or not they knew the depicted person ("Do you recognize this face? (Y or N)"). The task was self-paced, with no time limit, and each image remained on the screen until a response was made. Each participant completed both version A and version B of the test in separate, approximately 2-hour, sessions.

continued

Results/Discussion
The average number of famous faces recalled in this way was 290 (sd = 69; range = 169–407). We note that participants recalled significantly more personally known faces (M = 362) than famous faces (M = 290) ($p < 0.001$). This trend was present for 21 of our 25 participants. This indicates that participants who recalled many personally known faces also recalled many famous faces, and vice versa (r = 0.38). Participants were financially motivated to recall famous faces because they received per-item payment. Given that the recall rate was actually higher for personally known faces, and performance in the two tasks was positively correlated, we found no evidence that participants were less motivated when recalling personally known faces.

References
Jenkins, R., Dowsett, A.J., & Burton, A.M. (2018). How many faces do people know? *Dryad.* https://doi.org/10.5061/dryad.7f25j43

Question 2: Evidence-Based Question (EBQ)

2. This question has three parts: Part A, Part B, and Part C. Use the two sources provided to answer all parts of the question.

   For Part B and Part C, you must cite the source that you used to answer the question. You can do this in two different ways:

   - **Parenthetical Citation:**
     For example: ". . . (Source A)"
   - **Embedded Citation:**
     For example: "According to Source A, . . ."

   Write the response to each part of the question in complete sentences. Use appropriate psychological terminology.

   Using the provided sources, develop and justify an argument related to the ways in which schemas affect memory.

   (A) Propose a specific and defensible claim based on psychological science that responds to the question.

   (B) (i) Support your claim using at least one piece of specific and relevant evidence from one of the provided sources.

   (ii) Use a psychological perspective, theory or concept, or research finding learned in AP Psychology to explain how your evidence supports your claim.

   (C) (i) Support your claim using an additional piece of specific and relevant evidence from a different source than the one that was used in Part B (i).

   (ii) Explain how the evidence from Part C (i) supports your claim, using a different psychological perspective, theory, concept, or research finding learned in AP Psychology than the one used in Part B (ii).

Source A

Introduction
The War of the Ghosts study, conducted by Frederick Bartlett in 1932, is a classic experiment in the field of cognitive psychology. Bartlett wanted to investigate how memory is influenced by cultural schemas and individual interpretation. He used a Yup'ik folk tale called "The War of the Ghosts" to explore the role of schema in reconstructive memory processes and the retrieval process.

Participants
The participants in Bartlett's study were primarily British undergraduates from Cambridge University.

Method
Participants engaged in two types of reproduction. In serial reproduction, the participant reads "The War of the Ghosts" story and writes it down from memory. This reproduced version is read by another participant who writes down all they can recall, and the cycle repeats until 6 or 7 people have read and written a version of the story. The second type of reproduction was repeated reproduction. The same participant reads the story and after 15 minutes writes it down from memory. In both groups, the story got progressively shorter and more consistent with the participant's cultural background. Bartlett found that as participants recalled the story over time, they tended to distort and alter it to fit their own cultural schemas and expectations. The general information about the theme of the story, a fight, and death remained, but details that were inconsistent with Western cultural norms were often omitted or modified. For example, elements like "canoes" were often remembered as "boats," and supernatural aspects of the story were rationalized or omitted altogether. Additionally, participants tended to shorten the story and make it more coherent according to their cultural expectations.

Results and Discussion
Bartlett's findings suggest that memory is not a verbatim recording of events but rather a reconstructive process influenced by individual schemas and cultural norms. The study highlights the constructive nature of memory, as participants reconstructed the story based on their own cultural background and experiences. This has important implications for understanding how memory works in everyday life and how it can be influenced by factors such as culture, language, and personal beliefs. Bartlett contended that our perceptions and understanding of the world came from pre-set cultural understandings. Bartlett's study laid the groundwork for research on schema theory and reconstructive memory, which has since become a fundamental concept in cognitive psychology. It demonstrates the malleability of memory and the importance of considering cultural factors in memory research. However, it is important to note that the study has been criticized for its lack of diversity in participants and its reliance on a single story. Later research has expanded on Bartlett's work by examining the role of culture and individual differences in memory processes across a variety of contexts. Later researchers have taken issue with these findings, noting that the encoding process is the main point at which schemas affect memory. Furthermore, more modern research with schema theory has questioned whether schemas always come from deeply rooted cultural references or if they can be established in the moment by directing people to attend to specific elements of a situation.

Reference
Bartlett, F. C. (1932). *Remembering: A study in experimental and social psychology.* Cambridge University Press.

Source B

Introduction

Anderson & Pichert (1978) set out to explore the impact of schemas in memory processing. Schema theory suggests that people organize information into mental categories known as schemas. These schemas are created by prior experiences in the world. Schemas affect expectations and can affect the perception, encoding, and retrieval of information. Anderson and Pichert believed that schemas affected the encoding aspect of memory rather than the retrieval component, as earlier researchers into schema theory suggested.

Participants

The study included 80 participants (40 male and 40 female) from a local community college. The participants ranged in age from 20 to 30 years old. Participants were recruited from various academic, cultural, and ethnic backgrounds to ensure diversity in prior schemas.

Method

Participants were randomly placed into one of two groups and then read a story about a house. They were asked to listen to the story from the perspective of the group to which they had been assigned. In the first group, participants were asked to take on the role of a burglar, and in the second, they were asked to take on the role of a home buyer. The story referred to information about an external door that was always left open, bikes in the garage, a leaky roof, privacy from the neighbors, jewels left in a desk drawer, a color television, and a damp basement. There were 72 points covered in the story (36 that might appeal to a homebuyer and 36 that might appeal to a burglar). At the conclusion of the story, all participants were given a 12-minute distraction task. Participants recalled everything they could from the initial story, which was coded by four researchers to ensure inter-rater reliability. The coding was based on how many items they recalled out of 36 in each group (burglar or homebuyer). Next, the roles of the participants were switched and they heard the story again but from a different perspective. For example, if the participants had been in the role of the home buyer, they were now assigned the role of the burglar.

Results and Discussion

After the first reading of the story, four raters identified the participants' scores on the 72-point scale. Researchers found that participants recalled more components of the story that were consistent with their prior schema. Those assigned to the burglar group were more likely to remember details about the story that related to how to enter the house easily and undetected and how to quickly find valuables in the house. Those participants placed into the home buyer group were more likely to recall information consistent with home buying, such as how many bedrooms the house had, what the privacy from the neighbors was like, and aspects of the home that would either raise or limit the value of resale of the home (leaky roof, damp basement). Results were statistically significant with a p-value of <.01. The results demonstrate that encoding does affect schemas, as the participants were randomly placed into one of the two groups. Regardless of their previous background, participants recalled more information that was consistent with the schema provided at the start of the story. In the second condition, participants recalled more items from the new schema they were assigned, demonstrating that schemas are not predetermined and can be changed and modified to direct attention to certain parts of a situation. Schemas seem to provide a context and scaffold on which new learning can be based. Schemas can come from prior experiences or be provided at the moment, as was the case in this study, thus creating an expectation about how to filter information in the story.

Reference

Anderson, R. C., & Pichert, J. W. (1978). Recall of previously unrecallable information following a shift in perspective. *Journal of Verbal Learning and Verbal Behavior, 17*(1), 1–12.

UNIT 3: Development and Learning

Unit Overview

You might wonder what development and learning have to do with each other. At first glance, it seems like a stretch. Development is about the process of growth throughout life, and learning is about how we come to incorporate new information into our lives or make a new association. For psychologists, learning is a process that produces a permanent change in behavior. Development and learning are similar in that they track changes. Development tracks changes in physical, linguistic, social, and cognitive realms. Learning tracks changes in how people gain information by associating, observing, and thinking.

The discussion of development begins with prenatal development—growth during the months before a baby is born—and continues with the physical, cognitive, linguistic, and social changes that occur from birth through adulthood. Development across the lifespan is influenced by biological, environmental, and cognitive factors, so you will have many opportunities to apply what you learned in Units 1 and 2. As you read this unit, keep in mind the perspectives of *continuity and discontinuity (stages), nature and nurture,* and *stability and change*—three themes in developmental psychology. These are issues that developmental psychologists follow across the lifespan.

Like development, learning is influenced by biological, environmental, and cognitive factors. This unit will address three forms of learning: learning by association, learning by consequence, and learning by observation. You will see that, regardless of the form, repetition is a large part of most learning.

LEARNING OBJECTIVES

- Explain how enduring themes inform developmental psychology. (3.1.A)
- Describe ways cross-sectional and longitudinal research design methods used in developmental psychology inform understanding of behavior and mental processes. (3.1.B)
- Explain how physical development before birth applies to behavior and mental processes. (3.2.A)
- Explain how physical development in infancy and childhood applies to behavior and mental processes. (3.2.B)
- Explain how physical development in adolescence applies to behavior and mental processes. (3.2.C)
- Explain how physical development in adulthood applies to behavior and mental processes. (3.2.D)
- Describe how sex and gender influence socialization and other aspects of development. (3.3.A)
- Explain how theories of cognitive development apply to behavior and mental processes. (3.4.A)

- Explain how key components of language and communication apply to behavior and mental processes. (3.5.A)
- Explain how language develops in humans. (3.5.B)
- Explain how social development relates to behavior and mental processes. (3.6.A)
- Explain how classical conditioning applies to behavior and mental processes. (3.7.A)
- Explain how operant conditioning applies to behavior and mental processes. (3.8.A)
- Explain how social learning applies to behavior and mental processes. (3.9.A)
- Explain how cognitive factors in learning apply to behavior and mental processes. (3.9.B)

STUDY LIKE A CHAMP WITH DR. G. | REWARD AND PUNISHMENT

You may wonder how you got to be the way you are. Why are your levels of attention what they are? Why do you seem to like to study some subjects and not others? In this unit, you are going to be adding to your understanding of yourself and will also be focusing on two important concepts that can change your studying behavior: reward and punishment.

Together with learning how you develop cognitively, morally, and physiologically, you will also learn about operant conditioning. The basic concept, our associating behaviors with what follows, can be very helpful for you to modify your studying behaviors. If one kind of studying is followed by an outcome you like (say a good grade), that reward is likely to make you study more. If the behavior of procrastination or distraction (say scrolling reels on your phone for 20 minutes) results in your not going to meet your friends, this punishment (not seeing your friends) is likely to make you procrastinate less. You can use these fundamental processes to prune and tweak your studying behaviors. Identify the behaviors you want to do more off (such as practice retrieval, pretest, and spaced practice) and then pick how you can reward yourself when you do them. For example, for every time you practice test, give yourself a treat, whether it is mental or physical.

The use of reward and punishment, which you will learn more about in this unit (so pay close attention), can be some of the most powerful ways of changing behavior. You can use them for any behavior, but they are particularly useful to change your study behavior. There are many ways we avoid studying. There are also many activities that we like and dislike. You can now use the latter to change the former. Pick pleasurable activities and reward yourself with them when you study according to your plan. Likewise, be prepared to punish yourself if you do not study according to plan. Given that people gravitate toward rewards and away from punishment, these two techniques are powerful ways to change your study behavior.

Topic 3.1

Themes and Methods in Developmental Psychology

"The child's world is alert and alive, governed by rules of response and command, not by physical laws: a portentous continuum of consciousness, endowed with purpose and intent, either resistant or responsive to the child itself."

—Joseph Campbell

Essential Questions: How do enduring themes inform developmental psychology? How do longitudinal and cross-sectional research design methods used in developmental psychology inform understanding of behavior and mental processes?

Developmental psychology is a branch of psychology that examines how people evolve from infancy through adulthood and into old age, focusing on physical, cognitive, emotional, and social development. Developmental psychologists seek to understand how and why people change over time as well as how they remain the same. Developmental psychologists study both the chronological order of developments and the **enduring themes** that continue across the lifespan: continuous and discontinuous development, nature and nurture (see Topic 1.1), and stability and change.

Enduring Themes

Many developmental theorists have proposed stages of **discontinuous development** that are marked by age-specific periods of time. You can think of these stages like steps in a staircase—when you leave one step, you move to the next but spend little time on two steps at once. The stepwise *discontinuity* approach, however, is viewed by some developmental theorists as being more theoretical than real. As children develop, they may exhibit some aspects of one stage while also exhibiting aspects of the next stage. As you learn more about theories such as Piaget's stages of cognitive development or Erikson's stages of psychosocial development, this stage theory idea will make more sense.

In contrast, **continuous development** is a relatively even process without distinct stages. The *continuity* approach suggests that development is more like riding an escalator than climbing a staircase, with gradual changes over time.

The **nature and nurture** debate, as you read in Unit 1, is one of the oldest ongoing arguments among psychologists. Is a person's development a factor of

DNA? Or is it influenced more by environment and life experiences? Psychologists continue to compare the developmental impact of genetics with that of the environment, though they now know that some combination of these factors best explains development, and the combination may be different for each trait and each individual. Researchers also study the heritability of a given characteristic within a specific population. *Heritability* is the extent to which variations of a trait or behavior can be attributed to genetics for a group. We can talk about the heritability of height for the population and know that genes play a large role. We cannot, however, discuss heritability for an individual. (See Topic 1.1.)

The **stability and change** debate is related to both other debates. It centers on whether the traits an infant displays are enduring or whether they change as the growing person interacts with other people and the culture in which they are reared. In other words, to what extent can defining aspects of our lives change over the life span? Early theorists, including Sigmund Freud, believed that very little change happened in the adult years. (For Freud's view of psychodynamic development, see Topic 4.4.) Other theorists, including Erik Erikson, held that change continued throughout adulthood, into old age.

Longitudinal Design

To study developmental themes such as discontinuous and continuous development, stability and change, nature and nurture, and heritability, psychologists have devised specialized research designs.

In a method known as **longitudinal design**, researchers study individuals at several points during the lifespan. Some longitudinal (long-term) studies last a few months or years, while others last many decades. This method would be useful for studying the impact of a degenerative illness over many years or for studying language development in children. Some case studies also employ this design because they investigate an individual in depth over a long period of time.

One well-known and long-lasting longitudinal study, the Minnesota Longitudinal Study of Parents and Children, has been looking at attachment between babies and their mothers over about five decades. *Attachment* is the physical and emotional connection between infants and their caregivers. (For more on attachment, see Topic 3.6.) The study began in 1975, with 267 first-time mothers-to-be, and has now followed 180 individuals from 3 months before they were born until they were in their 30s. To eliminate variables, researchers focused only on children who were born into poverty. Researchers used a variety of assessments to determine the characteristics and expectations of the mother, the children's temperaments, and parent-child interactions. The mothers and children were assessed six times during the child's first year of life, every 6 months until the child was 2^1/$_2$ years old, and then at increasing intervals throughout the individuals' lives into their late 20s. This long-lasting study is now even looking at the offspring of the people who were children when the study began.

In the 1970s, many professionals doubted that early childhood experiences had much impact on behavior later in life, believing that new experiences "recorded over" old experiences. The Minnesota Longitudinal Study used a different model, summarized in several reports of the study. One report concluded that "development turns at each and every stage of the journey on an interaction between the organism as it has developed up to that moment and the environment in which it then finds itself." Although development grows from cumulative interactions with the child's environment, early experiences determine the framework for those interactions. The study has found strong evidence that early experiences, especially patterns in parent-child attachment, are predictive of certain behaviors later in life.

For example, the study looked at two groups of preschool children who showed poor adaptation on several of the study's assessments. One group had experienced secure attachment (a healthy balance between attachment and autonomy) and emotional support while they were infants and toddlers; the other had not. Those in the first group bounced back by the time they were in elementary school, while those in the second group continued to have adaptation problems. Similarly, depressed adolescents or those with conduct disorder who had positive early experiences were less likely than those who didn't to show continuing clinical problems as adults. These early life experiences seem to improve resiliency to obstacles later in life.

Although longitudinal research can generate in-depth and potentially interesting results, it has significant limitations. The longitudinal design can be very expensive to conduct. After many years, researchers may no longer be interested in their topic. Some unforeseen factors can affect the results of a longitudinal study. For example, over time, participants could drop out of the study or die. Some longitudinal studies are taken over by a different researcher or research team, which may change the direction of the study.

THINK AS A PSYCHOLOGIST

Apply Psychological Perspectives, Theories, Concepts, and Research Findings to a Scenario (Practice 1.A)

Consider the finding from the Minnesota Longitudinal Study of Parents and Children that one group experienced secure attachment and emotional support while they were infants and toddlers and the other group did not. Both groups experienced adaptation problems. Those in the first group bounced back by the time they were in elementary school, while those in the second group continued to have adaptation problems.

Practice Applying Psychological Perspectives, Theories, Concepts, and Research Findings to a Scenario

Complete the following activity.

Describe how the findings above from the Minnesota Longitudinal Study of Parents and Children relate to discontinuous and continuous development, nature and nurture, and stability and change.

Cross-Sectional Design

Instead of a longitudinal design, researchers often choose a **cross-sectional design.** In a cross-sectional design, researchers compare different groups based on such variables as age, socioeconomic status, and gender. This method is usually less expensive and faster than a longitudinal study. However, because it compares different groups at a single point in time, it can sometimes suggest differences that are not truly causal but are due to confounding factors or the limitations of one-time observation. Therefore, careful study design is crucial, including the use of statistical methods to control for potential confounders and cautious interpretation of results, especially when making causal claims.

For example, the results of one cross-sectional study about intelligence scores determined that intelligence declined as one aged. In fact, the differences were the result of *cohort effects*, the influences of being part of a group bonded on the basis of a time period or certain life experiences. Because young people today are tested far more frequently than in the past and have access to more information through technology than their predecessors, it appeared that young people were more intelligent, yet most research suggests that intelligence remains relatively steady throughout life. (See Topic 3.4.) For another example of the cohort effect, consider the results you might get if you were trying to measure school spirit and affiliation between cohorts (usually people in the same grade level) from different years. Students who graduated during the year when classes were held remotely because of COVID would likely have a lower level of school spirit and affiliation than students who were on campus every day.

The results of cross-sectional studies that measured intelligence levels across different age groups indicated that intelligence declines with aging, but results of a longitudinal study (long-term study) found that differences between age groups were eliminated when compared over individuals' lifetimes. Differences between age groups in the cross-sectional research seemed to reflect differences in access to information. The study also demonstrated the *Flynn effect*, a sustained increase since the 1930s in the intelligence test scores of people all around the world. (See Topic 2.8.) The increase in intelligence with each generation, not a decline in intelligence as one ages, no doubt explains why older people's test results were lower than younger people's.

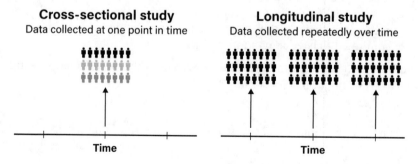

Figure 3.1.1 A Comparison of Cross-Sectional and Longitudinal Studies

THINK AS A PSYCHOLOGIST

Determine the Type of Research Design(s) Used in a Given Study (Practice 2.A)

Suppose a team of developmental psychologists are interested in how people perceive themselves across different ages. To begin studying this question, they decide to evaluate whether individuals of different ages perceive themselves to be the same person they were when they were 5 years old. They recruit individuals aged 10, 15, 20, 25, 30, 35, and 40, equally representing different genders and socioeconomic backgrounds.

Practice Determining the Type of Research Design(s) Used in a Given Study

Answer the following question.

Are the researchers setting up a longitudinal study or a cross-sectional study? Explain your answer.

REFLECT ON THE ESSENTIAL QUESTIONS

Essential Questions: *How do enduring themes inform developmental psychology? How do longitudinal and cross-sectional research design methods used in developmental psychology inform understanding of behavior and mental processes?* Make a chart like the one below. Use the Key Terms to complete the chart and answer the essential questions.

Enduring Themes	Developmental Research Design Methods

KEY TERMS

continuous development	discontinuous development	nature and nurture
cross-sectional design	enduring themes	stability and change
developmental psychology	longitudinal design	

1. Harvey is a university professor who researches personality. He has found that for most people, their temperament at age 6 is a fairly good indicator of what their temperament will be at age 60. Dr. Harvey's findings best represent which of the following developmental themes?

   (A) Change

   (B) Continuity

   (C) Nurture

   (D) Discontinuity

Questions 2 through 4 refer to the following.

A medical team wants to determine whether colon cancer is caused primarily by genetics or by environmental factors and if the causes change over the course of a person's life. They recruit people who have a history of colon cancer in their family and do a deep investigation of the individuals' work life, home life, diet, stressors, and blood tests, as well as genetic testing. They track this information from the time the participants are in their early 20s until they turn 40.

2. What type of research design is the medical team using?

   (A) Cross-sectional

   (B) Longitudinal

   (C) Structured interviews

   (D) Nonnumerical

3. Of the 50 people in the study, 10 people develop some type of colon cancer. The ages at which each of these individuals was first diagnosed are listed below. What is the mean age at which the individuals began to show symptoms?

| 32 | 30 | 38 | 23 | 27 | 31 | 32 | 24 | 27 | 34 |

   (A) 28.5

   (B) 15

   (C) 29.8

   (D) 32

4. If the medical team finds that colon cancer is often passed down through families and they next try to determine how much of developing the disease is attributable to genetics, they are investigating which of the following?

(A) The heritability of the disease

(B) The Flynn effect

(C) Eugenics

(D) Epigenetics

Questions 5 and 6 refer to the following.

Knute works for a firm that investigates people's political habits. He wants to determine if female and male registered voters of various age groups have different voting habits and considerations when they vote. Knute finds that, because of recent federal legislation, women voters in recent elections have different behaviors from those of women in the past.

5. What kind of research will help Knute answer these questions?

(A) Case study

(B) Longitudinal study

(C) Meta-analysis

(D) Cross-sectional study

6. That new legislation may indicate misleading trends in voting due to which of the following?

(A) Primacy effect

(B) Cohort effect

(C) Recency effect

(D) Continuity

7. Lorraine has just taken an intelligence exam. She scored well and wants to know how her scores compare to those of her parents and grandparents. Which of the following limits the legitimacy of comparing IQ scores across generations?

(A) Longitudinal studies indicate that IQ drops over the lifespan.

(B) Heritability research shows that IQ is largely determined by the environment in which one grows up.

(C) Cross-sectional research shows that IQ drops with each successive generation.

(D) The Flynn effect shows that IQ scores have continued to rise over the past few generations.

Topic 3.2

Physical Development Across the Lifespan

"Play is the highest expression of human development in childhood, for it alone is the free expression of what is in a child's soul."

—Friedrich Froebel

Essential Question: How does physical development from before birth through infancy, childhood, adolescence, and adulthood apply to behavior and mental processes?

From the earliest stages of life—spanning from before birth through infancy, childhood, adolescence, and into adulthood—our physical development profoundly shapes our behaviors and mental processes. During infancy and early childhood, the rapid growth of our bodies and the maturation of our brains provide the crucial foundation for our cognitive abilities, sensory perceptions, and motor skills. Think of the milestones of crawling, walking, and mastering fine motor control; not only do they empower infants to explore their physical world, but they also serve as catalysts for cognitive growth, allowing them to engage more actively with their surroundings.

Moreover, the intricate network of neural connections formed during this period lays the groundwork for language acquisition, social understanding, and the regulation of emotions, influencing our behaviors and mental processes well into later stages of life. As we progress through childhood and adolescence, ongoing physical changes continue to intertwine with behavioral and mental development. Puberty marks a period of profound physical transformation, which not only shapes secondary sexual characteristics but also affects brain structure and function—our internal landscape of thoughts and feelings.

These physiological changes contribute to the emergence of complex social behaviors, identity formation, and the regulation of emotions. Additionally, the importance of physical health and fitness becomes increasingly apparent during adolescence, since regular exercise not only boosts physical well-being but also enhances mood, cognitive function, and stress management—an essential consideration that carries forward into adulthood.

The aging process brings its own set of physical changes, from declines in muscle mass and bone density to alterations in sensory perception. These changes influence not just our physical abilities but also our lifestyle choices, social interactions, and cognitive functioning. Topic 3.2 reviews the details of these ongoing interactions among physical development, behavior, and mental processes throughout the lifespan.

Prenatal Development

The prenatal period begins with conception and ends at birth. A full-term pregnancy is typically about 40 weeks, with a baby considered full-term at 39 weeks. Conception occurs when a male sperm joins with a female egg to create a single cell—the beginning of a new life. The fertilized egg implants itself in the uterine wall, where growth occurs through rapid cell division.

By about 3 weeks, organ development begins in the embryo as cells continue to divide, replicate, and create new growth. At about 4 weeks, the heart develops and begins to beat, and the lungs, eyes, ears, palate, and central nervous system develop. The blood vessels of the placenta transfer nutrients from the mother to the embryo to foster growth. Basic brain development occurs by the end of the first month, including differentiation of the forebrain, midbrain, and hindbrain. By the end of 3 months, arms, hands, legs, and feet begin to develop, the kidneys begin to produce urine, and the pancreas begins to produce insulin.

By 20 weeks, the brain and nervous system are developed enough to enable movement and digestion. By around 24 weeks, the sucking reflex has developed, and by around 28 weeks loud sounds will produce a startle response.

Between 5 months into the pregnancy and 38 weeks, most fetuses will have reached the age of viability, allowing them to live outside the womb; however, the youngest preterm newborns cannot survive without medical intervention. Depending on development of the lungs, heart, and other organs, the newborn may still need external support until breathing is normal and body temperature is maintained independently. The fetus gains much weight and strength, especially in the last few weeks of a term pregnancy. The nervous system begins to build neural networks that will allow transmission of information back and forth between the brain, organ systems, and other parts of the body. The circulatory and musculoskeletal systems are fully developed, and the brain and nervous system will be almost completely formed by the time of birth.

Prenatal Susceptibility

During embryonic development, which occurs in weeks 3 through 8 of a pregnancy, the embryo is particularly susceptible to harmful agents called **teratogens**, such as tobacco, certain drugs, and infections, that can damage the cells and tissue of the developing embryo, resulting in physical or functional defects. Harmful exposure may also happen later during fetal development, which occurs from weeks 9 through 38. Alcohol consumption by the mother during pregnancy may result in the infant's developing *fetal alcohol syndrome (FAS)*. Severe cases of FAS can result in low birth weight, facial deformities, and limited intellectual abilities.

Many factors can influence the extent to which exposure to harmful substances during this critical stage of development might affect either the fetus or newborn child, including the following:

- Duration and dosage of the substance
- Time of exposure during pregnancy (the first half of pregnancy is most critical)
- Genetic makeup of the unborn child (some children may be more susceptible)
- Exposure of the mother to environmental factors before or during pregnancy or during nursing after childbirth

In addition, factors such as maternal illness, genetic mutations, hormonal imbalances, and environmental influences can significantly affect prenatal development, especially during the first 3 months.

Mother's Illness During pregnancy, **maternal illness** or infections can have detrimental effects on the developing fetus. Illnesses such as gestational diabetes and high blood pressure can interfere with the normal development of the fetus, potentially leading to birth defects, growth restrictions, or other complications.

Genetic Mutations Whether inherited from the parents or occurring spontaneously during embryonic development, **genetic mutations** can cause a wide range of genetic disorders and birth defects. These mutations can affect the way the fetus develops and can lead to conditions such as Down syndrome, cystic fibrosis, sickle cell anemia, and many others.

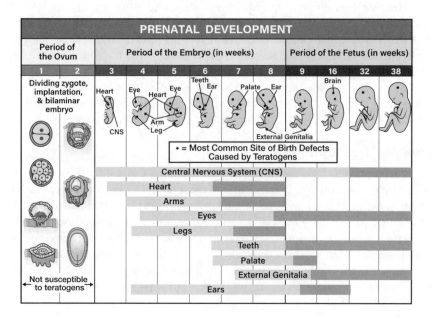

Figure 3.2.1 The lighter shade indicates periods of high sensitivity to teratogens.

Hormonal Imbalances Hormones play a crucial role in regulating the processes of prenatal development. Imbalances in the levels of hormones such as estrogen, progesterone, and human chorionic gonadotropin (hCG) can disrupt the normal growth and development of the fetus, leading to such complications as miscarriage, preterm birth, or birth defects.

Environmental Influences The environment in which the fetus develops can also have a significant impact on prenatal development. Factors such as exposure to toxins (lead, mercury, and certain chemicals, for example), radiation, tobacco smoke, and certain medications can interfere with the normal growth and development of the fetus, leading to birth defects, developmental delays, or other adverse outcomes. Maternal stress can also pose risks to prenatal development.

THINK AS A PSYCHOLOGIST

Interpret Quantitative or Qualitative Inferential Data from a Given Table, Chart, Diagram (Practice 3.C)

Practice Interpreting Data from a Given Chart

Complete the following activity.

Using Figure 3.2.1, write the major biological systems shown in the graphic (central nervous system, heart, arms, eyes, and the rest) on note cards or sticky notes. Organize the cards according to when each system is most in danger of damage from harmful substances or maternal illness during prenatal development. Write on each card what would happen to a developing embryo or fetus if that system were damaged. Try to be specific about what behaviors or mental processes would be affected after birth. Check your ideas with research after you finish the activity.

Infancy

Infancy lasts from birth until about 18 months of age, a period of great changes in the infant. The order in which an infant's brain, body, and socialization develop involves the interaction of both nature and nurture, although the child's biological development will be determined largely by nature. This orderly, sequential biological growth pattern is called *maturation*. The process of maturation is primarily determined by genetic makeup, but it can also be influenced by extreme environmental factors, such as lack of adequate nutrition early in life or exposure to teratogens.

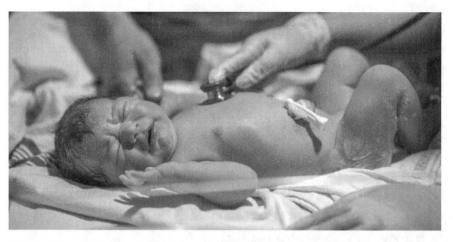

Within minutes of birth, all healthy newborns are given the APGAR test, which assesses breathing effort, heart rate, muscle tone, skin color, and reflexes. Virginia Apgar created this test in 1952 to quickly identify problems that could threaten a baby's chance of survival in the first 24 hours. It is credited with reducing infant mortality rates.

Reflexes

The healthy newborn exhibits many remarkable reflexes. A **reflex**, or *reflex action*, is an involuntary physical response (without conscious control) to a stimulus. (See Topic 1.2.) It is usually instantaneous upon receiving the stimulus and is established, or fixed, at birth.

- The *grasping reflex* occurs when newborns curl their fingers around objects when their palms are touched. This reflex will disappear at about three or four months but will be replaced by a voluntary grasping action.

- The **rooting reflex** occurs when babies are touched on the cheek and turn their faces toward the stimulus. This generally occurs along with a sucking reflex. It disappears at about five months.

- The *sucking reflex* drives a baby to suck objects placed in the mouth. The rooting reflex and sucking reflex work together to allow infants to receive nourishment. The sucking reflex is permanent but will change through learning and experience.

- The *Moro reflex* is a response to a sudden absence of support, producing a feeling of falling. It is the only unlearned fear in newborn babies. The response may be generated by a sudden loud noise or a change in an infant's body position. The arms and legs will be thrust out away from the body (abduction) and then pulled in closer to the body (adduction), the back may be arched, and the baby will usually cry. It is not the same as a *startle response,* a learned response to unexpected noises that occurs later in development and may replace the Moro reflex. Although the startle response still causes sudden body movements, they are less dramatic than those of the Moro reflex.

- The *stepping reflex* is the appearance of taking steps when the baby's feet touch a flat surface. Although this is not an indication that the baby is ready to walk, it may be a precursor to walking. It generally fades by about eight weeks.
- The *Babinski reflex* is the splaying of the baby's toes when the bottom of a foot is stroked. The toes will then curl inward. It will last through the baby's first year and with the stepping reflex may be beneficial to walking.

Many of these reflexes—because they allow infants to receive food or to cling to a caregiver in the early days of their lives—are considered survival reflexes and may be holdovers from our evolutionary past. They are also seen as milestones that indicate on-track physical and psychological development. Most of these reflexes disappear within the first 6 months of life, and some will be replaced by learned or voluntary responses that involve similar behavior.

NEWBORN INFANT REFLEXES			
Infant Reflex	**Stimulation**	**Innate Response**	**Duration**
Grasping	Palms touched	Grasps tightly	Disappears at 3–4 months, replaced with voluntary grasping
Rooting	Cheek stroked or side of mouth touched	Turns toward source, opens mouth, and sucks	Disappears at 5–6 months
Sucking	Mouth touched by object	Sucks the object	Permanent but changes through learning and experience
Moro	Sudden move or loud noise	Startles; thrusts arms out and then pulls them back in	Disappears at 3–4 months
Stepping	Infant held upright with feet touching the ground	Moves feet in walking motion	Fades after about 2 months
Babinski	Sole of foot stroked	Splays toes and twists foot in	Disappears at 9–12 months

Table 3.2.1

Motor Development

Eventually, reflexes will be replaced by the development of **gross motor coordination,** the voluntary movement and coordination of the large muscles of the body to perform full-body movements such as sitting, crawling, and walking. Although the timing may vary, most children will begin sitting independently at about 5 months, crawling at about 7 months, and walking near their 1st birthday. Unlike the timing, the sequence of babies' motor development is relatively consistent. Babies' motor development progresses from the body's midline outward. Children learn to control areas closer to their midsections before they learn to control their arms and legs, which explains why babies sit before they walk.

Children will also develop *fine motor skills,* the coordination of small muscle movements, typically involving the hands, fingers, and arms, in performing precise and refined movements. They gain the ability to use a simple pincer grasp—holding something between their thumb and index finger or their thumb and middle fingers—at about 5 months, allowing them to pick up a cookie or hang on to a toy or Daddy's expensive glasses. More specific hand-eye coordination improves dramatically between ages 3 to 5 years.

Children also exhibit developmental progression from head to toe. At birth, babies' heads are nearly the same size they will be at adulthood and take up about 30 percent of their total height. Unlike the head, children's extremities grow considerably in the first years of life. Children will be roughly half of their adult height when they become toddlers at about 2 years old.

INFANT MOTOR DEVELOPMENT		
Average Age Achieved	**Gross Motor Skill**	**Fine Motor Skill**
4–8 weeks	Lifts head	Grasps rattle briefly
8–10 weeks	Lifts self by arms; rolls from side to back	Glances from one object to another
16–18 weeks	Sits with support	Carries object to mouth; can hold two objects
5–7 months	Sits without support	Transfers object from hand to hand
7–9 months	Crawls	Pincer grasp
10–12 months	Stands holding on; walks holding on	Pushes car along; hits cup with spoon; shows hand preference; scribbles with crayon
12–18 months	Stands alone; walks alone	Builds up to 3-cube towers; opens book; turns 2–3 pages at a time
2–3 years	Runs; jumps; climbs	Turns single pages in book; cuts with scissors; pours drink

Table 3.2.2

Development of Perceptual Skills

Developing *perceptual skills,* a facet of cognitive development, involves learning to perceive, organize, and interpret sensory stimuli. Infants use perceptual information to make choices about using their newly acquired motor skills. In 1960, developmental researchers Eleanor Gibson and Richard D. Walk tested young children's ability to perceive depth by placing them near a **visual cliff**, a table with one half of the top opaque and appearing solid and the other half made of clear Plexiglas®. The meeting of the opaque side with the clear side represented the drop-off of a cliff. (See Topic 2.1 for more on this experiment.) Only 3 of 36 infants tested by Gibson and Walk crawled independently to the "deep" side of the cliff, presumably because they feared the danger posed by the drop-off. The same behavior was seen in infants up to 7 months old; however, 12-month-old infants learned to use their mothers' facial expressions as a guide to behavior. A mother's smile indicated safety and permission to crawl over the cliff, while a frown indicated a mother's fear and the infant avoided the cliff.

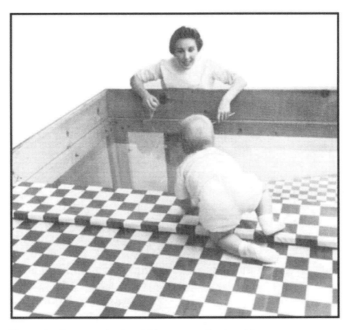

The mother is encouraging her child to cross to the clear side.

The visual cliff experiment has been criticized on several grounds. One is that, although the glass made the appearance of a drop-off, it was actually solid, so that babies could feel it under them. A second is that infants $6^1/_2$ months old and younger crossed the "cliff," but infants older than that did not. That difference suggests that the older ones may have had experiences the younger ones did not and that the decision to cross or not cross might have more to do with experience and learning than innate depth perception.

Critical or Sensitive Periods

Research with both humans and animals shows that critical or sensitive periods in infancy and childhood can exert profound effects on vision, hearing, motor development, social and emotional development, and language acquisition. A **critical period** is a specific time window during which a physical, emotional, or social milestone is developed that will not or cannot occur at a later date. During these critical or sensitive periods, the brain exhibits heightened plasticity, making it more receptive to environmental stimuli and experiences that shape neural circuits. For instance, studies have shown that children who are exposed to a rich linguistic environment during critical periods typically demonstrate superior language proficiency compared to those who experience language deprivation. You will learn more about language development in Topic 3.5 of this unit.

Critical periods extend beyond language acquisition to other domains, such as sensory perception, social cognition, and motor development. Studies investigating visual development have found that early visual experiences play a crucial role in shaping visual acuity, depth perception, and visual processing abilities. For example, infants who are born with cataracts can develop vision closer to normal provided that the cataracts are removed during early infancy. Similarly, children who are born deaf benefit more from receiving cochlear implants before age 2. The findings from research on critical periods show the connections between biological predispositions and environmental influences in shaping development during infancy and childhood.

Zoologist and ethologist Konrad Lorenz theorized that if attachment was important in human survival, as John Bowlby had demonstrated, then it may be important in other species as well. In the 1930s, Lorenz investigated the attachment of baby geese (goslings) to a mother figure. Birds, including geese, have a critical period for attachment to a mother-type figure. After hatching, goslings have an eighteen-hour critical period during which they will **imprint** on, or attach themselves to, a motherlike figure. As Lorenz discovered, the motherlike figure may even be of a different species. Instinctive bonding to the first moving object seen within hours after birth (or hatching) is described as *imprinting*. Lorenz presented himself shortly after the goslings had hatched, and they imprinted him as a motherlike figure. The goslings followed behind Lorenz in a straight line as he walked, responded to his calls (made through a duck call), and even pecked his face in what appeared to be an affectionate "kissing" behavior. Lorenz raised the goslings and, even as they grew older, they demonstrated a preference for him. While cross-species imprinting appears to work, a tendency to prefer to imprint upon one's own species has been demonstrated. Unlike certain animal species, humans seem to have a longer period—a **sensitive period** versus a critical period—during which attachment forms.

THINK AS A PSYCHOLOGIST

Evaluate the Appropriate Use of Research Design Elements in Non-Experimental Methodologies (2.C.3) | Interpret Quantitative or Qualitative Inferential Data from a Given Table, Graph, Chart, Figure, or Diagram (3.C.1) | Apply Psychological Perspectives, Theories, Concepts, and Research Findings to a Scenario (1.A.1) | Develop and Justify Psychological Arguments Using Evidence (4.A)

Developmental psychologists have long studied language acquisition in children. The graph below is derived from studies that explore the question, "When should children begin learning a second language?" Use the graph to answer the questions.

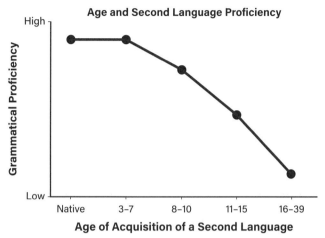

Age and Second Language Proficiency

Source: *From Kuhl (2010), based on Johnson and Newport (1989)*

Practice Foundational Skills

Complete the following activities and answer the question.

1. Identify the two variables of interest in the study presented in the graph.
2. Describe the relationship between the two variables in the study.
3. The research presented in the graph provides the strongest evidence for which of the following major themes in development?

   (A) Continuity and discontinuity

   (B) Stability and change

   (C) Critical period theory

   (D) Heritability

4. Based on the results of the study presented in the graph, make a defensible claim about when students should be exposed to a second language curriculum.

Changes in Adolescence

Adolescence is a time of great physical, biochemical, and psychological changes, all of which are intertwined. Adolescent milestones include puberty and a growth spurt. These, in turn, often bring psychological changes.

Puberty

Teenagers and some preteens experience **puberty**, a period during which they reach physical and sexual maturity and acquire the ability to reproduce. Puberty begins when the hypothalamus triggers the endocrine system to begin producing different levels of sex hormones.

Primary sex characteristics develop, including the testes in males and ovaries in females, which allow reproduction. Girls experience their first **menarche,** or menstrual period, a monthly cycle during which the uterus sheds its lining if an egg produced by the ovaries has not been fertilized. During puberty, boys experience **spermarche,** the first ejaculatory experience. While puberty generally occurs in early adolescence, the precise time frame may vary widely between individuals. Genetics and family history often determine whether the onset of puberty is early or late.

Puberty is occurring earlier than ever before, moving from an average age of $14^{1}/_{2}$ years one hundred years ago to roughly age $12^{1}/_{2}$ years today. Early onset of puberty has been attributed in part to increased body fat as a result of the consumption of animal hormones found in many modern foods, especially dairy products and meats.

Growth Spurt

During the early to mid-teens, a young person may be described as "filling out." Bone and muscle growth increase during this period and dramatic increases usually occur in height and weight. This rapid period of physical growth and development, triggered by hormones, is called a **growth spurt.** The growth spurt usually begins around age 10–11 for girls and 12–13 for boys, with a wide range of normal variation. During the peak of the growth spurt, adolescents can grow as much as 4–8 inches in height and gain as much as 20 pounds over a period of 1–2 years.

The growth spurt follows a specific pattern, with the legs and feet growing first, followed by the arms and hands, and finally the trunk. During the growth spurt, the bones elongate, leading to changes in body proportions and physical appearance. The growth spurt also affects the distribution of muscle and fat in the body, with boys typically gaining more muscle mass and girls gaining more fat around the hips and breasts.

Girls typically begin the growth spurt earlier than boys and reach their peak height velocity (or maximum rate of growth) around age 12. Some girls as young as 9 years old experience their first menstrual cycle and a growth spurt as signs of early maturation. Such early development, when their physical development is ahead of their cognitive development, can be a challenging time for girls, who are sometimes teased about their maturing bodies. Typically, boys experience a growth spurt later than girls; those who experience early growth may be lauded for their strength and physical stature. However, some boys may not experience puberty until their early to mid-teens. On average, boys reach their peak growth velocity around age 14.

Other Gender Differences

Secondary sex characteristics also develop during puberty, although they are not directly associated with reproduction. Development of body hair in both genders, breast development in females, and changes in voice and facial hair in males are secondary sex characteristics. These developmental changes, just like puberty itself, are influenced by genetics. Chromosomes differentiate sexes during prenatal development. Within their body cells, males display a *Y chromosome*, while females display two *X chromosomes*.

Physical and hormonal differences in sexes expand during and after puberty. Before puberty, both boys and girls have similar levels of sex hormones, but when sexual maturation is complete, males will have higher levels of *androgens,* the male hormones, while females will have higher levels of the female hormones *estrogen* and *progesterone*. *Testosterone* is the dominant androgen in males and is produced by the testes. It functions in prostate activity to support male reproduction and also helps strengthen muscles and bones. Females also produce testosterone—in the adrenal glands and ovaries—but display lower levels than males. Testosterone has been shown to be associated with aggressive behavior in both sexes. Estrogen is produced by the ovaries and influences the menstrual cycle and female sex characteristics. Progesterone is important for conception as well as maintaining pregnancy.

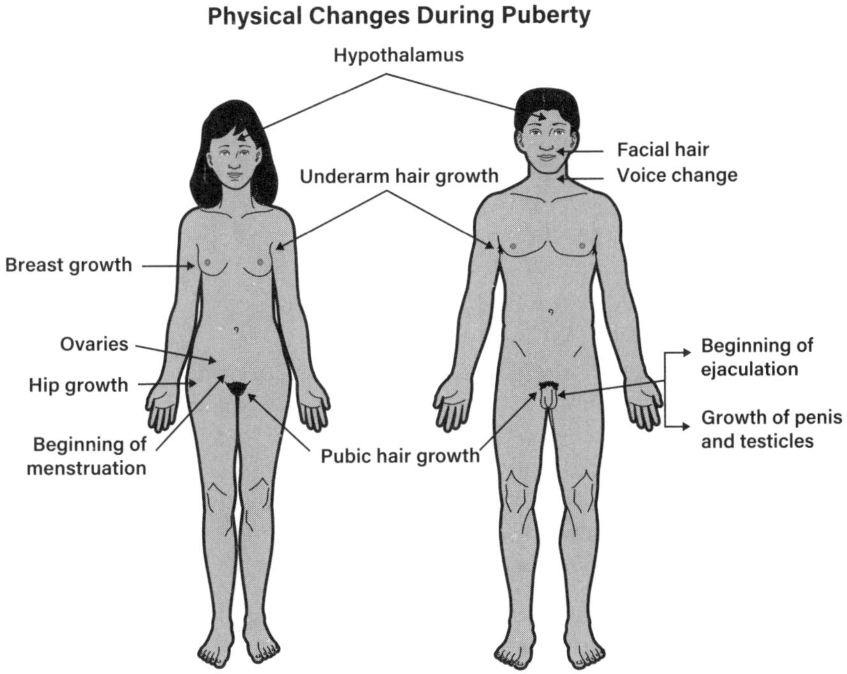

Physical Changes During Puberty

Figure 3.2.2 Physical Changes During Puberty

Psychological and Emotional Changes

Adolescents experience heightened emotions and mood swings, which can be attributed to hormonal changes, brain development, and the challenges of navigating social relationships and independence. Puberty may lead to changes in family relationships. Adolescents often become more independent as they mature and may desire more privacy, distancing themselves somewhat from other family members. Hormonal changes may also cause irritability and moodiness and contribute to redefining family social relationships.

Midlife and Beyond

Adulthood spans most of the lifespan and is characterized by gradual changes in reproductive ability and other physical signs of aging.

Reproductive Ability

In adulthood, the general leveling off and eventual decline in reproductive ability are significant biological milestones. During early and middle adulthood, individuals generally maintain a stable level of reproductive functioning. However, as they transition into later adulthood, women experience **menopause**, which is the cessation of menstruation and the end of a woman's natural fertility. Menopause typically occurs between the ages of 45 and 55.

For men, while there is no equivalent abrupt event such as menopause, there is often a gradual decline in reproductive abilities and sexual functioning with age. This process involves a decrease in testosterone levels, which can lead to changes in sexual desire, erectile function, and fertility.

These changes in reproductive ability are not only biological but also psychological and social. For instance, they can affect individuals' self-concept, sexual relationships, and family dynamics. Understanding and adapting to these changes is an important aspect of development during adulthood. However, study results report that people can remain sexually active into their 80s with good overall health. Generally, by middle age, people report having less sexual activity but greater satisfaction in their relationships.

Other Physical Changes

By the time people enter their forties, muscle mass, bone density, metabolism, visual acuity, and auditory acuity have declined to some extent. Generally, people in this age bracket pick up weight around their midsection. Excess abdominal weight in men and women is partly due to changes in hormones, which influence appetite, metabolism, and accumulation of body fat. The expanding waistline is also associated with dietary and exercise habits, lifestyle factors that may need to change.

Mobility and Flexibility A decrease in muscle strength and bone density can reduce an adult's **mobility,** the ability to move swiftly and smoothly. **Flexibility** also decreases because of the loss of cushioning cartilage in joints and the development of conditions such as arthritis, making movements that were once effortless, including such daily activities as bending and reaching, more challenging.

Reaction Time Older adults may experience a slowing down of cognitive processes and nerve conduction velocity (see Topic 1.3). In an older person, the brain takes longer to process information and send signals to the body, leading to slower reflexes and **reaction time**.

Visual Changes In older adults, **sensory acuity**, or the sharpness, keenness, or clarity with which a sensory system can perceive and discriminate stimuli, declines. Age-related changes in **visual sensory acuity** include a decline in the eye's ability to focus on close objects (presbyopia), a decrease in pupil size, and a reduced responsiveness to changes in light. The lenses of the eyes can become less clear, affecting the sharpness of vision.

Hearing Changes Aging can also affect **auditory sensory acuity.** Presbycusis is the gradual loss of hearing associated with aging, primarily affecting the ability to hear higher frequencies. It can make it hard to distinguish specific sounds or hear conversations in noisy environments.

As vision and hearing decline, people may need more light for reading and completing daily tasks. Age-related damage to the cilia in the inner ear may mean older people need to increase the volume on the radio or TV and ask people to speak up.

By middle age, somewhere between the mid-40s and age 60, hair may begin to gray and lines show up on the skin. Physical abilities may vary considerably in middle age and are strongly influenced by one's overall health status. Some men and women stay physically active through participation in such sports as running, tennis, golf, skiing, or pickleball. They may walk every morning, do yoga, or work out at a gym regularly on their own. Levels of activity will depend on one's interests, opportunities, and health.

REFLECT ON THE ESSENTIAL QUESTION

Essential Question: *How does physical development from before birth through infancy, childhood, adolescence, and adulthood apply to behavior and mental processes?* Using the Key Terms, complete a chart like the one below to gather details to help answer that question.

Developmental Stage	Behavior	Mental Processes
Prenatal		
Infancy		
Childhood		
Adolescence		
Adulthood		

auditory sensory acuity	maternal illness	rooting reflex
critical period	menarche	sensitive period
flexibility	menopause	sensory acuity
genetic mutation	mobility	spermarche
gross motor coordination	puberty	teratogen
growth spurt	reaction time	visual sensory acuity
imprint	reflex	

MULTIPLE-CHOICE QUESTIONS

1. Jack, the father of a newborn, gently strokes the bottom of his baby's foot. As he does this, the baby's toes move outward and then curl in. Which of the following newborn reflexes is Jack's baby demonstrating?

    (A) Rooting

    (B) Moro

    (C) Babinski

    (D) Stepping

2. Five-month-old Erin is able to crawl around the house with little difficulty. However, when it comes to other physical tasks, such as picking up a marble in a game, she struggles. These differences in ability demonstrate the differences between which of the following?

    (A) Gross motor coordination and fine motor coordination

    (B) Critical periods and sensitive periods

    (C) Reflex development and imprinting

    (D) Maturation and socialization

3. Luis is going through puberty. He is growing facial hair and becoming increasingly muscular in his upper body. These changes are most accurately described as which of the following?

    (A) Primary sex characteristics

    (B) Spermarche

    (C) Menarche

    (D) Secondary sex characteristics

Questions 4 and 5 refer to the following.

Developmental psychologists examined the height and weight of children in the first 25 months of life. They were interested in whether physical growth of a child progressed in a continuous or discontinuous manner. Their results are displayed in the scatterplot below.

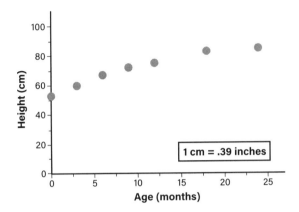

4. What type of research have these developmental psychologists conducted?

   (A) A meta-analysis

   (B) A correlational study

   (C) An experiment

   (D) A case study

5. What conclusion can be drawn from the data presented in the above graph?

   (A) There is no correlation between height and age in newborns.

   (B) There is slight positive correlation between height and age in newborns.

   (C) There is a strong negative correlation between height and age in newborns.

   (D) There is a causal relationship between height and age in newborns.

6. The type of measurement used in the above study is most accurately classified as which of the following?

   (A) Qualitative

   (B) Quantitative

   (C) Cross-sectional

   (D) Statistical significance

7. Some say that the younger a dog is at adoption, the more likely the dog is to have a strong attachment to the owner. Which developmental concept explains this phenomenon?

   (A) Sensitive periods

   (B) Imprinting

   (C) Menarche

   (D) Maturation

STUDY LIKE A CHAMP WITH DR. G. | TREAT YOURSELF

How do puppies learn to fit into the homes of the people who adopt them? They know when they've done something right because they'll hear those treasured words, "Good dog!" So they will keep doing that behavior and reap the reward.

How is your study plan going? Have you been quizzing yourself? Schedule some time to quiz yourself on the end-of-topic questions in one topic in Unit 1 and one topic in Unit 2. Before you do, though, decide how you will reward yourself for your efforts. Keep that reward in mind as you answer the questions. The reward will encourage you to stick with your plan.

Topic 3.3

Gender and Sexual Orientation

"I never feel confined by gender, by labels, by expectations, by stereotypes. I'm free to be myself."

—Princess Nokia

Essential Question: How do sex and gender influence socialization and other aspects of development?

Sex and gender are fundamental aspects of who we understand ourselves to be and have a profound impact on physical development and socialization throughout the lifespan. From early childhood, individuals are socialized into gender roles both implicitly and explicitly. This socialization occurs through interactions with family members, peers, media, and knowledge of social and cultural institutions. Gender norms dictate behaviors, interests, and attributes based on an individual's perceived sex, and they shape the development of self-concept, identity, and interpersonal relationships. Gendered socialization processes influence individuals' perceptions of themselves and others and affect their opportunities, aspirations, and experiences within society.

Sex and gender play a crucial role in shaping cognitive development, academic achievement, and career choices. Research suggests that gender stereotypes and biases can influence teachers' expectations and classroom interactions, contributing to disparities in educational outcomes between boys and girls. Societal expectations regarding gender roles may influence individuals' academic interests and career aspirations. For instance, fields such as science, technology, engineering, and mathematics (STEM) are often perceived as more masculine domains, leading to underrepresentation of women in these fields. Similarly, societal norms regarding caregiving and work-life balance may influence men's and women's career choices and trajectories. Topic 3.3 will help you understand the connections among sex, gender, and socialization as they affect development across the lifespan.

Influence of Sex and Gender on Socialization

The definitions of *sex* and *gender* are easily confused. **Sex** refers to the physical and biological differences between males and females, while **gender** refers to the social construction of roles for males and females. When they are born, babies are assigned the gender that corresponds to their biological sex: male babies are assigned as boys and female babies are assigned as girls.

A very small percentage of babies are born with disorders of sex development (DSD), which is also referred to as *intersex*. These babies have biological characteristics that don't fit the textbook definitions of male or female. Factors that contribute to DSD include varying combinations of sex chromosomes, external genitalia, internal sex organs, and hormones. For example, a group of genetic conditions known as congenital adrenal hyperplasia (CAH) is the most frequent cause of ambiguous genitalia in newborns, accounting for about 60 percent of all DSDs. Sometimes DSD is only diagnosed as the child enters puberty. Some DSDs require either surgical intervention or hormonal therapy (or both).

Sexual orientation addresses one's sexual attraction to male or female partners or, in some cases, both or neither. *Heterosexual* individuals are attracted to the opposite sex. *Homosexual* individuals are attracted to the same sex. Those who are attracted to both males and females are said to be *bisexual,* and those attracted to neither are *asexual.*

Gender identity is an important component of identity development, especially during and after puberty. *Gender identity* is an individual's internalized belief about masculinity or femininity, which may or may not be the same as the biological sex at birth. People whose gender identity corresponds to the sex they were assigned at birth are referred to as *cisgender*. Those whose gender identity is different from the sex they were assigned at birth are referred to as *transgender*. Other terms, such as *genderqueer, genderfluid, androgynous,* and *nonbinary*, are used by individuals who do not identify as either a man or a woman. Instead, they identify as existing somewhere along a spectrum or continuum of genders, or outside it altogether, often in a way that is continuing to evolve.

Both biological and cognitive factors shape gender identity. Genetics and prenatal hormones may have an effect on gender identity, and research suggests that there are structural and functional differences in the brains of males and females. In addition, certain areas of the brain differ in size between cisgender and transgender individuals, aligning more closely with their experienced gender than their biological sex. For some individuals, there is a significant disconnect between their assigned gender at birth and their experienced gender. This conflict can lead to *gender dysphoria*, a condition marked by distress. Understanding and addressing gender dysphoria involves considering both biological predispositions and cognitive experiences.

Cognitive factors influencing gender identity include the *gender schema theory*, which suggests that children develop a framework of knowledge about what it means to be male or female through their interactions with the world. These schemas influence their perception of themselves and their gender identity. As children grow, they form a sense of self, which includes gender identity. This process involves integrating information from their environment, including family, peers, and media. The ways in which parents respond to and encourage gender-typical or atypical behavior can affect the development of a child's gender identity. Societal norms and media representations of gender roles also influence gender identity. Exposure to diverse gender expressions and roles can expand a child's understanding and acceptance of different gender identities.

One's gender identity also involves incorporating *gender roles*—behaviors, traits, and attitudes associated with males and females—into one's self-concept. While gender identity begins to form early in life, adolescents may question whether they fit in with traditional gender roles, which vary by culture and society. Social pressures influence young people to play the part of their respective gender, regardless of how they feel about themselves.

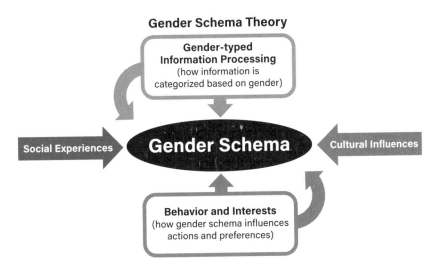

Figure 3.3.1 Gender Schema Theory

Socialization in Childhood

Gender typing is the process by which children become aware of the expected roles associated with their gender. Societies demonstrate these roles both implicitly and explicitly, and gender typing often takes place even before birth.

At baby showers, for example, if the parents know they're expecting a boy, shower guests will give gifts of blue clothing and toys. Pink gifts are given for girls and, if the sex of the child is unknown, gifts often are given in yellow or white. Boys are often allowed to cry for longer periods of time before parents pick them up, and they may be described as "tough." On the other hand, girls are often described as "delicate."

The pattern of gender typing continues into childhood as toys and activities are geared toward the roles that have often been associated with a given gender. Girls are often enrolled in ballet or cheerleading, and boys often play football or wrestle. While physical differences between girls and boys may contribute to differences in gender behavior, the impact of socialization cannot be overlooked. While efforts have been made recently to offer more diverse sports and activities for all genders, gender typing still exerts strong influence.

Socialization in Teenagers and Young Adults

During adolescence and young adulthood, individuals start to embrace their gender identity. At this stage, they may use gender typing as a benchmark to assess if their interests and behaviors align more closely with societal expectations for males or females. Someone with an *androgynous personality* may display both male and female characteristics. Dressing in clothes that are ambiguous—not clearly male or female—is dressing in an androgynous fashion. Androgynous traits also apply to personality and interests, covering a wide array between extreme masculine and feminine roles.

Those who differ in gender identity from their biologically defined sex are known as *transgendered*. This is an umbrella term, and the behaviors associated with it may vary considerably. Some transgendered individuals prefer to dress like those of the opposite sex and, at the same time, are sexually attracted to the opposite sex. Others seek gender reassignment surgery and find themselves sexually attracted to those of their birth sex. Still others do not find themselves physically attracted to either sex.

Some individuals may be unconcerned about whether their gender identity conforms to societal expectations or if they display roles inconsistent with their traditional gender roles. Others may remain unconcerned, even if they experience punishments, such as ridicule or lack of acceptance. For example, stay-at-home dads who take care of the house and children while their wives work are often comfortable in that role and not at all concerned about the opinions or expectations of others. Women who choose to be employed as construction workers or plumbers may enjoy this work, even though they face critiques from others about their choices.

Gender roles vary significantly in different cultures and populations, and expectations may also differ. For example, in Samoan culture, the terms *Fa'afafine* and *Fa'afatama* are used to describe gender roles existing in the space between male and female worlds. These are accepted third and fourth genders in which, for example, biological males may dress in feminine clothing and perform traditionally feminine roles in the household. These gendered behaviors are unrelated to their sexual preferences.

Ideas of gender roles are evolving slowly as society recognizes that an individual's interests and strengths may not be consistent with those associated with gender.

Roots of Gender Identity

Gender identity seems to evolve from a combination of nature *and* nurture. *Social learning theory* suggests that gender role behavior is developed through the observation of others and through rewards and punishments. Developmental psychologist Albert Bandura (see Topic 3.9) relies on the cognitive and social principles of social learning theory to explain how individuals learn and display gender behavior. Bandura believed that we learn from observing and imitating the behaviors of those around us. If you grew up in a household in which a father or older brother took out the garbage and a mother or older sister made dinner each night, you might imitate the behaviors that were consistent with traditional gender roles.

Psychologists learned much about the issue of nature and nurture in gender development from the case of David Reimer, who was born in 1965 and raised as a girl after a circumcision went terribly wrong. The parents were encouraged to raise their son as a daughter because their doctor believed that gender was determined exclusively by nurture. David underwent surgery to construct female genitalia and was raised as "Brenda" without being told about his birth sex. The parents were encouraged to dress their (now) daughter in female clothing and encourage her to participate in "female" activities. However, Brenda identified more with males and masculine behaviors and was often ridiculed for her interest in masculine behaviors. Brenda experienced significant psychological distress during high school. She struggled with her assigned gender identity and experienced depression, isolation, and confusion. During her teenage years, Brenda was informed of her birth sex and the nature of her surgeries. This traumatic revelation intensified her psychological struggles. She decided to undergo surgery to become male because this was consistent with her own gender identity. David's case shed much light on gender transitions and the importance of genes in the roles of gender development.

While adolescence can be a challenging time overall, it may be more challenging for those who do not clearly fit into the confines or roles that society has determined suit their gender. Researchers have come to see gender and sexual orientation as less binary and more fluid. Many individuals do not clearly engage in singularly male or female activities. Others cannot clearly identify their sexual orientation as a single gender.

Evidence from sexual orientation research has established that genetics plays a strong role in sexual orientation. Sexual orientation is also influenced by the prenatal environment (second to fifth months of pregnancy) and sexual differentiation of the brain that occurs during fetal and infant (neonatal) development. Differences in the brain's structure and function, including sex-differentiated activation of the hypothalamus, are thought to contribute to gender identity and sexual orientation. Nevertheless, no definitive conclusions have been reached, and research continues. Sexual orientation for some individuals is variable and may change over their life span. However, programs aimed at modifying an individual's sexual orientation have had little success, and the American Psychiatric Association is opposed to them because they rest on the false assumption that nonheterosexuality is a mental disorder.

THINK AS A PSYCHOLOGIST

Determine the Type of Research Design(s) Used in a Given Study (2.A.1) | Evaluate the Appropriate Use of Research Design Elements in Non-Experimental Methodologies (2.C.6)

Are parents' gender schemas related to their children's gender-related cognitions? Researchers[1] examined 43 studies, comprising 48 different samples, to explore the correlation between parents' gender schemas and their children's gender-related cognitions. The children, spanning from infancy to early adulthood, were assessed on various factors, including gender self-concept, attitudes toward gender, gender-related interests, and occupational attitudes. The analysis revealed a modest yet significant correlation ($r = .16$) between parent gender schemas and offspring measures. Specifically, parents holding more traditional gender schemas tended to have children with more gender-typed cognitions about themselves or others compared to those with more nontraditional schemas. These findings cautiously suggest a potential impact of parental influence on the development of their children's gender-related cognition.

Practice Determining the Type of Research Design and Evaluating the Use of Design Elements in Non-Experimental Methodologies

Answer the following questions.

1. The research conducted in this study is best characterized as which of the following?

   (A) Meta-analysis

   (B) Naturalistic observation

   (C) Experimental

   (D) Case study

2. Many of the results from the 43 articles used surveys in the collection of data. Briefly explain how social desirability bias may have influenced these results.

---

1   Tenenbaum, H. R., & Leaper, C. (2002). Are parents' gender schemas related to their children's gender-related cognitions? *Developmental Psychology, 38*(4), 615–630. https://doi.org/10.1037/0012-1649.38.4.615

Essential Question: *How do sex and gender influence socialization and other aspects of development?* Using the Key Terms, complete a chart like the one below to gather details to help answer that question.

	Socialization	Other Aspects of Development
Sex		
Gender		

KEY TERMS

sex   gender

MULTIPLE-CHOICE QUESTIONS

1. Todd is fifteen. He plays baseball and enjoys video games. While he enjoys dancing, he does not practice often or take classes because he does not believe taking dance classes is consistent with how males should behave. Todd is demonstrating which of the following?

   (A) Gender identity

   (B) Gender stability

   (C) Sexual identity

   (D) Sexual orientation

2. As Reginald speaks to Jordan, he assumes that because of Jordan's long hair and higher voice, Jordan must have a feminine gender identity. Despite Jordan's displaying androgynous behaviors and statements, Reginald interprets these as consistent with his previous beliefs. Reginald is demonstrating which of the following cognitive biases?

   (A) Hindsight bias

   (B) Confirmation bias

   (C) Cognitive dissonance

   (D) Overconfidence

3. Marion is the mother of fraternal twins Jackson and Mabel. She often dresses Jackson in blue and Mabel in pink. What is Marion demonstrating?

(A) Gender identity

(B) Gender typing

(C) Androgyny

(D) Sexual orientation

4. Dr. Desai is interested in studying individuals who have gone through gender reassignment surgery. She is conducting an in-depth study of a group of eight individuals to determine how well they adjust to their new gender after the surgery. She conducts interviews with the patients, their friends, and family, and also uses a battery of self-report inventories and brain scans. Which research methodology has Dr. Desai used?

(A) Correlational

(B) Naturalistic observation

(C) Meta-analysis

(D) Case study

5. Dashka, a 14-year-old female, comes from a traditional family in which gender roles have been passed down through many generations and are well ingrained in the customs and traditions of the family. Which of the following roles would you anticipate being assigned to Dashka?

(A) It is likely that Dashka would be expected to work outside of the home to provide the main source of income for the family.

(B) It is likely that Dashka would make all financial decisions for the family.

(C) It is likely that Dashka would do much cooking and cleaning for the family.

(D) It is likely that Dashka would be expected to complete any construction projects around the house.

6. Maria was the kicker on her school football team, and she wrestled on the boys' team as well. She also likes to get dressed up and loves make-up and romantic comedies. Which best describes Maria's gender behaviors?

(A) Bisexual

(B) Transgendered

(C) Androgynous

(D) Gender types

Topic 3.4

Cognitive Development Across the Lifespan

"Thought and language are the two greatest powers on earth."
—Lev Vygotsky

Essential Question: How do theories of cognitive development apply to behavior and mental processes?

Cognitive development is the process of intellectual growth a child goes through to develop information-processing abilities, perceptual skills, language learning, understanding of concepts, and problem-solving abilities.

Several theories of cognitive development offer insights into how behavior and mental processes evolve over time. One, developed by Jean Piaget, focuses on how cognitive development occurs through a series of distinct stages, each characterized by qualitatively different ways of thinking. Another theory, developed by Lev Vygotsky, emphasizes the role of social interactions, cultural context, and language in cognitive development.

Although the most rapid period of change in cognitive development occurs during infancy through adolescence, cognitive changes occur during adulthood as well. The ability to solve problems, see relationships, and think abstractly begins to decline after middle age. At the same time, individuals' accumulated intelligence and ability to use skills, knowledge, and experience increase with age.

Piaget's Theory of Discontinuous Cognitive Development

Starting in the 1920s, Swiss psychologist **Jean Piaget** theorized that what a child is able to do intellectually depends on the age of the child and development of the brain. His approach was grounded in a *discontinuous perspective* or step theory of development. According to Piaget, children actively construct their understanding of the world. He believed that children were "little scientists." As they progress through cognitive development, their thinking abilities, including perception, memory, problem-solving, and abstract reasoning, become more sophisticated. In Piaget's theory, biological maturation and environmental experiences combine to shape cognitive development and influence behavior.

Piaget spent the early years of his career creating intelligence exams while employed at a school run by Alfred Binet, creator of the first contemporary IQ test. (See Topic 2.8.) Piaget noticed that children of a given age consistently answered the same questions incorrectly. He also noticed that young children answered some questions incorrectly because their thought process appeared to be different from that of older children. Piaget's life's work was inspired by these early observations. He wanted to develop a theory that traced the cognitive development of children in some orderly fashion. He studied his own children and grandchildren as references for his theory.

Piaget's Stages of Cognitive Development

According to Piaget, children use their experiences in the world to categorize and judge new events as they occur. They use **assimilation** to make sense of new situations by relating them to prior experience and their existing **schemas**, or frameworks for thinking. (See Topic 2.2.) For example, if a child sees the big red dog Clifford in a book, he may call him Elmo if he is already familiar with the fuzzy red character from *Sesame Street*. He assimilates the idea of fuzzy red objects, believing, based on his past experience and schema, that they are all Elmo. However, once the child learns the name for Clifford, a different fuzzy red object, he may no longer confuse the two. At this point, the child has learned the process of **accommodation**, a way to modify his schema to include the new information.

If a child sees the ocean for the first time and calls it a giant pool, she is *assimilating* prior experience. When she no longer makes this mistake and calls the body of water an ocean, she has *accommodated* by differentiating between situations and creating new categories. Children accommodate as they learn language that helps them differentiate among objects.

Even adults experience assimilation and accommodation because people are always experiencing new situations, new foods, new ideas, and new challenges. We try to place these novel experiences into our preexisting schemas, but sometimes we must create new categories because our current classification is inadequate. If, for example, you taste frog legs for the first time, you might say, "They taste like chicken" because you are assimilating, by searching your mind for something to help you classify and understand this experience.

To remember the difference between assimilation and accommodation, you might want to use this mnemonic device that focuses on the double letters in each word. In *assimilation*, the double *s*'s stand for the way the schema "stays the same." In *accommodation*, the double *c*'s stand for "creates change."

The First Stage The **sensorimotor stage** is the first of Piaget's stages. According to Piaget, it lasts from birth through roughly the first 2 years of life. During this stage, children begin to understand that their movements are tied to sensory satisfaction. A child engages in motor activities that bring a desirable result. For example, touching a musical mobile hanging above the crib will make a satisfying noise. If a baby girl cries in her crib, her mother may appear and comfort her. The child's motor activities are associated with sensory satisfaction, thus the name *sensorimotor stage*.

Until babies develop object permanence, they do not realize that even things they can't see can exist. Peekaboo holds a true fascination for babies.

At about 8 months of age, a child begins to understand that objects exist even when hidden. This discovery is known as **object permanence**. Before this discovery, if a child throws his stuffed animal out of the crib and it is out of his sight, he will believe that it no longer exists and will not try to find it. The child would feel the same way when his primary caregiver was out of sight and experience *separation anxiety*, a fear that the caregiver no longer exists. However, the child will come to realize that the thrown object is still there and he just cannot see it. It takes longer to grasp that the same applies to people.

Children in the sensorimotor stage also experience *stranger anxiety*, the fear or wariness of encountering unfamiliar people. Piaget believed that this fear of strangers stems from the infant's growing ability to differentiate between familiar and unfamiliar faces. Infants may perceive unfamiliar faces as potential threats or sources of discomfort, leading to stranger anxiety.

The Second Stage The **preoperational stage** is Piaget's second stage of cognitive development, lasting roughly from ages 2 through 7. It is called "preoperational" to express the state of mind that cannot yet perform such operations as combining or separating ideas or using logic. Children in this stage can begin to see objects as symbols and often demonstrate this ability by exhibiting pretend play. They may imagine that their playroom is a schoolhouse or that a piece of paper represents a plate or a pillow.

During this stage, children also exhibit **animism**, a belief that inanimate objects have feelings and humanlike qualities. For example, a child may become upset if a parent gives the child a kiss good night but does not kiss all of her stuffed animals. She may express to her parent that the stuffed animals' feelings have been hurt, not understanding that the toys are not living beings. Some may argue that such pretense, though false, allows children to develop empathy and understanding for others.

Children in the preoperational stage will also display **egocentrism**— seeing the world only through their own perspective. While adults may explain this as selfish behavior, it reflects the inability of the child at this age to understand a situation from another's point of view. Preoperational children believe others see the world from the same perspective by which *they* see the world. For example, if a family were to go to a carnival and the child had a wonderful time, the child would report that everyone had a great time when asked how the rest of the family enjoyed the carnival. Children at this stage may stand directly in front of the TV, blocking the views of others; because *they* can see the screen, they presume others can as well. Children in this stage also engage in **pretend play**, which helps to build social and emotional skills. Children in the preoperational stage may enjoy engaging in activities like "playing school" or acting like a fireman. These types of activities help build children's imaginations and often involve socialization with others in this stage.

At about age 4, most children begin to understand that their aunt is also their mother's or father's sister and their grandmother is their mother's or father's mother. Earlier, children would only have been able to understand their own connection to their aunt (or other family members) and not the connections with others. They now understand that relationships with others go in more than one direction, and they become less egocentric.

Later developmental psychologists have added to Piaget's theory. One of these concepts is the **theory of mind**, in which children understand that other people may see the world from a different perspective than they do. This shift is most evident as children transition to the next stage (the concrete operational stage) and begin to show an understanding of others' viewpoints, although they still struggle with abstract and hypothetical thinking until they reach the formal operational stage.

The Sally–Anne test is a popular way to help determine if children have yet acquired a theory of mind. In the test, a child is told a story in which a girl named Sally places a marble into a basket and then leaves for a walk. Another girl named Anne sees Sally put the marble in the basket. Anne takes the marble out of the basket and puts it into a box. Sally returns and wants to play with the marble. The child being tested is asked where Sally will look for the marble. A child without theory of mind will answer that she will look in the box, because the child knows from the story that the marble is in the box. In contrast, a child who has developed a theory of mind will say that Sally will look in the basket because that child understands that Sally was on a walk when the marble was placed into the basket and, therefore, will have a different perspective on the location of the marble, expecting it to still be in the basket.

Figure 3.4.1

Piaget emphasized that children in the preoperational stage exhibit *one-dimensional thinking*. While they understand that a glass is either "tall" or "short," they cannot understand that a tall, thin glass may hold the same amount of juice as a short, fat glass. Such one-dimensional thinking keeps preoperational children from understanding conservation, the principle that changing the shape or appearance of an object does not necessarily change the object's mass. If a young boy has a dime in his pocket, he would gladly trade it for a nickel because the nickel is larger and surely must be more valuable than the dime. Similarly, the same amount of modeling clay rolled out like a snake will appear to children in this stage more than the same amount rolled into a ball, simply because it appears to have more surface area. The preoperational thinker who cannot understand the transformation of shape in relation to mass is demonstrating the act of focusing on only one aspect of a problem when more aspects are relevant.

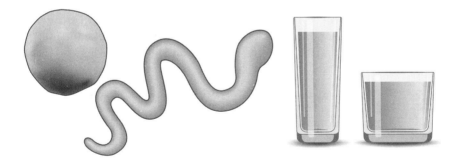

Figure 3.4.2 One-Dimensional Thinking

The Third Stage The **concrete operational stage** is Piaget's third stage of cognitive development, a period lasting roughly from ages 7 through 11. During the concrete operational stage, the child exhibits *two-dimensional thinking* and now understands that changing the shape of an object does not necessarily change the mass. During this stage, a child can understand **reversibility**, the idea that actions can be reversed, returning to their original state. A child can see the ball of clay changed into a snake and understand that the snake can be returned to its original state as a ball of clay.

Piaget determined that by the age of 8, children understand that a short, fat glass may hold the same amount of juice as a tall, thin glass, exhibiting the principle of **conservation**. The boy with the dime in his pocket should now be able to understand that a nickel is not worth more than a dime, even though it is larger. Piaget claimed that children acquire this skill at about age 8, but researchers today believe that children have this skill much earlier.

Children in the concrete operational stage also become less egocentric; they no longer think that the world revolves around them and understand that their parents and others have separate lives. They recognize that their parents may have jobs that do not involve them, even though they may not fully understand what their parents do in those jobs. Children in this stage begin to think logically about problems and about concrete objects that exist in their environment. However, challenges continue to arise in thinking and reasoning abstractly or thinking in three dimensions.

The Fourth Stage The **formal operational stage** is the fourth and final stage of cognitive development in Piaget's theoretical model. Beginning in early adolescence, children are able to think about constructs and ideas that do not physically exist in the world. They understand **abstract concepts** like virtue and honesty, even though these are not tangible objects, and they understand sarcasm, which requires the recognition that language used in that way does not convey its literal meaning. They can also reason through **hypothetical situations** and plan potential solutions for long-term problems. Children in this stage can move between scientific and intuitive thinking and select the appropriate mode of thinking for different tasks. However, even though children now have the ability to think abstractly, they may still benefit from educational instruction that provides concrete examples to make the material more robust and tangible. This mode of thinking allows growing children to create a sense of identity and begin to make plans for their own futures.

PIAGET'S STAGES OF COGNITIVE DEVELOPMENT		
Cognitive Stage	Approximate Age	Description
Sensorimotor	Birth to 2 years	Sensory and motor contact exploration; development of object permanence and separation anxiety
Preoperational	2 to 6 or 7 years	Symbolic and egocentric thinking; ability to pretend; child does not think logically
Concrete Operational	7 to 11 or 12 years	Can think logically about concrete objects and do simple math; conservation develops
Formal Operational	12 to adult	Abstract and hypothetical thinking emerges; strategy and planning become possible

Table 3.4.1

An easy way to remember Piaget's four stages of cognitive development is to think of the phrase "Students of Psychology Can Fly" (SPCF). The first letters create initials for **s**ensorimotor, **p**reoperational, **c**oncrete operational, and **f**ormal operational stages.

While Piaget's theory is widely known and accepted, it is not without critics and challenges. Many suggest that Piaget underestimated the cognitive abilities of children. Researchers have found that children as young as 4 months old may have object permanence in certain situations—they look longer when an object disappears in an unexpected way that may seem impossible to the child. Many children also develop conservation far earlier than age 8. Others criticize Piaget's stage theory because children can often demonstrate cognitive abilities from more than one stage at the same time. Further, Piaget did not make a clear distinction between competence and performance and, without that distinction, the abilities he ascribes to children in each stage fall into all-or-nothing categories. While most current research supports Piaget's order of childhood cognitive development, his idea that all children move through the cognitive stages at roughly the same age has also been disputed.

THINK AS A PSYCHOLOGIST

Explain How Cultural Norms, Expectations, and Circumstances, as Well as Cognitive Biases Apply to Behavior and Mental Processes (1.B.1)

As you have read, Piaget's four-stage theory ends with the transition from a concrete operational to a formal operational period, during which abstract and hypothetical thinking developed. Michael Cole and his and his colleagues (1971)[2] studied the Kpelle tribe in Africa, trying to see at what point they transitioned from the concrete operational period to the formal operational period. The Kpelle had oral language but little written language. Researchers asked members of this tribe to sort various words into different categories. The researchers expected the adults to be able to separate the words into categories familiar to Western thinkers, such as different kinds of fish together, different kinds of birds together, and both of these groups underneath the category of "animals." However, to the researchers' surprise, the Kpelle categorized objects functionally, such as categorizing fish, birds, and eat into one category because they ate fish and birds. After several attempts to get them to categorize these words into hierarchical structures but failing at these attempts, the researchers were about ready to give up. However, one of the researchers asked, "How would a foolish person separate these words into different categories?" The Kpelle immediately separated the words into the kinds of familiar categories that the researchers were expecting.

---

2   Cole, M., Frankel, F., & Sharp, D. W. (1971). The development of free recall learning in children. *Developmental Psychology, 4*(2), 109–123.

Vygotsky's Theory of Cultural and Biosocial Development

In 1934, Russian psychologist **Lev Vygotsky** introduced a theory of cultural and biosocial development which critiques Piaget's idea that all children develop cognitive abilities at essentially the same time. His **sociocultural perspective** suggests that the social and cultural environment allows children to progress through development stages either more quickly or more slowly, depending on the stimuli in that environment. For example, if children are in an enriching environment, in which they have access to cognitive stimulation through many resources and much social interaction, they may move through Piaget's stages more quickly than a child with minimal exposure to such stimulating situations.

Vygotsky believed that one's culture provided not only language but also problem-solving strategies and other educational tools that would foster children's cognitive development. He also stressed the importance of mentors who could teach children and refine their skills and knowledge. Because each culture differs, he suggested that universal guidelines for children's cognitive development were misleading. He viewed cognitive development as a social process, disagreeing with Piaget's view that children were independent explorers of their environment. Vygotsky also proposed the **zone of proximal development**—the difference between what a learner can do without help and what a learner can do with help—to suggest the steps to making children more independent. If children need assistance tying their shoes, for example, their parents may initially help them and then coach them as they attempt to tie their own shoes (what they can do with help), but as they become more capable of doing this independently, their parents should provide less and less assistance until the children can complete the task alone (what they can do without help). This process is called **scaffolding**, named for the structures that temporarily support builders as they work on new construction.

Piaget's and Vygotsky's theories are not the only ones that attempt to explain the process of cognitive development. Some recent work on the interaction of nature and nurture in forming one's level of intelligence seems to support a more eclectic view on the development of children's cognitive abilities.

THINK AS A PSYCHOLOGIST

Identify Reasoning That Supports, Refutes, or Modifies an Established or Provided Claim, Policy, or Norm (4.B.1)

Practicing Identifying Reasoning

Complete the following activity.

1. Support the following claim with two pieces of evidence from this topic. Label your evidence as **Evidence 1** and **Evidence 2**.

   Claim: Cognitive development relies on sociocultural factors.

Middle Age and Beyond

Developmental psychologists have spent much time studying the cognition of children, whose abilities develop so quickly. Understanding children's cognitive abilities also helps determine the continuity of these skills throughout the lifespan.

Many changes take place in the brain after middle age. For example, levels of neurotransmitters that affect the brain's **fluid intelligence**—the ability to solve problems, see relationships, and think abstractly—decline after middle age, thereby reducing the ability to solve new problems and process new information. Significantly reduced production of the neurotransmitter dopamine reduces levels of activity in the frontal lobe of the brain. For this reason, the brain's processing speed, reasoning, response time, and memory capacity may also be reduced. In addition, the weight of the human brain decreases after age 60, and the brain has fewer active neurons. Neurons atrophy with aging, and older adults may have up to 30 percent fewer functioning neurons than younger adults. The neurons that appear to be most affected by age are those responsible for sensory and motor activities. Blood flow and oxygen to the brain also decrease with age, resulting in the increased time older adults need to process new information. As a result of these gradual changes, older adults may have trouble learning unfamiliar technology, understanding how to set up new programs on their computers or use wireless devices, or responding to changes as quickly as they might have in the past. A general decline in *working memory,* the memory we use to take in information (see Topic 2.3), may also make it difficult to remember multiple pieces of information at the same time.

In contrast, crystallized intelligence generally increases with age. **Crystallized intelligence** represents an individual's accumulated intelligence over time and the ability to use skills, knowledge, and experience. Do you know older adults who can name all of the U.S. presidents who occupied the White House during their lifetime? Calling on accumulated knowledge, some older adults may be able to describe historical events in great detail or recall characters and stories from books they read years earlier. Long-term memory does not seem to decline at the same rate as working memory, so older memories can be retrieved more easily than new information. Healthy older adults with active cognitive and physical lives can delay the deterioration of mental capacities. As in other areas of psychosocial development, the intermingling of nature and nurture determines one's cognitive health status. While some individuals with inherited **cognitive disorders**, such as Alzheimer's disease or Lewy body disease, will see a clear decline in cognition after ages 65 to 70, others will remain cognitively astute well into their 80s and 90s.

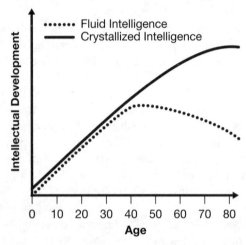

Figure 3.4.4

Some older adults develop a brain condition known as **dementia**, in which thinking, memory, and behavior begin to deteriorate. The frontal lobes of the brain begin to deteriorate to some extent in all adults over age 50. About 14 percent of Americans over the age of 71 are diagnosed with a specific form of dementia known as *Alzheimer's disease*, a degenerative disease in which memory loss is progressive and plaques accumulate in nervous system tissues. The age of onset is generally after 65, although some will experience early-onset Alzheimer's disease. Chances of developing Alzheimer's disease doubles every 5 years until age 85. Lower levels of the biochemical acetylcholine have been found to be associated with Alzheimer's disease, as well as the presence of a specific genetic trait (i.e., ApoE4 allele on chromosome 19). Signs of Alzheimer's may include problems speaking or writing, misplacing items, confusion with time or place, and the inability to complete familiar tasks. People with Alzheimer's disease also may experience extreme changes in personality and, in advanced stages, have trouble recognizing family and friends.

Some people who do not have any type of cognitive disorder may nonetheless experience a rapid decline of certain cognitive abilities known as the *terminal drop* in the weeks or months prior to death. Older adults may also experience small strokes that obstruct blood flow to the brain and can also reduce cognitive functioning. While some of this decline might be genetic, studies have found that the risk of developing dementia is reduced in those who remain cognitively and physically active.

THINK AS A PSYCHOLOGIST

Evaluate the Appropriate Use of Research Design Elements in Non-Experimental Methodologies (2.C.4)

Several studies have explored the link between fluid intelligence capabilities and the capacity of one's working memory. Below is a modified abstract from one such study.[3]

Abstract: Working memory capacity and fluid intelligence are known to be strongly correlated traits. Typically, high-working memory capacity is believed to aid reasoning by accurately maintaining relevant information. In this article, we propose a new perspective, suggesting that tests of working memory capacity and fluid intelligence measure complementary processes essential for complex cognition. These processes are the ability to maintain access to critical information and the ability to disengage from or block outdated information. In problem solving, high working memory capacity allows a person to accurately and stably represent and maintain a problem, enabling effective hypothesis testing. From this viewpoint, the strong correlation between working memory capacity and fluid intelligence arises not from one ability influencing the other, but from separate attention-demanding mental functions that, although sometimes contrary, are organized around top-down processing goals.

The above study demonstrates a strong correlation between working memory capacity and the level of fluid intelligence.

Practice Evaluating the Use of Research Design Elements in Non-Experimental Methodologies

Answer each of the following questions in one or two sentences.

1. Discuss how a directionality problem could be related to this research.

2. Discuss how a third-variable problem could be related to this research.

---

3 Shipstead, Z., Harrison, T. L., & Engle, R.W. (2016). Working memory capacity and fluid intelligence: maintenance and disengagement." *Perspectives on Psychological Science, 11*(6) 771–799. DOI: 10.1177/1745691616650647

REFLECT ON THE ESSENTIAL QUESTION

Essential Question: *How do theories of cognitive development apply to behavior and mental processes?* Use the key terms to answer that question and complete a chart like the one below.

Theory of Cognitive Development	Behavior	Mental Processes
Piaget's Stage Theory		
Sociocultural Perspective		
Adult Changes in Cognitive Capabilities		

KEY TERMS

abstract concept
accommodation
animism
assimilation
cognitive development
cognitive disorder
concrete operational stage
conservation
crystallized intelligence

dementia
egocentrism
fluid intelligence
formal operational
hypothetical situation
object permanence
preoperational stage
pretend play
reversibility

scaffolding
schema
sensorimotor stage
sociocultural perspective
theory of mind
zone of proximal development

KEY PEOPLE

Jean Piaget

Lev Vygotsky

1. Emily, who is $2^1/_2$ years old, is at the zoo. She points to a lion and calls it a dog because she has never seen a lion before. Emily's behavior demonstrates which of the following?

   (A) Accommodation

   (B) Object permanence

   (C) Conservation

   (D) Assimilation

2. Four-year-old Andrew now understands that even though he loved the new cartoon movie about cars, his sister Alexis did not feel the same way. The ability of Andrew to understand that others may not see the world in the same way he does shows his development of which of the following?

   (A) Accommodation

   (B) Theory of mind

   (C) Concrete operational thinking

   (D) Egocentrism

3. What would Lev Vygotsky find to be the most significant limitation of the work of Piaget in regard to children's cognitive development?

   (A) Piaget relied too much on interviews conducted with parents.

   (B) Piaget did not take into consideration the impact that one's social environment may have on cognitive development.

   (C) Piaget relied too heavily on the concepts of sex and aggression as motivating factors for behavior.

   (D) Piaget was wrong about the order in which children develop cognitive skills.

4. Bridget understands that even though her sandwich has been cut in half, she does not have twice as much sandwich as her friend who has an uncut sandwich. Which cognitive landmark has Bridget mastered?

   (A) Object permanence

   (B) Abstract thinking

   (C) Artificialism

   (D) Conservation

5. Charolette is 85 years old. Each morning, she successfully completes a crossword puzzle, and she enjoys reading and learning about presidential trivia and American history. She knows more about these topics than ever before. Which of the following is strong for Charolette?

(A) Emotional intelligence

(B) Fluid intelligence

(C) Crystallized intelligence

(D) Accommodation

6. Martha has recently turned 65. According to the graph below, how would developmental psychologists expect her intellectual abilities to change over the next decade?

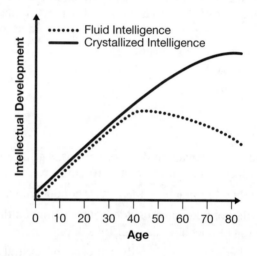

(A) There will be a decrease in Martha's accumulated knowledge and intelligence.

(B) Martha is less likely to experience neurocognitive disorders because of a decrease in plaques.

(C) Martha is likely to produce higher levels of acetylcholine than she did in her teens.

(D) There will be a decrease in Martha's ability to solve problems and think abstractly.

7. Dr. Rafeen is a developmental psychologist who studies cognitive issues in mature adults. He is trying to determine the average age of onset for Alzheimer's disease so he can introduce some interventions for those who are most at risk. The following chart represents the ages at which a group of Dr. Rafeen's patients were first diagnosed with Alzheimer's. What is the mean age of this group?

Patient #	Age of Onset
1	81
2	67
3	80
4	78
5	82

(A) 77.6

(B) 81.2

(C) 72

(D) 86.4

8. Roqaya knows that her dad goes to work each day as a pharmacist. She can understand that he has a life that is separate from her, even if she does not yet realize exactly what it means to be a pharmacist. What stage of Piaget's cognitive development is Roqaya likely experiencing?

(A) Sensorimotor stage

(B) Preoperational stage

(C) Concrete operational stage

(D) Formal operational stage

STUDY LIKE A CHAMP WITH DR. G. | RETRIEVAL PRACTICE

You just completed Topic 3.4—almost halfway through Unit 3—and probably have a pretty good memory of what you just read, though you may not hold onto it for long. Remember to test yourself repeatedly on current and earlier topics, and even earlier *units*, to get the greatest benefit from retrieval practice. The more you practice, the stronger your long-term memory of the material will be.

Topic 3.5

Communication and Language Development

"We speak not only to tell other people what we think, but to tell ourselves what we think. Speech is a part of thought."

—Oliver Sacks

Essential Question: How do key components of language and communication apply to behavior and mental processes?

In order to think about thinking, we need language, the primary means through which we communicate our ideas and reflect on our lives. "Humans are so innately hardwired for language," writes psychologist and linguist Steven Pinker, "that they can no more suppress their ability to learn and use language than they can suppress the instinct to pull a hand back from a hot surface."

Language is our spoken, written, or signed words and the ways we combine them to communicate meaning. Our language and its complexity represent one of the greatest differences between humans and other animals.

The Basics of Language

Language as a system is a social construct agreed upon by its users. That is, the meanings of words, the rules of grammar, and the structures of language are not inherent or natural but rather are established by convention and mutual understanding among people within a language community. For example:

- **Vocabulary:** The words in any language represent agreed-upon labels for objects, actions, and concepts. For instance, the word *dog* denotes a specific animal because English speakers have collectively agreed on this usage.

- **Grammar:** The rules for combining words into phrases and sentences are based on a shared understanding within the language community. **Grammar** structures how we express relationships between different concepts and actions and organizes meaning in a systematic way.

- **Syntax:** A set of rules, principles, and processes known as **syntax** govern the structure of sentences. Sentence structure is not arbitrary, but is based on an agreed-upon set of principles that members of a language group follow to ensure clear communication.

- **Semantics:** The meaning of words and sentences, or **semantics,** relies on shared understanding. Users of a language have a common agreement on what words signify, which allows them to communicate ideas and information effectively.

Without this collective agreement on language systems, communication would be highly inefficient and the transmission of culture, knowledge, and traditions across generations would be severely hindered. The consensus on language is, therefore, foundational to social interaction, cultural continuity, and individual expression.

Basic Units of Language

A **phoneme** is the smallest distinctive sound unit in a language. English uses about 40 phonemes. A few of the basic sounds in English are illustrated in Table 3.5.1. While the English language has only 26 letters, as you can see in the figure, an *o* can be pronounced in many different ways, leading to numerous phonemes that are connected to a single letter. Additionally, letter combinations such as *ch* or *sh* function as a single sound that is unique to these letter combinations.

Some Basic Sounds (Phonemes) in English	
S as in *sat*	**E** as in *egg*
T as in *tap*	**I** as in *ink*
P as in *pan*	**O** as in *other*
N as in *nose*	**Oa** as in *boat*
M as in *mat*	**Oo** as in *cook*
A as in *ant*	**Oo** as in *boot*

Table 3.5.1 Selected English Phonemes

A **morpheme** is the smallest unit that carries some meaning (semantic interpretation). It may be a word or a part of a word (such as a prefix). Some morphemes are also phonemes, such as *I* or the *s* that indicates a word is plural. The word *unkindness* has three parts: *un-* (the prefix), *kind* (the root word), and *-ness* (the suffix). Each one contributes meaning to the word, so each is a morpheme.

Generative Nature of Language

Language is **generative**, allowing users to create and understand an infinite number of sentences, including sentences that have never been spoken before. This generative quality is possible because of a language's rules, which can be applied in novel ways to generate new expressions. Even with a finite number of words and morphemes, the generative nature of language means that users can produce an unlimited number of unique phrases and sentences.

Psychologists have explored whether animals have the ability to learn language. One of the most famous of the animals studied is Nim Chimpsky. Nim lived with a family and was taught American Sign Language. He learned dozens of different signs, but there is disagreement on whether he actually had generative language because most of his signs were imitations of signs that he had seen his trainers or owners make. Sadly, Nim died of a heart attack at the Black Beauty Ranch after signing a worker who was bringing him snacks to hurry.

Language is not a fixed set of phrases. Instead, it allows for creativity and variation, enabling speakers to express a wide range of ideas, emotions, and thoughts. Just as speakers can generate new sentences, listeners can understand them, thanks to their knowledge of linguistic rules and the context in which the language is used.

Language Development

Babies are born with 100 billion neurons or more. However, the myelin sheath that protects the axons of the neurons—the channels neural signals travel—is not well developed. By 6 months of age, the neurons in Wernicke's area of the brain, where language comprehension is processed, have become myelinated. By 12 months of age, myelination is developed in Broca's area, the region responsible for speech production. Myelination is completed by age 2.

Nonverbal Language

Humans develop language skills in a predictable series of stages that are universal across cultures. **Nonverbal manual gestures**, such as pointing, are an intrinsic part of language development across many cultures. These gestures make communication possible, especially before verbal skills are fully developed. They not only precede language but also complement and reinforce verbal communication. Gestures are considered their own type of communication. You can see this when individuals who do not speak a common language can still communicate with one another using gestures.

Children first understand and then use gestures to communicate their needs, desires, or interests. For example, infants may reach out toward an object before they can express their desire for it verbally. This act of reaching or pointing can then evolve into more complex gestures that can signify different things, depending on the cultural context or the conventions established within a family or community.

Early Vocalizing

The **cooing stage** is one of the earliest phases in language development, typically emerging around the age of 2 months and lasting until about 4 months. During this stage, infants begin to vocalize and experiment with their vocal cords by producing soft, vowel-like sounds. This cooing is a baby's way of practicing the use of the tongue, lips, and palate to make noises, which later evolves into more structured babbling and eventually into actual speech.

Cooing sounds are often elongated vowels, such as "oo," "aa," and "ee." These sounds are produced at the back of the mouth and are usually a baby's response to a calm and content state, often occurring when they are comfortable, interested, or happy. This is not just random noise; it's the beginning of the process of learning how to control their vocal cords and mouth muscles. These sounds can be seen as the first "conversations" infants have and are crucial for their social development because they typically provoke responses from caregivers.

Parents and caregivers typically encourage cooing by cooing back, smiling, and talking to the infant, which helps with bonding and social interaction. This exchange is a fundamental part of the language-learning process, as it introduces the concept of turn-taking in conversation.

The cooing stage lays the foundation for later stages, starting with the **babbling stage**, which begins at about 4 months of age. This is the stage of speech development in which the infant spontaneously vocalizes various sounds, at first unrelated to the language spoken in the home. These are essentially nonsense sounds that have no meaning, such as "ba-ba-ba" or "da-da-da."

By the time a child is about 10 months old, the sounds take on the sounds of the home language. If children are not exposed to alternate languages, they tend to lose the ability to make and hear the phonemes of other languages. Therefore, an adult English speaker could not "hear" and discriminate among some of the sounds in Mandarin (a tonal language) or languages with clicks, such as Xhosa and Swazi.

Next is the **one-word stage** of language development that typically takes place between ages 1 and 2, during which a child speaks mostly in single words. This is sometimes called the *holophrastic* stage, since a whole idea can be expressed in one word. For example, "Go!" might mean "I want to leave now." "Car" could mean "There is a car."

The *two-word stage* of language development begins at about age 2. During this stage, a child speaks mostly two- or three-word statements, such as "car go" or "Daddy fall" or "Mommy silly" or "want cookie." In this stage, known as **telegraphic speech** because a child's speech is like a telegram, a child will use mostly nouns and verbs. **Overgeneralization**—the application of grammar rules in instances to which they do not apply, as in "Daddy buyed me a present"—is common as preschool children continue to develop language. In this case, the child is using the grammar rule of adding an *ed* to the end of a verb in order to make it past tense. They have not yet learned that there are exceptions to the rule, which they will gradually learn over the coming years.

By ages 6 to 10, children can speak in full sentences and master syllable stress patterns to distinguish among words. By this age, they have learned 80 percent of all the language they will ever need. Nearly all the rest is learning complexity, metaphors, irony, puns, simile, allegory, hyperbole, analogy, rhetoric, poetry, rhyme schemes, puns, euphemisms, and other linguistic subtleties.

Between the age of 5 and puberty, language acquisition becomes more difficult than during the first 5 years of life, but it is still more effective than learning a new language as an adult. Language learned after the age of 9, whether sign language or a verbal/written language, will generally result in communication less fluent than that of native speakers of that language. As with attachment, there seems to be a critical or sensitive period at which individuals are biologically prepared to learn language.

THINK AS A PSYCHOLOGIST

Explain How Cultural Norms, Expectations, and Circumstances Apply to Behavior and Mental Processes (1.B)

Researchers of language have identified two different processes people use when learning a second language: *additive bilingualism* and *subtractive bilingualism*. The additive bilingualism process takes place when the second language is learned in addition to the first language. Subtractive takes place when the second language replaces the original language.

People who have learned a second language may experience benefits and drawbacks socially. People who speak their language of origin on account of additive bilingualism may feel an instant connection with others who also speak that language. They may feel more strongly affiliated with their ethnic group. They may feel more useful helping their parents or grandparents in translating essential services (an act called "language brokering"), but this also comes at a cost when they feel burdened by having to be a translator for their parents or grandparents.

People who do not speak their language of origin on account of subtractive bilingualism may be ostracized by peers who speak their language of origin. They also may feel they are not "really" part of their ethnic group. They may not be able to be language brokers for their parents or grandparents, leading them to feel guilty about not being as useful as their siblings or peers who maintain their language of origin.

Practice Explaining How Cultural Norms, Expectations, and Circumstances Apply to Behavior and Mental Processes

Complete the following activity.

Write a few sentences explaining how the language (or languages) you speak shape your personal and cultural identity. Provide examples from your own life or observations and consider whether speaking multiple languages can alter or expand your sense of identity.

THINK AS A PSYCHOLOGIST

Evaluate Whether a Psychological Research Scenario Followed Appropriate Ethical Procedures (2.D.3) | Evaluate the Appropriate Use of Research Design Elements in Experimental Methodology (2.B.3)

"Wendell's stutterers" refers to a notable study conducted by Wendell Johnson, a psychologist, in the late 1930s. This study aimed to investigate the development of stuttering in children through a unique experimental design. Johnson recruited 22 orphaned children from the Iowa Soldiers' Orphans' Home, most of whom were initially nonstutterers. The study's procedure involved dividing the children into two groups: one group received positive speech therapy, where their speech was praised and encouraged, while the other group received negative therapy, where their speech was criticized and mocked.

Over the course of the study, Johnson observed significant changes in the speech patterns of the children. The children who received negative therapy began to develop stuttering symptoms and other speech impairments, while those who received positive therapy did not. This finding challenged prevailing beliefs about the root cause of stuttering, which had often been attributed to physiological or genetic factors. Instead, Johnson's study suggested that environmental factors and psychological influences could play a significant role in the development of stuttering.

Practicing Evaluating Ethical Procedures and the Use of Design Elements

Answer the following questions.

1. In the study, Dr. Wendell Johnson was applying concepts in discriminatory ways from which of the modern psychological perspectives? (See Practice 1.A to review these perspectives.)

   (A) Humanistic

   (B) Psychodynamic

   (C) Behaviorist

   (D) Evolutionary

2. Cite a specific ethical reason why a current IRB would be unlikely to allow this study today.

3. Identify the independent variable (IV) of this experiment.

REFLECT ON THE ESSENTIAL QUESTION

Essential Question: *How do key components of language and communication apply to behavior and mental processes?* Using the Key Terms, complete a chart like the one below to gather details to help answer that question.

What are the basic components of language?	How does language develop in human beings?	How do human beings acquire language?

KEY TERMS

cooing stage	nonverbal manual gestures	syntax
babbling stage	one-word stage	telegraphic speech
generative	overgeneralization	vocabulary
grammar	phoneme	
morpheme	semantics	

MULTIPLE-CHOICE QUESTIONS

1. Two-year-old Mica tells her grandmother that she "eated" her dinner already. Mica's language error is most clearly an example of which of the following?

   (A) Babbling

   (B) Telegraphic speech

   (C) Semantics

   (D) Overgeneralization

2. The Vietnamese language has a sound that goes with the letters *ng* at the beginning of words, including names. Americans have difficulty hearing and speaking that sound. The *ng* sound describes which component of language?

   (A) Semantic unit

   (B) Syntax

   (C) Morpheme

   (D) Phoneme

Questions 3 through 6 refer to the following.

The graph below represents the average number of words a child knows from 10 to 36 months of age. Children were divided into three groups, based on their family's status: professional families, working-class families, or families on government assistance.

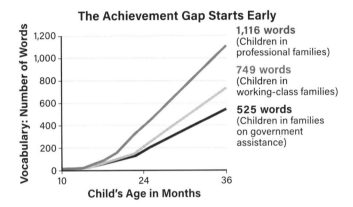

3. What type of research was conducted to gather the information displayed in the graph?

(A) Case study

(B) Correlational study

(C) Naturalistic observation

(D) Meta-analysis

4. What conclusion can be drawn from the results of this study?

(A) Regardless of family environment, children know roughly the same number of words.

(B) There is a negative correlation between age and number of words a child knows.

(C) A family's socioeconomic situation can influence the language development of children.

(D) There is no statistical significance in the difference found between working-class families and families on public assistance.

5. Why could this study not be conducted as an experiment?

   (A) Because it would not be ethical to purposely place children into a deprived environment if researchers anticipated a negative outcome

   (B) Because it is impossible to create an environment that affects how many words a child knows

   (C) Because even changing a child's environment would not affect the number of words they learned

   (D) Because children's language acquisition does not end at 36 months, and the children should be tracked in a longitudinal design

6. The following data set represents the number of words children in the study knew. In order to determine the average distance from the mean for the number of words children knew at 36 months, what would be the best statistical measure to use?

Group	Words at 24 Months	Words at 36 Months
Professional	405	1,116
Working-Class	222	749
Government Assistance	191	529

   (A) Statistical significance

   (B) Range

   (C) Standard deviation

   (D) Correlational coefficient

7. Kyra's parents are delighted that she is learning to speak and want to be certain that she stays on track with her language development. They have talked with their doctor and know the stages of language acquisition. Kyra is currently saying phrases such as "dog here" and "cookie me." What stage of language acquisition is Kyra currently experiencing?

   (A) One-word stage

   (B) Telegraphic speech

   (C) Babbling

   (D) Overgeneralization

Topic 3.6

Social-Emotional Development Across the Lifespan

"The bond between a child and their mother is the strongest and most important relationship in the animal kingdom."

—Konrad Lorenz

Essential Question: How does social development relate to behavior and mental processes across the lifespan?

Social development encompasses the acquisition of social skills, formation of relationships, and understanding of social norms and roles. As you saw from Vygotsky's sociocultural perspective, a child's social environment and cognitive development are closely intertwined. An enriched environment can accelerate cognitive development while a deprived environment can slow it down. During the early years of life, interactions with caregivers and other children help shape how a child forms emotional bonds, manages emotions, and develops social skills. Secure attachment during infancy lays the groundwork for healthy social and emotional development and forms the basis for later interpersonal relationships. As children progress through childhood and adolescence, peer relationships become increasingly important, influencing identity formation, self-esteem, social cognition, and emotional intelligence.

In adulthood, social growth affects how people act and think in close relationships, as parents, and at work. Social experiences and cultural standards shape important life events during this stage. Parenting presents new challenges and opportunities, and parenting styles have a strong influence on children's behavior.

This topic begins with an examination of the complex interactions between individuals and their social environments. It concludes by considering a comprehensive stage theory of psychosocial development across the lifespan, framing each stage as a "crisis" that needs to be confronted and resolved.

The Influence of the Social Environment on Development

The **ecological systems theory,** developed in 1979 by Urie Bronfenbrenner, proposes an explanation of how the social environment shapes human development. This theory emphasizes the interconnectedness between individuals and their surrounding contexts and highlights interconnections between various systems. The theory proposes five systems that begin with the environment that is closest to the individual and end with society, culture, and time. They provide a layered perspective on the influences that affect an individual's growth and behavior.

Microsystem The **microsystem** represents the immediate environment in which an individual lives and interacts daily. It includes the people and groups with whom the individual has direct contact, such as family, peers, school, and community organizations. These relationships are crucial because they directly influence the individual's experiences, beliefs, and behaviors. For instance, a supportive family or nurturing school environment can foster positive development. Or consider how your specific school environment, school climate, school spirit, and interactions between students and staff all contribute to how you experience a "typical" school day in that microsystem.

Mesosystem Microsystems do not exist in a vacuum. For example, your parents may work with parents of your friends or you may attend school with your teacher's children. The **mesosystem** refers to these and other connections and interactions between the different components of the microsystem. It involves the relationships between family and school, family and peers, or school and community, among others. The quality and nature of these interactions can affect the individual's development. For example, consistent communication between parents and teachers can enhance a child's academic performance and socioemotional well-being.

Exosystem The **exosystem** is made up of external environments that indirectly influence the individual's development, even though the individual may not be actively involved in them. These include factors such as parents' workplaces, neighborhood conditions, media, and social policies. Changes or events in these settings can have ripple effects on the individual's experiences and opportunities. For instance, a parent's job loss may lead to financial stress within the family and affect the child's well-being and academic performance.

Macrosystem The **macrosystem** encompasses the broader cultural, societal, and institutional contexts that shape individuals' lives. This includes cultural norms, values, beliefs, laws, and economic systems. Cultural events, historical trends, and social movements also fall within the macrosystem. These factors exert a profound influence on the individual's development by shaping the values, opportunities, and constraints within their environment. For example, cultural attitudes toward education or gender roles can significantly affect an individual's aspirations and behaviors. Some macrosystems value family over education. A child may be expected to drop out of school to help with family expenses because of the expectations of the broader culture.

Chronosystem The **chronosystem** recognizes the importance of time and historical context in human development. It refers to the changes and transitions that occur over the course of an individual's life, as well as the historical events and societal changes that shape different generations. Life events such as moving, marriage, divorce, or changes in economic circumstances can have varying impacts depending on the individual's age and stage of development. Additionally, societal shifts, such as technological advances or economic hard times, can influence opportunities and challenges across different life stages.

The ecological systems theory recognizes that human growth is shaped by a variety of influences over time. Through examining how different systems interact, researchers and those working in applied settings can gain more insight into what drives development throughout a person's life.

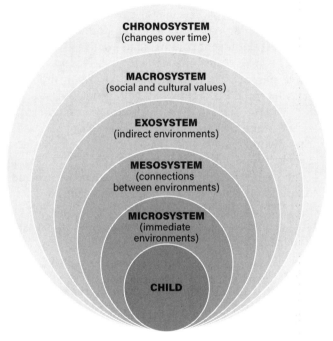

Figure 3.6.1 Bronfenbrenner's Ecological Systems Theory

Parenting Styles

Parents and other caregivers are key elements in the microsystem. Along with other researchers, clinical psychologist Diana Baumrind, noted for her research in the 1960s on parenting, investigated the influence of different parenting styles on children's behavior and developed categories of parenting.

Authoritarian parents are sometimes referred to as *dictatorial* because they enforce their rules without input from their children. They live by the philosophy of "my way or the highway." Authoritarian parents impose their will on their children, often behaving this way because they believe it will protect the children. Children of authoritarian parents often cannot make decisions for themselves and, when given some independence, may often make poor decisions. The children's decisions may appear to be especially immature for their age group. In addition, these children often display lower levels of self-esteem and are not well equipped to make independent choices because they have not had a say in setting rules and regulations.

Permissive parents may fall under the rejecting-neglecting parenting style, in which they are not involved with their children's lives and do not necessarily care to be involved. This style may occur because, for a number of reasons, a parent and child (children) do not live together, the parents work too much and are absent a lot, or parents are simply too concerned with events of their own lives to be interested in their children's lives. Children of rejecting-neglecting parents typically have little self-esteem and often act as adults prematurely because they have had to make decisions for themselves from a young age. Permissive parents may also be *indulgent*. These parents seek friendship with their children and set few boundaries for them. As a result, children of permissive-indulgent parents often are impulsive and demanding because they have become accustomed to getting their way.

Authoritative parents are responsive to the input and needs of their children and set rules and expectations, but they are not as rigid and demanding as authoritarian parents. These parents are warm, communicative, and open to discussions, including listening to their children's opinions and feelings. Importantly, they demonstrate a willingness to compromise, adjusting rules to better suit the maturity and circumstances of their child. This flexibility helps to foster a nurturing environment that encourages independence and emotional growth. Children of authoritative parents are well balanced, exhibiting good decision-making abilities and high self-esteem. Fortunately, Baumrind's work revealed that most parents fall into the authoritative style of parenting.

Regardless of parenting styles, children's behavior is not entirely determined by parental guidance. Some psychologists have suggested that a child's **temperament,** or disposition, is just as important as parenting style in determining parent/child relationships. Parents may also not fall neatly into a single parenting category and may be stricter in some areas and more lenient in others. Genetic factors may also play a role in both parenting behavior and children's behavioral responses. Some children may also be subjected to two different parenting styles, an area needing more research. Baumrind and other researchers conducted their studies primarily in Western societies, so study results may not reflect the parenting styles in different cultures. Future parenting research must therefore address a wider array of parenting styles displayed in other cultures.

Authoritative parents set reasonable rules and expectations and hold their children to living up to them.

THINK AS A PSYCHOLOGIST

Determine the Type of Research Design(s) Used in a Given Study (2.A.1)

Practice Determining the Type of Research Design

Complete the following activity.

Write two to three sentences briefly explaining why research on parenting styles is likely to be non-experimental rather than experimental.

Attachment

Newborns demonstrate an early attachment to their caregivers, showing preferences for their faces, scent, and language, even a few hours after birth. As the grasping reflex demonstrates, physical attachment to a caregiver is extremely important to a child's early development. The emotional bond between an infant and caregiver, or **attachment**, is considered to be just as important. Children as young as a few weeks old learn to recognize the facial expressions of their caregivers and may begin to imitate the facial expressions they see in others. Developmental psychologist John Bowlby was a pioneer in attachment research and the originator of *attachment theory* (1969). He claimed that attachment behavior in infants is innate. After observing infants' behaviors, such as wanting to remain close to a caregiver and raising their arms to be picked up when they were distressed or wanted comfort, Bowlby proposed that such behavior aids in survival and initiates nurturing responses from caregivers.

Secure and Insecure Attachment

Developmental psychologist Mary Ainsworth, noted for her work on patterns of attachment, designed a research method that allowed her to observe the behavior of infants and children covertly through one-way glass. Using this method, Ainsworth conducted what she called a *strange situation test* to investigate various forms of attachment and bonding between 1-year-old infants and their mothers (1970). In one type of experiment, a child and mother played together in a small room, and at some point, a stranger entered. At first, the child continued to play either independently or with the mother, seeming to be relatively indifferent to the presence of the stranger. However, when the mother exited the room, leaving the child alone with the stranger, the child cried and rebuffed the stranger's efforts to provide comfort. This behavior shows the child was experiencing **separation anxiety**, which is normal in babies when they cannot be with their caregivers. It also reflects **stranger anxiety**, the fear and uncertainty of an unknown person, especially in the absence of the caregiver. When the mother returned, the child settled down, made an effort to physically touch the mother, and went back to playing independently.

Infants like the one just described have a **secure attachment**. Although they show some level of distress when their caregivers leave, they eventually regain comfort knowing, based on their established bond, that the caregivers will return.

Researchers studying infants with an **insecure attachment** have found three different types of insecure attachments: avoidant, anxious, and disorganized. Each reflects distinct relationships between children and their caregivers.

Children displaying **avoidant attachment** tend to avoid or downplay closeness and intimacy with their caregivers. They may not seek comfort or support when distressed and often appear self-reliant. They may be indifferent to both the caregivers' departure and return. These children may approach the caregivers on their return but then turn away. This behavior can stem from past experiences in which caregivers may have been inconsistently responsive to the child's needs, leading the child to believe that closeness is not possible.

Children with **anxious attachment** are more likely to be distressed by the caregivers' departure and resentful when the caregivers return. Because the caregivers' behavior with these children may be inconsistent, the children's responses may be inconsistent, ranging from inconsolable when the caregivers return to clingy, refusing to leave their sides. They may seek constant reassurance and attention.

Disorganized attachment happens when a child's relationship with their caregiver is confusing and inconsistent. A toddler with a disorganized attachment may cry when the caregiver leaves the room. The child might run to the caregiver for a hug on the caregiver's return but then freeze or act strangely when the parent tries to comfort them. This behavior can be puzzling because the child seems torn between seeking closeness and feeling scared of the caregiver at the same time. This type of attachment often develops in situations where the caregiver behaves unpredictably or even harmfully. For instance, if a parent sometimes provides love and care but other times behaves aggressively or neglects the child's needs, the child will feel confused and fearful.

A child's preference for the mother as caregiver may have biological links but may also result from interactions between the mother and child that meet the child's needs consistently.

ATTACHMENT TYPES AND BEHAVIOR		
Attachment Type	**Behavior When Caregiver Left Baby with Stranger**	**Behavior When Caregiver Returns**
Secure	Upset; cries and refuses to be comforted by stranger	Makes effort to touch caregiver and returns to playing
Avoidant (Insecure)	Indifferent	Indifferent; may seek contact but then pull away
Anxious (Insecure)	Very distressed	May be inconsistent; hard to console or very clingy
Disorganized (Insecure)	May cry	May seek comfort but then freeze or fall

Table 3.6.1

Psychologist Harry Harlow continued the work of Konrad Lorenz, investigating attachment and maternal separation. At the time, most psychologists believed that a strong attachment bond formed between infant and mother because mothers provided food in the form of breastfeeding. Providing a child with the basic nourishment required for life created a strong mother/infant bond, they theorized. Harlow challenged this idea, suggesting instead that the strong attachment formed between infant and mother was due to *contact comfort,* or the physical comfort a caregiver provided to the infant.

Harlow focused his studies on primates because they are more similar to humans than are rats and pigeons, and their behaviors more closely paralleled human behaviors. In his experiments, controversial for their cruelty to the animal subjects, Harlow separated baby rhesus monkeys from their mothers and gave them two artificial, inanimate surrogate "mothers." One was made of wire and fixed with a bottle that provided milk to the baby monkey. The other was made of cloth-covered wood that would allow for cuddling, but this "mother" provided no food. While the monkeys did go to the wire mother when they needed food, they spent most of their time cuddling and clinging to the cloth mother. When the monkeys were afraid or threatened, they went directly to the cloth mother for protection and comfort. Harlow concluded that milk was not the key to bonding and that contact comfort contributed more to mother/infant bonding and to the health of infants. However, critics point to bias in the results, since the face of the cloth mother was natural looking, while the face of the wire mother was block-shaped and unappealing.

Harlow also conducted isolation experiments (also controversial) and discovered that monkeys raised in isolation without a real or artificial mother did not demonstrate a preference for either mother when afraid. Instead, these isolated monkeys withdrew, turned inward, and rocked back and forth when frightened. They also struck out frequently against other monkeys when they were given opportunities to socialize. Harlow's studies showed that the physical bonds between infants and caregivers may be just as important as the infants' biological dependency on mothers for food, if not more important.

Cultural Differences

Attachment styles differ greatly between cultures because of varying caregiving practices, social norms, and cultural values. In collectivistic cultures, caregiving often involves the whole community, where many family members or community members together take care of infants. This shared caregiving can lead to a more group-oriented attachment style, where

The Aka in Central Africa are known for their loving child-rearing, almost constantly holding, comforting, and playing with their children. Every community member plays a role in nurturing the next generation.

infants form secure connections not only with their primary caregivers but also with other important people in their social circle. In many African cultures, extended family members like grandparents, aunts, uncles, and older siblings play key roles in raising children, helping to create a strong sense of belonging.

On the other hand, cultures with individualistic values, like many Western societies, place a higher emphasis on independence and autonomy. Caregivers in these cultures might focus on nurturing self-reliance and emotional self-regulation in infants. For instance, in the United States, caregivers often encourage infants to explore on their own and form secure attachments with their primary caregivers through consistent and responsive caregiving.

Even within individualistic societies, cultural differences can affect attachment styles. Research shows that attachment patterns may vary between European American and Asian American families, influenced by differing cultural views on emotional expression, closeness, and interdependence.

THINK AS A PSYCHOLOGIST

Evaluate the Appropriate Use of Research Design Elements in Experimental Methodology (2.B.7, 2.B.3) | Apply Psychological Perspectives, Theories, Concepts, and Research Findings to a Scenario (1.A.1)

Dr. Chase is a graduate student who wants to conduct follow-up studies to Mary Ainsworth's strange situation test to see if there is a difference in how children attach to mothers versus fathers. She plans to ask 100 parents in her community to volunteer with their child. She then plans to randomly assign 50 children to do the strange situation test with their father and 50 children to do the same test with their mother. She plans to use an established scale to classify each child's attachment style as secure, avoidant, anxious, or disorganized. Once these data are collected, she will compare the two groups to see if the attachment styles were consistent across mothers and fathers.

Practice Evaluating Design Elements and Applying Concepts

Answer the following questions.

1. To what extent will Dr. Chase be able to generalize her results?

2. In this study, what is the independent variable (IV)?

3. Dr. Chase found that about 3 percent of the children responded to their parent's return with very little interest. Many simply continued playing and ignored their parent. Based on Ainsworth's research, these children would be classified as having which of the following attachment styles?

   (A) Avoidant

   (B) Anxious

   (C) Secure

   (D) Disorganized

The Development of Peer Relationships Over Time

Peer relationships evolve through various stages, starting from early childhood interactions, where friendships are formed based on shared activities and physical closeness. As children grow, these relationships become more complex, with school-age children selecting friends based on common interests, mutual respect, and trust. During adolescence, peer relationships gain further importance as teenagers seek independence from their families and develop stronger bonds with friends, often influenced by shared values, beliefs, and social goals. This period is crucial for social identity formation, with peer groups providing a platform for exploring self-identity, norms, and social roles. Into adulthood, peer relationships often reflect life stages and shared experiences, such as college, career paths, or parenting, with friendships becoming more selective and based on deeper connections and mutual support. Throughout life, these relationships play a vital role in personal development, offering opportunities for social interaction, emotional support, and personal growth.

Engagement with Peers During Childhood

During childhood, peer interactions play a crucial role in social and emotional development as children learn to navigate relationships, negotiate conflicts, and develop a sense of belonging within their peer groups. Parallel and pretend play with peers are significant vehicles for socialization and learning.

During **parallel play**, which typically occurs in early childhood, children play alongside each other without direct interaction or shared goals. This form of play allows children to observe and imitate their peers while engaging in similar activities independently. For instance, on a playground, one child may be building a sandcastle, while another nearby child builds their own castle, each absorbed in their task without direct collaboration. Through parallel play, children develop social awareness, observational skills, and the ability to coexist in shared spaces, laying the groundwork for more interactive forms of play later on.

By the time children enter preschool, they begin to engage in **pretend play**, in which they create imaginary scenarios, roles, and narratives, often incorporating props and costumes to enhance the make-believe experience. You read about pretend play earlier in this unit as part of Piaget's preoperational stage, which extends roughly from ages 2 to 7 years. This type of play allows children to experiment with social roles and norms, practice

Two girls riding their imaginary rocket ship.

communication skills, learn to cooperate with others, and develop creativity and problem-solving skills. For example, a group of preschool children playing doctor in a pretend medical clinic might take turns assuming the roles of doctors, nurses, and patients, improvising dialogue and actions. Pretend play not only fosters imagination and creativity, but also encourages cooperation, communication, and perspective-taking as children negotiate roles, share ideas, and collaborate to bring their imaginary worlds to life.

Peer interactions during older childhood often involve cooperative activities and shared interests that foster bonding and camaraderie. Participating in team sports, group projects, or collaborative games helps children learn the importance of teamwork, communication, and compromise. For instance, older children may work together in a classroom to complete a science experiment or solve a math problem, requiring them to communicate effectively, listen to each other's ideas, and contribute to the group's success. These collaborative experiences help children develop social skills such as leadership, cooperation, and conflict resolution, which are essential for building positive and supportive relationships with peers.

Social Changes During Adolescence and Early Adulthood

Adolescents often experience a reemergence of what Jean Piaget described as egocentrism (see Topic 3.4)—seeing the world from one's own perspective. Teens who experience **adolescent egocentrism** often believe that their experiences are unique and that their parents or others could not possibly understand what they are going through. For example, a teenage girl breaking up with her boyfriend may believe that her parents could never understand the pain of losing one's "first love." In reality, parents will likely recall similar events in their own history and could actually be a source of comfort.

Teens also tend to create **personal fables**, stories of their lives that are idealized and special and that make them feel invincible. Such fantasizing may cause them to engage in risky behaviors and create an overly optimistic sense of the future. For example, if a teenage boy knows the career path he wants to pursue, he may envision himself rising easily to the top of his profession. Teens do not often consider that things may not go as planned. However, such optimism may serve teens well in supporting active pursuit of their interests.

Teens may also experience being the center of attention for an **imaginary audience** that listens enthusiastically to their ideas and beliefs. Posts made by teens on social media sites may be expected to attract a lot of interest and agreement by all who read them.

Healthy parent-teen relationships are especially important in support of adolescent development. Overall, while much attention is given to possible conflicts between parents and adolescents, most teens report having relatively positive relationships with their parents. Although these relationships are not entirely without conflict, teens often realize that parents or guardians have their best interests in mind, even when they don't agree with all their decisions. Positive parent-teen relationships often pay great dividends, providing advantages such as the following:

- Teens who report having a positive relationship with their parents can help peers by giving good advice.
- Parents in healthy parent-teen relationships are more likely to address tough topics such as drug use and sexual activity with their teenage children and guide them when navigating these issues.
- Supportive parents play a larger role than peers in helping teens develop responsibility, gain education, and plan for the future.
- Having a good relationship with parents often carries over to positive relationships with peers.

Peer influence becomes very important during adolescence, as teenagers spend more time with peers than parents. Teens often spend most of the day at school, and after school they may be involved in school or community activities with their peers. Parents or adults are not present to direct group behavior, and teens must navigate activities and relationships on their own. Relationships with peers allow children and teens to learn to negotiate with others of their own age to resolve conflicts and make friends. Peer pressure may sometimes persuade teens to engage in behaviors parents would not approve of, but positive peer pressure can also guide teens to engage in more productive behaviors.

The increased influence of technology and social media sites gives teens a larger potential network of friends, but it also exposes them to potential online bullying. Cyberbullying is a prevalent problem that allows anonymous bullies to harshly shame other people online. Teens may find criticism or negative comments from an unknown source exceptionally difficult to deal with. Bullied teens may become increasingly self-conscious and self-critical in response to comments from someone they don't even know. Teaching preteens and teens to engage with technology safely has become an important consideration for parents in the information age.

Adult Social Development

The concept of **emerging adulthood** has evolved because teens are no longer jumping into adulthood and achieving complete independence from their parents as they leave their teenage years. Although adolescence is the transition period from childhood to adulthood, traditionally ending as young adults entered their 20s, increasingly young people in their 29s finish college and return home to live with their parents, sometimes depending on their parents to pay health insurance premiums or car payments.

The Social Clock and the Influence of Culture Culture helps shape the concept of adulthood and the timing of major life events, acting through a mechanism known as the **social clock**. This cultural construct dictates a typical age for reaching specific milestones, such as completing education, entering the workforce, marrying, and starting a family. The expectations can vary significantly from one society to another, shaping individuals' life paths and their sense of personal achievement relative to peers.

In many Western cultures, the concept of "emerging adulthood" has been recognized as a distinct phase that bridges adolescence and full-fledged adulthood. Typically occurring from the late teens through the twenties, this period allows for greater exploration of identity, career paths, and personal beliefs. Emerging adults may pursue higher education, experiment with different job roles, explore diverse romantic relationships, and often delay marriage and parenthood compared to previous generations. This phase is characterized by a sense of exploration and instability, as well as the opportunity for significant personal growth and self-discovery.

Conversely, in cultures with more traditional or structured societal roles, the transition to adulthood may be more abrupt and closely tied to specific rites of passage or the attainment of certain milestones, such as completing education or entering into an arranged marriage. These cultures might have a more defined and less flexible social clock, with less emphasis on personal exploration and more focus on fulfilling familial and societal roles.

Healthy friendships between teens often reflect healthy parent-teen relationships.

In some societies, teens go through a *rite of passage* that indicates a transition into a new stage of life. The transition may be associated with achieving a significant life event or being recognized for a particular accomplishment—a graduation, christening, or bar or bat mitzvah, for example. Often these rituals coincide with the onset of puberty, at which time teens may be recognized as adults in their communities.

While arrival into adulthood varies considerably by culture and region, true adulthood has been pushed back in Western societies. Young adults are putting marriage and children off until after they establish their careers and adult identities. This delay may require extended support from parents for a period of time, at least until the goals are met.

Some observers have been critical of this transition into adulthood, claiming that it represents a lack of focus and direction; others defend the prolonged process because it allows individuals to decide what they want to do rather than simply comply with what society expects. They argue that taking the time to make thoughtful decisions about a career or marriage may lead to greater success and happiness

A father congratulates his daughter on her *quinceañera*, a celebration with Hispanic cultural roots of a girl's fifteenth birthday and passage into adulthood.

in the future. Falling divorce rates are one concrete measure that suggests delaying marriage may make for happier and longer-lasting marriages.

The Formation of Families

Adult relationships often evolve into the formation of families or family-like bonds, characterized by mutual support and care. These connections, whether through biological ties, marriage, or chosen connections, serve as the cornerstone of adult social networks, offering emotional support, companionship, and practical assistance. The process of forming and maintaining these adult relationships is significantly influenced by childhood attachment styles, those patterns of bonding formed in early life with primary caregivers.

Childhood attachment styles—categorized broadly as secure, anxious, avoidant, and disorganized—lay the groundwork for how individuals approach relationships in adulthood. Those with a secure attachment style, having experienced consistent care and responsiveness from caregivers, are likely to form stable and trusting relationships with others. They tend to believe that they are worthy of love and that others can be relied upon, which facilitates the development of healthy, supportive adult relationships. Hazan and Shaver (1987)[4] conducted a large-scale self-report measure in a local newspaper and found that those who reported having secure relationships as children also reported having happier and stronger relationships as adults.

Conversely, individuals with anxious attachment styles may have experienced inconsistent caregiving, leading to fears of abandonment and feelings of unworthiness. In adulthood, this can manifest as clinginess or a constant need for reassurance from partners or peers. Avoidant attachment styles, often resulting from dismissive or emotionally distant caregiving, can cause adults to maintain emotional distance from others, struggle with intimacy, and prioritize independence over close relationships. The disorganized attachment style, stemming from chaotic or frightening caregiving, can result

---

4 Hazan, C., & Shaver, P. (1987). Romantic love conceptualized as an attachment process. *Journal of Personality and Social Psychology, 52*(3), 511–524. https://doi.org/10.1037/0022-3514.52.3.511

in adults having difficulty managing emotions and forming stable relationships, often alternating between seeking closeness and pushing others away.

The influence of these attachment styles on adult relationships demonstrates the importance of early emotional bonds in shaping the capacity for forming families or family-like networks that provide mutual support and care.

Psychosocial Development Across the Lifespan

Developmental psychologist and psychoanalyst Erik Erikson introduced a comprehensive theory consisting of eight stages of **psychosocial development** during the 1940s. His theory proposes that people must resolve psychosocial conflicts at each stage of the lifespan. **Psychosocial conflicts** refer to internal struggles faced by individuals at various stages of their life, stemming from the interaction between their psychological needs and the social demands or expectations placed upon them. This concept is central to Erikson's theory of psychosocial development, which proposes that an individual goes through eight distinct stages from infancy to late adulthood. At each stage, the person faces a unique conflict that represents a critical turning point in development. Successful resolution of these conflicts results in acquiring essential virtues or psychological strengths that contribute to healthy personality development.

Each stage of psychosocial development builds on the previous stage. The stages may unfold somewhat differently based on an individual's unique environmental influences and sociocultural experiences. An individual may not resolve this crisis in a certain stage, resulting in problems that emerge later in life, but lack of completion does not prevent moving to the next stage. Experiences that occur during any one stage may be modified later, and learned virtues or attributes may also persist through later stages.

Erikson's Stage Theory of Psychosocial Development

Erikson was inspired by the work of Sigmund Freud and worked with his daughter, Anna Freud. Erikson is known as a neo-Freudian or new Freudian because he modified and updated Freud's work to make it his own and address what Erikson believed to be limitations in Freud's theory. Erikson placed less emphasis on the sex drive (libido) and less focus on the unconscious than Freud. Erikson identified his theory as psychosocial development as opposed to Freud's **psychosexual approach**. Erikson's stage theory begins at birth and extends into adulthood and old age (unlike Freud's, which ends at puberty), and Erickson was more optimistic about human behavior than Freud, who was quoted as saying "People are cesspools of hidden desires." Erikson explained each of eight stages of psychosocial development as a "crisis" to be confronted and resolved. The resolution of each stage allows an individual to face the next crisis.

Childhood Stages Erikson proposed the following four stages of development for children from birth to age 12:

- **Trust and mistrust** is the first stage of psychosocial development, beginning at birth and continuing through the first year of life. During this stage, the child learns to depend on parents or a caregiver for support, comfort, and responsiveness to needs. Having a responsive caregiver encourages the infant to believe the world is a safe, secure place, worthy of trust. Having a rejecting or neglectful caregiver may make a child unable to place trust in others later in life. A successful resolution to this stage is the development of hope.

- **Autonomy and shame and doubt** is the second stage of psychosocial development. It lasts from ages 1 through 3, defining the child's toddler period. Children in this stage gain a sense of independence from their caregivers and begin to complete activities such as feeding and dressing themselves (*autonomy*). Toddlers begin to demonstrate their own will by asking for items they want, such as "cookie!" They may also deny requests, responding with an adamant "no" to show how they feel about taking a nap. If parents continually interrupt children's independent behaviors, toddlers may question whether they can act on their own (*shame and doubt*). The stage resolves with a sense of will.

- **Initiative and guilt** is the third stage of psychosocial development, which Erikson claimed lasts from ages 3 through 6 to define a child's preschool years. During this stage, children begin to take on even more independent activities and can begin to explore activities that capture their interest. A child may attempt to resolve the crisis of whether he can do something successfully. If a young child plans a tea party for her toys and everything goes well, she may engage in more self-initiated activities (*initiative*). However, if she views the tea party as falling apart or others refuse to play along, she may question whether she can carry through on such tasks. Morality also begins to develop when children feel guilty for mistakes they have made (*guilt*). The resolution of this stage is the development of a sense of purpose.

In the autonomy and doubt stage children begin to exercise their willingness (or unwillingness) to take part in certain activities.

- **Industry (competence) and inferiority** is stage four of psychosocial development. It tracks children from ages 6 through 12, defining their primary school years. During this stage, children begin to understand how others view them and how their performance compares to that of others. They also begin to identify tasks at which they excel and those for which they need more practice. If a child is successful at reading out loud in class and does better than his classmates on this task, he or she may begin to develop a sense of industry. If a child falls behind on many tasks in comparison to others of the same age, he or she may develop a sense of *inferiority*. This stage resolves with a sense of competence.

ERIKSON'S STAGES OF PSYCHOSOCIAL DEVELOPMENT			
Age	Conflict	Resolution	Description
Birth to 1 year	Trust and Mistrust	Hope	If infant needs are met, a sense of basic trust develops; if trust is not attained, child becomes fearful of others
1 to 3 years	Autonomy and Shame and Doubt	Will	Child develops sense of independence or self-doubt develops
3 to 6 years	Initiative and Guilt	Purpose	Child begins to initiate tasks and plans in play or initiative is held back by guilt
6 to 12 years	Industry and Inferiority	Competence	Child discovers their academic abilities and social relationships or develops feelings of inferiority

Table 3.6.2

Adolescent and Adult Stages Erikson's stages of psychosocial development continue into adulthood. His last four stages represent psychosocial development in adolescents and adults.

- **Identity and role confusion,** Erikson's stage five, is associated with adolescence and represents individuals from ages 12 through 18. During this stage, teens (or preteens) begin to discover their own identity, see how it differs from others, and understand what makes them unique and special. As teens attempt to discover how they fit into society and what their role will be, they may try out different types of dress, music, and activities. Teens may adopt the views, opinions, and interests of their peers, parents, or role models, or they may try playing different roles until they find one that best suits their individual interests. Those who do not develop a clear sense of who they are may experience role confusion and an identity crisis. James Marcia (page 435) expanded on this work of Erikson's and delved further into how an identity is eventually embraced by the individual.

- **Intimacy and isolation** is stage six in Erikson's model. It coincides with early adulthood, usually representing the 20s to 40s. According to Erikson, the young adult is looking for a potential life partner. While young adults do not necessarily need to get married in order to successfully overcome this crisis, they do need to find and develop emotionally close relationships. If they do not develop close, intimate friendships or relationships, they may feel isolated and alone. As you read earlier in this topic, emerging adulthood is a challenging time, and many young adults today are not seeking a long-term relationship until later in life.

- **Generativity and stagnation**, stage seven of Erikson's theory, represents middle adulthood. During this stage, individuals begin to reflect on their life's work and determine whether they are providing something beneficial to younger generations. Individuals who feel productive and sense that they are adding value to society are described by Erikson as experiencing *generativity*. In other words, they are "generating" value and satisfaction. Generativity may be achieved in different ways: contributing knowledge to the next generation, inventing something useful, creating a safer or more just society, or raising children to carry on one's legacy. If they are not feeling productive or satisfied with the value they are bringing to others, they experience *stagnation*—the feeling that they are not moving forward and are just going through the motions of life. Stagnation is the result of viewing one's work as meaningless or feeling that one has contributed neither talents nor children to benefit society.

- **Integrity and despair** is the eighth and final stage of Erikson's psychosocial development, and it represents later adulthood (late 60s and older). During this stage of development, older adults reflect on their overall life satisfaction. They evaluate whether their life has been well lived and whether they have contributed something beneficial to leave as their legacy. Those who possess integrity and see their lives as productive and meaningful may leave the world feeling that they have left it a better place. However, when older adults do not feel they have made a contribution and instead view their life as having no meaning, they are filled with regret and sadness, leading to despair.

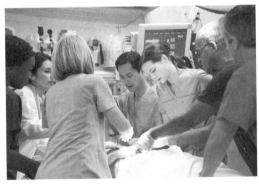
Adults who work in medical fields are likely to experience generativity—the sense of adding value to society.

Erikson's research is well known, but it has received criticism for a lack of empirical support. Questions have been raised about whether these stages can occur simultaneously rather than sequentially, as proposed by Erikson. Feminists have also critiqued Erikson's theory for representing the psychosocial crisis in males more than in females. Another criticism is that changes in societal expectations since Erikson's original theories were introduced may have shifted the ages at which these crises occur.

PSYCHOSOCIAL DEVELOPMENT IN ADOLESCENCE AND ADULTHOOD (See Table 3.6.2 for the first four stages in Erikson's model.)			
Age	**Conflict**	**Resolution**	**Description**
12 to 18 years	Identity and Role Confusion	Fidelity	Teenagers develop a sense of identity, or confusion about self occurs
18 to 35 years	Intimacy and Isolation	Love	Young adults develop intimate relationships, or they experience isolation
35 to 65 years	Generativity and Stagnation	Care	Adults seek to generate a legacy that can be passed to future generations, or they struggle with stagnation
65 years to death	Integrity and Despair	Wisdom	Older adults contemplate their life and either feel a sense of integrity and happiness or they feel despair and failure

Table 3.6.3

The Effect of Adverse Childhood Experiences

While Erikson addressed the conflict that occurred in each stage of development, not everyone can move through their childhood with the positive outcome Erikson associated with each stage. Some children face negative experiences early on that may affect them throughout their lives. **Adverse childhood experiences (ACEs)** encompass a range of traumatic events or stressors that occur during childhood, including abuse, neglect, household dysfunction, and other adverse circumstances. These experiences can have profound and long-lasting effects on individuals. Research indicates that individuals who have experienced ACEs are more likely to struggle with forming and maintaining healthy relationships, both in childhood and adulthood.

During childhood, ACEs can disrupt the development of secure attachments. Children who have experienced abuse, neglect, or inconsistent caregiving may struggle to trust others and form secure emotional bonds. As a result, they may have difficulties with social interactions, exhibit behavioral problems, and experience challenges in forming friendships or relationships with peers. Children who grow up in households characterized by dysfunction, such as substance abuse or domestic violence, may internalize unhealthy relationship patterns, leading to difficulties in establishing healthy boundaries and communication skills.

As individuals transition into adulthood, the effects of childhood trauma can continue to affect their relationships in significant ways. Adults who have experienced ACEs may struggle with intimacy, vulnerability, and trust in romantic relationships, often grappling with feelings of insecurity and fear of abandonment. The emotional and psychological consequences of ACEs, such as depression, anxiety, and low self-esteem, can further hinder their ability to form and maintain healthy relationships. Moreover, individuals who have experienced ACEs may be at greater risk of engaging in behaviors that jeopardize their relationships, such as substance abuse, self-destructive tendencies, or perpetuating cycles of violence and abuse.

Sociocultural Factors Cultural differences play an important role in how often adverse childhood experiences (ACEs) happen and their effects on people. What counts as an ACE, and how these events are seen and dealt with can vary widely between communities because of differences in cultural beliefs, values, and social systems. For instance, issues like racial discrimination, stresses from immigration, or trauma passed down through generations might be more common in certain groups, leading to more ACEs in those communities. Also, cultural views on family life, discipline, and asking for help can influence whether and how ACEs are recognized and managed by families and their communities.

The way people deal with ACEs, and the support they can get, also depend on cultural factors. Communities with strong social ties, cultural practices, and access to mental health services that understand and respect their culture might help people recover better from ACEs. On the other hand, problems such as poverty, racism, and limited healthcare can make the negative effects of ACEs worse and make it harder for people to get past these challenges, negatively affecting their personal well-being and relationships with others.

Creating a Sense of Identity

During adolescence, many teens try out different roles to determine the best fit. Dressing differently, changing groups of friends, and engaging in a range of different activities may help them begin to identify who they will become and what they might like to pursue. Developmental psychologist James Marcia expanded and refined the theories of Erik Erikson, which identified adolescence as a period of psychosocial crisis between identity and role confusion. Erikson explained that society permitted teenagers and college students to have a period of time in which they were free to explore different activities, interests, and potential career paths to find their identity. Marcia took this idea and proposed four stages in developing a sense of identity based on the criteria of crisis— "who am I?"—and commitment to resolving the identity/role crisis.

Many adolescents experience the first of Marcia's stages, **identity diffusion**, as a time in which they have not yet undergone an identity crisis and have made no commitment about their own identity. In this stage, teens have not truly considered their own beliefs or who they want to become. They do not seem particularly concerned with the outcome of a specific identity, perhaps thinking they will address the issue later. If they have some idea of who they want to become in the future, it is not well considered or perhaps not consistent with their talents and strengths.

Young teens may go on to experience the second stage, **identity foreclosure**, in which they have a sense of their core beliefs (e.g., political, moral, religious), but rather than considering these beliefs seriously and allowing them to shape their lives, they often simply adopt the views of their parents or society, especially about who they should become. For example, if asked which political party they identify with, they may answer "Republican," knowing that their parents are registered Republicans. The young person has made a commitment, it seems, without ever having explored or followed his or her own beliefs.

Adolescents in the third stage, **identity moratorium**, are struggling with their sense of identity. They experience the identity crisis without having made a commitment to its resolution. College students who explore many different possible major subjects or teenagers who make dramatic changes to their looks may be experiencing the identity moratorium while attempting to determine which identity is right for them. The development of these identities often involves the exploration of **possible selves**, which are the various identities an individual can envision for themselves in the future, considering their hopes, fears, and the range of life paths available to them. They may explore different activities or question long-held religious or political beliefs to determine if they are really committed to the ideals associated with these positions.

Toward the end of adolescence and into early adulthood, young people enter the fourth stage, **identity achievement**, a postcrisis phase during which individuals have identified and acknowledged who they are or want to be. These young people are not struggling with their identity; they have made a commitment. They may still adhere to the religious or political beliefs of their parents, but now it is because they have reflected on what those beliefs mean and have decided that they reflect their own ideals and beliefs as well.

Many factors may contribute to the formation of identity, including cognitive development, relationships with peers and parents, and the expectations of society and family. Even though one's identity is established more or less in the teens and early 20s, many young people have not completed the process and may continue to question their identity into adulthood. Lack of identity may contribute to changes in careers, political affiliations, or divorce later in life. Some adults continue to question who they are and may change course and reevaluate their choices as their lives unfold.

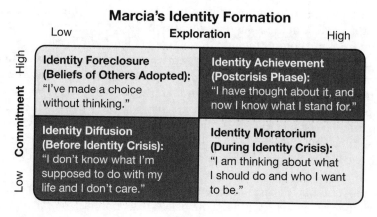

Marcia's Identity Formation

	Low Exploration High	
High Commitment	**Identity Foreclosure (Beliefs of Others Adopted):** "I've made a choice without thinking."	**Identity Achievement (Postcrisis Phase):** "I have thought about it, and now I know what I stand for."
Low	**Identity Diffusion (Before Identity Crisis):** "I don't know what I'm supposed to do with my life and I don't care."	**Identity Moratorium (During Identity Crisis):** "I am thinking about what I should do and who I want to be."

Figure 3.6.2

Identity formation is a complex process, particularly from a multicultural perspective. Individuals often navigate multiple layers of identity, including ethnicity, nationality, culture, gender, and personal experiences. These layers interact in dynamic ways, shaping how people view themselves and are perceived by others. For example, someone of mixed heritage might grapple with balancing aspects of their different cultural backgrounds while also fitting into the broader society they live in. This balancing act can lead to a rich, but sometimes challenging, sense of self, where multiple cultural norms, values, and expectations must be integrated.

James Marcia's theory of identity formation, which expands on Erik Erikson's work, provides a useful framework for understanding these layers. Marcia identified four identity statuses: identity diffusion, identity foreclosure, identity moratorium, and identity achievement. These statuses describe different ways individuals deal with the process of exploring and committing to various aspects of their identity. From a multicultural perspective, individuals

may experience these statuses in relation to their ethnic or cultural identity. For instance, an adolescent from an immigrant family might be in a moratorium status, actively exploring both their family's cultural heritage and the dominant culture of their new country before making a committed decision on how to integrate these identities.

Additionally, multicultural individuals often experience a unique blend of external pressures and internal conflicts that influence their identity formation. They might face societal expectations to conform to dominant cultural norms while also feeling a deep-rooted connection to their heritage. This duality can create tension, but also offers an opportunity for a richer, more layered identity. For example, a person might navigate the challenge of being seen as "other" in their daily interactions, while embracing the strengths and values derived from their cultural background. These experiences can foster resilience and a more profound understanding of one's multifaceted identity.

Navigating these layers of identity is crucial for developing a coherent sense of self. Multicultural individuals often face unique challenges and pressures that can affect their identity formation process. These can include dealing with discrimination, feeling the need to conform to different cultural norms in various contexts, or reconciling conflicting values between their home culture and the broader society. However, successfully integrating multiple cultural identities can lead to greater empathy, adaptability, and a more nuanced understanding of the world.

Develop a Claim

After reading about aspects of identity development through this multicultural lens, develop a claim about the relative benefits and challenges of a layered identity.

REFLECT ON THE ESSENTIAL QUESTION

Essential Question: *How does social development relate to behavior and mental processes across the lifespan?* Using the Key Terms, complete a chart like the one below to gather details to help answer that question. Note that not every concept applies to every life stage.

	Neonatal Through Infancy	Childhood	Adolescence	Adulthood
Parenting Styles				
Attachment				
Temperament				
Peer Relationships				
Social Changes				
Psychosocial Development				
Identity Formation				

MULTIPLE-CHOICE QUESTIONS

1. According to Mary Ainsworth, which of the following children would be considered to have a secure attachment, ?

   (A) Allen, who cries when his mother leaves but does not seem to care when she returns

   (B) Sam, who cries when his mother leaves and seeks physical contact from her when she returns before beginning to play independently

   (C) Bradley, who is indifferent to his mother leaving and returning

   (D) Szymon, who cries when his mother leaves and clings to her when she returns

2. Eesha was ecstatic about the opportunity to participate in a science project at her elementary school. She meticulously constructed a model of the solar system that she couldn't wait for her peers to see. However, as she compared her creation to those of her classmates, she wondered if her project was as good as theirs, fearing that she might not have as much talent as they do. Despite her initial enthusiasm, she began questioning her abilities and comparing herself unfavorably to her peers. Eesha's experience is most consistent with which of the following psychosocial stages?

   (A) Trust and mistrust

   (B) Autonomy and shame and doubt

   (C) Industry and inferiority

   (D) Initiative and guilt

3. Harry Harlow disagreed with many psychologists of his time about how a strong bond formed between mother and child. What did Harlow believe was the most important component in developing that bond?

(A) Identity achievement

(B) Temperament

(C) Contact comfort

(D) Food as a reinforcement

4. Demarcus is in his mid-40s. He has been in a career for the past 20 years but finds he no longer enjoys the work. He feels conflicted because he does not know how to make a change, and he feels like each day he goes through the same monotonous routine with little to look forward to. Which of Erikson's stages of psychosocial development is Demarcus likely experiencing?

(A) Identity and role confusion

(B) Intimacy and isolation

(C) Formal operational stage

(D) Generativity and stagnation

5. Marsha is 26, and she has many friends from college. She has just started a job as an accountant, which she enjoys and for which she is well suited. She is living at home with her parents and pays them a small amount of rent. She also has recently taken on her own car and insurance payments. She has plans to look for an apartment in the next few years. Which of the following is Marsha likely experiencing?

(A) Identity and role confusion

(B) Emerging adulthood

(C) The personal fable

(D) Industry and inferiority

6. Achad, like many other teenagers, has experienced significant struggles with forming an identity. As a result, he has tried out many different roles to figure out which best represents his individuality. Achad's experience is most consistent with which of the following?

(A) Identity foreclosure

(B) Identity moratorium

(C) Identity diffusion

(D) Identity and inferiority

Topic 3.7

Classical Conditioning

"Don't become a mere recorder of facts, but try to penetrate the mystery of their origin."

—Ivan Pavlov

Essential Question: How does classical conditioning apply to behavior and mental processes?

Psychologists define **learning** as a relatively permanent change in behavior resulting from experience or practice. Some behavior changes are not learned but, instead, are either the effect of a temporary biological change (e.g., using substances that alter behavior) or behavior that occurs naturally as a part of development and reflexive actions. For example, you do not learn to flinch when an object approaches your face or to blink when something blows into your eyes. These responses tell us that learning does not include instincts, reflexes, and maturation. However, we now know that you can have the same responses to learned stimuli; Ivan Pavlov was the first to explore this association.

The learning theorists, known as the **behaviorists** (adherents to the behavioral perspective), theorized that thoughts, or cognition, played no role in the study of behavior. Only **observable behavior** had meaning to them. The behaviorists' thoughts were strongly influenced by those of 17th-century political philosopher John Locke. According to Locke, to be born human was to be born with a *tabula rasa*, Latin for "blank slate." In this view, everything an individual becomes is the result of experience. In other words, our environment shapes every aspect of who we were, are, and will become. This view is known as *environmental determinism*. It allows us to understand the world in a way that makes the world controllable and suggests that we can change who people become by manipulating the circumstances in which they develop. John Watson, who founded the psychological field of behaviorism, claimed:

> Give me a dozen healthy infants, well-formed, and my own specified world to bring them up in and I'll guarantee to take any one at random and train him to become any type of specialist I might select—doctor, lawyer, artist, merchant-chief and, yes, even beggarman and thief, regardless of his talents, penchants, tendencies, abilities, vocations, and race of his ancestors.

Such confidence in the ability of the environment to shape who a person became was characteristic of early behaviorism.

Behaviorists believed that learning was done through conditioning. **Conditioning** is a key psychological process that involves learning new behaviors, changing existing ones, or stopping unwanted ones by forming connections between stimuli and responses. This process is sometimes known as *associative learning*. A **stimulus** is any event or situation that evokes a response from an organism. A stimulus could be anything from a sound to a visual cue or even a change in the environment. A **response** is the action or behavior that is triggered by the stimulus. For example, hearing a phone ring (stimulus) might prompt someone to answer it (response). Seeing the love of your life in the hallway (stimulus) might cause your heart to race (response). Conditioning shows how behaviors can be influenced and altered over time through these stimulus-response associations, allowing individuals to adapt to their surroundings by learning from their experiences.

Classical Conditioning: Pavlov's Dogs

Russian physiologist Ivan Pavlov provided experimental support for the views of behaviorists—but with dogs, not people. Between the late 1890s and 1930, Pavlov studied digestion and the salivary reflex in dogs. While conducting this research, Pavlov established the process now known as **classical conditioning**, a type of learning that links a *neutral stimulus*—one that causes no special response except to call attention to it—to another stimulus that elicits a natural or involuntary response in a given organism. The association between the two stimuli is one form of **associative learning**—a learning mode in which ideas and experiences are mentally linked and thereby reinforce each other.

Stimulus-Response Learning

The conditioning concept is based on the premise that behavior can be learned or modified through a stimulus and a response. For example, dogs salivate when they are presented with food—an unconditioned (unlearned) stimulus-response mechanism. However, while observing this process, Pavlov noticed that the dogs in his experiments began to salivate *before* being presented with food; they salivated as soon as they saw a person in a white lab coat, because it was a person in a white lab coat who brought them food. Obviously, this was a learned response. The dogs experienced an association between the lab coat and the food, which, in turn, induced salivation. The steps in the stimulus-response learning process were as follows:

1. White coat → food → salivation

2. Repeat many times

3. White coat → salivation

The dogs learned that seeing the white coat signaled that they were about to receive food—a learned stimulus-response. The formation of a learned association is called **acquisition**. The labels below identify the stimuli and the responses in this type of associative learning. Because the dogs would not naturally have salivated to a white coat, learning had to occur for them to salivate in response to it.

- **Unconditioned Stimulus** (US or UCS): any stimulus that causes an autonomic/automatic/reflexive response to the presentation of food to dogs
- **Unconditioned Response** (UR or UCR): behavior that is a reflex or autonomic response to a stimulus (e.g., blinking of the eyes, nausea, muscle tension, salivation, blood pressure or heart rate increase, or other involuntary response); in Pavlov's study, dogs salivating to the meat
- **Conditioned Stimulus** (CS): former stimulus that eventually causes a response because it has been partnered with the UCS, such as the white coat in the Pavlov study that was associated with the meat
- **Conditioned Response** (CR): behavior that is considered a reflex or autonomic response to a CS; in Pavlov's study, dogs salivating to the white coat

Once Pavlov noticed the lab coat → food → salivate pattern, he tried using a tuning fork as the conditioned stimulus. (The tuning fork is often replaced by a bell in discussions of classical conditioning, but this does not change the process.) The pattern switched to tuning fork → food → salivate; tuning fork → food → salivate; tuning fork → food → salivate; and after a number of repeated trials, the learned pattern became tuning fork → salivate, with the food portion of the pattern eliminated. The tuning fork was the conditioned stimulus (CS), the food was the unconditioned stimulus (US), and salivation was both the unconditioned (UR) and conditioned response (CR). Take a look at Figure 3.7.1 to see a visualization of each step in this classical conditioning process.

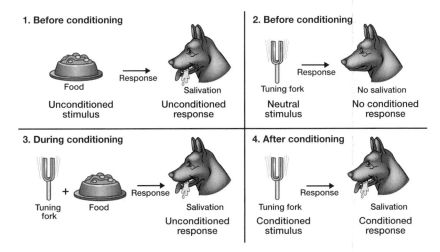

Figure 3.7.1

Pavlov noticed that the shorter the time between the conditioned stimulus and the unconditioned stimulus, the quicker and stronger the learned association. The closeness in time between the CS and US is called *contiguity*. Pavlov also found that other tuning forks worked as a CS for salivation. When the pitch was closest to that of the original tuning fork, the dogs' response to it was stronger.

Learned Responses in Everyday Life Advertisers routinely take advantage of learned responses. They link an attractive US with a CS (the product being sold) so consumers feel as good about the product as they do about the US. Psychologist Robert Cialdini reports that in a study about car commercials, men who were shown a commercial featuring an attractive woman rated the advertised car as faster, more appealing, and better designed than did the men who were shown a commercial for the car without the attractive woman. A similar process unfolds when companies license music to be associated with their brands. If a beloved song is associated with a product, advertisers hope that the positive feelings stirred by the song become associated with the product. Celebrity endorsements work much the same way. A well-known and admired celebrity or athlete may be paid millions of dollars to promote a product. People who like that celebrity or athlete want to be associated with them and may be more likely to purchase those products.

Stimulus Discrimination and Stimulus Generalization

Stimulus discrimination is a response to only the specific stimulus that has been conditioned. For example, if Pavlov's dogs were conditioned only to the specific tone that was associated with the meat, this would demonstrate stimulus discrimination. Similarly, if you got food poisoning after eating spoiled shrimp, and thereafter felt nauseated at the sight of shrimp but not at other types of seafood, you are discriminating between the stimuli you have been conditioned to and other similar stimuli. **Stimulus generalization** is a response to another stimulus that is similar to the original conditioned stimulus. For example, if a dog is conditioned to respond to a plastic bowl as a conditioned stimulus but not to a metal bowl, the dog exhibits stimulus discrimination if it does not salivate when a metal bowl appears. If a dog responds with salivation regardless of the material of the bowl, then the dog has generalized its response, exhibiting stimulus generalization.

Military veterans who had been exposed to bombs and their associated injuries

Many vets returning from war experience posttraumatic stress disorder (PTSD), a condition in which a sound once paired with danger triggers intense fear even when the vet is safe at home.

and destruction in war zones have often experienced classical conditioned responses. After they return home, sudden sounds from a branch snapping or a loud explosion may elicit intense fear or emotional responses in these veterans, despite their being in relatively safe situations. The initial fear response to land mines has been generalized to cars backfiring or sudden loud sounds.

THINK AS A PSYCHOLOGIST

Apply Psychological Perspectives, Theories, Concepts, and Research Findings to a Scenario (1.A.1)

Practice Applying Psychological Theories and Research Findings to a Scenario

Here are some other examples of stimulus discrimination and generalization. Identify the US, UR, CS, and CR in each example and determine if the example relates to stimulus discrimination or stimulus generalization.

1. A young woman listening to a popular song while driving is suddenly hit by another car, pushing her headlong into oncoming traffic. Although she survives the crash, the song later elicits an emergency response of the sympathetic nervous system, mimicking her experience in the accident. Other songs by the same artist do not cause the same response.

2. Alcoholism is sometimes treated medically by administering a drug called Antabuse®. If the individual being treated ingests any alcohol at all, serious vomiting will develop. The objective of the treatment is to pair, or associate, the vomiting with drinking alcohol and thus prevent or eliminate alcohol abuse. The intent is for the user to have this reaction to alcoholic drinks but not to other types of drinks such as soda or sports drinks.

Classical Conditioning: Watson and Little Albert

John Watson, who is often considered the founder of the behavioral approach to psychology, started one of his studies with an interesting research question. Can we condition fear in young children? He decided to use a loud noise as the stimulus in this study. Loud noises startle us and make us focus our attention on the source of the sound. However, people are often less afraid of the noise itself than of the circumstances associated with the loud sounds.

Imagine the sound of a hammer hitting a heavy metal bar. While it would definitely be startling for an adult, imagine the impact on a 9-month-old infant. In 1919, John B. Watson and his assistant, Rosalie Rayner, tested that impact on a 9-month-old baby nicknamed Little Albert. The research goal was to determine whether people—like Pavlov's dogs—could be classically conditioned.

Before beginning the classical conditioning process on Little Albert, Watson performed baseline readings to see Albert's responses to a variety of different objects. Watson tested a white rat, a rabbit, a dog, a monkey, masks (with and without hair), cotton, wool, and burning newspapers, and Albert showed no fear of any item but special interest in the white rat. Watson decided that the white rat would become the stimulus in the study. On a number of occasions, Watson presented Little Albert with the white rat and then created a loud noise. After exposure to several pairings with the loud sound of a hammer on steel while he played with the rat, Albert began to respond to the rat with fear, crying and pulling away. Albert had begun to anticipate the loud sound (US) and the feeling of fear that accompanied it (UR). The rat was paired with the loud sound and became the conditioned stimulus (CS). After the initial fear exhibited toward the rat, Albert began to respond to all furry objects (a rabbit, a mask with a cotton-ball beard, a dog, and a monkey) in a fearful way, exhibiting stimulus generalization. This series of experiments with Little Albert clearly showed the ease with which people can learn fears and phobias.

Little Albert's fate and actual identity remain somewhat uncertain. One team of researchers believed Little Albert's real name was Douglas Merritte, his mother was paid $1.00 for her baby's participation in the experiment, and he died at the age of six from hydrocephalus. More recent research suggests he was William Barger, whose nickname was Albert and who lived to the age of 87. Barger exhibited no special fears of furry white things, though he was afraid of dogs.

Now he fears even Santa Claus

This is a still from a movie taken of the Little Albert experiment. You can see the entire film on YouTube.

THINK AS A PSYCHOLOGIST

Evaluate Whether a Psychological Research Scenario Followed Appropriate Ethical Procedures (2.D.3, 2.D.6)

Practice Evaluating Research Ethics

Complete the following activity.

John Watson faced significant criticism for the research that he conducted with Little Albert. Based on modern ethical guidelines, identify two reasons why an IRB would not allow this research to be conducted today.

Higher Order Conditioning

Higher order conditioning, also called *second order conditioning*, is classical conditioning with an extra conditioned stimulus. Think about the model of Pavlov's dogs: first the tuning fork (CS), then the presentation of food (US), and finally the dogs salivating (UR). Second order conditioning adds another layer to this model. For example, if Pavlov's dogs already salivated to the tuning fork, a light might be added to the mix, changing the sequence from tuning fork → food → salivation to light → tuning fork → food → salivation. If the dogs have been successfully conditioned, the dog will salivate at the light. With higher order conditioning, a new neutral stimulus becomes associated with the conditioned stimulus.

For a personal example, let's say you have a favorite grandmother who always makes you feel warm, wanted, and loved. Her loving behavior elicits warm feelings. Although everyone's experience is different, many grandmothers' homes have a particular grandma smell—maybe from the food cooking on the stove or the furniture polish or Grandma's lavender soap. So you associate the aroma with your loved one: smell (CS) → grandmother (CS) → loving behavior (US) → feeling loved (UR). The image of your grandmother's house may trigger feeling loved. Or perhaps driving onto her street creates those feelings of being loved.

Higher order conditioning extends the conditioning concept to more complicated reflexive human responses and to seemingly unrelated stimuli. We are not typically aware of when we are being classically conditioned or when we experience higher order conditioning. However, these psychological concepts likely explain many experiences we have had, especially those involving fears. We may not recall an experience from our early childhood, but we may have been conditioned to respond in a fearful way that was extended into a higher order conditioning response.

Extinction and Spontaneous Recovery

Extinction is a process that leads to the gradual weakening, and eventual disappearance, of the conditioned response to the conditioned stimulus by presenting the CS repeatedly without pairing it with the UCS. Over time, presenting the CS without the US will weaken the association. The association eventually becomes **extinct,** or extinguished, and the conditioned stimulus may once again become a neutral stimulus, causing no particular response. That is, the conditioned stimulus no longer produces the conditioned response.

Occasionally, after a stimulus-response has been extinguished, it recurs without any obvious reason. Reappearance of the stimulus-response is known as **spontaneous recovery**. During spontaneous recovery, suddenly, and seemingly without cause, the learning reappears after a period of time, during which the organism did not respond to a previously learned stimulus (extinction). The reappearance indicates that the learning has not disappeared at all but has been inhibited in some manner or temporarily suppressed.

You can find examples of spontaneous recovery in almost everyone's life. As a child, you may have paired the sound of calliope music coming from an ice cream truck with your salivation in preparation for a treat. After not hearing those sounds for a while, you may no longer salivate when the truck and its music appear. However, even after years have passed, you may suddenly hear the music again and salivate. Similarly, in Pavlov's experiments with his dogs, after salivating was extinguished, the dogs recovered the salivating spontaneously when they heard a certain tone. The tone in some cases served as a primer to bring back the dormant response.

Using Classical Conditioning with Emotional Responses

As you have read, classical conditioning occurs when a neutral stimulus pairs with a naturally occurring stimulus to create a conditioned response in an organism. However, biology limits what an organism can be classically conditioned to learn. Moreover, psychologists and behavioral scientists have discovered that certain biological principles that help control body functions can also be applied to modify behavior. For example, conditioning principles and biological factors can work together to influence emotional responses, like fear and anxiety.

Recall from the Little Albert study conducted by John Watson and Rosalie Rayner that Little Albert was conditioned to fear the rat at first, and he then generalized the fear to other objects that were white, furry, or both (dog, monkey, and Santa Claus mask, among others). Psychologist Mary Cover Jones wondered if the process could work in reverse. Could classical conditioning reduce a fearful or phobic response, rather than bring it on? Her reasoning was that, if fears could be conditioned, they could also be counterconditioned. After conducting studies of her own on various phobias, or irrational fears, and developing a form of therapy to treat them, Jones published her findings in 1924 and became known as "the mother of behavior therapy."

Counterconditioning involved introducing a series of stimuli similar to a person's phobia. Her most famous subject was Peter, a 3-year-old with a fear of rabbits. During her treatment of Peter, she exposed the child to a rabbit, gradually moving Peter and the rabbit closer together while she simultaneously presented Peter with his favorite sweet—candy. Eventually, as the visits with dual stimuli progressed, Peter was able to touch the rabbit without manifesting a fear response.

Like Little Albert or Peter, you might have fears or anxiety as a result of conditioning. Do you remember math tests from your elementary school days? If you are like many students, being tested on math facts under time pressure produced anxiety for you, and possibly you were conditioned from those early experiences to feel anxiety, even today, in the form of a more generalized test anxiety. In timed testing situations, you may feel your heart race and experience shortness of breath. Your mind may be filled with negative thoughts. How can you relieve yourself of that anxiety?

One-Trial Conditioning and Biological Preparedness

If you have ever experienced food poisoning or even the onset of a stomach bug, then you have likely experienced taste aversion. **Taste aversion** is a unique conditioned response that occurs after a single pairing of an illness or symptoms such as nausea with eating a specific food. This is known as *one-trial conditioning*. Repeated pairings do not strengthen the association.

While studying radiation effects in rats in the mid 1950s, psychologist John Garcia discovered that initial exposure to flavored water followed by a toxic reaction to radiation (even several hours later) made rats averse to the water. Radiation made the rats feel sick (radiation → illness), and the sickness was paired with the taste of the flavored water (CS). The animals learned to avoid the flavored water because it had been associated with the radiation.

The taste aversion experiments modified previous assumptions about classical conditioning. First, they showed that the time gap between the conditioned stimulus and the biological response (the unconditioned stimulus) can be much longer than originally thought. Garcia's experiments demonstrated that aversion can be learned, even if nausea occurred hours after exposure to radiation or drugs, and that the aversion response can occur after only one trial, rather than multiple trials. Taste aversion appears to be a survival mechanism because it allowed the rats to learn quickly how to avoid poisonous food and to retain the aversion, and thus avoidance, of the potentially poisonous food, over time.

Taste aversion is especially common in cancer patients who associate post-chemotherapy nausea with the taste of a food they ate after treatment rather than with the chemotherapy. Cancer patients have also been shown to learn an "anticipatory nausea" associated with chemotherapy treatments. Before the treatment is started, patients are typically given medications to reduce nausea and vomiting. Studies have shown, however, that a large percentage of patients still become nauseated because the antinausea treatment given just before the start of chemotherapy itself acts as a stimulus that becomes associated with the chemo-induced nausea.

Taste aversion was put into practical application to protect sheep from coyotes. Sheep carcasses were laced with a poison that would sicken but not kill coyotes who ate it. The response was so strong that the coyotes not only stopped preying on sheep but they also ran away from them in fear.

Aversions may differ from one species to another and are learned differently. Humans cannot always visually notice that food has been contaminated and may learn taste aversion later after becoming sick. Most birds hunt by vision alone and appear biologically primed to establish aversions at the sight of tainted food. Other animals may learn to identify potentially poisonous food through its smell.

Biological preparedness is the notion that evolutionary mechanisms have hardwired animals, humans included, to swiftly establish connections between specific stimuli and responses. This natural tendency facilitates rapid learning, particularly when these connections are crucial for survival. Proposed by the psychologist Martin Seligman, the theory asserts that such learning is not merely accidental, but a strategic adaptation, equipping organisms to adeptly navigate and overcome the perils presented by their environments.

For example, many people and animals quickly learn to fear snakes and spiders. This rapid learning could be the result of evolutionary pressures in which ancestors who quickly learned to avoid these potentially dangerous animals had a survival advantage. Despite the low risk posed by most snakes and spiders in today's environments, the potential to fear them may be an evolutionary holdover.

Phobias offer another example. Phobias often center on objects or situations that posed historical survival threats, such as heights, darkness, or large predators. People can develop intense, irrational fears after a single negative experience, or sometimes with no experience at all, suggesting a predisposition to fear certain things more than others. Of course, fears can also be learned. We know from the studies on Little Albert that fears can be learned, even if they are not inborn, so there are several potential explanations for how people develop fears or phobias.

Habituation

Habituation is the process by which an organism becomes accustomed to a repeated stimulus, resulting in a decreased response over time because learning has taken place. In classical conditioning, responses that have been habituated may cause a decreased response. For example, if Little Albert eventually learned that the loud noise associated with the white rat posed no real danger, his heart rate might no longer have risen to the level it first did when he initially heard the noise. This phenomenon demonstrates the organism's ability to adapt to its environment by learning to ignore or become less responsive to stimuli that are perceived as nonthreatening or irrelevant.

In Pavlov's experiments, initially the sound of a tuning fork (NS) did not elicit any significant response from the dogs. Once the dogs showed a conditioned response (CR) of salivating to the sound of the tuning fork, they eventually became habituated to the sound, and their salivation response decreased over time.

Human infants have similar responses to auditory stimuli. For instance, when infants are exposed to a loud noise in their environment, such as the sound of a vacuum cleaner, they may initially startle or cry in response. However, with continued exposure to the noise without adverse consequences, infants gradually habituate to the sound, and their reaction diminishes over time as they learn that this object or event poses no real harm. Habituation allows individuals to filter out repetitive or nonthreatening stimuli, enabling them to allocate their attention and resources to more relevant or novel environmental cues.

THINK AS A PSYCHOLOGIST

Identify Psychology-Related Concepts in Descriptions or Representations of Data (3.A)

The chart below represents a hypothetical set of trials with dogs that had been conditioned to salivate to the sound of a bell. Gradually the bell was rung with no food presented.

Five Trials with Dogs Conditioned to Salivate

(Bar graph. Y-axis: "Amount of Saliva in Cubic Centimeters" ranging from 0.00 to 1.00. X-axis: Trial 1, Trial 2, Trial 3, Trial 4, Trial 5. Bars: Trial 1 ≈ 1.00, Trial 2 ≈ 0.70, Trial 3 ≈ 0.50, Trial 4 ≈ 0.31, Trial 5 ≈ 0.00)

Practice Identifying Psychology-Related Concepts in Representations of Data

Choose the correct answer.

1. The graph most clearly depicts which of the following concepts in classical conditioning?

   (A) Habituation

   (B) Extinction

   (C) Spontaneous recovery

   (D) Stimulus generalization

2. Which of the following behaviors represents the same concept as the one depicted in the graph?

   (A) A student develops anxiety when speaking in front of the class because of a previous embarrassing incident.

   (B) A student feels anxious even when just thinking about participating in class discussions because of the association with public speaking.

   (C) Over time, as a student repeatedly participates in class discussions without any negative experiences, the anxiety response diminishes.

   (D) After a long summer break with no public speaking, a student feels anxious again the first time they speak in class when the new school year begins.

MULTIPLE-CHOICE QUESTIONS

1. Chloe the dog likes going on walks, being petted, and eating. Every time she sees her owners place her food dish on the ground she starts to salivate. Over time, Chloe starts to salivate any time she sees a food dish. In this scenario, the food dish represents which of the following?

   (A) Unconditioned stimulus

   (B) Conditioned stimulus

   (C) Conditioned response

   (D) Unconditioned response

2. In Watson's Little Albert experiment, Albert became fearful of furry masks, rabbits, and furry dogs in addition to the white rat he was conditioned to fear. Which classical conditioning concept does this best illustrate?

   (A) Higher order conditioning

   (B) Counterconditioning

   (C) Stimulus generalization

   (D) Stimulus discrimination

3. Bailey had to get allergy shots weekly when she was a child. Before administering them, the doctor would put rubbing alcohol on her skin. Now Bailey's heart starts to race every time she smells rubbing alcohol. Bailey's heart racing to the smell of rubbing alcohol represents which of the following?

    (A) Conditioned response

    (B) Conditioned stimulus

    (C) Aversion conditioning

    (D) Biological preparedness

4. Rachel ate a salad with spoiled chicken three years ago. She became extremely sick and has not eaten chicken since. Which aspect of learning has allowed Rachel to learn this after only one trial?

    (A) Stimulus discrimination

    (B) Extinction

    (C) Counterconditioning

    (D) Biological preparedness

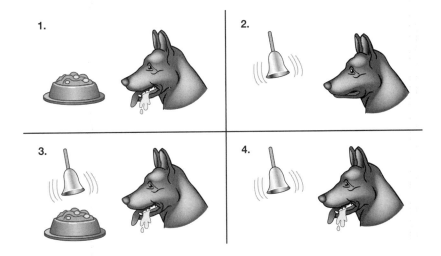

5. If the figure above represents the sequence in classical conditioning, what does the bell represent in panel 2, prior to the partnership of the bell and the meat?

    (A) Unconditioned response

    (B) Conditioned stimulus

    (C) Conditioned response

    (D) Neutral stimulus

6. The chart below depicts the heart rate of individuals presented with a loud noise a number of times (*x*-axis). The *y*-axis shows the strength of the response. What learning concept is displayed in these data?

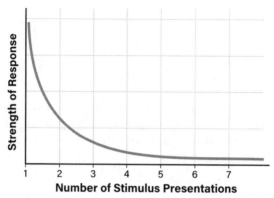

Source: Social Cognitive and Affective Neuroscience 2016

(A) Habituation

(B) Stimulus generalization

(C) Spontaneous recovery

(D) Higher order conditioning

7. If the 20 participants in the study above were randomly selected from a general population of undergraduate students, which would be true?

(A) The study would have successfully achieved random assignment.

(B) The researchers could determine cause and effect.

(C) The researchers could generalize to the population of undergraduate students.

(D) The study would likely have regression towards the mean.

STUDY LIKE A CHAMP WITH DR. G.

Remember to plan, monitor, and assess. If you are not sticking to your plan, develop another one and do your best to stick to that one. If you *are* sticking to your plan, reward yourself to reinforce your behavior.

Topic 3.8

Operant Conditioning

"I never teach my pupils; I only attempt to provide the conditions in which they can learn."

—Albert Einstein

Essential Question: How does operant conditioning apply to behavior and mental processes?

After Watson left psychology to work in advertising, psychologist B. F. Skinner assumed the behavioral mantle and rose to such prominence that he is considered the founder of the modern behavioral perspective. While Skinner understood the existence of mind, he viewed it as unworthy of study, since observable behaviors could be measured objectively. Skinner thought Watson's view of classical conditioning was too simplistic to fully explain human behavior and only applied to involuntary behaviors. Skinner hypothesized that an organism "operates" in its environment. He believed that every behavior has a consequence, pleasant or unpleasant. Behaviors that elicit a pleasant response are more likely to be repeated than those that are neutral or unpleasant. In the 1930s, these observations led Skinner to develop **operant conditioning**, a type of learning in which voluntary behavior is modified by the **consequences** that follow the behavior. Behavior is strengthened when followed by reinforcement—a reinforcing stimulus or reward—or diminished when followed by punishment.

Operant Conditioning and the Law of Effect

Skinner built upon the learning theory of Edward Thorndike. One of Thorndike's major contributions to psychology is the **law of effect** (1905), which states that any behavior followed by pleasant consequences is likely to be repeated, while any behavior followed by unpleasant consequences is likely to be reduced or stopped. Take a minute to consider how this might apply to your own life. What are some of the behaviors in your life that you have been rewarded for and have done again as the result of the reward? What are some things that you have been punished for, therefore decreasing the likelihood that you will engage in that behavior again? Also, consider whether you believe reinforcements and punishments are always successful; in other words, do reinforcements always strengthen a behavior and punishments always weaken one?

Thorndike devised an experiment using cats as his subjects. He designed a "puzzle box," a cage with a lever inside that would open a door for the cat to get out. He placed a cat in the puzzle box and placed a piece of fish outside of the box. The cat would attempt to escape and reach the fish.

The cat used trial and error, attempting various ways to escape the box to reach the fish until it found a way that worked. The cat would scratch at the bars, push at the ceiling, and dig at the door as the most common behaviors, but the only way out was to press the lever that opened the cage. Thorndike measured both the behaviors the cats used and the time it took for the cats to escape the box. After escape, a cat would be rewarded with the fish and then returned to the box, and the process was repeated. Over successive trials, the cat would learn that pressing the lever had more positive consequences than the other behaviors. In time, those other behaviors reduced as the cat learned to press the lever (see Figure 3.8.1). You can see in the graph within the figure that the more trials, the quicker the cat was able to escape from the puzzle box. The cat had clearly learned something through the reinforcement (fish) it received after escaping from the box.

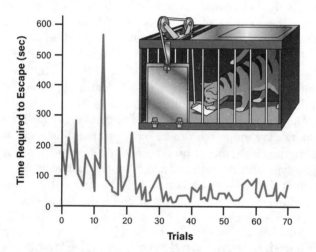

Figure 3.8.1

Thorndike successfully demonstrated that responses that produce a satisfying effect in a certain situation are likely to occur again in that situation, and responses that produce a discomforting effect are less likely to occur again in that situation. In other words, when good things happen after we do something, we are more likely to do it again. This pattern can sometimes lead people or animals to engage in **superstitious behaviors**—actions that are randomly tied to good results. For example, if you use a certain pen on a test and get a good grade, you might start using that pen for every test, even though it was your studying that earned you the good grade. Athletes may go through a certain ritual before a game or wear a specific piece of clothing that they are convinced brings them good luck. A victory or a great game then strengthens the superstition, even though the ritual or the clothing had nothing to do with the performance.

Reinforcement and punishment can be interpreted differently by different organisms. What seems pleasant to one organism may not be pleasant to another. Some people cannot stand hugs, while other people love them. The allure of cash may outweigh all other consequences for some individuals, even dangerous and deadly consequences.

While both classical and operant conditioning are types of associative learning, classical conditioning deals with involuntary behavior while operant conditioning addresses learning from the consequences of our own behavior. In classical conditioning, a response/behavior is *elicited* from an organism when an association is made. In operant conditioning, an organism *emits a* behavior that is linked to a consequence, and the consequence influences the likelihood of repeating the behavior.

Learned Helplessness and Control

In his book *Learned Optimism: How to Change Your Mind and Your Life* (1990), psychologist Martin Seligman recounts that, as a student, he conducted experiments in 1965 involving dogs and a mild shock. Seligman observed dogs that had no way to stop the shock because a lever in their cage that would turn off the shock was designed *not* to work. The dogs finally gave up and lay down whimpering on the shock plate. After struggling with the ethical and practical issues, Seligman began to investigate further using dogs in a cage with a partially electrified floor. In the second part of the study, dogs that in previous experiments had been able to control the shock by pressing a working lever that successfully stopped the shock learned fairly quickly that jumping over a short barrier allowed them to escape the shock, while the dogs that in previous experiments had no control over the shock lay down on the electrified floor and did nothing. Seligman and his research partner hypothesized that dogs in the second group had learned that nothing they did mattered, so they would just become helpless, lying down on the electrified floor. After running variations and replications of the research, Seligman concluded, "Clearly, animals can learn their actions are futile, and when they do, they no longer initiate action; they become passive."

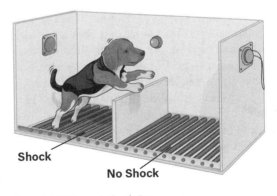

Figure 3.8.2 Seligman's Shuttle Box

Seligman and others continued to research **learned helplessness**, a mental state in which an organism continues to experience a painful, unpleasant, or aversive stimulus. Their assumption was that organisms become helpless because they have learned that, regardless of their actions, they have no ability to change the outcome.

Psychologist Donald Hiroto attempted a variation of these studies with humans, using a loud noise rather than an electric shock. He observed that people who were part of an experimental group in a situation in which they were unable to turn off the noise did not even try when they were later in a situation in which they *could* turn it off. They, too, had learned helplessness.

What about in real life? Can people learn to become helpless and then stop trying to accomplish something? Consider national politics. When people feel that they are unable to affect the development of public policy or to change unfair practices, they may stop voting. Similarly, some students who have experienced failure in school may come to think they will never succeed and will stop trying—and, as a result, they experience more school failure, reinforcing their belief. Unemployed people may search for jobs for a period of time, eventually giving up if they lack skills and connections or if they perceive some bias against them associated with age, gender, sexual orientation, or race. Humans and other animals who experience a sense of powerlessness after repeated failure to avoid aversive stimuli have essentially lost control. Many will give up after acquiring learned helplessness.

Skinner's Experiments

The results of Thorndike's studies—the cats' behavior responding to positive reinforcement—led directly to B. F. Skinner's development of operant conditioning, a key component of behaviorism. In his experiments, Skinner conditioned rats, birds, and people. Videos have captured Skinner training pigeons to play ping pong, pull toys, and play the piano. Skinner once said, "I don't deny the importance of genetics. However, the fact that I might be altruistic isn't because I have a gene for altruism; the fact that I do something for my children at some cost to myself comes from a history that has operated on me." The attitude expressed by Skinner derives from environmental determinism, a point of view holding that all behavior is the result of our interactions with our environment. In the nature and nurture debate, Skinner falls decidedly on the side of nurture. Behaviorism acknowledges the existence of genetics and the mind, but sees them as incidental to or nonfactors in behavior because they cannot be observed and, therefore, not objectively measured. In modern psychology, this extreme mindset is held by only a few, though the influence of behaviorism is still evident.

Reinforcement and Punishment

The terms used to describe the elements of operant conditioning usually refer to behavior that has already been exhibited.

- **Reinforcement** is a consequence that increases the likelihood of a behavior occurring again. Examples may include food, water, a hug, payment, and praise, such as "great job; nice improvement" from a teacher or coach.

- **Punishment** is a consequence that decreases the likelihood of a behavior occurring again. Examples may include a slap or punch, a traffic ticket, exclusion from a group, or having your phone confiscated.

- A **primary reinforcement** is an innately valued reinforcing stimulus, such as one that satisfies a biological need (e.g., food, drink, or sleep). **Secondary reinforcers** are learned through association (e.g., money and good grades). Money is not innately valuable, but it can be exchanged for other items that are closer to primary reinforcers. Secondary reinforcers are motivators that encourage behavior but do not fulfill a biological need.

The timing of a behavior and its following consequence must be close to the behavior to make it effective. For example, working people sometimes come home to a dog that has been inside all day and has relieved himself on the floor. A dog owner may grab the dog, take it to the scene, push the dog's nose near the waste, and yell, "Bad dog!" Since so much time has passed since the accident, however, the dog does not connect the scolding with relieving himself but can begin to make a negative association with the owner who is initiating the punishment. A time-based connection is missing between the dog's accident and the punishment. What the dog learns is to avoid people when they come home.

Both punishment and reinforcement can be either positive or negative. How can a punishment be positive? How can reinforcement be negative? To answer these questions, view positive and negative as they are used in mathematics. Positive means the addition of a stimulus, while negative means the removal or subtraction of a stimulus. All effective punishment, positive or negative, decreases the likelihood of a behavior occurring again.

A high five from a coach is a good reinforcement and will likely make you want to repeat whatever you did to earn it.

Table 3.8.1 shows how positive and negative apply to punishment and reinforcement. The stimuli described here are all consequences of behaviors emitted by an organism.

OPERANT CONDITIONING: REINFORCEMENT AND PUNISHMENT		
	Reinforcement (increase behavior)	**Punishment** (decrease behavior)
Positive (add stimulus)	*Positive Reinforcement* ADD pleasant stimulus/ consequence to increase behavior	*Positive Punishment* ADD aversive stimulus/ consequence to reduce behavior
Negative (remove stimulus)	*Negative Reinforcement* REMOVE aversive stimulus to increase behavior	*Negative Punishment* REMOVE pleasant stimulus to decrease behavior

Table 3.8.1

Positive Reinforcement A pleasant consequence that increases the likelihood of repeating a behavior, whether intentional or not, is a **positive reinforcement.** The reward occurs after a desired behavior. Spend time in a public park and you'll see many birds hovering near people, repeating behavior that was rewarded previously with handouts of food. Cats are creatures of habit, and if someone offers a cat a primary reinforcing stimulus of food, the cat will surely return to get more of that reinforcement. The behavior that has been reinforced is showing up on the person's doorstep. Similarly, when a young boy receives five dollars for every A he receives on his report card (desired behavior), the good grades will likely continue. A child who receives dessert after finishing the food on her plate (desired behavior) will continue to eat what she's served. A dolphin may be thrown a fish after performing a trick. Every time you give your pet food under the table from your plate, you are reinforcing begging for food at the table.

Negative Reinforcement The removal of an unpleasant/aversive stimulus to increase a behavior is called **negative reinforcement.** Since the goal is still to increase the occurrence of a specific behavior, the removal is still a reinforcement, but it is accomplished by eliminating something painful or annoying, which is the negative or subtraction component. Car technology applies this principle fairly often. If you start the car and do not fasten your seat belt, that annoying buzzer continues to sound until the seat belt is buckled. The desired behavior is achieved not by a pleasant consequence but by removing the aversive or irritating noise. Also, an itch is often considered an aversive stimulus. Scratching it removes the unpleasantness and simultaneously reinforces the behavior of scratching. A person with obsessive-compulsive disorder who has anxiety about their hands being dirty may feel compelled to wash their hands often. Handwashing removes the aversive stimulus (anxiety) and also makes it more likely that this person will wash their hands again in the future. In this case, the negative reinforcement can turn into a vicious cycle of handwashing.

Positive Punishment If you *add* an unpleasant or aversive stimulus to reduce a behavior, you are using **positive punishment**. An officer giving the driver of a speeding vehicle the consequence of a ticket reduces the speeding behavior by adding an unpleasant stimulus. If a student dresses inappropriately for school, he may receive a verbal reprimand and be less likely to violate dress code in the future. Parents whose young child dashes into the street without looking use positive punishment when they grab the child and raise their voices in a harsh tone (unpleasant consequence) to emphasize that running into the street is not a desired behavior. If this is effective, the child will not run into the street again. One of the clearest examples of positive punishment is the use of shock collars on dogs. Dogs can be fitted with collars designed to produce an electrical shock if they go beyond a specific area of a property bordered by an electrified underground "invisible fence." The undesirable behavior is leaving the specified area. When the dog moves beyond the invisibly fenced border, the shock is administered. The dog responds to the positive punishment by leaving the area less frequently.

Negative Punishment The removal of a pleasant stimulus to decrease or eliminate a specific behavior is called **negative punishment**. Fighting between siblings over a new toy may be stopped when the mother takes the toy away from one child, which effectively removes it from both children. Removal of the toy is the consequence for the behavior of fighting. If the fighting behavior decreases, punishment has worked. If a teenage girl stays out past her curfew and her parents ground her for a week during the summer, the pleasant stimulus of being with friends has been removed, most likely reducing the behavior of coming home late. If a soccer player receives two warnings for violations, they receive a red card and must leave the game permanently, and the team must play with one fewer member. The pleasant stimulus of playing the game was removed to reduce a behavior, making the removal a negative punishment if it decreases the likelihood that players engage in game violations. Both punishment and reinforcement are most effective when the consequence follows the response immediately and is applied consistently.

Humans may respond uniquely to punishment. For example, Ryan was getting in trouble in school almost daily, talking in class and bullying other kids. Teachers and administrators spoke with him and scolded him, sometimes loudly, for misbehaving. Strangely, such consequences, even though intended as punishment, turned into rewards or reinforcing stimuli. For Ryan, interaction with the teachers was reinforcement, even if it was in the form of punishment, and he increased his behavior. What was intended as positive punishment from the teachers actually turned into positive reinforcement for Ryan. Schools may also use suspension as a "punishment" for students. Quite often, however, it is the response the student is seeking. Being away from school can positively reinforce the undesirable behavior.

For reinforcement and punishment, "intention does not matter; outcome does." In other words, even if the *intention* of a suspension policy is to decrease undesirable behaviors, if it does not produce the desired *outcome*, it is ineffective.

The Operant Conditioning Chamber

Psychologist B. F. Skinner invented the operant conditioning chamber, often called a Skinner box (Figure 3.8.3). The box was designed to train research animals such as rats and birds. With the box and associated methods, Skinner created a revolution in conditioning research. His approach is still used by many investigators and is one of the most scientifically validated theories applied to understand behavior.

Skinner placed hungry or thirsty research animals in the operant conditioning chamber and trained them to do specific and sometimes amazing tasks. A hungry rat is obviously receptive to having food as a reinforcer. Hungry rats were placed in the chamber where they did what rats do—sniff around, explore every corner, put their paws on everything, including a lever constructed in the box, and generally operate within their new environment. As soon as Skinner noticed the lever being pressed, he would release a pellet of food—a positive reinforcement.

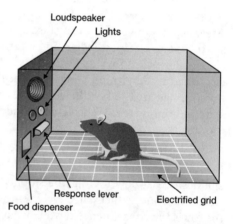

Figure 3.8.3 Operant Conditioning Chamber (or Skinner Box)

After several repeat trials, rats that pushed the lever made a clear connection between pressing the lever and the food. Skinner could then manipulate any natural rat behavior and have the rat running circles, doing multiple lever presses, and even more before obtaining food because, as you have read, if a behavior is followed with a desirable consequence, it is likely to be repeated.

Reinforcement Discrimination and Generalization

The study of reinforcement discrimination and generalization within the framework of operant conditioning has been foundational to understanding how behaviors are acquired, maintained, and modified. **Reinforcement discrimination** involves the ability to distinguish between situations in which a behavior will be reinforced and those in which it will not. This skill is crucial for adaptive behavior, since it enables individuals to modify their actions based on the context.

Consider a teenager who learns that their parents will reward them for completing homework before dinnertime but not for doing it late at night. Over time, the teenager discriminates between these two scenarios and is more likely to complete homework before dinner to receive positive reinforcement (e.g., praise, extra screen time). The teen is demonstrating reinforcement discrimination by recognizing that behaviors in specific situations are likely to be rewarded. Or, if you want your dog to come the first time you call, you will not reward her if you have to call her more than once.

Reinforcement generalization occurs when a behavior that has been reinforced in one situation elicits similar behaviors in different, but related, situations. People apply learned behaviors across various contexts, even without direct reinforcement in those new contexts.

For example, a child receives positive feedback and rewards at home for being polite, saying "please" and "thank you." As a result, the child begins to exhibit polite behavior not only at home but also at school and in other social settings, expecting similar positive outcomes. This is an instance of generalization, where the child applies a reinforced behavior across different environments. Or your dog may go get her leash anytime someone in the household puts on a pair of shoes, hoping that, like you when you put *your* shoes on, they want to go for a walk.

These findings have been repeatedly demonstrated in studies that have significantly contributed to our understanding of discrimination and generalization. Although much of the foundational research was conducted with animals, the principles have been applied widely in understanding human behavior, especially in educational settings, therapy, and behavior modification programs.

In one of these studies, Richard Herrnstein (1979) found that pigeons developed an ability to discriminate between pictures containing trees and not containing trees. They were rewarded with food when they pecked a picture that included a tree but not when they pecked a picture without a tree. Before long, they did not bother to peck the pictures without the trees and just paced around instead.

Schedules of Reinforcement

Skinner realized that, in day-to-day life, humans and animals are not reinforced each time they engage in a desirable behavior, so he created **schedules of reinforcement**. To help understand what would happen to behaviors that were reinforced only occasionally, Skinner posed five schedules of reinforcement, one continuous and four partial or intermittent schedules.

Continuous reinforcement occurs when each and every instance of a desired behavior is reinforced. Examples of continuous reinforcement include rats getting food every time they press a lever or monkeys getting food every time they insert a token into a slot. Each time they do the behavior, they get the reinforcement. At home, you may be reinforced with an allowance each time you unload the dishwasher.

A continuous reinforcement schedule is beneficial during the acquisition stage of learning. Your dog will learn pretty quickly that if he sits he will get a treat. A problem with this schedule is that, once the reinforcement ends, so does the behavior. If you stopped getting allowance, you would stop unloading the dishwasher.

Partial reinforcement, or not reinforcing a response every time, is a more common type of reinforcement. The intermittent format results in slower acquisition of a response but much greater resistance to extinction than continuous reinforcement. Intermittent response schedules can be carried out in four ways:

1. **Ratio schedules** are reinforcements based on the number of *behaviors* required.

2. **Interval schedules** are reinforcements based on the *passage of time*.

3. **Variable reinforcement** is reinforcement after a changing number of the desired actions or varying amounts of time.

4. **Fixed reinforcement** is reinforcement after a predetermined number of desired actions or a predetermined period of time.

Some reinforcing stimuli are immediate, and others are delayed. As in Pavlov's studies, longer delays are associated with a weaker connection between the stimulus and response, indicating that immediate reinforcers are more effective.

Interval Schedules Interval schedules can be fixed or variable, both of which relate to reinforcement related to time. A **fixed-interval schedule** of reinforcement provides reinforcement for the first behavior after a predetermined period of time. If the desired behavior is that the rat presses the lever every 30 seconds, then the rat will be rewarded the first time it presses the lever after 30 seconds. The reinforcer is dependent upon the organism performing the behavior, but the organism is reinforced based upon a definite, unchanging time interval. The organism will learn to time its activity to correspond to the reward. For example, the rat will relax after a reinforcement but start pressing the lever again at 28 or 29 seconds.

Think about fixed-interval schedules of reinforcement in your own life. If you have weekly music lessons, you might find yourself relaxing a bit right after a lesson but picking up your practicing as the next lesson approaches so that you can get the reinforcement of praise from your teacher. Or, if you finish your weekly chores by Thursday night, you will get your allowance for the week.

Variable-interval reinforcement is unpredictable reinforcement—that is, the first behavior after variable amounts of time is rewarded. You do not know when a behavior will be reinforced. For example, when you check your phone for text messages, you do not know if or when you will be rewarded with a message, but you will likely continue to check until you are. If a teacher tends to give pop quizzes, a steady rate of studying may develop, at least theoretically, because students cannot know when the quiz, which reinforces preparation, may occur. If you call a friend repeatedly and you keep getting the voicemail option (or a busy signal), you'll have to keep calling to finally speak to them. You will likely call at variable times because you cannot know when the line will be free.

Ratio Schedules Ratio schedules can also be fixed or variable. With a **fixed-ratio reinforcement schedule**, a behavior is reinforced after a specific *number* of behaviors. The classic example is a factory worker who receives a certain amount of money for each item they produce. A car salesperson on commission receives a payment after each car sold. A child receives her favorite candy every time she picks up all her toys. In some schools, students may be given a prize for reading ten books. Some restaurants offer a "buy ten, get the eleventh sandwich free" incentive. Sometimes when a college student completes an exam (e.g., 50 multiple-choice questions), they can leave the exam room (negative reinforcement).

With the **variable-ratio reinforcement schedule**, behavior is reinforced after a variable number of behaviors. The variable ratio is the most powerful reinforcement schedule, the one that most reliably produces desired behaviors. The organism does not know when reinforcement will occur. Since the variable-ratio form is based on a behavior that *has been* or *could be* reinforced, the organism must continue to exhibit the behavior to get any possible reinforcement. This is the power source behind variable-ratio reinforcement, a process that occurs around us every day. A salesperson doing cold calls must continue making the sales pitch to get the sale (reinforcement). The desired outcome is the sale, but the salesperson does not know which calls will lead to the sale.

Gambling is another classic example of the power of the variable-ratio schedule of reinforcement. An entire city—Las Vegas, Nevada—is founded on the variable-ratio schedule of reinforcement. A gambler will sit and feed nickels, quarters, dollars, or even more into a slot machine, with the chance of a possible payoff each time. If the guest does not play (playing is the casino's desired behavior), they cannot win (get reinforcement). The same can be said of those who play poker or blackjack. To win (reinforcement), a person must play (the desired behavior). The timing or number of hands a person must play to win is not established, so the possibility of winning is variable.

Dating may be an example closer to your experience. Asking someone out can be anxiety-producing, and it may or may not yield a positive response, but you must ask—i.e., do the behavior, ask—to receive the reinforcement of acceptance and a date. Checking social media for responses to something you posted is another example: You don't know when someone will provide the reinforcement of a "like," but you have to keep checking (behavior) to get the reinforcement.

Table 3.8.2 and Figure 3.8.4 provide an overview of the schedules of reinforcement. Notice that in Figure 3.8.4, each type of reinforcement behavior results in a distinctive pattern on the graph.

THE FOUR SCHEDULES OF REINFORCEMENT		
Type	**Ratio (based upon behavior)**	**Interval (based upon time)**
Fixed (number of behaviors or constant)	*Fixed Ratio* (e.g., reinforces every third lever press)	*Fixed Interval* (e.g., reinforces first lever press at 30-second intervals)
Variable (number of behaviors or length of time intervals is variable)	*Variable Ratio* (e.g., reinforces lever press after 3, 8, 2, 5, 3, 6 presses of the lever)	*Variable Interval* (e.g., reinforces lever press after 30 seconds, 12 seconds, 8 seconds, 33 seconds, 15 seconds)

Table 3.8.2

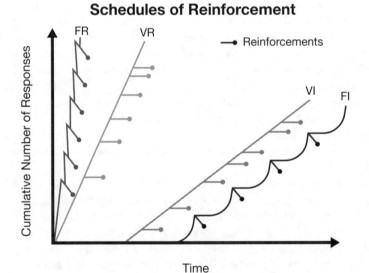

Schedules of Reinforcement

Figure 3.8.4 The fixed and variable ratios (FR and VR) reflect reinforcements in relation to the number of times a behavior is performed (the *y*-axis). The fixed- and variable-interval (FI and VI) reinforcements are based on time span (the *x*-axis).

Shaping

Shaping is a technique using a series of positive reinforcements to create more complex behavior. By rewarding **successive approximations**—steps toward a target goal—reinforcement can make a rat turn in a full circle to obtain food. First, when the rat makes a quarter turn, that behavior is reinforced. If the rat then turns a bit more, perhaps a half turn, that behavior is once again reinforced. That process continues until finally the rat is turning a complete circle. By doing this serially and properly, humans and nonhuman animals can be taught to do just about anything within their physical capability.

A familiar example in the classroom is a variation on the game of hot and cold. One student is asked to leave the room while the class decides on a desired behavior they want the student outside to perform. When the student returns, clapping is the reinforcer. The subject student must move about the room, being sensitive to which behaviors are being reinforced by the clapping and which are being ignored. As the student gets closer to the desired behavior (using successive approximations by the class), she changes her behavior accordingly. Whether the task is to open a window, sit in the teacher's chair, or pick up a book, it is learned relatively quickly. When changed to punishment, in which the class says "No!" to any behavior that is not the desired behavior, the subject may be left in a corner of the room, afraid to move, feeling helpless and foolish. The power of reinforcement over punishment is clearly demonstrated.

Nebraska Wesleyan University holds an annual Xtreme Rat Challenge, in which students exhibit their rats trained to jump hurdles, climb ropes, navigate an obstacle course, and more. Students use shaping to teach their lab rats to perform specific behaviors. But that's not all. After specific simple behaviors have been taught, a process known as chaining can be used to combine learned behaviors. Mastery of the process of chaining can make a rat run hurdles, climb a rope, jump from one platform to another, and then navigate a maze. Each behavior was taught separately, but behaviors were combined later to create the more complex course.

Biology in Operant Conditioning

Animals can be trained to adopt only those behaviors that are consistent with their biological predispositions. This fact indicates that biology limits what can be learned. For example, rats do not walk backward and cannot be trained to do so, because it's contrary to their natural inclinations.

Using food as reinforcement, psychologists Marian and Keller Breland trained raccoons to perform humanlike activities, such as putting a coin into a metal container. However, they could not train the raccoons to place *two* coins into the container. Rather than dropping the coins in, the raccoons held the coins, rubbed them together, and dipped them into the container. They essentially mimicked the natural raccoon behavior of washing food in a stream. This reversion to a natural behavior is called **instinctive drift**. The Brelands also trained the raccoons to put a large ball, too large for raccoons to wash, into a basketball hoop. Results of the experiment and others suggested that behaviorists must take species-specific behaviors into account when attempting to condition their behavior. The Brelands' focus on

The Brelands worked with animals' natural behaviors when conditioning them. They ran into instinctive drift when the raccoons they worked with reverted to their natural inclination to wash their food.

modifying animal behavior brought conditioning and biology together, changing the experimental methods applied in the field from primarily punishment of animals to reinforcement of naturally occurring animal behaviors.

Classical and Operant Conditioning Together

While we study classical and operant conditioning separately to understand the details behind learning, the reality is that they often occur within the same sets of behaviors. Humans and other animals are more complex than those represented by research animals in a laboratory environment.

The following scenario demonstrates that both operant and classical conditioning can be found in a typical classroom setting where a student is learning to present in front of peers.

Classical Conditioning Every time a student, Jensu, has to present in front of the class, the teacher uses a bell to signal the start of the presentation. Initially, Jensu has no particular feeling about the bell itself.

- Before conditioning, the unconditioned stimulus (US) is presenting in front of the class. The unconditioned response (UR) is nervousness, a natural response to public speaking.
- During conditioning, the neutral stimulus (NS) is the bell ringing. The bell rings (NS) just before Jensu starts presenting (US). The unconditioned response (UR) is Jensu's nervousness about presenting.
- After conditioning, the bell (CS) elicits the (CR), Jensu's nervousness, even before the presentation starts.

In this case, classical conditioning has occurred because Jensu has learned to associate the sound of the bell (CS) with the act of presenting (US), leading to nervousness (CR) whenever the bell rings, regardless of the context.

Operant Conditioning As part of the learning process, the teacher provides feedback and rewards for presenting in class.

- Before the behavior, Jensu knows that presenting well could lead to positive reinforcement.
- During the behavior, Jensu shows he has been working hard on his presentation skills, trying to improve each time he presents in front of the class.
- After the behavior, and after a particularly well-delivered presentation, the teacher provides positive reinforcement by praising Jensu and rewarding him with extra credit points. In another instance, to reduce Jensu's anxiety about presenting, the teacher assures him that he won't be graded on his next presentation, effectively removing the negative stimulus (fear of poor grades) if Jensu attempts the presentation.

In this operant conditioning aspect, Jensu's behavior of improving his presentation skills is shaped by the consequences that follow the behavior. Positive reinforcement (gaining extra credit) encourages Jensu to continue working hard on his presentations, while negative reinforcement (removal of the fear of being graded) encourages Jensu to present more confidently without the immediate pressure of being graded.

This scenario illustrates how classical and operant conditioning can coexist and interact within the same learning environment. While classical conditioning accounts for Jensu's emotional response (nervousness triggered by the bell), operant conditioning explains the modification of Jensu's behavior (improving presentation skills) through reinforcement. Both forms of learning contribute to the complex process of adapting and responding to educational settings, highlighting the multifaceted nature of human behavior and learning. Table 3.8.3 summarizes the characteristics of classical and operant conditioning.

CHARACTERISTICS OF CLASSICAL VS. OPERANT CONDITIONING		
	Classical Conditioning	**Operant Conditioning**
Terminology	CS, US, CR, UR	Response, reinforcement, consequence
How Behavior Occurs	Elicited involuntarily from organism	Emitted voluntarily by organism
Subject's Behavior	Does not control US	Controls reinforcement
Paired During Acquisition	Two stimuli (CS and US)	Response and reinforcement in the presence of certain stimuli
Responses Studied	Mostly involuntary reflexive and visceral (internal organs)	Mostly voluntary skeletal (movements)

Table 3.8.3

THINK AS A PSYCHOLOGIST

Apply Psychological Perspectives, Theories, Concepts, and Research Findings to a Scenario (1.A.1) | Identify the Variables in a Research Scenario (2.B.3) | Identify Psychology-Related Concepts in Descriptions or Representations of Data (3.A.1) | Calculate and Interpret Measures of Central Tendency, Variation, and Percentile Rank in a Given Data Set (3.B.3) | Propose a Defensible Claim (4.A)

Mr. Eden is a high school teacher who is trying to explore ways to get more voluntary participation from his students. He decided to test a strategy in which, each time a student voluntarily participated in class, that student would earn a "participation token." At the end of the semester, students would be able to exchange the tokens for various prizes. To see if this strategy was effective, he used the "participation tokens" with his period 1 class and used his normal strategies with his period 2 class. He then compared the rates of participation between the classes. The results are depicted below.

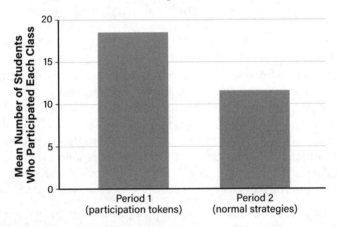

Practice Foundational Skills

Choose the correct answer.

1. In this study, Mr. Eden was using which of the following to encourage voluntary participation?

   (A) Secondary reinforcers

   (B) An unconditioned stimulus

   (C) Shaping

   (D) A fixed-interval schedule of reinforcement

Complete the following activities.

2. Based on the graph above, identify the dependent variable (DV) in Mr. Eden's study.

3. One week's worth of data from Mr. Eden's study is presented in the table below. Based on the data presented, which group had a higher standard deviation? Explain your answer.

Day of the Week	Group 1 (number of students voluntarily participating)	Group 2 (number of students voluntarily participating)
Monday	20	10
Tuesday	17	7
Wednesday	19	23
Thursday	21	2
Friday	18	12

4. Based on the results of Mr. Eden's study, what is a defensible claim that he could make about classroom participation?

REFLECT ON THE ESSENTIAL QUESTION

Essential Question: *How does operant conditioning apply to behavior and mental processes?* Using the Key Terms, complete a chart like the one below to gather details to help answer that question.

Topics	Behavior	Mental Processes
Key Experiments and Their Findings		
Terminology		
Relationship Between Stimuli and Behavior		

KEY TERMS

consequence
continuous reinforcement
fixed-interval schedule
fixed-ratio reinforcement
  schedule
fixed reinforcement
instinctive drift
interval schedule
law of effect
learned helplessness
negative punishment

negative reinforcement
operant conditioning
partial reinforcement
positive punishment
positive reinforcement
primary reinforcement
punishment
ratio schedule
reinforcement
reinforcement
  discrimination

reinforcement
  generalization
schedule of reinforcement
secondary reinforcers
shaping
successive approximation
superstitious behavior
variable-interval
  reinforcement
variable-ratio
  reinforcement schedule
variable reinforcement

1. Francesca often puts off doing her homework and ends up feeling extremely stressed the night before assignments are due. Her parents decide to implement a system by which Francesca has a strict study schedule, but with a twist: If she completes all her homework by Friday evening, she doesn't have to do any chores over the weekend. Francesca now finishes all her homework on Friday. Her change in behavior is due to which of the following learning principles?

   (A) Shaping

   (B) Secondary reinforcement

   (C) Negative reinforcement

   (D) Positive punishment

2. Service dogs are often trained to assist in such tasks as letting their person know someone is at the door, safely crossing the street, or pushing buttons on the elevator. To train these service dogs so precisely, their trainers use which of the following?

   (A) Shaping

   (B) Latent learning

   (C) Operant discrimination

   (D) Variable-interval schedule of reinforcement

3. Burrhus is training pigeons to peck at geometric shapes that occasionally appear on a screen. The pigeons will see several different shapes during the training, including squares, rectangles, circles, triangles, and trapezoids. However, Burrhus only reinforces the pigeons with a food pellet when they peck at squares. In the initial training Burrhus finds that the pigeons pecked at all shapes rather than just the square. The pigeons' behavior exemplifies which of the following?

   (A) Habituation

   (B) Discrimination

   (C) Instinctive drift

   (D) Generalization

4. After several attempts to change the circumstances with no success, a victim in an abusive relationship may give up hope of escaping because they perceive that their efforts have no effect on the outcome. If the victim eventually stops trying to leave the abusive relationship, it is most likely due to which of the following?

(A) Latent learning

(B) Avoidance conditioning

(C) Law of effect

(D) Learned helplessness

5. Once when Quentin saw his dog Judy sniffing around the new play structure, he gave her a tiny snack. Over the next week, each time Judy went outside and visited the play structure, Quentin gave her a treat, so she soon headed straight for the play structure whenever she went outside. Which idea best explains why Judy was more likely to repeat the behavior she had been rewarded for?

(A) Stimulus generalization

(B) Law of effect

(C) Insight learning

(D) Biological preparedness

Questions 6 and 7 refer to the following.

Lonnie is trying to use what he learned about conditioning to teach his pet rat a new trick as quickly as possible.

6. Which partial schedule of reinforcement should Lonnie use in order to train his rat so that the rat will most quickly learn the behavior?

(A) Fixed ratio

(B) Variable ratio

(C) Variable interval

(D) Fixed interval

7. Since Lonnie had so much luck training his first rat, he decided to also train his other four rats using the same schedule of reinforcement. The following represents how many trials it took each rat to acquire the behavior. What is the average number of trials it took Lonnie's rats to learn the new trick?

	Rat #1	Rat #2	Rat #3	Rat #4	Rat #5
Number of Trials	7	9	5	6	8

(A) 4

(B) 6

(C) 7

(D) 7.5

Topic 3.9

Social, Cognitive, and Neurological Factors in Learning

"People not only gain understanding through reflection, they evaluate and alter their own thinking."

—Albert Bandura

Essential Question: How do social learning, cognitive factors in learning, and neurological factors in learning apply to behavior and mental processes?

As the field of psychology evolved, scholars began to challenge the notion upheld by radical behaviorists that only observable behaviors merit examination. This shift in thinking acknowledged that, while thoughts may not be visible, they profoundly influence behaviors. Furthermore, it was recognized that behaviors and environmental interactions can, in turn, shape our cognitive processes.

Understanding human and animal behavior requires more than just observing actions; it requires delving into the internal cognitive mechanisms that drive these behaviors. Cognitive theorists have developed several methods to measure the impact of thought on behavior effectively. One theory suggests that we learn behaviors and attitudes by observing and imitating others, a process that plays a crucial role in shaping our behavior and social interactions. Another theory explains how learning can involve a sudden realization of a problem's solution without a trial-and-error approach. A third theory discusses learning that takes place without our making any focused effort and may not show immediately in our actions.

Social Learning

Learning takes place in a social context. **Social learning theory** explores the idea that we learn not just through direct experience, but also by observing the actions and outcomes of others' behaviors. It suggests that much of our knowledge is acquired by watching those around us—parents, teachers, peers—and modeling our actions based on those observations. This theory illuminates how individuals can learn new behaviors, attitudes, and even emotional reactions without experiencing reinforcement or punishment directly, but by watching and imitating the behavior of others. For instance, an athlete may learn to tackle properly in football by watching more experienced players and then imitating their position and technique. Or think about how you learned to drive. You probably watched others and had an idea of the process before trying it yourself. This framework focuses on the influence of our social environment on learning, connecting it directly to our interactions with others. Humans are social animals, and this observation-imitation partnership is part of the learning cycle.

Observational Learning

Psychologist Albert Bandura has influenced both behavioral psychology and social cognitive theory with his social learning theory (1977). The social learning theory proposes that people learn behaviors through **observational learning**—watching and mimicking **models.** A child may imitate the actions of her parents or older siblings. The idea of modeling behavior—showing how something is done—has profound implications in our media-driven world. YouTube presents thousands of tutorials on subjects ranging from using computer programs to applying makeup to painting with watercolors. If something can be learned, a how-to can probably be found online. The visual demonstrations are easy to access and ideal for imitation. First you watch, then you do.

As Bandura examined learning, he looked beyond Skinner's view that behaviors were learned only via stimulus and response. He suggested that learning can take place solely through observation or by direct instruction, without the use of punishments or reinforcements, and he discovered several social learning factors at work.

A key element of social learning is a model—a member of the same species exhibiting a behavior. A second element is an observer, an organism viewing the model. For example, a toddler can watch her older sibling pet the family dog gently and see how it is done. Learning something by watching someone model a behavior is called **vicarious conditioning.** *Vicarious* means "experienced in the imagination through someone else's actions." The model exhibits the behavior, and it is observed and interpreted by a viewer who can imitate it.

The viewer can also see the consequences of a behavior, an element of social learning called *vicarious reinforcement.* The toddler observing her mother praise the older sibling for being so gentle with the dog is an example of vicarious reinforcement. Although reinforcements are often observed, Bandura felt that they are not needed for learning.

Bandura does not regard an organism operating within its environment as a passive entity, but rather as an active creator of the environment. The environment influences the organism and its cognition, which in turn influence the environment. Bandura called this mutual influence *reciprocal determinism.* (See Topic 4.5.)

The social learning theory describes three possible models for imitation: live modeling, verbal instruction, and symbolic modeling. You imitate a live model when you learn how to use silverware by watching your parents and then replicating their behavior. You experience verbal instruction anytime someone explains something—at home, in a classroom, or anywhere else. You experience symbolic modeling through various media (e.g., television, movies, the Internet, and literature). You probably know firsthand how social media has influenced the behavior of many of your friends.

The Bobo Doll Experiments

Bandura reached many of his conclusions about vicarious learning by studying the behavior of children using a Bobo doll, an inflated plastic clown weighted at the bottom. When the doll was pushed over, it popped right back up.

The original experiment included four groups of children, two adults—one male and one female—and the experimenter. A child was brought into a playroom with an adult serving as a model. The experimenter instructed the child to play in one corner of the room with appealing toys while the adult was in another corner with other toys, including the Bobo doll, which the child was told were reserved only for the adult. In one scenario, the adult played with the toys for one minute and then played with the Bobo doll in an increasingly aggressive manner, including hitting, punching, and verbally assaulting the Bobo doll. In a second scenario, a nonaggressive adult played with the other toys in their corner for ten minutes and didn't play with the Bobo doll at all. After ten minutes, the experimenter returned and took the subject child to a different playroom. The experimenter told the children they could play with any of the toys in that room, but after two minutes, the experimenter took away that permission to increase the child's frustration. The experimenter told the child that they could instead play with all the toys in the original room, including the Bobo doll.

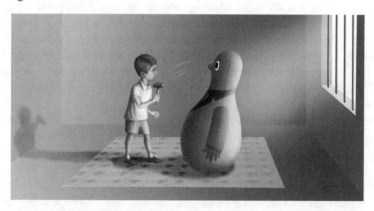

Figure 3.9.1 The Bobo doll experiments demonstrated vicarious learning. A video of segments of the experiment is available on YouTube.

Investigators observed the children from both groups (i.e., those exposed to the aggressive or nonaggressive models) and recorded acts of physical aggression, including kicking, punching, sitting on the Bobo doll, hitting it with a mallet, and tossing it around. They also recorded verbal aggression, including how many times the children imitated the adult model and/or used the phrases the model had used against Bobo, and they recorded any forms of aggression exhibited by the children but not modeled during the study.

Bandura found that children exposed to the aggressive model were more likely to act in a physically aggressive manner than those who were exposed to the nonaggressive model. Gender differences were also noted, with boys acting more aggressively than girls overall. Bandura predicted accurately that the children were more influenced by same-sex models than opposite-sex models.

By the 1980s, Bandura had expanded his research and his explanation of human behavior beyond social learning, integrating it into a **social cognitive theory** resting on the idea that part of what people know results from observing others. Bandura's approach to the processes that influence learning identifies four steps:

1. Attention—noticing that something is happening in the environment

2. Retention—recall of what was noticed

3. Reproduction—a producing action that mimics what was noticed

4. Motivation—a consequence from the environment that changes the likelihood of the behavior recurring (reinforcement and punishment)

Implications of Observational Learning

Bandura's numerous studies have attempted to understand the causal factors of aggressive and violent behavior as well as prosocial behavior (e.g., helping and altruistic behaviors). Studies by other researchers have shown that exposing children to aggressive and violent behavior in television, movies, and video games leads them to adopt more aggressive behavior themselves. Social learning theory indicates that children and teens learn aggression by imitating modeled behavior seen in specific media. However, not all aggressive or violent children have learned the behaviors from watching their parents or media sources. Genetics and individual biological factors (such as levels of testosterone) also play a role in determining levels and frequency of aggression.

Since Bandura's research, other studies have supported his findings and have even added a biological explanation for why observational learning takes place. Studies of primate species have led to the discovery of mirror neurons—nervous system cells that fire both when an organism itself is doing a behavior and also when it is observing another organism doing the behavior. The neurons "mirror" what is happening in the environment. The presence of mirror neurons can explain the internal "ouch" we feel when witnessing someone else's sudden injury. But, after repeated exposures to violence, the mirror neurons show decreased activity, suggesting desensitization.

THINK AS A PSYCHOLOGIST

Provide Reasoning That Is Grounded in Scientifically Derived Evidence to Support, Refute, or Modify an Established or Provided Claim, Policy, or Norm (Practice 4.B)

The Bobo doll test is a famous and influential experiment in the field of psychology. However, another doll test, one devised by psychologists Kenneth Clark and his wife Mamie Clark in 1939, became the basis for a landmark study exerting influence far beyond the field of psychology. In fact, it became the first psychological study to be used as evidence in a Supreme Court case.

The Clarks designed the experiment to test the effects of segregation on African American children—in other words, to measure the influence of a child's environment on self-image. The test was simple. An African American child was shown two dolls that were identical except for the color of their skin. They were then asked to pick a doll in response to such directions as

- Show me the doll you like best or that you'd like to play with.
- Show me the doll that is the "nice" doll.
- Show me the doll that looks "bad."
- Give me the doll that looks like you.

Most of the children chose the white doll as the "nice" one and the black doll as the "bad" one. When asked to explain why, the children often said "because it is white" or "because it is black."

Children overwhelmingly chose the white doll as the "nice one" in the Clarks' study. How might observational learning have played a role in their choice?

The Clarks repeated the experiment over a number of years in different settings, including the segregated schools of Clarendon County, South Carolina, in 1954. They found that African American children in segregated schools were more likely to choose the white doll as the "nice" one.

Professor Kenneth Clark was called as a witness in the consolidated legal cases known as *Brown v. Board of Education* (1954) that challenged the "separate but equal" ruling in *Plessy v. Ferguson* (1896), which had made segregation legal. When asked in court what conclusion he drew from the experiments, he replied: "The conclusion which I was forced to reach was that these children in Clarendon County, like other human beings who are subjected to an obviously inferior status in the society in which they live, have been definitely harmed in the development of their personalities; that the signs of instability in their personalities are clear, and I think that every psychologist would accept and interpret these signs as such." The Clarks' experiments were cited in a footnote in the Supreme Court decision striking down the concept of "separate but equal" as evidence of the harm segregation caused to African American children, marking the first time a Supreme Court decision included evidence from a study in the social sciences.

Practice Providing Scientifically Derived Evidence to Support, Refute, or Modify an Established Claim

Complete the following activity.

Although Professor Clark said that "every psychologist would accept and interpret these signs" as he did, in fact, the science behind the Clarks' doll test has been questioned and criticized by many. Research the critiques of the Clark doll test experiment. Find critiques based on sample size, methodology, and conclusions. Evaluate those criticisms and the original test and draw a conclusion about the landmark value of the experiment.

Cognitive Factors in Learning

While social factors in learning look outward at the impact of societal and cultural contexts, cognitive factors turn inward, examining the mental mechanisms that enable learning and comprehension. In the exploration of cognitive factors in learning, the concepts of insight learning and latent learning stand out as theories about the human mind's capacity to acquire, process, and use knowledge in complex and often subtle ways.

Insight Learning

In 1912, German psychologist Wolfgang Köhler cofounded the school of psychology known as Gestalt psychology, which is based on the view that perceptions are organized wholes (*Gestalts*) rather than a summary of their constituent parts. (See Topic 2.1.)

Köhler's work with apes helped demonstrate **insight learning**— the term for a sudden realization that

Sultan demonstrated that unobservable cognitive processes are at work in stimulus-response conditioning.

"just came to you" of how to solve a problem. In one study, Sultan, a chimpanzee, was given two sticks in his cage with bananas placed outside the cage just beyond the reach of each stick. After trying each stick unsuccessfully, Sultan fashioned the two sticks together to pull the bananas into his cage successfully. The experiment demonstrated once again that stimulus-response conditioning alone is not responsible for behavior—that some level of unobservable cognitive processes is at work.

Latent Learning and Cognitive Maps

Sometimes learning is not exhibited when it is first acquired. In other words, one can learn something but not show the behavior right away. This kind of learning is called **latent learning**. Animal studies conducted in the 1940s by psychologist Edward Tolman attempted to teach rats to run a maze during a series of one-day trials. The rats were divided into different groups, each group with a different reinforcement schedule. During the trials, Tolman noticed that one group did not exhibit the learned behavior until after it was reinforced. Although the rats had learned the maze, they were not compelled—or had no reason—to run it correctly until the behavior was reinforced with food. The rats had learned the behavior but lacked the motivation to demonstrate the learned behavior. The results of Tolman's research suggest two important aspects of learning:

- Learning can take place in an organism without the presence of a reinforcer.
- Organisms that display latent learning have formed a **cognitive map**, a mental representation that allows an organism to acquire, store, and recall information in both a real spatial world and in a metaphorical spatial environment.

The mental representation, or cognitive map, of the rats in Tolman's experiment was of the spatial layout of the maze. An example of stored spatial information for humans might be the verbal instructions you provide a friend when going to a new restaurant in town. If she is familiar with landmarks, you can refer to these and she should be able to follow along with your instructions to create a route in her head to get to the restaurant. If, however, your friend uses the GPS on her phone, she does not have a cognitive map because the spatial layout does not exist in her brain.

Learning is a phenomenon shared by all animals that are not completely governed by instinct. Humans are social beings who are constantly learning and refining their knowledge, whether through classical conditioning, operant conditioning, observational learning, cognition, or some combination of these learning modes.

Neurological factors in learning involve the brain's structure and function, including how neurons communicate, how neural connections are formed and strengthened (neuroplasticity), and how different brain areas are activated during learning processes. These factors are fundamental in understanding how we acquire, store, and retrieve information, and they play a critical role in shaping our ability to learn and adapt to new experiences, no matter which learning mode we use.

THINK AS A PSYCHOLOGIST

Apply Psychological Perspectives, Theories, Concepts, and Research Findings to a Scenario (1.A.2) | Develop and Justify Psychological Arguments Using Evidence (4.B.3)

For several decades, psychologists have debated the effect of children playing video games that contain violent acts and violent content. The following is a conclusion taken from research that explored several scenarios related to video gaming and aggressive behavior.[5]

> Violent video games provide a forum for learning and practicing aggressive solutions to conflict situations. The effect of violent video games appears to be cognitive in nature. In the short term, playing a violent video game appears to affect aggression by priming aggressive thoughts. Longer-term effects are likely to be longer lasting as well, as the player learns and practices new aggression-related scripts that become more and more accessible for use when real-life conflict situations arise. If repeated exposure to violent video games does indeed lead to the creation and heightened accessibility of a variety of aggressive knowledge structures, thus effectively altering the person's basic personality structure, the consequent changes in everyday social interactions may also lead to consistent increases in aggressive affect. The active nature of the learning environment of the video game suggests that this medium is potentially more dangerous than the more heavily investigated TV and movie media. With the recent trend toward greater realism and more graphic violence in video games and the rising popularity of these games, consumers of violent video games (and parents of consumers) should be aware of these potential risks.

Practice Applying Psychological Theories and Developing Arguments Using Evidence

Choose the correct answer.

1. Which type of learning is most clearly reflected in the above scenario?

    (A) Latent learning

    (B) Classical conditioning

    (C) Observational learning

    (D) Secondary reinforcement

---

5 Anderson, C. A., & Dill, K. E. (2000). Video games and aggressive thoughts, feelings, and behavior in the laboratory and in life. *Journal of Personality and Social Psychology, 78*(4), 772–790. DOI: 10.1037// O022-3514.78.4.772

Complete the following activity.

2. Using the preceding text, provide two pieces of evidence to support the following claim. Label them **Supporting Evidence 1** and **Supporting Evidence 2**.

   Claim: Parents should limit their children's exposure to violent video games.

REFLECT ON THE ESSENTIAL QUESTION

Essential Question: *How do social learning, cognitive factors in learning, and neurological factors in learning apply to behavior and mental processes?* Using the Key Terms, complete a chart like the one below to gather details to help answer that question.

Topic	Behavior	Mental Processes
Social Learning		
Cognitive Factors in Learning		

KEY TERMS

cognitive map	models	social learning theory
insight learning	observational learning	vicarious conditioning
latent learning	social cogitive theory	

MULTIPLE-CHOICE QUESTIONS

Questions 1 and 2 refer to the following.

In a variation of Bandura's studies with the Bobo doll, children were randomly assigned to watch a video that showed an adult model playing in the toy room. One group watched an aggressive model who repeatedly hit, kicked, and taunted the Bobo doll. The other group watched a video with a nonaggressive model playing in the toy room. After watching the video, each child got to go play in the toy room, and the researchers recorded how many acts of aggression the child committed. The results indicated a statistically significant difference in how many acts of aggression were committed between the two groups.

1. Which of the following most accurately characterizes why Bandura's research design is experimental?

 (A) The study compared two different groups of participants.

 (B) The researchers defined and measured a dependent variable.

 (C) Participants were randomly assigned to receive an independent variable.

 (D) Researchers used a double-blind procedure to eliminate possible experimenter bias.

2. Which of the following statements most accurately captures what it means to say that the results of Bandura's study were statistically significant?

 (A) The difference in aggressive acts between groups was not likely due to chance.

 (B) There is a strong positive correlation between the two variables.

 (C) In future replications, it is 95 percent likely that researchers would find the same results.

 (D) The results used qualitative measurements, thereby strengthening the validity of the research.

3. In one variation of the Bobo study, a group saw a video of the model receiving candy and praise for being aggressive to the Bobo doll. When that group of children went into the toy room, their rate of aggressive acts increased significantly over that of children who had only seen an aggressive model (without receiving positive reinforcement). This finding most clearly demonstrates the role of which of the following?

 (A) Vicarious reinforcement

 (B) Latent learning

 (C) Insight learning

 (D) Learned helplessness

4. Fred the dog has been placed into an enclosure while his owners are out. This fencelike structure keeps Fred in the living room because his owners do not want him wandering around the house when they are not home. Fred initially believes that he will be stuck in this enclosure all day but then suddenly realizes that he can push his body against the enclosure to move it enough to eventually provide room to escape. Which learning concept has Fred experienced?

 (A) Cognitive map

 (B) Vicarious conditioning

 (C) Latent learning

 (D) Insight learning

5. Deepak and Manisha would like to raise their children to be socially aware and helpful people. Social learning psychologists would recommend that the strongest way they can influence their children is to do which of the following?

(A) Read prosocial books to their children

(B) Avoid reinforcing the aggressive actions of the children

(C) Model the desired behaviors

(D) Begin the modeling once the children reach puberty

6. Monkeys raised in labs showed no fear of snakes. Monkeys raised in the wild showed strong fear of snakes. Lab-raised monkeys shown a video of wild monkeys responding with fear to snakes began acting fearfully after being exposed to a toy snake. This illustrates the power of which of the following?

(A) Insight learning

(B) Observational learning

(C) Cognitive maps

(D) Shaping

7. You lost your phone at school one day. In order to track it down, you go through your whole schedule in your mind to remind you of every place you had been since you arrived at school that morning. By doing so, you eventually realize that you left it in the cafeteria when you stopped to talk to your friends. Which learning concept has helped you locate your phone?

(A) Modeling

(B) Social learning theory

(C) A cognitive map

(D) Insight learning

8. Peter was the understudy in a play. He watched rehearsals every day but rarely had an opportunity to practice his lines in front of the audience or to find the proper placement on stage. The evening of the premiere, the lead in the role was sick and Peter had to perform. Despite never having received reinforcement for anything related to the role in the past, he performed beautifully and received a standing ovation at the end of the performance. How had Peter learned the lines?

(A) Classical conditioning

(B) Operant conditioning

(C) Latent learning

(D) A fixed-interval schedule of reinforcement

STUDY LIKE A CHAMP WITH DR. G | REWARDING YOURSELF

The sections on observational learning, classical and operant conditioning, and even cognitive development from this unit no doubt gave you many insights into your behaviors and perhaps explained some of your study habits as well. Did you find rewards that motivated you to study? Did you decide to use punishment to reduce maladaptive behaviors?

Operant conditioning can be a powerful way to change your studying behaviors, but be prepared to experiment with different rewards and punishments. This unit shows that rewards are better for long-term changes in behavior, and you may want to focus on what you find really rewarding. A key trick is to make sure you are not picking rewards you will give yourself anyway. For example, saying you will reward yourself with some screen time when you know you will give yourself phone time anyway is not going to be a good strategy. However, saying you will **not** get to use your phone and then sticking to that is!

Try not to use physiological needs as rewards either. Do not say you will only sleep or exercise if you get your studying done. Sleeping well and getting physical activity are important to your health and should not be used as rewards. On the other hand, treating yourself to something you do not eat regularly or do regularly (tried paintball?) can be a good reward. Find what will work for you!

Rewards involving physical activity can be especially satisfying. They can be special events, like paintballing, for when you reach certain study milestones. But everyday activities— shooting hoops, playing with your dog, rollerblading, practicing at the batting cage, even just going for a walk—can reward you with all the benefits of physical activity, including the "endorphin rush" (see Topic 1.3), and motivate you to keep working toward your study goals.

MULTIPLE-CHOICE QUESTIONS

Questions 1 through 3 refer to the following.

Dr. Suren is trying to determine if there is a relationship between age and different types of intelligence. She gathers the data shown in the graph by asking her local hospital to share the results of cognitive assessments of crystallized and fluid intelligence for 1,000 local patients from various age groups.

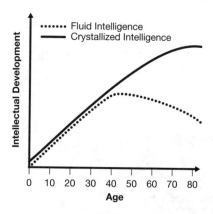

1. Which research technique has Dr. Suren used to gather this data?
   (A) Cross-sectional
   (B) Longitudinal
   (C) Experimental
   (D) Naturalistic observations

2. Dr. Suren wants to be certain that her study meets all of the necessary ethical guidelines. Which must she be certain to address?
   (A) Contact the families of the participants and ask their permission to use the results of the assessments
   (B) Do nothing; the hospital has the right to share patient information
   (C) Make sure personal information about the patients cannot be identified
   (D) Get permission only from the doctors of the participants in the study

3. What conclusion can be made from the data collected in this study?

   (A) Aging causes fluid intelligence to decrease.

   (B) There is a positive relationship between age and crystallized intelligence.

   (C) Individuals cannot learn new information past the age of 50.

   (D) People's intelligence decreases with age.

Questions 4 and 5 refer to the following.

The Johnson family has just added a new member to their family: Fuzzy, an adorable, white Maltese puppy. They are looking forward to using their knowledge of psychology as they implement behavioral techniques in training their new puppy and having him fit into the household.

4. The Johnsons begin training with classical conditioning concepts. They teach Fuzzy to associate receiving a treat with a clicking sound. After several trials, Fuzzy's heart races each time he hears the clicking noise. In the scenario, the clicking noise serves as which of the following?

   (A) Conditioned stimulus

   (B) Unconditioned response

   (C) Unconditioned stimulus

   (D) Conditioned response

5. If Fuzzy's heart also races when he hears a doorbell or the tick of the clock, this would serve as an example of which of the following?

   (A) Discrimination

   (B) Spontaneous recovery

   (C) Acquisition

   (D) Generalization

6. Which of the following is an example of observational learning?

   (A) Students in a classroom have their recess taken away until they are quiet.

   (B) A baseball player works in the batting cages until she becomes skilled at hitting.

   (C) A worker learns to fear the phone ringing because of a boss who yells over the phone.

   (D) Young women wear a clothing style similar to that of a popular singer.

7. In an experiment with young children, Dr. Saka showed the children a long tube of clay, then broke an exact-sized tube of clay into three segments. He asked them, "Does the single piece have more clay, do the three segments have more clay, or do they both have the same amount of clay?" Dr. Saka was testing which cognitive ability?

(A) Insight learning

(B) Theory of mind

(C) Conservation

(D) Egocentrism

8. Many types of social media are addictive because they provide rewards in the form of "likes" and views that serve as reinforcements. Which of the following perspectives on psychology best explains why it is so difficult to stop using these sites?

(A) Social learning theory

(B) Insight learning

(C) Operant conditioning

(D) Classical conditioning

9. When he was 14, Deandre began to sit in the front seat while his dad drove their car. He enjoyed watching the scenery as they drove around the city. One day, when his aunt was visiting from out of town, she asked Deandre to ride with her and then asked him how to get to a restaurant. Even though no one had told him to pay attention, Deandre knew how to get to the restaurant, based on this previous experience as a passenger, and he directed his aunt perfectly. Deandre's knowledge can be explained by which concept related to learning?

(A) Extrinsic motivation

(B) Latent learning

(C) The law of effect

(D) Instrumental conditioning

10. John and Mary have been dating for three years and hope to get married in the summer. They are considering having children in the next few years and are happy in their relationship with one another. They support each other in their careers and with personal issues. According to Erik Erikson, they are experiencing which aspect of psychosocial development?

(A) Identity

(B) Industry

(C) Intimacy

(D) Integrity

11. A dog retrieves slippers every day because, in the past, he received a food reward for this behavior. The dog's behavior is an example of which concept?

(A) A classically conditioned response

(B) An operantly conditioned response

(C) An unconditioned response

(D) An unconditioned stimulus

Questions 12 and 13 refer to the following.

Researchers are conducting a follow-up study on the occurrence of adverse childhood experiences (ACEs). They begin gathering data in a crime-ridden area in which many of the children come from homes with addiction issues and low socioeconomic status. They are initially alarmed by the number of ACEs the children experience. As they gather data from other neighborhoods with lower crime rates, more stable home environments, and high socioeconomic status, they find that their data more closely match the results of the earlier study.

12. Which best explains how the data have changed over the length of the study?

(A) Regression towards the mean

(B) Statistical significance

(C) A bimodal distribution

(D) A positive skew

13. What is the most likely hypothesis for the study described above?

(A) Individuals with ACEs who have proper counselling will not experience any adverse effects as adults.

(B) There is a negative correlation between ACEs and functioning in relationships later in life.

(C) There is no correlation between ACEs and trauma.

(D) ACEs cause people to have destructive relationships.

Questions 14 and 15 refer to the following.

You are opening a new daycare center and want to be sure that you are able to meet the needs of all of the children in your care. The daycare center will be set up to have children of different ages in separate rooms focusing on different cognitive and social tasks.

14. Which of the following cognitive landmarks is most likely to be demonstrated in your class that has 1-year-old infants?

(A) Object permanence

(B) Animism

(C) Conservation

(D) Imaginative play

15. If the researchers tracked the development of a specific cohort of students from the time they entered the daycare as infants to the time they left as four-year-olds, what type of research design would the researchers have used?

(A) Cross-sectional design

(B) Meta-analysis

(C) Longitudinal design

(D) Experimental design

FREE-RESPONSE QUESTIONS

Question 1: Article Analysis Question (AAQ)

1. Your response to the question should be provided in six parts: A, B, C, D, E, and F. Write the response to each part of the question in complete sentences. Use appropriate psychological terminology in your response.

Using the source provided, respond to all parts of the question.

(A) Identify the research method used in the study.

(B) State the operational definition of the dependent variable.

(C) Describe the meaning of the differences in the means of the group in relation to the study.

(D) Identify at least one ethical guideline applied by the researchers.

(E) Explain the extent to which the research findings may or may not be generalizable using specific and relevant evidence from the study.

(F) Explain how at least one of the research findings supports or refutes the researchers' hypothesis that rats raised in enriched environments would exhibit structural differences in their brains compared to those raised in deprived environments.

Introduction

The researchers were motivated by John Bowlby's attachment theory, which suggests that early attachment experiences influence individuals' romantic relationships in adulthood. Hazan and Shaver aimed to explore whether there were identifiable patterns of attachment in romantic relationships and whether these patterns related to individuals' experiences with caregivers in infancy. They believed that those with a strong attachment to parental figures early in life would have stronger attachments in romantic relationships later in life.

Participants

The study involved a random sample of 630 individuals chosen from 1,200 who responded to an advertisement in a local paper. The data collection was then repeated with 108 first-year university students. All participants provided informed consent before taking part in the study.

Method

Participants were asked to complete a "love quiz" in a local paper, which included questions about their romantic attitudes and behaviors. First, participants were asked to identify which of three paragraph-long descriptions about current relationships best applied to them. The descriptions can be summarized as "I am somewhat uncomfortable being close to others," "I find it relatively easy to get close to others," or "I find that others are reluctant to get as close as I would like." Additionally, they were asked to reflect on their early relationships (35 questions) with parents or primary caregivers and to indicate the extent to which these relationships resembled specific attachment styles, such as secure, anxious-ambivalent, or avoidant. Participants' responses were kept confidential, and they were assured of anonymity.

Results and Discussion

Hazan and Shaver found that most people were securely attached early in life (64%), and this led to happier and more trusting relationships as adults. The findings revealed that participants' responses to the "love quiz" were associated with their self-reported attachment styles. Specifically, individuals who reported secure attachments tended to have positive attitudes toward love and relationships, while those with anxious (anxious-ambivalent) attachments reported a fear of abandonment and a desire for closeness. Participants with avoidant attachments tended to have negative views of love and relationships, often emphasizing independence and self-sufficiency. It was found that those with a reported secure attachment style also reported higher overall satisfaction in relationships with a mean for securely attached participants at 4.53, anxious/ambivalent 4.15, and avoidant 4.19 (out of 6). The results supported the idea that adult attachment styles are influenced by early attachment experiences. The results were statistically significant ($p<.001$). The study provided evidence for the continuity of attachment across the lifespan and highlighted the importance of early relationships in shaping individuals' romantic behaviors and attitudes.

Reference

Hazan, C., & Shaver, P. R. (1987). Romantic love conceptualized as an attachment process. *Journal of Personality and Social Psychology, 52*(3), 511–524. https://doi.org/10.1037/0022-3514.52.3.511

This question has three parts: Part A, Part B, and Part C. Use the three sources provided to answer all parts of the question.

For Part B and Part C, you must cite the source that you used to answer the question. You can do this in two different ways:

- Parenthetical Citation:

  For example: ". . . (Source A)"
- Embedded Citation:

  For example: "According to Source A, . . ."

Write the response to each part of the question in complete sentences. Use appropriate psychological terminology.

Using the sources provided, develop and justify an argument on the extent to which models in media influence behaviors of young people through observational learning.

(A) Propose a specific and defensible claim based in psychological science that responds to the question.

(B) (i) Support your claim using at least one piece of specific and relevant evidence from one of the sources.

    (ii) Explain how the evidence from Part B (i) supports your claim using a psychological perspective, theory, concept, or research finding learned in AP Psychology.

(C) (i) Support your claim using an additional piece of specific and relevant evidence from a different source than the one that was used in Part B (i).

    (ii) Explain how the evidence from Part C (i) supports your claim using a different psychological perspective, theory, concept, or research finding learned in AP Psychology than the one that was used in Part B (ii).

Source A

Introduction
The Bandura Bobo Doll study (1961) was conducted to determine if children who witnessed aggressive acts were more likely to engage in aggressive acts themselves. Bandura was concerned by the increase in the number of violent cartoons to which children had access. He hypothesized that just the act of watching violence would make children more likely to engage in violent acts themselves.

Participants
The study involved a sample of 72 school-aged children between the ages of 3 and 6 who were drawn from the population at the Stanford University Nursery School. Parents of the children were provided with an informed consent about what would occur in the study. The children who participated were randomly divided into three groups.

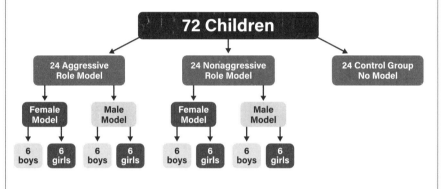

Method
All of the children witnessed one of the three conditions. In the first group, the children observed an adult model engaging in aggressive behavior toward a Bobo doll (an inflatable doll that will pop back up when knocked down). The adult kicked the doll, hit it with a mallet, and flung it into the air. In the second condition, the children witnessed an adult interacting with the Bobo doll in a nonaggressive manner and playing with other toys. In the third condition, children did not witness any adult interacting with the Bobo doll. After the observation period, children were placed into a room containing a variety of different toys including a Bobo doll. Their behavior was recorded, and the number of aggressive acts observed was identified in each group. Additionally, the data were broken down by the gender of both the participant and the model.

continued

Results and Discussion

The results of the study demonstrated that the children exposed to the aggressive model exhibited far more acts of violence toward the Bobo doll than the other groups. These aggressive acts included many of the same actions (hitting the Bobo doll with a mallet) that were exhibited by the adult during the observation period. Additionally, the children exposed to the aggressive model engaged in novel acts of violence. They created new ways to harm the Bobo doll, such as threatening the doll with a toy gun or hitting it with a baby doll.

The implication of the Bobo doll study suggests that children's behavior is influenced by the behavior of others. This behavior is then imitated by the children. The role model does seem to affect the likelihood that the behavior is imitated. Adults and peers who are leaders in the class are more likely to affect the behavior of other children in the class. Those who had few important social connections did not influence the children's behavior. The results also demonstrate the dynamic role of social learning. In addition to imitating the aggressive acts they witnessed the adult model engage in, the children were able to create their own ways of hurting the doll. The study has been criticized because some suggest that engaging in aggressive acts toward a doll that is intended to be hit does not translate into aggressive actions in day-to-day life. Additionally, some believe it was not appropriate to intentionally expose young children to overt acts of aggression, especially if the belief was that the aggression would be imitated.

Response Category	Experimental Groups				Control Groups
Imitative Physical Aggression	F Model	M Model	F Model	M Model	
Female Subjects	5.5	7.2	2.5	0.0	1.2
Male Subjects	12.4	25.8	0.2	1.5	2.0

Table 1 Mean Aggression Scores for Experimental and Control Subjects

Source

Bandura, A., Ross, D., & Ross, S. A. (1961). Transmission of aggression through imitation of aggressive models. *The Journal of Abnormal and Social Psychology, 63*(3), 575–582.

Source B

Introduction
Charlton et al. (2002) conducted a study on aggression in St. Helena, a remote island in the South Atlantic that is part of a British territory, to investigate the prevalence and nature of aggressive behavior in the population. The researchers aimed to understand the factors contributing to aggression in this unique context because St. Helena did not have access to television until 1995. The study intended to determine if the aggressive models that children were exposed to on television would increase acts of aggression as found in the Bandura and Ross (1961) study.

Participants
The study involved a sample of 300 individuals ages 3–8, from varied socioeconomic backgrounds, residing in St. Helena. Participants were recruited from schools, community centers, and other public spaces across the island.

Method
Charlton et al. (2002) employed a mixed-methods approach, combining surveys, interviews, and observational techniques to gather data on aggression. Participants completed questionnaires assessing their experiences with and perceptions of aggression, as well as factors such as family dynamics, peer relationships, and exposure to violence. Additionally, the researchers conducted structured interviews with a subset of participants to gain deeper insights into their experiences with aggression. Cameras were set up in the schoolyard and researchers coded any acts of violence. This was a longitudinal study that began before the introduction of television to the island and continued over the next two years.

Results/Discussion
The study revealed that aggression was relatively low in the population of St. Helena compared to mainland settings and remained low after the introduction of television. Those children who exhibited higher acts of aggression were drawn to watch more violent programming such as violent cartoons. This may suggest that a stronger biological predisposition to violence made children more drawn to violent programming. The researchers identified cultural norms and tight-knit social support networks as protective factors that limited aggression in the community. The findings suggest that while aggression is present in St. Helena, it is influenced by individual, familial, and societal factors. The television models did not override the underlying risk factors, such as family conflict and exposure to violence. Engaging in aggressive behavior is not necessarily the outcome of exposure to television violence.

Reference
Charlton, T., Gunter, B., and Hannan, A. (2002). *Broadcast television effects in a remote community*. Mahwah. NJ: Lawrence Erlbaum Associates.

Source C

Introduction
Becker (2002) conducted a study in the South Pacific island nation of Fiji to explore the role of observational learning in the development of eating disorders. The researcher aimed to investigate how individuals may acquire disordered eating behaviors through observing and modeling the behaviors of others, such as family members, peers, or media figures. Fijian culture had long revolved around generous amounts of food, and a robust, round shape was seen as attractive among both men and women.

Participants
The study recruited 63 female participants between the ages of 16 and 18. All girls were randomly selected from a school in Fiji near the capital of Nadroga. All spoke English.

Method
The first group of 31 girls was studied just before television was introduced to the island. A second group of 32 was studied three years later, after television had been introduced. The girls were given the EAT-26 inventory, which is a standardized test to determine eating attitudes and eating habits. Semi-structured interviews were also conducted, along with measurements of height and weight, to enhance the credibility of the data from the EAT-26 inventory. Interview questions related to the identification of potential binging and purging behaviors and questions about dieting practices.

Results/Discussion
The study found significant differences between the two groups' scores on the EAT-26 inventory. In the first group (before television), the average score was 12.7; the second group (after television) had an average score of 29.2. Scores above 20 are correlated with dieting and self-induced vomiting, although reported binging did not differ between the groups. In the first group, reports of dieting were rare. In the second group, 69% admitted they had dieted to lose weight and 77% said television made them feel differently about their body weight. Becker's findings highlight the importance of observational learning in understanding the cause of eating disorders. Fijian girls' exposure to thin television models replaced the model of a heavier Fijian woman, which had been the standard before the introduction of television. The females portrayed on television became models for teen Fijian girls and influenced their dieting behavior. The study shows the strength of imitation in the presence of models and underscores the need for interventions aimed at promoting positive role models and reducing exposure to harmful media messages to prevent the transmission of disordered eating behaviors. The study is difficult to replicate, since there are few places without access to television or the Internet. There may have also been other factors at play in the three-year interim between groups that affected the eating behaviors of teenage girls.

Reference
Becker, A., *et al.* (2002, June). Eating behaviors and attitudes following prolonged television exposure among ethnic Fijian adolescent girls. *British Journal of Psychiatry, 180,* 509–514.

UNIT 4: Social Psychology and Personality

Unit Overview

Imagine yourself at a school dance. You hang out with a few close friends and wonder what everyone else is thinking of you. You get some punch and immediately spill a little, making you even more self-conscious. You hear people laughing and are sure they are laughing at you. But you look around and see that no one is paying attention to you. You relax and "people watch." Football players are hanging out together, talking and laughing. Janice and Pedro are holding hands, deep in conversation. On the dance floor, Yolanda is teaching friends a new dance, and her followers are laughing at their mistakes.

A social psychologist would look at this scene and identify different elements of **social psychology**—a branch of psychology that uses a scientific approach to understand how and why social groups influence individual behavior and attitudes and how, in turn, individual attitudes and behaviors affect social groups.

In addition to relating to others in a group, Janice, Pedro, and Yolanda also operate as individuals with unique personalities, motivations, and emotions. The study of **personality** explores the diverse characteristics that make people unique, assessing these traits through various methodologies that capture the complex web of factors—some internal and some external—that shape personality. **Motivation theory** delves into the driving forces behind human behavior and mental processes, examining how both internal desires and external pressures shape actions. The psychological perspective on **emotions** investigates how feelings are experienced, regulated, and expressed, influencing everything from personal decision-making—such as deciding to go to the school dance—to social interactions—such as holding hands or leading a dance lesson. Together, these areas form a foundational triad in understanding human behavior, providing insights into how individuals perceive, interact with, and respond to the world around them.

LEARNING OBJECTIVES

4.1.A Explain how attribution theory applies to behavior and mental processes.

4.1.B Explain how locus of control (internal and external) applies to behavior and mental processes.

4.1.C Explain how personal perception applies to behavior and mental processes.

4.2.A Explain how stereotypes and implicit attitudes contribute to the behaviors and mental processes of prejudice and discrimination.

4.2.B Explain how belief perseverance and cognitive dissonance apply to attitude formation and change.

4.3.A Explain how the social situation affects behavior and mental processes.

4.3.B Explain how being in a group can affect an individual's behavior and mental processes.

4.3.C Explain how prosocial behavior affects behavior and mental processes.

4.4.A Explain how the psychodynamic theory of personality defines and assesses personality.

4.4.B Explain how the humanistic theory of personality defines and assesses personality.

4.5.A Explain how the social-cognitive theory of personality defines and assesses personality.

4.5.B Explain how trait theories of personality define and assess personality.

4.6.A Explain how theories about motivation apply to behavior and mental processes.

4.6.B Explain how eating and belongingness motivate behavior and mental processes.

4.7.A Explain how theories of emotion apply to behavior and mental processes.

4.7.B Explain how social norms and experiences influence the expression of emotions.

STUDY LIKE A CHAMP WITH DR. G. | INTERLEAVE

With three units already behind you, I bet you are thinking, "There sure are a lot of concepts to learn in psychology!" Yes, that is true, but we can use some more psychological science to help you remember it all. So far, with pretesting, practicing retrieval, and spaced practice (successful use of which you are rewarding, right?), you are already using the most effective techniques to study. Now to take it up a notch.

There is another key technique if you want to study like a champ. Technically, it is called **interleaving**. Try this. Put both your hands out in front of you and spread your fingers wide apart. Now bring your hands together and have the fingers of each hand mesh with each other. You have now interleaved your fingers. The key is to do the same thing with studying. The fingers of your left hand represent one unit (e.g., Unit 2, Cognition), and the fingers of the other hand represent material from another unit (e.g., Unit 3, Development and Learning). Instead of studying just one unit, you study topics from one unit interleaved with topics from another unit.

By forcing your mind to pay attention to more than one type of material, you create better structures for absorption of the material. By testing yourself on different material all in one session, you are challenging your retrieval process. Many research studies show that interleaving leads to better recall of material. You can even interleave different subjects (study psychology for a bit, then study biology for a bit) or if studying math—where the research on how best to study was first done—mix up solving numerical problems with word problems. Try interleaving as you test yourself on material from this unit.

Topic 4.1

Attribution Theory, Locus of Control, and Person Perception

"When we expect certain behaviors of others, we are likely to act in ways that make the expected behavior more likely to occur."

—Robert Rosenthal

Essential Question: How do attribution theory, locus of control, and personal perception apply to behavior and mental processes?

The school dance scenario at the beginning of the unit is fairly typical in high schools all over the country. First, we worry about what others think of us, and then we begin to make assumptions about others around us. Social psychologists call this *social cognition* because it involves how we think about ourselves and others in social situations. The term *social situation* refers to behaviors and mental processes that occur in a group of two or more people, or it may also describe an individual who *thinks* that others are observing them. For example, you may be driving on a highway and come across a sign that says "Speed Controlled by Radar." You immediately take your foot off the accelerator and look at the speedometer, whether or not you are driving over the speed limit. You want to make sure that you do not get a ticket. So, even if no one is *actually* observing your speed and, in reality, you are alone, you adjust your behavior because you *think* you are in a social situation.

At the center of social cognition is our effort to make sense of what is going on around us and inside us in social situations. Psychologists have developed theories about how individuals perceive and interpret their behavior and that of others. They involve cognitive processes such as perception, judgment, and interpretation of social stimuli. Each of the concepts explored in this topic considers the role of internal and situational factors in shaping individuals' perceptions, behaviors, and ways of understanding.

Attribution Theory

If you have a friend who tries all the scariest roller-coaster rides, you might think, "I wonder why he likes roller coasters?" You might conclude that he is a sensation seeker. In psychology, such a conclusion is called an attribution. An **attribution** is the way in which we explain the cause or causes of behavior. You attributed your friend's fondness for roller coasters to his tendency to be a sensation seeker rather than to some other explanation. Attributing his roller coaster-riding behavior to his being a sensation seeker is a **dispositional attribution**—an assumption that behavior is driven by internal characteristics such as intelligence or personality (or a person's disposition). If you attributed his behavior as responding to a friend's dare, you would be making a **situational attribution**, explaining the behavior as a result of an external source (a person's situation).

Attribution theory was first developed by Fritz Heider in 1958 and was later expanded by other researchers who, even into the 21st century, have used attribution theory as a tool to investigate the causes of behavior.

The table below shows attributions that might be made about a student who did well on an exam.

Attributions	
Dispositional: Driven by Internal Traits	**Situational: Driven by Circumstances**
The student must be smart.	The test must have been easy.
The student must have studied hard.	The teacher must have been in a good mood.

Table 4.1.1

Explanatory Style

People have a predictable way of explaining the causes of events to themselves, which is called an **explanatory style**. You can think of an explanatory style as the pattern of attributions that people assign to events in their own and others' lives. When someone has a *global explanatory style*, they tend to attribute negative events to causes that they see as affecting many areas of their life. If something bad happens, a person with a global style might say, "This always happens to me," or "Everything always goes wrong." If a person with a global style fails a test, they might think, "I'm bad at everything."

In contrast, a *specific explanatory style* involves attributing negative events to causes that are limited to particular circumstances. Individuals with a specific style are more likely to see negative events as isolated incidents that don't necessarily predict other negative outcomes in different areas of their lives. For example, if such a person fails a test, they might think, "I didn't study enough for this particular subject," attributing their failure to a specific, controllable cause rather than a global flaw in their capabilities.

When people have an **optimistic explanatory style**, they attribute negative events to external and specific causes and attribute positive events to internal and global causes. A **pessimistic explanatory style,** in contrast, involves attributing negative events to internal and global causes and attributing positive events to external and specific causes. Explanatory styles can have a significant impact on an individual's motivation, emotional well-being, and overall mental health.

Research has shown that individuals with an optimistic explanatory style tend to be more resilient and persistent and have better overall mental health compared to those with a pessimistic explanatory style. Pessimistic individuals are more prone to experiencing learned helplessness (see Topic 3.8), depression, and other negative psychological outcomes. Explanatory styles and attributions can be influenced by various factors, such as cultural background, personal experiences, and cognitive biases.

Cognitive Biases and Attribution

In the 1960s, researchers found that we have a tendency to attribute dispositional explanations of behaviors when we observe other people's behaviors, but we attribute situational explanations of behaviors when we explain our own behaviors. This concept is called the **actor-observer bias**.

Consider this scenario. There's a big math test coming up. On the day of the test, one of your classmates, Marco, arrives late and ends up rushing through the exam. When Marco gets a lower grade than usual, you think, "Marco did poorly because he's always disorganized and never plans ahead."

A week later, you find yourself running late on the day of another important test because your alarm didn't go off. Despite rushing, you also don't do as well as you usually do. However, instead of blaming your organizational skills or preparation, you think, "I only did poorly because my alarm failed, and I had to rush. It was just bad luck."

In this scenario, the actor-observer bias is evident in how you attribute the reasons for poor performance differently depending on whether you're observing someone else (Marco) or reflecting on your own experience. For Marco, you attribute the poor performance to a dispositional personal flaw (being disorganized), while for yourself, you attribute it to an external situation (the alarm not going off). This bias shows how people tend to attribute their own actions to external factors but often blame others' actions on their personal qualities or character.

In the 1970s, Stanford University professor Lee Ross termed this tendency the **fundamental attribution error**. People tend to attribute the behaviors of others to dispositional factors and ignore other explanations, such as situational or external factors. For example, if you observed a man hitting another man, you might tend to believe that the hitter was an aggressive person rather than consider that the other man may have struck the first blow.

When we observe the behavior of individuals from a minority group or underrecognized group (e.g., ethnic, sexual, and religious minorities), we tend to apply that same attribution error to the entire group. For example, if we witness a member of a minority hitting someone, we may believe that everyone from that ethnic group is aggressive, rather than considering it is just one person or that situational factors may account for the behavior. (See Topic 4.2 on discrimination, prejudice, and stereotyping.) Psychologist Thomas Pettigrew called this the *ultimate attribution error*.

Most people like to think of themselves as being good, moral individuals without evil intent or a lack of caring about others. These positive views of the self are maintained through **self-serving biases**, tendencies to see ourselves in a positive light. Many studies investigating this phenomenon have found that people see themselves as having above-average intelligence and high moral standards and as being more helpful than they are in reality. When a student does well on a test, for example, the student will likely attribute the success to their intelligence or hard work (a dispositional cause). If a student does not do well, they may blame an unfair test or unfair grading system (situational cause). People apply such biases to favorite teams and celebrities as well.

This tendency to evaluate ourselves in an overly favorable manner may create a problem-solving barrier. If we make only a few mistakes and do well on a test, we may tell ourselves, "I did well on this exam because I am smart." If we do poorly, we may tell ourselves, "The teacher did not prepare us well." This self-serving bias protects our own interests or self-esteem.

Attributional Biases			
Bias	Self	Other Person	Self attributes . . .
Actor-Observer Bias	✓	✓	. . . self-behavior to **external factors** . . . other person's behavior to **internal factors**
Fundamental Attribution Error		✓	. . . other person's behavior to **internal factors**
Self-Serving Bias	✓		. . . successes to **internal factors** . . . failures to **external factors**

Table 4.1.2

THINK AS A PSYCHOLOGIST

Explain How Cultural Norms, Expectations, and Circumstances Apply to Behavior and Mental Processes (1.B)

Meet Sara, an American college student; Kofi, a student from Ghana; and Ji-eun, an exchange student from South Korea. Sara invites Kofi and Ji-eun to join her study group meeting. When Kofi and Ji-eun both arrive 15 minutes late, Sara immediately feels frustrated and perceives their lateness as a sign of disrespect and irresponsibility. Growing up in an individualistic culture where punctuality is highly valued, Sara is quick to attribute their tardiness to their characters, rather than considering any situational factors that might have caused the delay.

Upon their arrival, Sara cannot contain her frustration and sharply remarks, "I hope you can take this more seriously in the future." Her remark catches Kofi and Ji-eun off guard. In their cultures, arriving late because of important social or family obligations is often understood and accepted. On his way to the meeting, Kofi encountered a friend who needed help, and he chose to assist, believing it was the right thing to do. Ji-eun also comes from a culture that values collectivism and family obligations. On her way to the meeting, Ji-eun had to deal with a family matter over the phone, which she prioritized because of her cultural emphasis on familial responsibilities. Both Kofi and Ji-eun assumed Sara would understand the importance of these social obligations. Both are surprised by Sara's strong reaction, which led to a tense and awkward atmosphere for the study session.

Practice Explaining How Cultural Norms, Expectations, and Circumstances Apply to Behavior and Mental Process

Complete the following activity.

1. Explain how the actor-observer bias applies in this scenario. Then suggest what Sara might have said to Kofi and Ji-eun that would have helped to make the study session more productive.

Locus of Control

Psychologist Julian Rotter proposed in 1954 that people actively seek pleasant outcomes and avoid unpleasant ones by engaging in specific behaviors. His early research indicated that behavior was influenced by social context and related factors, not just psychological factors. One of the factors he studied is **locus of control**, the perception of where control over life events resides. An **internal locus of control** is the belief that people have the ability to control their lives, their choices, and the world. They direct their life—life does not just happen—and they can influence people and situations. Such inner-driven individuals tend to have a high motivation level and an orientation to success. Those with a high internal locus of control are equipped with proactive ways to handle life's stressors, including the following:

- Engaging in activities that will improve their situation
- Striving for achievement—working hard to develop their own abilities, skills, and knowledge
- Being curious and wanting to find out why things happen the way they do
- Using current information to act in an effort to create positive outcomes

However, people with an internal locus of control are also more likely to blame themselves for circumstances beyond their control, a tendency that can be damaging.

In contrast, people with a high **external locus of control** believe that they have little or no control over their lives or over what people do. They often believe that life is a "function of chance, luck, or fate, is under the control of powerful others, or is simply unpredictable" (J. Rotter). These people tend to be pessimistic, passive, and accepting. These beliefs may lead to learned helplessness (see Topic 3.8) because the person with an external locus of control does not believe that their actions will have any impact on their environment.

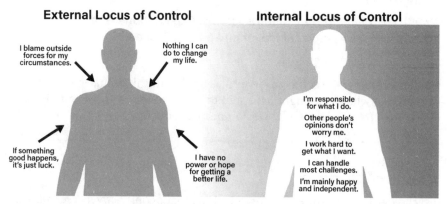

External Locus of Control

I blame outside forces for my circumstances.

Nothing I can do to change my life.

If something good happens, it's just luck.

I have no power or hope for getting a better life.

Internal Locus of Control

I'm responsible for what I do.

Other people's opinions don't worry me.

I work hard to get what I want.

I can handle most challenges.

I'm mainly happy and independent.

Figure 4.1.1

Person Perception

Imagine walking into a room where a heated discussion is underway. You notice one person speaking passionately, using grand gestures, while another listens quietly, nodding occasionally. Instantly, your brain starts to paint a picture of who these people might be: the speaker is bold and outgoing, maybe a bit aggressive, while the listener seems patient and thoughtful or maybe just shy.

This scenario highlights the process of **person perception**—our brain's ability to form impressions and make judgments about others based on limited information. Every day, whether we're watching strangers interact on a bus, choosing which posts to like on social media, or participating in classroom discussions, we are always evaluating and interpreting the world around us through this psychological lens.

These initial judgments and interpretations are not just passive observations. They actively shape our attitudes and behaviors toward ourselves and others. Three psychological concepts—the mere-exposure effect, self-fulfilling prophecy, and social comparison—illustrate how our perceptions can become a cycle of reinforcement, influencing how we think, feel, and even act, based on the impressions we form and the expectations we set.

The Mere-Exposure Effect

Imagine you hear a new song on the radio and you don't really like it at first. But after hearing it several more times during the week, it starts to grow on you, and soon it becomes one of your favorites. This is the **mere-exposure effect**, by which your preference for something increases the more you are exposed to it. In other words, people tend to develop a preference for things simply because they are familiar. The more we are exposed to a particular stimulus, such as a person, object, or idea, generally, the more favorable our attitude toward it becomes. This effect can manifest in various ways, from preferring certain brands or products to forming impressions about individuals based on repeated exposure. Advertisers use this effect to make consumers like their products by repeating commercials one after another or by establishing characters who appear repeatedly in commercials.

Person perception strongly shapes how we engage in social interactions and manage our relationships. When we see someone do something, our brain quickly tries to figure out why they did it. We might use shortcuts or heuristics (quick guesses—see Topic 2.2), or sometimes we even use stereotypes, which are predetermined ideas we have about certain groups of people. For example, if you see someone always wearing sports gear and spending time on the basketball court, you might think, "That person must love sports." That's an example of a mental shortcut that helps us navigate social landscapes more efficiently.

These quick guesses and ideas help us decide how to act and talk with others. If we perceive someone as approachable because they often smile, we're likely to respond warmly, smiling back and engaging positively. However, relying heavily on stereotypes and quick judgments can lead to misunderstandings and unfair treatment, underscoring the importance of thoughtful reflection on the reasons behind our perceptions and the actions they inspire.

Self-Fulfilling Prophecy

The term **self-fulfilling prophecy** refers to a psychological phenomenon in which an individual's belief or expectation about a situation or another person, positive or negative, influences their behavior in a way that causes those expectations to come true. For instance, consider a high school student who believes he is not good at math. This belief may cause the student to feel anxious about math classes or exams, leading to a lack of focus or avoidance of studying. Consequently, his performance in math may be poor, which in turn confirms his initial belief that he is not good at math. The student's belief influenced his behavior, leading to the expected outcome.

Similarly, a teacher who has high expectations for certain students may unknowingly provide those students with more attention and feedback, leading to improved performance from them. If a teacher believes that a student is not capable, they may not invest as much time or effort in that student, leading to poorer performance from the student. Whether we are focused on our own or someone else's behavior, beliefs and perceptions can shape our actions and the behaviors of others in a way that causes us to live up or down to our own or other people's expectations.

Social Comparison

Social comparison theory explores how individuals evaluate themselves by comparing their abilities, opinions, behavior, status, or attributes to those of others. Suppose, for example, you join a new sports team and notice that one of your teammates is really good at scoring goals. You start comparing your own skills to theirs and feel like you're not as talented. However, this comparison makes you practice more, and you eventually improve your skills significantly. This example of **social comparison** shows how comparing ourselves to others can affect our self-esteem and motivate us to change or improve.

Social comparisons can take one of two forms: upward social comparison and downward social comparison. **Upward social comparison** involves comparing oneself to others who are perceived as superior in some way, as the student athlete did in the example above. This comparison may lead to feelings of inadequacy and/or motivation for self-improvement. Social media often has this effect. If people post pictures on social media of their best moments, in picture-perfect scenes, they can create the illusion that they have an adventure-filled life. These impressions may cause people to feel bad about their own lives, even though social media portrays a highly filtered image of a life. Conversely, **downward social comparison** involves comparing oneself to others who are perceived as inferior in some respect, which may boost one's self-esteem. However, a downward social comparison could lead to anxiety because a person sees that they could be worse off.

People make social comparisons of wealth, status, appearance, and achievement. They often gauge their own success and happiness on how they stack up against others within their social circle. This comparison can shape individuals' perceptions of their own worth and influence their behaviors and aspirations.

Relative deprivation, a concept closely related to social comparison, refers to the feeling of dissatisfaction or resentment that arises when people perceive themselves as having less than they deserve compared to others. This perception of being deprived is often relative to the standards set by others in their social circles or society at large. People may feel relative deprivation even when their actual level of resources or achievements is abundant, highlighting the importance of social comparison in shaping subjective well-being.

THINK AS A PSYCHOLOGIST

Apply Psychological Perspectives, Theories, Concepts, and Research Findings to a Scenario (1.A.1) | Evaluate the Appropriate Use of Research Design Elements in Experimental Methodology (2.B.3) | Evaluate the Appropriate Use of Research Design Elements in Non-Experimental Methodologies (2.C.5) | Propose a Defensible Claim (4.A)

The following three studies were conducted by social psychologists investigating the same concept through very different scenarios.

Study 1: Researchers studied the development of affinity among students in a large college course. To do so, four women of similar appearance attended class sessions, posing as students in the course. The women did not talk to or interact with any of the other students. Each woman attended a different number (0, 5, 10, or 15) of class sessions. At the end of the term, students ($N = 130$) were shown slides of the women and asked to rate (using a Likert scale) the women's attractiveness and perceived similarity to them. The results showed that the woman who attended 15 class sessions was rated higher in perceived similarity and attraction than the women who attended fewer classes.

Study 2: Researchers designed a study in which participants were shown a series of Chinese characters (language symbols), some of which were presented more frequently than others. After three weeks, the subjects were shown the same set of characters again and asked to rate their preference for each character on a scale of 1 to 5. The results demonstrated that the participants consistently showed a higher preference for characters they had seen more frequently, even though they could not identify which characters they had seen the most in the first part of the study.

Study 3: College students volunteered for a study in which they were paired with another student of the same sex. The students did not know each other previously. The pairs were then randomly assigned to groups. One group was assigned to chat by email with their partner one time per week, another group four times per week, and the last group was assigned to chat by email with their partner eight times per week. The results showed that the more interactions the students had, the more they reported liking their partner and the more they were interested in staying in contact with their partner after the study concluded.

Practice Applying Concepts and Evaluating Research Design Elements

Answer the following questions and complete the activities.

1. The three studies above are investigating which of the following concepts?

   (A) Internal locus of control

   (B) Self-serving bias

   (C) Mere-exposure effect

   (D) Fundamental attribution error

2. Study 3 utilizes experimental methodology. Identify the independent variable in that study.

3. In Study 2, did the researchers use a qualitative or quantitative measure? Explain your reasoning.

4. Based on the findings in all three studies, make a defensible claim about research on this psychological phenomenon.

REFLECT ON THE ESSENTIAL QUESTION

Essential Question: *How do attribution theory, locus of control, and person perception apply to behavior and mental processes?* Using the Key Terms, complete a chart like the one below to gather details to help answer that question.

Concept or Theory	Behavior	Mental Processes
Attribution Theory		
Locus of Control		
Person Perception		

KEY TERMS

actor/observer bias
attribution
attribution theory
dispositional attribution
downward social
   comparison
explanatory style
external locus of control

fundamental attribution
   error
internal locus of control
locus of control
mere-exposure effect
optimistic explanatory style
person perception

pessimistic explanatory
   style
relative deprivation
self-fulfilling prophecy
self-serving bias
situational attribution
social comparison
upward social comparison

MULTIPLE-CHOICE QUESTIONS

1. Ethan is a wrestler on the high school team. He just finished wrestling in the conference meet, and things did not go well. His coach knows that Ethan has been dealing with many family issues lately and that his mind was not likely in the place it needed to be to wrestle well. Which of the following most accurately represents the coach's interpretation of this scenario?

   (A) Self-serving bias

   (B) Situational attribution

   (C) Actor-observer bias

   (D) Fundamental attribution error

2. Joyce has a writing teacher who encourages all her students to do their best every day. She often reminds them that they can all become the best scholarly version of themselves. At the end of the year, the teacher publishes pieces of all the students' work, and Joyce is amazed at not only her own writing ability but also that of the others in her class. The students' improvement throughout the year may have been due to which of the following?

(A) Social comparison

(B) Stable attribution

(C) Explanatory style

(D) Self-fulfilling prophecy

3. Larry's friend Isaac was in a car accident a few weeks ago. Larry claimed that Isaac was a terrible driver and an accident was destined to happen sooner or later. This week, Larry got into an accident himself but claimed that the roads were icy and the person in front of him suddenly applied their brakes. Which type of attribution best explains this situation?

(A) Actor-observer bias

(B) Pessimistic explanatory style

(C) Upward social comparison

(D) External locus of control

4. Lauren spends much time on social media and sees the posts of many of her friends and acquaintances in beautiful clothes and traveling to exotic locations. Lauren begins to feel that her life is boring and that she does not have any of these thrilling opportunities. Which social psychology phenomenon best explains how Lauren is feeling?

(A) Downward social comparison

(B) Self-serving bias

(C) Relative deprivation

(D) Stable attribution

Questions 5 through 7 refer to the following.

Ishika is taking the most demanding math class at her high school. She is struggling with some of the more challenging problems but believes that she can work hard and improve her grades. She creates a study group of students who get together three times a week to practice problems and review concepts from the class.

5. Which of the following does Ishika most clearly demonstrate in this scenario?

(A) Pessimistic explanatory style

(B) Internal locus of control

(C) Upward social comparison

(D) Mere exposure effect

6. The following data set represents the percentage grades for students in Ishika's study group on the first exam of the year and on the most recent exam (Test #4) after the study group had met for two weeks. The range of scores for Test #1 is 28. What is the range of scores for Test #4? r

Student	Test #1	Test #4
#1	62	78
#2	53	64
#3	77	81
#4	81	82
#5	59	67

(A) 18

(B) 15

(C) 14

(D) 78

7. Ishika plotted out the times the students spent studying and the improvement in their grades, which is seen in the figure below. What conclusion can be made from this data?

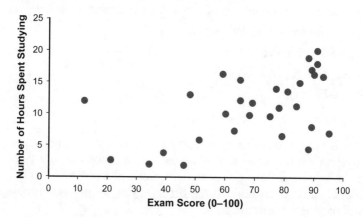

(A) There is a strong positive correlation between hours spent studying and exam scores.

(B) There is no correlation between hours spent studying and exam scores.

(C) There is a slight positive correlation between hours spent studying and exam scores.

(D) There is a slight negative correlation between hours spent studying and exam scores.

Topic 4.2

Attitude Formation and Attitude Change

"No one is born hating another person because of the color of his skin, or his background, or his religion . . . . If they can learn to hate, they can be taught to love . . . ."

—Nelson Mandela

Essential Question: How do stereotypes and implicit attitudes contribute to the behaviors and mental processes of prejudice and discrimination? How do belief perseverance and cognitive dissonance affect attitude formation and change?

How do you feel about the field of psychology? How do you feel about the person who sits to your right in your psychology class? To your left? How do you feel about your psychology teacher? All of these questions relate to attitudes. Attitudes are formed about everything we encounter—a presidential candidate, Niagara Falls, global warming, or even something as seemingly insignificant as the color green. Positive, negative, or neutral attitudes may arise toward any of these objects; we cannot help but feel and think *something* about them. Attitudes represent how you feel and what you think about objects, people, events, or issues.

Kurt Lewin, often called "the father of social psychology," thought that attitude was social psychology's most indispensable concept. Lewin and other social psychologists in the mid-1900s agreed that the three components of attitudes are (1) affects (feelings), (2) cognitions (thoughts), and (3) behaviors. These are sometimes referred to as the ABCs of psychology. However, while Lewin originally thought that attitudes closely predicted behaviors, later research showed that affects, cognitions, and behaviors are just parts within attitudes. Contemporary research proposes that attitudes do not necessarily predict behaviors.

In 1934, a classic study by Richard LaPierre, as well as later research it inspired, revealed the role of prejudice in attitudes. During a time of stark racism toward Asians, LaPierre traveled around the United States with a married couple of Chinese descent. Among 184 restaurants they visited, they were refused service by only one. Six months later, LaPierre wrote back to all 184 restaurants, asking them if they served Asian individuals. Owners of 129 restaurants replied, and 117, a full 91 percent, said they would never serve Asians. Of course, LaPierre knew that all but one restaurant had indeed served Asian customers just six months earlier. Because social norms change, people today sometimes claim to have no bias against a certain group, but their behaviors sometimes show otherwise.

Prejudice is one of the more troubling attitudes that people can hold. Social psychologists have found that two concepts, stereotypes and implicit attitudes, contribute to prejudice that may lead to discrimination.

Stereotypes

Stereotypes are generalized attitudes about a group of people—African Americans, women, gay people, transgender people, Whites, Asians, people with disabilities—based only on their membership in a group, not on any individual characteristics. These attitudes are often false or contain only an element of truth. Often, stereotypes serve the purpose of controlling or putting down the stereotyped group. For example, in the days of slavery, cotton plantation owners would call those they enslaved "lazy" because the owners wanted to make more money and wanted to give the enslaved workers a reason to feel they had to work harder.

Sometimes, however, stereotypes can contain an element of truth. For example, White Americans may see Asians as being quiet and passive. Many Asians *may* be quiet and passive, and on average, Asians may be quieter than other ethnic groups. However, *all* Asians are not quiet and passive. This form of stereotype either demands that all members of a group fit the image (there is no allowance for individual variation within the group) or exaggerates the differences among groups. There is always much diversity within a given group, and stereotypes do not account for these differences.

While often criticized for their oversimplification and potential to perpetuate bias, stereotypes can serve as cognitive shortcuts that streamline the decision-making process. They can lessen **cognitive load**—the amount of mental effort required to process information and make decisions—especially in situations in which people are faced with complex information or when time is limited. For example, imagine you are a college student in the United States attending an international student event on campus. You meet someone from Japan and, based on stereotypes as described above, you might expect them to be polite, reserved, and respectful. This understanding can help you adjust your behavior; maybe you bow slightly as a greeting or are more careful with personal space. In this case, the stereotype simplifies the interaction, allowing you to make a good first impression by respecting cultural norms.

However, this expectation might not apply to every individual from Japan. If the person is more outgoing or casual, the reliance on stereotypes could lead to awkwardness or misinterpretation. So, while stereotypes can provide a shortcut for determining how to act in certain situations, they can also lead to inaccurate or unfair assessments, and they overlook individual differences.

Stereotypes shape biased perceptions and experiences and often serve as the foundation for prejudiced attitudes and discriminatory behaviors. For example, consider a hiring manager at a tech company in California. A number of candidates have applied for a software engineering position. Among them is a candidate from India. A stereotype might suggest that candidates from India are highly skilled in software engineering and technology because of the country's reputation for producing IT professionals. This assumption could lead the manager to prioritize the Indian candidate over others, easing the decision-making process.

However, such stereotypes could lead to overlooking other qualified candidates or making assumptions about the Indian candidate's expertise based on nationality rather than individual skills. The result could be a biased and discriminatory selection process in which the hiring manager fails to see the unique qualities of other candidates, shutting down their opportunities.

Stereotypes not only shape perceptions of others but also influence self-perceptions and behaviors, since individuals may internalize negative stereotypes that lead to decreased performance. For example, a girl who internalizes the stereotype that boys are better at math and science than girls may avoid studying math and science and, therefore, receive lower grades in those subjects, creating a self-fulfilling prophecy.

Moreover, as the hiring manager at the tech company shows, stereotypes can fuel discriminatory behaviors, such as racial profiling by law enforcement and unequal treatment in healthcare, educational, and financial settings. Discriminatory behaviors in these areas can perpetuate inequalities.

THINK AS A PSYCHOLOGIST

Explain How Cognitive Biases Such as Confirmation Bias, Hindsight Bias, and Overconfidence Apply to a Scenario (1.B.2)

Stereotypes are persistent. Studies have shown that even when people try to overcome them, stereotypes continue to intrude. A recent study[1] looked at the neurocognitive science behind that persistence.

Underlying that science is a theory put forward by Donald Hebb that is often summarized by the sentence, "Neurons that fire together wire together." For example, if you see a drug dealer in a TV show who happens to be Hispanic, two neurons might fire at once—one for Hispanic (cell A) and one for drug dealer (cell B). If they fire at about the same time, their synaptic connection is established. Then, if you see a Hispanic person on the street, both cell A and cell B will fire, not only maintaining but further reinforcing the association, even if there is no evidence that this person is involved with any type of criminal activity.

1 Cox, W. T. L., Xie, X., & Devine, P. G. (2022, September). Untested assumptions perpetuate stereotyping: Learning in the absence of evidence. *Journal of Experimental Social Psychology*, *102*:104380. doi: 10.1016/j.jesp.2022.104380. Epub 2022 Jun 25. PMID: 35912164; PMCID: PMC9337700.

In the neurocognitive study on the persistence of stereotypes, undergraduates who volunteered and were almost all female and straight had to determine whether a male was gay or straight based on social media profiles (which were fictional, though the participants did not know that). The profiles listed some interests that could be equally relevant to both gay and straight men as well as some that are more stereotypically associated with one or the other. The raters received some training in the task and were randomly placed in three groups: one that received feedback confirming their selections, one that received feedback disconfirming their selections, and a third group that received no feedback. The raters were told that the profiles were about evenly divided between gay and straight men. Over time, the raters who received confirming feedback selected an even higher percentage of profiles as gay. Raters who were told their selections were incorrect still chose more profiles as gay, but not as many more as the first group. Raters who received no feedback selected a higher percentage of profiles as gay than those who were told their selections were incorrect.

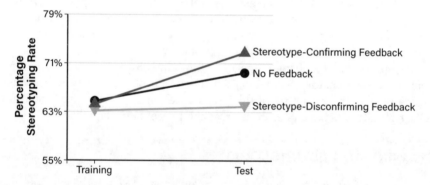

Practice Explaining How Cognitive Biases Such as Confirmation Bias, Hindsight Bias, and Overconfidence Bias Apply to a Scenario (1.B.2)

Answer the following questions.

1. All participants rated about 65% of the profiles as gay. Considering the directions the raters were given, what can you conclude about their preexisting stereotypes?

2. Apply the idea "When neurons fire together they wire together" to the results of the group who received confirming feedback. What role does confirmation bias play in this study?

3. How might the reward system in the brain have played a part in the results of the group receiving confirming feedback? What role does overconfidence bias play in this study?

4. What might explain why the group who received no feedback continued to increase their identification of gay profiles?

Prejudice and Discrimination

Stereotypes can serve as the cause of biased perceptions and experiences and result in prejudiced attitudes and discriminatory behavior. **Prejudice** is an attitude founded on unjustified, usually negative judgments, evaluations, or beliefs about a group of people based on their membership in the group. Prejudice usually involves bias or stereotypes. For example, some people may hold prejudiced views about teenagers and may assume that teenagers engage in more criminal acts or behave "wildly," even if these assumptions are unfounded.

While prejudice is an *attitude,* **discrimination** is negative *behavior* toward members of a target group based on their race, ethnicity, or other shared characteristic. Stereotypes and prejudices occur strictly in your head. Even though they may be negative perceptions, they don't directly hurt others. Because discrimination involves behavior toward others, however, it does or can hurt people. You might have a stereotype about mathletes (they study a lot), and you might have a prejudice against mathletes (you resent them), but your attitudes and feelings don't hurt them until you call them names, hit them, steal their notebooks, exclude them from activities, and bully them online. These negative behaviors discriminate against them.

Why is it important for us to know about the effects of negative categorization and discrimination? If you have ever been called a name or been discriminated against because of your membership in a group, you know it doesn't feel good. But the effects of discrimination go beyond feelings. Discrimination can lower a person's self-esteem and create stress that leads to mental and physical health problems for both adults and children.

THINK AS A PSYCHOLOGIST

Provide Reasoning That Is Grounded in Scientifically Derived Evidence to Support, Refute, or Modify an Established or Provided Claim, Policy, or Norm (4.B.1) | Determine the Type of Research Design(s) Used in a Given Study (2.A.1.b)

The following is an abstract of a study[2] that explored the extent to which workplace hiring discrimination has changed over time in the United States.

Abstract

This study investigates changes over time in the level of hiring discrimination in U.S. labor markets. We reviewed the results of every available field experiment ($n = 28$) of hiring discrimination against African Americans or Latinos. Together, these studies represent 55,842 applications submitted for 26,326 positions. We focused on trends since 1989 ($n = 24$ studies), when field experiments became more common and improved methodologically. Since 1989, whites receive, on

2 Quillian, L., Pager, Hexel, D., & Midtbøen, A. H. (2017). Meta-analysis of field experiments shows no change in racial discrimination in hiring over time. *Proceedings of the National Academy of Sciences, 114*(41), 10870–10875, doi:10.1073/pnas.1706255114

average, 36 percent more callbacks than African Americans and 24 percent more callbacks than Latinos. We observed no change in the level of hiring discrimination against African Americans over the past 25 years, although we find modest evidence of a decline in discrimination against Latinos. Accounting for applicant education, applicant gender, study method, occupational groups, and local labor market conditions does little to alter this result. Contrary to claims of declining discrimination in American society, our estimates suggest that levels of discrimination remain largely unchanged, at least at [hiring].

Practice Providing Evidence and Determining Research Method

Complete the following activities and answer the question.

1. Many people continue to claim that workplace discrimination is a thing of the past and rarely occurs in American society today. Using the abstract above, provide one piece of evidence to refute this claim.

2. Which research method was used to conduct the above study? Explain your answer.

Implicit Attitudes

Stereotypes, discrimination, and prejudice are often at the surface of our awareness. **Implicit attitudes**, in contrast, are *unconscious* evaluations of our biases toward certain objects, groups, or individuals. Unlike explicit attitudes, which are consciously held and easily expressed, implicit attitudes operate at an unconscious level and may not align with a person's stated beliefs. Research has revealed that implicit attitudes tend to lead to negative evaluations of others. For instance, the Implicit Association Test (IAT), a widely used measure of implicit attitudes, has consistently demonstrated that people show implicit biases toward certain social groups, such as racial minorities or communities marginalized for their ethnic background or gender expression.

Research using the IAT has shown that people tend to associate certain racial or ethnic groups with negative stereotypes, such as aggression or incompetence, even when those people explicitly reject such stereotypes. This discrepancy between explicit beliefs and implicit biases shows the variety of forces in play when people evaluate others.

Implicit attitudes can have real-world consequences. They can lead to discriminatory behaviors in hiring, housing, education, and criminal justice systems. Studies have shown that job applicants with stereotypically African American names are less likely to be called for interviews than those with stereotypically White names, indicating the impact of implicit biases on employment. These biases are implicit because those doing the hiring believe that they are honestly evaluating the candidates without consideration of race. Similarly, implicit biases among healthcare providers have been linked to unequal medical treatment and differing patient outcomes, with minority patients often receiving lower-quality care than their White counterparts.

The Just-World Phenomenon

The leaning toward negative implicit attitudes is apparent in the **just-world phenomenon**, the tendency to see the world as fundamentally fair and to believe that people get what they deserve based on their actions and behavior. Through this viewpoint, people see victims as having "asked for it" or "deserved what they got." For example, if someone believes that people experiencing poverty are lazy or unmotivated, they may implicitly evaluate them negatively, attributing their financial struggles to personal failings rather than economic barriers or social inequalities. In the same way, victims of discrimination may be implicitly judged as somehow deserving of their fate if they appear to be deviating from societal norms or expectations. This tendency to blame the victim and attribute negative outcomes to personal characteristics rather than external factors reflects the influence of the just-world phenomenon on implicit attitudes.

In-Group Bias and Out-Group Homogeneity Bias

A number of studies have shown many kinds of prejudice are strongly tied to in-group or out-group membership. An in-group is a group with which one identifies; an out-group is a group with which one feels no identification. These identifications are often described as an "us" versus "them" mentality.

While prejudice is a negative feeling toward an out-group, it is also a result of a strong **in-group bias**, reserving positive feelings such as admiration and trust, only for other members of the in-group. This bias can show in implicit attitudes, leading people to unconsciously hold more positive evaluations of in-group members than out-group members. For example, research has shown that people may implicitly associate their own racial or cultural group with positive attributes, such as intelligence or trustworthiness, while implicitly associating out-groups with negative stereotypes or traits. This bias can influence various aspects of social behavior, including decision-making, resource allocation, and interpersonal interactions, contributing to in-group favoritism and out-group discrimination. Following are some examples:

- Decision-making: When Anna, the president of the student council, selects members for a new committee, she tends to choose her friends— like Raffy and Sara—because they share similar interests and get along well. This leaves out other students like Rachel, who might bring fresh ideas but isn't part of Anna's circle.
- Resource allocation: Coach Arlington, who coaches the soccer team, favors players he knows from previous seasons, like Marcus and Jenna. When new students Tom and Lucy join the team, they find it hard to get opportunities to play because they're not part of the familiar in-group.
- Interpersonal interactions: There's a popular clique at school led by Chelsea and Brandon. They always sit together at lunch and rarely invite others to join them. Noah and Grace, who are outside this group, are having a hard time finding friends or fitting in.

Out-group homogeneity bias is a phenomenon in which people see members of an out-group as more similar to each other than members of their own in-group. For example, if you are a member of the school band, you might think that members of school sports teams are all alike, but members of the band—your group—are diverse and interesting individuals. This bias can contribute to negative implicit attitudes toward out-group members, who may be seen as lacking diversity or individuality. If people hold negative implicit attitudes toward a certain ethnic or religious out-group, they may perceive all members of that group as sharing similar characteristics or behaviors, such as being aggressive or untrustworthy. This oversimplification and generalization of out-group members can reinforce stereotypes and prejudice and lead to discrimination. Out-group homogeneity bias fosters a sense of "us versus them" and worsens feelings of social distance and distrust between groups.

Ethnocentrism

While in-group/out-group bias often operates at the level of relatively small social circles (those with whom we have direct contact), **ethnocentrism**—judging other cultures based only on the values and characteristics of one's own culture—operates on larger social and cultural levels. William Sumner coined the term (1906), which reflects the idea that one's own culture is the center of everything and all other cultures are seen only in relation to the central culture. Ethnocentrism can lead to negative implicit attitudes toward cultures other than one's own. People in Western cultures, for example, generally judge arranged marriages as oppressive because they limit personal choice, something Westerners value. People in cultures in which arranged marriages are common may find choice undesirable, and arranged marriages may present a favorable, orderly way to make a match and strengthen social and familial bonds.

THINK AS A PSYCHOLOGIST

Evaluate the Appropriate Use of Research Design Elements in Non-Experimental Methodologies (2.C.5) | Calculate Measures of Central Tendency in a Given Data Set (3.B.1) | Identify Psychology-Related Concepts in Representations of Data (3.A.2)

A sports psychologist wanted to investigate how members of two different basketball teams (each with ten players) viewed each other. The two teams practiced against each other over the course of a week, and then the researcher asked them to fill out surveys about how they viewed their own teammates and how they viewed members of the other team. The questions explored how similar, likable, and unique athletes believed members of their team were. The researcher then had the athletes complete the same ratings for the opposing team. Each athlete answered the questions using a Likert scale from 1–7 (1 indicates "extremely dissimilar to me" and 7 indicates "extremely similar to me"). Researchers calculated a composite score that averaged how the athletes scored their own team vs. the opposing team. The table below represents data from the ten members of one of the teams.

Rating of Teammates	Ratings of the Opposing Team
6.3	3.7
6.8	4.8
6.2	5.4
6.9	4.9
7	2.8
5.5	1.9
4.8	6.2
6.2	4.7
5.1	5.9
6.2	3.8

Practice Foundational Research and Statistics Skills

Complete the following activities and choose the correct answer.

1. Is the researcher in this study using quantitative or qualitative methods? Explain your answer.

2. Based on the data presented in the table, identify each measure of central tendency for the "Rating of Teammates" data.

3. The data presented in the table most clearly support which of the following?

   (A) In-group bias

   (B) Ethnocentrism

   (C) The just-world phenomenon

   (D) Discrimination

Developing and Changing Attitudes

We know that an attitude represents how we feel and think about objects, people, events, or issues. And we know that attitudes can shape our perceptions and behavior. But how do attitudes form, and how do they change?

Attitude formation is influenced by a variety of forces. Your attitudes develop as a result of direct interactions with others and personal experiences. Your family, peers, and cultural norms also shape your attitudes through socialization and observation. Knowledge you gain in school or from the media also shapes beliefs and attitudes. Emotions play a role as well, especially feelings tied to specific events or stimuli. Your attitudes are also influenced by reasoning, logic, and personal beliefs. Sometimes, reasoning and logic can persuade you to change your attitudes, but some attitudes are hard to give up.

Belief Perseverance

Belief perseverance is the cognitive bias that causes people to cling to their initial beliefs even after the basis for them has been discredited or disproved. In some respects, belief perseverance is a form of denial. For example, if you support a certain political candidate and find out that she has been accepting illegal bribes, you may initially be inclined to believe that this must be an attempt by the opposition to discredit her. It is easier to believe this than to accept that your beliefs in supporting the candidate were misplaced. For the same reason, studies have shown that jurors' evaluations of eyewitness testimony are unaffected even when the evidence is discredited. The findings suggest that jurors have difficulty disregarding initial testimonies even after they are retracted or proven unreliable.

Underlying the experience of belief perseverance may be **confirmation bias**, which is the tendency to search for information that supports our preconceptions and to ignore or distort contradictory evidence. These processes happen at an unconscious level, but we are drawn to pay more attention to information that seems to indicate that our original beliefs were correct. "You hear what you want to hear" is a common phrase describing this bias. Our confirmation bias is at work when we are in love and ignore all the negatives about our potential life mate. We tend to see all the things we love about this person and none of the red flags that might have doomed the relationship from the start. It is at work when we see others through the filter of stereotypes and prejudice. It is at work when we accept information that justifies or confirms our bias and ignore or reject information that counters our belief. Confirmation bias is one of the ways we delude ourselves (or, more bluntly, lie to ourselves) to stay within our comfort zone. (See Practices 2.B and 2.C for information on confirmation bias in research.)

Cognitive Dissonance

Clinging to attitudes despite new evidence refuting them causes an uncomfortable feeling. Psychiatrist Frantz Fanon wrote, "Sometimes people hold a core belief that is very strong. When they are presented with evidence that works against that belief, the new evidence cannot be accepted. It would create a feeling that is extremely uncomfortable. That uncomfortable feeling is called **cognitive dissonance**. And because it is so important to protect the core belief, they will rationalize, ignore, and even deny anything that doesn't fit in with the core belief." This cognitive disconnect is common and comes into play every time we rationalize—that is, find a seemingly reasonable but actually false explanation for the evidence presented. We may even flat-out deny the evidence. If a core belief has become a part of an individual's identity, then that identity is threatened by a challenge to that belief, and rationalizing is a common defense.

Cognitive dissonance is at work whenever we need to justify our struggles in an endeavor. Psychologist Leon Festinger said that people tend to love the things for which they have to work more. Imagine two soldiers, one a volunteer, one a draftee. Both are experiencing the pains of basic training or being a soldier in a war zone. The draftee can easily justify his dislike of the experience—he had no choice in the matter. The volunteer must justify to themselves why they chose to be in such a dangerous and stressful situation. The explanation will often involve a statement about the importance of being a soldier or being in the military. The belief that "the harder we have to work for something, the more we love it" is known as *effort justification.* If we do not put much effort into a decision or belief, then we are not threatened if or when it does not work out. We must justify to ourselves that the result is worth the effort, whether we are involved in the military, sororities or fraternities, or even relationships.

Festinger introduced the theory of cognitive dissonance in 1957. He also noted that cognitive dissonance occurs when we act in a way that conflicts with our beliefs and feel guilt or tension as a result. To reduce the discomfort, we might change either our actions or beliefs so the two positions align. For example, someone exaggerating qualifications on a résumé might feel cognitive dissonance about lying. That person could resolve the dissonance by removing the exaggerations from the résumé or by concluding that "everybody does it anyway" and stop feeling guilty.

To demonstrate support for his theory, Festinger had research participants engage in a boring task, such as turning a set of wooden knobs a quarter turn over and over for an hour or transferring a jar of BBs with a pair of tweezers to another jar one by one. After this task, the experimenter asked the participants to tell a person in the waiting room (who was actually a confederate working with the researcher) that the task was very interesting. For their trouble, the researcher offered the participant either $1 or $20 to lie to the confederate. Who do you think reported feeling that the task was more interesting? Believe it or not, when asked later how interesting the experiment really was, the group that was paid only $1 changed their minds about the experiment more than the group that was paid $20. In order to believe they really did not lie to the confederates, they had to change their minds about the experiment and feel that it really was interesting. The participants who were given $20 to lie to the confederates still felt that the study was not very interesting. At the end of the study, Festinger told the participants that giving them either $1 or $20 was part of the study. He asked all of them to give the money back, and all of them did.

Numerous studies have been conducted since Festinger's original study. Most have concluded that, while psychologists originally thought that attitudes "caused" behaviors and people needed to change their attitudes in order to adopt positive behaviors, the more effective way to handle cognitive dissonance is to first change the behavior, and attitude change will follow.

Stages of Cognitive Dissonance Relief

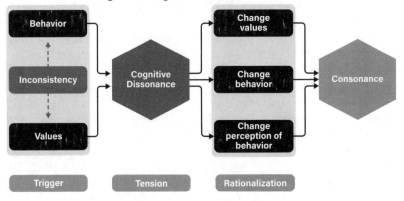

Figure 4.2.1 The inconsistency between behavior and values triggers cognitive dissonance. Rationalization is a way of relieving this tension: changing values, changing the behavior, or changing the perception of the behavior helps to reduce the dissonance.

REFLECT ON THE ESSENTIAL QUESTIONS

Essential Questions: *How do stereotypes and implicit attitudes contribute to the behaviors and mental processes of prejudice and discrimination? How do belief perseverance and cognitive dissonance affect attitude formation and change?* Using the Key Terms, complete a chart like the one below to gather details to help answer the questions.

Concept or Theory	Behavior	Mental Processes
Stereotypes		
Implicit attitudes		
Belief perseverance		
Cognitive dissonance		

KEY TERMS

attitude formation
belief perseverance
cognitive dissonance
confirmation bias
discrimination

ethnocentrism
implicit attitudes
in-group bias
just-world phenomenon

out-group homogeneity bias
prejudice
stereotypes

1. Marilyn believes that women are more nurturing and empathetic than men. As a result, she never hires any males to care for her three children, even though a number of qualified candidates have applied over the years. The fact that Marilyn intentionally refuses to hire males is most clearly an example of which of the following?

   (A) Prejudice

   (B) Discrimination

   (C) In-group bias

   (D) Implicit attitudes

2. Harold believes that the United States is the best country in the world and is always looking for evidence to demonstrate his point. His ethnocentric beliefs and behaviors most clearly represent which of the following?

   (A) Hindsight bias

   (B) Overconfidence

   (C) Belief perseverance

   (D) Confirmation bias

Questions 3 through 5 refer to the following.

Dr. Loren is researching cognitive dissonance. He requires his students to answer a survey about their political beliefs and the candidates they plan to support in an upcoming election. For his sample, he selects participants who indicated in the survey that they would NOT support a well-known national candidate who has been accused of embezzling money. Dr. Loren then randomly assigns the participants to one of two groups. In the first group, participants watched campaign commercials and read articles supporting that candidate. In the second group, participants read about the importance of volunteering to help that candidate's campaign, and then they spent three hours making phone calls encouraging voters to support the candidate.

3. Dr. Loren finds that the group who volunteered reported more cognitive dissonance than the group who read articles and watched commercials. Based on your understanding of cognitive dissonance, why did this likely occur?

   (A) Because the group that read and watched campaign commercials was acting in ways that were consistent with their beliefs

   (B) Because the group that made calls had to justify actions that did not align with their beliefs

(C) Because the group that made calls encouraging voters to support the candidate was not experiencing any tension or discomfort

(D) Because the group that read articles and watched commercials was unable to justify the time they spent reading about a candidate that they strongly opposed

4. Dr. Loren's research is best characterized as which of the following?

(A) Correlational

(B) Case study

(C) Experimental

(D) Naturalistic observation

5. An IRB would be unlikely to approve of Dr. Loren's research, based on which of the following?

(A) The professor is requiring that his students participate in the study.

(B) It is not appropriate to involve political views in research.

(C) There is too great a chance that participants will be harmed in the study.

(D) This study involves more deception than is allowed in a research design.

6. Jurgen went hunting in Africa and hired a guide to help him illegally hunt elephants for their ivory tusks. During the hunt, as they were tracking the elephant, Jurgen was trampled and seriously injured. He found that people were not very sympathetic to his injuries. What phenomenon best explains their response?

(A) Implicit attitude

(B) Just-world phenomenon

(C) Ethnocentrism

(D) In-group bias

7. Caitlin has long believed that her younger sister is not a very good soccer player. She recently attended one of her sister's games, and her sister scored four of the five goals in the game. Later in the season, her sister was named the most valuable player on the team. Despite these accolades, Caitlin continues to believe that her sister is not very good. What is Caitlin experiencing?

(A) Hindsight bias

(B) Self-fulling prophecy

(C) Belief perseverance

(D) Stereotyping

Topic 4.3

Psychology of Social Situations

"If you put good apples into a bad situation, you'll get bad apples."
—Philip Zimbardo

Essential Question: How do social situations, being in a group, and prosocial behavior affect behavior and mental processes?

In addition to social cognition and attitudes, social psychology also studies social influence—how we are influenced by others in a social situation. Think back to the group dancing in the gym at the beginning of this unit. Perhaps one or two people in Yolanda's group did not really want to dance, but they went along with the dance lessons, partly because they did not want to stand out but also because learning dance moves is often more fun with others. For one thing, there's safety in numbers—more people will make mistakes, so a person's individual mistake will not stand out.

Social influence might encourage people to find safety in numbers.

A third aspect of social psychology is social behavior—how we behave in social situations. Getting up to dance in Yolanda's group when you did not really want to is an example of *social influence*, while actually dancing in Yolanda's group is *social behavior*. The public display of affection between Janice and Pedro is also social behavior, performed to let others know that they are a couple. Rick also exhibits social behavior by being the center of attention in his group, telling jokes and entertaining his friends. Football players talking and laughing about their last game is also an example of social behavior.

The football players' behavior is actually a good illustration of a fundamental tenet of social psychology: the **social situation** influences, or even controls, behavior. On the football field, football players are expected to behave aggressively toward the other team to win the game. A defensive lineman runs over the player in front of him, anyone on defense tackles an opposing player with the ball, and offensive players elude defensive players, to name only a few behaviors both expected and accepted in a football game. However, though it's fine to *talk* about a game, obviously the actual football game behaviors would be inappropriate at a school dance. The social situation determines behavior.

Social Influences and Persuasion

Most social influence is good, helping people behave in ways that are acceptable within a culture. Have you ever visited another country and not known how to behave in a manner considered to be polite? For example, in the United States, we are taught as children to eat quietly, without mouth noises and with our mouths closed while eating. However, if you are eating noodles in Japan, it's polite to slurp the noodles noisily with gusto to show your appreciation. Eating your noodles quietly might suggest you didn't like them and might insult your host. Another norm in Japanese society is giving compliments three times because your host will refuse to accept your compliments the first two times. If you don't express the third compliment, you are considered impolite and insincere.

These examples provide insight into the concept of **social norms**, shared expectations and rules that guide behavior within a society or group. These norms are unwritten, but understood, codes of conduct that dictate how individuals should act in various situations. Social norms encompass the expectations placed on individuals, depending on their social positions or roles within a community or social structure, such as those of a parent, teacher, friend, or citizen. These roles come with specific societal expectations that dictate appropriate behavior, influencing how individuals interact with one another and conform to group standards. By adhering to social norms, individuals help maintain order and cohesion within their social environments. These behaviors also demonstrate respect for the culture or group.

Individualism, Collectivism, and Multiculturalism

In broad terms, how individuals behave in relation to the groups they belong to is largely governed by their cultural norms. In the United States, for example, as well as Australia, New Zealand, and the countries of Western Europe, **individualism** is the cultural norm. In these and other individualistic cultures, people place a high value on individuals over groups. They have a strong appreciation and need for autonomy, independence, and uniqueness, believing that individuals should be free to pursue their goals and make their own choices about how to achieve them. Competitiveness, hierarchy, social class, and independence are especially important. The individual is the focus and the group remains in the background. Norms in individualistic cultures tend to make equity a priority.

In contrast, people who live in cultures that value **collectivism** focus on the group to a great extent. The primary focus in collectivistic cultures is relationships, and individual needs remain in the background. Collectivistic cultural norms tend to focus on equality and cooperation.

Family structures differ, depending on the degree of collectivism or individualism in a culture. Collectivistic cultures emphasize extended family systems, whereas individualistic cultures emphasize the nuclear family system. Additionally, families that allow for easy separation among individuals promote individualism, and individualistic cultures more frequently have people who live farther away from and have less frequent contact with grandparents, aunts and uncles, and cousins.

Not all collectivistic cultures are the same, however, and individualistic cultures also vary. For example, India is a collectivistic culture that emphasizes conforming to approved beliefs and behaviors, in-group cohesion, tolerance for authoritarianism, submission to authority, and acceptance of hierarchy and social strata. Japan's collectivistic culture, in contrast, emphasizes cooperation and empathy.

A third cultural option, in addition to collectivism and individualism, is multiculturalism. **Multiculturalism**, the coexistence and acceptance of multiple cultural traditions within a society, influences how individuals perceive themselves and interact with others. Exposure to diverse cultures fosters a broader understanding and appreciation of different perspectives, lifestyles, and values, which can enrich one's worldview and increase the flexibility of one's thinking. People living in a multicultural environment often develop a more nuanced sense of identity that incorporates elements from various cultures around them. This multicultural identity can enhance empathy, tolerance, and open-mindedness toward others, reducing prejudice and stereotyping. How individuals see themselves in relationship to the larger group can vary widely. They may see themselves as independent individuals, as integral parts of one or more cultural groups, or somewhere in between, depending on the context and their personal experiences.

The concept of social norms implies that individuals' thoughts, feelings, and behaviors can be shaped by the social context. **Social influence theory** proposes that people tend to do what they perceive to be the norm and studies the mechanisms through which this influence occurs. Central to this theory are two primary types of social influence: normative and informational.

Normative versus Informational Social Influence

Normative influence stems from the human desire to fit in and be accepted by others, leading individuals to conform to the expectations and norms of their social group to avoid rejection or disapproval. It's about adhering to the group's standards to gain social acceptance and avoid standing out negatively.

Normative influence is at work when teenagers conform to group behavior even if they do not always agree with it. They are doing so to fit in with the group. For example, suppose a few popular students start wearing a new brand of sneakers. At first only these trendsetters wear them, but as more students notice that those wearing the new sneakers gain social approval and possibly admiration, the trend begins to catch on. Other students may start wearing these sneakers, not necessarily because they personally prefer them or find them more functional than other shoes, but because they recognize a pattern: wearing these sneakers is associated with a higher social status within the school. The desire to fit in, be accepted, or even elevate their social standing leads more students to conform to this emerging trend.

The normative influence is evident as students change their behavior (in this case, their choice of footwear) to align with the norms established by a subgroup within their peer community. They are motivated by the approval and acceptance of their peers, rather than by their own personal preference for the sneakers.

In contrast, **informational influence** arises from the desire to make correct decisions and interpret ambiguous situations accurately, leading individuals to look to the behavior and opinions of others as a source of information. For example, consider the problem of trying to make four triangles out of six toothpicks and some rubber bands without breaking the toothpicks. Suppose you are working on this toothpick problem by yourself and cannot solve the problem. Now, suppose, instead, that you are in a group and someone in the group asks, "Is it okay if we don't keep the toothpicks flat on the table?" and another person asks, "How many toothpicks will it take to make a pyramid?" You will immediately solve the toothpick problem! None of the members of the group is trying to coerce you into believing something you don't already believe or do something you don't want to do. They are merely providing information to solve the problem. In this case, you are more prone to go along with the group because you are unsure about how to proceed and assume others have more information than you do.

Informational influence is based on the assumption that others possess knowledge about what is appropriate or right in specific social contexts. Let's say you are at an amusement park for the first time. You see two rides ahead. There's a long line waiting for one of the rides and a shorter one for the other. You may assume that you should be in the long line because you assume the others know what they are doing.

By integrating normative and informational social influence, social influence theory provides a comprehensive framework for understanding how societal norms and the information available in one's social environment shape behavior that leads to conformity. The social pressure involved, however, is mostly internal. Other forms of social influence, for example persuasion, have more clearly identifiable external sources.

Persuasion

Have you ever gone into a store to buy a certain kind of cell phone but ended up being convinced to buy a more expensive model with more features? Salespeople are knowledgeable in the art of persuasion. **Persuasion** is the process of influencing someone's beliefs, attitudes, intentions, motivations, or behaviors through communication and reasoning, without coercion or force.

Reason versus emotion is an important distinction in persuasion. Two routes to persuasion, part of a model of attitudes and persuasion known as the **elaboration likelihood model**, were introduced in the mid-1980s by Richard Petty and John Cacioppo: the central route and the peripheral route. The **central route** involves reason and logic and an audience highly motivated to think and make decisions about the topic at hand. The **peripheral route** to persuasion relies on emotion or other superficial factors, such as bright colors, engaging music, celebrity endorsements, or nice packaging that has little to do with the item being promoted or sold. These can be effective if the audience is not especially motivated to think about the topic or to make good decisions. Studies have shown that people who experience the central route of persuasion are more strongly persuaded for a longer period of time. People who experience the peripheral route to persuasion may be convinced temporarily by the communication, but the persuasion may not last.

To understand the central route versus the peripheral route of persuasion, consider this scenario. If Mikayla is in the market for a new car, she might look at *Consumer Reports* to read up on positive and negative features of various cars and talk with many people about the cars they have. When viewing a commercial for a certain car, she might compare the message of the commercial with the various pros and cons she has examined. If the commercial resonated closely with positive aspects she studied, she might say that the commercial was persuasive, but if the commercial did not match what she studied, she might say that the commercial was weak. Her thinking followed the central route: she is persuaded by the information that relates directly to the subject at hand.

In contrast, if Mikayla is trying to decide what college to attend and bases her decision on what famous people attended and how beautiful the campus is, rather than whether the college excels in her intended major, she is being persuaded via the peripheral route, so named because it skirts the central message by offering catchy cues instead of addressing the issue head on. The next time you see a celebrity endorsement in an ad or a commercial, ask yourself what, if anything, you are really learning about the product itself. Chances are the advertisers are using the peripheral route to persuasion.

Often, if a person or product has one positive attribute, we will assume they have other positive attributes. This assumption is known as the halo effect. The **halo effect** serves as a shortcut for judgment and decision-making. It functions through the peripheral route to persuasion, which involves changing attitudes or beliefs through superficial cues or heuristics rather than through the deep processing of information. Mikayla engaged in deep processing when she formed her opinion about the car. If her friend is also looking for a car, she might use a shortcut: if Mikayla likes it, it must be okay. This is the halo effect in action.

When people are exposed to a persuasive message from a source they find attractive or credible, based on previous positive impressions, they are more likely to be influenced without critically evaluating the message's content. Marketers, advertisers, and influencers often leverage this by associating products with well-liked personalities or aesthetically pleasing imagery, thus persuading the audience to adopt favorable attitudes towards their offerings based on peripheral cues rather than substantive evaluation.

People who use persuasion often, such as salespeople, politicians, activists, or teachers, often have different strategies to help them persuade people. One technique, known as the **foot-in-the-door approach** (using the metaphor of a door-to-door salesperson), is based on the idea that if you ask people to agree to a small request first, they are much more likely to comply with a larger request later. For example, if you ask for a $1 donation to a charity, people will likely comply, because the amount is small. If you later ask them for a $10 donation or even more, they are more likely to comply, because they have already demonstrated support for the charity with their earlier $1 donation. Refusing the larger request would lead to the feelings of guilt or tensions associated with cognitive dissonance—if they did it once, why wouldn't they do it again?

Another technique, known as the **door-in-the-face approach**, is also effective. With this approach, you begin by asking people for a very large request—a $100 donation, for example—a request that most people will not only likely refuse but that also might make them slam the door in your face. However, if you later ask them for a much smaller request, a $10 donation, for example, they are likely to comply. Refusing to comply would challenge their sense of reciprocity—you adjusted your request, so it seems only fair that they should adjust their response. Telemarketers often use the technique, initially asking for an enormous donation which they expect to be denied (but they will accept if it is provided), and then they ask for a more reasonable donation.

SOCIAL PSYCHOLOGY AND PERSONALITY: *A MULTICULTURAL PERSPECTIVE*

One of the most studied areas in social psychology is persuasion. In the 1950s, Carl Hovland and his associates studied central aspects of what is persuasive.[3] These include the communicator, the content of the message, the medium or channel of communication, and the audience. If the *communicator* is a respected or influential individual, the message will be more persuasive. If the *content* of the message is of interest to the audience, the audience will pay more attention to the message. If the message is delivered in a flashy way via a popular *medium*—following the peripheral route—it may be more influential. Finally, the *audience* is a vital variable in persuasion. For example, using Taylor Swift or Beyoncé lyrics sprinkled throughout a message may be influential to a younger audience but fall flat for an older audience. Many studies since Hovland's original studies have confirmed the importance of these four central aspects.

Perhaps the most important aspect of persuasion is the communicator. If the audience believes the communicator to be credible, the message will be believed more than if the communicator is not believed to be credible. In Hovland's original study, research participants received a message regarding the dangers of nuclear weapons. This original study was conducted in the 1950s, not long after nuclear weapons were used on Japan to end World War II, and the United States and the Soviet Union were in an arms race to develop more and more powerful nuclear weapons. Therefore, Hovland's topic of study was of great importance to people of that era. Half of Hovland's participants were told that the anti-nuclear message they read came from J. Robert Oppenheimer, the American scientist identified as the "father of the atomic bomb," and the other half of the participants were told that the antinuclear message came from *Pravda*, the Soviet Union's main state newspaper. Not surprisingly, the research participants believed the message much more if they thought it came from Oppenheimer than if they thought it came from *Pravda*.

Additionally, the role of credibility and authority in persuasion can vary significantly across cultures. In cultures where hierarchical structures are deeply ingrained, people may be more easily persuaded by messages delivered by authority figures or experts. Conversely, in cultures where equality and democratic principles are emphasized, peer influence and consensus may play a more significant role in persuasion. Understanding these nuances helps in designing strategies that are culturally appropriate and more likely to achieve the desired persuasive outcomes. Hovland's findings on the impact of authority and expertise on persuasion further support the need to consider cultural context when assessing the effectiveness of persuasive messages.

---

3   Hovland, C. I., & Weiss, W. (1951). The influence of source credibility on communication effectiveness. *Public Opinion Quarterly, 15*(4), 635–660.

Multicultural perspectives on persuasion also highlight the importance of context and nonverbal communication. In many cultures, the context in which a message is delivered—including the setting, timing, and relationship between the communicators—can greatly influence its persuasive power. Nonverbal cues, such as body language, eye contact, and tone of voice, are also interpreted differently across cultures and can either enhance or undermine a persuasive message. For instance, maintaining eye contact is seen as a sign of confidence and honesty in some cultures, while in others it may be perceived as disrespectful or confrontational. Therefore, effective persuasion in a multicultural context requires a deep understanding of these cultural subtleties and an ability to adapt communication strategies accordingly.

Develop a Claim

After reading about persuasion from a multicultural perspective, develop a claim about how cultural values influence the effectiveness of persuasive messages in different contexts.

Conformity and Obedience

Conformity and obedience are fundamental aspects of social behavior that illustrate how individuals adjust their actions, attitudes, and beliefs in response to the influence of others. Conformity involves changing one's behavior to match the norms or behaviors of a larger group, often to fit in or gain social approval. Obedience, on the other hand, is about following orders or rules from an authority figure, even when personal preferences may differ. Both processes demonstrate the powerful impact that social environments and authority figures can have on individual behavior, creating a tension between personal autonomy and social influence.

Conformity

Whether unspoken rules, norms, and expectations influence a person's thoughts, feelings, and behaviors depends on a number of factors. Social psychologists revealed some of these factors through studying conformity. **Conformity** is behavior that is in accord with accepted group standards. Are you your own person, or do you follow the crowd? Most people say they act on their own ideas, and their own opinions will not be swayed by those of others who think differently. Solomon Asch set out to determine to what degree other people influence our opinions—or the external expression of our opinions. In his conformity experiments at Bryn Mawr College in the early 1950s, Asch claimed to measure differences in research subjects' visual judgments by asking groups of eight males to view sets of two cards, the first displaying one vertical line and the second displaying three vertical lines of different heights (Figure 4.3.1). When asked in separate experiments which one of three lines on the second card matched the height of the single line on the first card, seven subjects chose the wrong line unanimously. The eighth participant, always set up to go last, knew the answer was wrong and chose the real matching line at first. Eventually, however, he shifted his answer and went along with those who chose the wrong answer.

Unbeknownst to the real participant, the other participants in the group were confederates working with the experimenter. At first they gave correct answers and then began making "mistakes" uniformly. Although the real participant gave the correct answer initially, he began agreeing with the confederates and answering with the incorrect answer. Thirty-seven percent of participants conformed to the group judgment. The same results occurred in other groups.

When later interviewed about their answers, some real subjects said they knew that the others had chosen the wrong answers, but they didn't want to be different from the group. Others stated that they believed the others' answers were correct, but Asch did not believe them. He believed that they would rather indicate they did not know the correct answer to a simple question than to admit they were conforming to the group and giving up their individuality. The real subjects had conformed to the group without any overt pressure at all—no disapproving looks from the others. However, the majority of the participants did not conform, sticking to what they knew was correct.

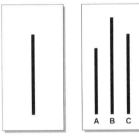

Figure 4.3.1 Asch Experiment

Obedience to Authority

The Asch studies make a statement about some people's willingness to "go with the crowd," but judging the lengths of different lines has no significant consequences. It is different when direct pressure from an **authority figure**— an individual who holds a position of power or influence and whose directives, decisions, or judgments are respected and followed by others—urges individuals to engage in an activity. In a landmark series of studies in the 1960s, Stanley Milgram randomly assigned one of two subjects to be the "teacher" and the other to be the "learner." The goal of the research was understanding **obedience**, the act of following the commands, instructions, or orders given by an authority figure or ruling body and involving compliance with established rules, laws, or social norms. Participants in the studies, all males, volunteered to take part after seeing an ad in a local paper offering $4.50 to take part in an experiment on "punishment and learning."

In these experiments, the real subject was always the teacher, and Milgram's confederate was always the learner. The teacher and learner were shown a panel with different levels of electrical shock (mild, moderate, severe—all the way up to 450 volts) that would be delivered to the learner for incorrect answers. The learner (confederate) was in a separate room and strapped to a chair from which he could reach four buttons to indicate his answer, one to four. The teacher was told that the learner was strapped down so he could not escape.

The teacher read a series of word pairs for the learner to remember. Later, when the teacher read the first word of each pair, the learner was to press the button for the correct paired word from the list. If the answer was correct, the teacher said "Correct" and moved to the next word. However, if the answer was incorrect, the teacher said "Incorrect," gave the correct answer, "shocked" the learner, and then moved to the next word. Levels of shock increased with each incorrect answer.

Although the learner was not really being shocked, the teacher heard recorded responses associated with the various levels of shock. These recordings started with mild "ouch" responses at the beginning and proceeded to horrible screams in the middle. Near the highest level of shock, the recorded voice yelled that his heart was hurting, and at the very end, there was nothing but silence and no responses to the words. While many of the real subjects protested that they did not want to continue the study, the researcher indicated that "the study must continue," and nearly two-thirds of the subjects complied with the researcher's demands and proceeded all the way to 450 fake volts. After all, the experimenter was the "authority." Many of the participants who continued with the shocks after protesting indicated that they would not be the ones responsible if something happened to the "learner." A similar experiment from 2009 found about the same percentage of people willing to comply with the researcher's demands.

Figure 4.3.2 Participants in Milgram's experiment did not know that the shocks they were administering were from a fake machine. Two-thirds of the participants obeyed instructions.

Certain conditions are shown to make people less obedient, however. One is the emotional distance of the victim. In variations of Milgram's study, compliance remained high in two-thirds of subjects when teachers could hear the learners through the wall. However, if the teacher was able to see the agony of the learner, obedience went down and decreased even further if the learner was right next to the teacher. Obedience went up when learners were in a soundproof room, and the teacher could not hear any protests.

Closeness and legitimacy of the authority figure also influence obedience. For example, if the experimenter communicated with the participant only by telephone and was not seen in a white lab coat, compliance went down. Obedience went down even further if the teacher never met the experimenter and only received instructions through a recording.

Institutional authority increases obedience to authority even further. Milgram's first experiments were conducted at Yale, a highly respected institution where well-known and respected research is conducted, but subjects' obedience decreased when Milgram moved his experiments to an undistinguished storefront near the campus.

Finally, remember the Asch studies on conformity? When Asch's participants were in a situation where all of the other confederates gave incorrect answers, some of the participants conformed to the group answers at least once. However, Asch also found out that if one of the confederates gave the correct answer, the real participants almost never gave incorrect answers and stuck with their own perceptions. Similarly, in conditions where the teacher was part of a group of people delivering shocks to the learner, if all of the other participants obeyed the authority's demands, the real participants also obeyed. However, if even one of the other group members refused to deliver shocks at the upper levels of the scale, the real participants also refused to go to the higher levels.

Milgram's studies showed *that* we obey; they do not explain *why* we obey, but Milgram had speculations about that. Recent studies, informed by Milgram's speculations, have shown there are several reasons why people might obey an authority figure.

- First, from an evolutionary perspective, we seem to have given up our responsibility to engage in a risky or dangerous activity if there is an authority figure to take on this responsibility. *We* are not shocking the learner; *the experimenter* is taking responsibility for the shocks.
- Second, we have been socialized from childhood to obey authority figures, such as our parents, our teachers, and the police.
- Third, the shocks were delivered incrementally by only 15-volt jumps. The difference between a 15-volt shock and a 30-volt shock is not that large, and the difference between a 165-volt shock and a 180-volt shock is less than 10 percent greater. As you read in the topics on sensation and perception, we tend not to notice stimuli that are less than 10 percent different from other stimuli. Additionally, this technique uses the foot-in-the-door technique by getting the learner to agree to issue a small shock and then gradually increasing the intensity.
- Finally, although all participants had a choice to continue with the experiment or not, they may not have *perceived* that they had the choice to discontinue. When they expressed concern about the experiment, the script of the experimenter was something like, "The experiment requires that you continue." Thus, even though a participant could have said, "Well, I don't care what the experiment requires, I am not going to continue to torture the learner," most of them did not refuse to go to the highest level of voltage.

You might not be surprised that the Milgram study was very controversial. In the Milgram study, research participants *thought* they were injuring or even killing the learners. At first, Milgram made sure to reintroduce the learner to the teachers after the study and debrief the teachers, so they knew they did not really harm the learner. As the study continued, however, to keep the word from getting out that no shocks were really issued, Milgram stopped debriefing participants, and some people did not find out until years later that the learner had not received any shocks. Even though they did not really hurt anyone, the teachers (participants) still had to live with the knowledge that they *could* have killed someone merely because the researcher asked them to do so.

Because of the potential harm done by this and many other studies in psychology and outside of psychology (e.g., medical research), researchers must have their research proposals evaluated by review boards at their home institutions to determine if participants will be properly protected. These review boards are called Institutional Review Boards (IRB), and every institution conducting research with human participants must have its research vetted through these IRBs (see Practice 2.D). The deception involved in Milgram's experiment led to the tightening of ethical standards for experiments with human subjects.

THINK AS A PSYCHOLOGIST

Explain How Cultural Norms, Expectations, and Circumstances Apply to Behavior and Mental Processes (1.B)

As you read, Solomon Asch conducted one of the more seminal studies in social psychology on conformity. Asch found that when confederates made wrong judgments in estimating the length of a line, most of the "true" research participants eventually conformed to the confederates at least once, with over one-third of the participants consistently conforming to the group by study's end. This occurred even though when people made these judgments by themselves, they were nearly 100 percent accurate. Moreover, none of the confederates applied direct pressure on the participants to conform, so the conformity occurred simply by self-imposed pressure. When interviewed about their performance later, these participants said that they knew the group's judgments were incorrect, but they did not want to "rock the boat."

Practice Explaining How Cultural Norms, Expectations, and Circumstances Apply to Behavior and Mental Processes

Answer the following question.

Bond and Smith (1996)[4] examined the Asch-like conformity studies over the years, and one of their findings was that collectivistic cultures had a higher percentage of those who conformed to the group than did individualistic

---

4 Bond, R., & Smith, P. B. (1996). Culture and conformity: A meta-analysis of studies using Asch's (1952b, 1956) line judgment task. *Psychological Bulletin, 119*(1), 111–137. DOI:10.1037/0033-2909.119.1.111Corpus ID: 17823166

cultures. Why might people from collectivistic cultures conform more to groups than do individualistic cultures?

Individuals' Behavior in Groups

Research on social influence makes it clear that being part of a group has a significant impact on an individual's behavior and mental processes. When people join a group, they often experience changes in how they think, feel, and act, primarily due to the presence and pressure of social norms, the desire for acceptance, and the influence of group identity. The need for social acceptance and fear of rejection can drive people to conform to group norms and participate in group activities, sometimes engaging in actions they would not consider as individuals.

Being in a group can affect an individual's mental processes through informational influence and social comparison. These can lead to shifts in attitudes and beliefs as individuals assimilate group viewpoints as their own to make sense of ambiguous situations or complex issues. Social comparison can affect self-esteem, self-concept, and motivation.

We join some groups, like school clubs, voluntarily. We are members of other groups because of circumstances, like where we are born. The culture we belong to has a profound impact on how we see the world and ourselves.

Group Polarization

Let's say a football game with your school's biggest rival is coming up. You have a plan to paint graffiti on the statue of your rival's mascot, even with the chance that you will get caught because of the increased security during the week of this historic rivalry game. If you were to get caught, you would likely be suspended from school and possibly endanger your future college plans. However, if you were successful, you would be a hero among your classmates and just might impress the classmate you want to date. Should you go ahead with your plan or not? Would it help to discuss this with some friends or not?

Most people would say that you should discuss this plan with your friends to really determine the positives and negatives and make a better final decision. However, research shows that a group discussion will almost always lead to a riskier decision. Group discussion does not lead to a straightforward 50/50 "do it or don't do it" result. Instead, the action the group discussion leads to is a riskier one than the original. This shift from a 50/50 decision to a riskier decision has become known as a *risky shift*. In other words, a risky shift is the tendency to shift from uncertainty about performing a task, or not, to making a decision with greater risk.

The risky shift phenomenon over time has been subsumed under what social psychologists call **group polarization**—the tendency for people to hold even more extreme views on topics after a group discussion of like-minded people. Social psychology researchers noticed that when people discussed things in a group, their opinions ended up being more extreme. In 1969, researchers identified some people in France who were minimally supportive of their president, Charles de Gaulle, who was in a dispute with the United States at the time. Those people also felt slightly negative toward Americans. However, when the researchers got these people together to discuss the positives and negatives of Franco-U.S. relations, at the end of the discussion, they were even more supportive of President de Gaulle and even more negative toward Americans. The same phenomenon—holding even more extreme views on a topic after group discussion—tends to be true across a number of different issues, such as feminism and racial attitudes.

You may not be surprised that the Internet has increased group polarization. Chat rooms or exclusive groups allow like-minded individuals to exchange ideas and radicalize one another's opinions. Moreover, because people may have screen names that are not their own, the Internet also gives individuals the opportunity to hide their true identities. Both group polarization and deindividuation can increase extreme and aggressive views. Even the cultivation of terrorism and terrorists has been attributed to group polarization principles.

Groupthink

You may have heard of an especially disastrous decision made by a supposedly intelligent group of people, and you may have found yourself wondering, "How could such intelligent people make such a shortsighted mistake?" Social psychologist Irving Janis wondered the same thing after President John F. Kennedy's decision to invade Cuba early in his administration, historically known as the Bay of Pigs invasion (1961). Janis labeled this phenomenon **groupthink**—referring to the tendency to make bad decisions because of the illusion that the plan of action is a good one and is supported by all members of the group. Janis described certain conditions under which groupthink may occur. These include the following:

- A respected and directive leader
- High cohesion among group members
- Isolation of the group from others
- Lack of procedures to seek information other than what is currently available to the group and to externally evaluate the group's information and decisions
- A highly stressful situation with perceived limited solutions

While deliberating the proposed plan of action, the group focuses on the "correctness" of this plan because of certain other elements:

- An illusion of invulnerability
- Rationalization
- Unquestioned belief in the morality of the group
- Stereotyped view of opponents

- Pressure to conform to the group
- Self-censorship
- An illusion of unanimity
- Mindguards—those who provide filtered or limited information to the group

President Kennedy was from the Boston area, home to Harvard University, and brought to the White House a number of Harvard-educated advisors he called "the best and the brightest." Therefore, the group had an *illusion of invulnerability*. How could such smart people ever make any bad decisions? They also rationalized that because they were so bright, their decisions were the best that could be made and that other decisions were flawed. Because their self-view included the position that they were working for the American people, who are basically moral, they had an *unquestioned belief in their own morality* in working toward decisions for the country. Their objective was to overthrow the Fidel Castro government in Cuba, a newly installed Communist government that took over the reins of power by force and by so doing fulfilled a *stereotypical view* of the Castro regime in the minds of the group. In their deliberations about the invasion, if anyone questioned whether or not the group's strategy should be pursued, the questioner was under *pressure to conform* to the rest of the group. Interviews after the ultimate failure of the invasion revealed that some group members had doubts but had engaged in *self-censorship*, feeling it would be out of line to express these doubts. Because no one overtly expressed these doubts, an *illusion of unanimity* was created around the plan to invade. If anyone had actually expressed doubts, that person would have

John F. Kennedy's "best and brightest" cabinet may have used groupthink to make important decisions.

been intercepted by *mindguards* to protect the leader, President Kennedy, from these views. While there did not appear to be any mindguards in the Bay of Pigs fiasco, there are such individuals in other cases of groupthink that Janis examined.

Many people have found groupthink to be a useful explanation for a number of decisions made since the Kennedy era. An analysis of the U.S. invasion of Iraq in 2003 concluded that groupthink was a major contributor to this decision. Groupthink also may have been a factor in financial fraud cases, certain forms of terrorism, and "pack journalism," a situation in which most journalists reach the same conclusions.

Diffusion of Responsibility

In 1964, a woman named Kitty Genovese was attacked multiple times late at night near her apartment building. She screamed when she was attacked by a man who stabbed her with a knife. A shout from a neighbor scared him away, but he waited nearby in his car until he saw that no police were coming. Then he came back, stabbed and raped her and stole $49 from her. One of her neighbors called the police nearly a half hour after the initial attack. Genovese died at the hospital from 13 stab wounds. A report of the murder in the *New York Times* inaccurately said that 38 witnesses stood by and did nothing to help her. Later reports said that neighbors did try to help her. Although reports of the murder in the *New York Times* were inaccurate and sensationalized, the Genovese case led to the creation of the 911 emergency call system and spurred social psychologists to study helping behavior and altruism.

Psychologists John Darley and Bibb Latané wanted to understand dynamics of situations like the Genovese case. In what is now a classic experiment designed to study whether people help in an emergency, Darley and Latané placed a research participant in a separate room and had the participant interact with another person through a communication system. The researchers led participants to believe that they were (1) the only person participating with one other person, (2) participating in a three-person group, or (3) one of six participants. Participants were to initially take two-minute turns discussing typical college student problems they faced. One of the participants, a research confederate, revealed that he sometimes has problems with seizures. When his turn to talk came again, the confederate started talking but then eventually stuttered and said that he was having a seizure. The only way participants could help the supposed victim was by leaving their room. Every one of the participants who believed they were the only one aware of the victim's seizure reported it right away, but only 62 percent who thought they were part of the group of six reported it.

Darley and Latané initially believed that people are less likely to help if there are other people watching because of a concept they called diffusion of responsibility. **Diffusion of responsibility** is the phenomenon that someone witnessing a problem is less likely to take action when others are also present because they assume that others are taking on the responsibility.

Social Loafing

If you've ever been on the losing side of a tug-of-war contest and thought, "If only we had pulled just a little bit harder, we would have won," your thought is actually close to the truth. A study conducted by Ingham, Levinger, Graves, and Peckham (1974) demonstrated that people pull harder on a rope simulating a tug-of-war contest when they believe they are alone than when they are in a group. Other researchers have called this phenomenon **social loafing**, referring to the tendency to exert less effort when working in a group if individual effort cannot be measured independently. In other words, not "the more, the merrier," but "the more, the lazier."

The key to social loafing is that a person's individual effort cannot be measured or detected. Whenever you buy new clothing, you may find a number on a little slip of paper in the pocket or somewhere on the clothing designating the person who inspected the piece. Before the inspectors were identified, however, many articles of clothing had defects that got past an inspector. Then, when inspectors were assigned numbers to place in each article of clothing they inspected, the inspectors became identifiable, which reduced the number of defective clothes dramatically. Making the inspectors individually identifiable nearly eliminated the effects of social loafing.

Deindividuation

While social loafing deals with issues of effort, deindividuation deals with issues of how we behave toward others and their property. **Deindividuation** is the loss of identity as a result of participation in a larger group, which lessens the sense of personal responsibility for one's actions and can lead to a higher degree of aggression.

Philip Zimbardo, a renowned social psychologist, revealed the effects of deindividuation, along with several other important social concepts, in his Stanford prison experiment. In the study, Zimbardo randomly divided student volunteers, who had agreed to participate in "a psychological study of prison life" and who had been screened for stability and psychological health, into prisoner and guard groups. A mock prison was set up in the basement of a university building, complete with an unlit closet used for solitary confinement. With the help of the local Palo Alto police, the students assigned to the prisoner roles were rounded up at their homes and brought to the police station where they underwent the usual booking procedures, including a strip search. They were then delivered to the mock prison. They were given ill-fitting smocks to wear marked with their prisoner number and had to wear chains around one ankle. The guards, meanwhile, were given uniforms and wooden batons to represent their authority. They were told they could not physically hurt the prisoners, but they could abuse them psychologically to convey the idea that the guards had all the power and the prisoners had none. They could refer to prisoners only by their number, and they wore sunglasses to avoid eye contact.

Within a few days, the student prisoners became docile and defeated, though one tried a hunger strike to gain some leverage, but he was placed in solitary confinement as a result. Other prisoners were ordered to bang on the door of the dark closet to harass the prisoner in solitary confinement. The guards became rough and aggressive. They demanded that the prisoners do humiliating acts, such as using a bucket in their cell instead of a toilet for elimination and not being able to empty the bucket. One-third of the guards were later judged to have carried out sadistic acts. The experiment was terminated after six days when a graduate student who came to the "prison" to conduct interviews strongly objected to the unethical treatment of the young men in the study.

In the Stanford prison experiment, one of the reasons the guards behaved aggressively toward the prisoners was that the guards lost their personal identities and became deindividuated. To further illustrate this point, Philip Zimbardo conducted a study in 1970 in which research subjects were divided into groups of individuals who either gave shocks or received shocks. Subjects in the shocker group wore either pillowcases with eye holes over their heads or their own clothes with name tags to identify themselves. Those with executioner-style pillowcases over their heads gave shocks of higher intensity and for longer periods of time than those who wore their regular clothes and name tags. The shock receivers were confederates of the experimenter and pretended that they were receiving painful shocks.

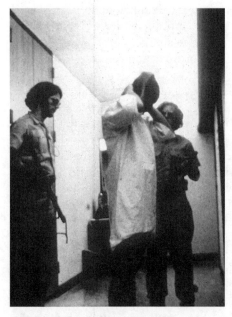

Guards in the Stanford prison experiment forced prisoners to wear pillowcases over their heads to depersonalize and demean them.

This was also the case with those "receiving" the shocks. When they had pillowcases with eye holes over their heads, they received shocks of higher intensity and for longer periods of time than when they wore their regular clothes and name tags. Thus, deindividuation can occur with either the victim or the aggressor.

Deindividuation can also occur as a result of group behavior. If everyone else is rioting or stealing or throwing rocks, individuals can lose themselves in the crowd and follow the crowd's behaviors.

Interestingly, higher aggression toward a victim can be counteracted under conditions of deindividuation. When researchers dressed up some of the "shockers" in nurse's uniforms, the level of intensity and duration of the shocks decreased. Since nurses are generally thought of as compassionate caregivers, losing oneself to a compassionate character leads one to act more humanely.

THINK AS A PSYCHOLOGIST

Propose a Defensible Claim (4.A, 1.A)

When prominent military and political leaders of defeated Nazi Germany faced military tribunals in Nuremberg, Germany, for their war crimes in 1945 and 1946, many invoked the "superior orders" defense—"I was given an order and had to obey it." However, the Nuremberg trials were the first cases in which such a defense could not be used to relieve someone from the responsibility of war crimes, although it could be used to reduce sentences. The superior orders defense, like the Milgram studies, cast participants as unthinking conformists who bowed to authority and simply "followed orders." The Milgram experiments seemed to explain or at least confirm the notion highlighted at the trials that Nazis committed atrocities in part because they were told to by an authority—that they were diligent servants of their superiors with little mind of their own. Political theorist Hannah Arendt coined the term "banality of evil" to express the idea that acts of evil do not require psychopaths—they can be carried out in the normal, boring course of a job, all in a day's work.

Hermann Göring (far left, first row) was the second-highest Nazi official to be tried and convicted at the Nuremberg trials. He was sentenced to death by hanging but committed suicide the night before he was to be hung.

Researchers S. A. Haslam and S. D. Reicher[5] dispute this idea. They have studied the behavior of Adolf Eichmann, a major organizer of the Holocaust, and found evidence that he was energetic, creative, and actively committed to carrying out the ideals of the Nazis, not an automaton mindlessly following orders. Haslam and Reicher conclude that tyranny is not caused by blind

---

5 Haslam, S.A., & Reicher, S. (2007, June). Beyond the banality of evil: Three dynamics of an interactionist social psychology of tyranny. *Personality and Social Psychology Bulletin, 33*(5), 615. originally published online April 17, 2007. DOI:10.1177/0146167206298570

TOPIC 4.3 PSYCHOLOGY OF SOCIAL SITUATIONS 543

obedience but, rather, by strong identification with authority, by "buying in" to the principles and goals of authority figures. Eichmann said his one regret was that he didn't kill more Jews. In a similar way, some of the participants in the Milgram study, when told that their participation helped advance scientific knowledge, saw their actions in the study as a contribution to a worthwhile cause, identifying with the authority. Haslam and Reicher conducted their own televised prison experiment in conjunction with the BBC, often referred to as the BBC prison study. That 2002 experiment, which had to be terminated early because of potential psychological harm to participants, gave the researchers the idea to further explore the issues of authority, obedience, and identification.

Haslam and Reicher argue that participants in tyrannical groups go through a predictable pattern. First, the individual is drawn to the group. Second, as the researchers say, "If people join the groups they like . . . , it is equally true that people come to like the groups they join." In other words, membership in the group transforms individuals. People who might have been on the fringes of a certain ideology will find their belief in that ideology strengthened by its repeated expression with the group. Finally, the groups are transformed by members who may have once been marginal but now assume a role of influence, which motivates them to expand the range of their influence over others through transforming the group by strengthening its power.

Practice Proposing a Claim

Complete the following activity.

Develop a claim about the extent to which the predictable pattern of participation in tyrannical groups proposed by Haslam and Reicher applies to either the Milgram obedience studies or the Zimbardo prison experiment. Defend your claim with at least one piece of evidence from the material you have just read about obedience and authority.

Other Dynamics of Individuals and Groups

The relationship between individuals and groups and the kinds of transformations that can occur within each have been the focus of a number of other psychological studies on how individuals and groups interact and influence each other in both social and organizational settings. These studies provide more insights into the complex dynamics that govern behavior in varied social and professional environments.

Social Facilitation

Have you ever performed in athletics, music, dance, or theater? If so, is your performance better when people are watching you, or is it poorer? When your performance is enhanced by the presence of others watching you perform, the effect is known as **social facilitation**; if your performance is poorer when you are watched by others, the effect is called *social inhibition*.

Social psychologists study two questions about social facilitation. Why does the presence of others sometimes facilitate and at other times inhibit performance? When does the presence of others enhance your performance, and when does it detract? The answer depends on the difficulty of the task and your level of preparedness.

A wealth of research found support for *both* the social facilitation *and* the social inhibition positions. In the 1960s, psychologist Robert Zajonc figured out why we were finding differences in the effect that the presence of others has on performance.

For difficult tasks or poorly learned tasks, just a small amount of arousal, such as that provided by the presence of others, can cause a decline in performance. Have you ever tried to perform a musical piece you did not practice much or missed a free throw in a basketball game because you had not practiced?

An easy or well-learned task is enhanced by the presence of others (social facilitation), while a difficult or poorly learned task is inhibited by the presence of others (social inhibition). Remember this the next time you have to perform in front of a crowd: the best thing you can do to help your performance is practice.

False Consensus Effect

The **false consensus effect** refers to the tendency of individuals to overestimate the extent to which their beliefs, opinions, preferences, and behaviors are common and shared by others. Individuals believe that their own responses are relatively common and representative of the majority, leading to a perceived consensus that may not exist in reality. This effect can be observed in various situations, from predicting the outcome of elections based on one's political preferences to assuming widespread approval of one's personal habits and ethical judgments.

Consider a situation in which students need to select a class project or group activity. Abebe is passionate about environmental conservation and believes most classmates share that concern. He confidently proposes a campaign to promote recycling within the school, assuming there is widespread enthusiasm for the topic. Abebe is surprised when his proposal receives a lukewarm response, with many classmates preferring a project on digital literacy or community service. Abebe's overestimation of shared environmental interests among his peers is a classic example of the false consensus effect; his personal biases led him to an inaccurate perception of the group's priorities. Research suggests that this effect is not merely a reflection of social desirability or wishful thinking, but represents a fundamental egocentric bias in how individuals process social information.

Social psychologists suggest that the false consensus effect stems from several psychological processes. One significant factor is the desire for belonging and the comfort in believing one is associating with others who share one's views and actions. The effect is reinforced by the social circles individuals typically inhabit, which often consist of like-minded people. This homogeneity, or similarity within personal networks, leads to an echo chamber effect, where the exposure to similar viewpoints strengthens the belief in a broader agreement. Moreover, the availability heuristic plays a role, as examples that confirm one's beliefs are more easily recalled than those that contradict them. (See Topic 2.2.)

Some theorists suggest that cognitive dissonance also plays a role. If an individual acknowledges that their opinions might be unpopular or in the minority, their self-esteem could be threatened. Assuming a consensus, whether or not it exists, acts as a defense mechanism to preserve a positive self-image and reduces cognitive dissonance.

The implications of the false consensus effect are far-reaching, affecting not only individual judgments but also interpersonal relations and societal dynamics. For instance, this bias can lead to misunderstandings and conflicts when individuals incorrectly assume agreement from others, potentially dismissing or underestimating the diversity of perspectives in a group. In the context of group decision-making, it can contribute to groupthink, where the presumed unanimity suppresses dissent and critical evaluation of alternatives. On a broader scale, the false consensus effect can influence the development and enforcement of social norms, as well as the design and implementation of public policies based on misjudged public opinion.

Conflicts and Social Traps

When conflicts within groups occur, the people involved are generally part of a community, so they are competing against those in their own community. What happens in conflicts beyond one's own community, such as rivalries, opposing teams, or even international enemies? Muzafer Sherif was among the first social psychologists to study this kind of conflict. In his 1966 study, Sherif studied competition between two boys' summer camps in Robbers Cave State Park in Oklahoma. During the first week, each camp was unaware of the other, so each group of campers spent the time getting to know one another and forming a group identity. One group named themselves the Rattlers, and the other group named themselves the Eagles. They participated in sports and other bonding activities within their groups.

After the first week, Sherif had the camp counselors slowly introduce the two camps and engage them in a series of competitions against one another, with the winning group receiving coveted Swiss army knives or medals. The competition degenerated into bad behavior, such as one group stealing the flag of the other group and throwing trash into the other's camp. Even fistfights took place in the second week, and one boy had his ukelele smashed.

In the third week, Sherif introduced **superordinate goals**—challenges that would benefit both groups and that required the two groups to cooperate with one another to complete a task. For example, Sherif sabotaged their water system by clogging the pipes. The two groups had to work together to fix this problem so that they would both have water. Additionally, a truck broke down, and both groups of boys had to work together to try and repair the truck. Sherif observed that the two groups, who had outwardly disliked one another during the second week of camp, ended up liking each other more during the third week. The superordinate goals helped unite the groups and reduced **negative affect,** which includes emotions such as anger, frustration, and fear, and **stereotyping.**

In contrast to superordinate goals, which unify groups and can lead to positive outcomes, **social traps** occur when individuals, groups, organizations, or whole societies act in their own self-interest and make choices that, cumulatively, lead to negative outcomes. This phenomenon can arise from a conflict between individual and collective interests, where the immediate benefits to individuals overshadow the long-term costs their actions impose on the group. It can also arise from situations in which short-term benefits reward a behavior that has long-term negative consequences.

A classic example of a social trap is the tragedy of the commons, where individuals must decide if they are going to compete or cooperate with someone else. This decision may arise when individuals overuse a shared resource, such as a public pasture, fishing ground, or even the atmosphere, to the point where it becomes depleted or damaged beyond repair. Each person, aiming to maximize their individual gain, contributes to a situation that eventually harms the group, including themselves, because of the degradation of the shared resource.

Social traps highlight the dilemma faced by individuals in making decisions that may benefit themselves in the short term but are harmful to the group in the long run.

Industrial-Organizational Psychology

The term *group dynamics* refers to the behavioral and psychological processes that occur within a social group or between social groups. Key elements of group dynamics include the roles and relationships among group members, the communication patterns, the group's cohesion or divisiveness, the emergence of leaders and followers, and the processes of decision-making and conflict resolution.

As young people, you often encounter group dynamics through school activities, such as group projects, sports teams, or clubs, where the focus is on learning, peer interaction, and personal development. These experiences teach you how to collaborate, handle conflicts, and contribute to a group's objectives, often under the guidance of a teacher or coach.

Adults, in contrast, encounter group dynamics mainly in the workplace, where employees work together to meet organizational goals, which requires a different level of professionalism and accountability. Workplace teams might deal with more complex tasks, requiring effective communication, leadership, and the ability to navigate organizational structures and professional roles.

Most adults in the United States work 8 hours a day, 5 days a week, with about 20 days off a year. That adds up to a little over 2,000 hours spent working, and that work usually happens in groups. The earliest psychologists to study work were interested in how to help make work more efficient.

Today, **industrial-organizational (I/O) psychologists**, a specialized subfield of social psychologists, focus more generally on studying people's behavior in the workplace. The field bridges the gap between psychological principles and the practical demands of the contemporary workplace, aiming to understand, predict, and enhance human performance, satisfaction, and well-being within organizational settings. I/O psychologists apply their expertise to a range of workplace issues, from individual employee well-being to the overarching structure of a corporation. This field is divided into two main areas: industrial psychology, which concentrates on individual or group performance and how to improve performances through practices such as training and evaluation, and organizational psychology, which focuses on organizational behavior, culture, and change to optimize workplace dynamics and health.

I/O psychologists study a wide array of topics that affect the workplace, including, but not limited to, employee selection, training and development, performance measurement, motivation, work-life balance, and leadership. They develop and implement assessment methods for selecting employees, design programs to train and develop talent within the workplace, and create strategies to boost employee engagement and performance. Furthermore, these psychologists work to identify the key traits of leadership and effective team collaboration, aiming to cultivate environments where employees can thrive. By scientifically analyzing these elements, I/O psychologists help organizations to not only select and retain the best talent but also to maximize the potential of their workforce.

Another critical area of focus for I/O psychologists is the quality of relationships among people working together. This includes examining how communication, conflict, and cooperation affect group dynamics and organizational outcomes. They study team structures, interpersonal relationships, and the social environment of the workplace to understand how these factors contribute to organizational success. I/O psychologists also develop interventions to improve team functioning, resolve conflicts, and enhance organizational communication. Their work ensures that the social and relational aspects of work are conducive to productivity, satisfaction, and overall organizational effectiveness.

A topic of great interest to employers and I/O psychologists is how people feel about their work, including aspects such as job satisfaction, commitment, engagement, and occupational stress, including burnout. **Burnout** is a state of chronic stress that leads to physical and emotional exhaustion, detachment, and feelings of ineffectiveness. It is a significant area of study within I/O psychology because of its impact on employee health and organizational productivity. By understanding the factors that contribute to job satisfaction and burnout, I/O psychologists can recommend changes to improve the work environment, such as modifying job roles, enhancing work-life balance, and creating support systems for stress management. Their goal is to create a work atmosphere that not only drives success for the organization but also promotes the well-being and personal satisfaction of every employee.

Prosocial Behavior

Whenever people help others, they are engaging in **prosocial behavior**, which can take many forms. For example, people donate their time and effort to help others by serving at a food bank, cleaning up a park, or assisting at a community event. They support charitable organizations or causes to benefit those in need. They engage in small acts of kindness, like helping a neighbor carry groceries, shovel snow, or mow their lawn. Prosocial behavior can also be participating in community efforts to restore a local landmark or organize a neighborhood watch. Providing emotional support to family and friends is another way to engage in prosocial behavior.

Altruism and Social Debt

A common belief is that a person who helps others is a good person who is motivated by **altruism**, which is selfless behavior performed out of concern for the well-being of others. Underlying altruism is a desire to help another person strictly for that person's benefit, without expecting any personal benefit. Significant research has focused on altruism as a reason underlying prosocial behavior.

A second major explanation for prosocial behavior is the concept of social debt. **Social debt** is the implicit expectation that arises in social relationships when one individual performs an action that benefits another, creating a perceived indebtedness. This concept is grounded in the social norms of reciprocity and responsibility, suggesting that when someone receives a favor or support, they owe a form of repayment or similar gesture of kindness in the future. Social debt underscores the interconnectedness of social interactions, where acts of generosity or assistance contribute to a cycle of mutual support and obligation within communities, thereby fostering social cohesion and cooperation. It is a fundamental aspect of human social dynamics, influencing behaviors and interactions across various cultural and social contexts.

The norms of social reciprocity and social responsibility contribute to the tendency of individuals to engage in prosocial behavior as a consequence of incurring social debt. The **social reciprocity norm** suggests that individuals are more likely to help those who have helped them in the past, thereby creating a cycle of mutual assistance. You may have heard this described as "paying forward." The reciprocity norm is consistent with the Golden Rule of "Do unto others as you would wish them to do unto you." The theory of *reciprocal altruism* expanded on this idea, suggesting that such behavior, while seemingly altruistic, is part of an evolutionary strategy to ensure mutual survival and benefit in groups.

In contrast, the **social responsibility norm** suggests that people act in prosocial ways out of a sense of moral obligation to support those who are in need and without any expectation of direct reciprocation. This norm is rooted in societal expectations that individuals will help those who cannot help themselves, such as children or the elderly. Research by Berkowitz and Daniels (1964), in their study "Responsibility and Dependency," found that the likelihood of individuals engaging in helping behaviors increases when they perceive the recipients as unable to reciprocate because of dependency or societal position.

Helping others provides benefits to the helpers.

At the same time, however, abundant evidence shows that helping others not only relieves the negative feeling resulting from seeing others in need but promotes a positive feeling so strong that it has been compared to the "runner's high," with its euphoric release of endorphins. The "helper's high," a phenomenon named by Allan Luks in 1988, is so powerful that it can have dramatic positive impact on both a person's happiness and physical well-being. Many self-reports and studies have confirmed the benefits of volunteering.

People who give their time to help others experience less depression, greater self-esteem, and even less physical pain than those who do not.

Helping Behavior and the Bystander Effect

Think back to the story about Kitty Genovese, who was attacked multiple times by the same individual late at night near her apartment building. In studying this type of situation, psychologists Darley and Latané observed that people are less likely to help someone in need if there are other people watching the distress. They called this phenomenon the **bystander effect**.

This counterintuitive behavior is influenced by a variety of situational and attentional variables, which can predict whether someone is likely to intervene in an emergency or a situation requiring assistance. One key factor, as you have read, is diffusion of responsibility. When people assume someone else in the group will take action, their own sense of responsibility to act is diminished. Additionally, fear of misjudging a situation and the desire to conform to the perceived reactions of others (normative social influence) can also deter people from helping. The presence and behaviors of others in a situation, called **situational variables,** can significantly affect an individual's decision to help.

Consider what you might do during a lunch break if a classmate suddenly appears to have a medical issue, such as a seizure. Students, including you, may freeze or look to others to take the lead, assuming that someone more competent or authoritative will step in. Or suppose you see a peer being verbally or physically harassed but hesitate to intervene or report the incident for fear of standing out, expecting that others who also witness the event will act instead. This hesitation can be influenced by the perceived social cost of intervention and the assumption that someone else will ultimately help.

Social psychologists have identified other factors that explain people's inaction in emergency situations. These other factors are known as **attentional variables** because they focus on how people pay attention to emergencies. Attentional variables include noticing the emergency, resolving ambiguity about whether the situation is an emergency, determining whether one has the ability to intervene, and determining if helping exceeds risks that might be present.

THINK AS A PSYCHOLOGIST

Calculate and Interpret Measures of Central Tendency, Variation, and Percentile Rank in a Given Data Set (3.B.3) | Evaluate Whether a Psychological Research Scenario Followed Appropriate Ethical Procedures (2.D.5) | Propose a Defensible Claim (4.A) | Explain How Cultural Norms, Expectations, and Circumstances, as Well as Cognitive Biases Apply to Behavior and Mental Processes (1.B.1)

Several follow-up studies on the work that Darley and Latané conducted demonstrate the bystander effect in several variations, including online forums.

In 2000, researchers investigated the extent to which the bystander effect might be present in online communications. In the study, 400 online chat rooms were observed. One of two confederates was used as a "victim" in each of the chat rooms: either a male victim whose screen name was Jake Harmen or a female victim whose screen name was Suzy Harmen. The purpose of the experiment was to determine whether the gender of the victim mattered, if the size of the chat group had any effect, and if asking for a person's help by directly using their screen name would have any effect on whether someone helped.

Results indicated that the gender of the victim had no effect on whether a bystander in the chat room assisted the victim. However, consistent with findings of Latané and Darley, the number of people present in the chat room did have an effect. The response time for smaller chat groups was quicker than in the larger chat groups. Importantly, this effect was nonexistent when the victim (Suzy or Jake) asked for help from a specific person in the chat group. The mean response time for groups in which a specific person was called out was 36.38 seconds (SD = 4.21 seconds). The mean response time for groups in which no screen name was pointed out was 51.53 seconds (SD = 13.51). A significant finding of the research is that intervention may, in part, depend on whether a victim asked for help by specifying a screen name. The bystander effect was inhibited when the victim asked a specific person for help.

Practice Foundational Skills

Complete the following activities and answer the question.

1. Briefly describe how the researchers used deception in this study and explain why it was necessary in this context.

2. What can you conclude from the differences in standard deviations (SD) between the two conditions?

3. Make a defensible claim about the following question: What differences might there be in bystander intervention between individualistic and collectivistic cultures?

REFLECT ON THE ESSENTIAL QUESTION

Essential Question: *How do social situations, being in a group, and prosocial behavior affect behavior and mental processes?* Using the Key Terms, complete a chart like the one below to gather details to help answer that question.

Social Influences and Persuasion	Conformity and Obedience	Individuals' Behavior in Groups	Other Dynamics of Individuals and Groups	Prosocial Behavior

altruism	foot-in-the-door approach	prosocial behavior
attetional variable	group polarization	situational variable
authority figure	groupthink	social debt
burnout	halo effect	social facilitation
bystander effect	individualism	social influence theory
central route	industrial/organizational	social loafing
collectivism	(I/O) psychologists	social norms
conformity	informational influence	social reciprocity norm
deindividuation	multiculturalism	social responsibility norm
diffusion of responsibility	negative affect	social situation
door-in-the-face approach	normative influence	social traps
elaboration likelihood	obedience	stereotyping
model	peripheral route	superordinate goals
false consensus effect	persuasion	

MULTIPLE-CHOICE QUESTIONS

1. Marissa is a highly effective salesperson at a local department store. She gets most of her sales by telling people about the materials and manufacturing of the products she sells, pointing out the warranty and explaining how to use the products most effectively. What type of persuasive technique is Marissa using?

   (A) Door-in-the-face

   (B) Foot-in-the-door

   (C) Peripheral route

   (D) Central route

2. In Solomon Asch's line comparison study, what response did the target participant typically give when all but one confederate gave an obviously wrong answer?

   (A) They conformed to what most of the group was saying.

   (B) They conformed to the confederate to whom they were most attracted.

   (C) They claimed to be confused about the correct response.

   (D) They stuck with their own perception of the correct answer.

3. If you were performing in a school play and had mastered your lines by practicing over and over again, your performance would most likely be enhanced under which of the following circumstances?

   (A) When you were alone

   (B) When you were in the presence of a large crowd

   (C) When you were with your best friend

   (D) When you were with a stranger

4. You are debating comprehensive immigration policy. One group is leaning in favor of this policy, and another group is leaning against it. You decide to divide yourselves into those in favor and those who oppose this policy to discuss your positions and then come back together as a whole group. What do you predict will happen?

   (A) The two groups will have the same positions, but there will be some subtle nuances to their positions.

   (B) The two groups will change to the opposite positions.

   (C) The two groups will feel even more strongly toward their original positions.

   (D) The two groups will feel more confused about which position to support.

5. Annie is an industrial-organizational psychologist. Which of the following is she most likely to do at work?

   (A) Survey employees about their satisfaction with their jobs

   (B) Examine the amount of profit the corporation makes

   (C) Investigate the productivity levels of the machines used by the corporation

   (D) Document the educational backgrounds of the management team

6. In many collectivistic cultures, villagers will come together to help care for children and the elderly. This behavior is an expected part of the culture. What social psychology phenomenon best explains this behavior?

   (A) Social responsibility norm

   (B) The halo effect

   (C) Altruism

   (D) Multiculturalism

Topic 4.4

Psychodynamic and Humanistic Theories of Personality

"I am what is mine. Personality is the original personal property."
—Norman O. Brown

Essential Question: How do psychodynamic and humanistic theories of personality define and assess personality?

Most people have wondered about personality at some time: Why am I the way I am? What makes that person tick? You have already read about some topics that relate to personality—the biological bases of behavior, consciousness, learning theories, cognition, and development. Even social psychology has something to say about personality because of the influence social situations have on what we think, feel, and do.

Personality is an individual's unique and relatively stable patterns of behavior, characteristics, thoughts, and emotions. If personality is like a completed puzzle, personality theories try to explain the mystery of the pieces and how they come together. Personality is so complex, however, that no single theory can claim to have all the answers. This complexity explains why there are many theories of personality. Each needs to be assessed on its own merits. Two influential theories are psychodynamic theories and humanistic theories.

Psychodynamic Theory

The **psychodynamic theory of personality** assumes unconscious forces determine behavior and influence personality. Psychodynamic approaches separate the mind into three levels of consciousness. Figure 4.4.1 depicts the mind as an iceberg, with **consciousness**, or our sense of reality, above the waterline. It is the smallest part of what goes on in the mind, even though consciousness is what we are most aware of. In the psychodynamic view, the forces that drive a person's personality operate under the surface. From the **preconscious** level, we can bring thoughts to conscious awareness with effort. For example, if you are wearing socks right now, you likely have not thought about them since putting them on this morning, but by calling attention to them, you can now feel them on your feet. You have moved that thought from the preconscious level to consciousness. The **unconscious** level, in contrast, is beyond our awareness. Freud believed that the unconscious held our wants and desires and was the driving force behind what motivates us to action.

Figure 4.4.1 shows that psychodynamic theory proposes that the mind contains three parts: the id, the superego, and the ego. This theory of the divided mind and how it works as a system to influence personality was developed by Sigmund Freud.

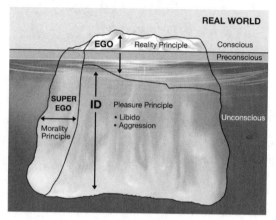

Figure 4.4.1 In Freud's theory, the conscious mind is just the tip of the iceberg.

Sigmund Freud and the Roots of Psychodynamic Theory

Sigmund Freud is probably the most recognizable name in the field of psychology. In the late 19th and early 20th centuries, he created a body of knowledge so influential that many concepts associated with it have become part of our culture. Freud termed his theory *psychoanalytic* because he considered it an analysis of the psyche, or mind. This approach to psychology encompasses a theory of personality, dream interpretation, and psychotherapy. Words such as *ego, denial, repression,* and *slip of the tongue* all owe their existence to Sigmund Freud and psychoanalytic theory. Underpinning Freud's theory is his core idea that humans are highly advanced animals struggling to cope with their animalistic urges. In psychoanalytic theory, all our animalistic biological drives, instincts, and urges—primarily sex and aggression—reside in the unconscious. The unconscious also contains memories of trauma, uncomfortable feelings, and thoughts that we repress, or block from conscious awareness because they are not appropriate or because they threaten our self-concept. These repressed feelings, thoughts, and trauma drive our personality and determine our behavior.

The Structure of Personality

Freud also proposed that personality is composed of the id, ego, and superego, which have different goals and perspectives that can cause conflict in the individual. The *id* exists at birth and contains all the instincts and energy, including sexual energy (libido), necessary for survival. According to Freud, the id operates exclusively at an unconscious level and has the goal of immediately satisfying instinctual impulses. Freud called this urge toward immediate gratification of impulses the **pleasure principle**.

Freud's focus on sexuality as one source of energy driving human behavior grew out of his training as a medical doctor and a biological researcher. He understood that humans are animals and, like all animals, are hardwired to reproduce. He proposed that human beings' high level of intellectual and social advancement causes adults to repress the basic biological impulse toward sexuality into the unconscious, but this repression was never complete.

Unlike adults, infants have no reason to repress the id's primitive physical urges. Infants are not only unashamed to load their diapers or feed from a breast, but they also derive pleasure from fulfilling the urges that assure their survival.

As an infant grows, the ego emerges. The **ego** is reality-based, residing in both the unconscious and the conscious and existing to take reality into consideration in satisfying the primitive needs of the growing infant. The ego operates based on the **reality principle**, a guiding principle that allows us to satisfy the id's primitive needs while also negotiating reality and the moral compass held in the superego.

The third part of the human mind is the superego. The superego develops as a result of the **morality principle**, which is the internalized need to comply with parental and other authority. Operating primarily at the unconscious level but also at the preconscious level, the *superego* is the moral sense of right and wrong, or a person's conscience. When the id expresses a want, the ego tries to address this want and the superego evaluates the ethical issues of the ego's expression. If the superego judges the expression to be socially appropriate, then the person is gratified. However, if the superego judges the expression to be socially inappropriate, it punishes the person through depression or anxiety. The superego is harsh and judgmental, shaming us to feel guilt about any number of things.

Parents' stories about potty training illustrate how growing children internalize their expectations. Parents often describe their little one, while still in diapers, sneaking behind a couch or chair to have a bowel movement. The child hides because the force of shame from the superego competes with the pleasure-seeking impulses of the id. The child has internalized parental and societal expectations that bowel movements are supposed to happen in private. The developing ego must find a way to satisfy both the id's desire for immediate gratification and the superego's shame-provoking sense of right and wrong. So the child enjoys the bowel movement without using the potty but does it privately, a choice driven by the practical options weighed by the ego.

For an everyday example, consider this. You're trying to eat healthier. If you go out with your friends for ice cream, you (or rather your id) may want to indulge in a giant sundae; your judgmental superego may remind you of your goals and the promise you made to yourself and convince you to have a glass of water; and your ego, based in the reality principle, may negotiate between the two and decide that you can get some low-fat yogurt.

The three parts of the mind constantly interact with one another. The ego is the reality-based referee between the primitive desires of the id and the ideals of the superego. The ego uses strategies to deal with and reduce the constant threat of anxiety that comes from this struggle between the id and the superego.

The Role of Defense Mechanisms

One strategy the reality-based ego uses is **ego defense mechanisms**, which distort or transform an urge arising from the unconscious to protect itself from anxiety and unwanted knowledge about desires and wants produced by the competing forces of the id and superego. The following eight defense mechanisms are the most common:

- **Repression** is the process of reducing anxiety by blocking impulses or memories from consciousness; it underlies all other defense mechanisms. The impulses or memories are threatening or painful. Some people who experienced terrible trauma as children have pushed those memories out of their mind to successfully live in the present without being haunted by those experiences.

- **Regression** occurs when the ego seeks to reduce anxiety by reverting to an earlier period of psychological development. For example, an adult faced with the stress of surgery may begin biting his or her fingernails or sucking on a thumb.

- **Displacement** occurs when aggressive urges are shifted toward a recipient other than the one who caused the feelings. For example, when you're angry at your parent or another authority figure but expressing that anger directly at them would cause too much anxiety, you yell at your brother or sister instead.

- **Projection** occurs when anxiety-producing feelings are repressed and then placed onto another person. For example, suppose a student feels insecure about their own popularity or social standing. Instead of acknowledging these insecurities, the student might start claiming that other students are overly concerned with being liked or fitting in. By projecting that insecurity onto others, the student manages the feelings without directly addressing their own concerns about acceptance and belonging. They can then navigate their social environment, while deflecting attention from their weak spots.

- **Denial** is the refusal of the ego to accept the reality of a situation, because doing so would produce unbearable anxiety. For example, a parent who hears that their child is causing trouble at school refuses to accept that their "angel" has engaged in such an activity.

- **Reaction-formation** defends against anxiety-producing thoughts or impulses by transforming the unacceptable urge into its opposite. For example, a person who harbors unconscious prejudice toward a group may preach the need for tolerance and inclusivity of that group.

- **Rationalization** occurs when excuses are created to justify or excuse an unacceptable impulse or behavior. For example, a person who wants to exercise regularly skips the gym because they have "had a really hard day."

- **Sublimation** occurs when a person channels an unacceptable urge into something with social value. Someone with an urge for aggressive behavior, for example, may turn it into a creative expression that gives social meaning to an act of aggression, as in a painting of a battle.

Assessing Freud's Theory

Freud developed his theory in the late 19th and early 20th centuries, when Victorian attitudes supporting sexual repression and a strong social ethic were widespread. There was also minimal scientific understanding of the brain and the field of psychology was still young; formulating theories of human behavior involved thoughtful speculation based on case studies rather than on modern empirical scientific methodology. Freud was also heavily influenced by the views of early philosophers on how to understand human behavior.

Major Criticisms of Psychoanalytic Theory Freud's research method, case studies, and theoretical interpretations are one area of major criticism of psychodynamic theory. The psychoanalytic theory is based on case studies that Freud developed from clinical therapy sessions with patients who were primarily troubled upper-class White Austrian women. These case studies lacked scientific methodology. From them, Freud developed biased theoretical explanations that fail to withstand modern scientific scrutiny using empirically based research methods.

A second major criticism is that the various elements of the mind—the id, ego, and superego—are impossible to verify with empirical research. There are no operational definitions of these concepts and no way to measure them. However, Freud never suggested they were literal. He created and used them as hypothetical ideas to illustrate how the mind works.

Freud's analyses of case studies were influenced by the accepted belief in male superiority during the Victorian era in which he lived. His views were, in large part, the product of an extremely male-dominated, paternalistic society. This male-centered and misogynistic worldview was the backdrop for various elements of the theory. When considering the merit of the psychoanalytic theory, you must consider the place and time in which the theory was developed.

A third major criticism is that the proposition that repression and other defense mechanisms prevent awareness of past trauma or current sexual urges is contradicted by current research on posttraumatic stress disorder (PTSD).

PTSD exists not because the trauma is repressed but because it is constantly and vividly remembered. Repressed memory of trauma is the exception, rather than the rule. Nonetheless, recent research does suggest that humans sometimes unconsciously attempt to protect their sense of self by distorting reality, forgetting or misremembering a trauma, although this appears to be the exception rather than the norm.

Last, Freud's theory constructs a closed world in which the theory can explain away any apparent counterexamples within itself. It is insulated from criticism from both within that world and without. For example, psychoanalytic theory can attribute a women's obsession with weaving and knitting to an unconscious motivation to conceal a physical deficiency. If the woman rejects this explanation, then according to the theory, she is employing the defense mechanism of denial. Constructed in this way, psychoanalytic theory allows no explanation to disprove the interpretation. Just as his hypotheses cannot be proved empirically, they can also not be falsified, and they thereby resist scientific scrutiny.

Four Major Criticisms of the Psychoanalytic Approach
1. Based on case studies lacking scientific methodology and drawn from only a small segment of people—mainly troubled upper-class White Austrian women
2. Influenced by male-dominated social norms
3. Thoughts on repressed trauma in PTSD contradicted by more research
4. Closed world allows no way to prove or falsify; everything can be explained away

Table 4.1.1

Strengths of Psychoanalytic Theory An unbiased assessment of psychoanalytic theory includes recognizing its positive aspects as well as its limitations. Despite its many shortcomings, Freud's body of work has enjoyed a lasting positive legacy. Freud's focus on the importance of early childhood has had a profound impact on how we view these early years. It is to his credit that most of the world recognizes that healthy adulthood stems, in part, from a healthy childhood.

In addition, research into both social psychology and attribution theory (see Topics 4.1 through 4.3) supports the theory of unconscious ego defense mechanisms. Some defense mechanisms, such as projection or rationalization, appear to be at work when people unconsciously distort the amount of agreement others share for their own beliefs (known as the false consensus effect). Defense mechanisms also appear to be at work when people attempt to preserve their self-esteem by using rationalization to resolve contradictory beliefs and actions (cognitive dissonance).

Last, though some argue that Freud placed too much emphasis on unconscious determinants of behavior, current research in neuroscience seems to partly validate this emphasis. Although modern neurology and neuroscience were in their infancy during the late 19th and early 20th centuries, Freud's description of the conscious mind as the product of unconscious forces appears to hold merit.

Neo-Freudians (new Freudians) have modified Freud's theory to focus on the impact of childhood events, early feelings of inferiority, and the role of the unconscious and to deemphasize the focus on sex and aggression. This more modern approach is known as the **psychodynamic approach**. And despite many advances in understanding and technology, when it comes to the mind and the physical brain that creates it, what we are aware of is, indeed, just the tip of the iceberg.

Psychodynamic Assessment of Personality

Because psychodynamic theories emphasize the role of unconscious forces in determining personality and behavior, they need tools that can access information that is outside of or beyond a person's conscious awareness. In psychoanalysis sessions, Freud used free association and dreams to gain information about unconscious feelings and influences. Based on these methods of clinical information gathering, researchers developed **projective tests**, which attempt to reveal the contents of the unconscious by getting people to verbally express unconscious issues in response to either an arbitrary or ambiguous shape or image. In projective tests, the person's response to the ambiguous image is assumed to be a *projection* of their unconscious thoughts, feelings, and impulses. (Remember the defense mechanism of projection, in which our own unacceptable thoughts or feelings are placed onto someone or something else.) Two projective tests are the Rorschach inkblot test and the Thematic Apperception Test (TAT).

Swiss psychologist and art student Hermann Rorschach created one of the most famous assessments in psychological history. The Rorschach inkblot test involves asking people to explain what they see in a set of ambiguous images called inkblots. An inkblot is formed by placing ink on paper, folding the paper in half, and then separating the halves. A standardized set of ten inkblots is used in assessments, and testers are trained to interpret responses to them. A person's response is scored by examining how many of the ten responses refer to the entire ink blot, major details of the inkblot that do not include the entire blot, minor details to which most people will not generally respond, the shading of the ink, the colors of the ink, and whether the figures discerned in the blot are static or moving. Those who analyze these assessments are looking for themes that may uncover unconscious wants and desires.

Inkblot

Personality theorist Henry Murray developed the Thematic Apperception Test (TAT) in the 1930s as an alternative assessment to the Rorschach test. This TAT involves presenting to people a standardized set of ambiguous photographs or illustrations. Images can show one, two, or more people in a setting. The nature of the setting may not be clear, and the relationship between the people is up to the viewer to decide. Individuals taking the TAT are asked to create a story in response to an image that explains who the people are and what they are doing. Additionally, they are asked what led up to the situation, what is happening in the picture, and what might happen later. The TAT provides more material to work with than typical responses to the Rorschach inkblot test.

These tests encourage individuals to say whatever comes to mind in response to the stimuli. This process is thought to tap into the preconscious—the thoughts that are not in immediate conscious awareness but can be accessed with some attention—and the unconscious, which houses repressed or socially unacceptable desires or emotions.

Both the Rorschach inkblot test and the Thematic Apperception Test are criticized for lacking validity, which means researchers cannot determine whether they measure what they are supposed to measure. Although a trained professional interprets the tests, scoring the test results is still subjective. Second, because of their subjective nature, the tests have low reliability, which means that the test results are not consistent when the same person repeats the test. Although projective tests can be useful in therapeutic situations and to encourage dialogue between psychologist and client, they should not be considered methodologically sound tools for testing hypotheses derived from a personality theory.

Humanistic Theories

Humanist psychologist Carl Rogers told a story of when he was a child living in an old house with a basement. There was a small window at the top of a basement wall. A bin of potatoes was stored against a basement wall for quite a while. One day his mother asked him to go down in the basement and fetch some potatoes. When he went downstairs, he saw something that stuck with him for life. In the darkness of the basement, the potatoes had begun to sprout, the vines clinging to the basement wall growing ever closer to the light from the small window. Carl Rogers believed the potatoes and their growing vines captured the essence of human growth, leading him to develop the humanistic approach to psychology. Those potatoes were growing toward the light, despite their desperate condition, and it is in our

Potatoes growing in a dark basement and reaching for the light inspired Carl Rogers to recognize the desire "to become."

very nature as human beings to reach for our own light. It is in our very nature, as Rogers expressed it, to *become*. The humanistic approach to personality stresses the positive qualities and potential inherent in all of us.

The humanistic approach emerged in the second half of the 20th century as a "third force" in psychology, contrasting with the negative view of psychodynamic theories and the overly mechanical and deterministic approach of behaviorism. Additionally, both the psychodynamic and behavioral theories are reactive models: In the psychodynamic model, the ego reacts to the demands of the id; in the behavioral model, a stimulus causes a response. Humanism's contribution was that it emphasized free will and continual growth, not reaction. In the humanistic perspective, individuals have the autonomy to make their own choices and are responsible for their actions. This belief in free will underlines the idea that people are capable of shaping their own destinies by making conscious decisions. The most well-known humanistic theorists are Carl Rogers and Abraham Maslow.

Carl Rogers

Carl Rogers is often credited with founding the humanistic approach. He was first and foremost a psychotherapist. The body of work he produced stemmed largely from case studies from his work with his clients, and it was from his experience first as a minister and then as a psychotherapist that he formed his humanistic views about personality.

Rogers believed that people have an innate drive toward *self-actualization*, which he defined as the ongoing process of realizing one's inherent potentials and capabilities. This drive is considered a fundamental part of human nature, pushing individuals to grow, develop, and achieve personal fulfillment. People on their way to self-actualization are characterized by openness to experience, a lack of defensiveness, the ability to be in touch with their deepest and most profound feelings, and a congruent alignment between their self-image and their everyday experiences. Rogers believed that people are naturally good and that a person is born perfectly congruent between the real self and the ideal self. The real self is the recognition and acceptance of one's natural self and the person they are in their day-to-day lives. To see a real self in action, watch a toddler interact with himself or herself in front of a mirror. There's no holding back the love and acceptance he or she has for that person in the mirror.

The ideal self emerges as the result of interactions with significant people in an individual's life, particularly parents. If all went perfectly, parents would have expressed **unconditional regard**, nonjudgmental acceptance of their children, without regard to their behavior. Such unconditional regard rarely happens, and some level of conditions of worth, implicit or explicit standards for acceptance and love, are in place in most relationships. These conditions of worth begin to separate the ideal self from the real self, which leads the two selves to become incongruent. The more the incongruence or separation, the more severe the impact on individuals' self-concept, or image of themselves. (See Figure 4.4.2.)

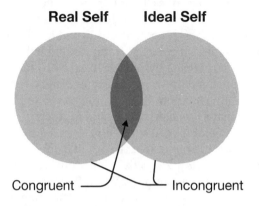

Real Self   **Ideal Self**

Congruent — Incongruent

Figure 4.4.2 Carl Rogers's Theory

A dysfunctional personality is a symptom of significant incongruence between the ideal self and the real self. For Rogers, this unhealthy state of incongruence could be resolved and a healthier personality achieved through exposure to genuine unconditional positive regard, which accepts a person in their current state without judgment. If a person were provided with genuine unconditional regard along with empathy, he or she would begin to become a fully functioning person, a person who strives to *become* and accept his or her genuine self. Many of Rogers's beliefs about unconditional positive regard and the ability of people to help move themselves toward their best selves have been incorporated into modern-day therapeutic approaches, which you will read more about in Unit 5.

Abraham Maslow

Abraham Maslow, like Rogers, embraced the basic goodness in human nature. Although Rogers's views were formed from his work as a psychotherapist, Maslow's theory of human behavior developed from his study of healthy personalities, such as Abraham Lincoln. Maslow observed the pessimistic nature of Freud's approach and the mechanistic approach of behaviorists. He took a different approach that views human personality as a reflection of the needs a person is striving to satisfy.

Maslow explained how people's motivations and behaviors reflect the physical or psychological needs they are trying to meet. Like Rogers, he theorized that all people are innately motivated by a **self-actualizing tendency**, fulfilling their natural desire to achieve their full potential. All levels above biological and safety needs are important contributors to personality, as people strive for belongingness, self-esteem, and self-actualization in different manners that relate to their personalities.

Maslow saw self-actualization as an ongoing process and becoming fully self-actualized as a rare event. According to Maslow, an unhealthy personality is one in which people are continually frustrated at the inability to satisfy their need to self-actualize. He attributed individuals' limitations to thrive to their environment rather than to a lack of desire and effort to become their best.

Assessing Humanistic Theories

The humanistic approach brought a much-needed positive outlook to theories of personality. It provided a new perspective of people as growing organisms rather than simply reactive beings, and it looked to the future rather than the past. The humanistic approach has found application beyond psychology in teaching and businesses. The approach has helped institutional management motivate and form more meaningful relationships with employees by recognizing and responding to their needs.

In spite of these contributions, humanistic theories have significant weaknesses. The theories are based on hypotheses that were not developed from empirical data or scientific observation. The concepts are vague and, therefore, extremely difficult to assess using sound scientific methodology, since they can neither be proved nor disproved. Additionally, critics point out that the humanistic view is overly optimistic about human nature and naïve in its prescription for a healthy personality.

Humanistic Assessment of Personality

Humanistic theories focus on the conscious mind and the belief that individuals are inherently capable of growth and fulfillment. The assessment of personality within this framework emphasizes understanding the person's view of themselves and their world, with particular attention to their feelings, thoughts, and experiences. Techniques such as open-ended interviews, self-report questionnaires, and narrative approaches are commonly used. One method, known as the self-image checklist, asks people to go through a list of characteristics and identify which of those applies to their personality now (real self). Next, they go through the same list of characteristics and identify those that represent the person they would like to be (ideal self). If there is much overlap between these, the person is congruent, and if not, they are incongruent and may need some help and focus to move closer to their real self. These methods allow individuals to articulate their self-perceptions, goals, and the obstacles they perceive in achieving self-actualization, providing a comprehensive and personal account of their personality.

Interviews—one-on-one conversations for the purpose of obtaining research information—are often used by humanistic theorists. While providing a wealth of personal information, the possibility of dishonesty is always a problem. Humanist theorists also use case studies (see Practice 2) involving in-depth analysis of a single subject.

THINK AS A PSYCHOLOGIST

Apply Psychological Perspectives, Theories, Concepts, and Research Findings to a Scenario (1.A.2) | Evaluate the Appropriate Use of Research Design Elements in Non-Experimental Methodologies (2.C.5)

Gina is a 20-year-old college student who is studying to become a surgeon. While generally a good student, she has on occasion missed classes and deadlines because she was out partying late the night before. Whenever this occurs, she feels guilty and is ashamed because she truly cares about school and wants to be successful in her academic pursuits. While she has good friends, she feels like her family is obsessed with her success. She often worries that she isn't living up to their high standards.

Practice Applying Perspectives and Evaluating the Use of Research Designs

Complete the following activities and answer the question.

1. Describe how a psychologist from the psychodynamic perspective would account for Gina's behaviors.

2. Describe how a psychologist from the humanistic perspective would account for Gina's behaviors.

3. If a psychodynamic psychologist wanted to further learn about Gina's personality, they would likely use a projective test (e.g. the Thematic Apperception Test). Would the use of a projective test be considered a measurement that is quantitative or qualitative? Explain your answer.

REFLECT ON THE ESSENTIAL QUESTION

Essential Question: *How do psychodynamic and humanistic theories of personality define and assess personality?* Using the Key Terms, complete a chart like the one below to gather details to help answer that question.

Theory	Definition of Personality	Assessment of Personality
Psychodynamic		
Humanistic		

STUDY LIKE A CHAMP WITH DR. G | INTERLEAVE

After answering the multiple-choice questions for Topic 4.3, choose a topic from an earlier unit and review the questions at the end. Interleaving consistently will help you better remember what you read.

KEY TERMS

consciousness	preconscious	reality principle
denial	projection	regression
displacement	projective tests	repression
ego	psychodynamic approach	self-actualizing tendency
ego defense mechanism	psychodynamic theory	sublimation
morality principle	of personality	unconditional regard
personality	rationalization	unconscious
pleasure principle	reaction formation	

MULTIPLE-CHOICE QUESTIONS

1. Freud said, "He that has eyes to see and ears to hear may convince himself that no mortal can keep a secret. If his lips are silent, he chatters with his fingertips; betrayal oozes out of him at every pore." To which aspect of psychoanalytic theory was Freud referring?

   (A) Defense mechanisms

   (B) Unconscious

   (C) Superego

   (D) The pleasure principle

2. Lauren was verbally reprimanded by her boss for dressing too casually at work and was told to go home during her lunch break and change into more professional attire. While driving home, Lauren gives the middle finger to a driver as he passes by. Which defense mechanism is most closely associated with Lauren's behavior?

   (A) Reaction-formation

   (B) Projection

   (C) Denial

   (D) Displacement

3. Which of the following is a consistent criticism leveled against Freudian psychoanalytic theory?

   (A) Freud relied too heavily on surface behaviors to infer causality.

   (B) Freud believed that humans are fundamentally animals with advanced intellectual capacities.

   (C) Freud believed the mind was made up of the id, ego, and superego, but these constructs are impossible to verify empirically.

   (D) Freud assumed that personality characteristics developed primarily from unconscious sources.

4. Why would a psychodynamic theorist prefer to use projective tests rather than interviews?

(A) Projective tests have higher validity and are more reliable.

(B) Interviews fail to take into consideration the underlying causes of a behavior.

(C) Projective tests, like the TAT, can reveal insights into unconscious motives.

(D) Interviews do not elicit honest responses regarding past events that formed aspects of the core personality.

5. "The curious paradox is when I accept myself just as I am, then I can change." This quotation most closely aligns with which of the following?

(A) Rogers's belief in the need for unconditional regard

(B) Rogers's belief in the importance of congruence

(C) Freud's belief in the importance of sublimation

(D) Freud's belief in the unconscious desires of the id

6. Freud wrote, "Instincts and their derivatives may be arranged as pairs of opposites: life versus death, construction versus destruction, action versus passivity, dominance versus submission, and so forth. When one of the instincts produces anxiety by exerting pressure on the ego either directly or by way of the superego, the ego may try to sidetrack the offending impulse by concentrating upon its opposite. For example, if feelings of hate toward another person make one anxious, the ego can facilitate the flow of love to conceal the hostility." This quotation is an attempt to explain which of the following ego defense mechanisms?

(A) Projection

(B) Reaction formation

(C) Denial

(D) Rationalization

7. Which of the following is a critique that a humanistic psychologist might level at someone who adheres to the psychodynamic approach to psychology?

(A) It places undue influence on the unconscious.

(B) It suggests that people have free will.

(C) It looks at how other people affect an individual's behavior.

(D) It focuses exclusively on what is happening in the brain and body.

Topic 4.5

Social-Cognitive and Trait Theories of Personality

"Personality is less a finished product than a transitive process. While it has some stable features, it is at the same time continually undergoing change."

—Gordon Allport

Essential Question: How do social-cognitive and trait theories of personality define and assess personality?

As the 20th century progressed, dissatisfaction with the psychoanalytic approach grew. The behavioral approach became an alternative to explaining the development and structure of personality. It rejected unconscious determinants of behavior and valued what can be empirically and objectively measured. The behavioral approach focused on the central role of learning, through rewards and punishments, in the development of personality. (See Topic 3.8 for more on operant conditioning.) The contributions of John Watson and B. F. Skinner established the behavioral school as an alternative to the more subjective and less scientific approach of Freud and the neo-Freudians. Initially, behaviorists rejected the idea of considering how thinking played a role in behaviors. However, it eventually became obvious that, if psychologists were to understand human and animal behavior and motives, thinking must become part of that equation.

Social-cognitive theories share the basic tenets of behaviorism—you are what you learn—but they also focus on the cognitive aspects of learning and forming behavioral patterns that come to shape personality. Like behavioral theorists, social-cognitive theorists reject explanations of personality based on unconscious forces that cannot be observed and measured.

Another response to the psychodynamic theorists' focus on the hidden forces behind behavior and personality is trait theory. Trait theories focus on observable and more measurable stable personality characteristics, including behavior, thought processes, and emotions.

Social-Cognitive Theory

The **social-cognitive theory** of personality suggests that cognitive processes play a role equal to the environment's role in determining the individual's behavior patterns and personality. To social-cognitive theorists, a combination of observational learning and mental processes lead to the long-lasting patterns of behavior called *personality*.

Albert Bandura proposed that three factors—person, environment, and behavior—interact to determine patterns of behavior and, thus, personality. Figure 4.5.1 illustrates Bandura's model of **reciprocal determinism**. In this model, a person's behavior (actions and decisions), environment, and personal factors (cognitive and biological processes, emotions, and competencies) interact with one another to determine behavior. For example, Rachel thinks she is funny and enjoys making people laugh (cognitive, emotional, and competency personal factors). These assessments lead her to join her school's improv team (behavior). Being on the improv team with other funny people (environment) leads to her making people laugh, which reinforces her beliefs that she is funny.

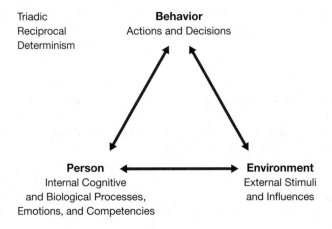

Figure 4.5.1 Albert Bandura's Reciprocal Determinism Model

Bandura came to believe that Skinner's exclusive emphasis on the environment was not enough to explain and understand the fine nuances of human and animal behavior. Instead, his theory assumes that a person's thinking (cognition), prior learning, and capacity to change the environment influence and determine behavior, not the environment alone.

Self-concept—the way one views oneself and in relation to others—is one of the key aspects of the "person" part of the triad. According to reciprocal determinism, an individual's self-concept both shapes and is shaped by their behavior and the environment. For example, a student who perceives themself as a strong leader (self-concept) may be more inclined to take on leadership roles in group projects (behavior), which, in turn, creates a social environment that reinforces their self-perception as a leader.

Both self-efficacy and self-esteem contribute to self-concept. **Self-efficacy**, the degree to which a person thinks (cognition) their efforts (behavior) will result in a desired outcome, illustrates the importance of thought on behavior and plays a crucial role in shaping self-concept within the framework of reciprocal determinism. High self-efficacy can enhance an individual's confidence in their capabilities on a certain task, motivating them to tackle challenges and persevere in the face of adversity. Self-efficacy on a task usually develops because of success on the same or similar task in the past. This self-assurance can have a positive effect on how one views oneself, contributing to a more positive self-concept. For instance, a student who believes they are capable of mastering difficult math problems (high self-efficacy) is likely to engage more persistently with challenging coursework, which in turn may lead to better performance. This success reinforces the student's belief in their competence, further strengthening their self-concept as a capable learner. According to the social-cognitive approach, people can develop high self-efficacy by changing their behaviors, thoughts, and social environment.

Self-esteem, or one's overall sense of self-worth or personal value, is another personal factor that contributes significantly to self-concept. Individuals with high self-esteem generally have a positive view of themselves, which influences their interactions with the environment and their behavior in ways that reinforce this positive self-perception. For example, a student with high self-esteem is more likely to participate actively in class discussions, seek leadership opportunities, and pursue ambitious goals, behaviors that can earn them further positive feedback from the environment (such as recognition from teachers and peers), affirming and enhancing their self-concept.

Assessing Social-Cognitive Theory

Social-cognitive theory provides valuable contributions to our understanding of personality, such as recognizing how social factors and mental processes contribute to behavioral outcomes. Most concepts in the social-cognitive theory are testable under scientific conditions. However, social-cognitive theory does not directly address biological influences on personality. It also seems overly critical of the concept and influence of unconscious aspects of the mind on behavior and personality and, perhaps, dismisses them too easily.

Assessment of Personality

In social-cognitive theory, personality assessment often involves a combination of methods that focus on understanding how individuals think, behave, and interact with their environment. These assessments tend to emphasize observable behaviors, cognitive processes, and situational responses. To reveal *cognitive processes,* self-report questionnaires may ask individuals to rate their agreement with statements that reflect their beliefs about their capabilities, their thoughts on the outcomes of their actions, or their general attitudes. To reveal *behavior* in different situations—either those designed to elicit certain behaviors or those taking place in everyday experience—observational methods can identify patterns of behavior that reflect underlying personality traits, such as how individuals respond to social pressures, handle stress, or pursue goals. To reveal *personality traits* such as perseverance, creativity, or resilience, performance tasks are administered. These are designed to simulate real-world challenges that require active problem-solving and decision-making and show how individuals apply their cognitive processes to manage and adapt to situations. Interviews and diaries are other ways to gather information that cognitive-social psychologists use to assess personality.

Trait Theories

While reciprocal determinism emphasizes the connections among individual behavior, environmental factors, and cognitive processes, trait theories present a different perspective by focusing on the consistent patterns in personality. Trait theorists focus on observable and more measurable **traits**, which are stable personality characteristics of behavior, thought processes, and emotions. According to **trait theories**, personality consists of observable and measurable traits that endure over time and across situations.

In 1936, Gordon Allport was the first psychologist to develop a comprehensive theory centered on traits. He rejected psychoanalysis as unscientific and impractical. Allport argued that explanations of behavior require determining a person's unique and enduring traits. He also rejected environmental influences. Instead, Allport proposed that personality is guided by about five to ten central traits, with which people are born. In addition, he went through the dictionary and identified thousands of words people commonly use to describe personality and traits.

Raymond Cattell used a statistical method called **factor analysis** to identify clusters of traits that are related to each other. Factor analysis analyzes multiple variables that are correlated and identifies how those correlations connect with each other. The technique allowed Cattell to find the overarching qualities that connect numerous different traits into clusters and, thereby, reduce the number of traits. The result was a more manageable and measurable way of studying personality traits.

Paul Costa and Robert McCrae developed a list of five traits or factors called the *five-factor model*, often referred to as the **Big Five theory** (see Figure 4.5.2). These five factors, which exist along a continuum described by adjectives at each extreme, are **agreeableness**, **conscientiousness**, **openness**, **neuroticism**, and **extraversion**. (A good mnemonic device for identifying the Big Five is OCEAN—**O**penness, **C**onscientiousness, **E**xtraversion, **A**greeableness, and **N**euroticism.) Costa and McCrae's Big Five model is currently the most widely accepted trait theory. The model is based on responses to various questionnaires and other research methods from a large pool of participants from around the world. Research has demonstrated that the Big Five traits are stable in adulthood, influenced by genetics, and predictive of behavior.

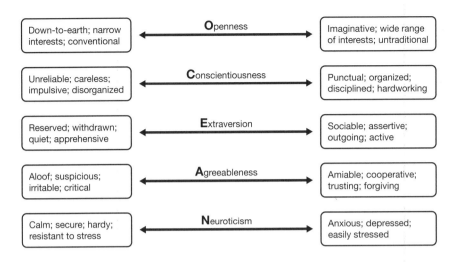

Down-to-earth; narrow interests; conventional	←── **O**penness ──→	Imaginative; wide range of interests; untraditional
Unreliable; careless; impulsive; disorganized	←── **C**onscientiousness ──→	Punctual; organized; disciplined; hardworking
Reserved; withdrawn; quiet; apprehensive	←── **E**xtraversion ──→	Sociable; assertive; outgoing; active
Aloof; suspicious; irritable; critical	←── **A**greeableness ──→	Amiable; cooperative; trusting; forgiving
Calm; secure; hardy; resistant to stress	←── **N**euroticism ──→	Anxious; depressed; easily stressed

Figure 5.4.2 Costa and McCrae's Five-Factor Model

Assessing Trait Theories

A strength of trait theories is the high degree of correlation among the traits defined independently by different researchers, no doubt because they were determined by observable behavior. When one aggregates a person's behavior over time and across different situations, patterns emerge. These patterns are what one might call a "personality" or "personality traits."

A criticism of trait theories is that it relies on the research method of self-reporting, which is accurate only to the degree that the subjects know themselves well and can assess themselves with a degree of objectivity. It also does not attempt to explain why certain behaviors and traits have developed. A major criticism of trait theories is that, while there are general consistencies across time and situation, situational variables are more accurate in predicting behavior than traits are. For example, if cheering for a sports team, an extraverted and an introverted person may both cheer because the situation dictates it, though an extraverted person may cheer more loudly than an introverted person.

Another major criticism of trait theory is that it does not do a good job in distinguishing "trait" from "personality." Most people would say that a personality is a constellation of traits, whereas trait theory tends to concentrate on single traits to describe a person.

Self-Report Personality Inventories

Researchers investigating trait theories use self-report personality inventories. **Self-report personality inventories** are questionnaires that consist of many closed-ended statements or questions that the test taker responds to with a yes/no or true/false response. Costa and McCrae developed the Neuroticism

Extraversion Openness Personality Inventory–Revised (NEO PI-R) to measure the dimensions of the five-factor model.

Well-designed self-reporting personality inventories tend to have higher reliability and validity than projective tests, but they also have problems. Participants may want to project a positive image and answer questions with some dishonesty, or they may unknowingly be deceiving themselves. They may also answer the questions too quickly and not think carefully about exactly how the question pertains to them.

THINK AS A PSYCHOLOGIST

Determine the Type of Research Design(s) Used in a Given Study (2.A.1) | Describe Trends in and Relationships Between the Variables as Depicted in the Data Presented, Such as Interpreting Correlational Data from a Scatterplot, Including the Correlation Coefficient (3.C.1) | Apply Psychological Perspectives, Theories, Concepts, and Research Findings to a Scenario (1.A.1)

Mrs. Griffey conducted a study to see if her class (N = 30) grades aligned with how students rated themselves on organizational skill (using a scale of 1–10). Her results are presented below.

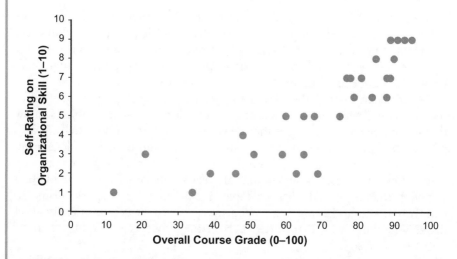

Practice Determining the Type of Research, Describing Trends in Data, and Applying Perspectives

Answer the following questions.

1. Briefly explain why Mrs. Griffey's study is not experimental.

2. Describe the relationship between the two variables in the above chart.

3. Which of the Big Five personality characteristics is being measured in this study?

Essential Question: *How do social-cognitive and trait theories of personality define and assess personality?* Using the Key Terms, complete a chart like the one below to gather details to help answer that question.

Theory	Definition of Personality	Assessment of Personality
Social-Cognitive Theory		
Trait Theories		

KEY TERMS

agreeableness	openness	self-report personality
Big Five theory	reciprocal determinism	inventory
conscientiousness	self-concept	social-cognitive theory
extraversion	self-efficacy	trait
factor analysis	self-esteem	trait theory
neuroticism		

MULTIPLE-CHOICE QUESTIONS

1. Trait theorists would most likely be criticized for which of the following?

   (A) Their emphasis on the importance of self-efficacy in the development of a healthy personality

   (B) Their belief that traits persist across all situations and are stable through the lifespan

   (C) Their belief that personality develops through early childhood conditioning and interaction with the environment

   (D) Their rejection of the notion that traits may be heavily influenced by biological factors

2. Reginald is a project manager who has many different tasks to juggle at work. He is often late to appointments and forgets to follow up with customers. Although he clearly knows the job and is capable, he often fails to complete projects on time. Based on this description, Reginald would rate low in which Big Five personality characteristics?

   (A) Neuroticism

   (B) Agreeableness

   (C) Conscientiousness

   (D) Openness

The following figure represents data collected about the Big Five personality characteristics gathered from around the world.

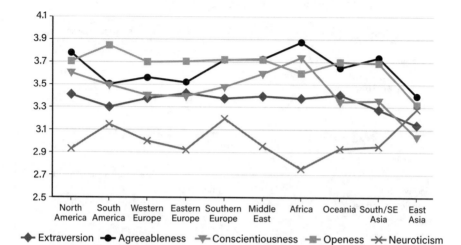

Source: Adapted from Schmitt, D. P., Allik, J., McCrae, R. R., & Benet-Martínez, V. (2007). The geographic distribution of big five personality traits: patterns and profiles of human self-description across 56 Nations. *Journal of Cross-Cultural Psychology, 38*(2), 173-212.

3. Based on the data displayed in the chart, which area of the world has the highest level of openness?

(A) North America

(B) South America

(C) Western Europe

(D) Middle East

4. Based on the data in the chart, which areas of the world has the highest levels of conscientiousness?

(A) Western Europe

(B) Eastern Europe

(C) Africa

(D) Southeast Asia

5. The scores below represent the mean for each area on the scale of neuroticism. What is the median score of the following data set?

Area of the World	Mean Score
North America	2.9
South America	3.1
Western Europe	3.0
Eastern Europe	2.9
Southern Europe	3.2
Middle East	2.9
Africa	2.7
Oceania	2.9
South/SE Asia	2.9
East Asia	3.3

(A) 3.3

(B) 3.0

(C) 2.9

(D) 2.7

6. Jamal recently took a personality inventory, but he did not know what concepts each question was asking him about. However, at the end of the test, all of the questions were clustered into categories and he was given an overall score representing his level in each of the Big Five personality categories. What method was used to organize these results?

(A) Factor analysis

(B) Inferential statistics

(C) Descriptive statistics

(D) Correlational coefficients

7. Caroline is a school counselor who talks to many students about issues they are having both in school and at home. She firmly believes that interactions among the child's thoughts, environment, and behaviors influence one another and impact the child's developing personality. Caroline's beliefs are most closely aligned with which of the following?

(A) Trait theory

(B) Self-efficacy

(C) Self-concept

(D) Reciprocal determinism

Topic 4.6

Motivation

"You may encounter many defeats, but you must not be defeated. In fact, it may be necessary to encounter the defeats, so you can know who you are, what you can rise from, how you can still come out of it."

—Maya Angelou

Essential Questions: How do theories about motivation apply to behavior and mental processes? How do eating and belongingness motivate behavior and mental processes?

Motivation is the drive that initiates, sustains, directs, and terminates actions—that is, motivation is the force directing a person to behave a certain way. Why do people fall in love, commit crimes, eat breakfast, run marathons, and perform a virtually limitless number of other behaviors?

Theories of Motivation

Several different theories attempt to explain motivation, but no single theory truly captures the complexity of what motivates all humans in all situations. Psychologists studying motivation, then, often focus on specific behaviors in their attempt to provide a more complete understanding of the factors that influence behaviors in general. This topic explores several theories of motivation and then takes an integrated approach to explain why we engage in a specific motivated behavior—eating.

Drive-Reduction Theory

Psychologist Clark Hull, focusing on *physical needs and desires*, argued that people are motivated by needs, drives, responses, and goals. He described the interaction of these four factors as the **drive-reduction theory** of motivation. Figure 4.6.1 shows how Hull believed that this model worked.

A person has a **need** when they have a biological need that has gone unmet. The need leads to the creation of a **drive**, an energized emotional state that pushes the person to do something. For example, hunger is an internal need that creates a drive, such as a push to eat. To reduce or eliminate that need, the person responds by trying to find food and stops responding only when the goal is met (i.e., the need has been satisfied; the person is no longer hungry). Drive reduction helps a person (or other animal) maintain a level of **homeostasis**, an internal balance in the body—somewhere between feeling very hungry and feeling overly full, for example.

The drive-reduction theory does well in explaining primary biological functions and needs, such as hunger and thirst, sleep and sex. However, critics of the drive-reduction theory believe it is too simple to explain all the varied behaviors of humans and animals. It also does not address topics such as ego, greed, love, commitment, compassion, attachment, and affiliation. By the late 1950s, motivational research headed in a different direction.

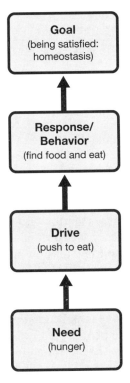

Figure 4.6.1 Drive-Reduction Theory

Arousal Theory

Arousal theory, like drive-reduction theory, focuses on physical needs and desires. **Arousal theory** proposes that people and other animals are motivated to perform because they are trying to maintain optimal levels of physiological arousal—the state of being awake and alert. If the arousal level is too high, they will be overstimulated and unable to concentrate, so they will be motivated to relax. If the arousal level is too low, they will seek out action or something that stimulates them.

Figure 4.6.2 shows how arousal influences performance. In general, people are motivated to behave so that they stay moderately aroused all the time.

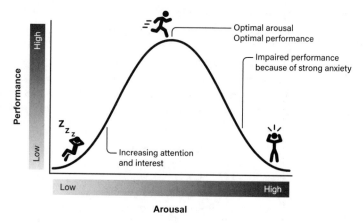

Figure 4.6.2 The Yerkes-Dodson Law of Arousal

When arousal is very low, people's performance suffers—they may be inattentive or uninterested (think about a boring lecture when you are tired; you probably won't remember much). When arousal is very high, however, people's performance also suffers—they may be anxious or overwhelmed. (People often report that they were overly excited/ambitious and "choked" in this situation. Think of an athlete who has made it to the state championship but is so nervous that they cannot perform to the best of their ability.) The idea that people need moderate levels of arousal to complete a task successfully is known as the **Yerkes-Dodson law** of arousal or the inverted-U theory of arousal, developed by psychologists Robert M. Yerkes and John Dillingham Dodson.

Of course, the "best" or optimal level of arousal for each person is determined by a combination of the individual's characteristics and elements of the situation or context. For example, some people prefer quieter environments and time alone to be able to think; they are motivated to find a lower level of arousal than someone who loves to be a regular part of large parties and celebrations. Task difficulty plays a role too. For example, most people need relatively lower levels of arousal to complete difficult tasks that require concentration, such as reading, and relatively higher ones to complete endurance tasks that require stamina, such as swimming.

A weakness of the arousal theory is that it is merely descriptive. It also does not explain complex social needs or indicate specifically what a person should do to obtain an optimal level of arousal in order to increase performance.

Self-Determination Theory

Self-determination theory (SDT), developed by psychologists Edward Deci and Richard Ryan, focuses on psychological needs. It is a broad framework for the study of human motivation and personality. It is centered on the belief that human beings have innate psychological needs that are the basis for self-motivation and personality integration. **Self-determination theory** identifies three fundamental psychological needs that must be satisfied to foster well-being, health, and behavioral effectiveness: autonomy, competence, and relatedness. *Autonomy* refers to feeling in control of one's own behaviors and goals; *competence* involves feeling capable and effective in one's activities; and *relatedness* means feeling a sense of belonging and attachment to others. Think about how affiliation in a club or sport at school might fulfill these needs. You are likely free to select the sport or club of your choice based on your own interests (autonomy). If you choose the math team because you like the subject, it is likely that you will perform well (competence), and you have an opportunity to meet and connect with others who share your interest (relatedness). SDT posits that greater fulfillment of these needs is associated with higher levels of intrinsic motivation and mental health.

Intrinsic motivation refers to doing an activity for its inherent satisfaction rather than for some outside reward. When students are intrinsically motivated, their behavior, persistence, and creativity are heightened. For example, high school students who enjoy learning about history because they find the subject genuinely interesting and rewarding are intrinsically motivated. This internal desire to explore, learn, and challenge oneself is the hallmark of intrinsic motivation. In contrast, **extrinsic motivation** involves performing an activity to achieve an external reward or avoid punishments. For instance, a student might study hard to get good grades, not because they enjoy the material or find it interesting, but because they want to gain approval from parents or teachers or because they see high grades as a pathway to college.

SDT suggests that while both intrinsic and extrinsic motivations are important, intrinsic motivation is generally associated with better learning outcomes, higher quality of work, and greater psychological well-being.

Incentive Theory

While drives can be seen as pushing behavior, **incentives** can be seen as pulling behavior (see Figure 4.6.3). In other words, drives are internal stimuli that motivate a behavior, whereas incentives are external stimuli that motivate a behavior—sometimes the same behavior. Consider, for example, an ice cream sundae or a pepperoni pizza or some other food that you find particularly tasty. You may be pushed to eat one of those appealing foods because of an internal drive—hunger. Or you might be pulled by an external incentive to eat the food because it's tasty, your friends are also eating and you want to join them, or there's a contest for how fast or how much you can eat, even if you are not being pushed by the internal drive of hunger.

People are motivated by incentives in all sorts of domains. A good grade is an academic incentive. A cash bonus for finishing a project at work is an economic incentive. A romantic relationship can be a social incentive. In each case, the incentive is something that a person is pulled toward and motivated to achieve. Incentives always have value to the individual striving to obtain them, but that value is based on a variety of factors beyond their ability to satisfy a need. For example, many Americans would find a chocolate sundae to be an incentive, but what about large fried caterpillars, which are a delicacy in parts of the world? What about balut, a partially developed duck inside its eggshell? For most Americans, eating caterpillar or balut probably has low incentive value.

Drives (Internal) and Incentives (External)

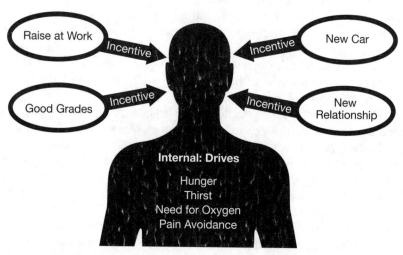

Figure 4.6.3 Incentive Theory

The incentive theory of motivation is based on the principles established by Edward Thorndike, B. F. Skinner, and others. (See Topic 3.8.) It can easily identify external pulls on behavior. However, the incentive model of motivation may not adequately explain altruistic behaviors or compassion.

Instinct Theory

In everyday conversation, people often use the word *instinct*—"listen to your instincts," "your first instinct is usually right," "if you want to win, you need to have that killer instinct." It's often used to mean a gut feeling about something, in place of or along with the word *intuition*, and sometimes it's used to mean a behavior that doesn't require any thought (e.g., a *reflex*). For psychologists, however, *instinct* has a more specific meaning. **Instinct** is an innate and consistent pattern of complex behavior that is performed the same way by every member of the species.

Human instinct-like behaviors include the drives to eat, drink, find shelter, and reproduce, though culture influences the ways in which these behaviors play out. The fight-flight-freeze response, a physiological reaction to threat that directs us to either fight, flee, or freeze for survival, is an element of human behavior closest to an instinct, though it is shared by other species.

Instincts can't explain most of the complex behaviors that humans engage in every day nor the diversity of behaviors people exhibit in response to the same stimuli. Some scientists argue that our complex behaviors have instinctive components, but humans also have a cerebral cortex for decision-making, which may override any predispositions to behave without thinking.

Other animals have instinctual fixed action patterns—behaviors in response to stimuli that, once started, continue to completion. Newly hatched sea turtles moving toward the ocean, honeybees dancing to communicate, baby kangaroos crawling up to get into the mother's pouch, and birds building nests are carrying out fixed action patterns. The turtles are motivated to get to the ocean, but they're not consciously aware of a need; their instinct is the reason they run for the water with all their energy.

Sensation-Seeking Theory

The **sensation-seeking theory of motivation**, developed by psychologist Marvin Zuckerman, describes a trait defined by the search for experiences and feelings that are varied, novel, complex, and intense. Individuals high in sensation-seeking are drawn to new, unusual, and thrilling experiences, often demonstrating a higher tolerance for risk and a lesser fear of potential dangers. Zuckerman identified four components that make up the sensation-seeking trait: thrill- or adventure-seeking, experience-seeking, disinhibition, and boredom susceptibility.

Thrill- or adventure-seeking involves a desire for outdoor activities and physically challenging pursuits that provide a high level of arousal. Thrill- or adventure-seeking might manifest as participation in extreme sports such as skateboarding, rock climbing, or mountain biking—activities that are physically thrilling.

Experience-seeking describes the pursuit of novel sensory or intellectual experiences through art, travel, music, and social nonconformity. Experience-seeking might be observed in people who are drawn to foreign exchange programs or cultural festivals, seeking new experiences that differ from their routine environment. People who are motivated by experience-seeking are often more open to exploring different cuisines, learning new languages, and immersing themselves in unfamiliar customs, driven by a deep desire for novel experiences that stimulate their senses and intellect. These behaviors will likely align to the personality trait of openness, which you read about in Topic 4.5.

Disinhibition refers to the tendency to seek release in social settings through partying, social drinking, or engaging in uninhibited social behaviors. For example, an individual with high disinhibition might be the first to volunteer for karaoke or dance contests, enjoying the feeling of letting loose among peers.

Last, **boredom susceptibility** is characterized by an aversion to repetition, routine, and predictable circumstances. Such individuals might find regular classroom settings stifling or traditional lectures tedious, often seeking ways to break the monotony with creative or unconventional responses to assignments. If you are motivated by boredom susceptibility, you might be more likely to challenge curricular norms, advocating for project-based learning or interactive educational technologies that provide the continual stimulation that keeps you engaged.

Motivational Conflicts

Kurt Lewin developed a theory based on how people see their "life space"— the arena in which they make social decisions. He theorized that people experience psychological tension until they fulfill their personal goals, and social behavior is motivated by the desire to resolve that tension. He went on to develop **motivational conflicts theory**, which describes the dynamics of human decision-making in the face of conflicting motivations. Lewin identified three primary types of motivational conflicts: approach-approach, approach-avoidance, and avoidance-avoidance.

These conflicting motives are engaged when we must make a choice between two things that pull us in different directions. If the choice is between two desirable options, it is called an **approach-approach conflict**. Do I go to one concert with my best friends or another concert with my significant other? Should I study abroad in Spain or in Italy?

A second type of conflict is called **avoidance-avoidance conflict**, the choice between two undesirable options. For example, do I want to do unpleasant homework or unpleasant housecleaning? Do I experience the anxiety of a dentist appointment or live with this mouth pain?

A conflict in which one event or goal has both attractive and unattractive features is called an **approach-avoidance conflict**. For example, you might aspire to a high-paying job that requires long, stressful hours.

Lewin's theory emphasizes that these conflicts can create significant psychological tension until we make a decision on how to resolve them. The conflicts and their resolutions lead to different strategies for conflict resolution depending on the individual's personal tendencies and the specific situation.

THINK AS A PSYCHOLOGIST

Evaluate the Appropriate Use of Research Design Elements in Non-Experimental Methodologies (2.C.2, 2.C.3)

Mr. Feldman wanted to evaluate which of Lewin's motivational conflicts caused his students more stress: approach-approach conflicts or avoidance-avoidance conflicts. He provided all his students ($N = 98$) with several real-life examples of each type of conflict and asked them to rate on a scale of 1–7 how much stress they would experience if they personally experienced that situation. The results are included in the table below.

Type of Conflict	Mean Student Stress Score
Approach-approach	5.1
Avoidance-avoidance	4.2

Motivation for Eating

Why do we eat? Clearly, hunger is not the only answer, although hunger plays an important motivational role in eating behaviors. Understanding hunger and **satiety**, the feeling of fullness, reveals the complexity of the interactions of physical and mental processes.

Biological Bases of Hunger

Hunger is often described as a biological drive, probably the most important drive for individual survival. In terms of the drive-reduction theory, hunger is a drive that pushes a person to behave in a way that fills a need. Nourishment is the need, and eating is the behavior that allows the person to fill that need. Where does this state of arousal come from?

The nervous and endocrine systems are both active in regulating hunger. The hunger signal has two parts: the "on" signal and the "off" signal. The "on" signal is triggered by something that stimulates the appetite. **Ghrelin,** often called the "hunger hormone," is primarily produced in the stomach and is released when the stomach is empty. It signals the brain, specifically the hypothalamus, to induce the feeling of hunger. The level of ghrelin increases before meals and decreases after eating, thus promoting food intake and stimulating appetite.

Leptin, on the other hand, is known as the "satiety hormone" (the "off" signal) and plays a contrasting role. It is produced by fat cells and communicates with the hypothalamus to suppress appetite. Leptin levels increase after eating and are generally higher in people with more body fat. By signaling the brain that enough food has been consumed, leptin helps to regulate energy balance by inhibiting hunger, which in turn helps to prevent excessive food intake.

The **hypothalamus**, a key part of the brain involved in regulating hunger and energy expenditure, uses information from these hormones to help balance food intake with the body's energy needs. The **pituitary gland**, under the control of the hypothalamus, also plays a role in this hormonal regulation. It releases various hormones that can influence the body's metabolism and can also affect the levels of ghrelin and leptin indirectly.

Disruptions in the levels of ghrelin and leptin or their signaling pathways may play a role in eating disorders and metabolic issues such as obesity or anorexia. Understanding the balance and interaction between these hormones is essential for developing treatments for such conditions and for promoting a healthy energy balance in the body.

External Factors That Influence Eating Behaviors

Sometimes, though, people eat even without the chemical signals indicating that food is needed for energy. Have you ever looked at the clock, noticed it was close to your regular mealtime, and suddenly felt hungry? The clock signaled a hunger response, serving as a learned environmental cue that you should eat.

External eating cues are signals and situations that come from outside of the body and promote eating behavior. Some examples of eating cues are smells and other sensory experiences, time of day, specific people, and social gatherings.

Learning plays a role too. Classical conditioning (described in Topic 3.7) often leads to otherwise neutral stimuli becoming motivators for eating. For example, the smell of food serves as an unconditioned stimulus—a person feels immediately hungry (the unconditioned response). If the person generally cooks and eats dinner at 6 p.m., the smell of the food will become associated with the time (the conditioned stimulus) and the person will begin to feel hungry as 6 p.m. nears

Ads for pizza companies are timed to be shown around dinnertime and are external cues triggering a taste for pizza.

(the conditioned response) even before the food is cooked. Do you eat your meals sitting in front of a TV or computer screen? If so, you may have learned to associate the screen with food, prompting hunger when watching.

Most people develop associations between food and certain environmental factors. For example, people whose environment contributes to stressful feelings reach for sweet foods. Sugars in the bloodstream provide energy to the body, and people experience a rush of energy after eating food containing sugars. Carbohydrates—foods such as candy bars, cookies, pasta, and breads—are among those foods that can lead to the "sugar high" feeling. Other foods, such as eggs, cheese, nuts, salmon, and tofu, trigger a release of serotonin, a chemical (neurotransmitter) in the brain that is involved in feelings of pleasure.

Culture, too, can significantly affect eating behaviors. What one culture considers a delicacy another might consider disgusting. Would you eat crickets, mealworms, or scorpions? What about that balut mentioned earlier or haggis, a Scottish "pudding" made from organ meat? You're probably more likely to reach for a bag of potato chips or chocolate chip cookies.

Many people in America prefer foods that are salty and sweet, and if they were not raised with spicy foods, they often dislike foods prepared with curries and peppers. In contrast, those flavors are common and preferred in many Latin American and Asian countries. Children raised in multicultural environments, who eat a variety of different cuisines, have more cultural cues motivating them to eat and are more likely to grow up to be adventurous eaters.

Some cultures have rules about which items are appropriate on certain occasions. For some, a cake is a common high-calorie dessert at celebrations of birthdays, graduations, and engagements. For some, certain foods are to be avoided, such as beef, pork, or insects.

Does your family sit down to a common table, focusing on the food and conversation? If so, how does that affect your eating? Being with others tends to motivate eating. People at a dinner party, for example, eat more than they would if they were alone. However, in some circumstances, being with others serves to decrease eating behaviors. In Western cultures in which being thin is portrayed as the ideal, women may eat less in social situations. Family and cultural practices related to parental control of eating and meal customs also exert influence on eating patterns. Many of us were raised with the "you must clean your plate" rule before we could leave the table. This attempt at control by parents over children can carry over into adult eating behavior.

THINK AS A PSYCHOLOGIST

Evaluate the Appropriate Use of Research Design Elements in Experimental Methodology (2.B.3) | Apply Psychological Perspectives, Theories, Concepts, and Research Findings to a Scenario (1.A.3)

After reading about controversy surrounding a study on calorie consumption and plate size, a researcher wanted to replicate that study. The researcher randomly assigned participants (N = 140) to either the "small plate" group or the "large plate" group and maintained the other conditions of the original study precisely. The researcher then tracked the calories consumed for each participant over the course of 10 days. The results of the study are below.

	Small Plate Group	Large Plate Group
Mean number of calories consumed at each lunch	583.7	601.2
Standard deviation	82.31	67.92

Practice Evaluating Research Elements and Applying Concepts

Complete the following activities.

1. Identify both the independent and dependent variables in this study.

2. Identify a logical conclusion that can be drawn from this study.

Essential Questions: *How do theories about motivation apply to behavior and mental processes? How do eating and belongingness motivate behavior and mental processes?* Using the Key Terms, complete a chart like the one below to gather details to help answer those questions.

Theory	Behavior	Mental processes
Drive-Reduction Theory		
Arousal Theory		
Self-Determination Theory		
Incentive Theory		
Instinct Theory		
Motivational-Conflicts Theory		
Sensation-Seeking Theory		
Eating		

KEY TERMS

adventure-seeking
approach-approach conflict
approach-avoidance conflict
avoidance-avoidance conflict
arousal theory
boredom susceptibility
disinhibition
drive
drive-reduction theory

experience-seeking
external eating cue
extrinsic motivation
ghrelin
homeostasis
hunger
incentive
instinct
intrinsic motivation
hypothalamus
leptin

motivation
motivational conflicts theory
need
pituitary gland
satiety
self-determination theory
sensation-seeking theory of motivation
thrill-seeking
Yerkes-Dodson law

1. Which of the following situations poses an approach-approach conflict for a person who listens only to classical music?

   (A) Having to sit through a friend's rehearsal for a violin recital or going out to your favorite restaurant

   (B) Choosing to study with one of two friends, both of whom listen to classical music while studying

   (C) Attending a classical music event or being forced to attend your cousin's first concert since taking up the electric guitar

   (D) Being offered a cash bonus for working a concession stand at a rap music festival

2. Andrew had a track meet directly after school and did not get home until 8 pm. He hadn't eaten anything since breakfast and immediately ran to the kitchen to get something to eat. Which motivational theory best accounts for this behavior?

   (A) Self-determination

   (B) Drive-reduction

   (C) Incentive

   (D) Arousal

The Yerkes-Dodson Law

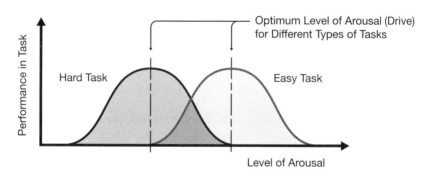

3. The graph above supports which of the following statements?

   (A) Optimal performance is influenced by task difficulty and level of arousal.

   (B) Difficult tasks require higher-than-usual levels of arousal for optimal performance.

   (C) Difficult tasks become easier when arousal is increased.

   (D) Easy tasks require lower-than-usual levels of arousal for optimal performance.

4. Wendy joined the volleyball team because her school was well known for having an outstanding team. She was mostly drawn to join because of the attention she would receive from being part of the team as well as the chance to win a state title, and she wanted the notoriety and all of the trophies. Which theory of motivation most clearly accounts for Wendy's behavior?

(A) Self-determination

(B) Drive-reduction

(C) Incentive

(D) Arousal

5. Rich is investigating the role of the hypothalamus in the regulation of appetite and food intake. Which of the following most accurately characterizes the impact of the hypothalamus on hunger?

(A) It produces a sense of satiety to counter hunger feelings that arise from stomach contractions.

(B) It monitors stomach contractions through the cranial nerves to determine the extent of hunger.

(C) It primarily responds to environmental cues such as the sight and smell of food.

(D) It works with the endocrine system to control hunger and satiety.

6. Natalia has been trying to lose weight lately. Even with a change in diet and exercise, she has only lost 5 pounds. What hormone may be driving Natalia's hunger levels and preventing her from losing weight?

(A) Ghrelin

(B) Glucagon theory

(C) Leptin

(D) Metabolic conversion

7. Kyra loves trying new foods and riding fast roller coasters. She travels frequently to explore new places and loves learning about new cultures. Which of the following best explains her motivation to have these new experiences?

(A) Drive-reduction theory

(B) Incentive theory

(C) Lewin's conflict theory

(D) Sensation-seeking theory

Topic 4.7

Emotion

"Human emotions have deep evolutionary roots, a fact that may explain their complexity . . . ."

—Robert Plutchik

Essential Questions: How do theories of emotion apply to behavior and mental processes? How do social norms and experiences influence the expression of emotions?

Robert Plutchik, one of the most influential theorists in the field of emotions, noted in a 2001 article that "the study of emotions is one of the most confused (and still open) chapters in the history of psychology." He points out that more than 90 definitions of emotion were proposed in the 20th century alone. Putchik writes, "It is no wonder that there is much disagreement among contemporary theoreticians concerning the best way to conceptualize emotion and interpret its role in life."

Theories of Emotion

Despite the confusion, many psychologists today agree on a few key components of emotion: **Emotion**, or **affect**, is a complex experience that begins with a stimulus **(external factor)** and includes physiological responses, subjective emotional feelings **(internal factor)**, and emotional expressions—the outward signs of what a person is feeling. The **physiological responses** include changes in heart rate, an increase in blood pressure and perspiration, and other involuntary responses in the autonomic nervous system, depending on the intensity of the emotion. Emotional expressions include certain facial expressions and posture, as well as such behaviors as crying or stomping one's feet. The ways in which people experience and express emotions are key to understanding emotions.

Early Theories of Emotion

One early explanation of the experience of emotion was proposed, independently, by two psychologists, William James and Carl Lange. Both men proposed that a stimulus in the environment leads to a physiological response (arousal of the autonomic nervous system) and that the emotional feeling arises from that response. This explanation, known as the James-Lange theory, reflects the idea that feelings are based on physiological arousal. The

James-Lange theory proposes a linear order—each step occurs in succession and causes the next step. For example, a person sees a bear (the stimulus) and then experiences autonomic arousal (increased heart rate, increased blood pressure, muscle tension) and then experiences the conscious feeling of fear. "I got scared, so my heart started to beat fast, and then I felt fear." In the James-Lange theory, the arousal comes before the feeling of fear.

Another view is that physiological arousal and emotional feelings emerge at the same time. This view was originally articulated by psychologist Walter Cannon and his doctoral student Philip Bard and is now known as the Cannon-Bard theory of emotions. They asserted that the stimulus (the bear) causes subcortical brain activity (in what we now know as the limbic system—see Topic 1.4). This brain activity creates the emotional feeling (fear) and the physiological arousal at the same time. In other words, it's the bear that simultaneously makes the person's heart race and makes the person feel afraid.

The Role of Cognition in Emotion

The theories and hypotheses just described include only physiological and emotional responses without a **cognitive** component. Other approaches to understanding emotions emphasize the role that people's thoughts play in their emotional feelings and behaviors.

Schachter's two-factor theory of emotions focuses on how people try to understand their physiological states of arousal. Psychologists Jerome Singer and Stanley Schachter argued that some environmental stimulus causes physiological arousal, but that the arousal itself doesn't lead directly to the emotional feeling. Rather, the person recognizes the arousal state and looks to the stimulus to explain it: "That is one big bear! He could eat me in one bite! My heart is beating out of my chest! I'm scared!" The person feels the arousal, appraises the situation, and responds based on that appraisal.

To test their theory that emotions result not only from physiological arousal but also from the cognitive appraisal of the situation, Schachter and Singer designed an experiment. They gave a shot of adrenaline to participants, which typically increases heart rate and induces a state of heightened physical alertness, and told participants it was for a vision test they were going to take. One group of participants was not told about the physiological effects adrenaline produces. Researchers placed that group of participants in a room with a confederate who was told to act happy. Researchers told another group of participants the real effects of the drug. That group, too, was placed in a room with a "happy" confederate. After the study, those in the group that was not informed of the effects of adrenaline reported feeling happy after being with the happy confederate, while those told the true effects of the drug attributed their physiological state to the drug and reported far less happiness. This experiment helped refute earlier theories that physiological arousal is the sole influence on emotions, because all participants were given the same shot of adrenaline. They reported different feelings based on their surrounding and interpretation **(cognitive appraisal)** of the situation.

You don't need to be part of an experiment to see the two-factor theory in action. If you've ever seen a toddler fall down hard, immediately look to the caregiver, and begin to wail if the adult has a look of fear on their face—but not if the caregiver laughs and says cheerfully, "You're okay!"—you've seen the two-factor theory in practice. This theory, emphasizing **cognitive labeling** of the physiology and appraisal of the situation, may reflect the complexities of human emotions more accurately than the earlier theories.

Joseph LeDoux argues that cognition is not always necessary in emotional experiences. If cognition is involved, emotional experiences take a slower pathway, which starts at the thalamus and then is routed to the cortical areas and finally to the amygdala, which triggers an emotional response. In scenarios involving frightening stimuli, the message follows a quick pathway traveling from the thalamus immediately to the amygdala and creating an instant emotional response. This "fast" unconscious pathway circumvents the cortex allowing an immediate response.

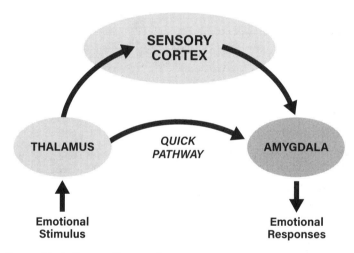

Source: Adapted from emotionresearcher.com

Figure 4.7.1 The Long and Short Pathways to Fear

In the late 1900s, Richard Lazarus flipped the order in which people experience emotions. Rather than the physical response driving cognition and emotion, Lazarus claims that the cognitive appraisal comes first. We appraise situations, and that appraisal causes an emotional response and then finally the physical response. Our understanding of emotions has seemingly come full circle from the days of the James-Lange theory.

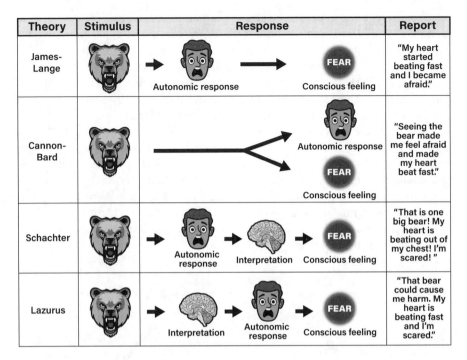

Theory	Stimulus	Response	Report
James-Lange		Autonomic response ➡ Conscious feeling (FEAR)	"My heart started beating fast and I became afraid."
Cannon-Bard		Autonomic response / Conscious feeling (FEAR)	"Seeing the bear made me feel afraid and made my heart beat fast."
Schachter		Autonomic response ➡ Interpretation ➡ Conscious feeling (FEAR)	"That is one big bear! My heart is beating out of my chest! I'm scared!"
Lazurus		Interpretation ➡ Autonomic response ➡ Conscious feeling (FEAR)	"That bear could cause me harm. My heart is beating fast and I'm scared."

Figure 4.7.2 Theories of Emotions Illustrated

Facial Feedback

While cognitive processes undoubtedly play a central role in how we understand and react to emotional experiences, the facial feedback theory introduces an additional layer, suggesting that the simple act of altering one's facial expression can directly impact one's emotional experience.

Parents often tell their unhappy children, "Just smile and you will feel better," and some research suggests that the parents may be right. The hypothesis for this practice is that specific facial expressions alter the blood flow to the brain, which in turn gives rise to emotional feelings. This idea, which was introduced in the 1960s but refined in the 1980s by psychologist Robert Zajonc and others, is known as the **facial-feedback hypothesis**. Like the earlier theories, the facial feedback hypothesis focuses on the relationship between a physiological response and subjective feelings.

Imaginative studies have been designed to test the facial feedback hypothesis. In one study, one group of participants held a pencil in their teeth with their lips not touching the pencil. Holding a pencil this way put each participant's face in a position resembling a smile. Another group of participants held the pencil on their upper lip, sandwiched between their lip and the base of their nose. This hold on the pencil put the participants' faces into what is commonly called a "duck face" pose, with lips pressed together in a pout and protruding—picture any number of selfies on social media to understand the duck face. While holding the pencil, each participant rated a series of cartoons based on how funny they were. If facial feedback influenced response, the "smiling" participants should feel happier and rate the cartoons as funnier than the "duck face" participants would. Although early studies did show this difference between the smiling and pouting groups, leading to the conclusion that facial expressions could impact the experience of different emotions, more recent replications of this work haven't consistently supported this idea.

The Broaden-and-Build Theory of Emotion

The **broaden-and-build theory of emotion**, proposed by psychologist Barbara Fredrickson, suggests that positive emotions broaden your awareness and encourage novel, varied, and exploratory thoughts and actions. Over time, these broadened thoughts and actions build skills and resources. For example, joy sparks the urge to play, which can help develop social skills and friendships. Curiosity about a subject leads to exploring and learning new information or mastering new skills, which increases personal resources like knowledge.

The broaden-and-build theory highlights how experiencing positive emotions can expand a person's awareness or perception of the world. This expanded awareness allows the person to see more possibilities and solutions during problem-solving situations. By broadening their attention and thinking, individuals are more likely to discover and build new skills, social ties, and knowledge, which contribute to their personal growth and well-being. This process forms a positive spiral where increased awareness leads to more positive emotions and further broadening and building of resources.

Consider this scenario. Jaime is very interested in art. One day, Jaime decides to join the school's art club, where students get to create and discuss art together. Initially, Jaime feels a bit nervous about sharing his artwork with others, worried about potential criticism. However, as Jaime participates more and receives positive feedback and support from peers, he starts feeling happier and more confident. This positive emotion of joy doesn't just make Jaime feel good; it also broadens his thinking and actions. Inspired by the club's encouraging environment, Jaime experiments with new artistic techniques and styles, which he wouldn't have tried before. As Jaime continues to engage in these new experiences, he builds new skills and forms deeper connections with fellow art club members. These changes not only enhance Jaime's artistic abilities, but also expand his social network and even career opportunities in the art world. This cycle of positive emotions leading to expansive actions and personal growth is at the heart of the broaden-and-build theory of emotions.

In practical terms, when someone feels positive emotions such as curiosity and interest while tackling a tough academic task, they tend to think more creatively and openly. This creative thinking can lead to new study methods or a better understanding of complex topics, enhancing their academic success and personal growth. Positive emotions not only make us more mentally flexible but also boost our interactions and connections with others, providing crucial emotional and psychological support. In contrast, frequent negative emotions, such as anxiety and frustration, can narrow our thinking. For example, worrying about failing an exam might focus our attention too much on negative outcomes, limiting our ability to study effectively or seek help from classmates or teachers, thus hindering our growth.

The broaden-and-build theory holds that there are long-term benefits of nurturing positive emotions in daily life. Over time, the expanded ways of thinking and behaving that positive emotions encourage can build on one another, leading to continued upward spirals of improved well-being and resourcefulness. This collection of resources becomes vital for managing future stressors and challenges. Ultimately, cultivating positive emotions contributes significantly to moving toward a more fulfilling and successful life.

Emotional Expression

Crying, smiling, punching a wall, holding hands, punctuating texts with emoticons—all are expressions of emotion. Some emotional expressions develop early in life and may be universal (e.g., smiles), whereas others are specific to a particular culture, age group, occasion, or time period. Emotional expression is so important to social interaction that infants become very distressed when their mother models a still face without any expression, and a lack of emotion is often a sign of a psychological disorder.

Facial Expressions

You have already read about the facial feedback theory in the context of what causes emotions (see page 594). Facial expressions, of course, also *convey* emotions. Early in his career, psychologist Paul Ekman became interested in identifying a set of universal emotions—that is, emotions that are common throughout every culture. Focusing on facial expressions, Ekman identified every muscle in the human face and then every possible combination of facial muscles. Ekman and his colleague Wallace Friesen developed the Facial Action Coding System (FACS), a tool for measuring movement of these muscles, which led them to create a taxonomy of facial expressions. The FACS can identify more than 5,000 distinct facial expressions.

Ekman found that the emotional expressions of anger, disgust, fear, happiness, sadness, contempt, and surprise were universal, present in every culture he studied. Ekman is well known for traveling to Papua New Guinea before villagers there had any connection to the outside world. He found that they had no problem identifying the facial expressions in a variety of pictures Ekman brought along, and after taking pictures in his travels like those shown below, people in the United States had no problem identifying the facial expressions displayed. Ekman and his colleagues have also identified emotions that are experienced but not expressed by changes in facial muscles.

In 2016, Ekman and his daughter Eve, a specialist in integrative medicine, helped create an interactive online map called the Atlas of Emotions that was commissioned by the Dalai Lama. The Tibetan monk wanted a tool people all

All these children would understand a smile in the same way.

over the world could use to develop compassion and inner peace, feeling that people have both destructive and constructive emotions and should focus on developing the constructive ones. Ekman surveyed 149 psychologists to try to find areas of agreement on the complex topic of emotions. Based on that survey, he identified five basic categories of human emotion—anger, fear, disgust, sadness, and enjoyment—each with many subsets and levels of intensity. To help people achieve a calm state, the atlas includes triggers of emotional responses and the behaviors that follow so people can learn to avoid the triggers and moderate their responses.

THINK AS A PSYCHOLOGIST

Apply Psychological Perspectives, Theories, Concepts, and Research Findings to a Scenario (1.A.1) | Calculate and Interpret Measures of Central Tendency, Variation, and Percentile Rank in a Given Data Set (3.B.1) | Evaluate Whether a Psychological Research Scenario Followed Appropriate Ethical Procedures (2.D.4) | Using Scientifically Derived Evidence, Explain How or Why a Claim, Policy, or Norm Is or Is Not Effective (4.B.3)

Read the following research summary.[6]

The glabellar region of the face contains the corrugator and procerus muscles. They are directly involved in frowning and thus play a key role in the facial expression of negative emotions, such as anger, fear, or sadness, which are

---

6   Wollmer, M. A., de Boer, C., Kalak, N., Beck, J., Götz, T., Schmidt, T., Hodzic, M., Bayer, U., Kollmann, T., Kollewe, K., Sönmez, D., Duntsch, K., Haug, M. D., Schedlowski, M., Hatzinger, M., Dressler, D., Brand, S., Holsboer-Trachsler, E., & Kruger, T. H. (2012, May). Facing depression with botulinum toxin: a randomized controlled trial. *Journal of Psychiatric Research*, 46(5):574–581. doi: 10.1016/j.jpsychires.2012.01.027. Epub 2012 Feb 24. PMID: 22364892.

highly prevalent in clinical depression. Correspondingly, a measurable over-activity of the corrugator muscles has been observed in cases of depression.

Muscles of the Glabellar Region

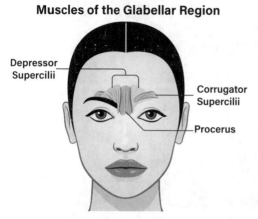

Researchers set out to investigate whether using Botox® (botoxbotulinum toxin) to inhibit movement of this set of muscles might affect the mood of people suffering from depression. They used a randomized double-blind, placebo-controlled trial to see if an injection of Botox® could help reduce symptoms of depression. Twenty patients were randomly assigned to receive an injection of Botox® ($n = 10$) or placebo (saline, $n = 10$). Before the study, all patients completed the 17-item version of the Hamilton Depression Rating Scale (HDRS) to establish their baseline score. Sixteen weeks after the treatment was given, both groups again completed the HDRS. Throughout the 16-week follow-up period, there was a significant improvement in depressive symptoms in the Botox® group compared to the placebo group as measured by the Hamilton Depression Rating Scale. The group receiving Botox® had a 47.1% reduction in their HDRS score, whereas the placebo group saw only a 9.2% reduction in their HDRS score. The table below shows the placebo group's HDRS score after 16 weeks.

Patient	#1	#2	#3	#4	#5	#6	#7	#8	#9	#10
Score	15	11	6	16	13	11	9	17	8	14

This study shows that a single treatment of the glabellar region with Botox® may provide a strong and sustained alleviation of depression in patients who did not improve sufficiently on previous medication. It supports the concept that the facial musculature not only expresses but also regulates mood states. In the published study, patients were referred to only by numbers.

Practice Foundational Skills

Answer the following questions.

1. The fact that Botox® improved patients' moods by inhibiting the facial muscles involved in frowning and negative emotions supports which of the following?

   (A) Broaden-and-build theory

   (B) Facial feedback hypothesis

   (C) Cultural display rules

   (D) James-Lange theory

2. Using the data provided in the table, identify the median and modal scores for the placebo group's ratings on the HDRS.

3. In terms of ethics, explain why the patients are simply identified by a number in the published report.

4. Similar research has replicated this finding, leading some to claim that Botox® can be an effective tool in the treatment of depression. Support that claim using one piece of statistical evidence from the study presented above.

Cultural and Social Differences in Emotional Expression

Although Ekman initially argued that facial expressions of anger, disgust, fear, happiness, sadness, and surprise were universal, research shows that emotions are not always expressed at the same times or in the same ways in every culture. Some researchers argue that cultural background heavily influences how people interpret facial expressions and how those emotions are shown (or not shown) to others. They found that different cultures may have unique ways of understanding the same facial expressions based on their own norms and emotional behaviors.

Display Rules

Expected or "appropriate" ways of expressing emotions that vary from culture to culture and situation to situation are known as **display rules**. For example, Japanese people are thought to be less likely than Westerners to show negative feelings such as anger and fear in their facial expressions; instead, they may mask them with a smile.

Display rules govern when, how, and to whom people show emotions and play a crucial role in social interactions by helping individuals manage their social image and navigate interpersonal communications effectively. For example, in many Western cultures, expressing joy and satisfaction in a job well done is encouraged and seen as a sign of confidence and competence. In contrast, cultures such as Japan's place a higher value on humility and modesty, often leading individuals to downplay their successes in public settings to avoid appearing boastful.

Research has shown significant variations in emotional display rules across different cultures, influencing not only how emotions are expressed but also how they are perceived and interpreted by others. For instance, the expression of anger may be more acceptable in individualistic cultures that value personal autonomy and direct communication, such as the United States, but less so in collectivistic cultures like South Korea, where maintaining group harmony is prioritized, and direct expression of anger can be seen as disruptive and disrespectful.

Elicitors

Factors or situations that trigger emotions are called **elicitors**. These, too, are shaped by the social and cultural context, and they regulate emotional expressions differently across various demographic groups. These differences in emotional expression and interpretation help maintain the social order and convey significant information about an individual's social identity and group memberships.

Within any given culture, display rules and emotional elicitors can differ according to gender, age, and socioeconomic status, reflecting the diverse roles and expectations that different groups may have. For example, research has indicated that women are often socially permitted and even expected to show more expressive emotions, such as joy and sadness, than men, who may be encouraged to display stoicism (self-control and fortitude) or control, particularly in professional settings. Age also plays a role, with younger children often given more leeway for emotional outbursts than teenagers or adults. Socioeconomic influences can dictate that people from higher social or economic classes maintain a composed and controlled demeanor, reflecting status, while those from lower classes may not face the same expectations and social norms.

Social norms significantly influence the expression of emotions by setting culturally specific guidelines on how, when, and where emotions should be expressed. These norms are ingrained from a young age and vary widely across different cultures and social contexts. For instance, in some cultures, displaying emotions like grief and sadness openly is encouraged as a sign of sincerity and a communal sharing of feelings, while in others, such displays might be considered inappropriate or a sign of weakness, prompting individuals to suppress or mask these emotions in public.

Cultural display rules guide not only how people show emotions outwardly but also how they experience them internally. People learn to adjust their emotional reactions to fit these social rules. Following these norms helps maintain social harmony and makes it easier for individuals to manage social interactions, since it aligns their personal feelings with what is expected by the community.

Personal history also significantly affects how people express emotions. How people see, understand, and respond to emotions is shaped by previous experiences and learned behaviors. For example, someone who has faced negative reactions for showing anger might learn to hold back that emotion in the future to avoid problems or punishment. Over time, this can become a conditioned response, an automatic behavior by which a person adjusts their emotional expressions based on what they expect the reaction to be. While this adaptation is a personal process, it is strongly influenced by the larger social environment. There is a continuous interaction between individual experiences and social norms that shapes how emotions are shown and understood in different settings.

THINK AS A PSYCHOLOGIST

Identify Psychology-Related Concepts in Descriptions or Representations of Data (3.A.2) | Determine the Type of Research Design(s) Used in a Given Study (2.A.1)

In a research study, men and women watched a scary 15-minute video while researchers observed their facial expressions through a one-way mirror. Researchers monitored the participants' facial expressions and tracked how many times each participant expressed fear. The results are in the bar graph below.

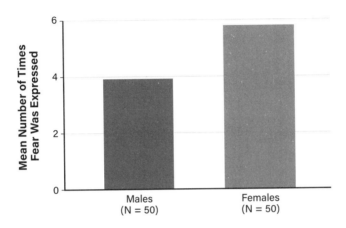

Practice Identifying Psychology-Related Concepts in Descriptions or Representations of Data

Answer the following questions.

1. Based on the description and bar graph above, what psychological phenomenon were researchers likely studying?

2. Using the description and bar graph above, explain why this research could not be conducted using a true experimental design.

REFLECT ON THE ESSENTIAL QUESTIONS

Essential Questions: *How do theories of emotion apply to behavior and mental processes? How do social norms and experiences influence the expression of emotions?* Using the Key Terms, complete a chart like the one below to gather details to help answer those questions.

Theory or Concept	Behavior	Mental Processes
Primary Emotions		
Emotions Arise from Physiological Arousal		
Physiological Arousal and Emotion Arise Simultaneously		
Cognition Plays a Role in Emotions		
Facial Feedback Hypothesis		
Broaden-and-Build Theory of Emotion		
	Expression of Emotion	
Facial Expressions		
Cultural Differences		
Social Differences		
Social Norms		
Display Rules		

KEY TERMS

affect	cognitive labeling	facial feedback hypothesis
broaden-and-build theory of emotion	display rules	internal factor
cognitive	elicitor	physiological response
cognitive appraisal	emotion	
	external factor	

MULTIPLE-CHOICE QUESTIONS

1. Thierry has been researching emotions for a year and believes strongly in the two-factor theory of emotion. What best represents Thierry's perspective regarding emotion?

(A) There is simultaneous arousal and emotional experience.

(B) The hypothalamus is the brain structure primarily responsible for emotional responses.

(C) Culture influences when it is appropriate to display various facial expressions of emotion.

(D) Cognitive appraisal is a critical component of any emotional experience.

2. Mark, a restaurant host, began his workday in a bad mood. However, by the end of the day, he felt much happier. According to the facial feedback hypothesis, what may have influenced the change in Mark's mood?

(A) The day was so busy that Mark did not have time to reflect on events that were troubling him.

(B) Because it is his job to be courteous to customers, Mark smiled at customers frequently, leading to an improvement in his mood.

(C) Mark helped several customers who then told his supervisor how nice he was.

(D) Mark is good friends with some of the wait staff, and seeing their friendly faces cheered him up during the shift.

3. Sarah recently took an inventory and identified her unique strengths. As she reflected upon the results, she noticed that her strengths were often tied to positive life events. She made a plan to engage in more of these types of activities and has since reported that her levels of depression have been considerably reduced. What theory of emotion best explains Sarah's experience?

(A) Cannon-Bard theory

(B) James-Lange theory

(C) Broaden-and-build theory

(D) Incentive theory

4. If you wanted to conduct research to determine if there was a relationship between a person's level of neuroticism and the experience of positive emotions, what would be the best research method to employ?

(A) Experiment

(B) Meta-analysis

(C) Longitudinal design

(D) Correlational study

5. Justine is learning about theories of emotion in her psychology class and strongly believes that the Cannon-Bard theory of emotion most accurately depicts how an emotional response unfolds. To help prepare for her upcoming exam, she is describing each theory to a friend. As she explains the Cannon-Bard theory, she'll need to include which of the following statements?

(A) Physiological arousal and the experience of an emotion occur simultaneously.

(B) The physiological state of arousal determines the emotional experience.

(C) Cognitively labeling physiological arousal plays a major role in the experience of emotions.

(D) The experience of an emotion is amplified by the brain interpreting which facial muscles are active during an emotion.

6. When Japanese students watched films that made them feel the emotion of disgust, they masked their expressions of disgust with a smile when an authority figure entered the room. However, when alone, they openly expressed disgust. American students maintained their expressions of disgust both alone and in the presence of an authority figure. Which of the following best accounts for the differences between the groups?

(A) Universality theory

(B) The two-factor theory

(C) The facial feedback hypothesis

(D) Display rules

 STUDY LIKE A CHAMP WITH DR. G. | SITUATION AND PERSONALITY

You now can better predict your behavior knowing about the influences of personal (i.e., personality psychology) and situational (i.e., social psychology) factors. Recognize any personality traits you may have to consider in modifying your study behavior. If you are already a conscientious student, conscientiousness being one of the Big Five traits (this unit), you will likely stay on track, keeping to your study plan. Likewise, knowing elements of your self-concept and self-esteem can also help predict why you study the way you do.

Also take some time to examine the situational factors that influence your studying. Do you study at a time or place that is free of distraction? When you study are you also streaming your favorite show or are your friends around chatting? Some situations are more likely to help you focus. Studying in a library where others are also studying helps you focus and study hard as well.

Whether you are interleaving or doing retrieval practice, both your personality and your situation can make a difference. While it's easier to control the situation than your personality, both can be modified. Remember, a key part of metacognition is monitoring how you're studying and assessing how well your plan is working. There is still time to modify your plan to truly study like a champ.

UNIT 4: Review

MULTIPLE-CHOICE QUESTIONS

1. Justine's driver education teacher has made a number of derogatory comments about "female drivers." At the end of the semester, he downgraded many of the women in the class because of their gender. Which of the following best refers to the teacher's grading practices?

   (A) Prejudice

   (B) Discrimination

   (C) In-group bias

   (D) Stereotype threat

2. Eduardo needed to get a good summer job but was worried that he wouldn't find anything. He felt that it didn't matter how good his application was or how well the interview went. He believed that you just had to be in the right place at the right time. Eduardo's views most clearly represent which of the following?

   (A) An external locus of control

   (B) An internal locus of control

   (C) High self-efficacy

   (D) Low neuroticism

3. Priya is a psychologist who conducts research to explore how people develop various personality characteristics. When testing personality, Priya uses a set of ten pictures that she presents to participants one at a time. For each picture, the participant is asked to tell a detailed and thorough story of what is happening in the picture, including the details that led up to the scene they are viewing. Based on the testing that Priya conducts, she is most likely to believe in which of the following psychological approaches?

   (A) Psychodynamic

   (B) Social-cognitive

   (C) Humanistic

   (D) Trait

4. Laureen experienced severe trauma as a child, but as an adult, she reports that she has no memory of the details of the trauma. A psychologist from the psychodynamic perspective would argue that which of the following has occurred?

(A) Repression

(B) Reaction formation

(C) Projection

(D) Regression

Questions 5 through 7 refer to the following.

Frieda is horrified by recent news reports that, over the past decade, a number of people in her large city have passed away because nobody helped them in an emergency situation. She gathers her team at the university where she works to conduct research on the topic. The team goes to a crowded part of the city to test a number of scenarios at different times of the day to see how people respond to situations that appear to be an emergency.

The first test was conducted at rush hour when many people were coming to and going from work. The research team staged an emergency in which a person suddenly fell to the ground clutching their chest. They timed how long it took someone to come and help the person in need.

5. What phenomenon is the research team testing?

(A) Mere exposure effect

(B) Bystander effect

(C) Social loafing

(D) Conformity

6. The research team is trying to determine if there is a link between the number of people present at the time of an emergency and the time it takes for a person in need to receive help. What type of research are they conducting?

(A) Experimental

(B) Case study

(C) Naturalistic observation

(D) Correlational study

7. The researchers plotted the data (depicted in the following chart). What conclusion can be made from the data gathered in this study?

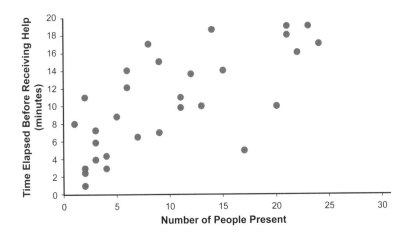

(A) More people present in an emergency causes a delay in the time it takes for a victim to receive help.

(B) When there were fewer people present, less time elapsed before someone received help.

(C) There is a negative correlation between the number of people present and the amount of time it takes someone to provide assistance.

(D) No clear conclusions can be made until the people present are interviewed to find out why they did or did not provide assistance.

8. Tyrese is a senior in high school who just received notification that he was not accepted into the university that was his first choice. In talking through the disappointment with his family, he tells them that he believes he'll never get into any college because he is an inferior student and that his future will be ruined because he lacks talent in everything he does. Tyrese's thinking most clearly demonstrates which of the following?

(A) Internal locus of control

(B) Pessimistic explanatory style

(C) Self-serving bias

(D) Reciprocal determinism

9. The drive-reduction theory of motivation is most useful in explaining which of the following behaviors?

(A) A student's desire to be competent in all of their courses

(B) A parent's attempts to provide unconditional positive regard for their children

(C) A teacher's need to put on a sweatshirt because their classroom is freezing

(D) An athlete's need to push themself to the limits of their physical capabilities

10. Ronaldo's soccer team just won the conference championship. They are a great team and have earned a spot in the playoffs. When asked why the team is so good, Ronaldo explains that he worked very hard in the off-season and this has allowed him to play strong defense and score many goals this year. Which of the following is Ronaldo demonstrating?

(A) Actor-observer effect

(B) Fundamental attribution error

(C) Self-serving bias

(D) External locus of control

11. With which statement is a trait theorist likely to agree?

(A) Personality characteristics are shaped primarily by adverse childhood events (ACEs).

(B) Personality characteristics are a result of the interaction between the person, the environment, and behavior.

(C) Personality characteristics are enduring characteristics that are stable across different situations.

(D) Personality characteristics are shaped by unconditional positive regard.

12. Despite her busy schedule, Sarah volunteers once a week at a local pet shelter. She does this because she truly enjoys spending time with the animals and lives in an apartment that does not allow her to have pets. Which of the following statements accounts for Sarah's behavior?

(A) She is facing an avoidance-avoidance conflict.

(B) She is conforming because of normative social influence.

(C) She is experiencing relative deprivation.

(D) She is intrinsically motivated.

13. Jonathan is finishing up his substantial lunch. What is likely happening in his body?

   (A) He is beginning to produce leptin.
   (B) He is beginning to produce ghrelin.
   (C) His levels of adrenaline are decreasing.
   (D) His levels of melatonin are decreasing.

14. Which of the following scenarios most clearly represents the false consensus effect?

   (A) Jane, a passionate environmentalist, assumes that most people in her community share her views on climate change because her social circle predominantly consists of individuals who hold similar beliefs.
   (B) John conducts a survey among his classmates about their favorite movie genre and confidently concludes that most people in his school prefer action movies because the majority of his respondents selected action as their favorite genre.
   (C) Caterina has several neighbors who voted for conservative candidates in political elections. Because of this, she assumes that her community is overwhelmingly conservative.
   (D) Mark, an avid sports fan, assumes that most fans who do not support the same team that he does are obnoxious and arrogant.

15. In regard to human emotion, which of the following is the best illustration of the impact of display rules?

   (A) Lars throws a dramatic tantrum in a public setting in a clear attempt to get his own way.
   (B) Odundo feels intense anger toward her professor and subtly displays that anger.
   (C) An elderly man insists that several youngsters at a movie theater are being inappropriately loud and aggressive.
   (D) A researcher discovers that students from some Asian cultures are more likely than American students to mask facial expressions of their emotions when in the presence of an authority figure.

QUESTION 1: ARTICLE ANALYSIS QUESTION (AAQ)

1. Your response to the question should be provided in six parts: A, B, C, D, E, and F. Write the response to each part of the question in complete sentences. Use appropriate psychological terminology in your response.

   Using the source provided, respond to all parts of the question.

   (A) Identify the research method used in the study.

   (B) State the operational definition of the dependent variable.

   (C) Describe the meaning of the differences between the groups in the study.

   (D) Identify at least one ethical guideline applied by the researchers.

   (E) Explain the extent to which the research findings may or may not be generalizable using specific and relevant evidence from the study.

   (F) Explain how at least one of the research findings supports or refutes the researchers' hypothesis that cognition plays a role in emotional experiences.

Introduction
Schachter and Singer wanted to challenge long held beliefs that people's physiological arousal was the sole reason they experienced different emotional states. They believed that in addition to physiological arousal, cognitive appraisal and one's surroundings played a role in our experience of emotions.

Participants
The study was conducted with 184 students at Columbia University. All participants were male. Participants volunteered for the study and a random sample was taken from these volunteers. Each participant was asked to sign an informed consent ahead of time, in which researchers asked permission to inject the participants with a vitamin "Suproxin" before having their eyesight tested.

Method
Part 1 of the study "Suproxin" was actually the hormone epinephrine, which triggers feelings of arousal such as racing heart, flushed skin, and trembling hands. Participants were randomly divided into four groups and given injections. Participants in three of the groups received epinephrine. One of these groups was correctly informed about the drug's effects, one was told nothing, and the third was misinformed about the effects. Those in the fourth, placebo, group received a neutral saline solution. **Part 2 of the study** Each participant was then placed in a room with either a "happy" or an "angry" confederate (research ally) acting like a participant. Both the participants and the confederates were told that before they could take the supposed vision test, they needed to complete a questionnaire and allow time for the drug to take effect. The confederate was instructed in each condition to behave in line with their supposed emotion: acting joyously in the happy condition—flying paper airplanes, bouncing a ball, etc.—and acting frustrated in the angry condition—complaining about the experiment, refusing to answer some items on the questionnaire, etc. At the conclusion of the study, the participants were asked about their emotional state.

Results and Discussion

Participants who were not told about the drug's true effects reported feeling like the confederates with whom they were placed. When participants were placed in a room with the happy confederate, they rated themselves as happy. They also engaged in more "happy" acts like those the confederate had modeled. When placed with the angry, irritated confederate, participants reported feeling angry. Although the participants were feeling similar physiological effects from the epinephrine, they labeled those effects as happy or angry, depending on the external cues in their environment, and they acted accordingly. Those in the informed group correctly attributed their arousal to the drug rather than to the environment. All participants were told the true nature of the study before leaving.

Expected Side Effects of the "Suproxin"

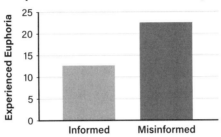

This study clearly indicates that emotional responses are not entirely physiological, because if they were, all participants who received the adrenaline should have responded similarly to one another. Instead, they cognitively appraised the situation and responded similarly to those around them.

Reference

Schachter, S., & Singer, J. (1962). Cognitive, social and physiological determinants of emotional state. *Psychological Review*, 69(5), 379-399.

QUESTION 2: EVIDENCE-BASED QUESTION (EBQ)

2. This question has three parts: Part A, Part B, and Part C. Use the three sources provided to answer all parts of the question.

   For Part B and Part C, you must cite the source that you used to answer the question. You can do this in two different ways:

   - Parenthetical Citation
     For example: " . . ." (Source A)
   - Embedded Citation
     For example: "According to Source A, . . ."

   Write the response to each part of the question in complete sentences. Use appropriate psychological terminology.

   Using the provided sources, develop and justify an argument related to the degree to which personality traits remain stable over a lifetime.

   (A) Propose a specific and defensible claim based in psychological science that responds to the question.

(B) (i) Support your claim using at least one piece of specific and relevant evidence from one of the provided sources.

   (ii) Use a psychological perspective, theory or concept, or research finding learned in AP Psychology to explain how your evidence supports your claim.

(C) (i) Support your claim using an additional piece of specific and relevant evidence from a different source than the one that was used on Part B (i).

   (ii) Explain how the evidence from Part C (i) supports your claim using a different psychological perspective, theory, concept, or research findings learned in AP Psychology than the one that was used in Part B (ii).

Source A

Introduction
The study, conducted by Mathew A. Harris and colleagues from the University of Edinburgh, investigated the long-term stability of personality traits across a span of 63 years. The research set out to determine whether personality characteristics measured in adolescence can predict those same traits in older age.

Participants
The study initially involved 1,198 participants from the Scottish Mental Survey of 1950 who were in their their early teenage years ($m = 13.9$). In 2012, researchers traced as many of the participants as possible through the United Kingdom National Health Service Register. 635 were located, and 171 agreed to participate ($m = 76.7$).

Method
Across the age trials, participants completed individually administered IQ tests (Stanford-Binet [SB] and Moray House Test [MHT]), followed by a series of home visits to assess a range of environmental factors. Participants completed several questionnaires related to personality and health and took part in a phone interview. Personality traits were originally assessed at age 14 using teacher ratings (1=lowest to 5=highest) on six characteristics. (The Big Five characteristics had not yet been developed.) At age 77, the same individuals rated themselves on the same characteristics and were also rated by someone who knew them well on these same characteristics in order to triangulate the data.

continued

The analysis revealed moderate correlations between self-ratings and ratings by others in old age, indicating some consistency in perceived personality traits over time. However, the correlation between the personality traits from adolescence to old age showed limited stability, suggesting significant changes in personality traits over the 63 years.

CHARACTERISTIC	1950_M	1950_SD	2013_M	2013_SD
N	1,198		171	
Gender (M/F)	585/613		82/89	
Age	13.9	0.6	76.7	0.4
Stanford-Binet IQ	102.6	20.7	115.7	19.7
Moray House IQ	100.00	15.0	110.1	11.2
(Personality Characteristics)	(Teacher ratings)		(Self and other's ratings)	
Self-Confidence	3.0	0,8	3.2	0.8
Perseverance	2.9	0.9	3.3	0.8
Stability of Moods	3.3	0.9	3.6	1.0
Conscientiousness	3.2	0.9	3.4	0.9
Originality	2.6	0.8	3.0	0.8
Desire to Excel	2.9	0.9	3.2	0.8

The study's findings challenge the notion of personality stability over a lifespan, showing significant evolution in personality traits from adolescence to old age. While certain traits such as "Stability of Moods" and "Conscientiousness" showed some degree of longitudinal stability, overall, the results suggest that personality may be more malleable over the life course than previously thought. Additionally, IQ scores were relatively stable but seemed to rise slightly over the 63-year period of the study.

Harris, M. A., Brett, C.E., Johnson, W., & Deary, I.J. (2016, December). Personality stability from age 14 to age 77 years. *Psychology and Aging, 31*(8): 862–874. doi: 10.1037/pag0000133.

Source B

This study explored the usefulness of changes in Big Five personality traits (extraversion, agreeableness, conscientiousness, neuroticism, openness) in predicting various life outcomes. Past research has confirmed the stability of these traits over time and their ability to predict life outcomes. This study investigates whether changes in these traits can also predict life outcomes, thus providing insights into the mechanisms linking personality changes to future life outcomes.

The research involved 81,980 participants from seven longitudinal data sets. Participants were drawn from diverse backgrounds and were tracked across various stages of their lives, providing comprehensive demographic and personality trait data.

continued

Method
The study employed a robust analytical framework using multilevel modeling—a type of modeling that is particularly useful when dealing with data that are nested, such as repeated measurements within individuals—to assess personality changes over time and their impact on static and changing life outcomes. It considered various control variables, such as baseline personality traits and initial levels of outcomes, to isolate the effects of personality changes.

Results and Discussion
The results indicated that changes in personality traits have significant predictive power for certain life outcomes. For instance, increases in agreeableness and conscientiousness were associated with improved relationship satisfaction and career achievements, respectively. The magnitude of these predictive effects varied across different life domains and was generally smaller than the effects of static personality traits. The findings suggest that, while static personality traits remain a strong predictor of life outcomes, changes in these traits also provide significant predictive value, supporting the notion of personality as a dynamic construct influenced by life experiences and changes. The study highlights the importance of considering both static and dynamic aspects of personality in predicting life outcomes.

Source
Wright, A. J., & Jackson, J. J. (2023). Do changes in personality traits predict life outcomes? *Journal of Personality and Social Psychology, 125*(6), 1495-1518. https://doi.org/10.1037/pspp0000472

Source C

Introduction
The study conducted by M. Brent Donnellan and Richard E. Lucas investigated the differences in Big Five personality traits (extraversion, agreeableness, conscientiousness, neuroticism, and openness) across different age groups. Using the British Household Panel Study (BHPS) and the German Socio-Economic Panel Study (GSOEP), it examines how these traits vary from adolescence to old age in two different national contexts.

Participants
The participants included 14,039 individuals from the British Household Panel Study and 20,852 from the German Socioeconomic Panel Study (GSPS), covering a wide age range from 16 to the mid-80s. These data sets provided a diverse demographic sample across both Great Britain and Germany, respectively.

Method
Participants answered a 15-item version of the Big Five Inventory in either 2005 or 2006. The study used a cross-sectional design, analyzing the data to identify trends in personality traits across different age groups.

Results and Discussion
The study found that extraversion and openness generally decreased with age, whereas agreeableness increased. Conscientiousness peaked in middle age. Notably, trends in neuroticism varied between the two samples: it decreased with age in the BHPS but increased in the GSOEP. The findings suggest significant cross-cultural consistency in how some personality traits change with age, with the exception of neuroticism. The study contributes to the broader understanding of personality development, indicating that certain traits do evolve in predictable patterns as people age that link to changes to adult life roles and experiences.

Source
Donnellan, M. B., & Lucas, R. E. (2008, September). Age differences in the big five across the life span: evidence from two national samples. *Psychology and Aging, 23*(3), 558–566. DOI: 10.1037/a0012897

UNIT 5: Mental and Physical Health

Unit Overview

You may have heard the Latin phrase *mens sana in corpore sano*, which is often used in both sporting and educational contexts. Or maybe you have heard an English version of it. It is usually translated as "a sound (or healthy) mind in a sound (or healthy) body." It emphasizes the importance of maintaining both mental and physical well-being for a balanced and healthy life. Although the phrase was coined by the Roman poet Juvenal nearly 2,000 years ago, it is still relevant today.

Mental health is closely interconnected with physical health. This relationship is bidirectional; that is, our mental health can affect our physical health, and our physical health can affect our mental health. Both contribute to our sense of well-being and quality of life. Our lifestyle choices, such as diet, exercise, sleep, and use of substances such as alcohol and drugs, affect both our physical and our mental health. For example, regular physical activity not only strengthens muscles and improves cardiovascular health but also elevates mood, reduces stress, and enhances cognitive function. Social connections and support networks play a crucial part in both mental and physical health and well-being. They provide emotional support, companionship, and a sense of belonging, which help protect against mental health problems. Social isolation and loneliness, on the other hand, have been linked to negative health outcomes, including increased risk of depression, anxiety, and physical illness.

LEARNING TARGETS

- Explain how health psychology addresses issues of physical health and wellness as they apply to behavior and mental processes. (5.1.A)
- Explain how stress applies to behavior and mental processes. (5.1.B)
- Explain how reactions to stress apply to behavior and mental processes. (5.1.C)
- Explain how the ways that people cope with stress apply to behavior and mental processes. (5.1.D)
- Explain how positive psychology approaches the study of behavior and mental processes. (5.2.A)
- Explain how positive subjective experiences apply to behavior and mental processes. (5.2.B)
- Describe the approaches used to define behaviors and mental processes as psychological disorders. (5.3.A)
- Explain how psychological perspectives define psychological disorders. (5.3.B)
- Explain how interaction models define psychological disorders. (5.3.C)

- Describe the symptoms and possible causes of selected neurodevelopmental disorders. (5.4.A)
- Describe the symptoms and possible causes of selected schizophrenic spectrum disorders. (5.4.B)
- Describe the symptoms and possible causes of selected depressive disorders. (5.4.C)
- Describe the symptoms and possible causes of selected bipolar disorders. (5.4.D)
- Describe the symptoms and possible causes of selected anxiety disorders. (5.4.E)
- Describe the symptoms and possible causes of selected obsessive-compulsive disorders and related disorders. (5.4.F)
- Describe the symptoms and possible causes of selected dissociative disorders. (5.4.G)
- Describe the symptoms and possible causes of selected trauma and stressor-related disorders. (5.4.H)
- Describe the symptoms and possible causes of selected feeding and eating disorders. (5.4.I)
- Describe the symptoms and possible causes of selected personality disorders. (5.4.J)
- Describe research in the treatment of psychological disorders. (5.5.A)
- Describe trends in the treatment of psychological disorders. (5.5.B)
- Describe ethical principles in the treatment of psychological disorders. (5.5.C)
- Describe techniques used with psychological therapies. (5.5.D)
- Explain how group therapy is different from individual therapy. (5.5.E)
- Describe effective uses of hypnosis. (5.5.F)
- Describe interventions derived from the biological perspective. (5.5.G)

Source: AP® Psychology Course and Exam Description

STUDY LIKE A CHAMP WITH DR. G. | TAKE CARE OF YOURSELF!

This last unit is perhaps the most anticipated and enjoyed section of any introductory psychology course. It also draws our attention to two extremely important factors that can influence our learning: mental and physical health. All my training tips for how to study like a champ have focused on key cognitive techniques. How you think and how you manage, monitor, and assess how you think is extremely important. Using effective study techniques such as pretesting, practice retrieval, spacing, and interleaving have all been shown to relate to better learning. None of that matters, though, if you are not in a mental and physical state to learn well.

Much of our functioning and our mental and physical health relies on some key health behaviors. The prescriptions for what to do are clear and well talked about, but how many of us follow them? Top of the list are physical activity, healthy eating, and sleep. You have learned the psychology behind what motivates such behaviors in earlier units and throughout this book. What you should know is that healthy behaviors and your mental health are not only important for your quality of life and well-being but they can also significantly influence how you study. In fact, these behaviors are so important, an entire chapter in my *Study Like a Champ* book (Gurung & Dunlosky, 2023) is devoted to healthy behaviors.

If you want to really study like a champ, then aim to get as close to eight hours of sleep a night as you can. Use learning techniques from Unit 3 (reward and punishment or classical conditioning) and Unit 4 (i.e., situational changes) to make your learning more effective. Get adequate sleep and you will feel more alert, be able to pay better attention, and remember more from every class. Likewise, try and get some physical activity every day. Even walking for 20 minutes a day is great; you do not have to run or go to the gym—just get active. Try to eat a balanced meal on a regular schedule to keep your circadian rhythm in sync (remember that from earlier in Unit 1?). Make some dramatic changes if you are not already sleeping well and being physically active. Start! See how good changes will feel.

Topic 5.1

Introduction to Health Psychology

"Stress, in addition to being itself, was also the cause of itself, and the result of itself."

—Hans Selye

Essential Question: How does health psychology address issues of physical health and wellness as they apply to behavior and mental processes?

Health psychology is a subfield in psychology that uses psychological and behavioral principles to study health, illness, and health care, including stress and coping. A related field is behavioral medicine, which applies psychology to manage medical problems. For example, asthma and diabetes are diseases that can be treated, in part, with psychological intervention. Together, researchers who study health psychology and behavioral medicine work to prevent illness, reduce stress, and promote health and well-being.

In addition to stress and coping, health psychologists study why people engage in health-promoting behaviors like exercising and eating nutritiously and in health-risk behaviors like smoking and excessive drinking. They work with people living with such chronic conditions as diabetes and heart disease to improve their quality of life and adherence to medical treatments. They also help people cope with acute and chronic pain, make necessary lifestyle adjustments, and deal with the emotional challenges and self-care demands associated with chronic illness.

Health psychologists collaborate with health care providers, policymakers, educators, and employers in diverse settings, such as health care facilities, workplaces, schools, and communities, to promote healthy lifestyles through education, counseling, and behavior modification techniques. They also collaborate with medical professionals to incorporate behavioral and psychological strategies into medical care. This collaboration focuses on areas such as making lifestyle changes, helping patients stick to their medication routines, and enhancing communication between health care providers and patients to achieve better health outcomes.

THINK AS A PSYCHOLOGIST

Determine the Type of Research Design(s) Used in a Given Study (2.A.1.b) | Interpret Quantitative or Qualitative Inferential Data from a Given Table, Graph, Chart, Figure, or Diagram (3.C.2) | Evaluate the Appropriate Use of Research Design Elements in Non-Experimental Methodologies (2.C.8)

Several studies have demonstrated that an optimistic explanatory style may contribute to positive health outcomes. (See Topic 4.1.) In one research design, psychologists combed through 15 different studies, which included 229,391 subjects who were followed for an average of 14 years, to evaluate whether optimism was associated with a lower risk of cardiovascular problems. Their results indicated that optimism was indeed linked to fewer heart attacks and a lower risk of premature death. Those with higher rates of optimism had a 35 percent lower risk for cardiovascular events and a 14 percent lower risk for an early death when compared to those who rated high in pessimism. In this study, $p < .001$, indicating that the findings were statistically significant.

Practice Foundational Skills

Choose the correct answer and complete the activities.

1. Which of the following research methods was used in the above study?

    (A) Experiment

    (B) Meta-analysis

    (C) Case study

    (D) Naturalistic observation

2. Briefly describe what statistically significant means.

3. This study demonstrates some health benefits of optimistic thinking. Briefly describe why replication would nonetheless be beneficial.

Stress

When people think about stress, images from films and television of people in catastrophic situations may come to mind. However, the media portrayal of stress is biased and incomplete. From a psychological point of view, stress is a mental and physical condition that occurs when a person encounters some demand or expectation and must adjust or adapt to the environment.

A **stress** reaction is the arousal of the autonomic nervous system that occurs in response to the stressor. Often, this arousal leads to the **fight-flight-or-freeze response** (see Topic 1.2), which occurs when people encounter something dangerous or even life-threatening and respond physiologically in a way that prepares them to potentially face and deal with the stressor in the safest possible way. These *acute stress* reactions—which last for only a short time until the danger is resolved—were highly adaptive when early humans experienced life-or-death situations daily as they struggled to survive. Today, however,

people often experience stress reactions to more typical daily events, such as seeing someone cut in line in the cafeteria, being stuck in traffic, having someone mispronounce a name, receiving a mean text, or getting behind on a deadline. These daily frustrations can alter mood and increase chronic stress levels, especially when the people involved react with the fight-flight-or-freeze response. Road rage, for example, is an emotional response to a stressor that occurs in situations that are usually not life-threatening.

Stress and Physiological Issues

Studies have consistently found that about 50 percent of teens feel stress in their lives every day.

Stress can have a profound effect on physical health, contributing to the development or worsening of various medical conditions. The following are just a few of the ways stress can affect physical health:

- **Hypertension** Prolonged stress can contribute to hypertension, or high blood pressure, and heart disease, increasing the risk of stroke by elevating heart rate and blood pressure. Over time, these can strain the heart and blood vessels, increasing the risk of cardiovascular events.
- **Headaches** Stress is a common trigger for headaches. The exact causes are not fully understood. Stress often leads to muscle tension in the neck, shoulders, and scalp, which can result in tension headaches. Stress can also affect blood flow in the brain, which can trigger migraines. And stress is often associated with psychological factors, such as anxiety, depression, and emotional distress, which can increase susceptibility to stress. This long list provides great reasons for trying to minimize levels of stress in your own life.
- **Immune Suppression** If the hormones produced by stress are consistently and persistently released, they can weaken the immune system, reducing the body's ability to fight off illnesses and infections.

In addition, stress can disrupt the digestive system, leading to symptoms such as stomachaches, diarrhea, and nausea. It can interfere with sleep quality, which in turn can worsen stress levels and contribute to a wide range of physical and mental health issues. *Chronic stress,* which is persistent and prolonged, can disrupt the balance of hormones in the body, affecting thyroid function and reproductive health. It can also contribute to weight gain and obesity. Stress hormones can increase appetite, while stress-related eating disorders such as emotional eating or binge eating can lead to overeating.

Health psychologists investigate the impact of stress on physical health and develop strategies to manage stress effectively through relaxation techniques, social support, and lifestyle modification.

Stressors

A **stressor** is a condition or event in the environment that challenges or threatens a person. Stressors have different intensities and effects on people's lives, and they combine to create an overall stress level for each person. Typical stressors include daily hassles, relationship troubles, and financial problems.

Stress can be negative (i.e., **distress**), but it can also be a positive motivating force. **Eustress** (pronounced "YOO-stress"), a positive form of stress, pushes people to achieve, to accomplish their daily and life goals. Exercise and travel are both examples of eustress. Eustress is a type of arousal that is beneficial and can lead to improved performance and well-being, according to the Yerkes-Dodson model (see Topic 4.6).

Less typical, but more stressful, are traumatic or unexpected events that are very intense, such as natural disasters, long-term chronic illness, or homelessness. Other examples include experiencing child abuse, witnessing a murder, or having one's home destroyed by fire. Traumatic stressors can cause psychological injury or intense emotional pain.

Adverse Childhood Experiences (ACEs) are traumatic events that occur during childhood and can have lasting negative effects on a person's physical and mental health. ACEs can be categorized into three major types: abuse, neglect, and household dysfunction.

- **Abuse** may be physical, emotional, or sexual in nature. Physical abuse includes hitting, beating, burning, or otherwise causing bodily harm to a child. Emotional or psychological abuse involves verbal abuse, threats, intimidation, rejection, or humiliation that undermines a child's self-esteem, emotional well-being, and sense of safety. Sexual abuse involves any sexual activity perpetrated on a child by an adult or more powerful person, including molestation, rape, and incest.

- **Neglect** may be either physical or emotional. Physical neglect involves the failure to provide for a child's basic needs, such as food, shelter, hygiene, and medical care. It can result in malnutrition, poor growth, and illness or injury. Emotional neglect involves the failure to meet a child's emotional needs, including love, affection, and support. It can lead to feelings of abandonment, low self-esteem, and difficulty in forming healthy relationships.

- **Household dysfunction** can be a result of domestic abuse, substance abuse, or mental illness in the home. Witnessing or experiencing violence between household members can cause fear, trauma, and emotional distress in children. Living with a household member who abuses alcohol or drugs can lead to instability, neglect, violence, and disruptions in caregiving. Living with a household member who has untreated or poorly managed mental health issues, such as depression, anxiety, bipolar disorder, or schizophrenia, can result in unpredictability and stigma.

ACEs can have profound and cumulative effects on children's development, shaping their cognitive, emotional, and social functioning. They can increase the risk of various physical and mental health problems later in life, including depression and anxiety disorders, posttraumatic stress disorder (PTSD), substance abuse, obesity, diabetes, chronic pain, and autoimmune disorders.

THINK AS A PSYCHOLOGIST

Explain How Cultural Norms, Expectations, and Circumstances Apply to Behavior and Mental Processes (1.B)

Health depends on a number of factors in addition to genetic predisposition. According to the Health Belief Model (HBM), a number of environmental factors can also contribute to susceptibility to disease and/or decreased life expectancy. Such environmental factors include *susceptibility, severity, barriers,* and, on the positive side, *benefits*.

- Susceptibility involves genetic propensities, but it also involves environmental factors such as stress (e.g., living in a high-crime area, bullying, or abuse), poverty, or living near a toxic dump site or in another unhealthy environment.
- Severity involves the intensity of a negative factor, such as if a family were just barely below the poverty line or extremely poor.
- Barriers involve obstacles to healthy behaviors, such as living in an area that does not have a lot of fresh fruits and vegetables available or not having reliable transportation to health care professionals.
- Benefits involve positive factors leading to a healthy lifestyle, such as the ability to exercise on a regular basis or access to healthy foods.

Practice Explaining How Cultural Circumstances Apply to Health

Answer the following question.

1. What are some ways cultural circumstances can affect one's health? Consider the following factors in your answers: neighborhood, income, transportation, and language differences.

MENTAL AND PHYSICAL HEALTH: *A MULTICULTURAL PERSPECTIVE*

As you have read, the Health Belief Model (HBM) is a psychological framework used to understand individuals' health behaviors and motivations. From a multicultural perspective, this model can provide insights into how different cultural backgrounds influence perceptions and actions related to health. Cultural factors strongly influence these beliefs and perceptions, affecting how people respond to health interventions. For example, in some cultures, traditional medicine and spiritual beliefs may play a key role in health decisions.

In multicultural contexts, the perceived benefits and barriers to taking health-related actions can vary widely. For instance, in collectivistic cultures, the decision to engage in health behaviors may be influenced more by family and community norms than by individual preferences. In contrast, individualistic cultures might emphasize personal responsibility and autonomy in health decisions. Health campaigns and interventions that align with these cultural values are more likely to be effective. For example, promoting vaccination in a collectivistic culture by emphasizing the protection it offers to the community can resonate more deeply than focusing solely on individual benefits.

Self-efficacy, or the belief in one's ability to take action, is another crucial component of the Health Belief Model that can be influenced by cultural factors. In cultures with an ingrained hierarchy, individuals might feel less empowered to make health decisions independently, relying more on authority figures or experts. In such contexts, health interventions may need to include efforts to build confidence and empower individuals. Additionally, understanding cultural attitudes toward health and illness can help in designing more culturally sensitive health messages. For instance, addressing stigmas associated with certain diseases in specific cultures can reduce barriers to seeking treatment and encourage proactive health behaviors. By considering these multicultural perspectives and the historical context of trust, health professionals can develop more effective, inclusive, and culturally appropriate health interventions.

Develop a Claim

After reading about multicultural issues in health care, develop a claim on how cultural competence in health care providers can improve patient outcomes and trust in the medical system among diverse communities.

Reactions to Stress

Stress has been a part of life as long as humans have existed. The term "fight or flight" refers to the choices our ancient ancestors had when they were faced with danger in their environment: they could fight or they could flee. In both cases, both physical and mental processes prepare the body to react to the danger. But, as we evolved, humans have also developed other ways of reacting to stress. We don't all react in the same way. In fact, researchers have found that men and women may react differently to stress.

General Adaptation Syndrome

Much of what psychologists know about the ways in which people respond to stress comes from the work of Hans Selye. Selye proposed the **general adaptation syndrome (GAS)**, a three-stage process that people go through in response to stressors. The first stage is *alarm*, in which the body detects stress and initiates the fight-flight-or-freeze response. This is similar to a fight-or-flight response but includes an additional reactive state in which a person may "freeze," or be unable to move, in response to a perceived threat. The second stage is *resistance*, during which those physiological indicators remain high as the person tries to cope with the stressors. *Exhaustion* is the third and final stage, during which the person's physiological resources are depleted. In this last stage, the body's ability to resist is compromised, leading to fatigue, burnout, and decreased immunity. Chronic stress can lead to long-term damage such as hypertension, heart disease, and other stress-related illnesses. It is during this stage that the greatest susceptibility to illness occurs as a result of immunosuppression—a lowered immune system. During catastrophes and significant life changes, people may move through the stages in a very short time.

Later researchers recognized that if there is long-term, repeated exposure to stressors, **burnout**—physical, mental, and/or emotional exhaustion—may occur. A person with burnout may get sick because the immune system is gradually worn down over time. Burnout is increasingly common in helping professions, such as human and veterinary medicine, nursing, and social work. Along with emotional exhaustion, in which the person feels "used up" and apathetic toward work, a person experiencing burnout often feels cynical and detached from the job. A burned-out person may also feel very little sense of personal accomplishment.

Tend-and-Befriend Theory

Psychologist Shelley Taylor studies social relationships and how they protect against stress. In response to the fight-flight-or-freeze response, which focuses on aggressive or evasive behavior in response to stress, she developed the **tend-and-befriend theory**. Her theory suggests that, in response to stress, people—especially females—come together with others for joint protection of self and offspring. The "tend" aspect of the theory refers to nurturing and protective behaviors aimed at caring for those in need. In response to stress, people may engage in caregiving behaviors, providing comfort, reassurance, and practical assistance to vulnerable members of their social group, such as children, family members, or friends in need. The "befriend" aspect of the theory emphasizes the importance of social connections and support in times of stress. Rather than withdrawing or isolating themselves when facing stress, people may seek out social support from friends, family, or community members. Befriending behaviors include seeking emotional support, sharing experiences, and collaborating with others to solve problems.

The tend-and-befriend theory has significant implications for understanding social behavior, health outcomes, and gender differences in the stress response. It highlights the importance of social support networks, nurturing relationships, and caregiving roles in promoting well-being and buffering the negative effects of stress.

The "tend" part of tend-and-befriend includes providing practical support, such as buying and delivering groceries.

Coping with Stress

Coping is the act of facing and dealing with problems and stressors, especially over the long term. When people have trouble coping with chronic stress, they often show emotional signs such as anxiety, apathy, irritability, excessive worry about illness, and mental fatigue. Unhealthy coping may take the form of avoiding responsibilities and relationships, engaging in extreme or self-destructive behavior, and neglecting basic self-care. For some people, unhealthy coping strategies include self-medicating with alcohol or drugs. While these counterproductive behaviors may distract from stress, in the long run they actually increase rather than reduce it.

Such cognitive factors as self-defeating fears and attitudes can make coping with stress difficult. Examples of statements showing self-defeating fears and attitudes include the following:

- "It would be terrible to be rejected, abandoned, or alone. I must have love and approval before I can feel good about myself."
- "If someone criticizes me, it means there's something wrong with me."
- "I must always please people and live up to everyone's expectations."
- "Other people should always meet my expectations."
- "I am basically defective and inferior to other people."
- "I'm hopeless and bound to feel depressed forever because the problems in my life are impossible to solve."

Psychologist Albert Ellis argued that when people create an unrealistic view of the world based on this irrational thinking, which he called "awfulizing," stressors seem more severe and are harder to manage.

Varieties of Coping Strategies

Successfully coping with stress is important for maintaining both health and a sense of well-being. People have different ways of coping, which vary depending on both the situation and the person. Since life does contain many stressors, multiple approaches have been developed to deal with the challenges.

Problem-Focused Coping One strategy for dealing with stress is **problem-focused coping,** which involves managing or fixing the distressing situation, either by changing our behavior or changing the situation. For example, a person stressed by being stuck in traffic on the freeway might exit at the next off-ramp and plot a new route on surface streets. Or if you have a fight with a friend, you go directly to your friend to work it out. These are examples of problem-focused coping because they involve taking steps to address and resolve the source of stress. You are not just managing the emotional fallout of the fight, you are actively working to resolve the issue that caused the stress in the first place.

Emotion-Focused Coping In some situations, a person engages in **emotion-focused coping,** controlling or replacing the negative emotional responses to the stressor (for example, "Okay, this is upsetting me, but I can stay calm and not lose my temper"). This may occur if we believe we do not have control over a situation or that we lack control over anything. When we engage in emotion-focused coping, we may seek out the support of others, try to find a positive side to the stressor, or take our minds off the problem. Some strategies that are emotion-focused include deep breathing, meditation, or taking medication aimed at reducing stressful emotional responses. Distractions like playing games or altering mood by using alcohol, drugs, food, or sex do not help us solve the problem at hand and are maladaptive.

 THINK AS A PSYCHOLOGIST

Calculate and Interpret Measures of Central Tendency, Variation, and Percentile Rank in a Given Data Set (3.B.3, 3.B.4) | Identify Psychology-Related Concepts in Descriptions or Representations of Data (3.A.2) | Evaluate Whether a Psychological Research Scenario Followed Appropriate Ethical Procedures (2.D.2)

A principal at a middle school wanted to investigate links between students' level of optimism and their overall stress level. He randomly selected 250 students to participate and had them take a survey to determine their percentile rank for an optimistic explanatory style. Each student then filled out a stress questionnaire (using a scale of 1–7 with 1 indicating very low stress and 7 indicating very high stress) to determine their overall stress level. Remarkably, the first two students' scores on the optimism survey were in the 99th percentile, but by the time he tested all of the students, the average percentile rank was 54th. The table below shows a sample of 15 students from the study.

Student	Optimism Percentile	Stress Score (1–7)
Student 1	99	1.0
Student 2	83	2.0
Student 3	19	6.5
Student 4	39	5.5
Student 5	77	2.5
Student 6	68	3.5
Student 7	21	7.0
Student 8	33	6.5
Student 9	94	1.5
Student 10	58	4.0

Practice Interpreting Data and Evaluating Ethical Procedures

Complete the following activities and choose the correct answer.

1. Briefly explain what it means for a student to score in the 99th percentile on their optimism score on this survey.

2. Briefly describe how regression toward the mean occurred in this scenario.

3. Based on the data presented in the table, which of the following is an accurate statement?

    (A) There is no relationship between optimism and stress.

    (B) There is a strong negative correlation between optimism and stress.

    (C) There is a strong positive correlation between optimism and stress.

    (D) Higher levels of optimism cause students to experience less stress.

4. Explain why informed assent is necessary in this study.

REFLECT ON THE ESSENTIAL QUESTION

Essential Question: *How does health psychology address issues of physical health and wellness as they apply to behavior and mental processes?* Using the Key Terms, complete a chart like the one below to gather details to help answer that question.

Environmental Influences on Health	Physical Impact of Stress	Prevention and Health Promotion

abuse	emotion-focused coping	household dysfunction
adverse childhood experiences (ACEs)	eustress	neglect
	fight-flight-or-freeze response	problem-focused coping
burnout		stress
coping	general adaptation syndrome (GAS)	stressor
distress		tend-and-befriend theory
	health psychology	

MULTIPLE-CHOICE QUESTIONS

Questions 1 through 3 refer to the following.

Dr. Boller conducted a study with her introductory psychology course to examine the stress level of her students and the frequency with which those students missed class because of illness.

Each student began the semester by filling out a computerized survey assessing their overall level of stress. Their results were reported on a scale of 1–10, with 10 representing the highest level of stress. She then tracked how often throughout the semester each student missed class because of illness. The results are depicted below.

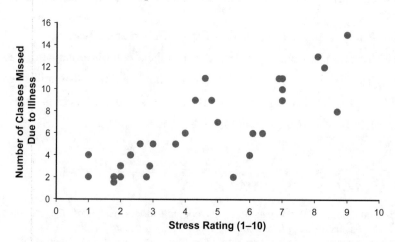

1. Which of the following is a sound conclusion based on these results?

(A) Stress caused students to miss more classes.

(B) Student stress was negatively correlated with the number of classes they missed.

(C) The two variables were positively correlated.

(D) There was no relationship between stress and illness in this study.

2. Dr. Boller tracked the number of classes missed for all the participants in the study, which can be found in the table below. What is the range of classes missed?

2	6	2	5	1	7	11	4	9	2
3	9	10	8	15	2	8	5	6	11
5	12	3	13	4	2	6	9	11	4

(A) 16

(B) 14

(C) 11

(D) 12

3. The findings in Dr. Boller's study most support which of the following?

(A) The alarm stage of the stress response

(B) The fight-flight-freeze stage of the stress response

(C) The resistance stage of the stress response

(D) The exhaustion stage of the stress response

4. Sayali is learning about various ways to cope with stress in her health class. Lately, she has had several disagreements with her best friend and decides to use a strategy she learned in class. If Sayali uses an emotion-focused coping strategy, she will most likely do which of the following?

(A) Talk with family to help reduce her distress

(B) Engage in problem-solving to brainstorm possible solutions

(C) Confront her friend directly in an effort to resolve the tension

(D) Develop a strategy to avoid further conflict with her friend

5. Taylor has been overwhelmed by work and her travel schedule over the past year. To relieve stress, she has made an effort to consistently reach out to her friends and family because they provide comfort and reassurance. Her response to dealing with stress exemplifies which of the following?

(A) Tend-and-befriend theory

(B) Problem-focused coping

(C) The resistance stage of general adaptation

(D) Social facilitation

6. Based on the following chart, which of the following is a logical conclusion that can be drawn?

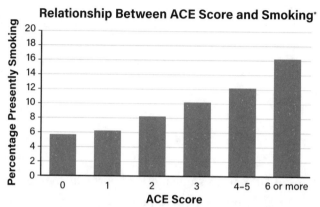

Relationship Between ACE Score and Smoking*

* Felitti, V. J. The Relation Between Adverse Childhood Experiences and Adult Health: Turning Gold into Lead. *Perm J.* 2002 Winter; 6(1): 44–47. doi: 10.7812/TPP/02.994. PMID: 30313011; PMCID: PMC6220625.

(A) Adverse childhood experiences cause people to smoke more frequently.

(B) Adverse childhood experiences are not correlated with negative health outcomes.

(C) Adverse childhood experiences increase the likelihood of substance abuse.

(D) Adverse childhood experiences increase when the rate of smoking increases.

7. The following graphic is most closely aligned with which of the following?

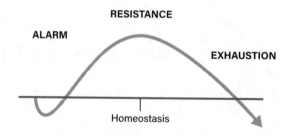

(A) Tend-and-befriend theory

(B) Fight-flight-freeze response

(C) General adaptation syndrome

(D) Problem-focused coping

Topic 5.2

Positive Psychology

"The aim of Positive Psychology is to begin to catalyze a change in psychology from a preoccupation only with repairing the worst things in life to also building positive qualities."

—Martin Seligman

Essential Question: How does positive psychology approach the study of behavior and mental processes?

Traditional psychology often focused on problems people have. Positive psychology, in contrast, shines a light on the good in life rather than just the bad. Positive psychologists are interested in answering questions such as these:

- What factors contribute to overall well-being and life satisfaction?
- How can people cultivate positive emotions such as joy, gratitude, and compassion?
- What strengths and virtues enable people to thrive and reach their full potential?
- How can resilience be developed to help people cope with adversity and bounce back from setbacks?
- What are the psychological benefits of activities such as mindfulness, meditation, and acts of kindness?

The field of positive psychology aims to explore the elements fostering well-being, resilience, psychological health, and positive emotions such as happiness.

The Emergence of Positive Psychology

Positive psychology emerged as a distinct field of study in the late 20th century, challenging traditional approaches that primarily focused on diagnosing and treating mental illness. Instead, it emphasizes promoting strengths and virtues that enable individuals and communities to thrive. At its most basic level, **positive psychology** is the scientific study of human flourishing.

Positive psychologists apply psychological theories and scientific research to promote well-being by emphasizing positivity in our emotions, characteristics, and social structures. They explore positive feelings like happiness, optimism, and hope, aiming to understand how these emotions contribute to a fulfilling life. They also examine personal traits such as courage and **resilience,** which help individuals overcome challenges and grow stronger, and seek to understand essential elements of creating supportive environments that nurture well-being. By focusing on these positive aspects of human life, they seek to enhance happiness and success.

Subjective Well-Being

Positive psychology is frequently called the "science of happiness," but this label is somewhat misleading. Happiness, typically construed as an emotion like joy, represents just one facet of the field. While happiness remains vital, positive psychology delves deeper into understanding and enhancing diverse human flourishing and dimensions of well-being. Instead of solely focusing on happiness, positive psychologists prefer the term *subjective well-being*. **Subjective well-being (SWB)** encompasses a broader spectrum, including life satisfaction, emotional affect, and a sense of meaning and purpose. It encompasses affective, behavioral, and cognitive dimensions, offering a more comprehensive perspective on human well-being. While the terms *subjective well-being* and *happiness* often seem interchangeable, positive psychologists argue that happiness is one of many contributing factors to overall well-being.

What factors do you think would enhance your well-being? It might be tempting to believe that more money, a different job, or admission into your dream college would significantly increase your well-being. While we often anticipate that these changes will make us "happier," their impact on overall well-being tends to be relatively small. Why do we struggle to accurately judge what will bring us happiness and increase our subjective well-being?

One explanation for this phenomenon is our susceptibility to **cognitive bias**. Cognitive biases are errors in thinking that occur as we process and interpret information from our surroundings, influencing our decisions and judgments. One common happiness myth revolves around the belief that money leads to lasting happiness. Many assume wealth or material possessions will significantly improve their well-being and life satisfaction. Often, this myth is strengthened by confirmation bias.

Confirmation bias (Topic 4.2) is our tendency to seek information confirming pre-existing beliefs or expectations. Someone who believes that buying new items leads to increased happiness might only focus on evidence supporting this idea while ignoring evidence suggesting otherwise, perpetuating their belief. In reality, research suggests that while money can contribute to happiness up to a certain point—providing basic needs such as food, shelter, and security—its influence on happiness diminishes beyond a certain income threshold. Once essential needs are met, additional wealth often has diminishing returns in terms of happiness. Instead, relationships, personal growth, and meaningful experiences play a more significant role in long-term happiness and fulfillment. Thus, while money can contribute to temporary pleasures and comfort, it is not the sole determinant of lasting well-being.

Factors That Influence Well-Being

Consider how, or if, this happiness misconception influences your personal experiences. How much lasting joy do you derive from a new outfit, video game, or phone? If these material possessions or events had a lasting impact on our well-being, our happiness would continually build up, leading to a steady increase in our happiness levels. Unfortunately, that's generally not the case.

Some people experience a temporary boost by achieving goals or acquiring possessions. This boost may lead them to continually pursue more in an attempt to maintain or increase their happiness, but they may find that lasting happiness remains elusive. This cycle implies that despite experiencing positive events or acquiring desirable items, our happiness returns to a stable baseline called the *happiness set point*. It reflects the notion that people maintain a consistent level of subjective well-being over time, regardless of temporary fluctuations caused by external circumstances.

Practicing Gratitude

Gratitude is a positive emotional response that emerges from acknowledging and appreciating the good aspects of life. It involves recognizing sources of goodness that extend beyond oneself. Gratitude can be an emotional state or a character trait. The practice of gratitude offers numerous benefits across social, physical, and psychological domains. Practicing gratitude elevates happiness and life satisfaction while fostering positive emotions such as optimism, joy, and pleasure.

Moreover, gratitude serves as a buffer against anxiety and depression, bolsters the immune system, lowers blood pressure, and mitigates symptoms of illness. Cultivating gratitude through interventions like gratitude journaling strengthens resilience, nurtures relationships, and fosters forgiveness, altruism, and compassion. Gratitude is not only an emotion or feeling but also a mindset and practice that increases subjective well-being.

THINK AS A PSYCHOLOGIST

Determine the Type of Research Design(s) Used in a Given Study (2.A.1.b) | Identify the Variables of Interest in a Research Scenario (2.C.3) | Propose a Defensible Claim (4.A)

Read the following abstract and conclusions of a research study.

Abstract: Many studies suggest a link between gratitude and life satisfaction, including various assessments of gratitude interventions. This paper presents a systematic review of recent literature on the influence of gratitude on life satisfaction. The aim of this research is to better understand the nature of the relationship between gratitude and life satisfaction and to evaluate the state of literature. In our study, we systematically reviewed 44 articles that focused on the link between gratitude and life satisfaction.

Conclusions: People who feel more gratitude tend to be more satisfied with their lives and sometimes report feeling more satisfied after performing gratitude-related tasks such as listing things they are grateful for. However, not all studies find these effects, and there is little evidence that these tasks work better than simply asking people to engage in other positive thoughts. It is also possible that people respond more positively to life satisfaction surveys after these interventions because of expectations or a social desirability bias rather than real changes in life satisfaction.

Practice Determining Type of Research Design and Variables of Interest and Proposing a Defensible Claim

Choose the correct answer and complete the activities.

1. Which of the following research designs was used in this study?

   (A) Experiment

   (B) Case study

   (C) Naturalistic observation

   (D) Meta-analysis

2. Identify the variables of interest in this study.

3. Based on the conclusion, make a defensible claim about the relationship between gratitude and life satisfaction.

Character Strengths

Character strengths are the psychological attributes or traits contributing to an individual's positive functioning and well-being. Positive psychologists Martin Seligman and Christopher Peterson identified and classified a set of core character strengths through their work on the Values in Action (VIA) classification of strengths. They believe it is essential to learn more about each person's positive qualities and, in doing so, help them gain tools that will help them put their strengths to work in their lives. This classification system outlines 24 universal character strengths organized into 6 broad virtue categories:

- **Wisdom and Knowledge**—Includes strengths such as creativity, curiosity, open-mindedness, love of learning, and perspective
- **Courage**—Encompasses strengths like bravery, persistence, integrity, and vitality
- **Humanity**—Involves strengths related to interpersonal relationships, empathy, kindness, and social intelligence
- **Justice**—Involves strengths such as fairness, leadership, teamwork, and citizenship
- **Temperance**—Includes strengths related to self-regulation, moderation, humility, and prudence

- **Transcendence**—Encompasses strengths like gratitude, spirituality, hope, humor, and appreciation of beauty and excellence

Source: CityU, Hong Kong, Department of Behavioral Sciences, Positive Education Laboratory

Figure 5.2.1 Character Strengths

Your defining character strength is known as your **signature strength**. You typically feel a sense of natural proficiency, engagement, and authenticity when using your signature strength. Character strengths can be nurtured and developed through deliberate practice. People who exercise their signature strengths or virtues report higher levels of positive objective experiences, such as happiness and subjective well-being. How you use your unique strengths may play a crucial role in their long-term impact on your well-being.

Cultural Norms

Cultural norms are rules about how people should behave in a society, while **cultural values** are the important beliefs of that society. The norms decide what is considered good or expected in a particular group. They affect how people in a culture view happiness by deciding what makes them happy and how they show it. For example, some cultures focus on working together and sharing (collectivistic societies), while others stress independence and personal success (individualistic societies).

Consider the VIA virtues—wisdom, courage, humanity, justice, temperance, and transcendence. Are these important everywhere? Not exactly. While some of these qualities are valued in many places, their meaning and importance can change depending on the culture. For instance, being fair might mean different things in different places, and being brave might be viewed differently in societies with ideas about courage that diverge from one another. So, while these qualities are important, how they are viewed can change from one culture to another.

THINK AS A PSYCHOLOGIST

Explain How Cultural Norms, Expectations, and Circumstances Apply to Behavior and Mental Processes (1.B)

For many years, psychologists have examined factors that made people feel good about their lives, and therapists have routinely asked clients about their social support system, which capitalizes on the strengths surrounding the clients. However, these areas of strength and sources of happiness were not systematically studied until the latter part of the 20th century.

Among the more prominent psychologists studying positive psychology is Martin Seligman. Seligman is most famous for his theory of learned helplessness, which proposed that people who are depressed have learned to be depressed from their surrounding circumstances and past experiences. After about 20 or 30 years of studying this theory, Seligman reasoned that if depression could be learned, happiness could also be learned, so he turned his attention to the growing field of positive psychology. Seligman and his colleagues examined five areas that "forced" people to acknowledge their own strengths and support systems: (1) show gratitude to others who have shown them kindness, (2) list three good things in life every day for an entire week, (3) identify what they did that showed them at their very best and evaluate their personal strengths that contributed to their best performance, (4) examine their own strengths and utilize one each day in a new way, and (5) integrate their own strengths as a daily routine.

Practice Explaining How Cultural Norms Apply

Answer the following question.

1. How might a collectivistic view of one's strengths differ from an individualistic view? Take into account what you know about the different cultures in relation to independence and equality, group dependence, and hierarchy.

Posttraumatic Growth

Posttraumatic growth (PTG) refers to the positive psychological changes that can emerge from grappling with trauma or challenging circumstances. While encountering crises is common in adulthood, many individuals struggle to recover. Although trauma can lead to adverse outcomes like posttraumatic stress disorder (PTSD; see Topic 5.4), not everyone develops PTSD after experiencing trauma. PTG challenges the prevailing view of trauma as exclusively harmful by acknowledging the potential for positive psychological changes stemming from navigating difficult life circumstances. This paradigm shift recognizes the multifaceted nature of human experiences, acknowledging that adversity, while undoubtedly painful, can spark growth and transformation.

Recent research has begun to explore PTG, highlighting how specific individuals undergo profound psychological shifts following traumatic experiences. Studies suggest that traumatic events can spur personal growth, leading individuals to perceive themselves as stronger and more resilient. Instances of PTG can be found in responses to events such as terminal illness, death, and loss, where people report newfound self-confidence, improved relationships, increased compassion, and a deeper philosophical outlook on life. PTG emphasizes the resilience of the human spirit, highlighting individuals' capacity to find meaning and growth in the aftermath of trauma. Although trauma is not downplayed or glorified, recognizing the possibility of posttraumatic growth provides hope during difficult periods, reaffirming people's inherent resilience in overcoming challenges.

REFLECT ON THE ESSENTIAL QUESTION

Essential Question: *How does positive psychology approach the study of behavior and mental processes?* Using the Key Terms, complete a chart like the one below to gather details to help answer that question and to compare and contrast positive psychology to other psychological theories.

	Focus/ Orientation	View of Human Nature	Therapeutic Approach
Psychodynamic Perspective			
Humanistic Perspective			
Positive Psychology Perspective			

KEY TERMS

character strengths	cultural values	resilience
cognitive bias	gratitude	signature strength
confirmation bias	positive psychology	subjective well-being
cultural norms	posttraumatic growth (PTG)	(SWB)

MULTIPLE-CHOICE QUESTIONS

1. Which of the following statements best captures how positive psychology differs from previous psychological approaches?

   (A) It emphasizes the innate drive toward self-actualization.

   (B) It explores factors that contribute to well-being and resilience.

   (C) It studies how trauma creates debilitating and lasting effects.

   (D) It attributes most human growth and thriving to environmental factors.

2. Bella is a high school student who wishes to increase her overall well-being. Based on research in positive psychology, which of the following would most help Bella achieve her goal?

   (A) Spending more time connecting with people on social media

   (B) Treating herself to an indulgent meal that she has been craving

   (C) Buying something new to take her mind off of the stressors in her life

   (D) Attempting to express gratitude to family and friends on a daily basis

Questions 3 through 5 refer to the following.

Dr. Jones conducted a study in which 30 volunteers agreed to track the number of times over the course of a year that they practiced using their signature strength in a new way. At the end of the study, Dr. Jones had each participant take the Beck Depression Inventory (BDI), which is scored on a scale of 0–63 (lower numbers indicate fewer depressed symptoms). The results of the study are presented below.

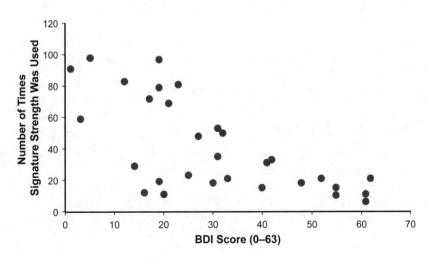

3. Which of the following research methods did Dr. Jones use in his research?

(A) Experiment

(B) Correlation

(C) Meta-analysis

(D) Case study

4. Dr. Jones has many studies running simultaneously. He is trying to match the results to each respective study. Which of the following most closely aligns to the results of this study?

P < .05	R = -.43	R = .61	N = 30
A	B	C	D

(A) A

(B) B

(C) C

(D) D

5. Which of the following is an appropriate conclusion that Dr. Jones can draw from the results of his study?

(A) Higher levels of depression caused participants to use their signature strength less frequently.

(B) Regular use of signature strengths has no relationship to participants' level of depression.

(C) The more participants used their signature strength, the more likely they were to develop depression.

(D) Increased use of participants' signature strength was linked to fewer depressed symptoms.

6. Aashna was a participant in Dr. Jones's study who regularly found new ways to nurture her existing friendships and show kindness to friends and strangers alike. Aashna's signature strength is most likely in which of the following categories?

(A) Wisdom and Knowledge

(B) Curiosity

(C) Humanity

(D) Temperance

7. Which of the following is a finding consistent with research in positive psychology?
   (A) Trauma often leads individuals to become more resilient and can lead to newfound self-confidence, improved relationships, increased compassion, and a deeper philosophical outlook on life.
   (B) The signature strengths of wisdom and transcendence rank well above the other strengths in predicting a person's overall well-being.
   (C) Cross-cultural research indicates the six broad virtue categories are equally valued and expressed from one culture to the next.
   (D) When people experience a major positive life change—for example, winning the lottery—their long-term happiness is significantly increased.

STUDY LIKE A CHAMP WITH DR. G

Effective study habits based on proven techniques can enhance your love of learning, an aspect of the Wisdom and Knowledge category of virtues.

Topic 5.3

Explaining and Classifying Psychological Disorders

"Over the course of the past decade, there's been an increased willingness to recognize mental health as an essential part of one's well-being."

—Nicole Spector

Essential Question: What approaches are used to define behaviors and mental processes as psychological disorders?

Psychopathology is the scientific study of mental disorders and different types of **maladaptive** behaviors associated with various disorders. *Maladaptive* means failing to adjust well to the environment. A number of terms, such as *mental illness*, *mental disorder*, and *psychological disorder*, have similar meanings and will often be used interchangeably. On the other hand, *psychiatric disorder* is aligned with medical definitions and clinical conditions. Psychologists and psychiatrists diagnose and treat people with mental illness. However, as medical doctors, psychiatrists will use a medical/clinical approach to diagnosis and treatment more than behavioral or cognitive approaches.

Defining and Diagnosing Psychological Disorders

The American Psychiatric Association (APA) defines a **psychological disorder** as "a syndrome characterized by clinically significant disturbance in an individual's cognition, emotion regulation, or behavior that reflects a dysfunction in the psychological, biological, or developmental processes underlying mental functioning." In other words, a psychological disorder, also called a *mental disorder*, is a dysfunctional and maladaptive pattern of behavior.

Level of dysfunction, perception of distress, and deviation from the social norm—known as the "3 D's"—are three criteria commonly used in the identification and diagnosis of psychological disorders. These criteria help clinicians assess whether a person's thoughts, feelings, or behaviors indicate a mental health condition. Following is an explanation of each criterion:

- **Level of dysfunction** refers to the degree of impairment or disruption in a person's ability to function effectively in various areas of life because of psychological symptoms or difficulties. When evaluating dysfunction, clinicians consider the extent to which a person's thoughts, emotions, or behaviors interfere with their daily functioning, relationships, work or school performance, and overall quality of life. Dysfunction can manifest in various ways, such as difficulties in maintaining relationships, fulfilling responsibilities, or engaging in typical activities. The presence of significant dysfunction suggests the possibility of a psychological disorder.

- **Perception of distress** refers to the subjective experience of emotional or psychological discomfort or suffering associated with a person's symptoms or difficulties. Clinicians assess whether they perceive their symptoms as distressing, bothersome, or impairing their well-being. This subjective experience of distress is an important consideration in diagnosing psychological disorders, since it reflects the person's own perception of their mental health status and the impact of their symptoms on their overall sense of well-being. While distress is a common feature of many psychological disorders, the absence of distress does not necessarily rule out the presence of a disorder.

- **Deviation from the social norm** refers to behaviors, thoughts, or emotions that significantly diverge from societal or cultural expectations or norms. While deviation from social norms alone is not sufficient for diagnosing a psychological disorder, it may be indicative of underlying mental health concerns when accompanied by dysfunction or distress. Clinicians consider whether a person's thoughts, emotions, or behaviors are markedly different from what is considered typical or acceptable within their cultural or social context. However, cultural factors influence the expression and interpretation of psychological symptoms, and what may be considered normal behavior in one culture may be perceived as abnormal in another.

Diagnosing and Classifying Psychological Disorders

In clinical practice, the assessment and diagnosis of psychological disorders involve a comprehensive evaluation of multiple factors, including the presence of symptoms, their severity and duration, their impact on functioning and well-being, and the individual's cultural background and personal context. Clinicians use standardized diagnostic criteria to guide their assessment and diagnosis of psychological disorders.

Diagnosing and classifying psychological disorders can have both positive and negative consequences. While they can facilitate validation, access to treatment, and research advancements, they also risk contributing to stigmatization, misdiagnosis, and dependency on labels.

For severe and debilitating disorders, such as schizophrenia or major depressive disorder, accurate diagnosis can lead to timely access to treatment and support services, potentially improving long-term outcomes. Clear diagnostic criteria can provide clinicians with guidance for selecting evidence-based interventions and monitoring treatment progress. However, for less severe conditions, such as mild anxiety or adjustment disorders, diagnosis may lead to unnecessary medicalization. Overdiagnosis of certain disorders, particularly in children and adolescents, can result in unnecessary stigma, labeling, and exposure to psychotropic medications with potential side effects.

People from lower socioeconomic classes or from marginalized or underrepresented groups may face additional challenges in accessing accurate diagnosis and appropriate treatment because of systemic barriers, bias, and disparities in health care access. Diagnosis can worsen feelings of stigma, shame, and self-doubt, particularly for people whose identities are already marginalized or stigmatized (e.g., LGBTQ+ individuals or people from racial or ethnic minorities).

Approaches to diagnosis and treatment that are sensitive to cultural differences can lessen stigma, encourage more people to seek help, and improve treatment processes and outcomes for diverse groups. Taking cultural factors into account during diagnosis can build trust and cooperation between clinicians and clients, making the therapeutic relationship more effective. However, such issues as stigma, racism, sexism, ageism, and other forms of discrimination can worsen disparities in mental health diagnosis, treatment, and outcomes. This discrimination can lead to conditions being underdiagnosed or misdiagnosed and limited access to care for marginalized groups. Furthermore, diagnostic labels may reinforce stereotypes and continue social inequalities, especially when the criteria for diagnosis are culturally biased or overlook the various ways people show distress and resilience.

THINK AS A PSYCHOLOGIST

Propose a Defensible Claim (4.A) | Provide Reasoning That Is Grounded in Scientifically Derived Evidence to Support, Refute, or Modify an Established or Provided Claim, Policy, or Norm (4.B.2) | Evaluate Whether a Psychological Research Scenario Followed Appropriate Ethical Procedures (2.D.4)

To what extent is it beneficial or harmful to receive a diagnostic label for a physical or psychological ailment? Researchers did a meta-analysis in 2021 to examine that question and the findings are summarized below.[1]

Worldwide, there has been an increase in the use of diagnostic labels for both physical and psychological diagnoses. Diagnosis reflects the process of classifying an individual who presents certain signs and symptoms as having, or not having, a particular disease or disorder. However, often less considered are the problematic or negative consequences of a diagnostic label. These may include increased psychological distress, preference for invasive treatments, greater sick-role behavior (taking on a social role with certain rights, such as being excused from school), and restriction of independence. We conducted a meta-analysis to explore this topic. All patient information was kept confidential to protect participants' rights to privacy.

1 Sims, R., Michaleff, Z. A., Glasziou, P., & Thomas, R. (2021, December 22). Consequences of a diagnostic label: A systematic scoping review and thematic framework. *Frontiers in Public Health*, 9, 725877. doi: 10.3389/fpubh.2021.725877. PMID: 35004561; PMCID: PMC8727520.

The results suggest that receiving a diagnostic label is not solely beneficial. For example, of the studies in our review that reported a psychosocial consequence of a diagnostic label, 60 percent of these reported negative psychological impacts, compared with 46 percent that reported positive psychological impacts. The results of this review suggest that many individuals experienced changes in their relationships with health care providers (and the latter agreed), lost emotional support, and experienced some detrimental changes in behavior because of the diagnostic label.

Practice Proposing a Claim, Providing Reasoning, and Evaluating Ethics

Complete the following activities.

1. Based on the information presented above, make a defensible claim about the use of diagnostic labels and support your claim by citing one specific piece of evidence from the summary.

2. Identify the ethical guideline that was specifically discussed in the research summary.

Diagnostic and Statistical Manual of Mental Disorders

Today, one manual is used as the source of criteria for defining psychological disorders, the *Diagnostic and Statistical Manual of Mental Disorders,* 5th edition (commonly referred to as the *DSM-5*). For more than 70 years, the mental health field has come to rely on the *DSM* as the "bible" of psychiatric diagnosis. Each new edition, theoretically, introduces improved definitions and diagnostic criteria for psychological disorders.

The *DSM-5* was published in 2013, and like the previous editions, it introduced new diagnostic criteria. Although it removed some disorders and added others, those changes were not made without serious discussion and debate. For example, the issue of Internet addiction was hotly debated in prepublication discussions and was pushed by many to be included as an official disorder. In the end, it was not included, although Internet Gaming Disorder is listed in the *DSM-5*, Section 3, under Conditions of Further Study. However, in a number of Asian countries, especially China, families send their sons to inpatient treatment centers in hopes of curing them of Internet gaming addiction, because gaming wreaks havoc in their daily lives. Is it abnormal to spend 18 hours a day on the Internet? Yes, say psychologists. Is it harmful? Probably. Is it an official psychological disorder? Not until the *DSM* writers and publishers say it is.

The *DSM-5* includes a Cultural Formulation Interview (CFI) and Cultural Formulation Appendix to help clinicians assess cultural factors relevant to diagnosis and treatment. These tools encourage clinicians to explore cultural identity, cultural explanations of illness, cultural factors affecting treatment, cultural stressors and strengths, and the impact of acculturation and migration on mental health.

The *DSM-5* also now considers environmental events, medical conditions, and potential genetic links for behavior as part of the diagnostic criteria. In contrast to earlier editions, the *DSM-5* does not require that all criteria be met before a diagnosis is made. Altogether, 20 categories of disorders are identified, with symptom descriptions and diagnostic criteria for a professional diagnosis. An overview of categories and specific psychological disorders will be presented and discussed in Topic 5.4.

International Classification of Diseases

The first edition of the *Diagnostic and Statistical Manual of Mental Disorders* was based on the *International Classification of Diseases (ICD)*. The *ICD* has been published by the World Health Organization (WHO) since 1948, when they began collecting data for all known diseases and injuries. In addition to classifying an exhaustive range of medical conditions, the *ICD* contains a comprehensive classification system for mental disorders. The 1992 revision had a new title, the *International Statistical Classification of Diseases and Related Health Problems (ICD-10)*. One volume, *The ICD-10 Classification of Mental and Behavioural Disorders*, was devoted to clinical descriptions and diagnostic guidelines of mental disorders. The current edition, *ICD-11*, was introduced in 2022. Most countries outside of the United States use the *ICD* to classify and diagnose those with disorders, and the *DSM-5* has aligned criteria and coding to the ICD, which should help provide consistent diagnoses worldwide.

Psychological Perspectives

During the last 100 years, a number of perspectives or theoretical approaches have attempted to explain the causes, or etiology, of psychological disorders. Most mental health professionals today do not rely exclusively on one approach. Instead, they use an **eclectic**, or broad-based approach, trusting a combination of established approaches to diagnose and treat individuals with psychological disorders. You have been introduced to each of these perspectives throughout the book, so as you read this section, stop at each heading that identifies a perspective and test yourself to see if you can determine why a person from this perspective might believe someone is experiencing symptoms related to a mental illness.

Behavioral Perspective

The **behavioral perspective** is based wholly on the theory that all behavior, whether adaptive or maladaptive, is learned. (See Topic 3.7.) These theories explain how behaviors are acquired and maintained through associative learning. For example, behaviorists explain the development of a fear of buttons based on classical conditioning. Seven-year-old Natalie, for example, had a loose button on her sweater and put it in her mouth, and soon it became lodged in her throat and she began to choke. Unable to breathe, she began to panic.

Her mother found her just as Natalie was falling to her knees, about to pass out, and her mother was able to remove the button. Soon after the incident, Natalie began to cry and hyperventilate when she was putting on any shirt with buttons. At 17 years old, she still cannot have any article of clothing with buttons and starts to panic if she just touches a button. For Natalie, the button has become an unconditioned stimulus associated with the unconditioned response of choking.

Similarly, operant conditioning (Topic 3.8) can be used to explain illness anxiety disorder (IAD), a condition previously known as *hypochondriasis* or *hypochondria*. As a child, the person with illness anxiety disorder may have experienced prolonged periods of emotional isolation from parents. Then, when the child became seriously ill, the parents provided a good deal of attention. The child learned that experiencing illness was positively reinforced by receiving much-needed love and attention. As an adult, the learned association between stress (the trigger) and the feeling of being seriously ill is positively reinforced by receiving medical attention, which will encourage the behavior to occur again in the future.

Psychodynamic Perspective

The **psychodynamic perspective** is based on the Freudian belief that all psychological problems or disorders stem from repressing past trauma, memories, or thoughts in the unconscious mind to avoid anxiety. When these anxiety-producing thoughts try to break through to conscious awareness, they may cause mental distress and maladaptive behavior. To see the psychoanalytic approach in action, imagine a woman who has been diagnosed with the disorder once known as *multiple personalities* (but now called *dissociative identity disorder*). She is repressing the anxiety-producing traumatic memories of prolonged childhood abuse by developing alternate personalities that keep those painful memories in her unconscious, even though her alternate personalities are maladaptive and disruptive to her daily life.

The psychodynamic approach tries to get into the unconscious minds of individuals to understand how they view the world and their relationships within it. The psychodynamic approach, therefore, sees all human functioning as stemming from forces within the individuals themselves, particularly in their unconscious.

Humanistic Perspective

The **humanistic perspective** is based on the belief that mental illness stems predominantly from issues involving low self-esteem, a poor self-concept, and the feelings and maladaptive behaviors that result from the inability to be one's authentic self. The humanist school of psychology believes that each individual has a natural drive toward growth of the authentic self or best version of themselves, which is referred to as the *self-actualizing tendency*. This tendency encompasses the pursuit of personal growth, fulfillment, and self-improvement. When this natural tendency is blocked, often because of a bad environment, a person may experience stress, which in turn may distort their perception of reality.

For example, Ana's greatest desire is to pursue an acting career, but her family and cultural factors pressure her to abandon her authentic passion and pursue a more practical career as an accountant. This divergence between her authentic needs for personal growth and the conditions of worth—the conditions Ana believes she has to meet to be worthy of her family's love—makes her feel incongruence between her real and ideal self, which can lead to depression and anxiety.

Cognitive Perspective

The **cognitive perspective** proposes that psychological disorders originate from illogical, irrational, or maladaptive thought processes. For example, the cognitive perspective on depression emphasizes the role of negative thought patterns and cognitive distortions in the development of depression. Key elements include negative thinking patterns; cognitive distortions, such as viewing situations in black-and-white terms or blaming oneself for events outside of one's control; and maladaptive beliefs and schemas that shape how individuals interpret their experiences, such as thinking of oneself as being unlovable or incompetent. Cognitive therapy helps individuals develop healthier, more realistic ways of thinking, which can alleviate depressive symptoms.

The cognitive model looks at how a person thinks in order to better understand their behavior. To accurately diagnose a mental disorder, it assesses a person's perceptions, attitudes, what they pay attention to, their memories, and how they process information.

Evolutionary Perspective

The **evolutionary perspective** proposes that some mental health conditions may have developed as ineffective reactions to environmental challenges or as unintended outcomes of beneficial traits over many generations. It suggests that certain psychological disorders might have been advantageous in ancient settings but are now problematic in today's world. This viewpoint emphasizes the need to think about human evolutionary history and the disconnect between old adaptations and contemporary lifestyles to better understand why psychological disorders are common and how they manifest.

One example of applying the evolutionary perspective to treatment is in the context of anxiety disorders. From an evolutionary standpoint, anxiety can be seen as an adaptive response to danger, enhancing an individual's ability to survive by promoting vigilance and caution. However, in modern environments, these adaptive responses can become maladaptive, leading to excessive and chronic anxiety. Phobias are a type of anxiety disorder characterized by intense, irrational fears of specific objects or situations. From an evolutionary perspective, phobias may arise because certain stimuli such as snakes or heights posed significant threats to our ancestors, making a heightened fear response advantageous for survival.

Sociocultural Perspective

In recent years, mental health professionals have looked more closely at the role culture plays in the causes and variations of psychological disorders. Culture is a significant factor in the development and structure of personality. Culture also exerts a strong influence on the development of unique variations of defined psychological disorders. While other psychological perspectives focus more on the individual, the **sociocultural perspective** emphasizes societal, group, and cultural influences in the individual's environment.

The *DSM-5* reflects greater awareness and sensitivity to cultural influences in psychological disorders than did earlier diagnostic manuals. Three culture-specific concepts have been added to its appendix, as follows:

- Cultural syndromes are categories of similar symptoms and explanations of causes that occur in a culturally specific context and are recognized within the culture. See Table 5.3.1.
- Cultural idioms of distress involve expressions of distress that do not necessarily involve specific symptoms or disorders but provide shared ways of experiencing and expressing personal and social concerns within a culture.
- Cultural explanations of distress or perceived causes refer to labels, attributions, or explanations that point to culturally agreed-upon meanings for and causes of symptoms, illness, or distress.

Examples of Cultural Syndromes	
Taijin Kyofusho	This is a social anxiety disorder specific to Japan in which a man or woman experiences intense fear that their body, bodily function, or appearance will embarrass others.
Susto	Specific to areas of Latin America, this psychological condition includes severe anxiety, along with physical symptoms caused by what is believed to be a religious-magic traumatic event that separates the soul from the body. Symptoms may include apathy, insomnia, irritability, and physical symptoms such as diarrhea.
Amok	Originating in Southeast Asia, this condition begins as a period of brooding and manifests as a sudden and possibly homicidal explosion of rage, usually caused by a perceived insult.
Hwabyeong	Specific to the Korean peninsula, *hwabyeong* is an overwhelming feeling of anger related to perceived unfairness. It is often caused by the buildup of unresolved anger that has been suppressed for a long time. The trigger is usually a family-related event, and symptoms include heat sensation, respiratory symptoms, and heart palpitations.

Table 5.3.1

Cultural relativism is a concept that explains the intersection between mental disorders and culture. In this model, psychological disorders can only be fully understood within the context of the culture in which they occur. Sociocultural factors include gender, socioeconomic conditions, age, and the values, traditions, and societal expectations that contribute to the cultural context. The sociocultural context can help determine what is and is not considered within the range of normal. Such context can also determine how psychologists may handle universal psychological disorders such as depression, anxiety, and schizophrenia.

Cultural factors can also influence the treatment strategy. Gender is one factor. In most Western cultures, depression is more frequently seen in women than in men because it is more consistent with what the culture associates with women. Another factor is the educational level and socioeconomic status of the individual. Poverty can be a key element in the development of depression or anxiety disorders and also limit access to treatment, so the disorders are often undiagnosed and untreated. Additionally, cultural stressors such as violence are also highly correlated with stress-related disorders.

Sociocultural factors play a role in how frequently disorders appear in a given society. For example, anorexia nervosa and bulimia tend to appear primarily in Western cultures such as in the United States, Europe, and other cultures that hold thin, often unrealistic models as icons of beauty. Depression and anxiety disorders are much less common in Asian cultures such as in China and Japan. Cultural norms for specific disorders vary widely among countries. In Japan, for example, mental illness, particularly depression, is considered a taboo condition that can bring disgrace and dishonor to the family and extended family. For this reason, Japanese men, women, and children who experience depression will more often report physical illness or bodily ailments.

Biological Perspective

The **biological perspective**, also referred to as the medical approach, presupposes that psychological disorders have a biological origin. These models see such disorders as anxiety, depression, obsessive-compulsive disorder (OCD), and schizophrenia as being influenced by genetics, brain damage, dysfunction of the brain's neurotransmitter and hormonal systems, or a combination of these neurobiological factors. The medical/biological model has become the predominant model, as evidenced by the common language used to describe psychological disorders: *mental illness, patient, therapy,* and *symptoms.*

Another indication of the growing reliance on this approach is the increasing acceptance and use of pharmaceutical drugs for the treatment of a wide variety of psychological disorders. Prescription drugs are often an expected method of treatment for such disorders as anxiety, depression, OCD, and posttraumatic stress disorder (PTSD), among others. One common example is the treatment of major depressive disorder (MDD) using antidepressant medications. From the biological perspective, major depressive disorder is viewed as a result of imbalances in brain chemistry, genetic predispositions, and abnormalities in brain function and structure. Neurotransmitters such as serotonin, norepinephrine, and dopamine play a crucial role in mood regulation, and imbalances in these chemicals are linked to depressive symptoms. Antidepressant medications are a primary treatment option for major depressive disorder, based on the biological understanding of the disorder. These medications aim to correct the neurotransmitter imbalances that contribute to depressive symptoms.

Interaction Models

In recent years, the *network approach* to conceptualizing mental disorders has gained traction. It holds that mental disorders are the result of interactions between symptoms. At the heart of this theory is the idea that symptoms are connected through biological and psychological factors that interact with one another. Proponents of this approach have argued that environmental factors, including adverse life events, social relations, and even external objects that lead to addictive behavior, should also be considered.

Biopsychosocial Model

The field of psychology has been dominated by Western culture since its origins, but it has finally begun to recognize more fully the powerful influence of culture on human behavior, personality, and psychological disorders.

The **biopsychosocial model** is an integrated model that combines the biological (medical), psychological, and sociocultural models and is believed by most professionals to be a more thorough approach to use when explaining, diagnosing, and treating psychological disorders.

All three approaches combine to help understand the cause of psychological disorders and to improve treatment. (See Figure 5.3.1.) For example, consider this scenario: A young man, Robert, presents himself to a clinical psychologist with symptoms that indicate bipolar disorder, a psychological mood-related disorder characterized by swings between depressed and excited emotional states. The clinical psychologist working from a biopsychosocial approach recognizes that Robert's condition potentially has a *biological* component—that is, a genetic or neurological tendency toward it. The psychologist would also explore *psychological* factors that contribute to the illness and identify other possible causes such as poorly adjusted thought patterns, disordered behavioral patterns or habits, and possible issues involving a negative self-concept. Finally, the psychologist will consider the *sociocultural* component and look for any societal or cultural factors that could be

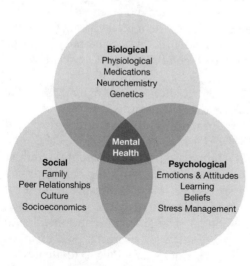

Figure 5.3.1 Biopsychosocial Model of Health

contributing to Robert's disorder. Societal/cultural factors may include gender issues, cultural expectations, work environment, education, and socioeconomic conditions.

Diathesis-Stress Model

The **diathesis-stress model** was developed in the 1960s by David Rosenthal, professor of psychiatry at Columbia University, when he was studying quadruplets who had all developed schizophrenia by their early twenties. Rosenthal was intrigued because there had been signs of psychological issues in their father and maternal grandmother. Because of the unusual nature of quadruplets, the girls also became minor celebrities, making for a very strange environment in which to be raised. The diathesis-stress approach recognizes a combination of biological and environmental causes of psychological disorders. Individuals who are genetically or neurobiologically predisposed to a psychological disorder may exhibit the disorder when exposed to environmental stressors that trigger characteristic symptoms of the disorder. This model assumes that people's genes put them at risk of developing a psychological disorder. For example, schizophrenia and clinical depression are viewed as biologically based disorders, but certain environmental events must occur in order for the disorder to manifest as symptoms. The environment almost serves as the impetus that turns on the genetic predisposition when conditions are right.

When applied together, three specific concepts help explain this approach. First, **diathesis** refers to the tendency or biologically based vulnerability to a particular mental illness. This vulnerability may occur in various degrees. Some people may be highly vulnerable, while others are less susceptible. The amount of environmental stress required to trigger the mental illness will vary depending on the level of biological vulnerability.

Second, **stress** develops from those environmental events that can trigger the onset of a biologically based disorder. If the diathesis potential is high and the individual's environment, including family, relationships, and social circumstances, presents a high enough level of stress, symptoms of the disorder are likely to show up.

The third concept, protective factors, refers to steps that can be taken to decrease the likelihood that a specific disorder will present itself. Protection involves modifying the environment to reduce exposure to stress or teaching the vulnerable person coping skills and building a strong support network to help reduce or eliminate symptoms of the disorder.

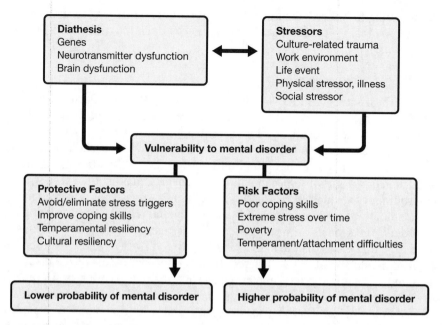

Figure 5.3.2 The Diathesis-Stress Model

THINK AS A PSYCHOLOGIST

Explain How Cultural Norms, Expectations, and Circumstances Apply to Behavior and Mental Processes (1.B)

The diathesis-stress model suggests that we have a propensity (or "diathesis") to develop a particular disorder, but that propensity will not be exhibited unless we are exposed to certain environmental stressors. This idea is akin to that of a monk named Mendel who grew and studied vegetables. He discovered that certain types of peas had a propensity to express certain characteristics, such as color or height. He called this the *genotype* of the plant. However, the exact color or height would be expressed only when the plant encountered certain environmental factors, such as how much water and sunlight it received. Mendel called these exact characteristics the *phenotype* of the plant. In the mental health domain, a person may have the diathesis to develop schizophrenia, but the schizophrenia will not be expressed unless the person is exposed to either an intense environmental stressor or sustained environmental stressors.

Practice Explaining Cultural Applications

Answer the following question.

1. In the diathesis-stress model, how might cultural differences affect mental disorder expression?

Essential Question: *What approaches are used to define behaviors and mental processes as psychological disorders?* Using the Key Terms, complete a chart like the one below to gather details to help answer that question.

Approach	Description

KEY TERMS

behavioral perspective	diathesis	perception of distress
biological perspective	diathesis-stress model	psychodynamic
biopsychosocial model	evolutionary perspective	perspective
cognitive perspective	humanistic perspective	psychological disorder
deviation from the social	level of dysfunction	psychopathology
norm	maladaptive	sociocultural perspective
eclectic		stress

MULTIPLE-CHOICE QUESTIONS

1. For the last several months, Brady has consistently felt low energy and doesn't enjoy things that he has typically enjoyed doing. His therapist believes he is suffering from depression and thinks that it stems from Brady's tendency to think pessimistically about most things in his life. The therapist's belief about what is causing Brady's depression is most closely aligned with which of the following perspectives?

   (A) Humanistic

   (B) Psychodynamic

   (C) Behaviorist

   (D) Cognitive

2. Dr. Shaver is a behaviorist who works with patients experiencing phobias. One of her patients has a phobia of bats and is reluctant to go out at night because of the bats flying around in her neighborhood. As a behaviorist, Dr. Shaver would most likely argue which of the following?

   (A) Bats are a symbolic representation of the patient's unconscious fear of her mother.

   (B) The patient was born with a genetic predisposition that makes her vulnerable to anxiety.

   (C) When the patient avoids going outside, she is being reinforced because her anxiety goes away.

   (D) Fearing bats is the result of evolutionary factors leading us to avoid things that may harm us.

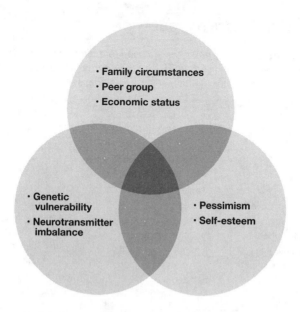

- Family circumstances
- Peer group
- Economic status

- Genetic
  vulnerability
- Neurotransmitter
  imbalance

- Pessimism
- Self-esteem

3. The above graphic best represents which of the following perspectives on the causes of depression?

   (A) The sociocultural perspective

   (B) The behaviorist perspective

   (C) The biopsychosocial perspective

   (D) The humanistic perspective

4. Which of the following best describes the purpose of the *DSM-5*?

   (A) The *DSM-5* provides diagnostic criteria that help clinicians determine whether someone is experiencing mental illness.

   (B) The *DSM-5* provides extensive analysis of the possible causes for each psychological problem.

   (C) The *DSM-5* provides detailed evidence-based treatment plans that align with each psychological problem.

   (D) The *DSM-5* allows patients to learn more about how disorders can affect individuals and society.

5. Which of the following statements most closely aligns with humanistic beliefs about what causes depression?

   (A) Lower than normal levels of serotonin result in higher levels of depression.

   (B) Depression results from repressed trauma in the unconscious mind.

   (C) Depression results when an individual experiences a gap between their ideal self and their real self.

   (D) Depression is a direct result of operant conditioning.

Questions 6 and 7 refer to the following.

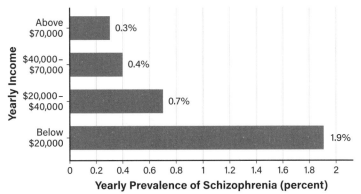

Yearly Prevalence of Schizophrenia (percent)

Source: Comer, *Fundamentals of Abnormal Psychology*, 8e, © 2016 Worth Publishers
Information from: Sareen et al., 2011

6. The evidence provided in the above chart best supports the views of which perspective?

   (A) Sociocultural
   (B) Diathesis-stress
   (C) Cognitive
   (D) Biological

7. This researcher also wants to investigate the average age at which participants in the study developed symptoms of schizophrenia. Below are the ages at which the symptoms first occurred. What is the mean?

Age of Onset of Schizophrenic Symptoms	19	22	20	20	24

   (A) 22
   (B) 21
   (C) 20
   (D) 19

Topic 5.4

Selection of Categories of Psychological Disorders

"I needed to put two critical ideas together: that I could be both mentally ill and lead a rich and satisfying life."

—Elyn R. Saks

Essential Question: What are the symptoms and possible causes of psychological disorders?

The DSM-5 provides the most up-to-date list and descriptions of more than 250 psychological disorders. Each one has a label—a name—and the *DSM-5* helps psychologists determine which disorder or disorders are potential diagnoses for a given patient. A diagnosis is done by evaluating patients' symptoms and matching them to characteristics, or criteria, of a labeled disorder. Labels in mental health can be both beneficial and problematic. While labels facilitate effective treatment and understanding, they must be used carefully to avoid stigma and maintain the person's holistic identity. Once a person is diagnosed with a serious psychological condition, they can lose their identity in the label, and people may view them as their illness rather than as the unique human they are.

The experts who compiled the *DSM-5* considered another aspect of psychological diagnosis: comorbidity, or the presence of two or more disorders at the same time. Some controversy surrounds comorbidity, because symptoms of some disorders overlap with symptoms of other disorders, potentially confusing treatment plans. For example, roughly one-third of people with obsessive-compulsive disorder experience depressive symptoms, often because they understand their obsessions are irrational but cannot stop them. If the OCD is causing depression, most would advise treating the OCD so the symptoms of depression eventually lift. If, however, a person is experiencing depressive symptoms so severe that they are in danger of harming themselves, the depression must be given priority.

Neurodevelopmental Disorders

Neurodevelopmental disorders—conditions associated with central nervous system functioning—begin in the **developmental period**, from conception to adolescence. These disorders usually include developmental deficits that affect social, intellectual, academic, and/or personal functioning. Symptoms of neurodevelopmental disorders focus on whether the person is exhibiting behaviors appropriate for their age or maturity range. The symptoms can be very specific, such as mispronunciation and articulation problems associated with a speech sound disorder, or more global, such as the learning and adaptive behavioral problems common to severe intellectual disability. Neurological developmental disorders, as a group, include intellectual developmental disorder, attention deficit/hyperactivity disorder, autism spectrum disorder, and tic disorder, among others.

Attention Deficit/Hyperactivity Disorder

Attention deficit/hyperactivity disorder (**ADHD**) is a neurodevelopmental disorder that leads to ongoing problems with paying attention or being overly impulsive, which affects everyday functioning and development. It's most commonly identified in childhood, more often in boys. Signs of ADHD in young children include difficulties with paying attention, staying organized, focusing, and completing tasks. Hyperactive behaviors might involve constant movement, like fidgeting or running around restlessly. Impulsive behaviors can include actions like suddenly hitting, interrupting conversations, or throwing things without thinking ahead.

To confirm a diagnosis of ADHD, these behaviors must be observed in more than one place, such as at school and at home. Diagnosing ADHD can be contentious because the behaviors used to diagnose it, like high activity levels or lack of focus, are often seen in many young children who do not have the disorder.

Autism Spectrum Disorder

Autism spectrum disorder (**ASD**) is a developmental condition characterized by repetitive behaviors and challenges with social communication and interaction. People with autism might face difficulties in several areas:

- **Social and emotional interaction:** They may struggle with back-and-forth conversations, fail to engage in typical social exchanges, and have difficulty understanding and responding to common social cues.
- **Nonverbal communication:** Understanding body language, maintaining eye contact, and interpreting facial expressions can be challenging.
- **Social relationships:** Developing and maintaining relationships can be difficult because of these communication barriers.

Behaviors associated with autism can include repetitive movements and speech, unusual ways of playing with objects, and a need for consistent routines. Additionally, individuals with autism often have a heightened sensitivity to sensory input from their surroundings. The severity of these symptoms can vary widely from mild to severe.

Noises and other sensory input can be overwhelming for children and adults with ASD.

Possible Causes of Neurodevelopmental Disorders

ADHD and ASD are complex conditions with multiple causes. Research suggests that a combination of genetic, neurological, and environmental factors play a role in their development. ADHD tends to run in families. Specific genes associated with neurotransmitter regulation, such as dopamine and norepinephrine, are tied to ADHD. Exposure to prenatal risk factors, such as maternal smoking and alcohol consumption, are linked to an increased risk of ADHD. Environmental factors, such as lead exposure and early childhood exposure to toxins or pollutants, may contribute to the ADHD risk.

Many genes may work together with environmental factors like air pollution, pesticides, and heavy metals, increasing the risk of ASD. Additionally, factors before birth, such as infections in the mother, certain medications she might take, and issues with her immune system, can also raise the risk of ASD. Older parental age, especially in fathers, is linked to a higher likelihood of having a child with ASD. Changes in how the brain develops early on and problems with how the immune system works may also play a role in developing ASD.

Schizophrenic Spectrum Disorders

Many consider **schizophrenia** the most profound and devastating of all mental disorders, and it is the most prevalent disorder among all psychotic illnesses. **Psychosis** refers to any disorder in which the affected person has lost contact with reality. The range of **psychotic disorders** includes delusional disorder, brief psychotic disorder, and schizophreniform disorder (essentially, short-duration schizophrenia).

The onset of schizophrenia usually occurs in the late teens to early 20s, and the severity of the symptoms can vary significantly from person to person. The spectrum of severity is described as the "rule of quarters." A quarter of those who develop schizophrenia will have one psychotic episode but will then recover and lead a relatively normal life. Another quarter will respond well to medication and be able to live relatively independently. The third quarter will need to live with supervision in a supportive facility. The last quarter will have the most severe symptoms and will require permanent care; 15 percent are unresponsive to medication.

Symptoms of Schizophrenia

Five symptoms are commonly associated with all **schizophrenic spectrum disorders**. These symptoms are classified as positive (additions) or negative (reductions) in relation to normal behavior. Positive symptoms are those not present in healthy individuals, which include delusions and hallucinations. Negative symptoms are characteristics that a healthy person possesses, but someone with schizophrenia is missing. The most typical negative symptom is diminished or complete lack of emotional expression. A diagnosis of schizophrenia requires at least two of the symptoms outlined below, and one of them must be delusions, hallucinations, or disorganized speech.

Delusions, or the persistence of false beliefs, are a positive symptom. They are usually held by affected individuals as ideas about themselves in relation to the world around them. A wide variety of delusions include paranoia, the idea of being harassed or spied on, and grandiosity, the belief that one has great abilities or is important or famous. Delusions are defined as bizarre if they are clearly beyond the realm of possibility. One common bizarre delusion is the belief of being in communication with God or Jesus; another is that the individual is missing an essential body organ. One schizophrenic patient reported that he had an x-ray showing that he had no heart. Another diagnosed schizophrenic was convinced that he was under surveillance by the Department of Defense, the FBI, and the CIA.

Hallucinations are false perceptions, sensory experiences without any external sensory stimuli. An authentic hallucination is involuntary and cannot be controlled by the individual. However, it is experienced as though it is as real as any other normal sensory perception. The most common type of hallucination is an auditory hallucination—hearing a voice that is totally separate from the individual. For example, someone with schizophrenia may report having an invisible person talking harshly straight into their ear, harassing them, or telling them to do something. Sometimes, the voices can be a source of comfort to the person having the experience.

Disorganized thinking or speech is a positive symptom that may manifest as combining thoughts or switching from one thought to another. A good way to explain this type of thinking is to imagine your train of thought expressed in speech as a highway with on- and off-ramps. A nonpsychotic person can remain focused on one thought while keeping the on- and off-ramps closed. In contrast, in a psychotic person or someone with diagnosed schizophrenia, the on- and off-ramps are wide open, and unrelated thoughts can suddenly intrude. The person can switch from one topic to a totally unrelated one—sometimes linking words together because they rhyme (called *clang association*) or spewing out an almost completely nonsensical jumble of words (often referred to as **word salad**).

Disorganized motor behavior can show up in strange or unusual ways, like suddenly becoming agitated without a clear reason or struggling to stay focused on a task. This behavior can include both positive symptoms and negative symptoms. One type of disorganized motor behavior is called catatonia. **Catatonia** can vary widely. For example, the positive side might involve excited but unusual movement, such as pointless and repeated actions, like making the same facial expressions over and over or repeating words continuously. The negative side, known as catatonic stupor, might involve adopting strange positions or staying completely still for a long time.

Negative symptoms Negative symptoms present generally as the lack of typical behavior, such as diminished emotional expression. The experience of diminished emotions is described as the **flat affect** (*affect* here is a noun meaning "subjective mood" or "emotional state"). Sometimes, however, expressed emotions are highly inappropriate, such as laughing when others are sad or displaying anger or tears during a joyful event. More typically, emotions will be entirely absent. *Avolition* refers to a significant decrease in or absence of any purposeful activity. The individual may simply sit or stand for hours in a **catatonic stupor** (described above), without moving or showing interest in participating in any activities.

Possible Causes of Schizophrenia

Schizophrenia is a brain disease whose exact cause is not yet known, although studies have suggested that a combination of genetics and environmental factors may contribute to its development. High levels of the neurotransmitter dopamine have been linked to schizophrenia (referred to as the **dopamine hypothesis**), and enlarged fluid-filled ventricles of the brain are also associated with neurological aspects of the disorder. Schizophrenia is more common in people whose fathers were older when they were born, and in those who have autoimmune diseases or were exposed to viruses and malnutrition during the second trimester before they were born. About 1 in 270 people globally have schizophrenia, and it is slightly more common in males. The risk of getting schizophrenia is higher—about 10 percent—if a sibling or close relative has the condition. If one identical twin has schizophrenia, the other twin has a 50 percent chance of developing it too. This shows that both genetics and environmental factors play significant roles in causing schizophrenia.

THINK AS A PSYCHOLOGIST

Identify Psychology-Related Concepts in Descriptions or Representations of Data (3.A.2) | Propose a Defensible Claim (4.A)

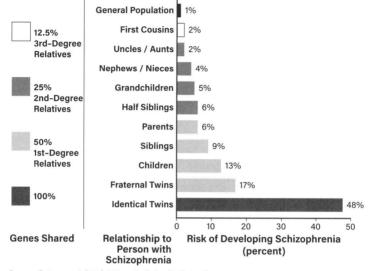

Source: Gottesman, I. (1991) A Meta-Analysis of Twin Studies

Practice Identifying Psychology-Related Concepts in Representations of Data and Proposing a Defensible Claim

Choose the correct answer and complete the activity.

1. The evidence presented in the above graph best supports the view of which of the following psychological perspectives?

    (A) Humanistic

    (B) Biological

    (C) Psychodynamic

    (D) Behavioral

2. Make a defensible claim about the evidence presented in the graph.

Depressive Disorders

The most common features of **depressive disorders** are significant feelings of sadness, emptiness, fatigue, and irritability that are accompanied by sleep and thought disruptions that significantly affect daily function. While the DSM-5 describes several types of depressive disorders, you will read about two of the most common disorders: major depressive disorder and persistent depressive disorder.

Major Depressive Disorder

Major depressive disorder, also known as *unipolar depression*, includes severe symptoms like feeling extremely tired, being in a depressed mood most of the time, losing interest in activities you used to enjoy, eating less, losing weight, sleeping poorly, feeling worthless or guilty, having trouble focusing, and often thinking about death or suicide. To be diagnosed with this disorder, a person must have at least five of these symptoms for two weeks or more. One of these symptoms must be either a depressed mood or a loss of pleasure or interest in activities. Depression often runs in families, which suggests a genetic link. However, usually something in a person's environment needs to trigger the depression for it to appear. Depression often occurs alongside other mental or physical health issues. If the depression is very severe, the person might also experience psychotic symptoms such as delusions or hallucinations.

Persistent Depressive Disorder

Persistent depressive disorder is a depressed mood that has lasted for at least two years. It is considered a milder form of depression with no suicidal thoughts. Someone with persistent depressive disorder may experience two or more of the characteristic symptoms: poor appetite or overeating, sleep disturbances, fatigue, low self-esteem, poor concentration, feelings of hopelessness, and a lack of interest in activities they had previously found interesting.

Possible Causes of Depressive Disorders

The causes of depressive disorders vary from person to person, but neurological factors may be involved, including deficits in the production of one or more of the neurotransmitters in the brain—serotonin and norepinephrine. Antidepressant drugs that affect levels of these neurotransmitters are frequently prescribed. Genetic links are also suggested; if one parent has depression, the risk for their child to develop it as a teen or adult is increased significantly.

Social and cultural factors also play a significant role in the development of depressive disorders. Individuals from lower socioeconomic backgrounds or minority groups may face chronic stress, which can contribute to depression. Cultural expectations regarding emotional expression, gender roles, and coping strategies affect how depression is perceived and experienced. Cultures that stigmatize mental illness may discourage individuals from seeking help for depressive symptoms.

Additionally, cognitive factors contribute to depression. The negative cognitive triad—negative self-view, negative worldview, and negative future outlook—play a significant role. Depressed individuals often see themselves as worthless, inadequate, or unlovable. They may view the world as unfair or hostile, and they may see future events as bleak and hopeless. These unhealthy patterns of thinking, or maladaptive schemas, are deeply rooted and are reinforced when individuals focus only on information that supports their existing negative beliefs. This focus can make people feel helpless and hopeless.

Constantly thinking about negative thoughts, memories, or problems keeps depressive feelings alive. Setting excessively high standards and unrealistic goals can also make someone constantly feel like a failure or not good enough. People who are perfectionists often harshly criticize themselves and blame themselves for any mistakes or perceived flaws. Intense and prolonged stress, traumatic events, and the loss of a close family member can trigger the onset of the disorder.

Bipolar Disorders

Undoubtedly, at some point you have experienced a sad day. You had "the blues." You may also remember a time when you had a really "up" day. Everything was clicking; you were really happy and excited to be alive. You did not have a mood disorder, obviously, but if your depressed or excited moods were so extreme and prolonged that they led to disruptions in your daily life, then they could be an indication of a **bipolar disorder**. (See Figure 5.4.1.)

The American Psychiatric Association clearly differentiates among schizophrenia, bipolar disorders, and depressive disorders. The importance of these distinctions is explained in the DSM-5 as follows:

> Bipolar and related disorders are separated from the depressive disorders in the DSM-5 and placed between the chapters on schizophrenia spectrum and other psychotic disorders and depressive disorders in recognition of their place as a bridge between the two diagnostic classes in terms of symptomatology, family history, and genetics.

—DSM-5, p. 123

The overlap in symptoms among these diseases does not mean that someone with bipolar or depressive disorder will develop schizophrenia or vice versa. Instead, it means

- the spectrum of symptoms can overlap in certain cases of schizophrenia, depressive disorders, and bipolar disorders.
- the etiology, or origins, of these disorders may also overlap; genetic links have been demonstrated for all three diseases.

The *DSM-5* outlines several bipolar-related disorders. **Bipolar I** is a mood (or affective) disorder in which an individual has experienced at least one manic episode (mania) as well as episodes of major depression. **Mania** is a state of abnormally elevated mood and intensely high energy that disrupts daily life. Mood in a manic episode is often characterized as either excessively euphoric, like "feeling on top of the world," or extremely irritable and dysphoric, experiencing profound unease. Manic episodes can lead to impairment in functioning at school or work and in daily responsibilities. People experiencing them may engage in risky or reckless behaviors that can have serious consequences. The extreme mood elevation and erratic behavior associated with mania can strain relationships with family members, friends, and colleagues. Mania can also pose significant safety risks, leading to accidents or injuries.

During a manic episode, people may experience feelings of grandiosity and begin many projects that are often beyond their skills or talents. Or they may go on spending sprees with money they do not have, leading to financial problems, legal consequences, and damage to their reputation. They often require significantly less sleep, maintaining high levels of energy with only 2 or 3 hours of sleep per night. People with bipolar I may display flight-of-ideas, a pattern of rapid, continuous speech where the person jumps quickly from one idea to another. The connection between thoughts may make sense to the person speaking, but it can be hard for others to follow because the transitions between topics are abrupt or seemingly unrelated. This symptom reflects a high level of mental distraction and a rapid flow of thoughts that race faster than they can express coherently.

An individual with bipolar I may also experience **hypomania**, a condition that is similar to mania but less severe. It is characterized by a pattern of episodes alternating between hypomania and major depression. To be diagnosed with bipolar I, however, the individual must also have experienced a full manic episode. The major difference in diagnosing bipolar I and **bipolar II** is that in bipolar II an individual would have experienced hypomanic episodes that never quite reach the severity of a full-blown manic episode (Figure 5.4.1).

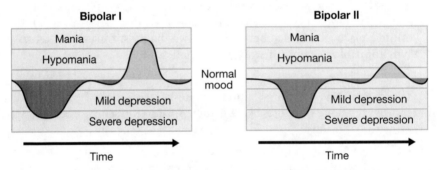

Figure 5.4.1 Bipolar I and II. In between mood extremes, people with bipolar disorders experience normal states.

The severity of depression for both bipolar I and bipolar II is classified as major depression, which, as you may recall, includes severe symptoms that can include fatigue, sustained depressed mood, diminished interest or pleasure in activities, decreased appetite, weight loss, sleep disturbances, feelings of worthlessness, guilt, diminished ability to concentrate, and persistent thoughts of death or suicide.

Bipolar and related disorders are a class of mood disorders that involve both poles of moods—ups and downs. Bipolar I is the more severe disorder. In bipolar I, individuals experience full-blown manic episodes characterized by significant impairment in functioning, including severe mood disturbance, increased energy, racing thoughts, reckless behavior, and potential psychotic features such as hallucinations or delusions. In contrast, bipolar II disorder involves hypomanic episodes, which are less severe than manic episodes. While hypomania shares some symptoms with mania, such as elevated mood and increased energy, the symptoms are milder in intensity and do not cause marked impairment in functioning or require hospitalization.

Possible Causes of Bipolar Disorders

The potential causes of bipolar disorders are diverse, encompassing a range of biological, genetic, social, cultural, behavioral, and cognitive factors, as shown in Table 5.4.1.

Contributing Causes of Bipolar Disorders	
Biological Factors	Research suggests that changes in certain neurotransmitters, especially norepinephrine and serotonin, may play a significant role in bipolar disorder. Additionally, hormonal imbalances and structural or functional abnormalities in the brain related to emotional processing could also contribute.
Genetic Factors	Bipolar disorder has a strong genetic component, indicating that it can run in families. Specific genes and genetic mutations are linked to the likelihood of developing the disorder, though no single gene causes the condition.
Social Factors	Life events and interpersonal relationships can influence the onset and course of bipolar disorder. Stressful life events, traumatic experiences, or unstable living situations can trigger episodes of mania or depression.
Cultural Factors	Cultural background can affect how individuals express symptoms of bipolar disorder, their willingness to seek help, and how they respond to treatment. Cultural stigma surrounding mental health can also affect the diagnosis and management of the disorder.
Behavioral Factors	Certain behaviors may exacerbate bipolar disorder or trigger episodes. For example, irregular sleep patterns and substance abuse have been known to provoke manic episodes in some individuals.
Cognitive Factors	Patterns of thinking and perception can also play a role in bipolar disorder. For example, an individual's cognitive style, such as how they process and respond to information, can influence their mood swings and susceptibility to episodes of mania or depression.

Table 5.4.1

Anxiety Disorders

Nearly everyone has experienced a feeling of nervousness from time to time— maybe about relationships, health, work, or financial issues. Anxiety, a feeling of unease, fear, or worry that something bad is about to happen, is something each of us will experience in life. However, what elevates common nervousness to an anxiety disorder is the intensity and persistence of symptoms and their interference with daily life. The DSM-5 outlines criteria for twelve anxiety disorders, several of which are described below.

A **phobia** is an irrational and debilitating fear. **Specific phobia disorder** is an anxiety disorder encompassing an overwhelming, unreasonable, and persistent sense of fear of a specific object or situation that provokes the fear response and sometimes leads to a panic attack. Any contact with the object or situation may produce an intense and immediate fear, and usually the person will actively avoid that fear-eliciting stimulus. Sometimes, even the thought of the object or situation may result in an unreasonable fear response. The individual may recognize that the fear is excessive and even unwarranted but still be unable to control it. The DSM-5 reports that about 6 to 8 percent of all people have specific phobias and the rate is higher (about 16 percent) among teens. Common phobias include **acrophobia**, or fear of heights, and **arachnophobia**, or fear of spiders (Table 5.4.2).

PREVALENCE RATE OF SPECIFIC PHOBIAS (UNITED STATES, 2022)	
Specific Phobia	**Prevalence**
Animals	40%
Insects	15%
Dark	12%
Public Speaking	10%
Fear of Unknown	8%
Blood	8%
Heights	4%
No phobias	3%

Table 5.4.2 Prevalence of Specific Phobias
Source: EnterpriseAppsToday

Agoraphobia, an intense fear of open, crowded, or enclosed spaces such as shops or movie theaters, is a common phobia. Agoraphobia may also include a fear of being outside the safety of one's home, being in open spaces, riding on public transportation, or standing in line in a crowd. Many people diagnosed with agoraphobia have a history of panic attacks, and the fear of having more of these panic attacks leads them to avoid places and situations. The frequent panic attacks of agoraphobic individuals are often associated with specific places in which such panic attacks occurred in the past. In extreme cases, even leaving their homes for the uncertain space outside can bring on a panic attack.

Panic disorder is an acute, or sudden and severe, feeling of extreme anxiety or fear that something terrible will happen at any minute. A **panic attack** can come on quickly and reach its peak within minutes. The trauma involved in a panic attack can be exacerbated by the simultaneous worry that the panic is associated with a life-threatening condition, such as a heart attack. Symptoms associated with panic disorder may include accelerated heart rate, chest pains, tremors, feelings of choking, shortness of breath, nausea, or numbness. The person may also experience a feeling of unreality, or a feeling of being detached from oneself. Some anxiety disorders are culture-bound, such as **ataque de nervios** (**ADN**), or "attack of nerves," which is prevalent among people of Caribbean or Iberian descent, including Hispanic populations, especially Puerto Ricans. Symptoms include trembling, shaking uncontrollably, uncontrolled crying, a feeling of heat rising from the chest to the head, and verbal and physical aggression. ADN is frequently brought on by a stressful event in one's family, such as a death or divorce or witnessing an accident involving a family member. Unlike a true panic disorder, ADN does not normally involve fear.

Social anxiety disorder (social phobia) involves the intense fear of being judged or watched by others. It causes some people to become overwhelmed with anxiety and fear when in social situations. They have an intense fear of being criticized or embarrassed, so they avoid such social situations as large events or parties, public speaking, being on stage, or using public restrooms. It is distinct from, but may include, agoraphobia.

One culture-bound social anxiety disorder, **taijin kyofusho (TKS)**, or "the disorder of fear," primarily affects people in Japan and Korea. In this case, it is fear of offending or displeasing others by one's appearance or bodily functions. Symptoms include a fear of social contact, extreme self-consciousness, and fear of contracting diseases. People experiencing TKS are afraid of offending others by blushing, staring inappropriately, presenting an improper facial expression or physical defect, or by emitting offensive odors. It is estimated that TKS affects 10–20 percent of Japanese people. Unlike other anxiety disorders, this one is more prevalent among men than women.

Generalized anxiety disorder (GAD) is defined as prolonged (six months or longer) feelings of unspecified worry and unease. Individuals with GAD are unable to stop the constant feelings of dread without a clear cause, and these feelings disrupt their daily lives. Other specific symptoms may include fatigue, restlessness, irritability, sleep disturbances, and muscle tension. Physical symptoms associated with heightened levels of distress, including headache, gastrointestinal problems, or diarrhea, are common in people with GAD.

Possible Causes of Anxiety Disorders

The possible causes of anxiety disorders can be broadly categorized into learned behaviors, cognitive and emotional responses, and biological or genetic factors. Anxiety disorders can develop through **learned associations,** a concept rooted in behavioral psychology. For instance, if a person experiences a panic attack in a particular setting, they might begin to associate that setting with anxiety and fear, leading to avoidant behaviors. This process is known as conditioning. Over time, the individual may start to fear not just the original setting but similar ones, expanding the scope of their anxiety.

Cognitive theories suggest that anxiety disorders arise from maladaptive thinking and emotional patterns that fail to adjust well to the environment. Individuals may exaggerate the threat of certain situations (known as *catastrophizing*), engage in "either-or" thinking, or constantly predict negative outcomes (fortune telling). These cognitive distortions can perpetuate a cycle of anxiety and fear, making everyday situations seem daunting or dangerous.

Anxiety disorders can stem from genetic predispositions. Research indicates that these disorders can run in families, suggesting a hereditary component. Additionally, imbalances in neurotransmitters that regulate mood and behavior can also contribute to the development of anxiety disorders. For example, disruptions in serotonin and dopamine levels are often observed in individuals with anxiety. Further, studies have shown that structural and functional abnormalities in brain areas associated with emotion regulation and threat perception can predispose individuals to anxiety disorders.

Understanding the causes of anxiety disorders involves looking at how these various factors—behavioral, cognitive, and biological—interact and influence each other. For instance, a person with a genetic predisposition to anxiety might be more likely to develop maladaptive thinking patterns in response to stress, which could further exacerbate their condition. Conversely, learning to modify these thought patterns and responses through therapeutic techniques can help manage or reduce the symptoms of anxiety disorders.

Obsessive-Compulsive and Related Disorders

Many people experience symptoms associated with obsessive-compulsive disorders and related disorders, possibly including checking a wristwatch repeatedly to verify the time, washing hands frequently to avoid germs, holding on to useless material things too long, or checking multiple times to be certain a door is locked or a window is closed. However, as with anxiety disorders, the difference between having a few compulsive habits and having a disorder is the persistence and intensity of those symptoms. In addition to the general obsessive-compulsive disorder, this category includes related disorders with specific obsessions, including hoarding, obsessive skin picking, obsessive hair pulling, a preoccupation with one's appearance, and others. Brain imaging has revealed differences in the basal ganglia in people with OCRDs, though whether it is a cause or effect is not yet certain.

Obsessive-compulsive disorders (OCDs) are characterized by the presence of **obsessions** (intrusive thoughts) and **compulsions** (intrusive, often repetitive, behaviors intended to reduce obsessions). For example, someone with obsessive-compulsive disorder might have an obsession with even numbers, feeling the need to adjust the volume on a car radio to an even number if it was set at an odd number. Or someone with OCD might insist on standing or sitting only on the right of someone at the dinner table or in a theater or almost anywhere because not doing so would cause anxiety to spike to an uncomfortable level.

Temporary Relief — Obsessive Thoughts — Increased Anxiety — Compulsive Behavior

Figure 5.4.2 The Obsessive-Compulsive Cycle

It is helpful to understand the relationship between obsessions and compulsions (see Figure 5.4.2). The obsessive thought increases anxiety, and engaging in the compulsion reduces the anxiety, thereby reinforcing the need to engage in the compulsion once anxiety arises. The obsession may be rooted in a neurochemical imbalance, or it may have psychological origins, such as observing similar behavior in parents or having a negative experience because something was not checked or cleaned.

In severe cases, OCD behavioral patterns can be burdensome and time-consuming. For example, a man was constantly obsessed with the idea or image that he had hit a small child while driving his car, which is a type of OCD categorized as *harming*. Any bump felt while driving would spike the obsessive anxiety-producing thoughts, and then he would begin compulsively checking and rechecking his route. He would drive around the block to the place where he thought he might have hit someone, checking repeatedly to make sure no one had been hit. He might repeat the compulsive behavior dozens of times in an effort to reduce his anxiety. Once, he was stopped by the police for exhibiting suspicious behavior. His OCD cycle was so severe that he eventually gave up driving.

Another form of OCD is **hoarding disorder**, in which someone accumulates an excessive number of things and stores them in a disorganized manner, often resulting in cluttered and unsafe living environments. People with hoarding disorder have difficulty discarding possessions, even those with little or no value, because they believe they need them or feel emotionally attached. Hoarding behaviors cause great distress, difficulty in functioning, and interference with daily activities, social relationships, and the responsibilities of work or school. People with hoarding disorder may have limited insight into the severity of their hoarding behavior and its impact on their lives, although some recognize the problem and feel ashamed or embarrassed.

A woman with hoarding disorder, for example, knows it is ridiculous to refuse to throw away used bandages, but inside her mind is the obsessive thought that something profoundly important is connected to that used bandage and throwing it away could lead to tragedy. The thought of throwing it away sends her anxiety soaring. So, she saves it, along with everything else—used teabags, price tags from purchased items, and shoes beyond repair. One woman saved all the hair that accumulated in her hairbrush because she felt like getting rid of it was getting rid of a part of herself.

People suffering from severe OCD may express thoughts of suicide or fantasize about contracting a fatal disease. Thoughts of death stem from the individual's awareness of the irrational nature of the obsession and compulsive behavior and inability to stop it, and they may see no other way out.

Possible Causes of Obsessive-Compulsive and Related Disorders

As with anxiety disorders, the causes of OCD are complex and include learned behaviors, problematic thinking and emotional patterns, and biological or genetic factors.

Learned Behaviors OCD can develop from habits formed by repeated actions. For example, someone might start washing their hands excessively because it temporarily reduces their anxiety about germs. Each handwashing event reinforces the behavior.

Problematic Thinking and Emotions People with OCD often struggle with unhelpful thoughts, like believing that failing to perform a ritual could lead to disaster, and the feeling of fear that accompanies them. These thoughts and feelings lead to intense anxiety, which people with OCD try to manage by repeating specific actions. Perfectionism and intolerance of uncertainty are associated with an increased risk of OCD.

Biological or Genetic Factors Genetics play a role; having family members with OCD increases the likelihood of developing it. Differences in brain structure and function also contribute, particularly in areas that involve controlling behavior and processing emotions. Some research suggests that hormonal changes or immune responses, especially from infections, might trigger OCD symptoms. Imbalances in neurotransmitters such as serotonin, dopamine, and glutamate may also play a role. Medical conditions such as autoimmune disorders or infections affecting the brain may be associated with the onset of OCD symptoms.

This blend of factors helps explain why OCD varies so much from person to person and informs treatments that include therapy to change habits and thoughts, and sometimes medication to help manage biological aspects.

Dissociative Disorders

Dissociative disorders are characterized by dissociations, or feelings of disconnection, from key aspects of mental functioning. These disruptions can affect consciousness, memory, identity, emotions, perception, body representation, motor control, and behavior, often leading to significant distress and impairment in daily life. The following table explains these common areas of dissociation.

Areas of Disconnectedness in Dissociative Disorders	
Consciousness	People may experience disruptions in their awareness, resulting in a foggy or disconnected sense of reality. This might include feeling detached from their surroundings or experiencing periods where time seems to stop or skip.
Memory	Memory loss, or amnesia, is common, particularly for certain time periods, specific events, or personal information. This isn't the typical forgetfulness people might experience; it's more severe and can significantly disrupt one's life.
Identity	Dissociative disorders can involve a fragmented sense of identity. In cases like dissociative identity disorder (DID), formerly known as multiple personality disorder, there might be two or more distinct personality states or identities within a single individual, each with its own way of interacting with the world. See below for more information on DID.
Emotion	Emotional responses can become disconnected or numbed. Individuals may feel an emotional detachment from situations that would typically elicit strong emotions, or they may experience emotions that seem inappropriate or unexplained, given the context.
Perception	Disturbances in perception can occur, such as feeling detached from one's body (depersonalization) or experiencing the world as unreal or dreamlike (derealization). These symptoms can be distressing and may interfere with a person's ability to interact with their environment.

Body Representation	Some people may struggle with body representation issues, feeling as though parts of their body do not belong to them or experiencing distortions in how they perceive their body in space.
Motor Control	In some cases, individuals may lose control over their movements, feeling like they can't move normally or feeling that they are moving in ways they did not initiate.
Behavior	Dissociative disorders can lead to erratic or unusual behavior that a person may not remember performing. This can include anything from mundane tasks performed during a dissociative state to more complex behaviors that seem out of character.

Table 5.4.3

Dissociative disorders are often triggered or made worse by trauma and are thought to be a coping mechanism, helping individuals escape from the reality of traumatic experiences. Treatment typically involves psychotherapy, with the goal of integrating the dissociated parts of memory, identity, and experience into a cohesive whole with the goal of improving functional ability and reducing distress. The two most common dissociative disorders are dissociative amnesia and dissociative identity disorder (DID).

Dissociative Amnesia

Dissociative amnesia is the inability to remember parts of the past as a result of trauma. The loss of these memories is triggered psychologically rather than by physical damage and is often associated with traumatic events, such as rape or child abuse. *Localized amnesia*—the inability to remember events during a specific time, such as the period from age 5 to age 7—is the most common type of memory loss. *Selective amnesia* involves the loss of only certain specific memories. For example, a soldier may remember what he was doing before and after an explosive device blew up near him and killed his fellow soldier and friend, but he cannot remember the actual event. *Generalized amnesia*—the total loss of memory of one's life, including learned skills and acquired knowledge—is rare. People with generalized amnesia are often referred to law enforcement and psychiatric care because they are found to wander aimlessly.

This behavior is also characteristic of a dissociative fugue experience. (*Fugue* is derived from the Latin word for "flee.") **Dissociative amnesia with fugue** is a rare and severe dissociative disorder characterized by sudden, unexpected travel or wandering, during which individuals experience memory loss of their identity, personal history, and past events. This dissociative state typically involves an abrupt departure from one's usual environment, accompanied by confusion about the circumstances of the journey. An individual with dissociative fugue may create a new identity and may be very distressed.

One of the first cases of dissociative amnesia with fugue ever documented was that of Ansel Bourne, a respected and well-known preacher and store owner in Rhode Island. Bourne suddenly disappeared without a trace in 1887. He was later discovered in Norristown, Pennsylvania, more than 200 miles away, living under the name A. J. Brown and working as a day laborer. He

had adopted a completely new persona and had no recollection of his identity, his past life, or how he ended up in Pennsylvania. Eventually, Bourne's true identity was discovered through a series of newspaper articles, and he was reunited with his family. His experience highlights the sudden onset and profound impact of dissociative amnesia with fugue on an individual's identity and behavior.

Generally, a person with this disorder will remember bits and pieces of their identity and past, nearly always returning to their life. Like a musical fugue, which starts with a particular melodic theme and journeys through transformations, a person with dissociative amnesia with fugue will change and ebb but will eventually come back to where they started.

For two months of his life, Ansel Bourne lived as A. J. Brown, with no memory of his previous life. After psychologists, including the renowned William James, helped him recover the memory of his real life, he had no memory of the months he lived as A. J. Brown.

Dissociative Identity Disorder

Dissociative identity disorder (**DID**), formerly called *multiple personality disorder*, is the presence of at least two distinct identities (*alters*) that appear along with impaired memory beyond mere forgetfulness. For example, Clara walks with her husband and three young daughters in the aisles of a grocery store. When they get to the children's cereal section, Clara the wife and mother is no longer there. In her place is a six-year-old child named Bridgette. Her speech is that of a little girl, and she quickly takes off the glasses that Clara had been wearing because the little girl has no vision problems and sees better without the glasses. She whines about the choice of cereal. At dinner time, while the father and three daughters are at the dinner table, a twenty-two-year-old single woman named Hannah sits in the living room rolling her eyes and muttering that she feels like she is in prison and just wants to go out and party. Hannah, Bridgette, and Clara are the same person but are different personalities, different alters. Seven other personalities appear as well. Clara is the core identity, but when any of the other identities take over, they live the life that Clara has disappeared from, at least temporarily. Clara blacks out and has no memory of her actions during this time. Clara has dissociative identity disorder and, like others with the disorder, experienced prolonged physical and/or sexual abuse at an early age, in her case between the ages of 7 and 15. The core personality "separates" as a way of protecting itself from the past traumas, but it comes out in the alters who may hold some of those memories.

In DID, the two or more separate identities, or alters, are completely different—they may be different ages, have different mannerisms, and display unique brain functioning when traced. For example, some individuals diagnosed with DID display different evoked potentials (responses to stimulus) for each alter. Using an electroencephalograph (EEG) to measure the brain wave response to a common stimulus, the evoked potential for each alter is shown as a different pattern on the EEG graph.

Disparity between diagnoses of DID in different regions and cultures around the world is a controversial topic among psychology and psychiatry professionals. Although many psychological disorders are found relatively consistently throughout the world, DID seems to be specific to Western cultures. More than 80 percent of DID cases are concentrated in Western cultures. The inconsistent rate of diagnosis has raised questions about the prevalence and validity of the disorder. While the rate of schizophrenia diagnoses has remained relatively consistent around the world, DID diagnoses peaked in the early 21st century and have decreased since then.

Treatment for DID is complex and focuses mainly on dealing with the specific trauma in a therapeutic setting and reintegrating the various alters into the core personality. Reintegration can be difficult because each alter has developed a specific role or function in coping with stress and events and often holds painful memories from the past. The core personality must not only confront the traumatic memories from his or her past but must also learn to deal with the challenges of everyday life that are different for each alter.

Possible Causes of Dissociative Disorders

The most significant risk factor for dissociative disorders is experiencing severe psychological trauma, such as childhood abuse, neglect, or other forms of overwhelming stress. DID often serves as a coping mechanism to protect a person from the emotional impact of traumatic events. Early disruptions in attachment relationships, such as inconsistent caregiving or neglect, can contribute to the development of dissociative symptoms. These disruptions may impair a person's ability to regulate emotions and form stable, secure relationships. Certain personality traits, such as being impressionable and drawn to fantasy, may increase susceptibility to dissociative experiences. These traits may prompt individuals to dissociate in response to stress or trauma, where some individuals who experience similar trauma may not separate.

Trauma and Stressor-Related Disorders

Imagine being in lower Manhattan on September 11, 2001, and seeing people jumping out of windows a hundred stories above you. Or imagine parents waiting outside a hospital room for word about whether their child who had been hit by a car would live or die. Imagine surviving when all the other members of a platoon died in a bomb explosion or a plane crash. The *DSM-5* includes a chapter focused on trauma- and stressor-related disorders, exploring the cause of psychological symptoms that result from exposure to such overwhelming traumatic events. These events can result in symptoms of hypervigilance (heightened awareness and watchfulness), severe anxiety, flashbacks to traumatic or stressful experiences, insomnia, emotional detachment, and hostility.

Posttraumatic Stress Disorder

Posttraumatic stress disorder (**PTSD**), which was once known as *shell shock*, is characterized by symptoms that begin to develop shortly after people experience or witness a traumatic event. They may include uncontrollable flashback memories and nightmares, dissociative symptoms, sleep disturbances, hypervigilance, and problems processing the traumatic event. Traumatic events are often violent. Common examples include sexual or physical assault, kidnapping, violent crime, military combat, and natural disasters such as earthquakes, hurricanes, or tornadoes. Children who are victims of inappropriate sexual contact or sexual assault with or without violence or who experience a traumatic medical event are also susceptible to PTSD.

Symptoms of PTSD last for more than a month or develop six or more months after the traumatic event. This disorder became a familiar topic in the media after the Vietnam War and again after the war in Iraq, as returning veterans, mostly men, were diagnosed with the disorder in veterans' hospitals around the United States. Yet women are actually reported to be affected by

Roughly 9 to 16 percent of veterans of the wars in Afghanistan and Iraq are estimated to have PTSD.

PTSD at a higher rate than men and across a wide range of traumatic events. The *DSM-5* also distinguishes between diagnoses of PTSD for adults and children. Children suffering from PTSD may experience developmental regression, reverting to a more childlike state, such as the loss of language ability, and their symptoms may manifest in play behavior.

In adults, the common symptoms of PTSD include re-experiencing the traumatic event through flashbacks and nightmares. Such memories are frighteningly intense and include the quality of actually reliving the traumatic experience. Environmental triggers, such as viewing a similar event on television, seeing a person in uniform, or perceiving certain sounds and smells, can cause intense psychological distress.

As a result, sufferers of PTSD may often avoid certain individuals or activities associated with these triggers.

Cognitive distortions and the avoidance mechanism of amnesia may also be symptoms of PTSD. Sufferers may develop negative thoughts, including irrational levels of distrust. They may also blame themselves for the traumatic event. Some individuals with PTSD may become highly aggressive with little or no provocation; they may also startle easily and have trouble concentrating.

Fortunately, the majority of people who experience traumatic events do not develop PTSD. Researchers continue to evaluate individuals who have experienced similar traumatic events, those with PTSD and those without, hoping to discover why some people are affected and some are not and identify those at risk. Understanding the underlying differences may lead to better treatment for people who do develop PTSD. Research suggests that people may be genetically or psychologically predisposed to having more debilitating responses to traumatic events, but no definitive conclusions have yet been reached. Research has shown that the trait of resilience may make people less vulnerable to PTSD after a traumatic experience.

Possible Causes of Trauma and Stressor-Related Disorders

As their label suggests, trauma and stressor-related disorders such as PTSD are primarily caused by exposure to traumatic or stressful events. Certain individual factors, such as genetics, temperament, pre-existing mental health conditions, previous trauma exposure, and coping mechanisms, may increase a person's susceptibility to developing trauma-related disorders. Following a traumatic event, a person may experience a range of psychological reactions, including intense fear, helplessness, horror, or dissociation. These reactions can disrupt normal cognitive and emotional processing and contribute to the development of trauma-related symptoms.

Feeding and Eating Disorders

Feeding and **eating disorders** are characterized by a change in the consumption or absorption of food that is harmful to physical health or psychological functioning. The most commonly diagnosed and treated eating disorders listed in the *DSM-5* are anorexia nervosa and bulimia nervosa.

Anorexia Nervosa

Anorexia nervosa (often referred to as *anorexia*) is a life-threatening eating disorder that involves intense fear of weight gain or becoming overweight, a distorted perception of one's weight or body shape, and persistent restriction of caloric intake, leading to extreme weight loss and increasing damage to physical health. It affects more females than males and occurs more frequently in young adults.

Typical symptoms of anorexia include abrupt and profound weight loss, coupled with exercise and constant weighing, compulsive and covert checking of one's body in mirrors or reflective surfaces, and increased verbalization

Figure 5.4.3 Anorexia Nervosa

of the fear of weight gain or being or becoming fat. Many people diagnosed with anorexia will also exhibit *body dysmorphia*—an increasing cognitive misperception of being overweight despite evidence to the contrary (Figure 5.4.3). These individuals may have a strict daily calorie-counting regimen, develop phobias to certain foods, hoard food, and become preoccupied with images of food and recipes. They may also develop an obsessive interest in preparing food for others but refuse to eat with them, have ritualistic eating behaviors, and exhibit symptoms such as increased social isolation, depression, and anxiety.

Of all the mental disorders, anorexia poses the greatest risk of death. The risk of suicide is significantly higher among those struggling with anorexia than among the general population. The short- and long-term medical consequences of the disorder can also be life-threatening as a result of damage to the cardiovascular system (heart and blood vessels), which may include irregular heart rhythms, congestive heart failure, or acute heart failure. Other medical complications associated with anorexia include renal (kidney) damage, gastrointestinal damage, cessation of the menstrual cycle leading to infertility, osteoporosis (bone damage), tooth damage or loss, and skin complications.

Treatment often involves immediate medical care, including hospitalization, for those who are significantly underweight or experiencing severe complications of anorexia. Inpatient care is often the preferred treatment because it offers a combination of medical supervision, dietary and nutrition education, and group and individual psychotherapy to address the underlying psychological issues that led to the anorexia.

Bulimia Nervosa

Bulimia nervosa (commonly referred to as *bulimia*) is a potentially life-threatening eating disorder that involves secretive binging—eating large or excessive amounts of food that is generally dense in calories in a short period of time. Binging is usually accompanied by a feeling of lack of control, followed by some form of compensatory behavior such as purging—self-induced vomiting, misuse of laxatives or diuretics (medications that increase urination to remove excess fluid from the body), and fasting or excessive exercise to compensate for the high calorie intake. Signs of bulimia include relieving one's bowels with the use of laxatives immediately after eating, callouses or wounds on the knuckles or hands resulting from frequent self-induced vomiting, discolored or damaged teeth, and major fluctuations in weight. Many people with bulimia are at or slightly above an average body weight. Medical issues associated with bulimia are similar to those for anorexia—cardiovascular and gastrointestinal problems, cessation or irregularity of the menstrual cycle, and osteoporosis. Like anorexia, bulimia affects mostly females, though its incidence among males is increasing, and it also occurs more frequently in young adults.

Some people with bulimia struggle with exceptionally low self-esteem, which is responsible in part for their preoccupation with weight and body image. People with bulimia are prone to such cognitive distortions as awfulizing (cognitive perceptions that things are much worse than they really are) and rigid thinking. Binge-purge episodes may be followed by a sense of shame and increased feelings of depression and anxiety.

People with bulimia usually follow a binge-purge episode with dieting, a process described clinically as the "bulimic cycle" (Figure 5.4.4). Treatment focuses on the underlying self-esteem issues and emotion management of bulimia, along with behavioral therapy. Therapy also involves addressing issues that perpetuate the bulimic cycle. Immediate attention is typically given to any medical problems that have developed as a result of the disorder.

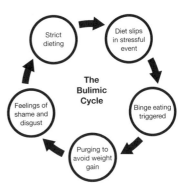

Figure 5.4.4 The Bulimic Cycle

Possible Causes of Feeding and Eating Disorders

Eating disorders are complex mental health conditions influenced by a combination of factors. Feeding and eating disorders can arise from biological, genetic, social, cultural, behavioral, and cognitive sources.

- **Biological causes:** These can include abnormalities in brain structure and function, hormonal imbalances, and neurotransmitter irregularities. For instance, disruptions in the hypothalamus, which regulates hunger and satiety (feeling of fullness), can contribute to disorders like anorexia nervosa and bulimia nervosa. Hormonal factors, such as those involving cortisol and serotonin, also play a role in these conditions.

- **Genetics:** Genetics play a significant role in the development of eating disorders, with family history being a strong predictor. People with relatives who have experienced eating disorders are at higher risk. Genetic factors can predispose individuals to feeding and eating disorders. Specific genes related to mood regulation, appetite, and metabolism may increase the risk of developing these conditions. Twin studies further support the genetic influence, as identical twins are more likely to both develop eating disorders compared to fraternal twins.

- **Social and cultural influences:** An example of these influences is societal pressure to attain unrealistic standards of beauty and thinness, which can contribute to the development of eating disorders. Exposure to media images that promote thinness and dieting behaviors may increase dissatisfaction with one's body and trigger disordered eating patterns. When television was introduced in 1995 to the island country of Fiji, many adolescent girls demonstrated increased levels of body dissatisfaction as they were inundated with images of thin models who looked unlike the typical Fijian women. Cultural norms and practices around food, dieting, and exercise in Fiji before then favored the idea of fuller-bodied women and an abundance of food as a sign of health and prosperity. The sociocultural influence of perceived beauty shifted quickly, resulting in increased rates of eating and feeding disorders on the island. Family dynamics, peer influences, and interpersonal relationships can also trigger eating disorders.

- **Behavioral causes:** These include chronic dieting, restrictive eating, and excessive exercise, any of which can increase the risk of developing eating disorders. These behaviors may start innocently as an attempt to improve health or lose weight, but can escalate into disordered eating patterns over time, especially if they are reinforced through cycles of reward and punishment.

- **Cognitive factors:** These include distorted thinking patterns and beliefs about food, weight, and body image. People with feeding and eating disorders often have a heightened focus on perfectionism, control, and self-criticism. Cognitive distortions, such as viewing things as all good or all bad, can lead to unhealthy attitudes and behaviors related to eating and body image.

Eating disorders frequently occur along with other mental health conditions, such as depression, anxiety disorders, obsessive-compulsive disorder (OCD), and substance abuse. These comorbid conditions can contribute to the complexity of eating disorder symptoms and complicate treatment.

Personality Disorders

People with personality issues that are so problematic, abnormal, and enduring that they lead to distress or impaired interactions with others suffer from personality disorders. **Personality disorders** are enduring patterns of thinking and behavior that can greatly interfere with social and occupational functioning. The diagnosis of personality disorder is somewhat controversial because of the subjectivity in determining symptoms and the wide variety of symptoms that are involved in different types of personality disorders, but five characteristics are associated with personality disorders:

- Enduring patterns of inner experience (thoughts, feelings, and perceptions), as well as behavior that deviates from one's cultural norms
- Pervasive and rigid symptoms
- Onset in adolescence or early adulthood
- Stability of symptoms over time
- Personal distress or impairment of normal functioning

A diagnosis is made only if the symptoms cause significant functional impairment or distress for the individual and are not better explained by other conditions.

Personality disorders are grouped into three clusters, based on common features.

Cluster A: "Odd, Suspicious, and Eccentric"

Cluster A disorders include disorders that show patterns of paranoia, social isolation, cognitive or perceptual distortions, and eccentric behaviors.

Paranoid personality disorder, for example, is just what the name implies. It is a pattern of distrust and suspicion about other people's motives, and usually those motives are believed to intentionally cause harm. It is different from paranoid schizophrenia because it does not present any of the psychotic features characteristic of that disease or loss of touch with reality. This unfounded and constant suspicion of others often causes difficulties in relationships with others, which often fall apart amidst false claims of acts of wrongdoing.

Schizoid personality disorder is characterized by a pattern of detachment from social relationships and a limited range of emotional expression in interpersonal settings. People with this disorder often prefer solitary activities and have difficulty forming close relationships. They may seem indifferent to praise or criticism and typically exhibit a restricted range of emotions, appearing emotionally cold or detached. Despite their lack of social interest, they may still experience loneliness and often engage in solitary pursuits or hobbies.

Schizotypal personality disorder (STPD) is characterized by eccentric behavior, unusual beliefs, and difficulties with social interactions. People with this disorder may exhibit eccentric or peculiar behavior, including unusual mannerisms and dressing inappropriately. They may have unusual beliefs or magical thinking, such as believing in telepathy or superstitions. And they may experience perceptual distortions, such as sensing an unseen presence or hearing whispers that aren't there. They often have odd thinking patterns, such as having paranoid ideas or suspicion. People with STPD often feel anxious or uncomfortable in social situations and may have few close relationships. They may have difficulty with social functioning and may appear eccentric or odd to others, but typically do not experience full-blown psychotic symptoms.

Cluster A Disorders	
Paranoid Personality Disorder	• Distrust and suspicion of others' harmful intentions • Lack psychotic features • Make interpersonal relationships difficult
Schizoid Personality Disorder	• Detachment from social relationships • Limited range of emotional expression • Often prefer solitary pursuits
Schizotypal Personality Disorder	• Eccentric behavior and dress • Magical thinking • Perceptual distortions (sensing things that are not there)

Table 5.4.4

Cluster B: "Dramatic, Emotional, Erratic"

Cluster B disorders, as their descriptive name implies, are disorders that cause significant disruption, and even harm, to self and others.

Antisocial personality disorder (APD) is most frequently associated with criminal behavior. A person with APD often is unable to feel empathy or guilt, and that inability leads to a pattern of disregard for the rights and well-being of others, along with rampant manipulative behavior. People with APD constantly lie and engage in behaviors that are deceitful, manipulative, and harmful to others, without experiencing remorse or guilt. Although people with APD may not ever commit a crime, about 50 percent of serious crimes are committed by people with APD. People with APD are predominantly male, and with their ability to put a façade on their lack of empathy and even appear charming, people with antisocial personality disorder may use their ruthlessness to land themselves in powerful positions in business or other careers. Individuals with APD tend to like risky behaviors and have little regard for obeying social norms of behavior.

Research suggests that APD has a significant biological basis. People with APD have a weaker autonomic response to fear and show less recognition of emotion in facial expressions. Twin studies have confirmed a genetic basis for a tendency to APD, and when that is combined with environmental stressors, the disorder is more likely to develop. A study of APD in prisoners has also demonstrated that some individuals with APD do not respond in their brain to physical punishment like others. Therefore, punishment may not serve as a deterrent for engaging in illegal or evil and immoral acts.

Histrionic personality disorder (HPD) is characterized by a pattern of excessive attention-seeking behavior, dramatic emotional expression, and a need to be the center of attention. People with this disorder often display theatrical or flamboyant behaviors, seeking validation and admiration from others. They may have shallow or rapidly shifting emotions. They often experience dramatic mood swings, going from being ecstatic and euphoric to crying uncontrollably over a minor inconvenience. They may exhibit exaggerated emotional responses to everyday events, or they may use their emotions to draw attention to themselves. Their relationships may be characterized by intense but fleeting connections. People with histrionic personality disorder may use their physical appearance or sexuality to draw attention to themselves and may have difficulty forming deep, meaningful relationships due to their tendency to prioritize attention and excitement, even at their own personal risk.

Some studies have found that about 21 percent of top business executives likely have antisocial personality disorder.

Narcissistic personality disorder is characterized by a pervasive pattern of grandiosity, a constant need for admiration, and a lack of empathy for others. People with this disorder often have an inflated sense of self-importance, exaggerate their achievements, and seek constant attention and validation. They may struggle with maintaining healthy relationships because of their manipulative or exploitative behavior, and they may have difficulty accepting criticism or acknowledging the feelings and needs of others. Despite their outward confidence, they often have deep-seated feelings of insecurity and may be highly sensitive to perceived slights or rejection. People with this disorder may not see their behavior as problematic.

Borderline personality disorder is characterized by unstable emotions, self-image, and relationships. People with this disorder may experience intense mood swings, have difficulty regulating emotions, and engage in impulsive behaviors such as self-harm or substance abuse. They may also have a fear of abandonment and struggle with unstable relationships, often alternating between idealizing and devaluing others. People with borderline personality disorder may also have a poor sense of self and may experience feelings of emptiness or identity disturbance.

Cluster B Disorders	
Antisocial Personality Disorder	• Manipulative and deceitful • Unable to feel remorse or guilt • Associated with crime and positions of power
Histrionic Personality Disorder	• Attention-seeking, often flamboyant, behavior • Dramatic mood swings • Shallow relationships
Narcissistic Personality Disorder	• Sense of grandiosity and need for admiration • Exaggerate accomplishments and seek validation • Highly sensitive to perceived criticism
Borderline Personality Disorder	• Unstable emotions • Impulsive behaviors, including substance abuse and self-harm • Fear of abandonment and poor sense of self

Table 5.4.5

Cluster C: "Anxious and Fearful"

Cluster C disorders include avoidant, dependent, and obsessive-compulsive personality disorders. In contrast to some of the self-aggrandizing symptoms in Cluster B disorders, symptoms of Cluster C disorders include inadequacy, submission, clinginess, hypersensitivity, and orderliness.

Avoidant personality disorder is characterized by feelings of inadequacy, extreme sensitivity to negative evaluation or rejection, and avoidance of social situations due to fear of embarrassment or criticism. People with this disorder often wish for social connection, but may avoid it because of fear of being judged or rejected. They may struggle with forming close relationships and may appear shy, timid, or socially withdrawn. People with avoidant personality disorder may also have low self-esteem and may be overly sensitive to perceived criticism or disapproval from others. Treatment typically involves therapy to help build confidence, improve social skills, and challenge negative thought patterns.

Dependent personality disorder is characterized by a pervasive and excessive need to be taken care of, leading to submissive and clinging behavior, fear of separation, and difficulty making decisions without reassurance from others. People with this disorder often rely heavily on others for emotional support, guidance, and decision-making, to the extent that it interferes with their ability to function independently. They may have difficulty expressing their own opinions or asserting their needs and may fear rejection if they do not comply with others' wishes. Treatment typically involves therapy to promote independence, build self-esteem, and develop healthier coping mechanisms.

Obsessive-compulsive personality disorder (OCPD) involves a disruptive preoccupation with orderliness, perfectionism, and personal and interpersonal control. People with this disorder may have an excessive devotion to work and productivity, at the expense of leisure activities and relationships. They may be overly conscientious, rigid, and detail-oriented, and they may set unreasonably high standards for themselves and others. People with obsessive-compulsive personality disorder may struggle with flexibility and may have difficulty delegating tasks because of their insistence on doing things their own way.

Obsessive-compulsive personality disorder should not be confused with obsessive-compulsive disorder (OCD), with its obsessive urge and a compulsive behavior to relieve the anxiety the urge produces. The main difference between the two is that OCD may be short-term and treatable, whereas OPCD is a lifelong disorder that disrupts thoughts, behavior, and mood. Individuals with OPCD generally don't recognize their behavior as problematic, whereas those with OCD are typically aware that their obsessions and compulsions are irrational and disruptive.

Cluster C Disorders	
Avoidant Personality Disorder	• Feelings of inadequacy • Avoidance of social situations for fear of being judged • Low self-esteem
Dependent Personality Disorder	• Excessive need to be taken care of, clingy • Difficulty functioning independently • Fear of rejection
Obsessive-Compulsive Personality Disorder	• Preoccupation with orderliness, perfectionism, and control • Overly devoted to work • Unable to delegate

Table 5.4.6

Possible Causes of Personality Disorders

Personality disorders are believed to develop from biological, genetic, social, cultural, behavioral, or cognitive sources. *Biological sources* are similar to those of other personality disorders: abnormalities in brain regions such as the prefrontal cortex and amygdala, which are involved in regulating emotions, decision-making, and social behavior; imbalances of neurotransmitters like serotonin, dopamine, and norepinephrine; and hormonal imbalances, especially those involving the stress hormone cortisol.

A *genetic component* is also likely in the development of some personality disorders, with certain personality traits and vulnerabilities being heritable. *Social factors,* such as adverse childhood experiences, bullying or social rejection during formative years, and dysfunctional families also play a role. Family can also contribute to *behavioral factors* such as maladaptive behaviors learned from and reinforced by family members. Such *cultural factors* as cultural norms, societal expectations, and media influences may shape the development of personality disorders. *Cognitive sources* of personality disorders include negative thinking, distorted self-image and self-esteem, and misinterpreting social cues. Whatever their source, the factors that lead to personality disorders result in difficulty in maintaining healthy relationships.

THINK AS A PSYCHOLOGIST

Apply Psychological Perspectives, Theories, Concepts, and Research Findings to a Scenario (1.A.3) | Evaluate Whether a Psychological Research Scenario Followed Appropriate Ethical Procedures (2.D.4)

James, a 25-year-old man, often felt like he was on an emotional roller coaster. His relationships were intense but short-lived, swinging from adoration to resentment within days. In his latest relationship, he lavished his girlfriend with flowers and jewelry, but days later felt like he could no longer stand to look at her. One moment, he would feel euphoric and confident; the next, he would plunge into despair, feeling empty and abandoned. His fear of being alone was so overwhelming that he would sometimes make impulsive decisions, like quitting jobs or ending friendships abruptly, just to avoid rejection. When stressed, he sometimes resorted to self-harm, cutting his arm as he had done since he was a teenager as a way to cope with his overwhelming emotions. Despite his outward charm and intelligence, James struggled with a chronic sense of instability in his identity and mood and sometimes thought of suicide as a way out of his pain.

Practice Applying Concepts to a Scenario and Evaluating Ethical Procedures

Choose the correct answer and complete the following activity.

1. James was evaluated by a team of psychiatrists who agreed upon a diagnosis and treatment plan. Based on the symptoms presented, which personality disorder was he likely diagnosed with?

   (A) Borderline

   (B) Schizotypal

   (C) Histrionic

   (D) Narcissistic

2. Identify an ethical guideline that psychiatrists must abide by when reporting a case study such as James's.

REFLECT ON THE ESSENTIAL QUESTION

Essential Question: *What are the symptoms and possible causes of psychological disorders?* Using the Key Terms, complete a chart like the one below to gather details to help answer that question.

Disorder	Symptoms

KEY TERMS

acrophobia
agoraphobia
anorexia nervosa
antisocial personality
  disorder (APD)
arachnophobia
ataque de nervios (ADN)
attention deficit/
  hyperactivity disorder
  (ADHD)
autism spectrum disorder
  (ASD)
avoidant personality
  disorder
bipolar I
bipolar II
bipolor disorder
borderline personality
  disorder
bulimia nervosa
catatonia
catatonic stupor
compulsion
delusion
dependent personality
  disorder
depressive disorder

developmental period
dissociative amnesia
dissociative amnesia with
  fugue
dissociative disorder
dissociative identity
  disorder (DID)
dopamine hypothesis
eating disorder
flat affect
generalized anxiety
  disorder (GAD)
hallucination
histrionic personality
  disorder
hoarding disorder
hypomania
learned association
major depressive disorder
mania
narcissistic personality
  disorder
negative symptom
neurodevelopmental
  disorder
obsession

obsessive-compulsive
  disorder (OCD)
obsessive-compulsive
  personality disorder
panic attack
panic disorder
paranoid personality
  disorder
persistent depressive
  disorder
personality disorders
phobia
posttraumatic stress
  disorder (PTSD)
psychosis
psychotic disorder
schizoid personality
  disorder
schizophrenia
schizophrenic spectrum
  disorder
schizotypal personality
  disorder
social anxiety disorder
specific phobia disorder
taijin kyofusho (TKS)
word salad

MULTIPLE-CHOICE QUESTIONS

1. Shana is a 32-year-old woman whose daily interactions are marked
   by constant drama. Her insatiable need for attention and constant
   reassurance, coupled with her exaggerated emotions and sexually
   provocative behavior, often leave those around her feeling overwhelmed
   and uncomfortable. These behaviors are consistent with a diagnosis of
   which of the following psychological problems?

   (A) Dissociative amnesia with fugue

   (B) Schizotypal personality disorder

   (C) Bipolar disorder

   (D) Histrionic personality disorder

2. In his early 20s, Alejandro started to hear voices that narrated his every action, and he began experiencing extreme paranoia, believing that anyone he encountered was plotting to harm him. Alejandro's problems are most consistent with which of the following disorders?

(A) Borderline personality

(B) Obsessive-compulsive

(C) Panic

(D) Schizophrenia

3. Lance is a 25-year-old male whose behavior is characterized by a reckless disregard for others, in which he shows no remorse or empathy when he has caused harm. His daily social interactions are marked by a constant need to manipulate and deceive the people he encounters. Lance's behaviors are most consistent with which of the following?

(A) Attention deficit/hyperactivity disorder

(B) Antisocial personality disorder

(C) Histrionic personality disorder

(D) Bipolar disorder

4. Taijin kyofusho is a culture-bound disorder that is experienced primarily by people in Japan. This disorder, in terms of symptoms, is most closely aligned with which of the following *DSM-5* disorders?

(A) Bipolar II disorder

(B) Borderline personality disorder

(C) Social anxiety disorder

(D) Obsessive-compulsive disorder

5. The dopamine hypothesis, prenatal virus exposure, and genetic predispositions are all thought to play a role in the development of which psychological problem?

(A) Schizophrenia

(B) Autism

(C) Generalized anxiety

(D) Agoraphobia

6. Alex is a 10-year-old who greatly struggles with social interactions. It is challenging for him to maintain eye contact and comprehend social cues. He likes to rigidly adhere to routines and is distressed when unexpected changes occur. Alex's behaviors demonstrate characteristics of which of the following psychological problems?

(A) Antisocial personality disorder

(B) Panic disorder

(C) Autism spectrum disorder

(D) Bipolar I disorder

Thoughts	Behaviors
Fear of contamination	Washing, cleaning
Need for symmetry	Ordering, balancing, straightening until "just right"
Doubts (e.g., door locked, stove off)	Repeated checking behaviors

7. The table above represents common symptoms associated with which of the following psychological problems?

(A) Dissociative amnesia with fugue

(B) Obsessive-compulsive disorder

(C) Hoarding disorder

(D) Paranoid personality disorder

Topic 5.5

Treatment of Psychological Disorders

"When we are no longer able to change a situation, we are challenged to change ourselves."

— Viktor Frankl

Essential Question: How are psychological disorders treated?

Psychotherapy is a general term for the treatment of mental health problems through interaction between trained psychologists and those seeking help. As you will see, one approach to psychotherapy may be better for treating depression, while another approach may be more effective for treating anxiety issues such as social phobia. Many mental health professionals use an eclectic approach, taking ideas from a variety of approaches to best serve the client. These approaches include both psychological and biomedical models, because psychological problems may stem from neurological abnormalities or from learning, childhood trauma, destructive habits of thinking, or sociocultural factors. This section explores many of those approaches, examining similarities and differences among them, as well as their effectiveness in addressing psychological problems.

Effectiveness of Psychological Therapies

Does psychotherapy work, and which approaches are more effective than others? The earliest attempt to determine the effectiveness of psychotherapies came in the 1950s when Hans Eysenck published research concluding that existing psychotherapies, especially psychoanalysis, were not any more effective than no treatment at all. Though controversial, Eysenck's work began a vital conversation about the effectiveness of psychotherapy that continues to this day. The field of psychology is stronger when it willingly subjects itself to the rigor of sound empirical research.

In the more than 70 years since Eysenck's eye-opening publication, thousands of studies have been conducted to answer the fundamental question: Does psychotherapy work? The current answer, based on empirical research, is a qualified yes. What has been determined through **meta-analysis**, in which multiple studies are statistically analyzed to determine a common result, is that most psychotherapeutic approaches seem to show effectiveness and they all share what are called *common factors*:

- **Therapeutic alliance:** This is a relationship between client and therapist that is caring, genuine, understanding, and empathetic. This approach was derived from the work of Carl Rogers, the founder of the humanistic perspective to psychology. This bond must be established first. To achieve this bond, the therapist must demonstrate **cultural humility** by acknowledging their own cultural biases and approaching each client with an open mind and respect for cultural differences.
- **Positive expectations:** The client begins to believe that the therapeutic process will result in positive outcomes. The client and therapist agree on goals and the tasks needed to achieve them.
- **Specific action plan:** The therapist prescribes a plan of action, and the client uses it and begins to form a sense of self-efficacy based on the new behaviors.

If a therapeutic approach includes the three factors above, the meta-analysis shows that it will be more effective in helping a person than no therapy at all. However, the meta-analysis shows some therapeutic approaches to be slightly more effective than others for specific psychological disorders. Behavioral therapy appears to be more effective for ADHD behavior problems, bed-wetting, marital dysfunctions, and phobias. Cognitive-behavioral therapy appears to be effective for anxiety disorders such as generalized anxiety disorder, phobias, panic disorders, PTSD, and depression. Psychodynamic interpersonal therapy is also effective for depression. Many anxiety and depressive disorders have the best long-term results when treated with a combination of psychotherapy and psychoactive medications.

To examine the empirical research yourself, you can visit two excellent sources: the American Psychological Association's (APA) *PsycInfo* site and the National Center for Biotechnology Information's (NCBI) PubMed site. Be wary of approaches that do not have empirical research to back them up. If you want to find out if equine therapy, adventure therapy, or rebirthing therapies are truly effective, find the empirical research that proves it.

Deinstitutionalization and Decentralization of Mental Health Care

By the mid-1950s, long-term institutionalization of people with mental illness peaked. When it became clear that long-term psychiatric hospitalization was doing more harm than good, a major shift called **deinstitutionalization** began, in which treatment shifted from inpatient psychiatric hospitalization to outpatient community mental health programs. Deinstitutionalization was propelled by forces that included the development of psychoactive medications, the introduction of federally funded welfare programs, and recognition that the poor care and mistreatment of the people with mental illness in psychiatric institutions was a denial of basic civil rights.

Today, mental health care is primarily community-based and outpatient, as opposed to inpatient hospitalization. Long-term psychiatric hospitalization is now more infrequent than it was a half-century ago. The 1963 Community Mental Health Act marked a national shift toward establishing community mental health centers across the nation. A number of programs and approaches to community mental health care developed, including the case-management model, community teams, support groups, assertive community treatment, outpatient commitment laws/programs, and community support programs.

Community-Based Treatment

Since the 1960s, care for people with mental illness has been greatly influenced by the community mental health movement. With the 1963 Community Mental Health Act and the introduction of psychoactive medications to reduce the symptoms of severe psychological disorders, the custodial care model (or warehousing) of people with mental illness was replaced by a model that brought people with severe mental illness back to their communities where they could be treated locally, at a lower cost, and on an outpatient basis.

Since the 1990s, community-based mental health care has been driven by two movements—evidence-based intervention and the recovery model. **Evidence-based intervention** uses research-based and outcomes-oriented data and other information to determine what works best. The recovery model is seen as an alternative to the long-term care model that emphasizes stabilization. The recovery model constitutes a new paradigm that stresses healing, social support, empowerment, and hope. From these two movements, improved mental health care has focused on a number of programs and treatment models to enhance care for people with mental illness at the community level.

Community support programs comprise a system of treatment of the severely mentally ill using a case manager who coordinates the services and treatments that each client needs to achieve or maintain healthy functioning in their community. Those who provide mental health services in these programs understand that severe mental illness often requires multidimensional care that includes services that go beyond the clinical setting (Figure 5.5.1).

Components of Community Support

Figure 5.5.1 Components of Community Support

By the 1980s, problems appeared that challenged the effectiveness of community support programs. Decreased state and federal housing subsidies, substance abuse and addiction, unemployment, poverty, and crime led to the need for a more intensive and comprehensive approach.

Assertive Community Treatment One such intensive approach is assertive community treatment. It was developed to address the weaknesses of community support programs and is a much more comprehensive and intensive approach to providing mental health services to those with severe mental illness, as well as such additional problems as substance abuse and lack of family support. Assertive community treatment teams provide specialized support, treatment, and whatever else is needed to enable the person to achieve and maintain community integration and to prevent homelessness or rehospitalization.

Assisted Outpatient Treatment A civil court order requiring community-based mental health services is known as assisted outpatient treatment (AOT). Such a court-ordered treatment plan usually includes psychiatric medication and/or attending treatment sessions but may also require abstinence from other drugs as well as the avoidance of certain places or people that may serve as triggers for negative experiences or behaviors. When used by community courts, AOT enables the community to ensure that treatment is provided when a lack of intervention could endanger the individual or the community.

Assessing Community Mental Health

Community-based treatment has shown mixed results. On one hand, meta-analyses of studies looking at the effectiveness of deinstitutionalization and community mental health programs show that evidence-based programs provide effective treatment. However, although treatment using the community mental health model is also much more cost-effective, the availability for that treatment has not kept up with demand. While emptying the huge psychiatric institutions is considered a success, many people suffering from severe mental illness, without the support necessary to cope beyond the gates of those institutions, have become homeless or incarcerated. The current estimate is that between 20 and 25 percent of homeless people suffer severe mental illness. Some people have argued that, in too many cases, life in psychiatric institutions was replaced by life on the streets or in a jail cell.

Severe mental illness often includes *comorbidity*, the diagnosis of two or more psychological disorders at once. Substance abuse is often the comorbid disorder among people with severe mental illness, since this is often perceived as a way of coping with the problem when, in fact, it often serves to exacerbate the illness. This factor has contributed to the dramatic increase in incarceration. As the rate of long-term psychiatric hospitalization decreased, by the late 1970s, the rate of criminal incarceration began to climb (Figure 5.5.2). Community mental health works, but only for those who have access to it. Most agree that more needs to be done to increase access to community mental health so that those suffering severe mental illness don't find themselves trapped in homelessness or incarceration.

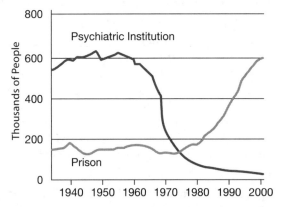

Figure 5.5.2 Effects of Deinstitutionalization

Ethical Principles in the Treatment of Psychological Disorders

The American Psychological Association (APA) published *Ethical Principles of Psychologists and Code of Conduct*, which enumerates the ways its members are to uphold high ethical principles. The general principles are intended "to guide and inspire psychologists toward the very highest ethical ideals of the profession." These general principles are summarized below:

- **Principle A: Beneficence and Nonmaleficence**
  Beneficence means "doing good," and **nonmaleficence** is the duty to do no harm. Psychologists strive to benefit those with whom they work and take care to do no harm. They aim to promote the welfare of their clients and to minimize harm through their professional activities. Psychology, as a discipline, is a helping science, and this ethical principle is a constant reminder of this overarching goal in the field.

- **Principle B: Fidelity and Responsibility**
  Psychologists establish and maintain trustworthy relationships with clients, colleagues, and the public. They fulfill their professional responsibilities with integrity, honesty, and reliability.

- **Principle C: Integrity**
  Psychologists strive to be honest, accurate, and truthful in all aspects of their professional work. They avoid engaging in deceptive practices and ensure the accuracy of their scientific and professional activities.

- **Principle D: Justice**
  Psychologists promote fairness and equality in their professional activities, including the distribution of resources, the treatment of clients, and the selection of research participants. They strive to be aware of and address biases and discrimination in their work.

- **Principle E: Respect for People's Rights and Dignity**
  Psychologists respect the rights, dignity, and worth of all individuals, regardless of factors such as race, ethnicity, gender, sexual orientation, age, disability, religion, or socioeconomic status. They strive to be aware of and address cultural and individual differences in their professional practice.

In addition, psychologists are expected to maintain high standards of competence in their professional work and strive to stay informed about new developments in their field. They should only provide services and use techniques for which they are adequately trained and experienced. Psychologists must obtain informed consent from clients before beginning any professional relationship or providing any services. They ensure that clients understand the nature, purpose, risks, and benefits of the services being offered and obtain their voluntary consent to participate. And finally, psychologists maintain confidentiality in their professional relationships and take steps to protect the privacy of their clients. They only disclose confidential information with appropriate consent or when mandated by law or ethical standards because the client or another may be in danger.

Techniques in Psychological Therapies

Therapy for mental illness can be divided into two general categories: the biomedical approach, with its primary focus on biological causes and medical treatment, and the psychological approach. The psychological approach (psychotherapy) is separated into four categories that are often selected because of the origin or cause of a mental illness: psychodynamic, cognitive, behavioral, and humanistic.

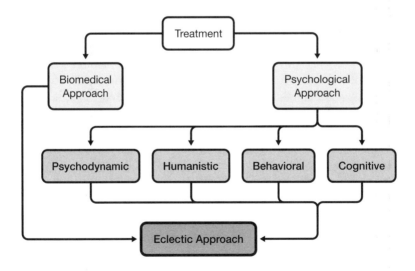

Figure 5.5.3

Psychodynamic Therapies

Psychodynamic and humanistic therapies are often referred to as *insight therapies* because the central goal is to help the patients or clients gain insight into the underlying causes of their mental distress or illness and use that insight and improved self-awareness to resolve psychological problems. **Psychodynamic therapies** aim to help patients gain insight into these underlying causes by tapping into the unconscious.

Psychoanalysis The original psychodynamic approach, known as *psychoanalysis*, was developed by Sigmund Freud in the 1890s. Its central goal was to create a trusting environment so that a patient would more easily reveal repressed unconscious conflicts causing emotional turmoil. Freud's psychoanalytic approach was based on the theoretical assumption that neurosis, mental problems in one's conscious life, stems from long-repressed childhood memories, trauma, feelings, or primitive biological urges involving the id and held in the unconscious.

In traditional psychoanalysis, often requiring two or three sessions a week for up to seven years, the patient reclines on a couch while the psychoanalyst sits out of direct view, listening carefully to what the patient says and taking notes. It is an unequal partnership with the psychoanalyst in a superior "expert" role.

The two main techniques Freud developed to help reveal the inner conflicts of the patient's unconscious were free association and dream analysis or interpretation. During free association, the patient is encouraged to say whatever comes to mind without blocking or filtering any content, even if it is seemingly unrelated to the issues they are currently facing. As the patient's trust in the psychoanalyst increases, the patient's ego will lower its guard, so that the true nature of the unconscious will begin bubbling up to the surface for the psychoanalyst to interpret. Freud believed that the unconscious would reveal itself in slips of the tongue (Freudian slips) or dreams, which Freud believed were a method of wish-fulfillment.

Dream interpretation was another significant aspect of psychoanalysis and, for the few that still practice strict Freudian psychoanalysis, it still is. Freudian analysis, or interpretation of dreams, is based on the theory that what is consciously remembered in a dream (manifest content) are the symbolic representations of the unconscious forces, urges, or conflicts (latent content). According to Freud, the number of things represented by symbols in dreams is not great, but they typically include the human body, parents, children, siblings, birth, and death. For example, houses may represent people. A house with flat walls represents a man, while a house with something projecting from it, like a balcony, represents a woman. Birth is usually represented by a reference to water, and death by taking a journey. The job of the patient is to report the manifest content, and the job of the psychoanalyst is to analyze this content to determine its latent meaning and provide insight for the patient into the unconscious roots of problems.

Freud's psychoanalysis has resulted in a number of terms and techniques that continue to be recognized as integral aspects of many other forms of psychotherapy. Freud realized that therapeutic rapport (a trusting relationship with the therapist) was essential in overcoming resistance, the unwillingness of the patient to reveal anxiety-provoking conflicts hidden in the unconscious. Freud also coined the term *transference* to describe the natural consequence of the therapeutic relationship when the patient transfers their emotional issues with people in their life unconsciously onto the therapist and develops strong positive or negative feelings for the therapist. A typical example of transference occurs when the patient begins to emotionally relate to the therapist as a parent figure or love interest. The job of the therapist is to detect when transference is happening and in an emotionally neutral manner communicate to the patient that it is taking place, then help the patient understand what it reveals. Freud can also be credited for introducing to the therapeutic process the concept of *catharsis*, which refers to the often aggressive emotional release a person can experience in therapy. Freud believed that the release of aggressive energy would help the person get rid of these aggressive feelings, but this has not held up in modern research on catharsis.

Psychodynamic Therapies Traditional Freudian psychoanalysis is not often used now, for a number of reasons. Psychodynamic therapies have largely replaced psychoanalytic methods from Freud's original approach. Modern-day psychodynamic therapies place much less emphasis on the id or superego and even less reliance on the central idea of sex or animalistic aggression as an underlying unconscious impulse. Instead, a psychodynamic therapist, though still believing strongly in the unconscious influences of the mind and the importance of childhood events, will conduct therapy face-to-face, focusing more on current relationships. Psychodynamic therapy usually only requires once-per-week sessions with a total duration measured in months, not years.

One type of psychodynamic therapy is interpersonal psychotherapy (or IPT). As the name suggests, the focus is on helping the client improve existing relationships rather than delving into deep-seated trauma from early childhood. The primary mental health issue that IPT addresses is depression.

Another type of psychodynamic therapy, object relations therapy, is based on the social psychoanalytic perspective that social relationships in early childhood lie at the heart of mental problems in adulthood. The object refers to the significant person in the client's life and the emotional problems stemming from that relationship. Therapists who use this approach will develop a very intense and nurturing relationship with the client with the aim to help heal the damage from earlier relationships that lacked the necessary nurturing.

Assessing Psychoanalysis and Psychodynamic Therapies Freudian psychoanalysis is not used much today because for many disorders it does not work as well as other approaches. For example, this approach has not demonstrated significant improvement for those experiencing symptoms of schizophrenia. It also lacks empirical research supporting its efficacy, so justifying many years of expensive psychoanalytic treatment is hard to do. Also, psychoanalysts' interpretations of patients' free associations or dreams are significantly subjective.

Additionally, traditional psychoanalysis runs the risk of fostering patient dependency because it takes so long and the therapist holds a very authoritative position. Modern psychotherapy emphasizes helping the client develop autonomous coping skills, an emphasis that runs counter to traditional psychoanalysis.

Psychodynamic therapies have moved away from the more controversial aspects of Freud's original theories and therapeutic approach. Interpersonal psychotherapy (IPT) has been shown to help alleviate depression and anxiety, but cognitive-behavioral therapy (CBT) is slightly more effective. Also, IPT's effectiveness is only slightly better than no therapy at all, but when combined with pharmacotherapy (antidepressive or antianxiety medicine) IPT shows more effectiveness.

Humanistic Therapies

Another branch of insight therapy is the humanistic approach. As you read in Topic 5.3, the humanistic perspective sees humans as fundamentally good. The central goal of humanistic therapy is to help people accept themselves through self-awareness and self-fulfillment. Although both psychodynamic and humanistic approaches are considered insight therapies, **humanistic therapy** focuses on the present and future rather than the past, and on conscious experiences rather than unconscious thoughts. The humanistic school of psychology has developed several influential approaches, including person-centered or Rogerian therapy.

Person-Centered or Rogerian Therapy A widely used form of humanistic psychotherapy developed by Carl Rogers was an outgrowth of his unwavering belief that all humans possess a fundamental drive to fulfill their unique and positive potential (a self-actualizing tendency). Rogers believed a person's psychologically troubled life was caused by the divergence of the real self from the ideal self (incongruence). If a child's upbringing is consumed by conditions of worth, the child will lose the sense of their real self and become emotionally troubled in the ideal self as an adult. The end result is a person who suffers emotionally from the loss of self, and this suffering can take many forms.

In **person-centered therapy** (also called *client-centered* or *Rogerian therapy*), the therapist honors the inherent human potential of the client by acting as a nonjudgmental facilitator of the therapeutic process. The therapist does not give advice or interpret the meanings of the client's thoughts or behaviors but acts as a sounding board in the hopes of leading the client to gain insight into their own challenges.

Four principles are central to the Rogerian person-centered approach: unconditional positive regard, empathy, genuineness, and active listening.

- **Unconditional positive regard** is nonjudgmental acceptance of the client, intended to reinforce for clients that they have value (without conditions) for who they really are. Directly emanating from unconditional positive regard is the practice of allowing the client, rather than the therapist, to steer the direction of the therapy. For this reason, this form of therapy is sometimes called *nondirective*.

- A Rogerian therapist must show the deepest level of understanding by trying to see things through the client's eyes. This should increase *empathy*, the ability to truly see, feel, and understand what the client is experiencing.

- *Genuineness* refers to the therapist's willingness to foster an honest and open relationship with the person. Rogers believed it is essential to model an authentic and genuine relationship so that the person will be more comfortable striving for congruence, or an overlap between their real self and their ideal self, in other relationships.

- **Active listening** by the therapist reinforces the principles of unconditional positive regard, empathy, and congruence through intensely and empathically listening to the client and paraphrasing what the client says, focusing on the specific emotions and feelings expressed. Active listening prevents the therapist from offering advice or judgments, which can unintentionally hinder clients from gaining their own insights. Active listening enables the therapist to create a sort of nonjudgmental mirror in which the client sees what he or she is saying and feeling and then gains insight, self-acceptance, and ultimately an empowering sense of self-awareness and the ability to change and grow.

Client: I just got so sick of his constant criticism, especially when he told me to "man up." It was like no matter how well I did in school or my career choices I was never good enough.

Therapist: M-hm. He kept putting you down. Even when you excelled.

Client: Yeah and that's why I gave up on sharing my success with him. But I still love him, I mean - he's my dad. How can I not? But I also feel like I hate him too, which makes me feel so guilty. (begins to cry)

Therapist: Your father's criticism hurt you terribly, and yet you never gave up on trying to share your success with him. You feel conflicted by your strong feelings, even now. I can see how painful this for you.

Client: Yes, and I know I'm an adult now so it shouldn't matter. But some how I kept expecting him to be different.

Therapist: Ho matter how old you are, he's still your father. And now that he's sick, you feel guilty that you haven't reached out to him.

Client: Yeah, the guilt killing me, but I still can't seem to make myself reach out. I just know I'll be rejected again.

Therapist: Maybe you will be. But what hurts more—right now? The guilt or the fear of being rejected?

Client: The guilt. Definitely... I think I should give him a call. Maybe just ask how's he doing and let him know I'm here for him.

Figure 5.5.4 Example of Active Listening

Assessing Humanistic Therapy The most significant challenge, when assessing the effectiveness of humanistic therapies, is the lack of empirical research. Most research is qualitative and derived from either client or therapist feedback, which tends to be positive, but inherently subjective and, therefore, biased. The positive attributes shared by all effective therapeutic approaches are those factors that are strongly linked to the outcomes of any form of psychotherapy. The common factors of **therapeutic alliance**, positive expectations, and a specific action plan are central to all humanistic therapies and, therefore, it is very difficult to isolate the unique techniques of a particular humanistic therapy in order to measure effectiveness, although it is clear that a large number of people benefit from this type of therapy. Many humanistic techniques, such as the importance of a trusting and nonjudgmental relationship between client and therapist, also have been incorporated into other therapeutic approaches.

Applied Behavioral Therapies

Insight therapies assume that with improved self-awareness comes a resolution of psychological problems. In contrast, action therapies focus on providing practical solutions, teaching coping skills, and modifying thoughts and actions to help resolve psychological problems. Behavioral therapy and cognitive therapy are the most widely used action therapies.

Behavioral psychology—or behaviorism—is based on the theory that all human behavior, healthy or unhealthy, is learned. So **applied behavioral therapy** uses classical conditioning or operant conditioning to help clients unlearn maladaptive behaviors and replace them with more adaptive or healthy behaviors. Behavioral therapists are not concerned with unconscious or repressed memories and do not believe that they hold the key to improving mental health. They see the problematic behaviors not as a symptom of underlying psychological issues but as the problems themselves. Behavioral therapy offers a number of methods of solving behavior problems, including exposure therapies, aversion therapy, operant conditioning, and modeling.

Exposure Therapies Classical conditioning is a learning theory that explains how involuntary (automatic) responses such as feelings of fear or disgust become associated (connected) with new stimuli. That person you know who is deeply afraid of heights got that way because at some point the neutral stimulus (being in a high place) became associated with a natural or unconditioned stimulus (falling from a height), which caused a great deal of fear. Behavior therapies that use classical conditioning to reduce anxiety are called **exposure therapies**. Mary Cover Jones, often called "the mother of behavioral therapy," developed the earliest form of exposure therapy in 1924 when she demonstrated the principles of desensitization (or *counterconditioning*) by eliminating a little boy's fear of rabbits by associating a pleasant stimulus (food) with the learned stimulus (a rabbit). As the little boy was given yummy food to eat, Jones slowly moved the caged rabbit closer and closer to the little boy until eventually the boy was eating and petting the rabbit at the same time. Fear gone; psychological problem solved!

Years later, after giving up on the psychoanalytic approach to treating anxiety disorders, Joseph Wolpe developed an exposure therapy for reducing anxiety, primarily phobias, called *systematic desensitization*. Wolpe continued where Mary Cover Jones left off. His method includes three steps:

- The client learns to practice deep relaxation.

- The client creates a hierarchy of anxieties from lowest anxiety-producing stimulus to highest.
- Led by the therapist, the client is introduced to the least-feared object or situation while practicing deep relaxation. When able to deal with this first stimulus without experiencing anxiety, the client is introduced to the next fear-producing object or situation while practicing relaxation until the client is successfully able to deal with the object or situation at the top of the hierarchy, which is the most intense fear.

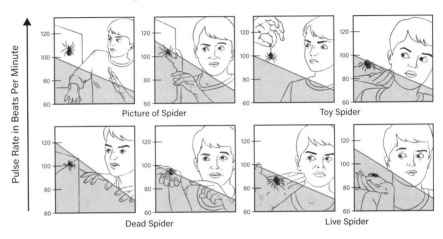

Figure 5.5.5 Systematic Desensitization

Today, with the introduction of computer technology, a form of systematic desensitization called virtual reality graded (or gradual) exposure is sometimes used. The client wears virtual reality goggles that provide a visual experience of the feared object or situation. This approach is obviously more practical than providing real-life exposure to situations such as airplanes or heights. This technology has been used successfully to treat anxiety disorders, including social phobia and post-traumatic stress disorder (PTSD).

Aversion Therapy Combining the principles of both classical conditioning and operant conditioning is aversion therapy. As the name suggests, **aversion therapy** is a form of behavioral therapy in which an unwanted behavior is associated with a stimulus to which the client has a great aversion. Aversion therapy is based on classical conditioning—when the unwanted behavior, such as drinking alcohol, is associated with an unpleasant stimulus (vomiting, for example), a newly learned (conditioned) response (fear/disgust) is elicited. The use of operant conditioning in aversion therapy is essentially punishment. If you experience an unpleasant consequence when behaving a certain way, you will eventually stop the behavior. An example of aversion therapy is the medication Antabuse, which is used to treat alcohol use disorders. The unpleasant side effects when it is combined with alcohol in the body—including fast heartbeat, chest pain, dizziness, nausea, and thirst—help keep people from drinking.

Operant Conditioning Behavioral therapists use behavior modification based on **operant conditioning** principles developed by B. F. Skinner, by which learning (or unlearning) voluntary behaviors results from positive or negative reinforcement or punishment. For example, intellectually disabled children, children with autism spectrum disorder (ASD), or institutionalized adults can learn more appropriate social behaviors and life skills by being positively reinforced each time they display an approximate behavior or by being punished when they display undesirable behaviors. If the ethical punishment is effective, extinction will occur and undesirable behaviors will be replaced by more appropriate behaviors.

Token economy systems use positive reinforcement and are often used in institutional settings such as prisons, psychiatric hospitals, or schools. Tokens are earned for desired behaviors and exchanged for rewards, like using the computer, playing video games, or eating desirable food. Some are skeptical of token economies because they do not prepare individuals for a typical life, in which they will not be rewarded for each behavior. It is best to move someone to a variable-ratio schedule of reinforcement (see Topic 3.8) before they leave the institutional setting because this will encourage the behavior to continue even after the reinforcements have ended.

Modeling In some situations, the most practical behavioral therapy method is modeling, in which the therapist demonstrates the desired behavior to help clients learn the behavior themselves. An excellent way to extinguish irrational fears is for the client to observe the therapist or some other person handling the feared object without any bad consequence. Modeling can also be used in the same way to help clients overcome anxiety over social situations.

Biofeedback In **biofeedback**, electronic monitoring equipment measures and provides feedback about physiological processes in the body, such as heart rate, muscle tension, skin temperature, and brainwave activity. By providing real-time information about these bodily functions, biofeedback enables individuals to learn how to control them voluntarily. Biofeedback is often used as a component of behavioral therapy for various health conditions, including anxiety, chronic pain, headaches, high blood pressure, and insomnia. It enables individuals to gain greater awareness and control over their physiological responses, leading to improved health and well-being.

Assessing Behavioral Therapy Behavioral therapy can be a quick and efficient way to deal with certain behavior problems. For example, behavioral therapies are effective in treating anxiety disorders, such as social phobia and many specific phobias. They also show positive results for children diagnosed with attention deficit hyperactivity disorder (ADHD) when coupled with medication or biofeedback therapy.

Certain behavioral therapies should be used with caution. Aversion therapy and flooding could be harmful if done carelessly, because the client is subjected to negative situations that may backfire and reinforce the very undesirable behaviors intended to be removed. And behavioral therapy is not effective in eliminating the symptoms of major depression, bipolar disorder, or schizophrenia.

Cognitive Therapies

After extensive research into the causes of depression, psychiatrist Aaron Beck concluded that the symptoms of depression grew as a result of cognitive distortions and that these can be replaced through therapy with more positive, accurate, and realistic ways of thinking. By the early 1960s, Beck's **cognitive therapy** was introduced as an effective way of treating depression by helping the client recognize dysfunctional, self-defeating, and maladaptive thought patterns. Cognitive therapy is now considered effective for other disorders, including anxiety, eating, and personality disorders.

Central to cognitive therapy is Beck's cognitive triad, which comprises three interrelated and dysfunctional types of automatic thinking: (1) negative thoughts about self, (2) negative thoughts about the world, and (3) negative thoughts about the future (Figure 5.5.6). Each of these cognitive distortions, or errors in logic, feeds off the others in a self-reinforcing negative cycle. A cognitive therapist's goal is to help clients recognize their negative thoughts as unrealistic, reject them, and replace them with more realistic functional thoughts. Some cognitive distortions coined by Beck include catastrophizing (*If I don't earn a 5 on my AP Psychology exam, my life will be ruined*), all-or-none thinking (*He never called me back; I must be a total loser*), and personalization (*The teacher didn't call on me because she hates me*).

Cognitive restructuring is aimed at identifying and challenging maladaptive or distorted thinking patterns and replacing them with more

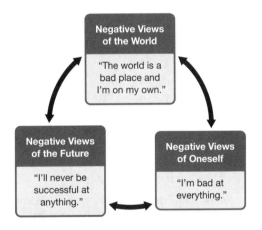

Figure 5.5.6 Cognitive Triad

balanced and rational thoughts. This therapeutic process is a core component of cognitive therapy and is used to treat a variety of psychological disorders, including depression, anxiety, and stress-related issues. The first step is to recognize and identify the negative or irrational thoughts that contribute to emotional distress. Once this has been accomplished, the next step is to critically evaluate and challenge these thoughts. This step involves examining the evidence for and against the thought, considering alternative perspectives, and assessing the thought's accuracy and helpfulness. The final step is to replace the distorted thoughts with more balanced, rational, and constructive thoughts. This step involves formulating thoughts that are realistic, based on evidence, and conducive to emotional well-being and problem-solving. Replacing "I always mess up everything" with "I made a mistake this time, but I can learn from it and do better next time" is an example of cognitive restructuring.

Assessing Cognitive Therapy Cognitive therapy takes much effort on the part of the therapist and the client. It has been shown to be highly effective in treating psychological problems and disorders, including depression, anxiety, PTSD, eating disorders, and substance abuse. It is so effective that some people need as few as six sessions to achieve their goals.

Cognitive-Behavioral Therapies

A type of therapy closely related to both cognitive and behavioral therapy is **cognitive-behavioral therapy** (**CBT**). Cognitive psychology emerged from the behaviorist school because behavior is almost always linked to cognition (thinking). Cognitive-behavioral therapists approach psychological problems based on the assumption that cognition leads to emotional responses and behavior.

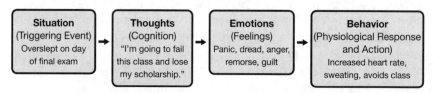

Figure 5.5.7 Cognitive-Behavioral Therapy

The guiding principle of CBT is that depression, anxiety, or any other psychological problems are caused by maladaptive or illogical thinking. To solve these problems, the cognitive-behavioral therapist helps the client reframe the maladaptive thought processes. Cognitive-behavioral therapies, such as rational-emotive behavior therapy and dialectical behavior therapy, combine techniques from the cognitive and behavioral perspectives to treat mental and behavioral disorders.

Rational-Emotive Behavior Therapy In the early 1950s, Albert Ellis rejected Freudian psychoanalysis and developed **rational-emotive behavior therapy** (**REBT**) based on his belief that the reason behind most psychological problems was irrational thoughts. Ellis believed that people cognitively perceive themselves and their world in their own particular way, and those perceptions (cognitions) guide reactions to events and people. Psychological problems arise when those thoughts are irrational and lead to behavioral consequences that cause distress. Ellis thought that the therapist should be more of a teacher, challenging the client's irrational thoughts in a straightforward and rather impersonal, and some would say aggressive, way.

The key challenge confronting a client in REBT is understanding that the activating event does not cause the emotional and behavioral consequences—the client's irrational way of thinking does. Ellis coined the term *awfulizing* to refer to the tendency to irrationally overestimate or exaggerate a situation or event. During a typical REBT session, the therapist will carefully observe the client's thought processes and emotional reactions and then directly challenge the absurdity of those thoughts.

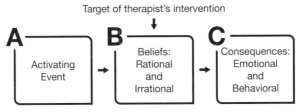

Figure 5.5.8 Albert Ellis's ABC Technique

Ellis believed that the cause of emotional and behavioral problems was not an Activating event but rather the Beliefs and thoughts of the person interpreting it. The Consequences could be healthy if the interpretation is rational.

Dialectical Behavior Therapy While working with chronically suicidal individuals with borderline personality disorder, Marsha Linehan realized that standard behavior therapy was not particularly effective. Through trial and error, she developed a new form of cognitive-behavioral theory. **Dialectical behavior therapy (DBT)** combines elements of cognitive-behavioral techniques. It focuses on individuals' skills to manage overwhelming emotions, improve interpersonal relationships, and cope with distressing situations. DBT generally helps people focus on the development of four types of skills:

- **Mindfulness:** Mindfulness skills help individuals become more aware of their thoughts, emotions, and sensations in the present moment, without judgment. Techniques such as mindfulness meditation, deep breathing, and observing thoughts nonjudgmentally are taught in order to enhance self-awareness and reduce emotional reactivity.

- **Distress tolerance:** Distress tolerance skills teach individuals how to tolerate and survive crises and distressing situations without making impulsive or harmful decisions. These skills include distraction techniques, self-soothing activities, and accepting reality as it is without trying to change it.

- **Emotional regulation:** Emotional regulation skills help individuals identify, understand, and manage their emotions more effectively. Techniques such as identifying triggers, increasing positive emotions, and reducing vulnerability to negative emotions are taught in order to improve emotional stability and resilience.

- **Interpersonal effectiveness:** Interpersonal effectiveness skills focus on improving communication, assertiveness, and relationship-building abilities. Techniques such as assertive communication, setting boundaries, and resolving conflicts are taught in order to enhance interpersonal relationships and reduce relationship problems.

Dialectical behavior therapy is typically delivered in individual therapy sessions, skills training groups, and phone coaching between sessions. It is a structured and goal-oriented therapy that emphasizes collaboration between the therapist and client. While originally developed for borderline personality disorder, DBT has been adapted and found to be effective for treating a range of mental health conditions, including mood disorders, eating disorders, substance-use disorders, and PTSD.

Assessing Cognitive-Behavioral Therapy Cognitive-behavioral therapy has a substantial evidence base demonstrating its effectiveness in treating various mental health conditions, including depression, anxiety disorders, PTSD, OCD, and eating disorders. It has strong empirical support, focusing on identifying and changing patterns of thinking and behavior that contribute to distressing symptoms. It typically involves setting specific treatment goals, developing individualized treatment plans, and using structured techniques to achieve those goals.

Cognitive-behavioral therapy emphasizes collaboration between the therapist and client, with clients encouraged to take an active role in therapy, learn new skills, and apply them in their daily lives. This collaborative approach fosters a sense of empowerment and self-efficacy. In addition, CBT is typically time-limited and focused on achieving specific treatment goals within a relatively short period. This makes it a cost-effective and efficient treatment option, particularly for individuals with limited resources or time constraints. Because CBT focuses on teaching people the skills they need to help change their thoughts and improve interactions with others, this method also is often the longest lasting of all of the therapeutic approaches.

While CBT is effective for many individuals, it may not be suitable or sufficient for everyone. Some clients may prefer or benefit more from other therapeutic approaches that emphasize different techniques or theoretical orientations. CBT primarily targets cognitive restructuring and behavioral change, which may not address underlying emotional or interpersonal issues for some clients. Individuals with complex or longstanding mental health problems may require a more comprehensive treatment approach. Also, CBT requires active participation and engagement from the client, which may be challenging for individuals with low motivation, cognitive impairment, or limited insight into their problems.

THINK AS A PSYCHOLOGIST

Apply Psychological Perspectives, Theories, Concepts, and Research Findings to a Scenario (1.A.2)

Practice Applying Perspectives

In one or two sentences, complete the following activity.

Explain how a cognitive therapist and a humanistic therapist would differ in their treatment of a client with chronic anxiety.

Modes of Therapy

The term *modes of therapy* refers not to the various psychotherapeutic approaches, such as psychodynamic, cognitive, behavioral, and humanistic, but to the differing ways to deliver these therapeutic approaches. The most recognizable mode is individual psychotherapy. Other modes include group, self-help groups, family, and couples/marriage counseling. Therapists who practice these other modes of therapy still use one or more of the psychotherapeutic approaches, depending on what best serves their clients and which modes of therapy are available.

Group Therapy

Group therapy provides what can be a vital element to mental healing: knowing you are not alone. In a small group, usually around 6 to 12, people with similar problems come together under the direction or facilitation of a trained therapist or counselor to discuss their psychological issues.

Group therapy offers a number of benefits that individual therapy lacks. First, group therapy provides members with the beneficial realization that they are not alone in their suffering and struggles. That knowledge reduces the sense of isolation and hopelessness. Second, the counselor can monitor the interactions between group members and encourage healthy interpersonal behaviors. Third, with proper guidance by a trained therapist, the dynamics of the group itself can serve to address healthier coping skills such as problem-solving, self-confidence, assertiveness, listening skills, and empathy. Group therapy also enables a therapist to treat more clients at the same time and is less expensive for the clients than individual therapy. Group therapy is perhaps most well-known for helping those with substance-use disorders, but can be used for a variety of psychological disorders and provides a strong support network that is beneficial for those trying to change long-standing habits or thought processes.

THINK AS A PSYCHOLOGIST

Evaluate the Appropriate Use of Research Design Elements in Non-Experimental Methodologies (2.C.1) | Propose a Defensible Claim (4.A) | Provide Reasoning That Is Grounded in Scientifically Derived Evidence to Support, Refute, or Modify an Established or Provided Claim, Policy, or Norm (4.B.3)

The following abstract[1] is from a peer-reviewed journal.

Abstract: Cognitive-behavioral therapy (CBT) has demonstrated favorable long-term outcomes in youth with anxiety disorders. However, long-term outcomes of CBT delivered in a group/community setting are uncertain. This study examined the long-term outcomes of individual (ICBT) and group CBT

---

1   Kodal, A., et al. (2018, January). Long-term effectiveness of cognitive behavioral therapy for youth with anxiety disorders. *Journal of Anxiety Disorders. 53*: 58-67.

(GCBT) in youth with anxiety disorders treated in community mental health clinics. A total of 139 youth (mean age at assessment 15.5 years, range 11–21 years) with a principal diagnosis of separation anxiety disorder, social anxiety disorder, and/or generalized anxiety disorder were evaluated, on average, 3.9 years post-treatment (range 2.2–5.9 years). Outcomes included loss of all inclusion anxiety diagnoses, loss of the principal anxiety diagnosis, and changes in youth- and parent-rated youth anxiety symptoms.

In the long term follow-up of the 139 youth, 53% ($n = 73$) of the sample no longer met the DSM criteria for any anxiety disorder; 63% ($n = 87$) of the sample no longer met the DSM criteria for the anxiety disorder for which they had originally been diagnosed. Additionally, most participants in both the ICBT group and GCBT group experienced significant reductions in all anxiety symptom tests or measures. Statistical analysis on all measures explored showed no statistically significant differences between the ICBT and GCBT groups ($p < 0.05$).

Practice Evaluating Design Elements, Proposing a Claim, and Providing Reasoning

Complete the following activities.

1. State a possible hypothesis for the above research study.

2. Based on the information provided in the abstract, make a defensible claim, and provide one piece of evidence to support your claim.

Hypnosis

You may have seen an old movie in which a hypnotist or performer holds up a pocket watch, lets it swing slowly, and asks another person to concentrate on the watch. The victim surrenders her will to the hypnotist and is then told to do something illegal like rob a bank. Or perhaps you have been to a county fair or a stage show in which a hypnotist makes volunteers from the audience squawk like chickens, flap their arms, run around, or do some other strange behavior. Practitioners of hypnosis have been fighting such mythical depictions of hypnosis for years. Stage hypnotists are known to screen possible collaborators among their audiences to find people who can focus well and who are exhibitionists who like to perform in front of crowds. True hypnotism is a science—the induction of a state of altered consciousness that uses the power of suggestion to change specific mindsets but does not make individuals behave contrary to their core principles.

Modern hypnosis was devised and introduced by Franz Mesmer, from whose name the terms *mesmerism* and *mesmerize* are derived. Although trance states and forms of hypnosis have been around for as long as humans, Mesmer brought hypnosis from the realm of magic into the realm of science. While he did not bring it very far, researchers in the fields of medicine and psychiatry began to study hypnosis. In current views, **hypnosis** is an induced altered state of consciousness that heightens a person's suggestibility—openness to responding to suggestion—without losing his or her sense of self or control. People do under hypnosis only what they would be willing to do in their usual, fully conscious state of mind, nothing more.

In the past, hypnosis was thought to be able to help someone recover repressed memories—overwhelming emotional experiences that are consciously or unconsciously forgotten. However, research has shown that hypnosis is ineffective in memory recovery. Most recovered memories are nothing more than falsely created memories made at the suggestion of an overeager hypnotherapist. Similarly, research shows that age regression therapy—inducing through hypnosis the state of mind of a younger version of the client—is also not a viable technique, lacking empirical support.

In therapeutic hypnosis, a state of suggestibility makes someone more able to respond positively to recommendations, such as those for reducing a smoking habit or feeling no pain during a visit to the dentist. Hypnosis is especially effective at reducing pain. Some people have used hypnosis successfully to treat anxiety, depression, gastrointestinal disorders, skin conditions, and many other troublesome conditions, though the positive results may be nothing more than the placebo effect. Therapists can use posthypnotic suggestion to encourage a client to respond to desired outcomes. Hypnosis is a useful tool that trained therapists can use effectively, but it is not appropriate for everyone.

Biologically Derived Interventions

Advances in medicine and psychiatry and knowledge of how the brain functions have made profound strides in the last half of the 20th and first part of the 21st centuries. Unlike psychologists, who are not medically trained, physicians and psychiatrists, whose training focuses on biology, are inclined to view biological abnormalities as the cause of mental illness, and they therefore offer treatment using a biomedical or biological approach. Biomedical therapy involves the use of pharmaceutical medications to treat psychological disorders and is ideally used in combination with different types of psychotherapy. Psychopharmacology is the study of how medications affect the mind and behavior. Medications used to treat psychological disorders are called **psychoactive medications**. There are also other biomedical treatments that are much less frequently used and much more controversial, including electroconvulsive therapy and psychosurgery.

Psychoactive Medications or Pharmacotherapy

Many types of psychoactive medications treat the symptoms of different psychological disorders. They do not cure the disorders; they only aim to alleviate the symptoms. The drugs are divided into classes: antianxiety, antidepressant, mood stabilizers, stimulants, and antipsychotics (Table 5.5.1). All of these psychoactive medications are more effective when used in conjunction with psychotherapy.

Psychoactive Medication	Used for	Brand Names	Effects
Antianxiety	PTSD, panic disorder, social phobia, OCD	Xanax® Valium®	Depresses central nervous system; reduces apprehension and nervousness
Antidepressants	Depression (recently, for long-term treatment of anxiety disorders)	Prozac® Zoloft®	Improves mood by reducing absorption of neurotransmitters serotonin and norepinephrine
Mood Stabilizers	Bipolar disorders	Lithium Lamotrigine	Reduces manic episodes and depressive episodes
Stimulants	ADD/ADHD	Ritalin® Adderall	Improves focus and attention by preventing absorption of dopamine and norepinephrine
Antipsychotics	Schizophrenia	Haldol® Thorazine®	Reduces positive psychotic symptoms such as delusions and hallucinations through inhibiting the neurotransmitter dopamine

Table 5.5.1

Antianxiety drugs are drugs that reduce symptoms related to anxiety, such as tension, fear, apprehension, and nervousness. There are two common approaches to treating anxiety using drugs—short term and long term. For acute anxiety, such as that associated with phobias or panic disorders, *benzodiazepines* are often used. Benzodiazepines are tranquilizing drugs that depress the central nervous system by increasing the effects of a brain chemical called *gamma-aminobutyric acid* (GABA), which depresses neural activity in the brain. Commonly prescribed benzodiazepines include Xanax® and Valium®.

Antidepressants elevate mood by affecting neurotransmitters such as serotonin, which is believed to play a role in depression. Recently, antidepressants have been found to reduce the symptoms associated with anxiety disorders, PTSD, and obsessive-compulsive disorder as well.

Different types of antidepressant drugs have different effects on certain neurotransmitters. As you read, SSRIs also act as agonists for the neurotransmitter serotonin. Other types of antidepressants include serotonin and norepinephrine reuptake inhibitors (SNRI) and norepinephrine and dopamine reuptake inhibitors (NDRI).

Mood stabilizers are drugs prescribed for people diagnosed with bipolar disorders because they reduce dramatic mood swings. They are also used for mood problems related to schizophrenia and schizoaffective disorder. The best-known mood stabilizers are **lithium** and Lamotrigine. Lamotrigine was initially created to treat seizure disorders and epilepsy but has also been effective in the treatment of bipolar disorder.

Stimulants are psychoactive medications that do what the name implies: They stimulate the central nervous system. Stimulants are not antidepressants. The most common use for stimulants is for the treatment of attention deficit disorder (ADD) and attention deficit hyperactivity disorder (ADHD). It has been hypothesized that the brain of a child with ADD/ADHD is unable to fully utilize two particular neurotransmitters—dopamine and norepinephrine. These two neurotransmitters get absorbed back into the neurons before they can do their stimulating work. Some believe that a child with ADD/ADHD lacks the neurological ability to stimulate, so the child will self-stimulate if his or her external environment is not stimulating enough. That may explain why the ADD/ADHD child fidgets, talks out of turn, darts about, and seems unfocused. Children with ADD/ADHD need stimulation that the brain is not providing, and that is why stimulants reduce the symptoms of ADD/ ADHD. The most common stimulants prescribed for ADD/ADHD are Ritalin®, Adderall, and Dexedrine®, all of which are reuptake inhibitors. They stop the absorption of dopamine and norepinephrine and allow the brain to experience more stimulation. The child then is able to stay more focused and pay attention for longer periods of time.

Antipsychotic medications are used to reduce positive symptoms of schizophrenia and, in extreme circumstances, of bipolar disorder. As you read in Topic 5.4, schizophrenia includes positive symptoms, such as delusions of paranoia and auditory hallucinations, and negative symptoms (behaviors that stop happening), such as a lack of normal emotional reactions and social interaction. Examples of common antipsychotic drugs are Haldol®, Prolixin®, and Thorazine®. Atypical antipsychotic drugs not only reduce positive symptoms but also target such negative symptoms as withdrawal and apathy.

Assessing Psychoactive Medications

Psychoactive medications are only prescribed after a careful diagnosis by a medical doctor. They all carry the possibility of serious side effects. **Tardive dyskinesia (TD)** is a neurological disorder caused by long-term use of antipsychotic drugs. TD is characterized by uncontrolled facial and tongue movements or uncontrolled arm or leg movements. The condition may go away if the antipsychotic drug is removed soon enough, but sometimes the condition is permanent.

A great deal of research indicates that a psychoactive medication used in conjunction with psychotherapy is more effective in treating psychological disorders than is a drug alone. These drugs reduce the symptoms of a disorder, but they do not treat the underlying causes.

Electroconvulsive Therapy

Electroconvulsive therapy (ECT) is used in the most serious cases of depression. ECT involves the administration of a short-duration electric current between the temples that causes a seizure. (The patient is anesthetized so the seizure does not cause physical convulsions.) ECT is used when medications have failed to alleviate the symptoms.

ECT was first introduced in the 1930s and became widely used but, by the 1950s, its popularity waned. Recently, its use has not only increased, but some psychiatrists are employing a repetitive or frequent application to permanently relieve the symptoms of depression. Modern-day ECT therapies are much more controlled than those from nearly a century ago. ECT has a number of side effects, with memory loss among the most prevalent. Most memory loss is temporary and goes away within a few months.

Psychosurgery

Psychosurgery is the intentional surgical destruction of part of the brain in order to reduce symptoms of mental illness. This was typically used on schizophrenic patients prior to the release of antipsychotic medications. While it did occasionally stop psychotic episodes, this was primarily because the person had been thrown into a state of shock. Many were left unable to speak or communicate.

Psychosurgery was first used in the 1930s in a surgical procedure called a *prefrontal lobotomy*, or simply **lobotomy**, in which the frontal lobes are separated from the rest of the brain by cutting the connecting nerve fibers. This brutal procedure is fortunately a relic of the past. Modern neurology has introduced a much more selective method of destroying brain tissue in order to treat the most severe forms of depression and obsessive-compulsive disorder. The procedure is called a *bilateral anterior cingulotomy*. It involves inserting an electrode into the brain and carefully guiding it to specific neurons that connect the frontal lobe to the limbic system, the seat of basic emotional responses. With a controlled electric current, small areas of selected brain cells are destroyed. This procedure can also be used to destroy tumors or to treat Parkinson's disease or epilepsy.

Deep Brain Stimulation and Transcranial Magnetic Stimulation

Neuropsychiatrists have recently begun treating severe cases of depression that are resistant to medications through deep brain stimulation, in which a thin wire is surgically implanted in the area of the brain associated with depression. The wire is connected to a battery and supplies a slight electric current that stimulates neuronal growth that appears to reduce the symptoms of depression.

Another neurological technique that avoids destruction of brain tissue or inducing convulsions through electric shock is the use of noninvasive magnets called **transcranial magnetic stimulation** (TMS). An electrified coil placed very near the skull delivers an electromagnetic pulse to a specific area of the brain. Research seems to indicate that after repeated exposure to the electromagnetic stimulation, specific neurons appear to grow in a way that reduces the symptoms of depression.

Assessing the Biomedical Approach

The discovery in the mid-20th century that drugs could reduce the symptoms of severe psychological disorders is rightly considered one of the most important turning points in the treatment of mental illness. No longer was a person with schizophrenia destined to suffer from the psychotic symptoms in an institution, nor was a person with severe depression doomed to perpetual sadness. Additionally, as more and more psychoactive medications have been developed, more and more people who suffer from anxiety, obsessive-compulsive disorder, PTSD, or other disorders have been able to find relief from their symptoms.

But there are important caveats. Psychoactive medications reduce the symptoms but do not cure the illness, and they can also produce serious side effects. Another important concern is the increasing reliance upon such drugs as the first or only treatment. People diagnosed with bipolar disorder, depression, or anxiety and prescribed antidepressant or antianxiety drugs should get psychotherapeutic treatment as well. While drugs often reduce symptoms quickly, psychotherapy can take much time and effort before seeing results. Unfortunately, too many people take the medications without undertaking psychotherapy. They become dependent on the drug to relieve the symptoms but miss the opportunity that psychotherapy affords to treat the underlying psychological causes of the disorder. Research has shown that a combination of psychopharmacological drugs and psychotherapy produces the best long-term results.

THINK AS A PSYCHOLOGIST

Evaluate Qualitative and Quantitative Research Methods and Study Designs (2.A.1.a) | Evaluate the Appropriate Use of Research Design Elements in Experimental Methodology (2.B.4, 2.B.8, 2.B.10, 2.B.9, 2.B.12) | Evaluate Whether a Psychological Research Scenario Followed Appropriate Ethical Procedures (2.D.1, 2.D.4) | Interpret Quantitative or Qualitative Inferential Data from a Given Table, Graph, Chart, Figure, or Diagram (3.C.2)

The following is adapted from a study designed to evaluate the effectiveness of fluoxetine (Prozac®) in reducing symptoms in adolescents experiencing major depressive disorder.

Methods: Ninety-six adolescents (aged 13–17 years) with major depressive disorder were randomized (stratified for age and sex) to take 20 mg of fluoxetine or a placebo daily for 8 consecutive weeks. Participants met weekly with a psychologist to examine changes in the severity of symptoms that each participant experienced. The tool for measuring the severity of symptoms was the Children's Depression Rating Scale (CDRS). Following are the results.

	Fluoxetine Group	Placebo
Percent assessed as "much" or "very much" improved on the CDRS $p = .02$ (indicating statistically significant results)	56%	33%

Practice Evaluating Research Methods, Elements, and Ethics and Interpreting Data from a Table

Complete the following activities and answer the questions.

1. Describe why this research would be classified as experimental.
2. Identify the sample of participants used in this study.
3. Identify the experimental and control groups in this experiment.
4. Was the measurement of the dependent variable quantitative or qualitative? Explain your answer.
5. Why would a double-blind procedure be necessary in this study?
6. Explain the value of attempting to replicate this study.
7. What considerations would an IRB need to take into account for this study that would differ from other studies that do not involve drugs?
8. The data reported in the table indicate that the results were statistically significant. What does that allow us to conclude?

REFLECT ON THE ESSENTIAL QUESTION

Essential Question: *How are psychological disorders treated?* Using the Key Terms, complete a chart like the one below to gather details to help answer that question.

Type(s) of Disorders	Treatment

MULTIPLE-CHOICE QUESTIONS

1. Which statement best describes the difference between psychodynamic therapy and behavioral therapies?

   (A) The main tool in psychodynamic therapy is active listening, while the main tool in behavioral therapies is free association.

   (B) Behavioral therapies help clients develop insights, while psychodynamic therapies help clients change behaviors.

   (C) Psychodynamic therapy attempts to reveal trauma that is buried in the unconscious, while behavioral therapies attempt to counter-condition problematic patterns of behavior.

   (D) Behavioral therapies focus on realizing one's full potential, while psychodynamic therapy stresses the need to alter maladaptive thoughts.

2. After several years of taking mediation, Keanu began to experience uncontrollable facial and tongue movements as well as uncontrollable movements in his fingers. Which of the following psychological problems was Keanu most likely taking medication for?

   (A) Narcissistic personality disorder

   (B) Major depressive disorder

   (C) Schizophrenia

   (D) Generalized anxiety disorder

3. Professor McLane is interested in conducting research to try to determine the extent to which therapeutic interventions lead to positive outcomes for patients suffering from psychological problems. Which of the following research techniques should Dr. McLane use to investigate this topic?

(A) Cross-sectional

(B) Meta-analysis

(C) Naturalistic observation

(D) Case study

4. "We think we listen, but very rarely do we listen with real understanding, true empathy. Yet listening, of this very special kind, is one of the most potent forces for change that I know." This quotation most represents beliefs that underlie which of the following therapeutic approaches?

(A) Person-centered therapy

(B) Object relations therapy

(C) Dialectical behavior therapy (DBT)

(D) Systematic desensitization

5. Rowan has an intense fear of being in small, enclosed spaces such as elevators. In therapy, his psychologist teaches him various relaxation techniques and then works with him to create a hierarchy of steps that will incrementally help him get closer to being able to be in a small space without feeling panic. Rowan's psychologist is using a technique most associated with which of the following perspectives?

(A) Humanistic

(B) Psychodynamic

(C) Behaviorist

(D) Cognitive

Questions 6 and 7 refer to the following.

A study was conducted to determine the long-term efficacy of using lithium to treat bipolar disorder. Volunteers who had been diagnosed with bipolar disorder were randomly assigned to either take lithium or a placebo. The data below were collected five years after the study concluded.

	Recurrences of Depression or Mania
Lithium Group	30%
Placebo Group	70%

6. Which of the following research methods was used in the above study?
   (A) Correlational
   (B) Cross-sectional
   (C) Naturalistic observation
   (D) Experimental

7. The method of treatment used in the above study most closely aligns with which of the following perspectives?
   (A) Sociocultural
   (B) Biological
   (C) Cognitive-behavioral
   (D) Psychodynamic

STUDY LIKE A CHAMP WITH DR. G.

As semesters end, we all have more deadlines and more assignments due. Unfortunately, many of us start sleeping less, eating poorly, or skipping our physical activity engagements. This is exactly the opposite of what helps us get the work done better. For the best mental and physical health, sleeping, eating well, and getting physical activity are just what the doctor ordered (and no, I'm not that kind of doctor, although I do have a Ph.D.). Healthy behaviors are not only one of the best ways to cope with stress, but they are essential to learning and doing well at school.

The effectiveness of your retrieval practice, spacing, pretesting, and interleaving all increase if you are sleeping well, eating well, and getting physical activity. Even if your attempts over the last few weeks have not worked completely, do not give up. Revise your plan. Try again. Monitor your success, and revise your plan again if need be. All these techniques, both for mental and physical health and for learning well, need practice. They are worth the effort, since they will serve you well, not just for your exams, but for the rest of your life as well. Now that is something to cheer for! All the best.

UNIT 5: Review

Questions 1 through 3 refer to the following.

Dr. Seefeldt is a clinical psychologist who treats patients experiencing major depressive disorder. He uses several techniques in his approach to treatment, but wanted to explore whether the techniques were equally effective. Dr. Seefeldt received informed consent from 100 patients who were diagnosed with depression and were willing to participate in a study. The patients were randomly assigned to one of two groups. Group 1 received treatment that was nondirective, in which Dr. Seefeldt listened reflectively and provided unconditional positive regard. Group 2 received therapy in which Dr. Seefeldt would help the patient identify, confront, and alter maladaptive, irrational, self-defeating statements. At the end of the three-month trial, patients' symptoms were assessed using a depression scale with ratings from 1 to 7. A low score on the scale indicated few symptoms of depression and a high score indicated significant symptoms of depression. The results are in the table below.

	Average Score on Depression Scale at the Conclusion of the Treatment
Group 1	5.62
Group 2	3.14

1. Dr. Seefeldt's research is best classified as experimental due to which of the following?

    (A) The use of random assignment

    (B) The use of confounding variables

    (C) The use of a measurable dependent variable

    (D) The use of a convenience sample

2. What is the independent variable in this study?

    (A) The length of time that patients received therapy (three months)

    (B) The severity of depression that patients had at the beginning of the study

    (C) The score that patients received on the depression scale

    (D) The type of therapy the patient received

3. The treatment that Group 2 received most closely aligns with which of the following therapeutic techniques?

(A) Exposure therapy

(B) Rational emotive behavior therapy

(C) Person-centered therapy

(D) Object relations therapy

EXPOSURE HIERARCHY	
Anxiety-Producing Situation	**1–10**
Imagine the feared situation for 5 minutes	1
Imagine the feared situation while describing it out loud for 10 minutes	2
Watch a video or look at pictures of the feared situation	3
Watch a live demonstration of the feared situation	4
Participate in the feared situation in a controlled environment with a trusted person present	5
Briefly encounter the feared situation in real life (e.g., for 1 minute)	6
Gradually increase the duration of exposure to the feared situation (e.g., for 10 minutes)	7
Fully engage in the feared situation for an extended period (e.g., for 1 hour)	8
Participate in the feared situation for a significant amount of time (e.g., for 30 minutes)	9
Regularly participate in the feared situation as part of daily life	10

4. The above table is most closely related to which of the following therapeutic techniques?

(A) Systematic desensitization

(B) Person-centered therapy

(C) Free association

(D) Cognitive restructuring

5. Jayson is incredibly stressed about an argument he had with his girlfriend. After brainstorming possible ways to alleviate the problem, he decides the best approach is to directly work with his girlfriend on a tangible plan to resolve their dispute. Jayson is utilizing which of the following?

(A) Emotion-focused coping

(B) Problem-focused coping

(C) Tend-and-befriend coping

(D) General adaptation coping

6. Louise experienced a panic attack several years ago when she was shopping at a store. Ever since that episode, she has great anxiety about going to any place where she might have a similar experience. This has created a debilitating situation and led her to avoid almost any situation in which she would need to leave her house. These problems are most consistent with which of the following?

    (A) Dependent personality disorder

    (B) Bipolar disorder

    (C) Agoraphobia

    (D) Obsessive-compulsive disorder

7. Yana is experiencing a profound and debilitating sense of anxiety centered on her fear that her physical appearance will cause embarrassment to others around her. Yana's problems are most consistent with which of the following?

    (A) Social anxiety disorder

    (B) Dissociative amnesia

    (C) Posttraumatic stress disorder

    (D) Bipolar I disorder

8. Dr. Lindenberg conducts a study on several college campuses to see if there are patterns of illness when students come into the campus health center during a semester. She finds that the illness rates at all campuses were highest in the week after final exams. Which of the following statements likely accounts for this finding?

    (A) The pressure of the semester exam period creates the need for more emotion-focused coping, which makes students more likely to get sick.

    (B) Students aren't able to practice and engage with their signature strengths as much over that time, which can lead to illness.

    (C) The prolonged stress of the semester likely causes students to experience some level of immunosuppression, leaving them more vulnerable to illness.

    (D) During such stressful times, students are likely to engage in more tend-and-befriend behaviors that amplify exposure to other people, making it more likely they will get sick.

9. Which of the following most clearly reflects an eclectic approach to the treatment of a psychological problem?

(A) A psychoanalyst interprets the latent content of a patient's dream and analyzes transference taking place between the patient and the therapist.

(B) A therapist uses a token economy to reinforce appropriate behaviors of her patients.

(C) A therapist uses exposure therapy to treat a phobia, along with active listening, in an effort to show the patient unconditional positive regard.

(D) A therapist challenges the client to consider the illogical premise of a belief and educates the client regarding the cognitive triad.

10. Over the past several years, Jerry's life has been a roller coaster of extreme highs and lows. There have been weeks when he experienced feelings of boundless euphoria, which often resulted in him behaving impulsively, spending beyond his means, and abusing substances. These episodes were often followed by months where Jerry could barely muster the energy to get out of bed and had deep feelings of hopelessness and worthlessness. Jerry's experiences are most consistent with which of the following?

(A) Persistent depressive disorder

(B) Attention deficit/hyperactivity disorder

(C) Bipolar I disorder

(D) Narcissistic personality disorder

11. A behavioral therapist would likely criticize the psychodynamic approach on the grounds that psychodynamic therapists do which of the following?

(A) They spend too much time restructuring the self-defeating thoughts of the patient.

(B) They overemphasize the impact societal expectations have on an individual's dysfunctional behavior.

(C) They rely too heavily on the use of medication without trying to discover the root of a patient's disorder.

(D) They expend too much effort trying to uncover problems rooted in the patient's unconscious mind.

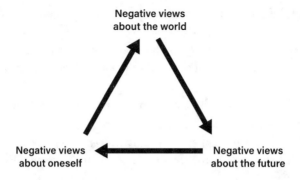

Negative views about the world

Negative views about oneself

Negative views about the future

12. The graphic above represents an explanation about what leads people to experience depression and anxiety. This viewpoint is most representative of which of the following perspectives?

(A) Humanist

(B) Evolutionary

(C) Diathesis-stress

(D) Cognitive

13. Angel's therapist does not offer interpretations of their comments or give them specific directions as to how to improve their life. Instead, the therapist listens and supports Angel with nonjudgmental acceptance. Angel's therapist is using techniques linked to which of the following therapies?

(A) Free association

(B) Person-centered therapy

(C) Cognitive restructuring

(D) Aversion therapy

14. Which of the approaches to psychology emphasizes that learning more about your character strengths and practicing gratitude are core to increasing your subjective well-being?

(A) Positive psychology

(B) Humanistic psychology

(C) Psychodynamic psychology

(D) Behavioral psychology

15. For the past several months, Nikola has experienced a complete lack of emotion. He doesn't feel happy, sad, angry, etc. He has also stopped engaging in any goal-oriented behavior, including taking care of his basic hygiene needs. Nikola's experience is most consistent with which of the following?

(A) Positive symptoms of schizophrenia

(B) Negative symptoms of schizophrenia

(C) Manic symptoms of bipolar disorder

(D) Compulsions of obsessive-compulsive disorder

SECTION II: FREE-RESPONSE QUESTIONS

Question 1: Article Analysis Question (AAQ)

Your response to the question should be provided in six parts: A, B, C, D, E, and F. Write the response to each part of the question in complete sentences. Use appropriate psychological terminology in your response.

Using the source provided, respond to all parts of the question.

(A) Identify the research method used in the study.

(B) State the operational definition of depressive symptoms.

(C) Describe the statistical results from the study.

(D) Identify at least one ethical guideline applied by the researchers.

(E) Explain the extent to which the research findings may or may not be generalizable using specific and relevant evidence from the study.

(F) Explain how at least one of the research findings supports or refutes the researchers' hypothesis.

Introduction
The goal of this study was to assess the impact of group therapy on participants with depressive symptoms, compared with those with symptoms who received no treatment. Researchers believed that group therapy would be a more cost-effective treatment than cognitive-behavioral therapy.
Participants
Participants included adult patients with depressive spectrum disorders ($n = 2,218$). The mean age of participants was 44 years old, and 70 percent were women. The participants were volunteers recruited through media advertisements. Participants in each study were provided with informed consent prior to the onset of treatment, with the right to discontinue treatment at any time.

continued

Method
The 48 studies examined reported pre- and post-test treatment scores of depression. Of these 48 studies, 18 included an untreated control group. The studies included brief group therapy interventions with an average of 19 hours of therapy over 12 sessions. The group therapy session included an average of 7 people. Multiple theoretical approaches were used in group therapy. Studies that the Beck Depression Inventory (BDI), which is based on self or interviewer report, were eligible for inclusion.

Results and Discussion
Of the 48 studies, 45 concluded that group therapy for depression was effective, and that this treatment significantly reduced depression. In the 18 studies with a control group, depression decreased in both the treatment and control conditions, but the improvement was more dramatic in the treatment condition, as the table below shows.

Group	N of Studies	Mean BDI	SD
Treated Clients (Group)			
—Pretreatment	35	23.90	5.32
—Posttreatment	35	12.30	3.44
Untreated Controls			
—Pretreatment	13	24.90	3.54
—Posttreatment	13	20.90	4.20

The study showed an average effect size of 1.03 after treatment, suggesting that those in treatment were better off than about 85% of those in the non-treatment group. No differences were found in the effectiveness of group therapy and that of cognitive-behavioral therapy. However, cognitive-behavioral therapy, which is most often conducted in individual sessions, is considerably more expensive. The study allows for a better understanding of the potential benefits of group therapy to a broad spectrum of individuals with depressive symptoms. Similar studies can be conducted and then compared regarding the efficacy of different types of therapeutic interventions.

Reference
McDermut, W., Miller, I. W., & Brown, R. A. (2001). The efficacy of group psychotherapy for depression: A review of the empirical research. *Clinical Psychology: Science and Practice*, 8(1): 98–116.

Question 2: Evidence-Based Question (EBQ)

This question has three parts: Part A, Part B, and Part C. Use the three sources provided to answer all parts of the question.

For Part B and Part C, you must cite the source that you used to answer the question. You can do this in two different ways:

- Parenthetical Citation:
  For example: ". . . (Source A)"

- Embedded Citation:
  For example: "According to Source A, . . ."

Write the response to each part of the question in complete sentences. Use appropriate psychological terminology.

Using the provided sources, develop and justify an argument related to the benefits of positive psychology exercises in various settings.

(A) Propose a specific and defensible claim based in psychological science that responds to the question.

(B) (i) Support your claim using at least one piece of specific and relevant evidence from one of the provided sources.

   (ii) Use a psychological perspective, theory, concept, or research finding learned in AP Psychology to explain how your evidence supports your claim.

(C) (i) Support your claim using an additional piece of specific and relevant evidence from a different source than the one used in Part B (i).

   (ii) Explain how the evidence from Part C (i) supports your claim using a different psychological perspective, theory, concept, or research findings learned in AP Psychology than the one used in Part B (ii).

Source A

Introduction
The study "Do positive psychology exercises work?" aims to replicate and expand on a landmark study by Seligman et al. (2005). The original study demonstrated the long-term benefits of positive psychology exercises (PPEs) on depression and happiness. The current work follows the same methodology with enhancements in the control conditions to test the effects of expectancies for success and cognitive access to positive self-relevant information. The study seeks to determine if practicing PPEs will increase reported levels of happiness, while decreasing reported levels of depression.

Participants
The study involved 1,447 participants, primarily White (78%) and Canadian (84%) females (83%), with ages ranging from 18 to 72 years and an average age of 33. Participants were recruited through Facebook advertisements targeting Canadian users over 18 years old. The sample included individuals with clinically significant levels of depressive symptoms, with 64% having some college or university education, and 30% being married, with 44% having children.

continued

Method

The study used a random-assignment, placebo-controlled design. Participants completed a battery of tests, including baseline measures of happiness (Steen Happiness Index – SHI) and depressive symptoms (Center for Epidemiologic Studies Depression Scale – CES-D). They were then randomly assigned to one of four conditions:

1. **Expectancy control (early memories):** Participants wrote about early memories every night for a week.

2. **Positive placebo (positive early memories):** Participants wrote about positive early memories every night for a week.

3. **Three good things:** Participants listed three good things that happened each day and why they happened.

4. **Using signature strengths in a new way:** Participants took an online inventory of their character strengths and used one of their top strengths in a new way each day for a week.

All exercises required approximately 10 minutes a day, and participants were reminded to complete follow-up assessments at 1 week, 1 month, 3 months, and 6 months.

Results and Discussion

Attrition: Of the 1,447 participants, 344 (24%) completed all requirements, including the 6-month follow-up. Those who dropped out by 6 months were more depressed and less happy at baseline.

Happiness: A repeated measures ANOVA (Analysis of Variance, a statistical method used to compare the means of three or more groups to determine if there are any statistically significant differences among them) indicated that participants increased in self-reported happiness over time. The PPEs led to significant increases in happiness compared to the expectancy control group but did not surpass the positive placebo condition. Both "Three good things" and "Using signature strengths in a new way" resulted in lasting increases in happiness at 1 week, 1 month, 3 months, and 6 months.

Depressive Symptoms: The PPEs did not lead to significantly greater reductions in depression over time compared to the control groups. Changes in depressive symptoms did not differ across conditions.

The study replicated the findings of Seligman et al. (2005) in terms of happiness, but not depression. The PPEs produced greater increases in happiness than the expectancy control group, confirming their effectiveness beyond creating "high hopes." However, the positive placebo (positive early memories) had effects as significant and long-lasting as the PPEs, suggesting that the access of positive, self-relevant information is a common factor with a substantial therapeutic effect. The lack of significant effects on depression may be due to differences in control groups and participant characteristics, compared to the original study. The study highlights the importance of rigorous methodological designs and the need for further research to provide insight into the specific mechanisms responsible for improvements in mood and flourishing.

Reference

Mongrain, M., & Anselmo-Matthews, T. (2012). Do positive psychology exercises work? A replication of Seligman et al. (2005). *Journal of Clinical Psychology*, 68(4), 382–389. https://doi.org/10.1002/jclp.21839

Source B

Introduction

The study of character strengths is a significant aspect of positive psychology, focusing on traits that promote positive functioning and flourishing. Signature strengths, which are central to an individual's identity, have been linked to subjective well-being (SWB). This study aimed to explore various hypotheses explaining the relationship between signature strengths and SWB, such as the perceived ability to use these strengths, recognition by others, and the value placed on them by one's school, workplace, and country.

Participants

The study involved 2,875 adults who participated through the VIA Institute on Character website. The final sample consisted of 2068 individuals who completed all measures. Participants were predominantly female (78.3%), with ages ranging from 18 to 82 years (M = 43.40, SD = 12.43). The majority were from the United States, with others from Australia, Canada, the United Kingdom, and various other countries. Many held a bachelor's degree or higher, with few reporting high school education or lower.

Method

The study used the Signature Strengths Survey (SSS) to assess signature strengths. Participants completed several measures, including the Authentic Happiness Inventory, Brief Job Satisfaction Measure, Center for Epidemiologic Studies Depression Scale, New General Self-Efficacy Scale, Relationship Assessment Scale, Rosenberg Self-Esteem Scale, and Satisfaction with Life Scale. Data were collected on the perceived enactment and recognition of signature strengths and their valuation by one's country and workplace or school.

Results and Discussion

Participants identified an average of 5.43 signature strengths. The study found that the identification of signature strengths alone was not a strong predictor of subjective well-being. Instead, the perceived recognition and valuing of these strengths by others, especially in workplace or school settings, were better predictors of subjective well-being. Enactment of signature strengths and recognition by others also contributed to subjective well-being, but to a lesser extent.

The study concluded that the relationship between signature strengths and subjective well-being is primarily driven by the recognition and valuing of these strengths by others in one's environment. This suggests that interventions aiming to enhance subjective well-being should focus on creating environments that recognize and value individuals' signature strengths. The findings highlight the importance of communal and relational aspects in fostering well-being.

Reference

Blanchard, T., Kerbeykian, T., & McGrath, R. E. (2019). Why are signature strengths and well-being related? Tests of multiple hypotheses. *Journal of Happiness Studies*, 21(6), 2095–2114.

Source C

Introduction

This study investigates the cultural differences in the endorsement and association of character strengths with well-being in two distinct Israeli communities: religious female youth leaders and secular (non-religious) male police investigators. The research is grounded in positive psychology and sociological theories, exploring how social contexts influence the expression and impact of character strengths. By examining these differences, the study aims to provide insights into how specific strengths contribute to well-being within different sociocultural settings.

continued

Participants

The study involved two distinct groups

1. **Religious Female Youth Leaders:** 97 participants aged 18–20, serving as volunteer leaders in the religious youth organization Bnei Akiva.

2. **Secular Male Police Investigators:** 100 participants aged 23–50, working in investigative roles for the police and the Israel Ministry of Defense.

These groups were chosen to represent different demographic characteristics, including gender, occupation, religiosity, and age.

Method

Participants completed the Virtues in Action Inventory of Strengths (VIA-IS) to assess their character strengths and the Mental Health Inventory (MHI) to measure their well-being. The VIA-IS evaluates 24 character strengths across six virtues: wisdom, courage, humanity, justice, temperance, and transcendence. The MHI focuses on psychological well-being, assessing feelings and evaluations over the past month. Data collection occurred during formal work-related gatherings, adhering to ethical guidelines.

Results and Discussion

Significant differences emerged in the endorsement of eight character strengths between the two groups. The police investigators rated six strengths (social intelligence, persistence, honesty, self-regulation, modesty, and humor) higher than the youth leaders. In contrast, the youth leaders rated gratitude and spirituality higher.

In terms of signature strengths, 46% of investigators identified honesty as a top strength, while 75% of youth leaders identified spirituality. Significant differences were also found in the bottom-ranked strengths, with spirituality and appreciation of beauty being the lowest for investigators, and modesty and self-regulation for youth leaders.

Correlation analysis revealed that most strengths were significantly associated with well-being in both groups. However, some strengths (e.g., love of learning, creativity) were not correlated with well-being in the investigator group, while others (e.g., prudence, appreciation of beauty) were not correlated in the youth leader group. The strengths most highly associated with well-being for investigators included self-regulation, honesty, zest, leadership, and teamwork. For youth leaders, the top strengths were hope, zest, social intelligence, love, and bravery.

The findings suggest that sociocultural contexts significantly influence the endorsement and impact of character strengths on well-being. The youth leaders' higher endorsement of transcendence and humanity strengths reflects their religious and ideological environment. Conversely, the investigators' higher endorsement of self-regulation and honesty aligns with the demands and values of their occupation.

The study highlights the complexity of the relationship between character strengths and well-being, suggesting that strengths highly valued in a community are more likely to enhance well-being. However, not all highly endorsed strengths (e.g., spirituality for youth leaders) significantly contribute to well-being, indicating potential effects of social comparison and relative deprivation.

These results underscore the importance of considering sociocultural factors when developing interventions to promote well-being. Tailoring interventions to match the values and characteristics of specific communities can enhance their effectiveness.

Reference

Littman-Ovadia, H., & Lavy, S. (2012). Differential ratings and associations with well-being of character strengths in two communities. *Health Sociology Review, 21*(3), 299–312.

AP® Psychology Practice Exam

SECTION 1—MULTIPLE-CHOICE QUESTIONS

75 Questions—90 Minutes

Directions: Identify the choice that best completes the statement or answers the question.

1. Researchers want to determine if deinstitutionalization has helped those who were once confined to mental health facilities. They receive permission and obtain a list of names of individuals who have gone through the deinstitutionalization process and are now working and living outside of a facility. Next, they ask employers to disclose each individual's attendance and rate their job performance compared to other employees. Even with permission, what ethical considerations must be taken into account?

   (A) The employers may treat the employees differently if they are aware of their prior experiences.

   (B) It would be impossible to track individuals to their places of employment.

   (C) This research study could only be carried out with the use of confederates.

   (D) The researchers must obtain informed assent before the study.

2. Rafael and his friend are having a staring contest. Rafael has selected to stare as long as he can at a red bulletin board just behind his friend's head. His friend has decided to stare at a blue poster on the wall behind Rafael. According to the opponent-process theory of color vision, which of the following afterimages will Rafael and his friend experience when they look at a neutral surface after one minute of the staring contest?

   (A) Rafael will see green; his friend will see yellow.

   (B) Rafael will see yellow; his friend will see blue.

   (C) Rafael will see blue; his friend will see white.

   (D) Rafael will see red; his friend will see yellow.

3. Jarrod is working hard to improve his artistic skills so that he can get into art school. He is painting a landscape and wants to make it as realistic as possible. He draws a river that gradually narrows in the distance. Which of the following monocular depth cues has Jarrod used to draw the river?

(A) Interposition

(B) Retinal disparity

(C) Relative size

(D) Linear perspective

4. Last year Nadia suffered a rupture to her eardrum and since that incident, she finds that she needs to turn the volume up significantly louder on her television in order to hear it clearly. Nadia is most clearly experiencing which of the following conditions?

(A) Inability to hear high frequency sounds

(B) Synesthesia

(C) Conduction deafness

(D) Sound localization

5. Hans recently had a seizure, and now he is experiencing loss of feeling in his limbs and difficulty moving them. Which of the following brain area has most likely been affected by this seizure?

(A) The right occipital lobe

(B) The left parietal lobe

(C) The right temporal lobe

(D) The left occipital lobe

6. Maureen is taking a yoga class. Her instructor tells her to focus on a point in the front of the room and place her foot on her knee while she raises her hands above her head in a tree pose. Which sense allows Maureen to stay balanced in this pose for the next two minutes?

(A) Olfactory

(B) Kinesthetic

(C) Gustatory

(D) Vestibular

7. Jasmine just parachuted out of an airplane for the first time. While she was terrified, she also enjoyed the experience. Now that Jasmine is safely on the ground, which of the following will bring her breathing and heart rate back to normal?

   (A) Central nervous system

   (B) Somatic nervous system

   (C) Sympathetic nervous system

   (D) Parasympathetic nervous system

8. Samantha is trying out for her school's dance team. After her performance, one of the judges is very vocal and advocates for Samantha to make the team. Even though the others are not sure this is the right decision, to keep from causing conflict they go along with the vocal judge. Which of the following types of group dynamics has occurred?

   (A) Group polarization

   (B) Social facilitation

   (C) Groupthink

   (D) Social loafing

9. Cecilia had an incredibly difficult childhood. Her mother had a severe mental illness, and her father had a substance use disorder. Cecilia finds herself forgetting large parts of her past. Cecilia has no physical problems, and she does not seem to have any desire to recover those memories. Which of the following best explains Cecelia's condition?

   (A) Schizophrenia

   (B) Dissociative amnesia

   (C) Generalized anxiety disorder

   (D) Dissociative identity disorder

10. Ellie wanted to improve her practice SAT score, so she took the same test a second time under the same conditions but scored noticeably lower the second time. Which of the following concept best explains Ellie's experience?

    (A) Bias in testing

    (B) Poor test-retest reliability

    (C) Problems with test standardization

    (D) Problems with predictive validity

11. Haiden is playing a concert when suddenly the lights go off on the stage, leaving him in pitch blackness. He is able to see a stagehand out of the corner of his eye but cannot see the audience straight ahead of him. Which of the following best explains Haiden's experience?

   (A) The blind spot in Haiden's eye is directly behind the lens causing blindness in that area of the retina.

   (B) The cones are primarily located in the optic disc.

   (C) The rods are primarily located in the peripheral vision and are active in dim light.

   (D) The ganglion cells are activated by light and therefore not working.

12. Marvyn was in an accident that severely damaged his medulla. Which of the following may occur?

   (A) Marvyn may experience difficulty with his hearing.

   (B) Marvyn may have trouble processing sensory signals from his body.

   (C) It may affect Marvyn's balance, movement, and coordination.

   (D) It may result in respiratory failure, paralysis, and even death.

13. James, a young adult with autism, has an extraordinary talent for memorizing and accurately reciting historical dates and events. Researchers wanting to identify differences in both the structure and function of his brain would likely use which of the following scanning techniques?

   (A) Electromagnetic stimulation

   (B) Lesioning

   (C) EEG

   (D) fMRI

Questions 14 through 16 refer to the following.

Dr. Kumar wants to find out if perceptual sets influence a person's perceptions. He plans on recruiting 60 participants and then randomly assigning them to groups: one that sees nothing before they are presented with the ambiguous drawing featured below, and the others who are presented with pictures of ducks prior to seeing the ambiguous stimulus. Dr. Kumar then asks each subject to identify what animal they see in the ambiguous picture. The participants who had previously seen pictures of a duck were significantly more likely to identify the ambiguous drawing as a duck.

14. What type of research is Mr. Kumar conducting?

    (A) An experiment

    (B) A correlational study

    (C) A naturalistic observation

    (D) A meta-analysis

15. How could Mr. Kumar best operationalize the dependent variable in this study?

    (A) The group that receives no pictures prior to seeing the ambiguous drawing

    (B) The percentage of participants who report seeing a duck in the ambiguous drawing

    (C) The group that saw the duck prior to seeing the ambiguous drawing

    (D) The number of pictures that are presented prior to the presentation of the ambiguous drawing

16. The graph depicts the number of people in each group who initially saw the rabbit in the ambiguous drawing versus those who saw the duck. Based on the findings of this study, what conclusion can be drawn?

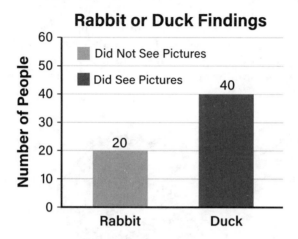

Rabbit or Duck Findings

(A) It does not matter if the participants were primed with a picture prior to seeing the ambiguous drawing.

(B) Priming with duck pictures prior to seeing the ambiguous drawing made it more likely that participants interpreted the ambiguous picture as a duck.

(C) The control group was more likely to identify the picture as a duck rather than a rabbit.

(D) The experimental group was more likely to identify the picture as a rabbit rather than a duck.

17. Catherine has taken a drug that is causing her heart to race and her pupils to dilate. Which of the following psychoactive drug categories likely includes the drug she has taken?

(A) Stimulant

(B) Hallucinogen

(C) Opioid

(D) Depressant

18. Partha went on a date that did not go well. Later, when her friends ask her about the person, she indicated her date was selfish, short-tempered, and narcissistic. However, the restaurant they went to was overcrowded and short staffed, but Partha did not consider these as reasons for her date's behavior. Partha is demonstrating which of the following?

(A) Self-serving bias

(B) Actor-observer bias

(C) Fundamental attribution error

(D) Belief perseverance

19. Daphne has had turbulent relationships with her family and many of her friends over the years. She is manipulative and often lies or exaggerates how much she needs those around her. She often makes dramatic accusations if someone challenges her comments or threatens to end a relationship. While many people are frustrated by her actions, people do not take action because Daphne often threatens to hurt herself if they leave. Which of the following best explains Daphne's behavior?

(A) Antisocial personality disorder

(B) Borderline personality disorder

(C) Avoidant personality disorder

(D) Narcissistic personality disorder

20. Syani gathers data to help target specific populations to encourage them to vote in local and national elections. Recently, she has been investigating how people in different ethnic groups have voted in presidential elections to help the candidate she works for understand where to spend time recruiting new voters. Which research design best explains what Syani has done?

(A) Experiment

(B) Cross-sectional

(C) Longitudinal

(D) Meta-analysis

21. Alex's math teacher repeatedly tells his class that he believes in them even though they have mediocre grades. Eventually, Alex's grades improve. Which of the following best explains this phenomenon?

(A) Hindsight bias

(B) Belief perseverance

(C) Self-fulfilling prophecy

(D) Stereotype threat

22. Agueda is a sleep researcher who has discovered that, if a person sleeps for eight hours, the last four hours look different from the first four. Which of the following best explains the difference between these segments of sleep?

    (A) The first four hours of sleep will contain more stage 2 sleep.

    (B) The first four hours of sleep will contain more stage 3 sleep.

    (C) The first four hours of sleep will contain more REM sleep.

    (D) (D) The first four hours of sleep will contain fewer sleep terrors

23. Rachel's grandmother is 96 years old. She is physically and mentally healthy but has recently moved into an adult retirement home. Each week the home holds a trivia contest, and Rachel's grandmother knows nearly every answer when given enough time to think about it. Which of the following represents her collective knowledge of the answers to these questions?

    (A) Fluid intelligence

    (B) Practical intelligence

    (C) Analytic intelligence

    (D) Crystallized intelligence

24. Franklin had terrible seizures as a young child. To limit the seizures, he had a hemispherectomy at age 8. Franklin is now 20 years old and has few difficulties in day-to-day life. Which of the following best explains this ability to recover?

    (A) Plasticity

    (B) Split-brain research

    (C) Long-term potentiation

    (D) Neural pruning

25. Kristen is looking to adopt a puppy, but she is not certain which one she wants. She keeps going to shelters' websites until she finds one she thinks is really cute. She returns to the website each day for two weeks and finally decides that she will adopt the cute puppy. Which of the following has likely influenced Kristen's decision?

    (A) Foot-in-the door phenomenon

    (B) Mere exposure effect

    (C) Central route to persuasion

    (D) Framing effect

26. Frederick was working in a large factory when several floors collapsed. A number of Frederick's coworkers were killed, while he made it out of the building with only minor injuries. Frederick has not been able to return to the building and often finds himself reliving the event. Which of the following best explains what Frederick is experiencing?

(A) Panic disorder

(B) Dissociative identity disorder

(C) Posttraumatic stress disorder

(D) Dissociative amnesia with fugue

27. Jorge wants to stay in good shape, but he does not enjoy exercising. His decision to work out each day (or not) is driven by which of the following?

(A) Sublimation

(B) Approach-approach conflict

(C) Approach-avoidance conflict

(D) Avoidance-avoidance conflict

28. Some researchers believe there may be ethical considerations that limit psychodynamic therapists from trying to retrieve people's repressed memories. What ethical considerations may be a limitation on this type of research?

(A) There is no way to know if the information is confidential or if other people are also aware of this information.

(B) Reliving these painful memories may be traumatic for the individuals.

(C) There are not enough samples of individuals with repressed memories to draw meaningful conclusions.

(D) It is impossible to randomly place participants to groups.

29. Wesley is a social media influencer. Every time he makes five posts on his site, he is paid $100 by the company whose product he is advertising. Wesley is being reinforced on which schedule of reinforcement?

(A) Continuous

(B) Fixed-ratio

(C) Fixed-interval

(D) Variable-ratio

30. Annabelle's mother told her that the large tree in the backyard is an elm. Annabelle is out for a walk with her father. She sees a maple tree and calls it an elm and then sees a fir tree and calls it an elm. Which of the following terms explains what occurred?

 (A) Prototype

 (B) Assimilation

 (C) Animism

 (D) Accommodation

Questions 31 through 33 refer to the following.

Mr. Newman is conducting a study with 20 tennis athletes. He believes that running three miles a day will improve their overall cardiovascular health as measured by heart rate. Mr. Newman randomly assigns half of the athletes to run three miles a day while the others continue with their normal routines. Unbeknownst to Mr. Newman, some of the participants in both groups have been running outside of the research time.

31. Which of the following best describes the additional running among the participants?

 (A) Independent variable

 (B) Third variable

 (C) Dependent variable

 (D) Confounding variable

32. In Mr. Newman's study, which of the following is the dependent variable?

 (A) Running three miles

 (B) Extra running

 (C) Heart rate

 (D) Normal exercise routine

33. The table contains the heart rates of the athletes measured in beats per minute. What is the mode of this data set?

62	84	75	68	77
88	77	81	88	82
68	68	72	73	68
71	70	68	69	85

(A) 16

(B) 77

(C) 74.7

(D) 68

34. Even though he is punished for digging holes in the backyard, Snoopy the dog continues to engage in this behavior. Which of the following best explains why this behavior continues?

(A) Instinctive drift

(B) Taste aversion

(C) Learned helplessness

(D) Extrinsic motivation

35. Priya has volunteered her time and donated much money to support a local political candidate. Recently, the candidate has been accused of embezzling money, and many people have testified that this has been occurring for many years. Despite this evidence, Priya continues to support the candidate and thinks the accusations are lies created by political opponents. Which of the following best explains Priya's views?

(A) Representativeness heuristic

(B) Belief perseverance

(C) Confirmation bias

(D) Availability heuristic

36. Daniel hit his hand with a hammer, causing the sensory neurons to fire. Which of the following is happening in Daniel's sensory neurons as they carry an action potential to his brain?

(A) Neurotransmitters return to the soma of the cell.

(B) The neurons stop receiving neurotransmitters.

(C) The neurons become active as sodium ions enter.

(D) Potassium ions exit the neurons during repolarization.

37. Norman is at an amusement park for the first time. A ride he wants to go on has two lines. One line is short, and the other is long. Norman joins the long line because he assumes the other riders have more information about how the lines work for the rides. Which of the following has guided Norman's behavior?

   (A) Informational social influence

   (B) Cognitive dissonance

   (C) Normative social influence

   (D) Deindividuation

38. Drew's tennis camp brought in a professional tennis player to help improve the students' serving. Drew watches the professional and later recreates the same form which ultimately improves his serve. Which of the following best explains Drew's behavior?

   (A) Operant conditioning

   (B) Cognitive learning

   (C) Classical conditioning

   (D) Vicarious conditioning

39. Ranata has a stressful job and finds comfort in eating food that reminds her of her childhood. She has gained quite a bit of weight over the past few years. She often binges on high-calorie foods and then purges those calories. Which of the following best describes what Ranata is experiencing?

   (A) Anorexia nervosa

   (B) Binge eating disorder

   (C) Bulimia nervosa

   (D) Dissociative disorder

40. Malin is learning to ski in a simulator. The simulator makes an irritating beeping noise until Malin is in the correct position. This feature helps Malin find the correct ski position quickly. Which of the following has helped Malin improve her skiing form?

   (A) Positive reinforcement

   (B) Negative reinforcement

   (C) Positive punishment

   (D) Negative punishment

41. Justin is experiencing a terrible fear of heights. He and other people with this condition have been working with a therapist who emphasizes a step-by-step process to get more comfortable in higher and higher places. Which of the following techniques is Justin's therapist using?

(A) Cognitive therapy

(B) Active listening

(C) Free-association

(D) Systematic desensitization

Questions 42 and 43 refer to the following.

Christina is enrolled in a very challenging engineering program. Her professor indicated that females in this program often score lower than males. Even though the females in the program are quite capable, after their professor's comments, their scores were lower than expected.

42. What best explains the lower scores of the females?

(A) Self-fulfilling prophecy

(B) Stereotype lift

(C) Social comparison

(D) Pessimistic explanatory style

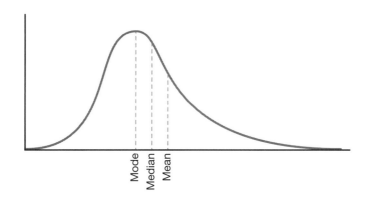

43. The graph represents the results of the females on this exam. What type of distribution is displayed in the graph above?

(A) Scatterplot

(B) Negative skew

(C) Positive skew

(D) Normal distribution

44. Valent is an architect who has been commissioned to design a new office building in a very small space. The client has requested many individualized aspects to the project, and Valent has been struggling with how to proceed. Suddenly, one evening while working late, he comes upon a solution to build up and out while still flooding the many offices with light from above. Which of the following best explains this solution?

    (A) Insight
    (B) Functional fixedness
    (C) Algorithm
    (D) Mental set

45. Reginald is doing research to determine if all the hundreds of research studies published on intelligence tests over the past decade support Charles Spearman's theory of a general intelligence (g-factor). Which of the following research techniques would be best to study this phenomenon?

    (A) Case study
    (B) Meta-analysis
    (C) Experiment
    (D) Correlational study

46. Professor Lutz is running rats through a maze. He has injected the rats that live together in one cage with acetylcholine. Rats that live together in separate enclosures were not given any injection. After running the rats through the maze multiple times, Professor Lutz determined that the injection of acetylcholine caused the rats to learn the maze more quickly. What is wrong with this conclusion?

    (A) There was no proper independent variable.
    (B) There was no random assignment to groups.
    (C) There was no dependent variable.
    (D) This is a correlational study.

47. Muzafer Sherif conducted studies on using superordinate goals to help people overcome biases toward other groups. Which of the following would help to increase confidence in these findings?

    (A) If random assignment were used in the study
    (B) If the study was conducted as a single-blind study
    (C) If different researchers were able to replicate the findings
    (D) If this was conducted as a case study

48. Ruby has made it to the Olympic trials in ice skating. She always performs well, but she is so nervous because of the significance of this event that she falls twice during her routine, essentially eliminating herself from qualifying. Which of the following best explains why Ruby performed poorly in this instance?

(A) Drive reduction theory

(B) Incentive theory

(C) Instinct theory

(D) Arousal theory

49. Ranelle is a sophomore in high school. She recently made the varsity basketball team and plays mostly with juniors and seniors. While she was surprised initially by making the team, over the course of the season she started to believe in her abilities and knows that this is where she belongs. Which of the following best explains Ranelle's belief?

(A) Reciprocal determinism

(B) Agreeableness

(C) Self-concept

(D) Self-efficacy

50. Deepak recently took an IQ test, and his score was one standard deviation above the mean. Using the diagram below, identify Deepak's percentile rank on this exam.

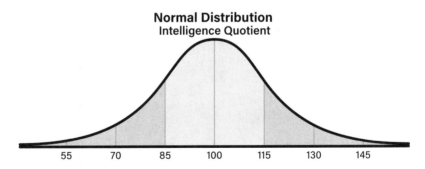

Normal Distribution
Intelligence Quotient

55   70   85   100   115   130   145

(A) 2.5

(B) 16

(C) 84

(D) 97.5

51. Aarya did well on her AP Psychology exam and also got an A in her psychology course in college. What conclusion can you draw about the AP Psychology exam?

    (A) It has a high test-retest reliability.

    (B) It has predictive validity.

    (C) It has construct validity.

    (D) It is standardized.

52. Dr. Katan is a zoologist who is investigating the behavior of chimps and wants to study conformity in the chimp population at the zoo. Which of the following types of studies would be best used to explore this phenomenon?

    (A) Naturalistic observation

    (B) Correlation

    (C) Meta-analysis

    (D) Experiment

53. Jansen has been feeling sad. He has lost his appetite and is having trouble sleeping. Which neurotransmitter is likely contributing to Jansen's experience?

    (A) Serotonin

    (B) Dopamine

    (C) Endorphins

    (D) Acetylcholine

54. Ryan has been experiencing flashbacks and is having trouble sleeping. He is seeking treatment from a therapist who uses a psychodynamic approach. Which of the following is the most likely treatment technique his therapist will use?

    (A) Counterconditioning

    (B) Dream interpretation

    (C) Active listening

    (D) A token economy

55. A marketing firm wants to determine if the foot-in-the door or door-in-the face technique is a more effective sales strategy. They randomly assign participants to use either the foot-in-the-door technique or the door-in the-face technique when making scripted phone calls. Consumers are then asked to rate, on a scale of 1–10, how likely they were to buy the product associated with the sales pitch. Which of the following conclusions can be made from this study?

(A) Whether or not there is a relationship between variables

(B) If the type of sales pitch affected the likelihood of buying

(C) If participants felt they could trust the sales person

(D) What the sales skill level is of the individual participant

56. Nadine's mother drank alcohol when she was pregnant and Nadine was born with fetal alcohol syndrome. Drinking alcohol during pregnancy is known to be which of the following?

(A) Epigenetics

(B) Predisposition

(C) Teratogen

(D) Imprinting

57. The following graph represents the prevalence of depression and positive childhood experiences. Which of the following conclusions can be made from these data?

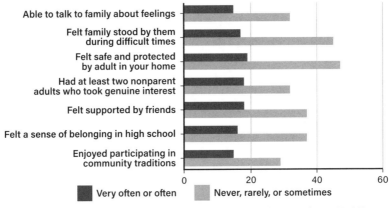

Prevalence of Depression and Poor Mental Health

Source: Pinetree Institute, ACEs & Trauma

(A) Positive childhood experiences do not have any influence on the prevalence of depressive symptoms.

(B) Depression is primarily caused by genetic influences.

(C) Positive childhood experiences can help to reduce the impact of depressive symptoms.

(D) Positive childhood experiences add to increased levels of anxiety.

58. Before conducting his research, Robert predicts that most teachers are extroverts. During the course of his research, he finds many variations in teachers' behaviors, but interprets the results to demonstrate that his hypothesis was correct. Which of the following may play a role in the conclusions Robert draws from his research?

(A) Representativeness heuristic

(B) Confirmation bias

(C) Social desirability bias

(D) Availability heuristic

59. Mateo is 4 months old. At which of the following stages in language development is Mateo likely functioning?

(A) Babbling stage

(B) One-word stage

(C) Telegraphic speech

(D) Morphemes

60. Henry had a difficult day at work. During his commute home, he just missed his train and yelled at another commuter on the train platform. According to Freud, which of the following defense mechanisms was Henry displaying?

(A) Projection

(B) Displacement

(C) Reaction formation

(D) Rationalization

61. Theodore, who is 45 years old, feels great satisfaction in the work he is doing in his career and in his family life. According to Erik Erikson, which of the following best describes Theodore's current psychosocial development?

(A) Autonomy

(B) Identity

(C) Intimacy

(D) Generativity

62. George has been taking antipsychotic medication to reduce the experiences of hallucinations and delusions. Which of the following best describes how antipsychotic medication works to inhibit these symptoms of schizophrenia?

(A) It acts as an agonist for serotonin.

(B) It acts as an antagonist for dopamine.

(C) It acts as an agonist for acetylcholine.

(D) It acts as an antagonist for glutamate.

63. Renaldo's mother is a therapist who works with adolescents who have experienced trauma. She is treating one of Renaldo's friends, but when he asks her what is happening during the sessions with his friends, she does not reveal any of the details. Which of the following best explains Renaldo's mother's response?

(A) Informed consent

(B) Right to withdraw

(C) Debriefing

(D) Confidentiality

64. Which of the following conclusions can be made from the data in the graph?

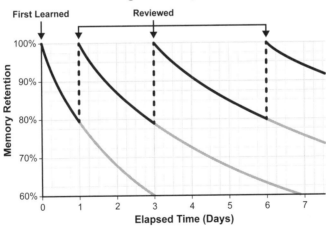

Ebbinghaus Forgetting Curve

(A) If we review material multiple times, we are less likely to forget.

(B) Despite our best efforts, we are likely to forget most of what we have learned.

(C) We remember more information when we are first exposed to it.

(D) Multiple points of review provide little increase in information retention.

65. After becoming ill from eating chicken nuggets at a fast-food restaurant in his teens, Markham never ate nuggets again. According to John Garcia, which of the following best accounts for the situation that Markham is experiencing?

(A) Instinctive drift

(B) Contingency theory

(C) Latent learning

(D) Biological preparedness

66. When Reema was 2 years old, she put her hand on the hot stove while her mother was baking a cake. Ever since, Reema feels fear anytime she is near the stove. Which of the following is the conditioned stimulus in this example?

(A) The kitchen

(B) The stove

(C) Reema's mother

(D) Fear of the stove

Questions 67 and 68 refer to the following.

Martin Seligman proposed a new policy in which people are tested for their ability to deal with traumatic situations. The American military adopted this system of testing, which will help determine who will be placed on the front lines in combat situations.

67. Which of the following best describes what this test is trying to measure?

(A) Learned helplessness

(B) Resilience

(C) Plasticity

(D) Stamina

68. If Seligman conducts one-on-one interviews to gather this data, what type of research is he conducting?

(A) Cross-sectional

(B) Qualitative

(C) Quantitative

(D) Longitudinal

69. Wendell is having suicidal thoughts and believes he is worthless and contributes nothing to society. He has recently started seeing a therapist who uses techniques from the cognitive perspective. Which of the following is this therapist most likely to use in the course of treatment?

(A) Rewarding positive behaviors

(B) Delving deep into a patient's unconscious

(C) Providing medication to help a person overcome illness

(D) Helping Wendell replace negative thoughts with productive ones

70. The following map represents extraversion scores in different parts of the United States. Which of the following conclusions best represents these findings?

Extraversion

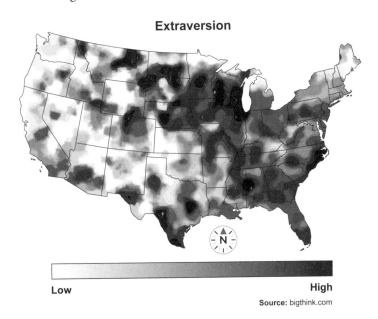

Low   High

Source: bigthink.com

(A) People in the Northeast have higher levels of extraversion than people in the Southeast.

(B) People in the upper Midwest have the highest levels of extraversion.

(C) People living in the West have higher levels of extraversion than those in the East.

(D) People along the northern and southern borders of the country have similar levels of extraversion.

71. Isaac sees his friend walking toward him down a long hallway. His friend appears to be smaller than people close to Isaac. The fact that Isaac does not perceive his friend to be tiny is likely due to which of the following?

    (A) Proximity

    (B) Relative height

    (C) Relative size

    (D) Interposition

72. When people are asked to picture a "house" in their mind, they usually picture their own home and assume that many people live in houses similar to their own. Even though there are many different types of housing around the world, this thought best aligns with which of the following?

    (A) An algorithm

    (B) A mental set

    (C) A prototype

    (D) Belief perseverance

73. Kai is 23 years old and has begun to have thoughts that there are bugs crawling on his skin and that his friends and family are trying to poison him. Kai's experiences are most consistent with which of the following psychological problems?

    (A) Schizophrenia

    (B) Antisocial personality disorder

    (C) Bipolar disorder

    (D) Dissociative identity disorder

74. Lena has gathered data on the impact of adverse childhood experiences (ACEs). She has 20 participants and has gathered the reported numbers of ACEs for each participant using the Behavioral Risk Factor Surveillance System, a standard assessment. Which of the following statistics would be used to report variability in this data set?

Adverse Childhood Experiences N=20				
0	4	1	0	2
1	0	0	1	1
2	3	1	1	2
1	2	2	3	4

(A) Mean

(B) Median

(C) Correlation coefficient

(D) Standard deviations

75. Which of the following best explains a view Lev Vygotsky held in contrast to Piaget?

(A) Biology determines when children will learn cognitive skills.

(B) Mentors and a positive environment can help children learn more quickly.

(C) Cognitive abilities will develop at the same rate in all children.

(D) Epigenetics determines how thinking unfolds in children.

2 Questions—70 Minutes

Directions: You have 70 minutes to answer BOTH of the following questions. For the Article Analysis Question, plan on 25 minutes, including 10 minutes reading time. For the Evidence-Based Question, plan on 45 minutes, including 15 minutes reading time.

QUESTION 1: ARTICLE ANALYSIS QUESTION (AAQ)

1. Your response to the question should be provided in six parts: A, B, C, D, E, and F. Write the response to each part of the question in complete sentences. Use appropriate psychological terminology in your response.

   Using the source provided, respond to all parts of the question.

   (A) Identify the research method used in the study.

   (B) State the operational definition of the dependent variable.

   (C) Describe the meaning of the differences in the means of the group in relation to the study.

   (D) Identify at least one ethical guideline applied by the researchers.

   (E) Explain the extent to which the research findings may or may not be generalizable using specific and relevant evidence from the study.

   (F) Explain how at least one of the research findings supports or refutes the researchers' hypothesis that the foot-in-the-door approach is effective even in the context of socially unacceptable behavior.

Source

Introduction

The "Foot-in-the-door" (FITD) technique is a well-documented compliance method in which a small initial request increases the likelihood of compliance with a subsequent larger request. This study explores the application of the FITD technique to deviant (socially unacceptable) behaviors, an area previously untested in the literature. Researchers believed the FITD technique would still be effective even in this new context of deviant behavior.

Participants

Two experiments were conducted involving different participant groups. In the first experiment, 74 pedestrians (33 men and 41 women) in Bordeaux, France, were approached by a male confederate posing as a sociology student. The second experiment involved 160 adults (80 men and 80 women) in a bookshop, where they were approached by a young male confederate.

Method

Both studies used a similar methodological framework but different setups. In the first experiment, the confederate asked pedestrians to participate in a public opinion poll (minor request) followed by a request to assist in stealing a road sign. The second experiment involved a request to retrieve (minor request) and then purchase a pornographic magazine under the pretense of the confederate's being underage. Control groups in both studies did not receive the initial minor request. Deception was used in both studies in which confederates were used to interact with potential participants. All participants were later debriefed and told the true intention of the study.

Results and Discussion

Analysis utilized a 2x2 model, an experimental design that involves two independent variables, each with two levels. This design results in four experimental conditions, as each level of one independent variable is paired with each level of the other independent variable. It allows researchers to examine the main effects of each independent variable and the interaction effect between the two variables. In this study the groups created were (1) stealing road sign/women, (2) stealing road sign/men, (3) buying pornographic magazine/women, and (4) buying pornographic magazine/men. In both studies, results highlighted a significant interaction effect between gender and experimental condition. All participants in both studies complied with the initial minor request. More participants (21.3%) agreed to the confederate's request in the FITD condition than in the control condition (6.3%). In the second condition, only men complied to the request to buy the pornographic magazine Notably, men showed higher compliance in the FITD condition compared to control (32.5%) than in the control (10%), while women showed the opposite effect or no significant difference.

The experiments revealed that the FITD technique might increase compliance with deviant requests among men but not women, suggesting a gender-specific response to this compliance strategy. The findings challenge existing theories on compliance, suggesting that the type of request (prosocial vs. deviant) and participant gender significantly influence the effectiveness of the FITD technique.

These results are significant in understanding gender differences in compliance behavior, especially in response to unethical requests. The study suggests that socialization and self-perception theories may explain why women are less likely to engage in socially unacceptable acts even when initially complying with a minor request.

References

Freedman, J. L., & Fraser, S. C. (1966). Compliance without pressure: The foot-in-the-door technique. *Journal of Personality and Social Psychology.* 4(2), 195–202.

Burger, J. M. (1999). The foot-in-the-door compliance procedure: A multiple process analysis and review. *Personality and Social Psychology Review*, 3(4), 303–325.

Pascual, A., & Guéguen, N. (2005). Foot-in-the-door and door-in-the-face: A comparative meta-analytic study. *Psychological Reports*, 96(1), 122–128.

2. This question has three parts: Part A, Part B, and Part C. Use the three sources provided to answer all parts of the question.

For Part B and Part C, you must cite the source that you used to answer the question. You can do this in two different ways:

Parenthetical Citation:

   For example: ". . . (Source A)"

Embedded Citation:

   For example: "According to Source A, . . ."

Write the response to each part of the question in complete sentences. Use appropriate psychological terminology.

Using the sources provided, develop and justify an argument on the extent to which models in media influence behaviors of young people through observational learning.

(A) Propose a specific and defensible claim based in psychological science that responds to the question.

(B) (i) Support your claim using at least one piece of specific and relevant evidence from one of the sources.

   (ii) Explain how the evidence from Part B (i) supports your claim using a psychological perspective, theory, concept, or research finding learned in AP Psychology.

(C) (i) Support your claim using an additional piece of specific and relevant evidence from a different source than the one that was used in Part B (i).

(D) (ii) Explain how the evidence from Part C (i) supports your claim using a different psychological perspective, theory, concept, or research finding learned in AP Psychology than the one that was used in Part B (ii).

Source A

Introduction

The study by Albert Bandura and Kay Bussey examines the influence of gender constancy and social power on sex-linked modeling. It explores how children's understanding of gender permanence and the perceived power of models affect their imitation of gender-typed behaviors. It specifically explores the competing predictions of cognitive-developmental theory and social learning theory concerning sex-linked modeling. Cognitive-developmental theory suggests that gender constancy is essential for emulating same-sex models, while social learning theory posits that sex-role development is influenced by a broad array of social influences, with modeling the method in which learning occurs. The study investigates whether children at different levels of gender constancy will emulate same-sex models and how social power impacts this emulation.

Participants

The participants in the first experiment were 36 children (18 boys and 18 girls) aged between 29 and 68 months, from Stanford University's Nursery School. In the second experiment, there were 32 children (16 boys and 16 girls) aged between 3 years and 5 years and 10 months, also from Stanford's Nursery School.

Method

The study used two independent variables: gender constancy (high vs. low) and social power of the model (high vs. low), resulting in four experimental conditions.

Participants' levels of gender constancy were assessed using a standardized interview technique. Children were classified as having high gender constancy if they understood that gender remains constant over time and situations, and low gender constancy if they did not have this understanding.

The social power of the models was manipulated by presenting them in different contexts:

- High social power: Models were introduced as teachers or authority figures.
- Low social power: Models were introduced as peers or individuals with no authoritative status.

Modeling Sessions Participants were randomly assigned to one of the four conditions:

1. High gender constancy - High social power
2. High gender constancy - Low social power
3. Low gender constancy - High social power
4. Low gender constancy - Low social power

Each child was individually exposed to two models (one male, one female) performing gender-typed activities. The activities were pre-determined and included tasks traditionally associated with either males (e.g., building with blocks) or females (e.g., playing with dolls).

Observation and Measurement After exposure to the models, the children's behavior was observed in a free-play session. Trained observers, blind to the children's gender constancy classification, recorded the frequency and type of gender-typed activities each child engaged in. The primary dependent variable was the extent of imitation of the gender-typed behaviors demonstrated by the models.

Data were analyzed to examine the main effects of gender constancy and social power, as well as their interaction on the children's imitation of gender-typed behaviors. This detailed methodology allowed the researchers to systematically investigate how cognitive understanding of gender and the perceived authority of models influence children's gender-typed behavior imitation.

continued

Results and Discussion

The analysis revealed a significant main effect of gender constancy on the imitation of sex-linked behaviors. Children with high gender constancy imitated same-sex models significantly more often than those with low gender constancy (p < .01).

There was also a significant main effect of social power on imitation. Regardless of gender constancy, children were more likely to imitate models with high social power compared to those with low social power (p < .01).

The interaction between gender constancy and social power was significant (p < .05). Specifically, the effect of social power was more pronounced in children with high gender constancy. These children showed the highest levels of imitation when exposed to high-power same-sex models.

Additionally, the results indicated gender differences in the pattern of imitation. Boys with high gender constancy showed a stronger preference for imitating male high-power models, while girls with high gender constancy were more likely to imitate female high-power models. However, in the low gender constancy group, these gender differences were less pronounced

The results support social learning theory's view that modeling is a crucial mechanism in sex-role development, operating independently of gender constancy. Children imitated same-sex models even at low levels of gender constancy, suggesting that gender constancy reflects general cognitive abilities rather than being a selective factor in sex-role development. The findings challenge cognitive-developmental theory, which suggests that gender constancy is a prerequisite for same-sex modeling.

The results also showed that social power influences modeling behavior, with boys more likely to imitate powerful female models, indicating that social power can override same-sex modeling preferences. This finding suggests that boys are more flexible in their modeling behavior when influenced by power dynamics, whereas girls' cross-sex modeling was less affected by power.

These results have practical implications for educational and parenting practices. Emphasizing the consistency of gender roles and presenting high-power, diverse role models can influence children's gender-typed behavior and expand their range of activities and interests.

Reference

Bussey, K., & Bandura, A. (1984). Influence of gender constancy and social power on sex-linked modeling. *Journal of Personality and Social Psychology, 47*(6), 1292-1302.

Source B

Introduction

This article examines how young children actively seek out and interpret gender cues in their environment. This process shapes their gender identity and stereotypes. The authors explore cognitive developmental theory and gender-schema theory, highlighting the role of children as active participants in their gender socialization.

Participants

The participants discussed in the studies reviewed in this article span various age groups, from infants to young children. The focus is on how children as young as six months begin to discern gender cues and how these perceptions evolve as they grow older. The studies reviewed include diverse samples of children from different backgrounds to understand the generalizability of the findings.

continued

Method

The article reviews multiple studies that use various methods to explore gender development. These methods include:

1. **Observation:** Researchers observe children's behavior and interactions in naturalistic settings to see how they respond to gender cues.
2. **Experiments:** Controlled experiments test children's reactions to gendered toys, activities, and roles.
3. **Surveys and Interviews:** Children are asked questions to gauge their understanding of gender roles and stereotypes.
4. **Longitudinal Studies:** These track children's gender development over time to understand how their perceptions and behaviors change.

Results and Discussion

The results from the studies reviewed highlight several key findings:

1. **Early Gender Recognition:** Infants as young as six months can distinguish between male and female voices. By nine months, they can discriminate between male and female faces. By 11 to 14 months, they can associate voices with the correct gender.
2. **Formation of Gender Stereotypes:** By age five, children have developed clear gender stereotypes. They categorize activities, toys, and roles based on gender.
3. **Impact of Gender Identity:** Once children identify with a gender, they show a preference for same-gender peers and activities. They also exhibit selective attention and memory for information relevant to their gender.
4. **Developmental Patterns:** Gender stereotyping follows a predictable pattern. Children initially learn about gender characteristics, then consolidate this knowledge rigidly between ages five and seven, and later become more flexible in their beliefs around age eight.

The discussion highlights the implications of these findings for understanding gender development:

1. **Active Construction:** Children are not passive recipients of gender norms. They actively seek out and interpret gender information from their environment.
2. **Cognitive Influences:** Cognitive developmental theory and gender-schema theory both emphasize the role of cognitive processes in gender development. Children use gender schemas to organize their experiences and guide their behavior.
3. **Developmental Changes:** Understanding gender involves a progression from rigid to more flexible beliefs. This progression is influenced by cognitive development and social experiences.
4. **Future Research:** The authors call for further research to explore the nuances of gender identity development, including how children with atypical gender experiences (e.g., those with ambiguous genitalia) navigate gender cues.

This summary provides an overview of the key elements of the article, focusing on how children actively construct their gender identities and the cognitive processes involved in this development. The reviewed studies illustrate the early emergence of gender perceptions and the developmental path of gender stereotypes. The discussion emphasizes the active role of children in their gender socialization and suggests areas for future research.

Reference

Martin, C. L., & Ruble, D. (2004). Children's search for gender cues: Cognitive perspectives on gender development. *Current Directions in Psychological Science, 13*(2), 67-70.

Source C

Introduction
This article introduces gender schema theory as a framework for understanding how individuals develop sex-typed behaviors and self-concepts. The theory states that sex typing arises from gender-based schematic processing, where individuals process information through the lens of culturally ingrained gender associations. This cognitive structure, or schema, influences how people perceive themselves and others, leading to sex-typed behavior and self-concepts.

Participants
The study described 48 male and 48 female Stanford undergraduates who were preselected based on their scores on the Bem Sex Role Inventory (BSRI), a 60-item self-reported survey to characterize people as masculine, feminine, or androgynous. The inventory was developed by the researcher in 1974.

Method
Bem's article details several studies designed to test aspects of gender schema theory: **Study 1: Gender Clustering in Free Recall**   • **Participants:** 48 male and 48 female Stanford undergraduates.   • **Procedure:** Participants were shown a sequence of 61 words, including names, animal names, verbs, and articles of clothing, with some items being gendered (e.g., masculine or feminine). Participants were asked to recall as many words as possible.   • **Measures:** The study measured the extent to which participants clustered words based on gender during recall.

Method
Study 2: Gender-Schematic Processing of the Self-Concept   • **Participants:** 48 male and 48 female Stanford undergraduates.   • **Procedure:** Participants rated 60 attributes from the BSRI as either self-descriptive (ME) or not self-descriptive (NOT ME). How long each response took was recorded to measure the speed of schema-consistent and schema-inconsistent judgments.   • **Measures:** The study examined how quickly participants responded to gender-consistent versus gender-inconsistent attributes.

continued

Results and Discussion

Study 1: Gender Clustering in Free Recall

- **Findings:** Sex-typed participants exhibited significantly more gender clustering in their recall than cross-sex-typed, androgynous, or undifferentiated participants. This finding supports the idea that sex-typed individuals are more likely to organize information based on gender.

Study 2: Gender-Schematic Processing of the Self-Concept

- **Findings:** Sex-typed participants responded more quickly to schema-consistent judgments and more slowly to schema-inconsistent judgments compared to other groups. This pattern indicates that sex-typed individuals process self-relevant information through a gender schema.

The article also references additional studies that support gender schema theory. For example, children with highly stereotyped views of sex-appropriate behavior were more likely to remember gender-consistent information. College students who were sex-typed showed greater differentiation between male and female stimuli. The results of the studies supported the central tenets of gender schema theory, demonstrating that sex-typed individuals process information, including self-relevant information, in terms of gender schemas. This gender-based schematic processing manifests in various ways:

- **Clustering in Recall:** Sex-typed individuals showed a greater tendency to cluster words based on gender, indicating that they organize information according to gender schemas.
- **Self-Concept Processing:** Sex-typed individuals were faster at making schema-consistent judgments (e.g., a sex-congruent attribute is self-descriptive) and slower at making schema-inconsistent judgments (e.g., a sex-congruent attribute is not self-descriptive).

Bem's discussion highlights the societal implications of gender schema theory. The theory suggests that societal emphasis on gender differences leads to sex typing and reinforces gender stereotypes. Bem argues that this cognitive processing is influenced by the pervasive social cues that stress the importance of gender differences. The studies reviewed demonstrate the pervasive impact of gender schemas on information processing and self-perception.

Reference

Bem, S. L. (1981). Gender schema theory: A cognitive account of sex typing. *Psychological Review, 88*(4), 354-364.

Works Cited

Introduction

xxxiii: Fisher, M., Goddu, M. K., Keil, F. C. (2015). Searching for explanations: How the Internet inflates estimates of internal knowledge. *Journal of Experimental Psychology, 144*(3), 674–687.

xxviii: Gilovich, T., Medvec, V. H., & Savitsky, K. (2000). The spotlight effect in soci\\al judgment: An egocentric bias in estimates of the salience of one's own actions and appearance. *Journal of Personality and Social Psychology, 78*(2), 211–222. DOI: 10.1037//0022-3514.78.2.211

xxxix: Crosby, J. R., King, M., & Savitsky, K. (2014). The minority spotlight effect. *Social Psychological and Personality Science, 5*(7), 743–750. DOI: 10.1177/1948550614527625

xl: Brown, M. A., & Stopa, L. (2007). The spotlight effect and the illusion of transparency in social anxiety. *Journal of Anxiety Disorders, 21*(6), 804–819. DOI: 10.1016/j.janxdis.2006.11.006

xlvi: Gurung, R. A. R., & Dunlosky, J. (2023). *Study like a champ: The psychology-based guide to "Grade A" study habits.* American Psychological Association.

Practice 1: Concept Application

25: Zimbardo, P., Haney, C., Banks, C. W., & Jaffe, D. (1971). Stanford prison experiment. https://web.stanford.edu/dept/spec_coll/uarch/exhibits/Narration.pdf

Practice 2: Research Methods and Design

35: Ahmad, S. F., Han, H., Alam, M. M., et al. (2023). Impact of artificial intelligence on human loss in decision making, laziness and safety in education. *Humanities and Social Sciences Communications, 10*(1), 311. https://doi.org/10.1057/s41599-023-01787-8

36: Echabe, A. E., & Castro, J. L. G. (1999). Group discussion and changes in attitudes and representations. *The Journal of Social Psychology, 139*(1), 29–43.

Practice 3: Data Interpretation

76: Brooks, A. W. (2014). Get excited: Reappraising pre-performance anxiety as excitement. *Journal of Experimental Psychology: General American Psychological Association, 143*(3), 1144–1158. 0096-3445/14/$12.00 DOI: 10.1037/a0035325

Practice 4: Argumentation

103: Jacob, C., Guéguen, N., & Boulbry, G. (2010). Effects of songs with prosocial lyrics on tipping behavior in a restaurant. *International Journal of Hospitality Management, 29*(4), 761–763. https://doi.org/10.1016/j.ijhm.2010.02.004

103: Kniffin, K. M., Yan, J., Wansink, B., & Schulze, W. D. (2017, March). The sound of cooperation: Musical influences on cooperative behavior. *Journal of Organizational Behavavior, 38*(3), 372–390. doi: 10.1002/job.2128. Epub 2016 Aug 9. PMID: 28344386; PMCID: PMC5347889

103: Ganser, J., & Huda, F. (2010). Music's effect on mood and helping behavior. *UW-L Journal of Undergraduate Research XIII.*

107: Collins, J. E. (2024). Education policy reform for the Hip-Hop era. *Kappan, 105*(7), 60–61.

109: Clark, S. S., & Giacomantonio, S. G. (2015). Toward predicting prosocial behavior: Music preference and empathy differences between late adolescents and adults. *Empirical Musicology Review, 10*(1), 50.

110: Jacob, C., Guéguen, N., & Boulbry, G. (2010). Effects of songs with prosocial lyrics on tipping behavior in a restaurant. *International Journal of Hospitality Management, 29*(3), 761–763. https://doi.org/10.1016/j.ijhm.2010.02.004

111: Ruth, N. (2016). "Heal the World": A field experiment on the effects of music with prosocial lyrics on prosocial behavior. *Psychology of Music, 45*(2), 298–304. DOI:10.1177/0305735616652226

112: Hong, M., Liang, D., & Lu, T. (2023). "Fill the world with love": Songs with prosocial lyrics enhance online charitable donations among Chinese adults. *Behavioral Sciences, 13*(9), 739. https://doi.org/10.3390/bs13090739

115: Sanfilippo, K. R. M., Spiro, N., Molina-Solana, M., & Lamont, A. (2020, February 6). Do the shuffle: Exploring reasons for music listening through shuffled play. *PLOS ONE, 15*(2): e0228457. doi: 10.1371/journal.pone.0228457. PMID: 32027672; PMCID: PMC7004375

115: Alexander, S. (1999, Fall). The gender role paradox in youth culture: An analysis of women in music videos. *Michigan Sociological Review, 13*, 46–64.

115: Andsager, J., & Roe, K. (1999). Country music video in country's year of the woman. *Journal of Communication, 49*(1), 69–82.

Unit 1: Biological Bases of Behavior

Topic 1.1

121: Thomas, A., Chess, S., Lerner, R., & Lerner, J. (1998). New York longitudinal study, 1956–1988. https://doi.org/10.7910/DVN/CIGGJY, Harvard Dataverse, V2.

122: Curtis, K. S., Davis, L. M., Johnson, A. L., Therrien, K. L., & Contreras, R. J. (2004). Sex differences in behavioral taste responses to and ingestion of sucrose and NaCl solutions by rats. *Physiology & Behavior, 80*(5), 657–64. doi: 10.1016/j.physbeh.2003.11.007. PMID: 14984799

122: Buss, D. M., & Schmitt, D. P. (1993, April). Sexual strategies theory: An evolutionary perspective on human mating. *Psychological Review, 100*(2), 204–232. https://doi.org/10.1037/0033-295X.100.2.204

129: Segal, N. L., & Hur, Y.-M. (2022, August). Personality traits, mental abilities, and other individual differences: Monozygotic female twins raised apart in South Korea and the United States. *Personality and Individual Differences, 194*(5), 111643.

135: Jang, K. L., Livesley, W. J., & Vernon, P. A. (1996, September). Heritability of the big five personality dimensions and their facets: A twin study. *Journal of Personality, 64*(3), 577–591.

Topic 1.2

140: Matsumura, K., Miura, K., Takata, Y., Kurokawa, H., Kajiyama, M., Abe, I., & Fujishima, M. (1996, November). Changes in blood pressure and heart rate variability during dental surgery. *American Journal of Hypertension, 11*(11 Pt 1), 1376–80.

163: Alexander, B. K., Coambs, R. B. & Hadaway, P. F. (1978). The effect of housing and gender on morphine self-administration in rats. *Psychopharmacology, 58,* 175–179. https://doi.org/10.1007/BF00426903 (one of a number)

164: SAMHSA, Center for Behavioral Health Statistics and Quality. National Surveys on Drug Use and Health (NSDUHs), 2002, 2005, 2006 to 2010 (Revised March 2012), and 2011–2014.

Topic 1.5

202: Jeon, M., Dimitriou, D., & Halstead, E. J. (2021, February 19). A systematic review on cross-cultural comparative studies of sleep in young populations: The roles of cultural factors. *International Journal of Environmental Research and Public Health, 18*(4), 2005. doi: 10.3390/ijerph18042005. PMID: 33669583; PMCID: PMC7922907

Topic 1.6

225: Lim, S. X. L., Höchenberger, R., Busch, N., Bergmann, M., & Ohla, K. (2022, March). Associations between taste and smell sensitivity, preference and quality of life in healthy aging—The NutriAct Family Study Examinations (NFSE) cohort. *Nutrients, 14*(6), 1141. 10.3390/nu14061141.

Unit 1 Review

240: Rosenzweig, M. R., Bennett, E. L., & Diamond, M. C. (1962). Effects of environmental complexity and training on brain chemistry and anatomy: A replication and extension. *Journal of Comparative and Physiological Psychology, 55*(4), 429–437.

242: Bouchard Jr, T. J., Lykken, D. T., McGue, M., Segal, N. L., & Tellegen, A. (1990). Sources of human psychological differences: The Minnesota study of twins reared apart. *Science, 250*(4978), 223–228.

Unit 2: Cognition

Topic 2.1

252: Simons, D. J., & Chabris, C. F. (1999). Gorillas in our midst: Sustained inattentional blindness for dynamic events. *Perception, 28*(9), 1059–1074.

258: Ahluwalia, A. (1978). An intra-cultural investigation of susceptibility to "perspective" and "non-perspective" spatial illusions. *British Journal of Psychology, 69*(2), 233–241.

258: Segall, M. H., Campbell, D. T., & Herskovits, M. J. (1966). *The influence of culture on visual perception.* Bobbs-Merrill.

261: Palmer, S. E. (1975) The effects of contextual scenes on the identification of objects. *Memory & Cognition, 3*(5), 519–526.

Topic 2.7

320: Bartlett, F. C. (1932). *Remembering: A study in experimental and social psychology.* Cambridge University Press.

Topic 2.8

343: Popa, C., Ciobanu, A. M, & Ionescu, B. (2017). Ethical dilemmas of using intelligence tests in practice and research. *Cercetări filosofico-psihologice, 9*(2), 67–69.

349: Brewer, W. F., & Treyens, J. C. (1981). Role of schemata in memory for places. *Cognitive Psychology, 13*(2), 207–230. https://doi.org/10.1016/0010-0285(81)90008-6

Unit 2 Review

355: Jenkins, R., Dowsett, A. J., & Burton, A. M. (2018). How many faces do people know? *Dryad.* https://doi.org/10.5061/dryad.7f25j43

357: Bartlett, F. C. (1932). *Remembering: A study in experimental and social psychology.* Cambridge University Press.

358: Anderson, R. C., & Pichert, J. W. (1978). Recall of previously unrecallable information following a shift in perspective. *Journal of Verbal Learning and Verbal Behavior, 17*(1), 1–12.

Unit 3: Development and Learning

Topic 3.3

390: Tenenbaum, H. R., & Leaper, C. (2002). Are parents' gender schemas related to their children's gender-related cognitions? A meta-analysis. *Developmental Psychology, 38*(4), 615–630. https://doi.org/10.1037/0012-1649.38.4.615

Topic 3.4

399: Cole, M., Frankel, F., & Sharp, D. W. (1971). The development of free recall learning in children. *Developmental Psychology, 4*(2), 109–123.

403: Shipstead, Z., Harrison, T. L., & Engle, R.W. (2016). Working memory capacity and fluid intelligence: maintenance and disengagement. *Perspectives on Psychological Science, 11*(6) 771–799. DOI: 10.1177/1745691616650647

Topic 3.6

429: Hazan, C., & Shaver, P. (1987). Romantic love conceptualized as an attachment process. *Journal of Personality and Social Psychology, 52*(3), 511–524. https://doi.org/10.1037/0022-3514.52.3.511

Topic 3.9

478: Clark, K. B. (1947). Racial identification and preference in Negro children, in T. M. Newcomb & E. L. Hartley (eds.) *Readings in Social Psychology.* Henry Holt.

481: Anderson, C. A., & Dill, K. E. (2000). Video games and aggressive thoughts, feelings, and behavior in the laboratory and in life. *Journal of Personality and Social Psychology, 78*(4), 772–790. DOI: 10.1037//O022-3514.78.4.772

Unit 3 Review

491: Hazan, C., & Shaver, P. (1987). Romantic love conceptualized as an attachment process. *Journal of Personality and Social Psychology, 52*(3), 511–524. https://doi.org/10.1037/0022-3514.52.3.511

494: Bandura, A., Ross, D., & Ross, S. A. (1961). Transmission of aggression through imitation of aggressive models. *The Journal of Abnormal and Social Psychology, 63*(3), 575–582.

495: Charlton, T., Gunter, B., and Hannan, A. (2002). *Broadcast television effects in a remote community.* Lawrence Erlbaum Associates.

496: Becker, A., et al. (2002, June). Eating behaviors and attitudes following prolonged television exposure among ethnic Fijian adolescent girls. *British Journal of Psychiatry, 180,* 509–514.

Unit 4: Social Psychology and Personality

Topic 4.2

513: Cox, W. T. L., Xie, X., & Devine, P. G. (2022, September). Untested assumptions perpetuate stereotyping: Learning in the absence of evidence. *Journal of Experimental Social Psychology, 102,* 104380. doi: 10.1016/j.jesp.2022.104380. Epub 2022 Jun 25. PMID: 35912164; PMCID: PMC9337700

515: Quillian, L., Pager, Hexel, D., & Midtbøen, A. H. (2017). Meta-analysis of field experiments shows no change in racial discrimination in hiring over time. *Proceedings of the National Academy of Sciences, 114*(41), 10870–10875, doi:10.1073/pnas.1706255114

Topic 4.3

531: Hovland, C. I., & Weiss, W. (1951). The influence of source credibility on communication effectiveness. *Public Opinion Quarterly, 15*(4), 635–660.

536: Bond, R., & Smith, P. B. (1996). Culture and conformity: A meta-analysis of studies using Asch's (1952b, 1956) line judgment task. *Psychological Bulletin, 119*(1), 111–137. DOI:10.1037/0033-2909.119.1.111Corpus ID: 17823166

543: Haslam, S. A., & Reicher, S. (2007, June). Beyond the banality of evil: Three dynamics of an interactionist social psychology of tyranny. *Personality and Social Psychology Bulletin, 33*(5), 615. (Originally published online April 17, 2007) DOI:10.1177/0146167206298570

Topic 4.5

576: Schmitt, D. P., Allik, J., McCrae, R. R., & Benet-Martinez, V. (2007). The geographic distribution of big five personality traits: Patterns and profiles of human self-description across 56 nations. *Journal of Cross-Cultural Psychology, 38*(2), 173–212.

Topic 4.7

597: Wollmer, M. A., de Boer, C., Kalak, N., Beck, J., Götz, T., Schmidt, T., Hodzic, M., Bayer, U., Kollmann, T., Kollewe, K., Sönmez, D., Duntsch, K., Haug, M. D., Schedlowski, M., Hatzinger, M., Dressler, D., Brand, S., Holsboer-Trachsler, E., & Kruger, T. H. (2012, May). Facing depression with botulinum toxin: a randomized controlled trial. *Journal of Psychiatric Research, 46*(5), 574–581. doi: 10.1016/j.jpsychires.2012.01.027. Epub 2012 Feb 24. PMID: 22364892

Unit 4 Review

610: Schachter, S., & Singer, J. (1962). Cognitive, social and physiological determinants of emotional state. *Psychological Review, 69*(5), 379–399.

612: Harris, M. A., Brett, C. E., Johnson, W., & Deary, I. J. (2016, December). Personality stability from age 14 to age 77 years. *Psychology and Aging, 31*(8), 862–874. doi: 10.1037/pag0000133

613: Wright, A. J., & Jackson, J. J. (2023). Do changes in personality traits predict life outcomes? *Journal of Personality and Social Psychology, 125*(6), 1495–1518. https://doi.org/10.1037/pspp0000472

614: Donnellan, M. B., & Lucas, R. E. (2008, September). Age differences in the big five across the life span: Evidence from two national samples. *Psychology and Aging, 23*(3), 558–566. DOI: 10.1037/a0012897

Unit 5: Mental and Physical Health

Topic 5.1

630: Felitti, V. J. (2002, Winter). The relation between adverse childhood experiences and adult health: Turning gold into lead. *The Permanente Journal, 6*(1), 44–47.

Topic 5.3

643: Sims, R., Michaleff, Z. A., Glasziou, P., & Thomas, R. (2021, December 22). Consequences of a diagnostic label: A systematic scoping review and thematic framework. *Frontiers in Public Health, 9,* 725877. doi: 10.3389/fpubh.2021.725877. PMID: 35004561; PMCID: PMC8727520

Topic 5.4

661: Gottesman, I. (1991). A meta-analysis of twin studies. In *Schizophrenia genesis: The origins of madness.* W. H. Freeman.

Topic 5.5

705: Kodal, A., et al. (2018, January). Long-term effectiveness of cognitive behavioral therapy for youth with anxiety disorders. *Journal of Anxiety Disorders. 53,* 58–67.

Unit 5 Review

721: McDermut, W., Miller, I. W., & Brown, R. A. (2001). The efficacy of group psychotherapy for depression: A review of the empirical research. *Clinical Psychology: Science and Practice, 8*(1), 98–116.

723: Mongrain, M., & Anselmo-Matthews, T. (2012). Do positive psychology exercises work? A replication of Seligman et al. (2005). *Journal of Clinical Psychology, 68*(4), 382–389. https://doi.org/10.1002/jclp.21839

724: Blanchard, T., Kerbeykian, T., & McGrath, R. E. (2019). Why are signature strengths and well-being related? Tests of multiple hypotheses. *Journal of Happiness Studies, 21*(6), 2095–2114.

725: Littman-Ovadia, H., & Lavy, S. (2012). Differential ratings and associations with well-being of character strengths in two communities. *Health Sociology Review, 21*(3), 299–312.

Image Credits

page 4: Thinkstock; page 8: Thinkstock; page 9: Thinkstock, Contentra; page 10: Biodiversity Heritage Library; page 16: Getty Images; page 18: Getty Images; page 25: Philip Zimbardo, CC by SA 4.0 International; page 28: Getty Images; page 35: U.S. Dept. of Justice; page 59: A. Bacall/Cartoonstock; page 63: Getty Images; page 69: CC by-SA 4.0 International: page 79: Getty Images; page 99: Getty Images; page 101: Getty Images, National Archives; page 107: Getty Images; page 113: B. F. Skinner CC by 3.0 Unported, Carl Rogers CC by SA 2.5; page 114: Carol Gilligan CC by SA 3.0, George I. Sanchez CC by SA 4.0 International, Courtesy of Derald Wing Sue; page 115: Getty Images, page 116: Getty Images; page 120: Alamy; page 117: Thinkstock; page 149: Thinkstock; page 157: Thinkstock; page 163: Thinkstock; page 181: Chris Hope, iStock; page 182: Courtesy of Mike Hamilton; page 183: © 2011 Ovaysikia, Tahir, Chan and DeSouza; Getty Images; page 184: US Dept. of Health and Human Services; page 200: Thinkstock; page 204: Thinkstock; page 221: Thinkstock; page 223: Thinkstock; page 248: Thinkstock; page 252: David Simons; page 253: Science Source/Getty; page 259: Thinkstock; page 261: Getty Images; page 267: Thinkstock; page 273: Getty Images; page 281: Thinkstock; page 280: Thinkstock; page 281: Getty Images; page 301: Getty Images; page 311: Getty Images; page 331: Thinkstock; page 350: Getty Images; page 372: Getty Images; page 375: CC by-SA 4.0; page 345: Getty Images; page 387: Thinkstock; page 395: Thinkstock; page 470, Science Source; page 420: Thinkstock; page 423: CC by SA 4.0 International; page 425: Getty Images; page 426: Getty Images; page 428: Thinkstock; page 429: Thinkstock; page 431: Thinkstock; page 402: Thinkstock; page 437: Getty Images; page 444: Thinkstock; page 459: Getty Images; page 460; Thinkstock; page 468: Thinkstock; page 478: Photograph by Gordon Parks, Courtesy of The Gordon Parks Foundation/Library of Congress; page 479: The Mentality of Apes by Wolfgang Köhler; page 241; page 485: Getty Images; page 502: Getty Images; page 534: Milgram Collection, Archives of the History of American Psychology, The Drs. Nicholas and Dorothy Cummings Center for the History of Psychology, The University of Akron, (right) Stanley Milgram papers, 1927-1993 (inclusive). Manuscripts & Archives, Yale University; page 539: Library of Congress; page 542: Philip G. Zimbardo, Inc.; page 543: Thinkstock; page 550: Getty Images; page 557: Thinkstock; page 561: Rorschach /Wikimedia Commons; page 562: Thinkstock; page 586: Thinkstock; page 597: Thinkstock; page 617: Getty Images; page 620: Getty Images; page 625: Getty Images; page 640: Getty Images; page 658: Getty Images; page 674: Thinkstock; page 681

Index

(f) = Figure

Assertive Community Treatment, 691

assimilation, 264

Assisted Outpatient Treatment (AOT), 691

associative learning, 442, 443, 457, 645

ataque de nervios (ADN)/ "attack of nerves", 666–667

Atkinson, Richard, 285

Atkinson and Shiffrin model, 286

attachment theory, 421

attention, 250–252, 477

attention deficit/ hyperactivity disorder (ADHD), 159, 657, 658, 689
children with, 700
diagnosis of, 657
stimulants, use in treatment, 709

attentional variables, 551

attitude formation, 511–524

attribution, 499
theory, 499–502

audition, 217

auditory sensory acuity, 381

auditory sensory system, 217–222
amplitude, 217
audition, 217
auditory cortex, 219
cochlea, 219
conduction, 218
echolocation, 218
frequency theory, 220
hair cells, 219
hearing, problems in, 221
hearing, theories of, 219–220
infrasound, 218
pitch, 217
place theory, 219–220
sound, theories of, 219–220
sound frequency, 217–218
sound localization, 220–221

sound waves, 217, 218
halamus (sensory relay station), 219
ultrasound range, 218
volley theory of pitch perception, 220

argumentation
established claim, 102
gathering scientifically derived evidence, 102–103
norm, 102
nuance, 102
plan, 102
policy, 102
reasoning, 102–103
reasoning that modifies a claim, 106
reasoning that refutes claims, 105
reasoning that supports claims, 104
reasoning that supports, refutes, or modifies, 103
scientifically derived evidence, 102

authoritarian parents, 419–420

authority figure, 533

autism
behaviors associated with, 657

autism spectrum disorder (ASD), 657
nonverbal communication, 657
social and emotional interaction, 657
social relationships, 657

autobiographical memory, 304

autonomic nervous system (ANS), 137–138

autopsy, 185

availability heuristic, 267, 268, 272, 546

aversion therapy, 699–700

avoidance-avoidance conflict, 584

avoidant attachment styles, 429

avoidant personality disorder, 682

awfulizing, 702

B

balance
vestibular sense, 228

Bandura, Albert, 121, 389, 475–477, 482–483, 493, 494, 570
Bobo Doll study, 493
model of reciprocal determinism, 570

bar chart (or bar graph), 73

barriers, 622

Beck's cognitive triad, 701

behavior, biological bases of
heredity and environment, interaction of, 119–135
nature and nurture, debate about, 117

behavior therapies, assessment of, 700–701
children with ADHD, 700
nervous system, 117

behavioral approach, 5–6
observable behavior, 5

behavioral perspective, 1, 645–646

behavioral psychology/ behaviorism, 698

behaviorism, 5, 458
stimulus and response learning, 5

behaviorists, 12, 442

belief perseverance, 520

benefits, 622

benzodiazepines, 160

bilateral anterior cingulotomy, 710

bimodal data sets, 83

bimodal distribution, 82

biofeedback, 700

biological approach, 7

biological perspective,
649–650
  antidepressant
    medications, 650
  major depressive disorder
    (MDD), 649
biological preparedness,
  449–450
biologically derived
  interventions, 707–711
biomedical approach,
  assessment of, 711
  psychoactive
    medications, 711
biomedical therapy, 707
biopsychosocial model,
  8, 650–651
  disease-causing behavior
    (biological), 8
bipolar disorders, 663–665
  mania, 663
  possible causes, 665
  severity of depression, 664
bipolar I disorder, 663, 664
bipolar II disorder, 664
blind spot, 214
Bobo Doll experiments,
  476–477
  social cognitive theory,
    477
Bobo Doll test, 478–479
body dysmorphia, 676
body senses, 226–228
  gate-control theory of
    pain, 227
  pain sensory system, 227
  phantom limb pain, 227
  touch sensory system, 226
borderline personality
  disorder, 681
boredom susceptibility, 583
bottom-up processing,
  245–246
brain, methods for
  understanding, 180–181
  case studies, 180–181
brain damage and vision
  disorders, 216

blindsight, 216
face blindness, 216
prosopagnosia, 216
brain plasticity/
  neuroplasticity, 176, 180
  hemispherectomy, 180
brain processing, 187–188
  adrenaline, 188
  amygdala, 188
  basal ganglia, 187
  Broca's area, 187
  cerebellum, 187
  cerebral cortex, 187, 188
  frontal cortex, 187, 188
  frontal lobe, 187, 188
  hippocampus, 187, 188
  lateral hypothalamus, 188
  left hemisphere, 187
  motor cortex, 187
  occipital lobe, 187
  parasympathetic nervous
    system, 188
  parietal lobe, 187
  RAS, 188
  somatosensory cortex, 187
  sympathetic nervous
    system, 188
  temporal lobes, 187
  thalamus, 187
  Wernicke's area, 187
brain scanning, 181–185
  computerized axial
    tomography (CT or
    CAT scan), 182
  damaging or stimulating
    parts, 184
  deep brain stimulation,
    185
  electroencephalogram
    (EEG), 182, 182(f)
  electroencephalography,
    182
  electromyography (EMG),
    184
  functional magnetic
    resonance imaging
    (fMRI), 183
  lesioning, 185
  magnetic resonance
    imaging (MRI),
    182–183

positron emission
  tomography (PET scan),
  184
prefrontal cortex, 184
prefrontal lobotomy,
  184–185
X-rays, 181–182
brain stem
  cross-lateral, 169
  medulla oblongata/
    medulla, 169
  midbrain, 169
brain waves, 195
  alpha waves, 195
  beta waves, 195
  electroencephalography
    (EEG). 195
  encephalogram, 195
brain, structures and
  functions of, 168–172
  brain stem, 169
  cerebellum, 170
  limbic system, 170–172
  procedural learning, 170
  reticular formation,
    169–170
  structure, 168
brain's reward center, 170
broaden-and-build theory of
  emotion, 595–596
Broca, Paul, 181
Broca's area, 181, 187, 410
Bronfenbrenner, Urie, 417
  Ecological Systems Theory,
    419(f)
bulimia nervosa/bulimia,
  676–677
  binge-purge episode with
    dieting, 677
  binging, 676–677
  signs of, 677
  treatment, 677
burnout, 549, 624
bystander effect, 551

C

caffeine, 158
Calkins, Mary Whiton, 4,
  114

convenience sampling,
40–41, 42

convergent thinking, 274

coping, 625

coping with stress, 625–626
varieties of, 626

cornea, 212

correlation, 30

correlation coefficient, 94, 95

correlational method of
research, 53

correlational studies,
51, 53–55
directional problem, 55
first variable, 34
positive correlation, 34
second variable, 34
third variable activity, 55

counterconditioning, 448

creativity, 273–275
expertise, 273
high intelligence, 273
intrinsic motivation, 273

criterion validity, 335

critical thinking, 263

cross-modal recruitment,
222

cross-sectional design, 364
cohort effects, 364
Flynn effect, 364
intelligence levels across
different age groups, 364

crystallized intelligence,
401–402

Csikszentmihalyi, Mihaly,
274

cultural bias, 48

cultural differences, 327

cultural display rules, 600

cultural expectations, 18–19

cultural explanations, 648

cultural factors, 649

cultural idioms, 648

cultural influence, 130
family environment, 130
individualism-
collectivism, 130

intelligence, 130

cultural norms, 17–18,
635–636, 649, 678
cultural values, 635
VIA virtues, 635

cultural relativism, 648–649

cultural syndromes, 648

cyberbullying, 427

D

Darwin, Charles, 3, 7–8, 113,
121, 192, 328
theory of evolution, 3

data, 71
chart, 71
diagram, 71
figure, 71
graph, 71
line graph, 72
line graph, value of, 73
sets, 81
table, 71
x-axis, 73
y-axes, 73

debriefing, 65, 536
participants, 67–68

deception, 65, 67

decision-making, 269–271
mental set, 269–270

deductive reasoning, 13–14

deep brain stimulation, 185,
710

deep processing, 288

defense mechanisms, role of,
558–559
denial, 558
displacement, 558
projection, 558
rationalization, 559
reaction-formation, 559
regression, 558
repression, 558
sublimation, 559

defensible claim, 99–101,
201, 222, 343, 470, 506,
543, 544, 551, 633, 634,
643, 661, 705

defensive forgetting, 319

deindividuation, 541–542
higher aggression toward a
victim, 542
Stanford prison
experiment, 542

deinstitutionalization, 689

delusions/persistence of false
beliefs, 659

demyelination, 152

dependent personality
disorder, 682

dependent variable, 29, 32

depressants, 159
alcohol, 159–160

depressive disorders,
661–663
cognitive factors, 662
possible causes, 662–663
social and cultural
factors, 662

developmental psychology,
361–367
enduring themes, 361

Dexedrine®, 709

*Diagnostic and Statistical
Manual of Mental Disorders*,
24, 644–645
Cultural Formulation
Appendix, 644–645
Cultural Formulation
Interview (CFI), 644
DSM-5, 644–645

dialectical behavior therapy
(DBT), 703–704

diathesis-stress model,
651–652
diathesis, 651
mental illness, 652
protective factors, 651
stress, 651

dichromatism, 215

diffusion of responsibility,
540

directionality problem, 51

discontinuous
cognitive development,
393–399
development, 361

emotional responses, 667

emotion-focused coping, 626

empathy, 697

encoding failure, 318

encounter group dynamics, 548

endocrine system and behavior, 155–156
adrenaline, 156
ghrelin, 156
hypothalamus, 155
leptin, 155
melatonin, 156
oxytocin, 156
pituitary gland, 155

endogenous opioid peptides, 161

endorphins, 154

environmental determinism, 441, 458

epilepsy, 178

epileptic seizures, 178

episodic memories, 279

Erikson's stage theory of psychosocial development, 430–434
adolescent and adult, 432–433
autonomy and shame and doubt, 431
childhood stages, 430–432
despair, 433
Freud's psychosexual approach, 430
generativity, 433
identity and role confusion, 432
industry (competence) and inferiority, 431–432
initiative and guilt, 431
integrity, 433
intimacy and isolation, 432
stagnation, 433
trust and mistrust, 430–431

estrogen, 378

ethnocentrism, 518

eustress, 621

evidence-based intervention, 690

evolutionary approach, 7–8
Charles Darwin, thoughts on natural selection, 7
physical adaptations of finches, 8

evolutionary perspective, 647

evolutionary psychologists, 121–122, 123

evolutionary psychology, 121–124
adaptation, 121
adaptive traits, 121
criticisms of, 123–124
discriminatory practices, 124
eugenics, 124
hindsight explanation, 123
natural selection, 121
overt eugenics movement, 124

excitatory neurotransmitters, 150

executive functions, 264–265

expectations, 17

experience-seeking, 583

experimental group (s), 32–33, 44

experimental methodology, 29, 32
design elements in, 37
laboratory experimentation, 37

experimental testing, 52

experimenter bias, 44

explanatory style, 500

explicit memory, 279
effortful processing, 279

exposure therapies, 698–699

external locus of control, 504

external validity, 42

extinction, 447

extrinsic motivation, 581

eye, structure of, 212–214
accommodation, 212
bipolar cells, 213
blind spot, 214

cones, 213
cornea, 212
dark adaptation, 213
fovea, 213
lens, 212
optic chiasm, 214
optic disc, 213
optic nerves, 214
pupil, 212
retina, 212
rods, 213

F

face validity, 335

Facial Action Coding System (FACS), 596

facial expressions, 596–597

facial feedback, 594–595
"duck face" pose, 594–595

facial-feedback hypothesis, 594

false consensus effect, 545–546
cognitive dissonance, 546
homogeneity or similarity within personal networks, 546

falsifiable hypotheses, 36–38

families, formation of, 429–430
adult relationships, 429
childhood attachment styles, 429
individuals with anxious attachment styles, 429

family studies, 126–127
Alzheimer's disease, 127
dementia, 127
intelligence and cognitive abilities, 126
personality traits, 126–127
schizophrenia and psychiatric disorders, 126
substance abuse and addiction, 127

farsightedness, 212

feeding and eating disorders, 675–678

behavioral causes, 678
biological causes, 677
cognitive factors, 678
genetics, 677–678
possible causes, 677–678
social and cultural
influences, 678
female psychologists, 2
fight-flight-or-freeze
response, 619, 623
Finnish education system,
131
fixed interval schedule, 464
fixed mindset, 345
fixed ratio reinforcement
schedule, 465
fixed versus growth
mindsets, 345
flat affect, 660
fluid intelligence, 401
fluoxetine (Prozac), 711
Flynn effect, 339–340
foot-in-the-door approach,
530
forebrain, structures and
functions, 172–176
association areas, 173–174
cerebral cortex, 173
cerebral cortex or
cerebrum, 172
corpus callosum, 173
frontal lobes, 175–176
left hemisphere, 173
lobes, 173
motor cortex, 176
occipital lobes, 174
parietal lobes, 175
somatosensory cortex, 175
temporal lobes, 174
forgetting, 317–320
curve, 317–318, 320
theories of, 318
forming and modifying
schemas, 264
Freeman, Walter, 185
"lobotomobile"
conducting lobotomies,
184

Freud, Sigmund, 5, 10, 113,
193, 62, 430, 556–557,
559–561, 564, 569,
694–696, 702
psychoanalysis, 694–695
theory of forgetting/
repression, 319
transference, 695
functional fixedness, 275
functionalism, 3, 4
fundamental attribution
error, 501

G

Gage, Phineas, 180–181
Gallup poll, 57
gambler's fallacy, 272
gambling, 465
gamma-aminobutyric
acid (GABA), 154, 159,
160, 708
Gardner, Howard, 329, 330
multiple intelligences, 329
gender, 385
gender dysphoria, 386
gender identity, 386, 387
roots of, 389
gender norms, 385
gender roles, 387
ideas of, 388
gender schema theory, 386
gender typing, 387–388
genderfluid, 386
genderqueer, 386
gender-typed cognitions, 390
gene-environment
interactions, 120–121
development of
personality, 121
reciprocal
determinism, 121
sensitive or critical
period, 120
temperamental
characteristics of the
children influence the
parent's behavior, 121

general adaptation syndrome
(GAS), 623–624
burnout, 624
chronic stress, 624
fight-flight-or-freeze
response, 623
generalized amnesia, 671
generalized anxiety disorder
(GAD), 667
genetic influence, 129–130
job satisfaction, 130
mental health, 129
personality traits, 129
self-esteem 129
genetics, 386
genuineness, 697
Gestalt, 248
Gestalt psychology, 4,
248–250
closure, 250
figure-and-ground
perception, 248–249
grouping, 249
proximity, 249
similarity, 249
ghrelin, 156, 585
glial cells, 144
global explanatory style, 500
glutamate, 154
long-term potentiation
(LTP), 154
good sleep habits, 202
grammar, 408
graphics, 72–81
bar chart, 72–73
diagram, 78
line graph, 73–74, 78–79
negative correlations, 76
pie chart, 74
psychological as
well as statistical
concepts, 77–79
reinforcement associated
with behaviorists, 79
scatterplot, 77
table, 79
visual representations, 77
gratitude, 633
group dynamics, 548

methamphetamine (MDMA),159

method of loci, 295

middle age and beyond, 401–403
Alzheimer's disease, 402
brain's fluid intelligence, 401
cognitive disorders, 402
dementia, 402
terminal drop in the weeks or months prior to death, 403
working memory, decline in, 401

midlife, 380–381
adult's mobility, 380
flexibility, 380–381
hearing changes, 381
menopause, 380
reaction time, 381
reproductive ability, 380
visual changes, 381

Milgram experiments, 543

Milgram's first experiments, 535

mind-altering chemicals, 157

mindfulness, 703

Minnesota Longitudinal (long-term) Study of Parents and Children, 362

misinformation effect, 321

mnemonic devices, 293–295
categories, 295
chunking, 295
hierarchies, 295
HOMES, 294
method of loci, 294
OCEAN, 294
SAME, 294

mode, 81, 83

modeling, 700

modern hypnosis, 706–707

modern neurology, 710

modes of therapy, 705

monochromatism/total color blindness, 215–216

monocular depth cues, 254

interposition, 254
linear perspective, 254
relative clarity, 254
relative size, 254
texture gradient, 254

monozygotic (MZ) twins, 125

mood stabilizers, 708
lithium, 708
lamotrigine, 708

mood-congruent memory, 312

morality principle, 557

morpheme, 409

motivated forgetting, 319

motivation, 578–590
theories, 497, 578–584

motivational conflicts, 584
theory, 584

motor neurons, 145

movement
kinesthetic sense, 228

Müller-Lyer illusion (ML), 257

multiculturalism, 527

multiple intelligences, 329–330
Gardner's theory, 329–330

multiple sclerosis (MS), 152
disruption of neural transmission, 152
immune system, 152

multi-store model, 285–286
long-term memory (LTM), 286
sensory memory, 286
short-term memory, 286

Murray, Henry, 561

myasthenia gravis (MG), 151
body's immune system, 151
hallmark of, 152

N

narcissistic personality disorder, 681

narcolepsy, 204

National Research Act 1974, 66

Native American tribes
learning, 131

natural selection, process of, 122–123
adaptive behaviors, 122–123
epigenetics, 123
fight-flight-or-freeze response, 123
genetic mutations, 122
human mate preferences, 122
outdated behavior, 123
universally adaptive response, 122

naturalistic observation, 30, 35, 62–64
non-experimental research methods, advantages and disadvantages of, 64
student behavior, 62

nature and nurture
debate, 361–362

nearsightedness, 212

negative cognitive triad, 662

negative correlation, 30, 51, 54
"bad" relationship, 54

negative punishment, 461–462

negative reinforcement, 460–461

negative symptoms, 660

negatively (left) skewed distribution, 89–90

neglect, 621

nerve deafness, 221

nervous system, 136–143
myelin, 147
neural structure, 146–147
neurotransmitters, 147
synapses, 147
terminal buttons, 146–147
treelike protrusions, 146

neural communication, 165

neural structure, 165

neural transmission, 147–155
  action potential, 148
  all-or-nothing principle,
    148–149
  depolarization, 148
  neural impulse, 149
  neuron, "peel" or
    membrane of, 148
  process of, 148–150
  refractory period, 149
  resting potential, 148
neuroanatomy, 144
neurocognitive science, 513
neurodevelopmental
  disorders, 656–658
  developmental period
    from conception to
    adolescence, 656
  possible causes, 658
  symptoms, 656–657
neurological developmental
  disorders, 657
neuron and neural firing,
  144–165
  cranium, 144
  nerve cells, structures and
    functions of, 144
  neural structure, 146
  reflex arc, 145, 146
neurons, 144
neuroplasticity, 176, 222, 241,
  304, 480
neuroscience, 176
neurotransmitters, 150–153
  functions of, 150–153
  reuptake, 150
neutral stimulus, 442
nicotinic receptor, 158
nominal, 84
nonbinary, 386
non-carpentered cultures,
  257
non-experimental
  methodologies, 30, 33, 52
  using qualitative
    data, 33–34
non-experimental research
  designs, 52

non-experimental
  researchers
  case studies, 52
non-experimental studies, 56
non-REM (NREM)
  sleep, 196–197
  high-frequency/low-
    amplitude theta waves,
    196
  stages 1 and 2, 196
nontasters, 225
nonverbal language, 410–411
nonverbal manual
  gestures, 410
norepinephrine, 153
  and dopamine reuptake
    inhibitors (NDRI), 708
normal behavior
  positive (additions) or
    negative (reductions),
    659
normal curve, or
  symmetrical bell curve, 81
normal distribution, 82,
  87–89
"normal" intelligence, 337
normative influence,
  527–528
nuances
  in findings, 109
  in process, 108–109
  in research, 108
  of claims, policies, and
    norms, 108
nurturing environment, 131
nurturing practices, 131–132

O

obedience, 533
  authority, 533–536
obedience to authority,
  533–536
  Asch studies on
    conformity, 535
  closeness and legitimacy
    of, 534
  mild "ouch" responses, 534
  Milgram's study, 535–536

obedience, 533
object relations therapy, 695
objective conclusion, 2,
  14–15
observable behavior, 441
observational learning,
  475–476
  implications of, 477–478
  social learning theory,
    475–476
obsessive thought, 668
obsessive-compulsive
  disorders (OCDs),
  668–670
  behavioral patterns, 669
  biological or genetic
    factors, 670
  compulsions, 668
  obsessions (intrusive
    thoughts), 668
  possible causes, 669–670
  problematic thinking and
    emotions, 670
obsessive-compulsive
  personality disorder
  (OCPD), 683–684
obstructive sleep apnea, 205
olfaction, 222
one-trial conditioning,
  448–450
operant conditioning, 6,
  455–473, 485, 700
  biology in, 467–468
  instinctive drift, 467–468
  reinforcement and
    punishment, 457
  superstitious behaviors,
    455
  Thorndike, 455
operant conditioning
  chamber/Skinner box, 6,
  462
operational definitions, 36,
  52
opioids, 160–161
opponent-process theory,
  215

optimistic explanatory style, 500

out-group homogeneity bias, 518

overconfidence bias, 17, 22

OxyContin®, 161

P

panic attack, 666–667

panic disorder, 666

paranoid personality disorder, 679

parasympathetic nervous system, 139

parenting styles, 419–420
child's temperament, or disposition, 420

parents' gender schemas, 390

partial reinforcement, 464

peer evaluation, 49

peer pressure and conformity test, 69

peer relationships over time, 425–430

peer review, 49

peers during childhood, engagement with, 425–426
interactions during older childhood, 426
parallel play, 425
Piaget's preoperational stage, 425–426
pretend play, 425

people with autism difficulties faced, 657

percentile rank, 82

perception, 245–261

perceptual constancy, 255

perceptual systems, 245–252
bottom-up processing, 245–246
cultural expectations, 248
emotional context, 247
expectations, 248
internal prior expectations, 246
perceptual set, 247

processing incoming information, 245–246
prosopagnosia, 246
schemas, 247
top-down processing, 246

peripheral nervous system (PNS), 137

permissive parents, 420

persistent depressive disorder, 662

person perception, 504–506

personal distress, 679

personal history, 600

personality, 497, 555
assessment of, 561–562
consciousness, 555
disorders, 678–683
Freud's focus on sexuality, 557
humanistic assessment of, 565
pleasure principle, 557
preconscious level, 555
psychodynamic assessment, 561–562
psychodynamic theory of, 555
social-cognitive theory, 569–570
structure of, 556–558
unconscious level, 555–556

personality disorders, 678–683
behavioral factors, 683
biological sources, 683
Cluster A: "Odd, Suspicious, and Eccentric," 679–680
Cluster B: "Dramatic, Emotional, Erratic," 680–682
Cluster C: "Anxious and Fearful," 682–683
cognitive sources, 683
genetic component, 683
possible causes, 683
social factors, 683

person-centered therapy/ client-centered or Rogerian therapy, 696

persuasion, 529–530
central route, 529
communicator, 531
credibility and authority, role in, 531
door-in-the-face approach, 530
foot-in-the-door approach, 530
halo effect, 530
multicultural perspectives, 531
peripheral route, 529

pessimistic explanatory style, 500

pessimistic individuals, 500
learned helplessness,500

PET (positron emission tomography), 222

Pettigrew, Thomas, 501

phantom limb pain, 227-228

phi phenomenon, 257

phobia(s), 450, 665

phoneme, 409

phonemic encoding, 288

physiological changes, 368

Piaget, Jean, 393

Piaget's four-stage theory, 399

Piaget's theory of discontinuous cognitive development, 393–399
abstract concepts, 398
adults experience assimilation and accommodation, 394
assimilating prior experience, 394
assimilation, 394
children, exhibit animism, 395–396
concrete operational stage, 397–399
egocentrism, 396
formal operational stage, 398–399

hypothetical situations, 398
in adults, 394
in children, 394
object permanence, 395
one-dimensional thinking, 397
Piaget's stages, 394–399
preoperational stage, 395–397
principle of conservation, 398
process of accommodation, 394
reversibility, 398
Sally–Anne test, 396
sensorimotor stage, 394–395
separation anxiety, 395
stranger anxiety, 395
theory of mind, 396
two-dimensional thinking, 397

pie chart, 74

placebo, 44, 45
effect, 44, 45
and experimenter bias, 45

plasticity, 180

Play-Doh, 323

pleasure principle, 557

population of
a study, 40
interest, 41

positive correlation, 30, 51, 54
correlation coefficients, 54

positive psychology, 631–640

positive punishment, 460–461

positive reinforcement, 460

positively (right) skewed distribution, 89

posttraumatic growth (PTG), 636–637

posttraumatic stress disorder (PTSD) / "shell shock," 559–560, 636–637, 674–675

avoidance mechanism of amnesia, 675
cognitive distortions, 675
possible causes of, 675
symptoms of, 674–675

predictive validity, 336

prefrontal lobotomy/ lobotomy, 710

prejudice, 515

prenatal development, 369–371
environmental influences, 371
genetic mutations, 370
hormonal imbalances, 371
maternal illness, 370
prenatal period, 369

prenatal hormones, 386

prenatal susceptibility, 369–370

primacy effect, 297

primary reinforcement, 459

principles of desensitization/ counterconditioning, 698

Principles of Psychology, 3

proactive interference, 318–319

problem solving, 265–267
algorithms, 265–266
confirmation bias, 268
heuristics, 266–267
problems in, 268
trial and error, 265

problematic thinking and emotions, 670

problem-focused coping, 626

procedural memories, 281

procrastination or distraction, 360

progesterone, 378

projective tests, 561

prosocial behavior, 549–551
helper's high, 550
runner's high, 550

prospective memory, 281–282

prototype, 263

psychoactive drugs,
effect on behavior and mental processes, 157, 165
dependence or addiction, 161–162
addictive behaviors, 161
adrenaline junkies, 162
brain biology, 162
prefrontal cortex, 162
psychological dependence, 161
rebelling against parental and societal norms, 162
sociocultural factors, 162

psychoactive medications, 709
assessment of, 709
or pharmacotherapy, 707–709

psychoactive substances, 158

psychoanalysis, 694

psychoanalytic approach, 5

psychoanalytic theory, 556, 559
criticisms of, 559–560
strengths of 560

psychodynamic approach, 5, 561

psychodynamic perspective, 646

psychodynamic therapies, 694, 695

psychodynamic therapist, 695–696

psychological assessments
principles for, 333–336
psychometric principles, 334
standardization, 334
standardized tests, 334
validity, 334–335

psychological disorders, 2, 641
diagnosing and classifying, 642–643
diagnosis and treatment, approaches to, 643

to refute a claim, 102
to support a claim, 102
recall, 311
recency effect, 297
reciprocal determinism, 475
recognition, 311
regression to the mean, 82
regression toward the mean, 93
  research and data analysis, 93
regular observations of training sessions, 34
Reimer, David, 389
reinforcement, 459
  discrimination, 463
  generalization, 463
  schedules of, 463–466
relative deprivation, 506
reliability, 336
  and validity of intelligence testing, 336
REM sleep behavior disorder, 205
replication, 50
representative sample, 40, 41
representativeness heuristic, 266
repressed memories, 707
reproductive ability, 380
research
  conduct, impact on, 48
  confederates, 65
  outcomes, impact on, 48
research designs
  empirical data, 31
  experimental research, 31
  non-experimental research, 31
  scientific method, 31–32
  types of, 31–36
response, 442
reticular activating system (RAS), 170
retrieval practice processes, 313
  testing effect, 313

retroactive interference, 318
retrograde amnesia/ forgetting events, 305
Ritalin®, 709
Rogers, Carl, 562–564
Rorschach inkblot test, 561–562
Rorschach, Hermann, 561

S

Sacks, Oliver, 181
sampling bias, 40, 41
scenario, 2
  practice applying concepts to, 11–12
Schachter's two-factor theory, 592
schema, 264
schizoid personality disorder, 679
schizophrenia, 658
  possible causes, 660
  rule of quarters, 658–659
  symptoms of, 659–660
schizophrenic spectrum disorders, 658–659
schizotypal personality disorder (STPD), 679
science, technology, engineering, and mathematics (STEM), 385
scientifically derived evidence, 109, 112
secondary reinforcers, 459
secondary sex characteristics, 378
sedatives/tranquilizers or hypnotics, 160
seizure disorders, 708
selective attention, 251
  cocktail party effect, 251
selective norepinephrine reuptake inhibitor (SNRI), 153
self-actualization, 563
self-determination theory (SDT), 580–581

autonomy, 581
competence, 581
relatedness, 581
self-fulfilling prophecy, 505
self-report bias, 51
self-report personality inventories, 573–574
  Neuroticism Extraversion Openness Personality Inventory–Revised (NEO PI-R), 573–574
self-serving bias, 1
self-serving biases, 501–502
Seligman, Martin, 449, 457, 636
semantic, 409
  encoding, 288
  memories, 280
semicircular canals, 228
sensation, 208–234
  absolute threshold, 208
  difference threshold/ just noticeable difference (JND), 209
  process of, 208
  sensory adaptation, 210
  signal (or stimulus) detection theory, 209
  transduction, 208, 209
  Weber's Law, 209
sensation-seeking theory, 583
  Zuckerman, Marvin, 583
sensorineural deafness, 221
sensory
  adaptation, 210
  conflict theory, 229
  habituation, 210
  interaction, 210
  memory, 286
  neurons, 145
separation anxiety, 421
serial position effect, 296–297
serotonin, 152
  and norepinephrine reuptake inhibitors (SNRI), 708
severity, 622

sex, 385
sex and gender, 385
   influence on socialization, 385–390
sexual orientation, 386
   genetics, role of, 389
   research, 389
shallow processing, 287
shape constancy, 255
shaping, 467
   successive approximations, 467
Shiffrin, Richard, 285
short-term memory (STM), 279, 283–284
single-blind study, 44
situational attribution, 500
situational variables, 551
size constancy, 255
skewed distributions, 89–90
skewness, 82
Skinner's experiments, 458
Skittles®, 210
sleep, 192–207
   consciousness, 192–193
   falling asleep, 196
   human consciousness, levels of, 193,
   hypnagogic sensations, 196
   stages of, 196–197
   suprachiasmatic nucleus (SCN), or "master clock," 196
   unconscious level, 193
sleep apnea, 204
sleep deprivation, 199
sleep disorders, 204–205
   insomnia, 204
   narcolepsy, 204
sleep disruptions, 199–200
   sleep debt, 199
sleep habits, 201–203
   and culture, 201–202
sleep/wake cycle, 194
   circadian rhythm, 194

slower-acting endocrine system, 155
smell, 223–224
   olfaction, 223
   pheromones, 223
   vomeronasal organ, 223
social anxiety disorder (social phobia), 667
social behavior, 525
social clock
   influence of culture, 428
social cognition, 499
social comparison theory, 506
social connections, 615
social debt, 549–550
social desirability bias, 51
social development, 417
social environment, influence on development, 417–419
   chronosystem, 418–419
   exosystem, 418
   macrosystem, 418
   mesosystem, 418
   microsystem, 418
social facilitation, 544–545
social influence, 525, 537
   theory, 527
social inhibition, 545
   positions, 545
social learning, 474–479
   theory, 389, 474
social loafing, 540–541
social norms, 526
social pressures, 387
social psychology, 497
social reciprocity norm, 550
social responsibility norm, 550
social situation, 499, 526
   and persuasion, 526–530
   psychology of, 525–554
social-cognitive theories, 569–572
   assessment of, 571
   personality assessment, 571–572

self-concept, 570
self-efficacy, 570–571
self-esteem, 571
social-emotional development, 417–440
   adulthood, social growth, 417
   attachment, 421–424
   cultural differences, 423–424
   cultures with individualistic values, 424
   individualistic societies, cultural differences, 424
   secure attachment during infancy, 417
   sense of identity, creating of, 435–436
   separation anxiety, 421
   shared caregiving, 423–424
   strange situation test, 421
   stranger anxiety, 421
socialization in childhood, 387–388
   Fa'afafine, 387
   Fa'afatama, 387
   gender identity, 387
   gender roles, 387
   gender typing, 387
   societal norms, 386–387
sociocultural
   approach, 7
   factors, 649
   perspective, 648–649
sociocultural perspective, 648–649
   cultural syndromes, 648
   DSM-5, 648
somatic nervous system, 137
somnambulism (sleepwalking), 205
sound, theories of, 219–220
sound localization, 220–221
source amnesia, 322
spacing effect/spaced repetition, 295–296
   distributed practice, 295

massed practice, 295

specific explanatory style, 500

specific phobia disorder, 665–666

split-brain, 178

split-brain research, 176, 177–180

  brain lateralization or cortex specialization, 177

  Broca's aphasia/ Broca's area, 179

  contralateral, 178

  contralateral hemispheric organization, 178

  corpus callosum, 178

  divided brain, 177

  left hemisphere as the "language side" of the brain, 177

  patients with a severed corpus callosum, 178

  right side, 177

  split-brain experiment, 179(f)

  visual field, 178

  Wernicke's aphasia/ Wernicke's area, 179

split-half reliability, 336

spontaneous recovery, 447–448

SRIs (selective serotonin reuptake inhibitors), 152

stability and change debate, 362

stage hypnotists, 707

standard deviation, 82

standardization, 334

Stanford prison experiment, 542

Stanford-Binet Intelligence Test, 332

state-dependent memory, 312

statistical significance, 94

stereotypes, 512–513

  biased perceptions and experiences, 513

cognitive load, 512

influence self-perceptions and behaviors, 513

neurocognitive study on persistence, 514

Stern, William, 333

stimulants, 158, 709

  attention deficit disorder (ADD), treatment of, 709

  attention deficit hyperactivity disorder (ADHD), treatment of, 709

  children with ADD/ ADHD, 709

stimulus, 442

  discrimination, 444–445

  generalization, 444–445

stimulus-response learning, 442–444

  acquisition, 443

  learned responses in everyday life, 444

stranger anxiety, 421

stream of consciousness, 3

stress, 619–626

  and physiological issues, 620

  cultural circumstances, 622

  headaches, 620

  immune suppression, 620

  reactions, 619, 623–625

stressors, 621–622

stroboscopic movement, 257

structural encoding, 287

structuralism, 3, 4

structuralists, 4

structured interview, 60

  data collected with, 51

  key features of, 60

"Students of Psychology Can Fly" (SPCF), 399

subjective well-being (SWB), 632–633

  cognitive bias, 632

  confirmation bias, 632

  and happiness, 632

influencing factors, 633

substance P, 154

subtractive bilingualism, 412

sunk-cost fallacy, 271

superego, 5, 557

"superior orders" defense, 543

supertasters, 224–225

supportive educational environment and genetic predispositions interaction between, 131

survey research random selection, 57

surveys, 56

susceptibility, 622

sympathetic nervous system, 138

synesthesia, 210

syntax, 408

systematic desensitization, 698

T

taijin kyofusho (TKS)/the disorder of fear, 667

tardive dyskinesia (TD), 709

taste, 224–225

  gustation, 224

  papillae, 224

  salty foods, 224

  supertasters, 224–225

taste aversion, 448–449

  experiments, 449

teenagers and young adults, socialization in, 388

  androgynous personality, 388

  transgendered, 388

tend-and–befriend theory, 624–625

teratogens, 369

testing effect, 313

testosterone, 378

test-retest reliability, 336

Thematic Apperception Test (TAT), 561–562

theoretical perspectives, 10

therapeutic hypnosis, 707

thinking and reasoning, 13

third variable problem, 51

thrill- or adventure-seeking, 583

time-based connection, 459

tip-of-the-tongue (TOT) phenomenon, 319

Titchener, Edward, 3

token economy systems, 700

tolerance, 157–158
to the drug, 157

top-down processing, 246

traditional psychology, 631

trait theories, 572–574
assessing, 573
big five theory, 572
criticism of, 573
factor analysis, 572
measurable traits, 572
OCEAN, 572

transcranial magnetic stimulation (TMS), 185, 222, 710

traumatic brain injury (TBI)
long-term effects of, 53

traumatic event, 674

trial and error, 265

triarchic theory of intelligence, 330

trichromatic theory, 214

tutoring program, 33

twin studies, 125–126

U

ultimate attribution error, 501

unconditional positive regard/nondirective therapy, 696–697

unconditional regard, 563

unconditioned response (UR or UCR), 443, 446

unconditioned stimulus, (US or UCS), 443, 446

upward social comparison, 506

V

validity, 334–335

variability, measures of, 85–90
bell curve, 87
score's percentile rank, 87
standard deviation (sd), 86
data set, variation of, 86
normal distribution, 87–89
outliers, 88–89

variable (s), 32
interval reinforcement, 465
of interest, 52
ratio reinforcement schedule, 465
trends and relationships in, 95–96

Venn diagram, 75

vicarious conditioning, 475

vicarious reinforcement, 475

violent video games, 481

visual perceptual constancies, 255–256
perceptual constancy, 255

visual perceptual processes, 252–254
binocular depth cues, 253
convergence, 253
depth perception, 253
retinal disparity, 253

visual sensory system, 211–217
eye, structure of, 212
infrared (IR) light, 211
night vision, 211
photoreceptor (light receptor) cells, 211
ultraviolet (UV) light, 211
visible spectrum, 211
visual processing, 211

vocabulary, 408

Vygotsky, Lev, 400
sociocultural perspective, 417

theory of cultural and biosocial development, 400

Vygotsky's theory of cultural and biosocial development, 400
scaffolding, 400
zone of proximal development, 400

W

wakeful consciousness, 193

war crimes, 543

Washburn, Margaret Floy, 4

Weber, Ernst, 209

Wechsler Adult Intelligence Scale (WAIS), 332

Wechsler Intelligence Scale for Children (WISC), 332

Wechsler Intelligence Scales, 332–333
digit-symbol coding, 333
symbol searching, 333

Wendell's stutterers, 413

Wernicke, Carl, 181

Wertheimer, Max, 4

Western cultures, 131

withdrawal, 158

word salad, 659

wording problems, 57–58
"either-or" nature of the question, 57
forbid and allow, 57
self-report bias, 58
social desirability bias, 58

working memory, 283

working memory model, 284–285
central executive, 285
elaboration, 285
episodic buffer, 285
long-term memory, transferring to, 285
phonological loop, 285
rehearsal, 285
retrieval, 285
visuospatial sketchpad, 285

Wundt, Wilhelm, 3

X

Y

Z